# Constructing Victims' Rights

CLARENDON STUDIES IN CRIMINOLOGY

Published under the auspices of the Institute of Criminology,
University of Cambridge, the Mannheim Centre, London School of
Economics, and the Centre for Criminological Research,
University of Oxford.

GENERAL EDITOR: ALISON LIEBLING (*University of Cambridge*)

EDITORS: MANUEL EISNER AND PER-OLOF WIKSTRÖM
(*University of Cambridge*)

PAUL ROCK, JILL PEAY, AND TIM NEWBURN
(*London School of Economics*)

LUCIA ZEDNER, RICHARD YOUNG, AND RICHARD ERICSON
(*University of Oxford*)

# Constructing Victims' Rights

The Home Office, New Labour, and Victims

Paul Rock

OXFORD
UNIVERSITY PRESS

# OXFORD
UNIVERSITY PRESS

Great Clarendon Street, Oxford OX2 6DP

Oxford University Press is a department of the University of Oxford.
It furthers the University's objective of excellence in research, scholarship,
and education by publishing worldwide

in Oxford New York

Auckland Bangkok Buenos Aires Cape Town Chennai
Dar es Salaam Delhi Hong Kong Istanbul Karachi Kolkata
Kuala Lumpur Madrid Melbourne Mexico City Mumbai Nairobi
São Paulo Shanghai Singapore Taipei Tokyo Toronto

Oxford is a registered trade mark of Oxford University Press
in the UK and in certain other countries

Published in the United States
by Oxford University Press Inc., New York

© P. Rock, 2004

The moral rights of the author have been asserted
Database right Oxford University Press (maker)

First published 2004

British Library Cataloguing in Publication Data

Data Available

Library of Congress Cataloging-in-Publication Data

Rock, Paul Elliott.
Constructing victims rights : the Home Office, New Labour, and victims / Paul Rock.
p. cm.
ISBN 0–19–927549–1
1. Victims of crimes—Government policy—Great Britain. 2. Victims of crimes—Legal
status, laws, etc.—Great Britain. 3. Reparation—Great Britain. I. Title.
HV6250.3.G7R6 2004
362.88—dc22
2004010777

ISBN 0-19-927549-1

1 3 5 7 9 10 8 6 4 2

Typeset by Kolam Information Services Pvt. Ltd, Pondicherry, India
Printed in Great Britain on acid-free paper by
Biddles Ltd., King's Lynn

*In Memoriam*

# General Editor's Introduction

Clarendon Studies in Criminology aims to provide a forum for outstanding empirical and theoretical work in all aspects of criminology, criminal justice, penology, and the wider field of deviant behaviour. The Editors welcome excellent PhD work, as well as submissions from established scholars. The Series was inaugurated in 1994, with Roger Hood as its first General Editor, following energetic discussions between Oxford University Press and three Criminology Centres. It is edited under the auspices of these three Criminological Centres: the Cambridge Institute of Criminology, the Mannheim Centre for Criminology at the London School of Economics, and the Oxford Centre for Criminology. Each supplies members of the Editorial Board.

Paul Rock's book, *Constructing Victims' Rights: The Home Office, New Labour, and Victims*, is a meticulous account of the world of criminal justice policy-making, of changing sensibilities, and of 'people doing things together', in the field of victims' interests. Rock examines how various critical events, and 'disparate passages of talk and writing', came together in the form of a Victims' Bill of Rights, later to become the Domestic Violence, Crime and Victims Bill in 2003, transforming the politics and formal identities of victims. The study began as 'a sociology of emerging policies for victims' and it ended as 'an essay in political history'. It is a close and complex account, showing how a modernizing government responded to, and shaped, escalating activity in this field. Rock's observations on the role of email in corroding institutional and documentary memory, like his observations of the ways in which policy-making 'goes on', and of the selective uses made of evaluation research in the face of political pressures, are perceptive and disquieting. He shows how the policy-making process is a 'contingent and emergent' process, ever exposed to 'possibilities of collision or convergence with other developments that could never originally have been foreseen'. This is an outstanding narrative account of those developments, and a fine sociological analysis of their role in the creation of a new place for victims in criminal justice.

The editors welcome this important addition to the *Series*.
Alison Liebling
Cambridge, May 2004

# Preface

*Constructing Victims' Rights* attempts to reconstruct something of what the politicians and policy-makers of the New Labour Government, 1997–2001, sought to achieve when they talked about 'placing the victim at the heart of the criminal justice system'. It dwells on the forms of criminal justice policy as they underwent change inside Government around the turn of the century, and on the substance of policy as those forms shaped political representations and activities centred on victims of crime. At its core is a description, in Howard Becker's deceptively simple phrase, of people doing things together—in this instance, officials, politicians, the non-governmental organizations, and representatives of the practitioners— and the joint activity upon which they were engaged was the production of written and spoken arguments in committees, submissions, letters, emails, and reports. This is a study of discussions, definitions, and accounts as they were given public and private expression by officials and politicians. It is talk about talk in an environment replete with talk (Andrew Rawnsley described the post of Home Secretary as 'the most paper-intensive job in the Cabinet'[1]) and what that talk heeded, created, and shaped became the topic and resource of this analysis. What it neglected will tend to be neglected here too.[2]

I lay emphasis on that concentration on argument inside Government because this book is not about material changes in the everyday treatment and experiences of victims in and around the criminal justice system. It would have been premature to explore such matters and the practical implementation of policy was another process altogether, off-stage, out of focus and too substantial to be managed within a single study. Neither could the book ever have been a

---

[1]  A. Rawnsley; 'Canny Blunkett moves a step closer to No. 10', *Evening Standard*, 30 October 2001.

[2]  An internal email in October 1997 about a draft speech on restorative justice to be made by a politician to an audience composed, in part, of a local victim support scheme remarked, tellingly, that 'surely this is not a PVU matter—[the private secretary] saw the magic words Victim Support and thought of us. The lead lies elsewhere.'

catholic history of the politics of criminal justice or a compendium of policies about victims in all the areas of life in which they appeared at the time: such a work would not only have been an impossibly large undertaking but would also have lacked structure and coherence.

*Constructing Victims' Rights* examines how very disparate passages of talk and writing about victims in the Government of England and Wales came in 2001 to converge and combine to form what could be treated by officials as a critical mass that required ordering and reconstruction as a Victims' Bill of Rights[3] that was later reincarnated as a proposal for a Victims and Witnesses Bill and, finally, as a Domestic Violence, Crime and Victims Bill that was announced in the Queen's Speech of 26 November 2003, and it is in effect a lengthy unpicking and explanation of those proposals and that Bill. Although, as I shall show, some of the rights that were promised were actually a little weak and tangential, the prospect of rights had begun to seem significantly more solid[4] and compelling, and the events leading up to them merit analysis as an important and interesting transformation of the politics of victims, as a course of action bringing about the construction of new formal identities for victims, and as a glimpse of how criminal justice policy-making was accomplished at the turn of the century.

Research started in the early summer of 1998, before those proposals were ever fully contemplated, and it tracked the policy process step by step as it unfolded inside Whitehall until just after the 2001 general election, rather than retrospectively when all would seem plain and its authors could take stock and tell me and each other what must after all have really happened. Like much other policy-making, work on victims at the turn of the century was sensed

[3] Aired, signally, by the Home Secretary at the Labour Party Conference in Glasgow on 17 February 2001: '... in the next few weeks, I will be publishing proposals to give victims of crime an enforceable bill of rights laying down the treatment which they can expect from the criminal justice system... this package of measures should finally begin to bring victims in from the cold—to put their interests at the heart of the criminal justice system'.

[4] Rights for victims were certainly aired before 2001, but they were insubstantial and ambiguous, as much aspiration as enforceable claim. Spencer called them 'more paper than practical'. J. Spencer; 'Improving the Position of the Victim in English Criminal Procedure', paper given at the International Conference on the Rights of the Accused, Crime Control, and the Protection of Victims', Hebrew University of Jerusalem, 19–23 December 1993.

before the event as largely open-ended, somewhat piecemeal, sometimes without clear overall design and foreknowledge (it would have
been impossible to have had a presentiment of any such pattern at
the time because the design itself was to be an emergent property of
processes yet to unfold), often moulded by events as they arose,
leading in uncertain directions, and capable of taking odd twists
that led into blind alleys. Of course, I too could not know what
would happen, and could only hope, like Mr Micawber, that something would turn up and I would have a story to tell. I too was unsure
about where events were tending—if indeed they were tending anywhere—and, lacking a clear system of relevance, could do little other
than play the magpie, keep my eyes and ears open and dismiss little
as unimportant. Unlike some analyses of the politics and policies of
criminal justice which endow action with clear intent, deeply embedded purposes or a disembodied rationality and organization, this
book is an effort to reproduce some of the '"messy actualities" of
"what actually happens"'.[5] To be sure, that sense of indeterminacy
had vanished by the time I came to write, and it was all too easy
retrospectively to bestow pattern on events (there could have been
no analysis without it), but there may still remain in this book some
lingering fidelity to the lived reality of the policy-making of a particular period.

Although *Constructing Victims' Rights* actually describes only a
small and rather peripheral slice of criminal justice policy-making, it
was vital to simplify what seemed a large enough task. A number of
lenses defined its theme. First, it illuminates a critical change in
political talk about victims' rights that took place inside the bowels
of the Home Office at the beginning of this century.[6] It explores
processes as they emerged and contributed to that change, and, in
particular, the very disparate representations of victims that were to
take shape and coalesce inside policy-making. It explains how victims
so represented came to acquire a special pragmatic significance

[5] P. O'Malley *et al.*, 'Governmentality, criticism, politics,' *Economy and Society*,
1997, Vol. 26, No. 4, p. 509.

[6] Walklate remarked in 1989 that the image of the victim was 'not powerful
enough ... to initiate the notion of victims' rights nor has it questioned in any way
the fundamental structuring of the role of the victim in the criminal justice process'.
S. Walklate; *Victimology: The victim and the criminal justice process*, Unwin Hyman,
London, 1989, pp. 128–9. It is the shift from that position to a rights-based politics of
victims that this book describes.

within Whitehall and Westminster[7] that bore few of the marks of mass public campaigning or moral agitation for victims *as* victims (indeed, very little such campaigning at all took place during the period although campaigns for other causes or for very particular sub-groups of victims certainly made their mark) or of the new ideological moralism that was said by a number of criminologists and others to be driving the politics of criminal justice and victims in the West.[8] And by implication, it touches on the repertoire of selves and identities which the criminal justice system permitted victims formally to assume, linking the State to private subjectivity.

The social anthropologist, Isaac Shapera, used to define ethnography as a history of the present. It was just so with this book. If it began as a sociology of emerging policies for victims, it inevitably ended as an essay in political history.[9] By the time the first draft was complete in the summer of 2003, the Home Office it describes had already begun to seem again like a foreign country whose occupants and topography had changed beyond knowing. For methodological, narrative, and analytic reasons, it is loosely centred in and around the deliberations of two key bodies. The first was the interdepartmental Victims Steering Group, the lead committee that met twice-yearly under the auspices of the Home Office, itself the Government's lead department and principal site of work in victims' matters. What came before that committee defined much of who passed for victims and what passed for policy at the time (and, for that reason, I have chosen not to give an independent definition of victims here, at the outset, but let their identity become revealed as this history proceeds).

---

[7] See A. Sanders; 'Victim Participation in an Exclusionary Criminal Justice System', in C. Hoyle and R. Young (eds.); *New Visions of Crime Victims*, Hart Publishing, Oxford, 2002, p. 209.

[8] See H. Boutellier; *Crime and Morality: The Significance of Criminal Justice in Post-modern Culture*, Kluwer, Dordrecht, 2000; D. Garland; 'The Culture of High Crime Societies', *British Journal of Criminology*, Summer 2000, Vol. 40, No. 3, pp. 357, 367. Similarly Gaucher and Elliott argued about the emergence of talk about victims' rights in the USA that the 'focus was ideologically consistent with and served to legitimize the shift towards a more punitive and retaliatory criminal justice philosophy and policy...' 'R. Gaucher and L. Elliott; "Sister of Sam": The Rise and Fall of Bill C-205/220', paper presented at the American Society of Criminology 51st Annual meeting, Toronto, Canada, 18 November 1999.

[9] According to Renée Fox, Paul Lazarsfeld used to say that if ethnography was any good, it would graduate to becoming a history of the past as well as of the present.

The second body was JVU, the Home Office's Justice and Victims Unit. JVU had formerly been the Procedures and Victims Unit, and earlier still, before April 1996, C4. JVU was so named in 1999 but later, after the period covered by this book, it was re-christened the Justice, Victims and Witnesses Unit and then, in 2003, it was split into a Victims Unit and a Justice and Witnesses Unit, and those names are evidence of the continual administrative flux and expansion of the policy area and of the Home Office itself at the turn of the century. JVU 'owned' a segment of one of the Home Office's seven aims, Aim 2,[10] being 'responsible for issues relating to procedure in the criminal courts, and for policy relating to victims of crime including compensation for victims'.[11] It was the major organizer, synthesizer, and site of the Government's policy work on victims between May 1997 and June 2001, and the pattern of its activities and the work of its staff gave structure to this book. The results may appear a little odd and distorted to the criminological eye because they focus on Rosencrantz and Guildenstern rather than Hamlet, on the victim rather than the suspect, offender, defendant, or prisoner, but that was my chosen task.

Two major pieces of policy-making will figure above all, and I shall touch on them intermittently for purposes of illustration, and even before they appear in the chapters that are specifically devoted to them. One was the activity of the Working Group on Vulnerable or Intimidated Witnesses that produced a report, *Speaking up for Justice*, published in June 1998, leading to the Youth Justice and Criminal Evidence Act 1999, that contained numerous recommendations about the treatment and protection of witnesses, including a prohibition on the personal cross-examination of complainants and a tighter control of evidence of sexual history in rape cases, and a greater use of screens, supporters, and video-recorded testimony. The other was the inquiry under the chairmanship of Sir William Macpherson of Cluny into the investigation of the death of Stephen Lawrence, a young black man killed in April 1993, whose report was published in February 1999 with a number of recommendations, *inter alia*, about the responsibilities of the police, Crown Prosecution

---

[10] 'Delivering justice through effective and efficient investigation, prosecution, trial and sentencing, and through support for victims'. *The Home Office—A Guide*, Home Office, London, October 2000, p. i.

[11] Home Office Criminal Policy Group 1999, internal memorandum.

Service and Victim Support to the families of people killed in racially-aggravated crime. It was an inquiry and a report that loomed
large over the politics of victims throughout the first New Labour
administration.

I received permission from the Home Office, Victims Steering
Group, and Victim Support to undertake research in July 1998,
and observed my first meeting of the Victims Steering Group in
December 1998. Thereafter, work followed a common-sense
course,[12] devoted, initially, to an omnivorous quest for leads and
bearings (remembering that Howard Becker had said that 'you
include anything that tells you it can't be left out by sticking its
nose up so that it can't be ignored'[13]); then to a rudimentary mapping of what lay before the Group and the Unit; to reading papers
and speaking to each member of the Victims Steering Group, the
Justice and Victims Unit and others to gain a view of victims as they
were ordered into groups, issues, and initiatives; attempting, in the
process, to establish their probable future trajectories; and pursuing
each of those movements in turn, sometimes into dead ends,[14]
sometimes into new areas, and encountering new groups of people
to consult and new materials to read as I did so.[15] A first draft of the

[12] It was a course not dissimilar to that enjoined by Peter Blau when he said that a
case study of bureaucracy can make use of interlocking research procedures, direct
observation, documents, and interviews. See his *The Dynamics of Bureaucracy,*
University of Chicago Press, Chicago, 1955, p. 4.
[13] H. Becker; *Tricks of the Trade,* University of Chicago Press, Chicago, 1998,
p. 56.
[14] One such dead end was the long-promised Freedom of Information Bill which
seemed for a time to promise changes in victims' access to information about the
progress of criminal investigations. Exemptions contained in the Bill would not have
made that access possible.
[15] As well as meetings of the Victims Steering Group, I observed meetings of Victim
Support's National Council, the Trustees of Victim Support, the interdepartmental
Racist Incidents Standing Committee, and other bodies. I also attended a Home Office
Special Conference on the role of victims in the criminal justice process in September
1999; the Tenth United Nations Congress on the Prevention of Crime and the Treatment of Offenders in April 2000; the Joint Home Office/Institute of Public Policy
Research seminar to discuss the Victim's Charter Draft Consultation Paper in January
2001, and other conferences and meetings, including the annual conferences and
annual general meetings of Victim Support. I conducted ninety seven formal interviews and many informal conversations, pursuing matters as they arose. Where
quotations are not ascribed to primary or secondary sources, it should be assumed
that they stemmed from interview. And I read the papers, minutes, reports, corres-

book was completed by the beginning of August 2003, and was then sent to principals and colleagues for comment. Within the Home Office itself, Ian Chisholm, the head of JVU during almost all the period covered by the book, took charge of distributing the draft, collating comments, and advising me about how to proceed. The remarks I received over the next few months were almost wholly constructive, relating principally to minor errors of fact or name, and they did not challenge the general tenor of my analysis. The sole stipulation laid down, and one I found not unreasonable, was that reference to and quotation from the then currently serving members of the Home Office should be anonymous (and the outcome will be that the narrative that follows will centre on the doings of an odd blend of the named and the nameless).

I was mindful that this was a study framed largely by the preoccupations of official and politician, that it was their sensibilities that informed my own, and that trying to appreciate those sensibilities should be an important end in its own right: after all, what was real to them was real in its consequences. But I also drew on stocks of sociological knowledge contained in the writings of others and in my own earlier experiences in the field on other occasions. It was chastening that those writings and experiences only occasionally seemed to illuminate problems at hand, and that it seemed to have been impossible to step into the same bureaucracy twice. The Home Office I had known in the 1980s[16] and mid-1990s[17] was not the modernizing Home Office of the late 1990s and early 2000s (and by 2003 it had radically changed once more). And many of the academic writings on government and 'governmentality' tended to smack of the outsider's account, overly-schematic and coherent in its modelling of decisions and processes, not quite capturing, as Rose put it, 'the actual configurations of

pondence, and hard copies of emails that were housed in the Justice and Victims Unit, the national office of Victim Support, and elsewhere. Some documents were incomplete or missing, and, no doubt, hard copies were not kept of all emails, although I was told that the more important were all recorded.

[16] See my *Helping Victims of Crime: The Home Office and the Rise of Victim Support In England and Wales*, Clarendon Press, Oxford, 1990.

[17] See my *The Social World of an English Crown Court*, Clarendon Press, Oxford, 1993 and *After Homicide: Practical and Political Responses to Bereavement*, Clarendon Press, Oxford, 1998.

persons, organizations and events at [a] particular historical period'.[18]

Even so, in trying to reconstruct those seemingly novel configurations, I am more than conscious that I never really was an insider; that documents were sometimes incomplete; that my attendance at the Home Office and Victim Support was at best sporadic; and that I was not privy to many conversations on the telephone or in corridors. There are, said Jack Katz with some understatement, 'times and places in the subjects' lives that are beyond the ethnographer's reach'.[19] So it was that I came to be reminded by a 'Grade 7' official and seasoned member of the Justice and Victims Unit, that 'files are interesting—for what they're worth—but an awful lot goes on outside the files', and by Teresa Reynolds, Policy Officer of Victim Support, that consultation with Helen Reeves, the Chief Executive Officer about policy decisions 'would be me . . . trying to catch Helen when she's around, it's often, . . . half past seven, eight o'clock in the evening, . . . when I go in there to say "I just need to check this out with you" . . . it might be in the kitchen, it might be in the corridor'. I too had gossiped in and around Home Office meetings and in the kitchen and corridors of Victim Support but I had not been there often, and certainly not in the evening, and had also missed a great deal. Again, and quoting one of the subjects of another, very different ethnographic study, 'any sociologist who simply believes that time spent in the field qualifies him as "one of the boys" is not only sadly mistaken but in grave trouble'.[20] I certainly was not one of the boys in the Home Office or Victim Support. Yet those who were this history's principals have moved on and memories fade,[21] this is an account based on extensive documentation,[22] observation, and interview, and research is no more than the art of the possible. And I was pleased and reassured to be told by Ian Chisholm at the end

[18] N. Rose; 'Government, authority and expertise in advanced liberalism', *Economy and Society*, 1993, Vol. 22, p. 288.
[19] J. Katz; 'Ethnography's Warrants', *Sociological Methods and Research*, May 1997, Vol. 25, No. 4, p. 399.
[20] H. Hasan; 'Afterword' in M. Duneier; *Sidewalk,* Farrar, Straus and Giroux, New York, 1999, p. 326.
[21] Indeed, by 2003, new officials at the new Home Office Victims Unit were curious to read this history in draft because they had no knowledge of what it contained.
[22] From time to time, I have merely paraphrased the more formal or technical passages of internal documents in the text, partly because I wished to convey the form of argument, partly to add verisimilitude.

that he believed that I had got things right. The principal subject's endorsement was for me an important phenomenological test of the work.

If the book does contain a central theme, it is that who victims were and the shape they were to take were pragmatic, contingent constructions; that talk about rights was an ordering response to a mass of quite discrete legal and political processes that accrued around problems that were only incidental to them; and that, because they were never to be recognized fully as formal participants in criminal procedure, their eventual standing was to be resolved by a clever and original *finesse* of the problem of rights that was to be floated as the possible kernel of new legislation. Let me now turn to the contexts in which that policy-making arose in the mid-1990s.

January 2004

# Acknowledgements

Work on this book began in mid-1998 after I had been given permission to study policy-making on victims during the period of the first Labour administration.[1] Those approving the project were the officials, Ian Chisholm, head of the Justice and Victims Unit, and John Lyon, then head of Criminal Policy at the Home Office; the then Home Office Minister, Alun Michael; and members of the interdepartmental Victims Steering Group, a gathering of the powers in Government and the criminal justice system whose deliberations touched on problems of victims and the *Victim's Charter*. No conditions were laid down on what I could do or write, save that officials should be allowed to comment on drafts before publication and that I should not disclose information passed to me in confidence (although very little such expressly confidential information was, in fact, passed on). Almost without exception, Home Office officials and Ministers agreed to be interviewed and allowed me to observe meetings and read papers, and I am deeply grateful to them for their patience, candour, and helpfulness. This book may be seen as a testament to the transparency of officials and politicians in the first New Labour administration.

Ian Chisholm was strategically placed in the developing politics of victims, and he came to act, in effect, as my native informant: he was endlessly kind, incisive, and supportive in steering me at critical junctures through what was to become an increasingly tangled thicket of policy initiatives. At the end, he was more than helpful in shepherding the clearance of the first draft of this book inside the Home Office.

Outside the Home Office, Dame Helen Reeves, Chief Executive Officer of Victim Support, the prime voluntary organization for victims in England and Wales, and the only such organization represented on the Victims Steering Group and ensconced in Government, was again extraordinarily helpful in advising me and allowing me to read papers and attend meetings of the National Council and

---

[1] In the event, the administration was to run between 1 May 1997 and 7 June 2001.

Trustees of Victim Support. She has been a consistently supportive guide in the work that led up to this and other studies over the years. I am grateful to her and her colleagues, and especially Jeremy Corbett, Robert Latham, Teresa Reynolds, and Anne Viney for their assistance.

The events centred on the inquiry into the investigation of the murder of Stephen Lawrence gave a special inflection and urgency to the politics of victims in the 1990s, and I am indebted to Peter Bottomley, at one time the Member of Parliament for Eltham, the constituency in which the Lawrence family lived, and to Lady Howells, a friend and adviser to the Lawrences, for talking to me and letting me see their papers.

Academic friends and colleagues supplied me with ideas and materials as the work evolved, and I thank them: Ben Bowling, David Downes, Janet Foster, Benjamin Goold, Katie Gould, Simon Holdaway, Carolyn Hoyle, Martin Innes, Nicky Lacey, Camille Loxley, Tank Waddington, Richard Young, and others. Ian Chisholm and Tim Newburn read and commented on the entire first draft; Judy Wajcman Chapter 2; Nikolas Rose an early draft of Chapter 4, Kate Akester and Kate Malleson Chapter 5, Howard Webber Chapter 6, Declan Roche and Heather Strang Chapter 7, and Janet Foster, Ros Howells, Coretta Phillips and Tank Wadding-ton Chapter 9, and their comments were invaluable.

I interviewed numerous people in and around Whitehall and Westminster, and many of their names will emerge as the book unfolds. This research would have been impossible without their co-operation. The interviews themselves were in their turn tran-scribed by Joyce Lorinstein, a tedious task which she undertook with cheerfulness and fortitude, and I owe her a great debt. All uncited quotations should be assumed to stem from those interviews unless they are otherwise described.

The research costs of the initial phases of the work were sup-ported by a grant from STICERD, the Suntory and Toyota Inter-national Centres for Economics and Related Disciplines based at the London School of Economics, and I must thank them again for their generous help. Partly because of the sheer bulk of the materials that were amassed as a result of the openness I encountered, one of the lengthiest phases of the work was centred on reading and editing papers, and I am grateful to the Nuffield Foundation, and to the Foundation's ever-helpful Assistant Director, Sharon Witherspoon, for funding two terms' leave of absence from the London School of Economics to concentrate on preparatory work for the book. In February 2003, at the culmination of that editing work, I retired to the Rockefeller Foundation's Bellagio Study and Conference Center at the Villa Serbelloni where, cosseted, I began to write. My thanks are to the Foundation and my fellow residents for such an idyllic and supportive environment in which to work.

# Contents

# 1

# Prelude: Crime and Victims at the Turn of the Century

I shall begin by setting the scene with a short tour of the world of crime and victimization as it came to bear on the evolution of policies for victims within the Home Office around the time of the General Election of May 1997. In Chapter 2, I shall then examine something of the formal organization of the Home Office and, in Chapter 3, explore the workings and propulsive force of its committees. Following the principle of parsimony, this will be an account framed more or less strictly by the need to understand the events that were to culminate in the floating of a Victims' Bill of Rights in 2001.

Crime had been an abiding political and social problem in England and Wales for several decades, waxing and waning in importance, not perhaps a matter of very urgent public attention during the election, but certainly a source of persistent concern and no longer regarded as under control. Crimes reported to and recorded by the police had risen fairly steadily throughout the greater part of the twentieth century, and particularly since the mid-1950s. England and Wales, countries that had once prided themselves on their gentling of the masses[1] and their successful suppression of disorder, crime, and incivility,[2] appeared to have become two of the most crime-prone countries in Europe, low in their rate of homicide (at 2.6 per 100,000 population compared with a European mean of 7.2 in 1996[3]); but high in assaults (440 compared with a

[1] See G. Durston; *Criminal and Constable: The Impact of Policing Reform and Crime in Nineteenth Century London*, PhD., London School of Economics, 2001.
[2] See T. Gurr, P. Grabosky and R. Hula; *The Politics of Crime and Conflict: A Comparative History of Four Cities*, Sage Publications, Beverly Hills, 1977.
[3] All figures are taken from *European Sourcebook of Crime and Criminal Justice*, Council of Europe, Strasbourg, 1999.

mean of 172 in 1996) and rape (11.1 compared with a mean of 6.6); robbery (143 and 63); theft (6,835 and 2,415); the theft of motor vehicles (951 and 307); and burglary (2,243 and 935). Identified as contributing quite disproportionately to those statistics were a small group of young, careering, high offenders,[4] reflecting in small measure, perhaps, the greater ineptitude and more public and exposed nature of their crimes,[5] and of their offences against public order in particular:[6] 40 per cent of offenders cautioned or convicted for an indictable offence in 1997 were under twenty-one, and the peak age of offending was eighteen.[7] It was the young, above all, who came significantly to be identified with the problem of crime in the political mind.

To be sure, those figures do require cautious interpretation: they reflect, *inter alia*, differences in how and what acts were defined as criminal; the greater visibility of certain crimes; the propensities of victims and witnesses to report crimes to the police; and police enforcement procedures, recording practices, and counting rules. One important source of qualification was to be provided by the findings of the British Crime Survey, inaugurated in 1982 and then applied at roughly two-yearly intervals thereafter, which calculated by mass survey how many private adults in England and Wales had been victims of crime in the previous year, whether or not they had reported their experience to the police. The crime surveys were themselves acknowledged to be in need of careful reading: they could record only what people *claimed* to have been crimes, and their respondents' interpretive practices required (but did not undergo) deciphering; they were beset by inevitable problems not only of memory loss and confusion but also of what was called the 'telescoping' of events which could distort estimates of when crimes had actually taken place; they were initially poor at securing information about embarrassing and stigmatizing crimes, particularly sexual offences, which people might have

---

[4] 7% of males who had been convicted of six or more offences accounted for 65% of all convictions. 'Criminal and custodial careers of those born in 1953, 1958 and 1963', Home Office Statistical Bulletin, 32/89.

[5] See I. Loader; *Youth, Policing and Democracy*, Macmillan, Basingstoke, 1996.

[6] See J. Foster; *Villains: Crime and Community in the Inner City*, Routledge, London, 1990.

[7] *Information on the Criminal Justice System in England and Wales: Digest 4*, Home Office, London, 1999, p. 21.

been hesitant to confide to the strangers who were interviewing them;[8] they neglected crimes against corporate victims, including shops and shopkeepers;[9] they at first neglected those under 16, a population heavily exposed to crime;[10] and they were inevitably poor at reaching other heavily victimized but elusive groups, including squatters, immigrants, and the homeless. Yet they did manage to unearth a substantial volume of unreported and unrecorded incidents of victimization—the estimate was that a mere 25 per cent of crimes were ultimately recorded in the official statistics—and they also served as a useful check and comparison in the making of attempts to assess trends in crime over time.

After a seemingly inexorable and prolonged rise in recorded crime, the rate of increase in official crime rates began to falter in 1994 and then fell. There was a drop of 8 per cent in 1996–7 alone. At first it was conjectured that the decline was perhaps more apparent than real, an artefact of shifts in computing practices,[11] but the complementary British Crime Surveys revealed that there had also been parallel changes in the population's experience of victimization. For instance, between 1995 and 1997, and for comparable offences, the number of recorded offences fell by 12 per cent whilst the British Crime Survey showed a fall of 15 per cent,[12] and similar falls were shown by many other countries,[13] including those in the European Union,[14] at much the same time. Although the decline in

[8] The problem was to be resolved by the use of machines which allowed respondents to answer questions discreetly.

[9] For a study of the high rates of victimization of commercial establishments, see, for instance, *Crime against retail premises in 1993*, Home Office Research Findings, No. 26; and *Crime against manufacturing premises in 1993*, Home Office Research Findings, No. 27.

[10] See S. Anderson *et al.*; *Cautionary Tales—A Study of Young People and Crime in Edinburgh*, University of Edinburgh, Edinburgh, 1992.

[11] The preferred explanation at the time of the election which was, for instance, offered by John Benyon in interview on Channel 4 News, 23 April 1997.

[12] *The 1998 British Crime Survey: England and Wales (Home Office Statistical Bulletin 21/98)*.

[13] *Tenth United Nations Congress on the Prevention of Crime and the Treatment of Offenders: Crime and Justice: Meeting the Challenges of the Twenty-first Century*, Vienna, Austria, 10–17 April 2000: 'The state of crime and criminal justice worldwide, report of the Secretary-General', 15 December 1999.

[14] See G. Barclay and C. Tavares; *International comparisons of criminal justice statistics 2000*, Home Office Statistical Bulletin, 05/02, July 2002, p. 3.

crime had not been widely noticed by those questioned in the 1998 British Crime Survey, it did appear that there had been a companion lessening of their concern about crime: the proportion of people reported to be 'very worried' about crime had also fallen between 1996 and 1998 from 22 per cent to 19 per cent for burglary, 19 per cent to 18 per cent for street robbery and 25 per cent to 21 per cent for theft of cars. Yet 18 per cent of women (31 per cent of women over sixty) and 3 per cent of men still said that they felt very unsafe on the streets at night.[15]

Falls there may have been, but the volume of crime and the fear of crime were absolutely and relatively large in the 1980s and early 1990s, and rates in England and Wales ranked high in international comparisons. Crime surveys conducted in eleven industrialized countries, and reported in 1997, revealed that the British confronted the highest risk of having one's car stolen, of having goods stolen from one's car, of burglary, and of contact crime. There was said to be in England and Wales a high anxiety about burglary, the highest fear of crime on the street, and highest consciousness of home security.[16] There was anxiety about public 'incivilities', exemplified by the public drinking of alcohol and by gatherings of adolescents,[17] that seemed to signal a loss of formal and informal control over public space. Moreover, the falls had not been uniform: whilst there had been a decline in the overall rate, some recorded crimes had risen, and, most worrying, they included violence against the person (by 5 per cent) and sexual offences (by 6 per cent).[18] So much political and media capital was to be made of those latter figures at the time of the election that it was quite possible on occasion to overlook the wider general trends altogether.

[15] *Concern about crime: findings from the 1998 British Crime Survey,* Home Office Research Findings No. 83, 1999.

[16] P. Mayhew and J. van Dijk; *Criminal Victimisation in Eleven Industrialised Countries,* Ministry of Justice, the Netherlands, 1997.

[17] See NACRO; *Nuisance Problems in Brixton,* NACRO, London, 1997 and T. Budd and L. Sims; 'Antisocial behaviour and disorder: findings from the 2000 British Crime Survey', Home Office, 2001. 32% of those questioned in the crime survey flagged 'teenagers hanging around' as a 'big problem' in their neighbourhood.

[18] *Criminal Statistics, England and Wales, 1997,* The Stationery Office, London, 1998.

Offending seemed to be no longer exceptional, having become part of the furniture of everyday life,[19] and the supreme, driving imperative of the politics of law and order at the time was to cut the crime rate through a mix of prevention programmes; enhanced technological surveillance; reforms of the workings of criminal justice agencies, and of the youth justice system especially; more severe sentencing; and the restoration of what was called 'public confidence in the criminal justice system'.[20] The 'attrition' of cases moving through the criminal justice system was a particular concern—under half of the offences known to victims were estimated to be reported; only half of those reported offences were recorded; a fifth of recorded offences were 'cleared up'; and only 3 per cent of those offences resulted in a caution or conviction in 1997[21]—and there was an insistent focus on increasing the number of convictions by coaxing victims and witnesses to report crime and testify in court. John Halliday, Director of Criminal Policy at the Home Office in 1997, recalled:

I mean I think there was a very powerful sense, I remember discussing with people in the very, in the early 1990s, of a loss of confidence in the criminal justice system across the piece. There was the erosion of confidence in it as a crime control mechanism which research had kind of brought home to a much wider audience, the attrition chart and all the rest...I think most people recognised whether by instinct, whether instinctively or intellectually or whatever, that the whole system depended on public confidence.

Partly as a result of the unremitting work of Victim Support[22] and its progeny, the Victims Steering Group, and its early allies, such as the Home Office official, David Faulkner,[23] who had been lodged inside

---

[19] See J. Young; *The Exclusive Society*, Sage, London, 1999, p. 30.

[20] For example, a draft paper for the Criminal Justice Consultative Council, Victims and Witnesses, 18 September 1996, talked about a 'growing recognition that victims of crime are vital to the effective operation of the criminal justice system'. Public confidence suffers otherwise, it was noted.

[21] *Information on the criminal justice system in England and Wales: Digest 4*, Home Office, London 1999, p. 29.

[22] In 1997–8, Victim Support's 15,310 volunteers were organized into 386 local schemes in England, Wales and Northern Ireland and offered support to 1,164,500 victims.

[23] Much of that history is given in my *Helping Victims of Crime, op. cit.*, and *After Homicide, op. cit.*

the core policy-making circles of the criminal justice system; partly as a result of dawning apprehensions about the consequences of alienating victims and witnesses from the criminal justice system;[24] partly as a response to international declarations about the rights of victims;[25] and partly as a result of the apparently unending discovery of hitherto little-recognized but suffering groups of victims, such as abused children, victims of racist attacks,[26] and battered and raped women; victims of crime had come gradually to occupy a position of greater symbolic and practical salience within the criminal justice system.[27] An official of the Lord Chancellor's Department remarked to me in July 1998 at the Victim Support Annual Conference, 'who'd have thought ten years ago we'd have been talking about victims and witnesses!'

---

[24] Evidenced by the spate of conferences organized on the theme. For example, the Home Office Criminal Justice Conference; Victim and Witness Care, 31 October-1 November 1995; and the Hampshire, Dorset and the Isle of Wight Criminal Justice Liaison Committee, Victims and Witnesses, Conference Report, 7 February 1997; and the Criminal Justice Consultative Council, Summary of Activities 1996–97. A major policy document was to be issued in response to a 1995 Efficiency Scrutiny by the Trials Issues Group in July 1996. The 'Statement of National Standards of Witness Care in the Criminal Justice System: Taking forward standards of witness care through Local Service Level Agreements', adumbrated a number of principles, including witnesses being asked to testify only if essential; trial dates being arranged for witnesses where possible; provision being made for the special needs of witnesses; and enhanced sensitivity. Where there were special needs, it was stated, the police and defence should consider how those needs should be addressed, for example, by the provision of a key worker or a support worker. Priority was to be given to cases of cruelty, sexual abuse, or violence involving children. There was a need to be responsive to the special needs of ethnic minority groups. Separate accommodation should be provided for defence and prosecution witnesses where possible.
[25] See A. Crawford and J. Goodey (eds.); *Integrating a Victim Perspective Within Criminal Justice: International debates*, Ashgate, Aldershot, 2000, p. 19.
[26] See *CJA Section 95: Race and the Criminal Justice System 1995*, Home Office, London, March 1996. Victim Support had supported 38% more victims of racist attacks in 1997 than in the previous year (Victim Support Annual Report 1998).
[27] The changes, said John Spencer, 'have been more paper than practical'. Law makers have been unwilling to give victims solid rights and a standing in the prosecution process. J. Spencer; 'Improving the Position of the Victim in English Criminal Procedure', paper given at International Conference on the Rights of the Accused, Crime Control, and Protection of Victims, Hebrew University of Jerusalem, 19–23 December 1993, pp. 1, 13.

The criminal justice agencies and their committees were beginning more fully to discuss victims.[28] So were politicians.[29] John Major, the Prime Minister, held a special seminar in 1995 on criminal justice and the citizen to identify ways of improving services to witnesses, victims, defendants, and others, and that was to have consequences that I shall trace in Chapter 1. Publishing a report of the Parliamentary All Party Penal Affairs Group in July 1996,[30] Alun Michael, its chairman, then in opposition but soon to be a Home Office Minister, declared that 'The position of the victim still gives rise for concern. More needs to be done to put the victim at the centre of the criminal justice process.'

## Committees

There were private and public stocktaking inquiries into the workings of the criminal justice system that reveal something of how the

[28] Helen Reeves was to tell the Magistrates' Association in 1996 that 'victims are very topical', and she proceeded to list how the Court User Committees, the Criminal Justice Liaison Committee, and the Trials Issues Group had recently considered the needs of victims and witnesses. 'All are now talking about victims and how they should be treated...' Helen Reeves; 'The Role of Magistrates in Relation to Victims and Witnesses', The Magistrates' Association; *Victims and Witnesses*, Summer Conference, July 1996.

[29] Press release on PAPPAG; *Increasing the Rights of Victims of Crime*, 23 July 1996.

[30] *Increasing the Rights of Victims of Crime* recommended, *inter alia*, that more money should be allotted by the Government to Victim Support to pay for the co-ordinators of local schemes; an annual review of awards made by the Criminal Injuries Compensation Board; a discontinuation of reducing criminal injuries compensation because of the applicant's unspent criminal convictions; that information given in mitigation should be disclosable to the prosecution; that the Crown Prosecution Service should inform victims directly of its decisions and the reasons for giving them; that Victim Impact Statements (to be discussed in Chapter 4) should be extended nationally; that the Victim Support-administered witness service to be extended to all Magistrates' Courts; that there should be a provision of television links for child victims of violent and sexual offences; that the relatives of homicide victims should receive expenses for attending court; and that victims should be allowed to make representations to decision-making bodies charged with releasing 'mentally disordered offenders'. David Maclean, the Home Office Minister, replied to say, amongst other matters, that preparations for victim impact statements were in train; that informing victims was a police responsibility, and not to be devolved on the Crown Prosecution Services, because of resource implications; that the Government was considering extending the witness service to the Magistrates' Courts, but that there were, again, resource implications.

victim was being constructed in official circles during that period. The position of victims was ill-defined and contested in the mid-1990s. Who were eligible to be treated as victims was undecided. What their entitlements should be was unsettled. How much encouragement should be given to their alleged demands was unresolved. Different segments of the criminal justice system were manifestly at odds about how best to respond, but they *were* in accord that it was imperative to exercise extraordinary caution whatever might be done. On the one hand, victims were taken to have expectations and demands that had to be met if the criminal justice system was to continue to function. On the other hand, it was understood that an imprudent response would carry risks of victims becoming over-mighty and upsetting the integrity of criminal justice. It is with the unfolding of that dilemma that much of the rest of this book will be occupied. Let me offer two illustrations, one brief and the other more extended.

The Criminal Justice Consultative Council met in conference in March 1995, presided over by its chairman, Lord Rose, a judge at the Criminal Division of the Court of Appeal, to publicize its work and the work of its twenty-four Area Criminal Justice Liaison Committees. Victims and witnesses surfaced with the other preoccupations of the moment. The Council and the Committees were reported by Lord Rose to maintain close contact with 'many different bodies such as Victim Support and NACRO . . . underlin[ing] the fact that, at the heart of the criminal justice system was the central requirement that it should cater for the different needs of, on the one hand, the victim and, on the other, the wrongdoer. The public expected that victims would be able to give their account in court without undue delay, that they would be kept informed of the progress of their case and that prior to, during and after the trial they would be treated with sensitivity.'[31]

Barbara Mills, the then Director of Public Prosecutions (and later, on her retirement, a trustee of Victim Support) told the conference that the criminal justice system could not work without co-operation and evidence from victims and witnesses: 'Over the last 10–15 years the importance of victims and witnesses had at last been recognised

---

[31] 'The Work of the Criminal Justice Consultative Council and Area Committees: A report of the conference hosted by Rt Hon Lord Justice Rose . . . 3 March 1995', Home Office Special Conferences Unit, London.

and steps taken to treat them properly.' The Crown Prosecution Service would, she said, challenge the unjust mitigation that victims could find so offensive. Considerations of bail recommendations would take the victim's 'concerns' into account. But the Service could not and would not act for individual victims or allow victims to decide whether a prosecution should take place: 'The decision was an objective one for the CPS, taken against legal criteria, and not a matter for the victim.'

Sir Louis Blom-Cooper, a barrister, the newly appointed Chairman of Victim Support and, for practical purposes, the victims' representative, recited Victim Support's statement of rights that had been published the month before:[32] the right to be 'free of the burden of decision making about offenders'; the right to provide and receive information; the rights to protection and compensation; and rights to respect, recognition, and support. But he laid no claim to the victim's right to be consulted or to play any part in the court process other than act as a witness. And he was quite equivocal about victim impact statements, at that time being 'piloted', wondering to whom it was that they should be issued, whether they could be challenged in court, and if they should be regarded as confidential.

## JUSTICE

Around the time of the General Election of May 1 1997, another body, JUSTICE,[33] was conducting a review of the position of the victim in the criminal justice system, calling it a thorough examination of all stages of the victim's interaction with the criminal justice process.[34] The review was to lack political and practical impact when it was published because it was eclipsed in 1996 by the issuing of a new *Victim's Charter* that had stolen its thunder and anticipated many of its recommendations[35] (Kate Akester of JUSTICE wrote to

---

[32] *The Rights of Victims of Crime*, Victim Support, London, 1995.

[33] JUSTICE, the British section of the International Commission of Jurists, was founded in 1957 after lawyers observed trials in Hungary and South Africa.

[34] JUSTICE annual report 1998, p. 20.

[35] An ACPO representative on the Victims Steering Group was to write in response to the Committee's request for evidence that he was surprised at the timing, given that the Victims Steering Group had been addressing the majority of issues raised for over a year. Much of the Committee's work would be superseded by the Charter, he concluded.

her colleagues in August 1996, 'The Victim's Charter has thrown us off-course. We should . . . produce a shorter report dealing with the main contentious issues raised by it. We risk being overtaken by events'[36]. But the review nevertheless constitutes a useful and timely exploration in cameo of the stances adopted by criminal justice agencies at precisely the point that a new Labour Government came into office.

The decision to undertake the review had taken place in 1994, when the activist groups of so-called 'angry victims' were objects of marked media interest,[37] it was designed to be a counterweight to what was feared to be a looming reactionary politics of crime and the victim, and it was yet another product of David Faulkner's enterprise.[38] Kate Akester of JUSTICE recalled in July 1998 that:

It was David Faulkner's idea originally. He was a member of the council, and he thought it would be a good area to move into. And when I came [in May 1994] I thought it would be too, that in a sense it would be important to try to make a contribution from another perspective because it looked at one stage as though, if you like, the Right were going to take over victims. I don't think that's happened. But you know, we thought it might be useful to put in a contribution from a different perspective . . . David in particular thought that it would be a good idea to go at it from a more moderate point of view, and from a point of view of actually trying to achieve practical change because, this is the sort of thing that JUSTICE is best at.

[36]  Letter from Kate Akester, 1 August 1996.
[37]  The peak year of media attention had been 1993. See *After Homicide, op. cit.*
[38]  David Faulkner had retired from the Home Office in 1992. His own conclusions, tendered to the Committee as 'Principles and Accountability' in August 1996, were that much had been done in the last fifteen years as a result of the influence exerted by Victim Support and other non-governmental organizations on Government; an increased awareness and sympathy from Government and from service managers; a spontaneous sympathy from services at operational level and increased media attention. The Victim's Charters had made a significant contribution. But change was easier to gauge in terms of procedure than victim satisfaction, public confidence, or social stability. Public satisfaction may actually have declined. Indeed, there were questions to be asked about the extent to which the criminal justice system could deliver satisfaction to victims. What might be needed was a proper structure of accountability and a framework of principles in which policy and practice could be developed; and a greater accountability to victims secured through the development of clearly stated objectives, standards, and expectations; performance monitoring, independent inspection, and audit; an effective means of remedying mistakes; a unified system of complaints; a commissioner for victims with powers to inspect and report; designated local liaison officers for each service; and formal rights of appeal.

The rise of victims, JUSTICE was to claim, had opened up fundamental, troubling and unchallenged prospects for the criminal justice system:

...and its nature, purpose, scope, structure and accountability. If victims are to be given formal rights, or formal opportunities to influence decisions which affect the defendant or the offender—as the Government seems to be suggesting—the means by which they are exercised, and the safeguards they require, will have a profound effect on the nature of the adversarial system...Few of these implications have so far been examined, or even appreciated, by the government or those who would be affected by them.[39]

The Committee held its first meeting in the beginning of December 1994, first called for evidence in August 1995, organized a series of seminars in 1996 and published its report in May 1998.[40] In that process, at first and second hand, it came to encounter a mass of discordant, wary, and sometimes hostile official representations of victims. Michael Naish, co-ordinator of the Victim Support Witness Service at the Central Criminal Court, described quite pithily, for example, how the courts were insensitive to their 'cannon fodder'.[41]

In the Committee's papers was a Probation Circular[42] requiring probation officers to make contact within two months of sentence with the victims of serious offences whose offenders had been incarcerated. Probation officers were above all required to approach the family when the release of a life sentence prisoner was being contemplated. The circular recognized members of the family as victims where the offence had resulted in death or incapacity or where age or personal circumstances made it advisable to contact a friend or kin. But it was also markedly cautious. Victims were to be addressed face to face to 'update information' and ascertain their views, but it was to be made clear that they were not being invited to contribute to the decision about the date of release. Not only might their contribution lead to intimidation of the victim but the decision

---

[39] 'The Role of the Victim in the Criminal Justice Process: Why JUSTICE formed the Committee', undated.

[40] *Victims in the criminal justice process*, JUSTICE, London, May 1998.

[41] Minutes of the JUSTICE Committee on the Role of the Victim in the Criminal Justice Process, 5 April 1995.

[42] 61/1995 of 23 August 1995 in conformity with paragraph 13 of the 1995 national standard for supervision before and after release.

itself was strictly a matter for the Parole Board and the Home Secretary[43] (for its part, the Parole Board told JUSTICE that some victims wanted to convey their views about release but it did not believe that they were objective enough to do so and there was a need to balance the victim's and offender's interests in the matter of disclosing information[44]).

The new involvement of the probation service with victims could be sensed as disquieting. The Association of Chief Officers of Probation declared in 1996 that the service should 'take the needs of victims seriously and work to the principles of restorative justice' but there should be no direct contact with victims as part of pre-sentence report preparation. Neither was it the responsibility of the 'pre-sentence report writer' to assess the degree of loss or harm suffered by specific victims.[45] Indeed, the Deputy Chief Probation Officer for Essex informed JUSTICE that the service was uncomfortable about victims playing any more decisive role in the criminal justice system: probation officers were not trained to comfort victims and feared that they could re-open old wounds. Probation was not the appropriate service to offer solace to a distressed victim. There were, it was claimed, two contradictory strands in probation thinking, that probation work was centred on offenders and liaison with victims muddled and confused that work, on the one hand, and, on the other, that victims got 'a raw deal' and the probation service and Victim Support had much to offer one another. Only very recently had those competing demands of offenders and victims even been considered at all.[46]

The Crown Prosecution Service talked to JUSTICE about the need to retain public faith in the criminal justice system and of its obligations to make provision for the 'proper care and treatment' of victims and witnesses. Those obligations required, in their turn, the gathering of information about victims and the effect which crime

[43] West Yorkshire Probation Service: 'Life Sentence Offenders; Practice Guidance for Implementing the Recommendations of the Victim's Charter', 15 October 1993.

[44] The JUSTICE Report on 'The Role of the Victim in the Criminal Justice Process': evidence of the Parole Board, 31 October 1995.

[45] Association of Chief Officers of Probation; ACOP Position Statement on Probation Services and the Victims of Crime, February 1996.

[46] The JUSTICE Report on 'The Role of the Victim in the Criminal Justice Process': Deputy Chief Probation Officer, Essex Probation Service, briefing for JUSTICE Working Party, 9 February 1995.

had had upon them, but the information resided in police files, witness statements, and compensation forms, and it was not the business of the CPS directly to collect or supply it. The Service was furthermore reluctant to afford the victim a greater role in the criminal process: 'For the victim to decide whether or not a prosecution should continue, would be to return to a system of private prosecutions, similar to that which existed in the 19th Century, where prosecutions depended on the attitude, fortitude and resources of the prosecutor. Prosecution and punishment by the Crown for criminal offences is recognition of the principle that crimes are offences against society as a whole, and not only against the individual victim. To return the decision to prosecute to the victim, would break that link.'[47]

*Pari passu*, the Law Society, the professional association of solicitors, the body of lawyers heavily engaged in representing defendants, told JUSTICE that prosecutions took place in the public interest and that victims' needs formed no part of that interest. The Society may have endorsed the recommendation of the 1993 Royal Commission on Criminal Justice[48] that victims should as far as practicable be kept informed of the progress and outcome of cases, but it also held that, where their views *were* ascertained, the victims' interest should always be overruled by that public interest. Indeed, the very standing of victims *as* victims could not be confirmed until a very late stage, and it was only then, when an accusation had been proved, that they could be treated with special favour.[49]

There was a paper in the Committee's files on the progress made in the 'piloting' of the victim statements that had emanated from the Prime Minister's seminar on criminal justice and the citizen of June 1995.[50] A working group conceived in that seminar and chaired by Barbara Mills, the Director of Public Prosecutions, reported that statements would give the victim an opportunity to be heard; enable professionals to take the victim's interest into account in decisions and cautioning, bail and charging; aid the prosecution management

[47] Crown Prosecution Service Submission of evidence to the 'Justice' Committee: 'The Role of the Victim in the Criminal Justice Process', undated, p. 4.

[48] *Report of the Royal Commission on Criminal Justice*, Cm. 2263, HMSO, London, 1993.

[49] The JUSTICE Report on 'The Role of the Victim in the Criminal Justice Process': response from the Law Society, 1 November 1995.

[50] 'Victim Statements', no date, no provenance.

of the case, including the refuting of misleading mitigation; and inform the court for sentencing purposes. Victim statements should be optional, partly because they had to be open to challenge by the defence. They were best written in the victim's own words, and not given orally: those upon whom the effect was the greatest were held to be least able to give an oral statement and there was a risk of an unduly emotive impact on the court. The very definition of a victim entitled to report the impact of crime was as yet unresolved: it was not clear, for instance, whether the bereaved should be allowed to describe the impact of murder or manslaughter. The working party went further. Victim statements were supposed to affect sentencing but that was only part of their purpose. Vulnerable to anxiety and the risk of intimidation, victims should not be required to share the burden of decision-makers (and here could be heard the voice of Victim Support and its statement of rights[51]).

JUSTICE was informed in December 1995 by Christine Stewart, at that time head of the then Procedures and Victims Unit, that the Home Office was so heavily occupied with work on victims, including revising the *Victim's Charter*, that it could supply only a short account of its activities. The Government, she said, was about to ensure that agencies would report on their achievement of standards of service to the Victims Steering Group (which I shall also discuss in the third chapter). It had produced a victims of crime leaflet, revised in October 1994; an information pack for families of homicide victims in November 1995;[52] a probation circular on contact with victims (which I have already noted); and a leaflet for witnesses attending court. There had been steady progress towards realizing the *Victim's Charter* standard on keeping victims informed, but more improvement was necessary. The new Charter would define more clearly what developments the victim could expect to be

[51] Teresa Reynolds of Victim Support joined the Committee on 3 July 1995. Victim Support had submitted the European Forum's Statement of Victim Rights, of which it was an author. Victims' rights, it was argued, should be more clearly defined and treated as of comparable weight to those of the offender. Victims should not be obliged to be responsible for decisions about the offender but their interests should be protected. Their rights included respect and recognition; the right to communicate with justice authorities, victims being able to provide the information they wanted to give in their own words to ensure that they have a right to be heard, for compensation purposes, to alert authorities to risk, to take victims' interests into account in decision-making, and to refute malicious mitigation.

[52] The history of the 'homicide pack' is given in my *After Homicide, op. cit.*

informed about: the decision to charge or caution; the substantial alteration or dropping of charges; the date and final outcome of trial; vulnerable victims would be told about bail; and how victims could get redress.

And so it went on. There were submissions from the Police Superintendents Association and NACRO; from the National Society for the Prevention of Cruelty to Children, which was opposed to the proposition that the term 'victim' be enlarged to include indirect victims, and in favour of allowing a child to provide information but not to take part in decisions about sentence or parole and conditional release;[53] the Magistrates' Association, which was opposed to victims being allowed to address the court during proceedings and the idea of a victim's ombudsman (it would be 'just another tier of administration');[54] the Association of Directors of Social Services, which argued that it was tempting to enlarge the definition of victim, but that the term should be restricted to identified victims of crime to ensure that the 'net' was not spread too far, and that victims should not be allowed to determine decision whether to prosecute, what pleas to accept, and what sentence should be imposed;[55] the Police Federation, supporting the idea of an ombudsman but averse to the proposal that victims should have a part in sentencing decisions;[56] and others.

Looking back, the Committee's chairwoman, Joanna Shapland, claimed that the position of the victim had been something of an anomaly in the 1990s, still apart from the criminal justice system and not subject to the public sector reforms that had swept through much of the rest of the State.[57] Hesitating to talk about rights, her report recommended that the treatment of victims should be regulated by transparent public standards like any other group subject to government policy; dominated by clear 'legitimate expectations' of what services they were entitled to receive, and, in particular, by measures

[53] Evidence by the NSPCC, 19 October 1995.

[54] The JUSTICE Report on 'The Role of the Victim in the Criminal Justice Process': evidence by the Magistrates' Association, North East Branch, 25 October 1995.

[55] Evidence by the Association of Directors of Social Services, 1 November 1995.

[56] The JUSTICE Report on 'The Role of the Victim in the Criminal Justice Process': evidence by the Police Federation, September 1995.

[57] J. Shapland; 'Victims and Criminal Justice', in A. Crawford and J. Goodey (eds.); *Integrating a Victim Perspective Within Criminal Justice: International debates*, Ashgate, Aldershot, 2000, p. 148.

to increase support and information so that victims could 'properly carry out their roles and responsibilities'; and a Commissioner for Victims of Crime to discharge 'key functions' such as reporting to Parliament, undertaking thematic reviews of the experiences of victims and witnesses, and acting as the ultimate point of reference for complaints. Many of those recommendations were remarkably prescient, and their echo will be heard in Chapter 10, but it is the evidence on which they were based that it is chiefly of interest here.

It may be seen that possible changes in the future standing of the victim were being approached gingerly, hedged about with reservations, checks, and doubts, and certainly with no zeal by criminal justice agencies in the 1990s. There was not even any assurance about who victims might be[58] and whether they should encompass members of the family or intimates of the 'direct' victim. A member of the Committee wondered at an early stage in its deliberations whether the term should include major public companies or victims of insider trading. It might be best, it was thought, to 'unfurl' dimensions as the Committee went along, looking perhaps at how victims defined themselves.[59]

Conceptions of proper order and procedure seemed to be under threat. Victims were viewed by most with an ambivalence, nervousness, and suspicion. They had to be wooed but were none the less newcomers, outsiders in the formal world of criminal justice, liable to outbursts of emotion and unreason, undisciplined by the restraints that controlled the professional,[60] and capable of disturbing the balance of forces and proper practice of the trial (captured by lawyers in their concept of the 'equality of arms'). The notion of rights occasioned especial unease: it was not in general vogue in the early 1990s,[61] and the prospect of endowing so problematic a group

[58] Later, the Ministers who entered the new New Labour administration would have added their own categories: Lord Williams, as a former advocate with defence experience, interested in human rights matters, would have included defendants and prisoners as victims of crime. Alun Michael would have added the families, neighbours and associates of 'direct' victims, particularly in high crime areas.

[59] Minutes of the meeting of the JUSTICE Committee on the Role of the Victim in the Criminal Justice Process, 23 January 1995.

[60] See my *The Social World of an English Crown Court*, Clarendon Press, Oxford, 1993.

[61] David Faulkner observed at a meeting of the JUSTICE Committee on the Role of the Victim in the Criminal Justice Process on the 4 August 1995 that priority should be

as victims with rights in such a delicate area as criminal procedure was especially fraught. Victims were as yet people with 'absolutely no locus standi'[62] who were still taken by many trial lawyers, legal advisers, and judges to be little more than *alleged* victims ('alleged', that is, until the delivery of a verdict of guilt), or mere witnesses to an offence committed against society conceived as the body politic, Crown, or State.[63] The JUSTICE Committee had itself been uncertain about what terminology it should employ, oscillating between 'rights', 'expectations', and 'duties',[64] and plumping in the end for 'legitimate expectations'. One member complained in May 1995 that 'The term ["rights"] has cropped up from time to time during our meetings, and the literature ... bandies the term around constantly with no real discussion as to exactly what is meant by it. The problem with lack of clarity in definition is that it raises false expectations, creates confusion, and sows doubt ... '.

There was the lawyers' fear that rights for victims could be purchased only by compromising defendants' rights[65] and the fastidiously balanced procedures of an adversarial system that pitted the State against the defendant.[66] There was the penal reformer's engrained fear of the spectre of the empowered and baleful victim-vigilante who would demand increased punishments.[67] The prisoners' campaigning group, the Howard League, for example, issued a position paper acknowledging that victims were what it somewhat

given to the process or rights questions rather than support or service questions but, he said, the Committee would have to remember that 'rights' are politically unfashionable at the moment, especially if not accompanied by duties or obligations, but, he remarked, 'we can let matters take their course'.

[62] M. Brienen and E. Hoegen; *Victims of Crime in 22 European Criminal Justice Systems*, Wolf Legal Productions, Nijmegen, the Netherlands, 2000, p. 285.

[63] The matter was put succinctly by a judge, the chairman of an area committee of the Criminal Justice Consultative Council in March 1995: 'The Crown acted for the State. Many victims were under the misapprehension that the Crown was acting for them.' *The work of the criminal justice system*, Home Office, London, 1995, p. 6.

[64] Draft Plan for Rest of Report—September 1996, p. 9.

[65] See A. Sanders and R. Young; *Criminal Justice*, Butterworths, London, 1994, p. 24.

[66] See H. Fenwick; 'Procedural "Rights" of Victims of Crime: Public or Private Ordering of the Criminal Justice Process?', *Modern Law Review*, May 1997, Vol. 60, No. 3, pp. 317–33.

[67] See S. Walklate; 'Victims, Crime Prevention and Social Control', in R. Reiner and M. Cross (eds.); *Beyond Law and Order: Criminal Justice Policy and Politics into the 1990s*, Macmillan, Houndsmills, Hants, 1991, p. 208.

disparagingly called 'a growth industry', declaring its apprehensions about the likely consequences of victim impact statements and concluding that it was 'concerned that the political, academic and media interest in the plight of and provisions for victims of crime is no more than clever posturing.... Victims of crime may be little more than a political tool. Indeed it may be that some of the measures taken in the name of enhancing victims' position simply justify a more punitive criminal justice response.'[68] Such fears about possible damage to due process and proper procedure had long been shared by officials and politicians, leading the United Kingdom Government to enter a reservation on the 1985 United Nations Declaration on the Rights of Victims to the effect that the rights of victims should not extend to sentencing, case disposal, or the course of trial.[69]

And Conservative politicians had had other apprehensions as well in the financially austere 1980s and 1990s about the implications of awarding greater prominence to support for victims. Acceding to victims' needs and demands could cost money, and there was some discussion within the Home Office towards the end of 1993 about whether it should be offenders rather than the State who could be made to pay compensation to the victim for property losses not covered by the Criminal Injuries Compensation Board and for injuries below the Criminal Injuries Compensation Board threshold. Indeed, just before the election, the Government decided to freeze its grant to Victim Support for two years at the level set for 1996–7, and it announced in November 1996 that the freeze would be extended for a third year, 1998–9.[70]

The environment of policy-making for victims would be continually shaped by the play of those dual forces: by the Home Office and agencies' larger quest for greater efficiency in securing convictions and reducing crime and the lesser quest for ameliorating the victims' lot, on the one hand, and by the mass of financial, conceptual, and procedural qualms about reform, on the other. Whilst the bulk of those working in the criminal justice system might have been prepared to acknowledge victims conventionally defined and concede

[68] *Information: Victims of Crime*, The Howard League, London, 1997, p. 11.
[69] The special outsider status of the victim in the Anglo-American adversarial system has always engendered such claims for exemptions from international treaties affecting victims and designed principally to deal with inquisitorial justice.
[70] Report by the Victim Support Local Funding Panel to the National Council and the Home Office on the year 1996–7.

that they were entitled to better treatment, they were uncertain about how widely that identity could or should be enlarged, and they were almost unanimous that victims should not have justiciable rights, be a party to proceedings, take a role in decision-making and consultation, and be heard in court unless it was as witnesses testifying under examination. Victims were, in effect, to be contained within a political *cordon sanitaire*.

## The 1997 General Election

Political debate during the 1997 election turned largely on the management of the economy, taxation, Britain's place in Europe, devolution, and public services.[71] There *was* some lesser talk about crime,[72] the two main parties attempting competitively to represent themselves as being 'tough on crime',[73] and especially on crime committed by the young (indeed Robert Reiner called the election 'a penal auction'[74]). Academic criminologists dwelt almost exclusively on what they called the 'authoritarian populism' of that talk,[75]

[71] See D. Downes and R. Morgan; 'Dumping the "Hostages to Fortune": The Politics of Law and Order in Post-War Britain', in M. Maguire *et al.* (eds.); *The Oxford Handbook of Criminology*, Second Edition, Oxford University Press, Oxford, 1997, p. 129; and D. Downes and R. Morgan; 'The Skeletons in the Cupboard: The Politics of Law and Order at the Turn of the Millennium', in M. Maguire *et al.* (eds.); *The Oxford Handbook of Criminology*, Third Edition, Oxford University Press, Oxford, 2002, p. 291.

[72] Downes and Morgan remarked that 'In neither the 1997 nor the 2001 elections did law and order issues assume a prominent place.' D. Downes and R. Morgan; 'The British General Election 2001', *Punishment and Society*, January 2002, Vol. 4, No. 1, p. 82. It is revealing that a content analysis of political stories featuring on the major television channels during the election campaign did not even list crime as a heading. P. Goddard *et al.*; 'Too Much of a Good Thing? Television in the 1997 Election Campaign', in I. Crewe *et al.* (eds.); *Why Labour Won the General Election of 1997*, Frank Cass, London, 1998, p. 156. And a number of the standard accounts of the election also ignore crime as an issue. See, for instance, P. Norris and N. Gavin; *Britain Votes 1997*, Oxford University Press, Oxford, 1997; and G. Evans and P. Norris (eds.); *Critical Elections*, Sage, London, 1999.

[73] The Conservatives' prime nostrums for crime were prison ('prison works') and the recruitment of more police officers, and Michael Howard promised that an additional 5,000 officers would be recruited if they were returned to power in an interview on Independent Television News, 23 April 1997.

[74] R. Reiner; 'Crime and Control in Britain', typescript, undated.

[75] See, for example, Loader and Sparks, who wrote 'In the Britain and the US . . . the last decade or so has seen the emergence of emotionally-charged and (ostensibly)

and, influenced a little by the writings of David Garland,[76] sub-
sumed the very few references that politicians made to victims[77]
within an analysis of what they identified as a new punitiveness.[78]
Theirs was a judgment endorsed by a number of senior officials in
the Home Office, one of whom said, 'I mean a lot of the rhetoric
around victims could mean being tougher on criminals or it could
mean being more sensitive to [them]. Actually when you look at the
justifications for the sentencing policy, I think you'll find it's more to
do with protecting the public, reduced victimisation and protecting
the public and less offending, less crime... the linkage was more
powerful there actually in terms of the given justifications for the
sentencing policies.'

But references to victims were sparse during the election. I could
discover a report of only one altercation between the Conservative
Home Secretary and his opponent about victims,[79] an instance,
perhaps, of what Butler and Kavanagh called Jack Straw's 'close
marking' of the Home Secretary, Michael Howard.[80] In the month
before polling, Michael Howard declared that a returned Conservative Government would give 'victims a greater role in the fate of

punitive lay sensibilities and media discourses towards crime, and of governments that
aim not to temper and tame such sentiments, but to give voice and—legislative—effect
to them.' I. Loader and R. Sparks; 'Contemporary Landscapes of Crime', in
M. Maguire et al. (eds.); The Oxford Handbook of Criminology, Third Edition,
Oxford University Press, Oxford, 2002, p. 86.

[76] Victims, claimed Garland have become emblematic of a strategy of 'punitive
segregation' within a new politics of punitive criminal justice: 'a privileged place [has
been given to] victims, though in fact that place is occupied by a projected, politicised
image of "the victim" rather than by the interests and opinions of victims themselves.
When introducing new measures of punitive segregation, elected officials now routinely invoke the feelings of "the victim" as a source of support and legitimation.'
D. Garland; The Culture of Control: Crime and Social Order in Contemporary
Society, Oxford University Press, Oxford, 2001, p. 143. Garland is thinking most
particularly of the United States, where he now teaches, but his thesis has been
generalized to the United Kingdom where it fits less comfortably.

[77] It is perhaps significant that the sub-categories under which law and order issues
were reproduced on the BBC's 1997 election web site were courts, prisons, juveniles
and police, but not victims or witnesses.

[78] See, for example, M. Ryan; Penal Policy and Political Culture in England and
Wales, Waterside Press, Winchester, 2003.

[79] Although there may have been more that had not been recorded on the web sites
and in the press.

[80] D. Butler and D. Kavanagh; The British General Election of 1997, Macmillan,
Basingstoke, 1997, p. 20.

criminals' through victim impact statements: 'I believe,' he said, 'it is right for the suffering of victims to be heard in our courts before sentences are handed down.' Jack Straw's *riposte* was that the Home Secretary's conversion to the needs of victims was 'belated': 'For years, Labour has stressed the need for the whole criminal justice system to be more victim focused. Victims of crime want real action, not warm words 18 years too late.'[81] It is notable, first, that Mr Howard was announcing as future policy that which, as we shall see, was neither belated nor new but had been in the making since 1995; that, second, the talk about victims had been instigated by the Home Secretary, and not by Jack Straw who, remaining 'on-message' as it was called, followed the New Labour party election strategy of concentrating only on a limited number of prescribed topics; and that, finally, the two politicians did not dissent about the need to improve the victim's lot.

The Conservative Party's election manifesto[82] devoted the final two of its twenty-nine pages to 'a safe and civil society' and 'law, order and security', reporting increased spending on the police and prisons and falls in recorded crime. It made no direct allusion to victims, but noted only that witness intimidation had been made a crime. There was no reference to victims in a Conservative Party election briefing on 'law and order'.[83] There was a very restricted treatment of victims in yet another publication, *Protecting the Public from Crime,* issued in January 1997:[84] just under two of its thirty six pages touched on the Government's contribution to Victim Support; its work on the *Victim's Charter*; and, at rather greater length, the treatment of rape victims, a problem that had been vividly and abruptly dramatized in the Ralston Edwards case in 1996 at precisely the time when the manifestos were being drafted. The response to that case was marked in the Conservative manifesto ('We will also allow a judge to stop a defendant personally cross-examining in rape cases') and was in time to give rise to *Speaking up for Justice,* a report whose history I shall narrate in Chapter 8.

[81] BBC web site, election97, 21 April 1997.

[82] *You can only be Sure with the Conservatives*, The Conservative Manifesto, 1997.

[83] Conservative Party briefing on Law and Order, no date, no provenance.

[84] 'Protecting the Public from Crime', *Politics Today*, No. 1, 31 January 1997, Conservative Research Department.

The New Labour party concentrated as little on victims in preparing its own election campaign.[85] Its eventual success in the election was to be attributed to caution, a firm discipline, and being 'ruthlessly on-message'[86] by maintaining an unwavering focus on a few pivotal issues. Butler and Kavanagh talked about 'the emphasis [being] on discipline, repetition and getting across key messages...'.[87] The 'five pledges', or what the adviser, Philip Gould, called 'small, concrete promises',[88] on which campaigners dwelt, inscribed on a 'pledge card' and 'used throughout the campaign',[89] were spread across the field of domestic policy, and they included but one criminal justice matter, 'fast track punishment for young offenders', which could be said only very obliquely to affect victims. The other pledges related to income tax (and the promise not to raise tax lest the party be thought improvident), cutting waiting lists for treatment by the health service, employment for the young, and, above all, education and the cutting of class sizes. Victims were not the subject of any of those pledges, and other statements and proposals were equally barren. A 1996 policy paper on crime prevention, written by Jack Straw, soon to be the incoming Home Secretary, and Alun Michael, the future Home Office Minister responsible for crime policy, made no mention of victims.[90] Another paper talked only of restorative justice,[91] about to become one of the new Home Secretary's 'big ideas' when in office,[92] and a theme I shall also pursue below in Chapter 7. When interviewed about law and order issues, and staying 'on-message', Jack Straw focused on the reform of the youth justice system, and principally on 'fast-tracking';[93] on

---

[85] I make no judgment at all about whether the balance was right.
[86] BBC News web site, Election battles 1945–1997.
[87] D. Butler and D. Kavanagh; *The British General Election of 1997, op. cit.*, p. 226.
[88] P. Gould; 'Why Labour Won', in I. Crewe *et al.* (eds.); *Why Labour Won the General Election of 1997, op. cit.*, p. 7.
[89] BBC News web site, Election battles 1945–1997.
[90] J. Straw and A. Michael; *Tackling the causes of crime: Labour's proposals to prevent crime and criminality*, October 1996.
[91] J. Straw and A. Michael; 'Tackling Youth Crime: Reforming Youth Justice', Road to the Manifesto, May 1996.
[92] See Jack Straw; 'Youth and Society Lecture', Royal Philanthropic Society, 27 November 1995, in which the shadow Home Secretary talked about reparation orders in promoting youth justice.
[93] In, for example, a speech delivered on 7 April 1997 in which he promised to halve the time currently taken up between the arrest and sentencing of young offenders.

increasing the numbers of police officers; reducing youth unemployment; and combining rehabilitation with punishment.[94]

The party allotted a short paragraph of its fifty-two page manifesto, *New Labour because Britain deserves better*, expressly to victims, a mere fifty-nine words out of a total of seventeen and a half thousand.[95] Claiming that victims 'are too often neglected by the criminal justice system', it promised to ensure that they would be kept fully informed of the progress of their case[96] and that there would be greater protection for victims in rape and serious sexual offence trials, and for those subject to intimidation.[97] Those proposals were very similar to policies already in train under the Conservative Government, a version of measures to keep victims informed stemming, as I have remarked, from John Major's 1995 seminar and known colloquially as the 'One Stop Shop',[98] greater protection from the political response to the Ralston

[94] Channel 4 News, 23 April 1997.

[95] Its summary of the manifesto was even more cursory: 'more crime means more victims. Under the Tories, everyone's a victim.'

[96] That recommendation had stemmed from the Labour Party's review of the work of the Crown Prosecution Service, *The Case for the Prosecution*, published in April 1997, which asserted that inadequate attention has been given to the victim's perspective in the preparation of cases and the prosecution of offenders. Victims were not, it was said, routinely informed about the progress of the case against the accused, dates of hearings, and the reasons for cases being dropped and downgraded. The Conservative Government may have belatedly set up pilot projects to enable victims to provide statements about the crime and will give them information on the progress of a case, 'but this is too little, too late'. The local Crown Prosecution Service should inform the victim directly of their decision as was recommended by the 1993 Royal Commission on Criminal Justice. It was not, the Labour Party held, the job of the police to tell victims about decisions made by another agency and with which they may not be in sympathy. Local Crown Prosecutors should be accountable for their own decisions and would be expected to explain to victims their reasons for discontinuing or downgrading cases. They should be more pro-active in meeting victims and witnesses, and there was a need for a greater emphasis on the impact of the crime.

[97] That commitment had stemmed from New Labour's concern about reports of neighbour disputes: see Labour; *A Quiet Life*, Tough action on criminal neighbours, 19 June 1995: 'Time and again, criminal elements avoid sanction by the court through intimidating victims and witnesses.' And it was to be echoed in a demand from the Local Authority Associations: 'Crime—the Local Solution: A Manifesto by the Local Authority Associations', 27 January 1997.

[98] The only difference being that the Labour Party believed it should be the Crown Prosecution Service and not the police who should provide information to victims.

Edwards trial,[99] and an offence of witness intimidation having been introduced in 1995. I shall deal with all those issues later in the book.

The manifesto had been drafted by Alun Michael, Jack Straw, and Lord Williams, and it reflected a systemic approach to problems of law and order in which crime reduction assumed overriding importance.[100] Alun Michael said:

I was very pleased with the approach that Tony [Blair] brought to it, which was really saying, 'this is a new area for me, I want to ask questions. Why? You know, what are the problems, what are the issues, what are we really trying to address?' And it was by asking those questions, I think, that the whole discussion moved onto the question of, instead of 'do the public want us to be tough on criminals,' you know, 'do we need heavier sentences'... looking at it purely in terms of selling policy. It was, 'what's it really about?' And that's what brought about the analysis that the continual argument about whether you are tough on punishment as the solution to crime or do you deal with the causes as the solution to crime was a total intellectual farce. And that what you had to say was that, if you're going to tackle crime, you have to deal with both the causes or the conditions which allow it to flourish and also make sure there are very clear signals about what happens if you offend are there. And that you need to do it quickly in terms of nipping things in the bud. And that the real reason for doing all this, is not because you want to reduce statistics but actually crime affects the victim. So it was actually very much an approach that was based on saying 'what's the reality?' The reality is that people's lives are being ruined. How do you stop people's lives being ruined... how do you stop that sort of offending happening? So it actually, you know, was a victim-centred approach really, although I'm not sure we would necessarily have categorised it as such right at the beginning...

[99] Labour politicians had been as disturbed by the Julia Mason case as had Michael Howard. Alun Michael told the Magistrates' Association in November 1997: 'Our manifesto included a specific commitment to provide greater protection for victims in rape and serious offence trials and those subject to intimidation. In Opposition, we were as shocked as anyone else to hear of cases collapsing because witnesses were fearful of giving evidence... We have recently seen the terrible case of a rapist who cross-examined his victims for several days, subjecting them to trauma and distress. I am appalled by this further victimisation, and I am determined that vulnerable witnesses should not have to go through this type of experience.'

[100] Lord Williams said 'I was also doing Home Affairs in the Lords. So obviously and significantly, conversations between Alun Michael, Jack Straw and myself. 'Cause I think we all had a very clear feeling that you looked, you need to look at the whole of the criminal justice system, including prisons as well, in my opinion, to see how, in inverted commas, victims are dealt with.'

Proposals for victims took much of their meaning from that phrasing: reducing crime would reduce the numbers of victims, and that end could be secured by enlisting their co-operation. Jack Straw observed 'Putting the public's protection first also means putting the needs of victims first. Offenders cannot be brought to justice unless victims and witnesses report crimes to the police and are willing, if necessary, to give evidence in court. Yet the criminal justice system has been too slow in recognising its responsibilities towards victims and witnesses.'[101] Of course, crime reduction and securing convictions were not the sole object of aiding victims, and New Labour (and Alun Michael and Jack Straw, in particular) had long enjoyed a cordial relation with Victim Support, but, in one fashion or another, they never seemed to be entirely absent where victims were discussed. Alun Michael had continued: 'On the other hand, when you're looking at support for victims, that needs to be much more narrowly targeted, you know, the support for victims, the work of Victim Support has to be about the direct help of victims in the trauma they experience or dealing with the practical consequences of loss of money or whatever. And secondly, in the help, to enable victims to be able to give best evidence in court through the court support services.'

Like much else in the world of policy-making, the New Labour commitments to victims had many parents: there had been the imperative to cut crime and promote the greater effectiveness of the criminal justice system (to be pursued in the next chapter); the politicians' responses to disturbing reports about life plagued by difficult neighbours[102] and young people milling about in areas of high crime (pursued in Chapter 7); the growing recognition that, in the words of Liz Lloyd, about to become home affairs policy adviser to the Prime Minister, that those whose lives were so plagued were 'poor and live in the poorest estates', 'our people', the people for whom the party had a duty of care; responses to the cross-examination of rape complainants (pursued in Chapter 8); and a third, complementary narrative that helps to explain a little more of the precise *content* of the commitments. Victim Support claimed that it

[101] *Government's Crime Reduction Strategy*, Home Office, 29 November 1999. Foreword by the Home Secretary.

[102] Presaged in a 1995 policy document, 'Labour's proposals for tough action on crime'.

had fed its 1995 *Statement of Victims' Rights*[103] directly into the
deliberations of the Parliamentary All Party Penal Affairs Group and
its report, *Increasing the Rights of Victims of Crime,* in 1996,[104] and
thence to New Labour[105] through the intercession of Alun Michael,
the Group's chairman, a friend of Victim Support and one of the
authors of the party's manifesto. The Chief Executive Officer of
Victim Support, Dame Helen Reeves, said in 1999:[106]

If you look at all the documentation on victims and all the international
work and various conventions, what you'll find I think is that our work on
victims' rights in '95 was the first... that actually identified protection as
one of the primary rights and that's reflected in the European Forum policy
on victims' rights as well... we're just bringing various strands together
and saying 'look this is a whole area, we've been looking at information,
and we've been looking at whether or not victims have a voice
or... whether they should be consulted...' Alun Michael was obviously

[103] Very few professionals seemed to have quarrelled with Victim Support's statement of rights. Robert Latham, the Chair of Victim Support's National Council,
remarked that it 'has become conventional wisdom throughout the criminal justice
agencies'. Chair's Report, *1999 annual report*, Victim Support, London, 1999, p. 8.
Indeed, very significantly, it had been endorsed by the Lord Chief Justice. Lord Taylor;
'Witnesses, victims and the criminal trial', 12 April 1996. Paradoxically, the major
dissenters were to be found within Victim Support itself. Oliver Wilkinson, the chief
executive of Victim Support Northern Ireland, held, for instance that, that the movement towards victims' rights was unfortunate because, if certain rights were subject to
legislation, others would be overlooked, and a two-tier system would evolve (Victim
Support; Regional Meeting Spring 2001, 26 April 2001, Region 9, Northern Ireland).
And others, like Teresa Reynolds, wondered whether stated rights would not merely
become minimal standards ('there is a danger, I feel that in order to be achievable—
and clearly standards do need to be achievable, and they need to be measurable—you
can end up with the lowest common denominator').
[104] 'The majority of reforms recommended are those which Victim Support put
forward in its paper *The Rights of Victims of Crime* published in 1995'. *Victim
Support*, No. 63, Autumn/Winter 1996, p. 4.
[105] Although it must also be noted that Victim Support claimed that the rights it
claimed in 1995 had already been incorporated in the revised, 1996 Victim's Charter.
Victim Support; *report '97*. The origins of the Victim Impact Statement, then being
'piloted' under the *aegis* of that Charter, were, for instance, ascribed by Victim
Support to its assertion of the victim's right to information. Notes of a briefing held
at Victim Support National Office, 28 August 1996.
[106] She and Kate Mulley were to comment later '*The Rights of Victims of Crime* set
the agenda.' H. Reeves and K. Mulley; 'The new status of victims in the UK: Opportunities and threats', in A. Crawford and J. Goodey (eds.); *Integrating a Victim
Perspective Within Criminal Justice: International debates*, Ashgate, Aldershot,
2000, p. 130.

the link. Remember he was Chairman of the All Party Penal Affairs Group and in... the year before the election, they'd had a whole series of meetings on victims' issues. I think there were 12 meetings. And of course we planned that series with him and nominated all the speakers and we identified the issues... and the people who would speak. And Teresa [Reynolds, the policy officer of Victim Support] actually worked on that whole programme... you'll find that everything that hadn't yet been done actually came into those recommendations. A lot of them then got picked up by the new government because of Alun really.

The three commitments informed speeches touching victims made before the election,[107] and they were to be cited repeatedly after the election. They appeared in submissions to Ministers, Cabinet Committees, and the Treasury as mandates, prefacing reviews of what had been done[108] and what yet remained to be done,[109] and driving policy.[110] They were to become part of the hub of the Home Office's post-election briefing to new Ministers on victims. Manifestos are the simplest and most unarguable kind of initiative, argued James,[111] and they have force. The decision to continue work on vulnerable and intimidated witnesses was a response to the commitments; so was the phrasing and formal adoption of the Home Office's Aim 2, which I shall discuss in the next chapter;[112] and so,

---

[107] For example, when Jack Straw spoke to the Howard League on 12 September 1995: 'The criminal justice system must give greater attention to the victims of crime. Confidence in the system as a whole is eroded when victims are treated in a thoughtless and insensitive way. They should be kept informed of the progress of the case against the accused, the charges brought, the dates of any court hearings, and the outcome. The CPS... should ensure that it has all the facts about the impact of the crime on the victim. Such an understanding should imbue the prosecution case. The courts should be more victim and witness friendly. Victims should not have to sit in the same waiting areas as the accused. And we should have a properly funded CICS for the victims of violent crime.'

[108] Thus, Ian Chisholm, talking on the treatment of witnesses at the Victim Support National Conference, on 5 July 1999, began by reciting the manifesto.

[109] In, for instance, a 1999 paper on better services for victims for the Ministerial Group, which began by citing 1997 Labour Party manifesto.

[110] See *The Government's Expenditure Plans 1999–2000 to 2001–2002, Vol. 1*— Home Office aims; Home Office Press Release: Youth Justice and Criminal Evidence Bill receives Royal Assent, 28 July 1999.

[111] S. James; *British Government: A reader in policy making*, Routledge, London, 1997, p. 9.

[112] Criminal Justice Conference: Vulnerable or Intimidated Witnesses, Training Issues, 17–19 November 1998, Summary of Proceedings.

more contentiously, were internal debates about the rights of victims of mentally-disordered offenders to receive information. Where there was a political commitment, Ian Chisholm told Victim Support, 'then that's where money will be found compared with where things are desirable without a specific commitment'.[113]

## The New Administration

After eighteen years in opposition, New Labour was elected to power in what was described as a 'rout' of its opponents.[114] It received over 44 per cent of the vote—with a swing of 10 per cent from the Conservatives—amassing 418 seats, compared with the 165 of the Conservatives, and the 46 of the Liberal Democrats.

Election campaigns form a political hiatus in which officials, waiting in the wings, prepare for the return to power of the existing Government or the accession to power of the opposition. New Ministers would have to be briefed about Home Office business so that they could make informed judgments about existing commitments and future plans. Victims were but a minor part of that field, but they also had to be covered.

Officials had begun early to collect a stock of New Labour election materials, speeches, papers, and newspaper cuttings, filing them in a 'Labour Party folder', and circulating them within the Office from the Spring of 1996 onwards. They had had sight of correspondence between the opposition front bench and Ministers. Even before the election, they had been invited by Conservative Ministers to review the statistical and economic bases of a number of New Labour's proposals. Being asked to tender such advice was not uncommon. It was a matter of convention, re-affirmed by Cabinet guidance on the eve of the general election, that Ministers requesting such an appraisal should identify the texts and be responsible for interpretations or assumptions, and that departments should provide factual material, drawing attention to qualifications and assumptions.[115] It was necessary, one official remarked, 'to avoid casting the net so widely as to stray into what [might be] judged to

---

[113] Meeting of Victim Support National Council, 21 March 2000, my notes.

[114] A. Rawnsley; *Servants of the People*, Penguin, London, 2001, p. 12.

[115] Supplementary memorandum submitted by the Home Office to the Treasury and Civil Service Committee, undated.

be political territory'. By early 1997, Home Office officials had already come to know a good deal about the policies and political tenor of New Labour.

Four days after the date of the election was announced on 17 March 1997, the Permanent Secretary requested directors and heads of agencies to start preparing briefs for the incoming administration. New Ministers were to be supplied with an organizational guide to the Office; advice about appointments and commitments to be kept during the taxing first two weeks in office; an account of the main strands of policy work that had occupied the Department up until the recess; and a catalogue of the principal decisions and submissions that had to be made, including those flowing from election commitments.

The business of drafting the more specialized sections of those briefings was delegated down step by step from the Permanent Under Secretary to Directors and heads of units, the 'Grade 5s', and thence to officials, the 'Grade 7s', who possessed detailed substantive knowledge of policy areas.[116] The segment on victims and witnesses was mapped chiefly by the Grade 7s of the Procedures and Victims Unit who discussed criminal injuries compensation, which, it was thought, might well require review in 1998; the *Victim's Charter* and its two pilot projects; the future funding and support of Victim Support and the possible advance of its Witness Service into the Magistrates' Courts (and it was noted that Jack Straw had been reported in *The Daily Mail* to favour such an extension); and the implementation of measures to support child[117] and other vulnerable witnesses, already presaged by the formation of a working group in 1996, quite possibly about to include witnesses with learning disabilities within its terms of reference, and almost certain, because of the Labour party manifesto commitment, to embrace the better protection of intimidated witnesses. Early approval would have to be sought from Ministers 'as a matter of urgency' for the continuation of the working group, whose 'wide-ranging

---

[116] I shall describe the formal organization of the Home Office fully in the next chapter. See, for instance the chart on page 70 which lays out the formal hierarchy of the Department.

[117] There had been pressures to implement what was known colloquially as the 'full Pigot', the bundle of technical and other measures for easing the delivery of evidence by child witnesses recommended by an advisory committee chaired by T. Pigot: *Report of the Advisory Group on Video Evidence*, Home Office, London, 1989.

review' of the treatment of vulnerable witnesses had been announced by the previous Government in January 1997, and which had already proposed a discretionary scheme to prevent defendants from cross-examining rape and other vulnerable victims in person (it was pointed out that the New Labour manifesto had itself called for an end to the personal cross-examination by defendants of rape and other complainants). Ministers were to be told about consultations with the Department of Health about how best to inform victims about the release plans of 'their' incarcerated 'mentally-disordered' offenders (consultations that would loiter on for years and which illustrated powerfully how very different conceptions of the victim could be). Jack Straw's interest in restorative justice and the young offender was noted[118] although, as a matter to be assigned within the Home Office's internal division of labour to the Juvenile Offenders Unit, it would not significantly involve either the Procedures and Victims Unit or the Victims Steering Group.

James observed that 'governments rarely write policy on a clean slate. You have to set out from where you are . . . '.[119] Most of those working in and around affected regions of the criminal justice system noted little substantive change in victims' policy at first. The only distinctively new initiative to feature in the briefing, thought Ian Chisholm, 'was in [the area of] vulnerable witnesses because the difference . . . here is more on the intimidated witnesses' front . . . although the rape victims were in the Tory Manifesto as well, so we've been doing it anyway . . . Intimidation is the new thing.' And Helen Reeves, watching from a slightly greater distance, said: '[There has been a] lot of continuity. The big thing I think that's happened to this government is protection issues have been taken up. That is very new—[the protection of] victims and witnesses. And there were no policies whatsoever for protection apart from children' (that new feature will, as I have remarked, be discussed in Chapter 8). An official of the Courts Service concurred: ' In fact I'd been about two years under each government and on the issue of victims and witnesses I wouldn't have said there'd been any change in policy.'[120] Perhaps those observers should also have added the new

---

[118] Evidenced, again, for instance, in News from Labour: Labour outlines plans for Radical Reform of Youth Justice System, speech by Jack Straw, 20 November 1996.

[119] S. James; *British Government: A reader in policy making*, op. cit., p. 3.

[120] Teresa Reynolds, the Policy Officer of Victim Support, a long-standing member of the policy network centred on victims, reflected: 'I don't think there's been a radical

emphasis on juvenile offenders making reparation to the victim, but it is possible that that emphasis was thought to fall administratively and descriptively outside the boundaries of victims' policies conventionally conceived, managed and pursued. (Reparative justice will be the focus of Chapter 7).

If the substance of policy remained relatively intact at first, what did alter was the vigour and alacrity with which the new Home Officer Ministers and, eventually, the Prime Minister, began to pursue policies for victims. Perhaps now that the election was over, they were at greater liberty to move 'off-message' and concentrate on other matters in which they had an interest, and they certainly appeared to have an interest in victims, although officials observed that the more prominent 'headline' commitments (on the reform of youth justice, for instance) did palpably constrain them. The Home Secretary, Jack Straw, was a barrister and MP for Blackburn, whose constituency party shared offices with the local Victim Support Scheme. Before[121] and after attaining power, he had spoken both formally and informally[122] about the place of victims in the criminal justice system. He was to enjoin practitioners: 'I want all criminal justice agencies to have victims at the forefront of their minds. I want them to "think victim" when crucial decisions are being made... [It is] amazing that such a basic regard for victims has not been part of the system for many years. We can at least ensure that the victim is told what is happening.'[123] In a letter to the editor of a newspaper, he was to say: 'Both in my years in Opposition and since taking on

change from the government, actually. I mean the last government did actually do a lot for victims, you know, they, the last Victims' Charter was put together under their administration, so they actually put victims well and truly on the map.'

[121] In a speech as shadow Home Secretary to the Howard League in September 1995, for instance, he said that 'The criminal justice system must give greater attention to the victims of crime. Confidence in the criminal justice system as a whole is eroded when victims are treated in a thoughtless and insensitive way.' It is interesting that, even two years before the general election, victims were being framed by what was to become one of the criminal justice system's two stated aims, the maintenance of confidence in criminal justice. Problems of legitimacy and effectiveness shaped how victims were represented.

[122] In interview with *The Times*, 25 April 2001, for instance, he said that the civil libertarians' 'record seems to have stuck on one track: they have plenty of excuses for offenders without doing anything for the victims'.

[123] Speech on the launch of the Victim Support Telephone Helpline, 19 February 1998.

the job of Home Secretary, I have always sought to look behind the headlines and statistics to try to understand a little better the shattering effect that crime, particularly very serious crime, has on the lives of real people ... I have carried on and increased the pace of reforms that the previous Government set in train to bring the interests of victims much closer to the heart of the criminal justice system.'

Alun Michael had been involved in establishing a victim support scheme in his Cardiff constituency and had chaired the Parliamentary All-Party Penal Affairs Group when it issued a report on *Increasing the Rights of Victims of Crime,* in July 1996. 'I have had a long interest in Victim Support', he told a plenary meeting of Victim Support's Annual Conference in July 1998. He and the Labour Party had had close connections with Victim Support before the 1997 election, and they were to 'confirm' the link thereafter.

As Members of Parliament, moreover, holding surgeries, visiting their own and others' constituencies during the election, learning about popular discontents, both Ministers had been reminded continually about the very general and corrosive impact of crime on people in everyday life. Alun Michael said:

I came to listening to what people were saying, you know, in South London or the Northeast or Wales. And ... you have a lot of people who are victims, not of a severe, not of the effect of a severe crime that's targeted on them, [but] they're the victims of the level of crime in their area which takes away their sense of security and takes away the sense of community and undermines public confidence. So ... people's lives are affected and diminished by crime generally.

Within the formal constraints of balance and due process, endemic to all professional talk about victims in England and Wales, the new Ministers displayed an interest that was emphatically not endemic to that talk. Immediately on coming to office, Ministers reminded one another about the higher priority they intended to award victims, and they arranged for it to be promoted in a flurry of gestures.[124] The secretary of the Victims Steering Group, a Grade 7, noted: 'I think [the political interest in victims is] very high, it's a very high profile area, it's an area where ministers take a lot of personal interest, and they are keen to get out and about to meet, certainly to go to set-piece Victims Support occasions like their conferences ... '. There were to be answers to parliamentary questions in which the reiterated phrase

[124] See *Home Office Annual Report*, 1997–98, Home Office, London, 1998, p. 83.

was 'we are firmly committed to helping victims and redressing the balance'.[125] Alun Michael was to tell the Magistrates' Association in November 1997, 'All the criminal justice agencies need to be fully committed to improving the services they provide to victims and to develop ways to ensure that this happens more consistently. We said in Opposition that care and concern for victims would be one of our priorities if we were elected.'[126] There were to be staged occasions linking the Government symbolically to Victim Support: Alun Michael visited the organization's National Office in June 1997, only a month after the election,[127] and he addressed its Annual General Meeting in *lieu* of the Home Secretary in November 1997. For its part, Victim Support saw the new Government as a 'fresh opportunity to promote the need for more resources and victims' rights'.[128]

To be sure, and as I shall argue in the next chapter, those speeches and letters were usually drafted by officials (even if sometimes heavily amended by politicians), but no word was artless, and they were designed very precisely to convey the politicians' sentiments and were to be reinforced by practical and political action. In 1999, some time after the election, Anne Viney, Assistant Director of Victim Support, remarked:

There's a lot happening on victims' issues. It really is a lot. Whether it's due to a change of government or there is continuing momentum, I wouldn't know, because after all, the first thing this new government did was to give Victim Support more money. And the second thing it did was to give Victim Support even more money. I don't know whether the other lot would have done that. They might have done for all I can say, because, after all, it was a Conservative government who took the initial decision to fund Victim Support in any shape or form and who established the Victim's Charter.

Within a few months of the election, the Home Secretary reversed the previous administration's decision to freeze Government funding for Victim Support, awarding it an extra £1m. in June 1997,[129] an act that was as much demonstrative as functional; encouraged the

---

[125] See, for instance, *Hansard*: Written Answers, 3 July 1997; and Oral Answers, 27 October 1997 and 24 November 1997.
[126] Speech to the Magistrates' Association, 30 November 1997.
[127] *Victim Support News Service* June 1997.
[128] Victim Support May News, 1997, p. 2.
[129] Home Office News Release 142/97, 13 June 1997.

expansion of the Witness Service into the Magistrates' Courts; allowed victims to attend hearings in the youth courts;[130] confirmed that the working group on vulnerable witnesses should not be disbanded; invited (through the Attorney General) Sir Iain Glidewell, who was then chairing a committee reviewing the work of the Crown Prosecution Service,[131] to consider the manifesto commitment about prosecutors informing victims about prosecution decisions; awarded, for the very first time, and exceptionally,[132] funding of £43,500 (later £100,000 *per annum*, a small sum but a significant gesture and probably irreversible commitment) to SAMM, Victim Support's *protégé*, the self-help group for the families of homicide victims; and promoted reparative justice in which victims were to play a somewhat equivocal role. More than once he defended an emerging conception of victims' rights against the doubts of colleagues inside and outside the Cabinet who wondered whether victims could legally be said to exist at all before a guilty verdict had been delivered at trial, and who believed that enhancing their rights would upset the proper balance of an adversarial system. The Home Secretary and Alun Michael, officials of JVU maintained, were two politicians personally 'very sympathetic to victim support'. Their letters to Victim Support more than once contained the phrase that they were doing 'all they can to promote the service you provide to victims'.

Reflecting on the changes since 1997, Ian Chisholm commented, 'basically victims have done quite well out of the Government... So in a way they've got the rhetoric about what they want to do but they've also got the money... and there have been significant increases in support for victims.' The remainder of this book will now proceed to consider the organizations and policies that took those significant increases forward.

[130] Home Office Press Release: 2 October 1997.

[131] His report was to be published as *The Review of the Crown Prosecution Service*, Chairman Sir Iain Glidewell, June 1998, Cm. 3972. Its principal terms of reference were 'to assess whether the CPS has contributed to the falling number of convictions for recorded crime'. His recommendations 31 and 32 were that, as soon as practicable, the CPS should have the overall responsibility for witness warning; the transfer to the CPS of the responsibility for giving information and, where desired, an explanation to complainants/victims should take place in each CPS Area as soon as the resources of that Area permit.

[132] Exceptionally, because the Procedures and Victims Unit was not 'resourced' to run a grants programme.

**2**

# The Home Office at the Turn of the Century

It is now appropriate more fully to introduce the Home Office, the principal institution in this history, and the Department of State that was to orchestrate the policies that are the subject of this book. Before the 1997 general election, the politics of victims in the United Kingdom in the twentieth century had unwound almost wholly under Conservative administrations: Victim Support, the foremost non-governmental organization in the area, had certainly known no other than a Conservative Government, having been established in 1979 and receiving critical Government funding in 1986, the time at which it joined with the Home Office to found the Victims Steering Group. John Major, the last Conservative Prime Minister before the New Labour administration, had interested himself personally in victims' matters, and it was his *Victim's Charter* initiatives on the 'One Stop Shop' and victim statements that were occupying Home Office officials in the Procedures and Victims Unit when the new Government took office and continued to occupy them for a time thereafter. Those measures will be described in Chapter 4. Parts of this book will accordingly touch on policy-making that proved to be uninterrupted across administrations.[1] One such continuity was a Treasury commitment under the new Government to remain within the limits on public expenditure laid down by the last Conservative administration, and policy development was to be somewhat curtailed at first.[2] But New Labour did also give a new inflection to

---

[1] Indeed, the two election commitments bearing on victims that were offered in the Labour Party's manifesto promised policies that were already in train in the Home Office. R. Corbett, a Labour MP, and Chair of the Home Affairs Committee, remarked in March 2000 on the absence of marked discontinuities between Labour and Conservative policies on victims.

[2] See, for instance, *The Times*, 30 September 1999.

government, and it was an inflection that, at times by design, at times by tangent, came importantly to affect images of victims and their problems.

## New Labour and Criminal Justice

New Labour entered office in May 1997. Out of power for eighteen frustrating and chastening years, unschooled in office, it nevertheless had had copious time in which to prepare for government (a senior Home Office Official talked about 'the kind of advantage which a new government has, especially after a long period in opposition, of actually standing back and looking right across the field and deciding what it might do'), and it entered with a keen purpose and a large portfolio of reforms to apply to the forms and substance of administration. It was anticipated that the new Home Secretary, Jack Straw, would order a judicial inquiry into the police investigation of the death of Stephen Lawrence, a young black man who had been murdered in 1993, with potentially wide implications for the politics of race, crime, policing,[3] and human rights[4] (and that decision will be reviewed in Chapter 9). There were proposals for radical constitutional and administrative change: a Human Rights Act which would newly endow subjects with 'positive' rights (and that will be discussed in Chapter 5); a Freedom of Information Act which would afford citizens access to information held by public bodies; the devolution of government in Scotland and Wales; reform of the House of Lords; and what was rather vaguely styled the 'modernisation' of government and public services (to be discussed in Chapter 4). All but the penultimate pair of reforms came to colour the politics of victims, and they will receive extended attention later in the book.

---

[3]  See *The Voice*, 23 June 1997 and the *Guardian*, 25 July 1997.

[4]  Robert Latham, a barrister and the chairman of the Victim Support Trustees, reflected that the decision to hold inquiries into the death of Stephen Lawrence and 'Bloody Sunday' was part of the broad human rights agenda of the new administration. On 29 January 1998, the Prime Minister announced '... that a Tribunal be established for inquiring into a definite matter of urgent public importance, namely the events on Sunday 30 January 1972 which led to loss of life in connection with the procession in Londonderry on that day, taking account of any new information relevant to events on that day'. The Tribunal was to be chaired by Lord Saville of Newdigate.

New Labour was untried, there were critics predicting it would fail as its predecessors had failed through party and trade union indiscipline, high taxation, and improvident spending, and it had to prove itself. Conspicuous financial prudence was one reply. The systematic reform of public administration, utilizing what has been variously called the 'new managerialism', 'modernization', the 'new pragmatics',[5] and 'governmentality' (upon which I focus elsewhere), was another. Giddens observed that 'to retain or regain legitimacy, states without enemies have to elevate their administrative efficiency',[6] and managerialist changes first introduced by the Conservatives were appreciably accelerated and amplified by New Labour. By 'modernisation', New Labour intended a bundle of measures, including an emphasis on named policy outcomes susceptible of measurement; 'partnership working'; a preoccupation with what was called 'what works'; cost effectiveness; pragmatism; a resort to information technology; and 'image development'.[7] It is an umbrella word, susceptible of many nuances of meaning and use, mostly laudatory, and it was to be applied liberally.[8]

Driving reform was the new Prime Minister, Tony Blair, the leader of a self-styled 'radical and modernising government',[9] taking a 'unified nation into the next millennium',[10] who declared in his foreword to a 1999 White Paper that 'The Government has a mission to modernise—renewing our country for the new millennium. We are modernising our schools, our hospitals ... and our criminal justice system.'[11] His project has been described as Napoleonic in its scale and rigour:[12] citizens were to be better informed; better able to secure rights against abuses of State power; better able to affect the

[5] See P. Drucker; *The New Realities*, Harper and Row, New York, 1989.

[6] A. Giddens; *The Third Way*, Polity Press, Cambridge, 1998, p. 74.

[7] See T. Newburn; 'Criminal Justice Policy', in N. Ellison and C. Pierson (eds.); *Developments in British Social Policy 2*, Palgrave, Basingstoke, 2003, p. 242.

[8] It is, said Hood, 'a rhetorically successful idea because when the powerful but implicit metaphor of technological development is carried over into human organization it is inherently ambiguous'. C. Hood; *The Art of the State: Culture, Rhetoric and Public Management*, Clarendon Press, Oxford, 1998, p. 194.

[9] Interview in *The Times*, 2 September 1999.

[10] BBC web site. Election 97 news.

[11] Foreword to *Modernising Government*, Cm. 4310, March 1999.

[12] See P. Hennessy; *The Prime Minister*, Penguin Books, London, 2000, p. 478.

quality of services delivered by State bodies; and better assured that comprehensive internal controls, communication, and monitoring would ensure a greater effectiveness, economy, efficiency and responsiveness of the public sector. In the criminal justice system itself, there was to be a commitment to co-ordinated, strategic planning and 'trilateral' management by the three criminal justice departments of Home Secretary, Lord Chancellor, and Attorney General; 'evidence-based' or 'knowledge-based' policy-making; agreed collective aims, objectives, and targets; and the methodical application of quantified performance indicators to gauge success.[13] It was no longer enough for officials to advise and warn Ministers. They were required to manage, and do so to demonstrable effect. A member of the Home Office Business Performance Unit said in 1999, 'there is much more now a feeling of having to actually manage resources. I think the feeling before was that we were all kinds of intellectuals, working in a room on our own, you know, doing these hard things. Sitting in a room on your own and writing a paper was what you aspired to.'

Two overriding aims were set for the criminal justice system as a whole, and all policy arguments and work were to be referred to them: to reduce crime and the fear of crime,[14] and their social and economic costs; and to dispense justice fairly and efficiently, and to promote confidence in the rule of law.[15] Victims and witnesses came ineluctably to take some part of their character from their relation to the twin imperatives of crime reduction and public confidence. Crime would be reduced, it was said, by 'providing better support for victims and witnesses'.[16] Thus it was that Alun Michael, the first Home Office Minister of the new Government to be charged with responsibility for criminal policy and, within criminal policy, for victims, talked simultaneously about support and crime reduction

[13] See D. Faulkner; *Crime, State and Citizen*, Waterside Press, Winchester, 2001, p. 133 *et seq*.
[14] Despite a new armamentarium of administrative measures, nothing could be assured. Indeed there were risks of a self-falsifying prophecy underpinned by apprehensions that demographic and economic pressures would cause crime to rise and that an increased emphasis on reducing fear of crime would lead to an increase in fear.
[15] See Home Office Press Notice 512/98. Public confidence became an object of policy and research interest in the Home Office of the time. See, for instance, C. Mirrlees-Black; 'Confidence in the Criminal Justice System: Findings from the 2000 British Crime Survey', HO Research Findings No. 137, 2001.
[16] National Policy Forum Report 1999: Crime and Justice, Labour Party web site.

in June 1999: 'I think firstly, that crime is about victims and therefore, where there is a crime, you need to consider the victim. And
secondly, that the more crime you have, the more victims you
have and therefore reducing crime is the best thing you can do for
the potential victims.' Thus it was too that Liz Lloyd, a political
adviser to the Prime Minister, remarked in February 2000 that
victims were seen largely as parts and beneficiaries of wider reforms
to the criminal justice system, not as policy targets in their own right:
'victims will be alright if other objectives such as crime reduction
are realised'.

What McLaughlin called 'the unrelenting managerialism of criminal justice',[17] with its ancillary procedures and protocols, came for
practical bureaucratic purposes to impose its stamp on who victims
were and what should be done to them. Indeed, one of the prime
themes of this book will be that victims never came to be defined
independently of frames that actually served other policies and
politics. They came to the fore in a range of guises, but never, it
seemed, in their own name. Helen Reeves, Chief Executive Officer of
Victim Support, reflected in January 1999:

We've always had difficulty getting people to see what we regard as a very
simple fact: ... that [the matter of victims] is actually a third strand. People
even now will try to say 'well, it's part of crime prevention or it's part of
restorative justice' or whatever. Unless you can actually separate [it] away
from those things and focus [on it] in its own right ... then you can come
back together and say 'yes, there's a lot of crime prevention in here as well
and yes, of course, it's part of restorative justice, [but] unless you've
actually focused on the need to reduce the harm done by crime ... you're
not going to achieve anything. You're just going to become ... hijacked by
other priorities.'

## The Home Office and Modernization

I described a little of the beginnings and later development of the
Home Office in *Helping Victims of Crime*: founded in 1782, the
department was, with the Foreign Office, one of the two original
administrative arms of the State, at first undertaking tasks that the
Foreign Office (managing external affairs) did not perform, known

---

[17] E. McLaughlin *et al.*; 'The Permanent Revolution', *Criminal Justice*, Vol. 1,
No. 3, August 2001, p. 301.

as the 'residuary legatee', and charged in consequence with diverse responsibility for internal affairs. In the late twentieth century, it still encompassed broadcasting, criminal legislation, the Magistrates' Courts, the fire service, police, prisons, probation, immigration, support for victims of crime and criminal injuries compensation, the awarding of honours, and other matters. In what Canadian federal officials would have called 'turf wars', it came to shed some of those duties during the first and second New Labour administrations,[18] principally to the Lord Chancellor's Department, conveying, perhaps, something of the rivalry and the disparity in influence, power, and structured principle between Home Secretary and Lord Chancellor that was to affect policy-making throughout the period.[19]

The Home Office managed the bulk of the Government's response to crime, but most movements in crime patently lay outside its control. The common public explanation of recent trends, supplied by the 'saloon-bar' criminology of the time, pointed to failures in the recruitment and organization of policing.[20] But, within the Government which came to power in 1997, there were to be more reflective and intricate analyses that cast doubts on the capacity of the State significantly to affect what were recognized as complex and intractable processes.[21] Crime, it was argued by officials, was the outcome of ramifying social changes, many of which lay outside the effective reach of the Home Office, and which included a growing lack of social discipline; a weakening of the communal sense of

[18] Including in time work on the fire service, animal welfare, liquor and gambling, summertime, electoral law, the Church of England, hereditary peers and Lords Lieutenant, broadcasting, contingency and emergency planning, and, critically for victims, the Magistrates' Courts, the Human Rights Act, data protection, and the Freedom of Information Act to the Lord Chancellor's Department. It gained a few petty powers too: in 2001, for instance, it acquired responsibility for work permits and the Anti-Drugs Co-ordination Unit. The process continued in 2003 when it was reported that 'Home Office may lose powers to justice ministry', *The Times*, 6 June 2003.

[19] See, for instance, *The Sunday Times*, 8 February 1998, which claimed that the Lord Chancellor wished to take command of the criminal justice system in its entirety in what would become, in effect, a Ministry of Justice. See also *The Times*, 19 June 2001.

[20] See R. Sullivan; 'The Politics of British Policing in the Thatcher/Major State', *The Howard Journal*, Vol. 37, No. 3, August 1998, pp. 306–18.

[21] See A. James and J. Raine; *The New Politics of Criminal Justice*, Longman, London, 1998.

wrongdoing; the workings of unemployment combined, perversely, with rising prosperity; the impact of drugs; reduced risks of apprehension; and the activities of a hard core of 100,000 persistent offenders responsible for the bulk of crime.[22] One might have added that crime is affected by demography; rates and forms of employment; social and economic inequalities; rates of social change; levels of urbanization and social diversity; changes in family structure and patterns of travel and residence; fashions in the consumption of alcohol and drugs; fashions in the production and consumption of goods; and much else. 'Most of the causes of crime,' David Smith was to conclude, 'are beyond control by the criminal justice system.'[23]

The criminal justice system for which the Home Office was accountable as 'lead' department[24] was not wholly under its command. The new managerialism may have begun appreciably to consolidate and articulate Home Office power through new networks of contract and regulation, but there was still much in the system that was loose-coupled, tacit, and negotiated. Home Secretaries could not, for instance, simply order chief constables or prison governors to comply with their policies in operational matters[25] (a Director of Criminal Policy observed in 1998, 'if a member [of ACPO] chooses to go a particular direction, he has that right') although the probation service was to become subject to much greater central control. And Government power over criminal justice was not concentrated solely in the Home Office. Its writ did not always run in Scotland, and Scots policy sometimes operated in parallel with, sometimes subordinate to, and sometimes independently of developments in England.[26] Two other departments of State

---

[22] Policy Unit Crime Project—Phase 1: Understanding the Data, 28 July 2000.

[23] D. Smith; 'Less Crime Without More Punishment', *Edinburgh Law Review*, 1999, Vol. 3, p. 296.

[24] The Criminal Justice White Paper, *Justice for All*, Cm. 5563, July 2002, recited that 'The Home Office is the government department responsible for internal affairs and leading on criminal policy in England and Wales . . . ' no page number.

[25] And the chief constables' deliberative organization, ACPO, the Association of Chief Police Officers, could not instruct its members how to act. One of its representatives announced at a meeting of RISC, the Racist Incidents Standing Committee in February 2000, that 'we don't issue codes of practice. We issue advice.' The Prison Service representative claimed also to advise rather than command prison managers.

[26] A *concordat* was agreed in 1999 between the Scottish Executive and the Home Office to guide officials on the division of labour between the two powers. Under the

had responsibility for major swathes of criminal justice in England and Wales: the courts, and the judges, and magistrates who presided over them, were substantially independent estates under what was often only the nominal supervision of the Court Service[27] and the Lord Chancellor;[28] and the Crown Prosecution Service fell under the *aegis* of the Attorney General. The Department was not liable for matters of civil law, although civil law could affect victims of crime, and victims of domestic violence above all (such victims also being taken to be as much people with problems of housing and economic support as of crime). The Department of Health administered the secure hospitals in which 'mentally disordered offenders' were housed. Rape crisis centres were funded by local authorities and local health authorities.[29] The defence bar and solicitors were virtually autonomous, regulated by their own professional associations, and not often to be seen in interdepartmental or inter-agency committee although they did hold regular consultations with Ministers. The Treasury controlled expenditure and thence strategic planning, and its presence was felt continuously as it vetoed and modified the Office's plans and proposals. From time to time, the Prime Minister and his advisers turned to criminal justice matters, particularly just before the 2001 election and when there appeared to be failures in

Scotland Act 1998, considerable areas for which the Home Office was responsible in England and Wales were the responsibility of the Executive in Scotland. The Home Office retained responsibility for constitutional matters, security services, national security, immigration and asylum, and the criminal law in relation to drugs. Amongst the list of devolved matters was victims' issues.

[27] An executive agency of the Lord Chancellor's Department.

[28] On the retirement of Lord Irvine, the last incumbent, it was announced in June 2003 that the office of Lord Chancellor would in time be replaced by a new post of Secretary of State for Constitutional Affairs. The decision was prompted in part because of the constitutional anomaly, at odds with Article 6 of the Human Rights Act, that the head of the judiciary was also a politician. It is interesting that, under the Phare horizontal programme of the Justice and Home Affairs Chapter of the *acquis*, one of the tests applied by a European Commission mission to the ten accession States was the independence of the judiciary, a test, I was told by the head of the mission, England and Wales would have had difficulty in satisfying because of the Lord Chancellor's dual role. See *Reinforcement of the Rule of Law: Final Report of the First Part of the Project*, Phare Horizontal Programme on Justice and Home Affairs, European Commission, published by The Centre for International Legal Cooperation, Leiden, the Netherlands, 2002.

[29] Although the Home Office eventually agreed to support financially the National Confederation of Rape Crisis Centres.

delivering what were identified as key performance targets, and they were heeded.

The criminal justice system remained, in short, an array of semi-detached, lesser and greater powers[30] whose relations required continual and conspicuous diplomacy, discussion, and accommodation. Ian Chisholm, head of the Home Office Justice and Victims Unit, a man who was to play a crucial role in the developments reported in this book, noted that 'the criminal justice system is a "system" in quotes...'. And, whilst for the most part, procedures were routine, and officials were schooled in the etiquette of meeting, consultation, and submission, although much decision-making was 'cleared' before committees ever met, there would also be episodes where agreement could not be reached and policy-making stalled for a while.

The civil service was to be 'modernized' by the new administration. Richard Wilson, then Cabinet Secretary and Head of the Civil Service, pronounced in May 1999 that '"no change" is not an option. The Civil Service has to face the continuing challenge of change and modernisation.... we now require senior officials to be good managers and good leaders and know how to get results.'[31] The Home Office had undergone continual re-organization and change since the late 1960s,[32] but the project of modernization was to be pursued by the new Prime Minister and his colleagues with a special vigour.[33] It had to yield palpable results.

---

[30] Speaking about but one institution, Geoff Hoon, then Minister in the Lord Chancellor's Department, said in September 1998: 'The range of organizations involved in the court process can make improvements harder to achieve. The police, the CPS, probation officers and social services are all working for different employers, with different objectives, and often answerable to different Government departments...', 'Reshaping the Criminal Courts', Lecture delivered at the University of Leeds, 22 September 1998. He might well have added the Bar, solicitors, judiciary, and members of the Court Service.

[31] R. Wilson; 'The Civil Service in the New Millennium', May 1999, pp. 1–2.

[32] See, for instance, K. Theakston; *The Civil Service since 1945*, Blackwell, Oxford, 1995, p. 20.

[33] The other Departments of State were of course to undergo modernization in the same manner as the Home Office. See, for instance, *Modernising Justice, A Summary of the Government's Proposals*, Lord Chancellor's Department, December 1998; and *Transforming the Crown Court: consultation document: The emerging proposals*, Court Service, September 1999.

'Modernization' borrowed in part from the reformed Australian Labour Party[34] and the American New Democrats[35] who had themselves borrowed from the Conservative Party of John Major[36] and elsewhere. Directly or in translation, it duplicated and re-imported some of the new American talk about changes in the culture of government, an ideology of performance and measurement, the empowered consumer and the information-based organization,[37] but the talk was unfamiliar and untested at first, and it will be noted in what follows that officials tended interchangeably to use a number of different terms and words as they worked towards a new practice and a new terminology.

A key component of the process was the effort to define the criminal justice system (and the Home Office, at a remove and somewhat more obliquely) in the business school language[38] of 'entrepreneurial government'[39] and the market as a supplier of services to populations defined by new practices as customers. 'We're supposed', said an official of the significantly re-named Home Office Business Performance Unit (formerly the Efficiency Consultancy Unit and, earlier still, M Division) in 1998, 'to be looking at customer service as part of our remit and how the Home Office is delivering its service as part of efficiency... there are loads of committees and groups all around the Home Office looking at every aspect of that, how it's going to affect everyone... every group

[34] See A. Scott; *Running on Empty: 'Modernising' the British and Australian Labour Parties*, Cornerford Miller, Sydney, 2000. I am grateful to Tim Newburn for help in this general area of policy transfers.

[35] There was, according to Andrew Rutherford, a strong affinity and commerce at first between the Democratic Party of Bill Clinton and the New Labour of Tony Blair. 'New Labour, New Democrats and the New Criminality', paper delivered at the London School of Economics, 20 January 1999. And see K. Baer; *Reinventing Democrats*, University Press of Kansas, Lawrence, 2000.

[36] See D. Kettl; *Reinventing Government: Appraising the National Performance Review*, Center for Public Management, The Brookings Institute, August 1994, p. 34.

[37] P. Drucker; 'The Coming of the New Organization', *Harvard Business Review*, January–February 1988, p. 45. A senior member of the research wing of the Home Office, remarked of the new Ministers, 'they've been brought up to believe that knowledge and information is the way to progress. That's what Fabianism is all about!'

[38] N. Flynn (ed.); *Change in the Civil Service*, Public Finance Corporation, London, 1994, p. 2.

[39] D. Osborne and T. Gaebler; *Reinventing Government: How the Entrepreneurial Spirit is Transforming the Public Sector*, Plume, New York, 1993, p. xi.

has got somebody... looking at customer service and service delivery and how we might do that.'

The Department was not perhaps the most amenable to radical reform. It had always been at the centre of a web of delicately negotiated, often tacit relations that could be left indistinct for good political reasons.[40] It was driven by legal judgment, statute, and convention in its management of a law-bound and precedent-observing system; and it engaged continually in managing the fraught, risk-strewn 'dirty work' of the police, immigration service, and prisons where situations can go awry and scandal and crisis erupt without warning to the possible discomfiture of politicians.[41] Jack Straw, the new Home Secretary, recalled in early 1999, 'one of my Conservative predecessors gave me a gypsy's warning about coming to this place... He told me the key thing to remember is that at any one time there will be 50 sets of officials working on projects that will destroy your political career.'[42]

'We've managed to hold the line', said an official. 'When you think of the things this country's gone through in the last thirty years, we've managed to hold the line quite well.' In the 1970s and 1980s it had managed to hold the line largely by re-action rather than action, watchfully reconciling contradictions, resolving tensions and responding to crises as they arose. It had an established reputation for caution and carefulness that could be defined at the outset of the new and energetic New Labour administration as fustiness and pusillanimity. The Home Office, it was to be said, was hindered by outdated working methods and infrastructure.[43] There had to be a 'major change programme' to ensure that it had the 'right IT', accommodation and working methods to 'deliver its new aims in a cost-effective way'.[44] A concentration on the resolution of short-term crises was to be replaced by more extensive, considered

[40] There were, for example, areas of the relation between the Home Office and Victim Support that were expediently left untouched. I shall return to them below.
[41] A 'former minister' was quoted in The Times of 23 January 2000 as saying 'At the Home Office crises blow up seemingly from nowhere and can leave a weak man jabbering... The department's job is to confront evil. You are dealing with drugs, drink, pornography, gambling, crime punishment, prisons, cults and heaven knows what else.'
[42] Sunday Times, 24 January 1999.
[43] The Government's Expenditure Plans 1999–2000 to 2001–2002, p. 13.
[44] Home Office Annual Report 1998, foreword by the Home Secretary.

planning, partly under the auspices of a Strategic Policy Group, set up in 2000, as one of its members said, 'to provide a kind of strategic, long-term, cross-cutting, outward-looking facility for the Home Secretary... [in] an attempt to release a small part of the Office from being caught up in crisis-driven, knee-jerk policy-making on the hoof, that is so much a part and parcel of the way in which the Home Office works'. This was, remarked Chris Nuttall, then head of RDS, the Research, Development and Statistics Directorate, in 1998, 'real revolutionary stuff for the Home Office'.

The Home Office was to be modernized to deliver 'seamless services' by means of a greater and more extensive collaboration with its partners in the criminal justice system and central and local government; decentralization, devolution and the 'delayering' of management that had started in 1996; the matching of policy outcomes to 'real changes' through the stipulation of objectives, targets and performance measures;[45] the raising of standards of service delivery and policy formulation;[46] and longer planning cycles tied to 'trilateral' interdepartmental co-operation and the funding arrangements and public service agreements of the new, Treasury-orchestrated, triennial Comprehensive Spending Review. Policy officials were to manage as well as advise,[47] working with new project management techniques[48] which relied on an explicit language of 'business change', 'business performance', and 'business and information systems' revolving around agreed objectives, strong project control, problem identification and risk-management, and milestones and timetables.[49] To deliver a new criminal justice system, the Home Secretary told the Prime Minister in 2001, every part of the existing system would be subject to reform and modernization.

[45]  Statement by the Chancellor of the Exchequer on the Comprehensive Spending Review, 14 July 1998.

[46]  Foreword by the Permanent Secretary to *The Home Office—A Guide, October 2000*, Home Office, London, p. 3.

[47]  An erstwhile Inspector of Probation, but later to be Head of JVU, observed at the CIPFA Conference in June 2000, 'one of the Home Office's great weaknesses among my policy colleagues is to assume they've done something when they've issued a...circular.'

[48]  Signally, as I shall show, with the implementation of the initiative for vulnerable or intimidated witnesses, *Speaking up for Justice*.

[49]  Taken from F. Smith; *Project Management—Keeping out of Trouble*, Home Office Modernisation Unit, July 1998.

## Aims and Objectives

Playing its part in 'joined-up' strategic planning and performance management across the criminal justice system as a whole; contributing to, and serving as 'co-owner' of, the system's two cardinal aims and eight objectives;[50] written into its own lesser public service agreement which formed part of the greater Criminal Justice System Public Service Agreement[51] that specified 'what the Government expects from the criminal justice system',[52] were the Home Office's own 'mission'[53] and list of seven corporate aims and attendant objectives established in late 1997. 'Aims are the highest level outcomes that the Home Office [was] working to achieve',[54] and they were laid out as something of a hierarchy. Aim 1, 'reduction in crime and the fear of crime' had 'top priority'[55] as, indeed, it had for the criminal justice system as a whole. Aim 2 was the 'delivery of justice through effective and efficient investigation, prosecution, trial and sentencing, and through support for victims'.

Aim 2 had been inserted late in the drafting process and as a result of a delayed recollection of the Government's three manifesto commitments to victims. A senior member of the Research and Statistics Directorate of the Home Office reflected in 1998, 'I don't think [victims] are particularly high profile...They're always written into Home Office aims, but they were written in as an afterthought. [The head of the Criminal Policy Division] said, after seeing the first draft, "where are victims? Oh yes, where are victims? We'll add them to Aim 2".' Unusually, given the working methods I shall describe, the Department's aims and objectives were set without consultation, and certainly without consulting Victim Support. They were phrased at what a Director of Criminal Policy called 'a very high level of generality.' Unusually, too, Victim Support, straddling the formal boundaries of the criminal justice system, neither a legally-constituted criminal justice agency nor a wholly private institution, had been

---

[50] *The Home Office—A Guide, October 2000*, Home Office, London, p. 6.

[51] Published on 17 December 1998.

[52] Letter from the three Ministers enclosing the Criminal Justice System Strategic and Business Plans, 31 March 1999.

[53] In 1998, it was stated that that mission was to 'build a safe, just and tolerant society in which rights and responsibilities are balanced'. *Home Office Annual Report 1998*, Home Office London, 1998.

[54] *Home Office Annual Report*, Cm. 5406, Home Office, London, 2002, p. 14.

[55] *Home Office Annual Report 2000–2001*, Home Office, London, 2001.

named in early drafts of the statement of Home Office aims as an
agency with formal responsibility for delivering aims, but had disappeared from the final version.[56] There was an evident tentativeness
that underscored victims' initial marginality as a policy issue (even in
1999, victims directly received only 1.5 per cent of criminal justice
expenditure, of which 92 per cent (or £220,000,000) was devoted to
criminal injuries compensation)[57] but, tentative or not, the inclusion
of support for victims in Aim 2 was to be a solid political fact that
would work continuously to guide policy over the years. It gave
a mandate.

The new regime brought about a comprehensive,[58] functional
restructuring of the Department's formal organization.[59] 'The start
of management by aims throughout the office means significant
changes in the way we do business,' emailed the Director of Criminal
Justice Policy to heads of units in March 1999. It was imperative[60] to
devise a three-year strategic plan and a one-year business plan,
provide links to public service agreements and the 'modernisation
agenda' (including the introduction of new business and information
systems), and to announce aims and set targets.[61] Every Aim was to
have its own named 'stakeholders' and an accountable 'owner' or
'leader', and Aim 2 was assigned to the Criminal Justice Policy
Group of which the Justice and Victims Unit, or JVU, was a component, and JVU led, *inter alia*, on support for victims and criminal
injuries compensation. 'Spun out', in the words of a senior official,
the sometime Deputy Director of the Criminal Policy Directorate,

---

[56] Based on my notes of the meeting of the Victims Steering Group, 21 May 1999.

[57] Aim 2 Business Plan, 1999–2000, 31 March 1999.

[58] 'Benefiting from the establishment in late 1999 of a new high level business planning mechanism, it covers every corner of Home Office activity... The last three years have been a period of rapid change in the Home Office. As well as seeing the arrival of new staff and new technology, we have changed how we work as a department.' Introduction by the Permanent Secretary; *Home Office Business Plan 2000–2001*, Home Office, London, 2001, p. 2.

[59] 'The Office structure and planning system sets the framework... and embraces—objectives or outputs needed; decisions on resource allocation; lower level targets or milestones; allocation of work; monitoring progress; performance management; providing office with infrastructure and resources.' 'Delivering the Aims: Performance Management in the Home Office'.

[60] So important were the changes deemed to be that the first meeting of the Public Expenditure Committee to review delivery of public service agreement commitments, fixed for April 1999, was to be chaired by the Prime Minister.

[61] Guidance for the PSX Meeting on 29 April 1999, 8 April 1999.

'from the high level aims [were] all these more specific objectives and Ian [Chisholm, the head of JVU] will have several of those hard objectives with matching performance indicators in the victims area ... '. Aim 2 required the supportive infrastructure of a dedicated programme management group to 'construct teams around the projects and sub-programmes needed to achieve the programme as a whole',[62] a business plan, 'targets, monitoring and local accountability systems, and ... a work programme'.[63] 'We face', emailed a senior official, 'the doctrine of continuous improvement.'

Progress in Aim 2's objective of ensuring better services for victims and witnesses was to be assessed. By early 2000, and after some faltering in devising appropriate performance indicators,[64] it acquired a target (and 'target-champion' or 'accountable target-owner'[65] in JVU) to comply with the demands of the Department's public service agreement and interim, internal monitoring system and quarterly reports to the Management Board, Permanent Secretary, and Ministers (the Home Office had 'to know whether things are going to plan'). There was, it was decided (and without 'baseline data') to be a 5 per cent increase in victims' and witnesses' satisfaction with their treatment by the criminal justice system by March 2002.[66] Some part of what would be done would necessarily depend on existing policy initiatives, some on the 'introduction of the new strategic direction for the criminal justice system'. Members of the JVU believed that their brief was reasonably feasible. Colleagues working on crime reduction, for instance, were having a 'very hard

---

[62] Aim 2 Business Plan, 1999–2000, 31 March 1999.

[63] Draft Aim 2 Business Performance Monitor Commentary, undated.

[64] Measures should have been agreed by the end of March 1999. They were supposed, *inter alia*, to examine why a service was being delivered, and why in a certain way, what were the service objectives, were they going to deliver outcomes, could they be cheaper, and could quality be improved?

[65] Strategic Planning Group for the Criminal Justice System; 'Accountability for delivery of Criminal Justice System objectives and targets', paper by the Criminal Justice Joint Planning Unit, June 1999. Target-owning is only a little different from aim-owning, it was said, because the aim-owner is also responsible for the delivery of targets.

[66] It transpired eventually that 76%, a high proportion, of a special survey of 4,000 witnesses reported that they were satisfied by their treatment in the courts. The target of a 5% increase, not to be reached, was described subsequently by the Chair of the Victims Steering Group as 'silly' because of its formulation without knowledge of the baseline.

time—they were being sand-bagged all the time' by extensive demands for increased performance in the attainment of virtually unreachable targets as if 'it was just like reducing hospital waiting lists'. In 1999, for example, new performance targets were set for the criminal justice system, including reductions in the proportions of people under 25 reporting heroin and cocaine use by 25 per cent by 2005 and by 50 per cent by 2008.[67] Over 8,500 new targets were set by the Government in March 2000 alone, 614 of which were for the Home Office.[68] In 2000, for example, it was laid down that there should be a reduction in street robberies by 15 per cent, of car crimes by 30 per cent, and of burglaries by 10 per cent over the next five years in the Metropolitan Police area.[69] Agencies and lesser bodies embedded in the criminal justice system devised their own targets and measures in tandem.[70] There were substantial pressures to tailor figures to comply with the new targets, creating a quasi-Soviet world of fictitious achievements in the attainment of production norms.[71] A senior official reflected that the stress on performance management in the Home Office was 'curious because all it was doing was preparing pits for Ministers in the future'. Indeed, it was not to be very long before *The Times* came to report that 'Labour's target mania ties Whitehall in knots'.[72] In 2002, especially, there was a partial collapse of the claims of performance management as hosts of targets were not met[73] (and by 2003, after

[67] Labour Party web site July 2000: National Policy Forum Report 1999: Crime and Justice.
[68] *The Mirror*, 6 March 2000.
[69] *Home Office Annual Report*, 1999–2000, p. 23 and *Evening Standard*, 14 February 2000.
[70] The Lewisham Community Safety Team; 'Tackling crime and disorder in Lewisham, plan of action 1999–2002', for instance, talked about having identified seven key areas of concern, including planning to reduce racial harassment and attacks and homophobic violence and abuse by 6% in the first year and by 20% in three years.
[71] See A. Solzhenitsyn; *The Gulag Archipelago*, Collins, Glasgow, 1974. Reiner observed that there was 'considerable evidence that the pressure to produce results in the new performance indicator driven culture of police management is driving the police into wholesale massaging of crime figures'. R. Reiner; Police Research, undated.
[72] *The Times*, 13 February 2000.
[73] See, for example, *The Times*, 18 November 2002, which reported that the Government had missed 75% of its performance targets, that only 30 of the 130 public service agreements set in 2000 had been met, and that 40% of public service agreements set in 1998 had failed.

the lapse of time covered by this book, New Labour appeared to have begun a limited retreat[74]).

Managerialism was something of an alien force which did not take Whitehall, the Home Office or criminal justice system[75] by storm in the late 1990s.[76] A member of the Business Delivery Unit remarked in 1998 that 'there are all sorts of ideas that are really strange to us and strange to our organization, like the idea of money being important. I was only reading something today about I don't know, we're now having to really face reality, all sorts of Treasury initiatives, and we're finding that really hard to sort of cope with the idea that an outcome like better drugs delivery, can be costed.' All organizations have a dual face, conventionally described as the formal and informal, but more usefully captured by Maurice Punch's distinction between the world of records and appearance, on the one hand, and that of the submerged but acknowledged, on the other.[77] Whilst the outer, paper realities of the Home Office may have undergone a sea change, some held that the reforms had been

[74] On 4 July 2003, Tony Blair delivered what was presented as a major speech in Liverpool, a self-proclaimed turning-point that started to re-cast the character of his Government: 'Sometimes in government we can become so focused on getting the change done that we explain what we are doing but we don't always talk about why we are doing it. It can come across as a bit technocratic, a bit managerial. For the public, and sometimes for the party, the reason for reform is not always clear. But the purpose of reform is precisely to give effect to Labour values. It is to open up opportunity, to provide high quality health care or education based not on wealth, but on need. It's very purpose is social justice but in a changed world.' His speech was prefaced by an appearance on the radio on the same day by his Cabinet colleague, Patricia Hewitt, the Secretary of State for Trade and Industry, who said 'The public services must not be reduced to the language of customer service. You can't deliver health care or education as if you're delivering pizzas.' But that was all to take place much later in the future.

[75] See J. Plotnikoff and R. Woolfson; *Policing Domestic Violence: Effective Organisational Structures*, Police Research Series, Paper 100, RDS, December 1998, which reports almost no trace in the police response to domestic violence of any of the practices conventionally associated with the new managerialism.

[76] According to Christopher Hood, much of Whitehall at the time was still regulated on a basis of trust and collegiality rather than auditing, and the core of policy-makers were not as subject to the new regulatory regime as the outlying organisations responsible for delivering services. C. Hood *et al.*; *Regulation inside Government*, Oxford University Press, Oxford, 1999, pp. 73, 92.

[77] M. Punch; *Dirty Business: Exploring Corporate Misconduct*, Sage, London, 1996, p. 218.

marked only by piecemeal implementation and reluctant participation.

The introduction of the new performance management led to a re-
organization of the structure, nomenclature, and procedures of the
Home Office. It was welcomed by a number of officials, and particularly by some Directors and others who saw in it a useful methodology for engineering change. One, Sue Street, remarked of the
new system of targets, 'I think they're new in the sense that they're
articulated. I mean you will find extremely distinguished and wonderful colleagues from twenty years ago who actually both will say,
and it would be right to say, they've always seen it that way and they
were always fighting to recognise that. But you know, it's not until
you articulate it, you publish it, you agree with the Treasury, you
know, what it is you're delivering, that you can be confident that the
whole department [is on course as one].'[78] But from time to time the
methodology was to encounter obstacles and ambiguities which
I shall touch on as this book proceeds. It seemed to have been most
serviceable as a reforming process to those in the most senior positions who were less fully engrossed in the everyday, detailed work of
the policy divisions, and who found in it a condensed and convenient
working model of practices otherwise distracting, complex, obscure
and massive in scale. One official, a head of unit, observed that 'the
Ministers seem comfortable with it... My view is that all this
language of performance is very much the language of senior officials... It depends on where in the Office one is. I think once you get

[78] There were others who made substantially the same point. One, an official in the
Lord Chancellor's Department, observed, 'one thing I think... we're getting better at,
and there is room for improvement I think, is first of all articulating what it is you want
to get out of a particular exercise policy decision, or whatever, in terms of outcomes as
opposed to treating it as a process, i.e. you know, we've introduced this bill, we've
implemented it, the rules have been done, and then how do we evaluate it? Now
evaluation's very much more part of the process than it ever used to be and we're
improving, I think, in determining what the outcomes are with the various people who
have an interest in what the outcomes are.' Another, working in the Crown Prosecution Service, sitting on the Victims Steering Group, said, 'what I would say is that I
think it's had to make everyone much more disciplined in terms of you know, focusing
on meeting the commitments, making sure that we are and that you know, managers
are actually monitoring performance to ensure that we are. So it's not to say that it's
actually changing what we do significantly. I'm not sure that that would be a correct
thing to say. But I think it certainly focuses everyone's attention onto making sure that
we fulfilled them properly. But I wouldn't go so far as to say that it's radically changed
anything that we do. I think it's perhaps made us all focus a little more.'

above unit level, they tend to be more in this [new managerialist] world because that's what they can... deal with in terms of detail.' Working with outcomes was not the same as mastering the complexities of the 'black boxes' in which outcomes were actually produced. The semantic and practical requirements of those at the 'top of the Office' were not quite those of people working with the local, embedded realities of policy work. Theirs was a wider sweep that required a higher level of abstraction and simplification. One so placed at the top, Sue Street, reflected:

I'm the 'owner' in quotes of two of the principal aims... So to get my head round all of that substantial area of responsibility—I'm not going to deliver any of that on my own—so I had to think 'well, what are we really trying to do here?' And I do find the public protection angle is absolutely core, and so I try to think in terms of a criminal justice service to the public, and what would make it coherent and what are the objectives? So the approach to victims then becomes much more central to the strategy (although I would make the distinction if you're thinking citizens, then they are not all victims). So I think of it as a kind of citizens-centric criminal justice service... I think we have to think about what coherently protects the public. It informs some sort of development of sentencing policy... And I think drugs fit: it's quite an interesting example in terms of who is the victim and who is the offender because in drugs cases typically it is the same person. I'm also talking about a balance. So I think it's all, it's so subtle and complex that I can only approach it in a rather simplistic way of saying, you know, what will be a coherent service to the public...

That was the pragmatic and administratively-shaped world-view of a person at the summit who superintended the activities of a number of dedicated units covering different detailed areas of policy. To an official below, working in just one such a unit, it was the necessary proxy knowledge of a person who could not, would not or did not need to grasp policy-making as lived reality: 'that's her angle on it, and she hasn't got the background of the policy knowledge in this area. So therefore she sticks to that because that's the theory...' And such reflections were not confined to heads of units and those who worked for them.

I am mindful that I write about an organization that was in flux, that processes experienced in a transitional time were not fixed, that I exaggerate for purposes of analytic effect, and that officials managed to work together perfectly competently with the novel *lingua franca* and practices of performance management. But the first years of the New Labour administration were marked in the Home Office by, on the one hand, an outward uniformity of compliance and, on the other, by small ripples of *sotto voce* dissent. Modernization worked unevenly through the fabric of the department, and its neo-liberal ideology, vocabulary and procedures were not always and everywhere well-received by educated, liberal, and sometimes sceptical[79] men and women in the Units whose working media were words fastidiously deployed, arguments critically reviewed, and policy manoeuvres subject to a careful choreography. The realities and aspirations of the managerialist and the middle-ranking official did not necessarily mesh: said one in the middle ranks, 'I think there's a real disjunction and it's noticeable that [an official at the head of the division] hasn't got sufficient experience and knowledge of the subject . . . we're talking different languages and it's quite tricky.' Managerialism could seem 'contrived', a deformation and reification of the experiential exigencies of problem-solving: 'you get stuck into artificialities . . . [and] the trouble is that you then get stuck on that and you see that as the whole story, whereas in fact it's really a rather artificial telling of the story for purposes of Treasury-type performance . . . It's a way for senior management to think they're running things without knowing the detail of the business.' There were at first problems of translating the contents of one universe of meaning into those of another ('there's a real disjunction now between people doing policy up to head of unit and above, because you are operating in a different game') and of cultural dissonance.[80] To those accustomed to working with words and arguments skilfully deployed, it was always possible to utilize the new language to apparently effortless effect, but it could seem a little alien for all that.[81]

[79] There were, I was told by a member of RDS, the research and statistics directorate, 'endless management changes to be introduced and mantras to recite'.

[80] For a different but not unrelated treatment of the *sotto voce* culture of American public administration, see P. Heymann; 'How Government expresses Public Ideas', in R. Reich (ed.); *The Power of Public Ideas*, Harvard University Press, Cambridge, 1990, esp. pp. 88–9.

[81] By 2003, beyond the period covered by this book, it seemed as if the transition had been accomplished. A generation of older officials had retired, either at the early mandatory age of 60 set by the Civil Service, or before, and little was left of the liberal Home Office. David Faulkner, who had himself retired as a Home Office Director in 1992, reflected in a seminar that 'in the Office [in the 1980s] most people felt they were part of a tradition, conforming to a set of values which Ministers largely

Problems were not only semantic. The materials of 'governmentality' and modernization were not necessarily to hand, and it could be difficult to cost and quantify phenomena in the world of criminal justice policy-making. Data had not hitherto been collected and compiled in ways that lent themselves to measuring performance;[82] the appropriate information technology was not immediately in place;[83] and agencies were sometimes obliged merely to announce that no statistics were available or that they had to rely on proxy indices such as the number of complaints they had received from 'customers', the highly ambiguous indicator at first cited by the Crown Prosecution Service[84] and Courts Service[85] in discussing

accepted, and that has now gone, and they have been replaced by a pragmatism of "will it work?" and "will it come out in the indicators?" ' D. Faulkner, talking about his paper, 'Taking Citizenship Seriously: Social Capital and Criminal Justice in a Changing World', London School of Economics, 12 June 2003.

[82]  *Victim Support News Service* June 1997 reported that there had been almost no previous work on performance indicators in the voluntary sector. Similarly, it was noted that statistics could be provided for no more than three of the *Victim's Charter*'s 27 standards in November 1997. The *Victim's Charter* meeting of Victims Steering Group, 6 November 1997, Chairman's brief. 6 months later, the same complaint was being rehearsed at the next meeting: 'after two years there are few statistics to show compliance with the Charter standards. Yet demonstrating compliance is the all important issue'. Meeting of Victims Steering Group, 22 May 1998, Chairman's brief.

[83]  For instance, Victim Support had to announce at an 'informal meeting' in the Home Office in June 1998 that it had found it difficult to change present information until its whole information technology system had been changed. As matters then stood, it 'could only repackage what's already available'. It was to spend over £200,000 on information technology to comply with the demands of the new performance management. Minutes of meeting of Executive Committee of Victim Support, 21 July 1998.

[84]  See Crown Prosecution Service Annual Report April 1998–March 1999, 21 July 1999, Annex 3: Victim's Charter standards. Examples were that, on one standard ('a Crown Prosecution Service representative will explain why there was a delay') 26 complaints were received; and on another ('while you are waiting a Crown Prosecution Service representative will tell you what to expect' ) there had been 18 complaints. The Report stated that it had failed to reach 8 of its 12 targets, but had improved performance in 7. It was, it said, 'an acceptable outcome'.

[85]  The Court Service did come to issue a leaflet: 'I want to complain: what do I do?' in which steps to make complaints were outlines. Even so, a member of the Victims Steering Group observed in November 2001 that an absence of complaints could signify little more than that 'people have no confidence in the complaints procedure. It is unlikely to mean that the Crown Court is perfect.' The Group's chair replied: 'I think it is something we should be looking at because absence of complaint is hopeless. Our

victim and witness satisfaction. Thus an official of the Courts Service stated in March 1999, 'we've had no complaints about courts failing to meet charter standards. Now I say that doesn't mean that it hasn't happened but by their very nature the only way to monitor most of those standards is by complaint. You know if somebody, if you asked to see the courtroom and were told you couldn't, and just walked away, well how would I ever know?'

Comparisons could be missing. For example, indicators measuring the 'cost effectiveness' of the work of bodies such as Victim Support would be near to void unless it was known what condition victims were in before they received support and how long after the event, if ever, recovery could be said to have taken place.[86] There was an apprehension amongst some that the pursuit of targets would displace other activity,[87] that 'easily measurable indicators... will drive out the less easily measurable' or that the measurable would dislodge the non-measurable[88] (Douglas Hurd, the former Home Secretary, complained of the new propensity to engage in 'measuring what is unmeasurable... [and] auditing managers rather than inspiring them.... Because government can be too difficult, people can become blinkered and think of politics in engineering terms'[89]).

society is not very good at complaining. We're good at grumbling. A lot of people wouldn't know how to complain and wouldn't be bothered.'

[86] One Victim Support official enquired, 'To put the fundamental problem, how do you measure whether the outcome of a crime is more tolerable? When do you do it? When do you ask whether people are prepared to go out at night? One year? Three years?' National Council Meeting, 20 October 1998, my notes.

[87] See P. Blau; *The Dynamics of Bureaucracy,* University of Chicago Press, Chicago, 1955, p. 34. In the Criminal Injuries Compensation Authority, for instance, there was some pressure at the end of the calendar year to process applications where an award would be made and set aside for processing later those awards, the 'nil' awards, that would not feature in the Authority's formal reporting.

[88] A member of the Victims Steering Group observed 'we tend to concentrate on them to the detriment of other matters'. Victims Steering Group: meeting of 12 June 2001, my notes. Similarly, a Victim Support policy paper commented that the 1996 Victim's Charter had been written with the intention of having standards that were measurable, leading to a possible distortion of activity and a stifling of innovation because target monitoring can become dominant and rigid. Meeting of Victim Support Trustees, 20 October 2000, New Victim Policies: Paper for the Trustees. Again, the Director of Criminal Policy reflected in late 1999 that the draft Home Office public service agreement 'concentrate[s] on hard statistical measures to the exclusion of other things not measurable in such ways'.

[89] Speaking in the opening symposium at the launch of David Faulkner's *Crime, State and Citizen,* 4 June 2001.

Targets could be set in ignorance of 'baseline data' and become practically unattainable in consequence.[90] Targets could conflict (would the Home Office regard an increase in the numbers of applications under the already hard-pressed and massively expensive Criminal Injuries Compensation Scheme as a satisfactory or unsatisfactory measure?, wondered members of the Victim Support National Council in 1998[91]). Should reports of racist crimes increase (as the police argued) or decrease (as the Prison Service argued) in the wake of the report of the Macpherson Inquiry in early 1999?[92] Following a version of Gresham's Law, the attainment of one target might well inhibit the attainment of another,[93] and it was conceded in discussions about the Criminal Justice System Public Service Agreement in July 2000 that 'a wrongly formulated target can produce perverse behaviour'.[94] Other targets—such as crime rates—were affected less by changes in the criminal justice system than by complex, sometimes opaque processes over which officials had little control ('We have to recognise that the economic and demographic factors are working against us', noted one briefing on the new performance

[90] One such target was to raise witnesses' satisfaction with their treatment by the criminal justice system by 5%. There was some dismay in December 2000 when it was discovered in a commissioned survey of witnesses that the baseline was actually 76%, and to raise it by a further 5% was thought to be 'very challenging'.

[91] Victim Support National Council Meeting, 20 October 1998, my notes.

[92] A decrease might indicate a decline in racist crime, an increase a growth of confidence amongst members of minority ethnic populations and others in the criminal justice system. The matter was debated at the meeting of RISC, 7 December 1999.

[93] For example, said a senior police officer sitting on the Victims Steering Group, '...the one about response times, how long it takes you to respond to the incident. There is such an obsession with fast response times at all cost, that the quality of service you deliver when you get there, is actually not of consequence because you want to deal with it as quickly as possible so that you're able to meet the next response time and so on. Now I'd much rather we took a little bit longer to get there and give a quality service when we actually turn up.'

[94] Andy May, a Deputy Chief Constable who sat on the Victims Steering Group as ACPO representative, said, 'take something like the one I often quote is delivery of a sudden death message. You can knock on the door and say, "hello Mrs Brown, your husband's been killed in a motor crash, sorry about that. I'll get the next door neighbour to come in." Or you can do it as it should be done and devote time and resource and research into it and deal with it properly. Now I can't imagine any kind of performance indicator around that. But if you squeeze the amount of available time within the Police Service so tightly that it in the form of model that exists, that will be the service we will deliver.'

management[95]), and they could as a result appear quite quixotic (a Chief Constable informed a meeting of Victim Support Trustees in July 1999 that Downing Street had made a prediction that crime would rise by 40 per cent by some time in 2001 whilst it was still insisting that it should go down by 30 per cent). And a resulting tension could develop between what might be described as the 'realists' of the Home Office and agencies and the 'optimists' relentlessly driving reforms from 10 Downing Street.[96] Despite its own remonstrations,[97] the Home Office sometimes found itself charged with a lack of will and imagination that laid it open to criticism and intervention from the Prime Minister. Outcomes in the victims area could be equivocal and resistant to interpretation.[98] And they could simply defy measurement. One instance was the standard set for the

[95] Briefing for the PSX meeting on the CJS, 29 April 1999.

[96] BBC News On-line, 30 November 1999, reported that Tony Blair was not 'defeatist' over crime. The Home Secretary had informed Members of Parliament that economic models suggested that crime was likely to increase between 1997 and 2001. In his turn, the Prime Minister told listeners that 'We don't accept that [crime] has to rise, which is why we are taking a whole series of measures on burglaries . . . tougher measures on rape and assaults, tougher measures on youth justice, but also a whole range of measures on crime prevention as well. This is a situation where we can't allow ourselves to be defeatist about it. Crime has been coming down for two years, we have got to keep it coming down.' There was talk about the Prime Minister making Permanent Under-Secretaries personally responsible for failures to deliver performance targets: 'The letter comes after mounting Downing Street frustration over the lack of progress in delivering some of the Government's key reforms.' *The Times*, 24 August 1999. And he was also reported to have summoned chief constables to Downing Street after there had been a 20% increase in the recorded crime rate. *Evening Standard*, 12 October 1999.

[97] The Home Secretary stated that 'The economists have made projections of what effect they believe this would have on the level of recorded property crime, assuming no positive intervention by the police, local authorities or Government. I want to emphasise that the projections are not forecasts of what we as Government believe will, or should happen. Criminal behaviour is wrong, and the model provides no excuse for it. There is nothing inevitable about the trend in the models.' Home Office news release, 383/99, 29 November 1999.

[98] There was reported in 2000 to be declining but still high satisfaction amongst victims with the police, dropping from 63% declaring themselves satisfied in 1998 to 58% in 2000, but there was a lower figure amongst minority ethnic groups (A. Myhill and L. Sims; 'Victim's Charter Standards—findings from the 2000 BCS', prepared for the Victim's Steering Group). Helen Reeves enquired at the meeting of the Victims Steering Group in April 2000 where the paper was presented whether reported long-term declines in victims' satisfaction with their treatment in the criminal justice system might not be due to a raising of their expectations. Their priorities seem to have

police under the *Victim's Charter* that 'The police will do their best to catch the person responsible for your crime and to keep you informed of significant developments in your case:'[99] Commander Campbell of the Metropolitan Police, then a member of the Victims Steering Group, called it 'woolly stuff' and asked 'how the hell can you measure that?',[100] and his misgivings were to be repeated in a report to the Victims Steering Group which stated baldly that 'it is impossible to produce a statistic which shows whether the police are doing their best'.[101] A 'top of the Office' official who had superintended the drafting of a strategic planning document, observed that the new performance indicators were vague and there were not the resources and people on the ground to implement them. Performance indicators were, he said, the burden which was breaking the educational system, but it had been impossible to say so in the submission. For him, in effect, speaking the language of modernization was something of a pious perjury.

Most perplexing of all, perhaps, in the years of the first New Labour administration, compliance with the *Victim's Charter* standards was still heavily reliant on self-reported[102] rather than 'objective' data, and there were almost no sanctions for failure to attain targets apart from what were termed 'indirect penalties', the adverse

changed, she said: 'at the beginning people felt insulted and ignored ... and they're not complaining about that any more'.

[99] *The Victim's Charter,* Home Office, London, 1996, p. 2.

[100] He went on to remark about another standard, 'we didn't even agree on that one, the police will respond to reports as quickly as they can. Does that mean the initial call if it was an emergency call, how long the first responding officer took to get there or did it mean that, once the investigating officer for that offence has been appointed, how long did it take that individual to make their first contact and get the investigation under way? We didn't agree on that even ... It's just too loose. It's very well intentioned. I applaud the intentions behind it but it really ought to be tightened up.'

[101] Victims Steering Group meeting, 24 November 1999, 1996 Victim's Charter: Monitoring Standards of Service Standard 4.

[102] A Police Commander on the Victims Steering Group reflected, 'Well we don't know if there's non-compliance. That's one of the problems. If you can't measure it, how can you ascertain whether the police are complying with it. You know, the police will give you the name and telephone number of the officer responsible for the case or the crime desk. That's a little bit better but how is that measured independently? The answer is it's not. We the police say "oh yes, we've sent these leaflets". Then along comes the British Crime Survey that finds perhaps only 15% of them remember anything about this. And where does that leave us? So it leaves us in a very unsatisfactory position.'

effects on the criminal justice system,[103] and mechanisms of shame and self-reproach. There was some speculation, prompted by my questioning, about the possibility of consequences for pay and promotion and on the prospect of being summoned by the Permanent Under-Secretary to explain, as a Deputy Director of Criminal Policy put it, 'why [say] there's been slippage on a particular sub-aim that contributes towards their rural crime aim—that is real and that is different really'. But, as I shall show in the next chapter, the Victim's Steering Group, monitoring standards in the world of victims' policies, could only rely on officials' desire to perform well and avoid the humiliation that might accompany the missing of targets:[104] Dame Helen Reeves' observation, 'I think people want to be seen as doing the right thing', was echoed by John Halliday, Director of Criminal Policy and Chairman of the Victims Steering Group: 'We don't have the sanction of going out of business.[105] I mean that's the big difference. But we can trade on people's desire to do well and do a good job, [and] that's what we have to do.' Yet these were incentives flowing from the older professional culture of self-motivation and self-regulation rather than from the new performance management marked by political mistrust and external control. And interest in what might happen should there be non-compliance seems not to have been intense at the time, reflecting, again, perhaps the survival of the older professional culture of the civil service.[106] It would, after

[103] Ian Chisholm argued, for instance, 'we know that one of the problems the system faces is witnesses are not turning up and one suspects, we have to do more work on it, but if you have been waiting around a couple of times, you may not turn up a third time. So there's an arguable effect on the system on the whole of not treating witnesses [properly].'
[104] An Inspector of Probation talked about reiterated inspections of probation services and 'possible local reaction, you know, MPs who could ask questions and do and there's sentencers who would ask questions and who do and the situation committee to call the services you know, to account'.
[105] Jan Van Dijk of UNICRI in Vienna, once observed that 'if criminal justice systems were private businesses, they would go out of business because of customer dissatisfaction'. *Crime: Tenth United Nations Congress on the Prevention of Crime and the Treatment of Offenders: Crime and Justice: Meeting the Challenges of the Twenty-first Century*, Vienna, Austria, 10–17 April 2000—'Offenders have Rights... but Do Victims?'
[106] An official in the Government's Better Regulation Task Force, said in March 2000, 'I would say we are at this stage as well because we are at a very early stage of our work and I wouldn't actually know what the result of non-compliance is. I do know that in you know, there are certain areas where it's very grey because some police

all, be difficult to assign precise responsibility for many outcomes in so complicated a world as crime and the criminal justice system[107] and a culture of blame and penalty had yet to take hold. A policy official of the Crown Prosecution Service remarked simply, 'I don't know what happens if the report comes up to VSG [the Victims Steering Group] and that they're not happy at VSG with what you're getting back. We haven't reached that point yet, have we? But I mean individual agencies are monitoring their own [performance] ... [The] wider question as to you know, what would happen if the information feeding up to VSG was unsatisfactory. We've not actually reached that.'

Middle-ranking officials sometimes believed, as the Russian peasantry in 1905 had believed, that the Tsar-ministers were privately sympathetic to their lot and that it was the boyar-senior officials who held most tenaciously to the new managerialism, but, in good or bad faith (and mostly in good faith[108]) Ministers publicly drove modernization on and resistance was not only foreign to the general civil service tradition of disinterested service but could also earn one a personal reputation as maverick.[109] At the outset, it was certainly the case that Ministers sometimes remonstrated that submissions laid before them adopted the outer show but not the substance of a modernizing system. So it was that one of the new regulatory mechanisms by which 'governmentality' began to operate, a contractual service level agreement, in this instance between the Government and Victim Support, was referred back to officials on more than one occasion in 1998 because it was an 'SLA' for the 'sake of being one' rather than a 'proper' SLA: its objectives, it was said, were weak, and based on quantity rather than quality.

forces comply 100%, some comply 110% but some only comply 70%. So there's very much inconsistency. What the consequence for non-compliance is, I don't know.'

[107] An official in Service First, the Charter Unit within the Cabinet Office, said 'the difficulty is that whenever you're talking outcomes, you're really talking about lots of different agencies and agents. So reducing crime is hard to pin down to any one.'

[108] Alun Michael told me standards 'are important in the sense that actually setting what your intentions are is very important, providing that you then carry it on. I'm a great believer in management by objectives as it used to be called, so that you, you sharpened out from your statements of principle to measurable in terms of objectives and delivery.'

[109] In the case of the prison service and the maverick governor, see P. Carlen; 'Governing the governors', *Criminal Justice*, February 2002, Vol. 2, No. 1, p. 31.

Different worlds and appearances then co-existed in the Home Office at the turn of the century. At one pole was the public, stylized, formal, externally-regulated, economistic, commercialistic, and utilitarian world of the 'modernised' civil service as a performance-driven deliverer of clearly-delineated aims and objectives. At the other was the more complicated, subterranean, contingent, flexible, and nuanced world of a professional and hitherto significantly self-regulating civil service that experienced much of the social reality of problem-solving as an emerging sequence of largely non-quantifiable actions in the public service.[110] Officials occasionally acted as if they were working in a foreign language that did not quite translate their intentions.

## Ministers

The organization that delivered those aims, mapped rather schemat-ically in the Chart on page 70, was divided between politicians and officials: the chief sphere of the politician being the exposed and highly illuminated public domain of Parliament and the mass media, and of the latter the more private and secluded inner domain of Whitehall and the criminal justice system.[111] At the beginning of the new administration, the new Home Secretary, Jack Straw, was served by two Ministers of State and three Parliamentary Under-Secretaries of State responsible for different regions of policy. Touch-ing policies for victims at a tangent was Lord Williams of Mostyn, QC, a Parliamentary Under-Secretary, responsible for constitutional issues (other than elections), leading on Home Office business in the House of Lords, and in charge of the implementation of the Data Protection and Human Rights Acts of 1998; and, more squarely, Alun Michael[112] with charge, *inter alia,* of criminal policy, crime prevention and reduction, and victims' issues. Both Jack Straw and

---

[110] Perhaps all complex organizations are thus. See M. Punch; 'Suite violence: Why managers murder and corporations kill', *Crime, Law and Social Change,* 2000, Vol. 33, p. 245. For a parallel treatment of disparities between the public and private realities of policy-making, see R. Reich; *The Power of Public Ideas,* Harvard Univer-sity Press, Cambridge, Mass., 1990.

[111] Officials would speak to audiences in and around the criminal justice system, being visible to non-governmental organizations, for instance, but their names and faces would not have been known to the wider public world.

[112] Until October 1998, when he was succeeded by Paul Boateng, and then, in July 1999, by Charles Clarke.

Alun Michael, it will be remembered, had had links with Victim Support, and demonstrated a strong desire to promote policies for victims.

Ministers faced at least three major audiences: first, the political world of the Prime Minister, colleagues in other departments, and Parliament upon whom co-operation depended to promote almost any venture that touched on interests beyond the Home Office; second, the bureaucratic world of officials which they directed but that had existed before their arrival and would continue after their departure, a world nurturing policies whose beginnings they might not personally have known and whose implementation they might not survive in office to see; and, third, the world of public representations and public demands framed by constituents, lobbies, and the mass media. On the interstices of three worlds, Ministers were not strictly bound by bureaucratic protocol, convention, and regulation, and, at once unconstrained but unusually accountable, we shall see how, more than once, they were to intervene to promote ideas which had not been ratified in the slow and patient work of committees, consultations, and submissions. They were in that sense unfettered by normal routines, and their officials were sometimes obliged to work hurriedly in their wake to repair or service what they had done.

I shall deal with the first world of Parliament and Government as this book progresses, and with facets of the mass media and non-governmental organizations when I discuss the dramatization of politics in chapters on the Stephen Lawrence Inquiry and the *Speaking up for Justice* report on vulnerable and intimidated witnesses. One of those non-governmental organizations, Victim Support, over-shadowed all others. It was the one officially recognized representative of victims at large, incorporated somewhat uncertainly on the borders of the criminal justice system, and I shall examine its place and influence, particularly on the Victims Steering Group, in the next chapter.

Here I shall linger only with victim-constituents and petitioners, known colloquially as the 'angry victims' who, organized or unorganized, could make a mark well beyond their numbers and apparent power. Ministers, said a former senior civil servant, 'heeded experts but were easily swayed by constituents' views which carried a heavy moral and political weight'. Constituents were as authoritative a body as any other for the Member of Parliament, and Ministers were Members of Parliament. It was constituents who defined their formal role as political representatives and to ignore them would be to betray their responsibilities and forfeit something of their parliamentary identity. Charles Clarke said:

Victims are angry for a good reason that something terrible's happened to them. And I think it's better, in my constituency surgery where I've had to meet people who've really had terrible things happen to them, if they can feel that their loss has served something for the future, that it wasn't all for nothing, that there was a change in the system or a change in the law or something, that their relative didn't die in vain, as it were. It's very import-ant in my opinion for them to feel that, otherwise their lives go into a complete dive. And that's why, I mean I'm not going to spend my time as a therapist as it were, but I do think it's important to acknowledge that their scream has a right to be heard...I took the view, and I think Ian [Chisholm] was very helpful in this, too, that we should...be prepared to meet other organisations and see how it moves and develop a dialogue even though it's very difficult sometimes because people are very angry. But there are things that you learn. I mean I learned as a minister what their experience has been and therefore, it helps inform me as to what I should be trying to do in the future.

The victims whose meetings and letters were recorded in the files were not the victims of what is called volume crime, the thefts, burglaries, robberies, and assaults that make up the vast bulk of reported offences: those victims did not campaign at all. They were those who had been traumatically bereaved by the death of a relative feloniously killed as a victim of murder, manslaughter, or road crash. They could not be dismissed. Neither could their representations be disparaged. They were validated, almost sanctified, in their own eyes and in the eyes of those who beheld them, by an intensity of suffering and an exceptional experiential knowledge which lent immediacy, authenticity, and authority to what they said.[113] They could be extremely persistent, angry, and determined campaigners who demanded a response, but, for that very reason, they were also to be treated cautiously, neither ignored nor too readily appeased ('the challenge', observed an official to a Minister, 'is to reply in a caring fashion'). They could, it was thought, be intemperate and partisan in their judgment, uncomfortable to confront, and unreliable as guides to action. Officials were prone to be wary of them and tried to keep

---

[113] See my *After Homicide, op. cit.*

them at bay. 'They can be difficult, prickly and abrasive, confrontational...' warned a key official in the JVU in his briefing about one
group to a Minister. Given that anything said by a politician would
be dismissed, it would be unwise, warned another, to meet them in
public. There were to be meetings, but they could be immoderate,
and a Minister threatened on at least one occasion to end discussion
prematurely if the members of a group did not stop hectoring him.

The 'angry victims' could be cited in speeches, often in perfectly
good faith, as a personification of sound political reasons for
action:[114] they were vividly effective condensations of more abstract
and general arguments, and their invocation could underscore the
compassion and humanity of the politician. No doubt they were
from time to time before politicians in the imagination as policies
were rehearsed. But they were part of a separate, parallel universe of
discourse, appropriate to its political time and place, a small minority, not often explicitly cited within the internal policy process of
Government itself, offering at most the contents of an emotional
subtext to ostensibly neutral exposition: Charles Clarke said 'I've
made it a practice to meet people rather than not. I've responded to
debates in the House in that way—victims of violent crime but also
the victims of road accidents and so on who[m] I've met—but
I wouldn't say that the pressure that comes from there—[although
it's] real and I encourage it—is a very significant policy and opinion
for me.' When an organization representing victims was to be taken
across that symbolic divide between the public political world and
the internal policy-making process, it tended almost invariably to be
Victim Support, not the 'angry victims'.[115] Charles Clarke's predecessor, Alun Michael, reflected:

I think each of us have approaches from different groups. I mean there are a
lot of groups that are set up by people who've been the victims of violent
and horrific events, who sometimes set it up because they say 'nobody
should have to go through what I went through without support and help'.
And sometimes it's almost a way of working through themselves, and being

---

[114] Addressing the Labour Party Conference in October 1998, Jack Straw said that
the Crime and Disorder Act 'was not born from the musings of some detached political
elite. The act comes instead from the anger and concerns of our constituents, fed up to
the back teeth about criminal anti-social neighbours and about gangs of young
offenders out of control.'

[115] Although, as we shall see, Neville and Doreen Lawrence were also taken across
that divide as individuals, as was RoadPeace after the period covered by this book.

able to handle the experience that they've gone through. And the fact that it's done for those sort of personal reasons doesn't always make it a bad thing. I'm not suggesting that. Certainly on a number of occasions, I met groups of people who are very damaged and angry and upset because they've been through traumatic events. And sometimes those groups would be more focused on a single solution... That's why I think that it was signally important that Victim Support, as an organisation, both actually tried to work with some of those groups in a positive way and was trying to take, if you like, a more objective view of the things, which it's actually very difficult to do... They remain both authoritative and persuasive and practical.

I have already remarked in the previous chapter on how the Home Secretary and his Ministers responsible for criminal policy actively involved themselves in policy-making on victims throughout the first New Labour administration. They had drafted the three promises about victims in the election manifesto which was to be studied and translated into a broad agenda for action by officials as they readied themselves for an incoming government. Within a month of the general election, they had deliberately signalled their interest by increasing the Government's annual grant to Victim Support by a million pounds. They intervened when ministerial colleagues in other departments were slow or unwilling to move. They urged their own officials on. They made promises and expressed unrehearsed views which were noted by the officials who served them. Submissions and briefs would return with their personal observations about possible ways forward. They spoke about victims in speeches, parliamentary answers,[116] letters, and news releases, creating new commitments, or lending influence or emphasis to commitments already established or in the making. In short, the politicians of the new Government were energetic in the matter of victims as in other matters. Said a seasoned official in 1998, 'there is a lot more involvement, direct involvement, by Ministers, ... not just in policy but in management... the tradition was that they didn't really bother themselves about management but certainly over the last five years they've become more involved...'.

[116] An instance is Alun Michael's reply to a parliamentary question about restorative justice in the Thames Valley from an opposition Member of Parliament on 31 July 1997. He stated that he had 'been impressed by a number of initiatives such as the retail theft initiative in Milton Keynes...'. A senior official told a colleague in October 1997, 'We revised the position since AM's Parliamentary to Mrs May...'.

Involvement was almost always less a matter of command and control from above than of a dialectic in which officials tried to anticipate the wishes of politicians (but also indicated options and possible hazards within a structure that the politicians had defined[117]) and received in return ministerial observations which amended or rejected their efforts to interpret and consider the political will. Officials did not draft speeches, letters, and papers for express party political occasions, but all else was drafted, and what politicians said and wrote publicly was usually a revised version of what officials read as their intentions; available to be quoted back to them on later occasions as evidence of what they had meant or promised; and interlaced with more neutral and impersonal passages about background and history. The public face of the politics of victims (and most other politics) was thus in effect the politicians' modification of officials' representations of their own views, those representations being based on interpretations of past expressions by the politicians, the whole being set within a larger framework of political and administrative commitment, constraints, and possibilities. To complicate matters, Ministers changed office frequently (there were to be three consecutive Ministers of State responsible for criminal policy and victims between 1997 and 2001), their responsibilities were broad and onerous, and they did not and could not know all the planning, history, and detail that had underpinned the briefs, drafts, and submissions set before them. They had in large measure to trust their officials to phrase what was to be done and said in their name.

## Officials

Officials composed the permanent establishment of the Home Office, serving successive politicians and administrations; subordinate to the politician's will;[118] avowedly neutral in their professional

---

[117] There was no overt questioning of the new performance management, for instance.

[118] There was to be an illuminating exchange between Helen Reeves and the Director of the Criminal Policy Directorate, chairing the meeting of the Victims Steering Group of 24 November 1999. At issue was whether there should be a second stage Victim Personal Statement, at which victims could inform the court in writing about matters, in the chairman's words, 'whose primary purpose is to affect sentencing' (a position that was later to be changed). Helen Reeves remarked, 'The issue is,

commitments;[119] and concerned to coax proposals through the maze of the policy-making process. They were moved from post to post by design and at regular intervals—usually of three to four years—partly to inhibit the formation of undue attachments to local systems of relevance (or 'going native' as it was called), and partly to encourage the development of that commanding overview of many local systems which would be required of one who might eventually administer large swathes of a complex organization.[120] Those who initiated policy might not expect to see its consummation; those who saw a consummation might not have been involved in its conception; and a certain detachment necessarily ensued.[121]

The head of the Justice and Victims Unit who succeeded Ian Chisholm in 2001 succinctly offered a formal, public (and somewhat self-parodying) version of that position in a seminar for representatives of the European Community accession States in Dublin in October 2002, when she discussed relations between the State and non-governmental organizations with Helen Reeves, Chief Executive Officer of Victim Support:

I'm clearly the lady with the money and I never give them enough. I am a civil servant and I have no opinions of my own. I only have my Ministers' opinions. I have no expertise with working with victims. I am responsible for making policy happen. Ministers will say 'I want this to happen'. I might have to say 'this needs a law', or 'we need to go to the Treasury', or 'yes Minister we can do this'.

who wants it?' and was told by the chairman, 'the ultimate issue for me is whether Ministers want it...'.

[119] 'Neutrality', wrote Dowding, 'means that civil servants are willing and able to serve different administrations with equal effectiveness.' K. Dowding; *The Civil Service,* Routledge, London, 1995, p. 108.

[120] Although officials might in their careers occupy closely-aligned positions so that they will have worked at different times on different aspects of substantive problems broadly defined. One who became deputy head of the Criminal Policy Directorate in 2000 had formerly been occupied with policies on compensation orders to victims in the 1970s. Ian Chisholm, head of the Justice and Victims Unit in the first Labour administration, had in the past worked in the Prison Department and the Crime Prevention Agency on matters touching victims. *TIG Update,* Issue 11, February 1999.

[121] It was thus typical that both Keith Bradley, a Minister, and the woman who became head of the Justice and Victims Unit after the lapse of the period covered by this book, said at the launch of an implementation phase of *Speaking up for Justice* in January 2002 that they could not claim any credit for the policy.

Her predecessor, Ian Chisholm, was in post for a relatively long period as head of the Justice and Victims Unit between April 1996 and the point at which this narrative effectively ends in June 2001, and he was to play a pivotal role in the developments on which this book dwells. Like David Faulkner before him in the 1980s,[122] he came to be identified by those with whom he had dealings as one who was particularly knowledgeable about, involved in, and attentive to, issues affecting victims. He came to form a close working relation with Victim Support[123] (as had many of his predecessors) in pursuit of what had become known in the late 1990s as 'joined-up government'.[124] He was doughty in what was known as 'fighting his corner', for instance in securing Home Office funding for the self-help group SAMM, Support After Murder and Manslaughter, in early 1998. Under his direction of the Justice and Victims Unit, a number of separate policies came to converge and coalesce to form a critical mass, and we shall see in Chapter 10 that it was in part his response to the management of that mass that led to talk about a Victims' Bill of Rights.

## Administrative Structures

The 'realigned'[125] management structure of the Home Office was functionally arrayed around its seven aims under the overall political charge of the Home Secretary and Ministers, and the administrative charge of the Permanent Under-Secretary of State. Each aim fell under one of fifteen Groups that were themselves divided into specialist units. The Criminal Policy Group under its director and deputy director comprised twelve units of which one, the Justice and Victims Unit under its own head, a Grade 5, was itself split into core areas of responsibility under 'key staff'. In what was called 'a brigading of functions' by the Director of the Criminal Policy Group, the JVU was charged with ensuring that law and practice in relation

[122] See my *Helping Victims of Crime, op. cit.*

[123] Victim Support was to thank him for his 'considerable contribution' when he changed position and was no longer responsible for JVU. Minutes of the meeting of Victim Support National Council, 18 September 2001.

[124] 'The Procedures and Victims Unit work', he wrote, 'is all about joined-up government and working with groups in the community, such as Victim Support and the NSPCC', *HOtline*, 13 October 1998.

[125] *Home Office Annual Report, 1999–2000*, Home Office, London, 2000, p. 64.

## The Organization of the Home Office in 1997

Home Secretary

J. Straw

Ministers of State

| Lord Williams of Mostyn (Minister in the House of Lords, Human Rights and other matters) | A. Michael. . . (Criminal Justice Policy, including victims) | Other Ministers |

Permanent Under-Secretary of State

D. Omand

Criminal Policy Directorate [and twelve other directorates]

J. Halliday

[and ten other units, including the Sentencing and Offences Unit, Criminal Justice Bill and White Paper Unit, Mental Health and Criminal Cases Unit, Criminal Policy Strategy Unit and Juvenile Offenders Unit]

Procedures and Victims Unit

Grade 5

I. Chisholm

| Compensation and Victims | Prosecution Policy and Procedure | Evidence and Procedure | Trials Issues Group |
| Grade 7 | Grade 7 | Grade 7 | Grade 7 |

to criminal procedure was effective and 'that services to victims, including the operation of the Criminal Injuries Compensation Scheme, [were] well managed';[126] and its seven key staff in the area of victims in the first New Labour administration supplied the secretary to the Victims Steering Group and to the later *Victim's Charter* review; took forward the relevant recommendations of the Stephen Lawrence Inquiry (which will occupy its own chapter); prepared information leaflets, drafted speeches and advice to Ministers; supported new policy developments; worked with the One Stop Shop and Victim Statements pilot projects (which will also occupy their own chapter); supervised a number of policies on witness care; administered Government funding to Victim Support and SAMM, Support After Murder and Manslaughter;[127] and managed policy on compensation orders by offenders and the criminal injuries compensation scheme. What the Unit did not do was systematically maintain a grants programme for victims, although it did come to support Victim Support in 1986; Victim Support's affiliate, SAMM, in 1997; and later, outside the period covered by this book, the Rape Crisis Federation.

Like its sister units, JVU was a 'policy owner', a repository of substantive knowledge about and control over a particular area of work. Its members would field questions and draft text on matters affecting victims and witnesses (although the text would not necessarily later appear under the name of its original author); and members of adjoining units and officials in strata above the unit would characteristically defer to its rights to property and expertise in that region. For reasons of experience, practicability, accountability, and protocol its neighbours would not need to claim to 'know' much about victims. Thus a planning document, colloquially known as *CJ2010*, contained a chapter on victims drafted by Ian Chisholm. When asked about its analysis of victims' issues, the formal compiler of the report said: 'you probably ought to ask Ian Chisholm that because he is the policy owner. My role is to bring together and co-ordinate all of these different policy strands and try to make some kind of coherent strategy out of it which encapsulates all of the issues that the criminal justice system faces and victims is only one small part of that. So, if you want to know about detailed policy development on the victims side,

---

[126] Criminal Policy Management Team, October 2000.
[127] The central organization charted in my *After Homicide*, op. cit.

it is much better to ask somebody like Ian.' The outcome was that members of each unit were, for many practical purposes, at the centre of a division of labour and a concomitant system of knowledge and relevance from which the work of other units would appear somewhat out of focus. Officials were purposive and informed within their sphere, but, in a sense, their knowledgeability was maintained by a bureaucratically necessary fiction of functional ignorance about what was happening elsewhere, a reflection of Kenneth Burke's dictum that 'a way of seeing is always a way of not seeing'.

Functional ignorance was recognized and remedied by formally including other 'policy-owners' in deliberations about 'cross-cutting issues' (although not all policy-owners *were* always included and gaps could ensue). But there were consequences for framing identities, connections, and problems.[128] I have already remarked that problems of domestic violence were out of focus as were, for the most part, child protection,[129] rape, and the role of victims in the looming area of restorative justice whose home was the Juvenile Offenders Unit.[130] Vaughan observed that 'The structure of organizations limits members' access to information. The components of specialization—division of labor between and within subunits, hierarchy, geographic dispersion, for example—segregate knowledge about tasks and goals.'[131] Who, as a result, passed for victims and

---

[128]   Of restorative justice, one official was to write to colleagues in October 1997: '[it] is an issue that a good many separate parts of the Home Office have suddenly found themselves having to address although there is little substantive knowledge. Many parts of the HO are duplicating similar ground unknown to one another and have to generate proposals with partial or imperfect knowledge...'. His allegation was not supported by colleagues in the area, but it does flag how anomalies may seem to arise outside the established division of labour.

[129]   Child protection issues, reported an official of the Sentencing and Offences Unit in March 1999, were a matter in which 'the Department of Health broadly speaking is in the lead'. Yet JVU did have an interest, partly because of its role in convening the working group on vulnerable or intimidated witnesses, a category that included children, and its involvement in the Steering Group on Child Evidence. In late 1998, the Policing and Reducing Crime Group also had a stake in sexual violence and child abuse in its Police Operations Against Crime Programme. The issues were on the margins of a number of spheres of interest.

[130]   Helen Reeves commented in October 1999 'I don't sit on committees that often talk about restorative justice or race.'

[131]   D. Vaughan; 'Regulating Risk: Implications of the Challenger Accident', in J. Short and L. Clarke (eds.); *Organizations, Uncertainties, and Risk*, Westview Press, Boulder, Co., 1992, p. 239.

what passed for the field covered by policies for victims were inevitably circumscribed in ways that could confuse the insider and outsider. Chris George, working for Victim Support, critically involved in the development of restorative justice in the Thames Valley, concerned about the role of the victim in new cautioning and conferencing procedures that were managed by the Home Office Juvenile Offenders Unit, remarked how difficult it was that JVU knew little about restorative justice, and the Juvenile Offenders Unit little about victims: 'they are different departments', she complained, 'looking at different issues...'. I shall return to that matter in the next chapter.

Modernized to comply with the new performance management, the Home Office nevertheless retained some of the etiquette and practices of a classic Weberian bureaucracy, control being exercised hierarchically and information tending to travel vertically, level by level between, and laterally within, strata differentiated by authority and role. There was a protocol which fixed the broad lines of response, defining who could talk and write formally to whom and when about what kinds of matter, with what content and in what form. A minor anomaly was presented by political advisers, lying outside the formal chains of communication and accountability, answerable directly to the Home Secretary, who, from time to time, intervened to make recommendations or insert texts without observing the protocol customarily followed by permanent officials. On one occasion in 1998, for instance, a speech delivered by the Home Secretary contained unheralded passages about radical changes in courtroom procedure, disconcerting the Lord Chancellor who asserted robustly that he should have been consulted about an important matter that affected his department and the European Convention on Human Rights. But such diplomatic lapses were rare.

The circulatory system of the Office was marked by trails of decisions recorded on paper and email, and its contents flowed from diverse sources. 'Policy triggers' included 'the election manifesto, public commitments, events and crises, Parliament, public opinion, think tanks and the media, [and] specialist lobbying';[132] reports of inquiries; letters from Ministers' constituents; Members of Parliament writing to Ministers on behalf of their constituents;

---

[132] Induction for new Home Office Recruits 1999: C. Barnes; 'What is Policy?'

voluntary organizations requesting money and meetings or inviting Ministers to inaugurate conferences; academics proposing research; specialists forwarding policy recommendations, and much else. Each trail of decisions had its routes, substantive questions characteristically being referred down stage by stage until they reached the appropriately knowledgeable key member of staff and answering drafts travelling back to a stratum at or just below that of the official or politician who was originally addressed (private secretaries, for example, would often reply to letters sent to Ministers or the Home Secretary). Communication from colleagues in other units, or from departments and agencies outside the Office, would typically be directed at an official on the same level as the source, to be forwarded up or down the hierarchy to an appropriate recipient.

Paper travelled in orderly fashion: agendas preceded and minutes succeeded meetings; Ministers were routinely briefed in set form about new developments; and reports moved at fixed intervals to established destinations ('aim owners' were, for instance, to report quarterly in a 'standard format' to the Department's Criminal Justice Strategy Unit, outlining the business plans for each aim, performance measures, officials responsible for each objective, and the like[133]). In their most extended journeys, trails would involve drafts passing from key staff to heads of units, thence through the director of a group to the Permanent Secretary for guidance to officials about wording *before* submission and for accompanying guidance *to* Ministers on submission (although there were exceptions: 'key staff' in the units, for instance, wrote directly to Ministers on rare occasions); and, finally, from Ministers to Cabinet. As communication moved across major boundaries, so its ostensible authorship would change.[134] Most drafting was undertaken in the lower strata, at the level of substantive expertise, but what could emerge was a much redrafted and multiple-authored speech, letter or *communi-*

---

[133] J. Simmons; Strategy Board, to Management Board, 18 March 1999.

[134] The Criminal Policy Directorate's Statement of Purpose and Practice of March 1997 laid down, *inter alia*, that its main responsibilities were advising and briefing Ministers, including handling of correspondence, speeches, and parliamentary questions. In one unusual instance, Home Office officials drafted a letter for a colleague in the Crown Prosecution Service to appear over the Attorney General's signature for despatch to the Home Secretary.

*qué* issued in the name of the official or politician by whom it was released.[135]

The content of communication would be subject to tried *formulae* and conventions that simplified, standardized, and effectively anonymized work, ensuring continuity over time and between personnel, accountability, inclusiveness, and control. New recruits were told that the composition of policy proposals should be informed by stock preoccupations : 'know your stuff, edit it down, what questions do others have, don't take anything for granted; is the briefing about you? your enthusiasm? the subject? the subject in respect to the person being briefed?; what effect should your briefing have? ... manage the briefing to achieve the effect...'.[136] Reports to senior staff should consider 'What's the message? Structure/logical and strong framework; clarity—message easily understood? Clear simple language? Free from jargon? Clear recommendations/conclusions; simple and brief—focus on main issues; essential words and phrases—plain simple English; short words, sentences, paragraphs,[137] accurate/correct—supported by clear evidence, free from grammatical errors, complete—all necessary information; all important questions answered—balanced and fair—both sides of the argument, moderate, non-provocative language, constructive; avoid—clichés and slang, long words where short will do, passive terms, foreign words/jargon; affectation and desire to impress...'. There was, in short, a pronounced house style, and officials observed it. Theirs, said the head of RDS who succeeded Chris Nuttall, was the last bastion of literate English.

There was a strict template for documents. Thus the most important, 'submissions' laying policy proposals before Ministers, set out the 'issue', the 'background' (which would give a history and might point, say, to the keenness of public and media interest in the problem at hand), possible courses of action, 'handling' and 'timing issues'; annexes of pertinent correspondence, recommendations

---

[135] Indeed, the new head of RDS, Research Development Statistics, and formerly a Professor of Law, expressed some surprise when it was at first assumed that his speeches would be drafted by others. As an academic, he was accustomed to writing his own talks.

[136] Induction for new Home Office recruits, 1999: Modernising the Policy Process.

[137] One who was present at the induction took the following notes: 'extra detail can be annexed if necessary; business-like workmanlike; you're not working on an essay or an entry for a literary prize'.

and legislation; and a draft letter for the Minister's signature.[138] The preparation of submissions affected the phrasing of the arguments and action that anticipated them, requiring officials to give their minds to specific matters of context, urgency, presentation, target, and choice of action. And there was an equally strict mode of reply: Ministers would not characteristically write in person to those who had made a submission but through their private secretaries who might report quite perfunctorily that what had been proposed had been noted, that the Minister was content or that he or she had found the submission wanting in some or every particular. The private secretary's approving note was vital, the *laissez passer* that allowed matters, as it was said, to 'be taken forward'.

There was an etiquette to the public proclamation of new initiatives. The least initiative would be publicized by news release; the more important through arranged parliamentary questions; and the most important through news release, parliamentary question and a formal launch by Minister or Home Secretary to which might be invited journalists and 'stakeholders' (for instance, Victim Support, VOICE UK,[139] and the National Society for the Prevention of Cruelty to Children flanked the Home Secretary to yield the symbolic support of the private sector for the publication on 10 June 1998 of *Speaking up for Justice,* the consultation paper stemming from the vulnerable or intimidated witnesses initiative which will occupy its own chapter).

Most communications were 'copied in' to long lists of those in and about the Office who might have a 'key interest' or stake (the 'stakeholders') in the issue at hand, the lists tending to extend to relevant others on the level from which the communication issued, to key staff, and to officials to whom the writer was accountable. Those so 'copied in' were licensed to comment on what was afoot, and it was a licence that tacitly implicated them in proposals and initiatives: it was less easy to disclaim responsibility or profess astonishment when they had had their chance to intervene before matters came to a head or had reached Ministers or a wider audience. It was in this fashion that submissions to Ministers about any significant

---

[138] Even apparently slight matters could 'go to ministers'. In October 1997, for instance, the relevant Minister was asked to approve a new leaflet to be given to victims of crime.

[139] An organization devoted to witnesses with learning difficulties.

policy developments affecting the criminal justice system were supposed to indicate the extent to which other departments had been consulted and describe their views: 'Consultation should take place early with the aim of ensuring "no surprises".'[140] Travelling papers could then become transformed into a kind of public property containing ideas from many hands, editing and synthesizing thought, erasing that which might impede progress or compromise relations, and becoming increasingly anonymous, tactical and collective as they progressed. They might lose some of their original force, focus, or incisiveness as proposals, but their political prospects could be improved. In that sense, they were collaborative accomplishments although public accountability lay always with the named author if he or she were a politician.

There were other precautions and devices to ward off surprise and conflict: if, for instance, it appeared that there was an *impasse* or looming disagreement in discussions between equals in different agencies or departments, matters might be referred up to a more senior official or politician who might agree to prevail upon his or her counterpart in the other organization to intervene or settle matters personally ('wheeling out' a senior official or a politician was a term in local use). Such mechanisms for resolving disputes were vital if the conventional order of policy-making was to be maintained. After all, 'The bureaucratic preoccupation tends to be the avoidance of disturbance, the securing of a stable environment or negotiated order.'[141] Concord and resolution should prevail in committee, and particularly in committees containing outsiders who should not be exposed to shows of dissent: disputes between Ministers, in particular, were better resolved in person and not publicly or through proxies sitting in committee because, as an email put it on one occasion, 'it is wrong to air an internal Government dispute publicly. If the Home Secretary disagrees with X [another Minister] he should pursue it with X and say merely that the Government is addressing the ... issues.'

Emails, telephone calls and letters were devoted in large part to preparing the ground to guarantee that meetings, minutes, and written communications were managed efficiently and appeared

---

[140] Guidance on Trilateral Consultation, 1999.

[141] A. Jordan and J. Richardson; *British Politics and the Policy Process*, Unwin Hyman, London, 1987, p. 175.

harmonious and consensual.[142] As little as possible of a difficult decision, it followed, should go before important committees or figures before consultation or briefing and preparatory meetings behind the scenes had established a prospect of agreement[143] or, indeed, had vitiated the need for formal discussion at all,[144] and there was a busy commerce between people with 'lead responsibility' for critical areas of policy development in adjoining directorates, units, departments, and agencies. It was as imperative in a mobile environment continually to check territorial boundaries lest 'areas of overlap' and contradiction led to confusion and dispute. It was part of the emergent quality of the policy process focused on victims that developments in one region could encroach on those in another (most notably, in the period covered by this book, in the realm of data protection and the right to privacy under the Data Protection Act and the Human Rights Act of 1998). Officials were consequently obliged to devote themselves to forestalling clashes or repairing policies in collision. And matters of timing could be a complication. Events did not always march helpfully in step with one another: we shall see in Chapter 4 that in one instance, occurring in 1997, the progress of evaluating what were known as the *Victim's Charter* pilot projects, the One Stop Shop and the Victim Personal Statement, was out of joint with promises publicly delivered to implement initiatives nationally by particular deadlines, and repair work was required.

Just as monarchs once called one another cousin, so Ministers writing to Ministers would usually, but not always, address one another not only by first name but also under their own name. On the entry of new Ministers or a new administration, there would be some communication from the private office about the Ministers'

[142]  See M. Wright; 'Policy community and policy network' in P. Barberis (ed.); *The Whitehall Reader,* Open University Press, 1996, p. 55.

[143]  An ACPO representative's staff officer said of the Victims Steering Group, 'we do get calls from Victim Support about they're considering tabling an item, would we be in a position to contribute to that argument on the day. So we almost get a pre-warning about some issues and we go from there with it really and give them our position beforehand . . . We do a lot of negotiations about Victim's Charter issues out of the Steering Group and then they normally get signed off at the Steering Group.'

[144]  An ACPO representative on the Victims Steering Group stated that 'my focus would be on the problem outlined and what I needed to do to achieve a solution. Now sometimes that could be the Victims Steering Group, more often it would be a 'phone call or a chat with Ian Chisholm, people in the Home Office maybe . . .'.

preferred style of writing, and drafts corrected and edited in the Minister's hand could be distributed for the edification of officials ('to indicat[e] ... preferences in terms of content and style when writing ... '). Initiatives affecting expenditure, the work of other departments, or a significant facet of government policy required the approval of Cabinet colleagues through an appropriate committee. Officials with 'lead' responsibility having already been consulted, sometimes at considerable length, before the formal approach, the standard reply from a Minister would stipulate almost ritually but one condition or make one observation as if to confirm his or her Department's special interests and right to be acknowledged.[145] In the case of the Treasury, for instance, that observation would almost certainly touch on ensuring that new expenditure, if any, remained within agreed limits.

The *volume* of business was controlled by the spending limits set by the triennial Comprehensive Spending Review which stipulated budgets year by year and in advance for the funding of activities. The review allowed for a measure of planning in the medium term, and there was a small reserve, but the new, overlooked, or unanticipated might either have to be deferred to the next planning cycle or funded from existing budgets approved for other purposes. We shall see in Chapter 6 that, in the beginnings of the new New Labour administration in 1997–8, for instance, and as a result of a legal judgment in 1994, the final batch of awards that were still being made under the old 1990 common law damages model of the Criminal Injuries Compensation Scheme cost more than had been expected, and there was an anxious scrutiny of what other activities could be curtailed or postponed to pay for such unanticipated and unregulated, 'demand-led' expenditure.

Volume was controlled by the amount of parliamentary time and space afforded the Home Office in the Government's legislative programme. The proposed Victims' Bill of Rights, later the Victims and Witnesses Bill, and then the Domestic Violence, Crime and Victims Bill, which is to be the culmination of this history, was deferred in 2001 and at intervals thereafter in part because of the pressure of other parliamentary business. And volume was also regulated by the sheer administrative and physical capacity of

---

[145] From time to time, exceptionally, a submission would travel to the Prime Minister where it touched matters of known interest to him or her.

officials and others to transact business: decisions had continually to
be made about the numbers of working groups and committees that
people could bear at any time (an ACPO representative wrote to Ian
Chisholm in December 1998: 'Servicing the needs of the government
change programme is making life extremely difficult for a number of
senior police officers . . . '). Meetings could be rationed by spacing
(there was a limit to what the Victims Steering Group could accomplish, for instance, because it met only twice-yearly). Meetings could
be rationed by duration (although many of the meetings dwelling on
victims were long indeed, lasting in the Home Office and Victim
Support for two and a half hours or more, often without respite).
And items for discussion would be ranked in importance, the lesser
matters being subject to Chairman's action, postponed or excluded
altogether from the agendas of meetings.

The outcome was an orderly, controlled, almost stately, progression of proposals, decisions, submissions, and meetings conducted
within the greater and the lesser cycles of legislative programmes and
financial scrutiny, 'bilaterals' between the Home Secretary and
Prime Minister, meetings with Ministers and parliamentary committees, consultations and public commitments, on the one hand, and
the key intervening 'target outturns',[146] 'priority outcomes', 'milestones', and 'stages' that punctuated the policy process, on the other.
It was, for instance, usually impossible to embark on a substantial
new initiative without a proposal being made in good time for the
triennial Comprehensive Spending Review, and that, in its turn,
entailed lengthy prior internal deliberation about the likely political,
legal, and economic repercussions of policies, talks with external
agencies and organizations,[147] and trilateral and other consultations
with officials and Ministers from interested departments before
submission to the Treasury. Timetables were intricate, interdependent, and demanding; they could converge, collapse, or dovetail into
one another; their management required attentive co-ordination,
preparation, and servicing; and the papers accompanying them invariably conveyed an impression of unremitting urgency. Officials

[146] The language is taken from Aim 2 Business Performance Monitor, October
1999 and correspondence of the Strategy Unit with its reliance on the terminology of
SMART (Specific Measurable Achievable Relevant Times).

[147] There were, for instance, extensive discussions with the legal managers of
newspapers and with the Guild of Editors in 1999 about proposed reporting restrictions in the Youth Justice and Criminal Evidence Bill.

were preoccupied continually with the need to despatch what lay before them in good time.

It was, largely by design, a recursive process that folded back on itself. What was done and said inside and outside the Department created facts that could become politically constraining, compromising, or enabling, and officials had ever to be mindful of what they and politicians said. What was stated could be seized upon as a commitment or as a refusal to act, and commitments could not be made casually. It was sometimes as if officials and politicians produced their own political pressures, enacting an environment, in Weick's phrase,[148] that was capable of eliciting particular courses of behaviour.

A much underscored prerequisite of modernization was the comprehensive installation of information technology,[149] and emails and the Internet were being introduced somewhat patchily and tardily[150] to Whitehall and the agencies throughout the late 1990s and during the time of my research.[151] Computers were to speed and collate communication and information in the new, knowledge-based, evidence-led policy world, organizing intelligence about the functioning of the criminal justice system through the transmission of intelligence about trends in behaviour and performance,[152] and currents in victims' behaviour were themselves also measured to 'monitor' the work of criminal justice agencies. New information systems, claimed Richard Sennett, provide a comprehensive picture

---

[148] The joint criminal justice Victims and Witnesses Spending Review 2000 bid to the Treasury, for example, recited that the resources demanded reflected public commitments to the Stephen Lawrence and Glidewell Inquiries (which will be touched on below); publicly declared targets and public announcements by the Home Secretary.

[149] See *The Government's Expenditure Plans 1999–2000 to 2001–2002*, Vol. 2., p. 51.

[150] In February 1998, a request for information by a Home Office official to a colleague in the Canadian federal Ministry of Justice was accompanied by an apology for her not yet being on email. The *Victim's Charter* was placed on the Internet in early 1997. Victim Support acquired its own web site in September 2000 (although an earlier, pirate web site had opened a year before).

[151] Richard Wilson, the head of the Civil Service, claimed in May 1999 that it was only then that a proper IT system was being put in place across government departments. 'The Civil Service in the New Millennium', *op. cit.*, p. 2.

[152] The Board of Trustees of Victim Support were informed, for instance, at their meeting of 14 January 2000 that new forms of work and funding depended on a new accountability to the Home Office, and that that, in turn, required new and better

of the organization to top managers in ways which few individuals could elude.[153] But it might also be added that there was much that was not and could not be pictured by the new technology, and only the measured was visible.

Computers also speeded the transmission of messages and an outcome was that the visible and apparently stately progression of papers and meetings was actually lodged in a wider, more private, environment of gossip, informal discussion and, increasingly, a busy traffic in emails. I heard a little of the talk and saw much of the emails, and they constituted a series of parallel conversations and commentaries that were neither wholly unofficial (they were generally to the point and had their own, quite conventional presentational style) nor wholly official. When last I had studied the Home Office in the 1980s, its prime medium had been the carefully-nurtured and centrally-housed file, each file dedicated to a topic, identified by serial number and title in the Department's registry, containing the principal papers touching on an issue arrayed and numbered chronologically, accompanied by a running narrative of decisions taken, people consulted and considerations weighed. Praise was given to those who were 'good on paper', the officials who could write elegantly, logically, effectively, and succinctly. And the cumulative effect was that officials new in post, or wishing to learn the history of a problem, could refer to the file and learn what could serve—with the passage of time, the movement of staff and the inexorable tendency of officials to forget—as a good enough repository of well-ordered practical knowledge about a subject. All that had changed when I returned to the Home Office at the end of the twentieth century. 'Nobody ever, ever, ever does that now' said a member of RDS. Internal email had been in use for some two years, external email was being introduced, and 'being good' on paper had been displaced (or at least joined) by another admired skill: 'Nowadays,' said Ian Chisholm, 'what people want is a quick, fast response—quick thinking.'

performance measures as a condition of a grant in aid and, by extension, a major review of IT systems. Victim Support was to spend three years of lottery funding to buy some 350 new machines at a cost of £210,000 for distribution to its local schemes. In June 1999, only seven local victim support schemes had email addresses.

[153] R. Sennett; *The Corrosion of Character*, W.W. Norton and Co., New York, 1998, p. 55.

Two streams were beginning to run parallel to one another: one was the well-orchestrated and open progression of formal and weighty arguments, the 'machine', which remained the preserve of those good on paper; the other a voluminous buzz[154] of semi-private electronic exchanges, commentaries and drafts phrased more informally, but certainly not ungrammatically or colloquially,[155] reflecting capacities for rapid thought; the 'froth'. Ian Chisholm continued:

The internal stuff is beginning to affect our work, things are much faster, things move much quicker, everyone sorts of communicates . . . including all the politicians, and you just have to act more informally. . . This [emailing] is the quick stuff ('okay, that's not a good idea, blah, blah') but if you get something really complicated, in the legal area [for instance], you do then have to have the considered argument. So there is the parallel thing. It gets rid of a lot of the froth quickly, but if you wanted something really right ('this is what we're thinking about . . . '), the machine is still working, it has to go through the machine still, the machine still works . . . I think you can have them in parallel. It's a good sort of way of quickly exchanging ideas but you still need to go through the process and have a decent consideration.

The streams affected one another, lending each other momentum, content, and context, that amounted sometimes to virtual conferences and meta-narratives that supplanted the corporeal conference. 'If we need to talk', complained one official by email, 'let's have a meeting rather than more e-mails.' Yet the press of emails actually left less time to meet, write letters and briefs, and some officials

---

[154] An official of the Lord Chancellor's Department who had a lead on victims talked about 'a pattern, . . . daily, almost hourly contact, with them, with my counterparts. We do work very closely together within the criminal justice areas.' Another official talked about receiving 200 emails a day.

[155] Emails in the Home Office were quite evidently a form of talk regulated by the wider etiquette of the grammatical, orderly, and well-presented argument. A senior official said 'the Home Office is still maybe a bit more wordy and paperish even in its electronic versions than some other departments'. Officials were still presenting themselves one to another as competent, educated men and women, and there was almost none of the impersonal, linguistically impoverished, colloquial, context-independent and non-hierarchical communication that writers about electronic communication have flagged in, for instance, M. Brigham and J. Corbett; 'E-mail, power and the constitution of organizational reality', *New Technology, Work and Employment*, March 1997, Vol. 12, No. 1, p. 26; I. Peckham; 'Capturing the Evolution of Corporate E-Mail: An Ethnographic Case Study', *Computers and Composition*, 1997, Vol. 14, pp. 343–60; and M. Castells; 'Materials for an exploratory study of the network society', *British Journal of Sociology*, 2000, Vol. 51, No. 1, p. 19. Perhaps the character and consequences of email are more culture-bound than analysts have supposed.

complained that they now discovered themselves more often responding to others' messages than creating their own. (Of course,
others claimed that that press reinforced a not unwelcome reclusive-
ness: 'some people, given half the chance, will sit at their desk all day
and send emails to other people even if they're just around the
corridor').

There was an impact on interpretive procedures: the written page
and the formal utterance achieved a quality of 'indexicality', their
full meaning depending on an informal and unexplicated background of understandings and conclusions reached through the
medium of emails and private conversation. There was an impact
on the organization and retention of knowledge. In the archetypal
nineteenth century bureaucracy described by Weber, management
was 'based upon written documents (the "files") which [were] preserved in their original or draft form'.[156] By the late 1990s that
system had changed beyond recall. In the modernized Home Office,
files were no longer meticulously kept by a central agency (Chris
Nuttall, head of the RDS in 1998, said that 'the breakdown of the
file pre-dated email...email may have exacerbated it, but it isn't
email that's done it'), paper was but one medium of communication,
and there were no permanent, well-tended, and widely accessible
histories on disk or paper.

Analysts of the new electronic media appear to have expected the
very reverse: an intensification and enlargement of collective memories.[157] For example, Brown and Lightfoot asked a little grandly
'what happens to historical consciousness in the time of modern
technology?...remembering as a practical accomplishment exists
in the midst of two sets of interdependent activities. On the one side,
the weft of language, on the other, the ordering of things and equipment...people forget things. The archive helps them remember.'[158]
But the want of order and centralization in the paper and electronic
filing systems and the unregulated spread of emails in the Home

[156]  In P. Blau; *The Dynamics of Bureaucracy, op. cit.*, p. 33.

[157]  See, for example, R. Sproull; 'A lesson in electronic mail', in L. Sproull and S.
Kiesler (eds.); *Connections: New Ways of Working in the Networked Organization*,
MIT Press, Cambridge, Mass, 1991, p. 19; L. Markus; 'Finding a Happy Medium:
Explaining the Negative Effects of Electronic Communication on Social Life at Work',
*ACM Transactions on Information Systems*, April 1994, Vol. 12, No. 2, p. 140.

[158]  S. Brown and G. Lightfoot; 'Performing the past in the context of electronic
archives', unpublished paper, December 1999, pp. 3, 8, 11.

Office had disrupted the organized accumulation of an archive: emails were often ephemeral (an official remarked 'I wipe out scores a day'); too informal always to become public; occasionally quite personal to those who sent and received them;[159] and haphazardly collated and preserved. A senior official, the sometime Deputy Director of the Criminal Policy Directorate, complained to me in July 1998 that there was no obligation to keep hard copies of emails or consign them to disk, and the effect was that there was no written record or accretion of knowledge about decisions, no way of gaining full access to decisions, and no way of individuals tapping information. He had, he said, no idea of what the impact of those innovations would be and no one seemed to have attended to the problem.[160]

But some consequences were becoming transparent. An equally senior colleague complained over two years later that he was worried by the loss of the well-kept file with its narrative: he had no idea how people managed to step into new posts without a well-prepared brief in the form of a file. An instance was furnished by the lack of proper files on a major policy document, the 2001 European Framework Decision on the Standing of Victims which I discuss in Chapter 10: the decision had been managed by emails which the 'key' official in JVU had deleted because his computer's memory was overfull. It shows, reflected a colleague, 'some of the consequences of the new electronic management of information'.

As filing became less meticulous and as electronic communication grew in scale, so there was a loss of a corporate memory and the piling-up, instead, of ad hoc 'hybrid assemblies'[161] of paper and electronic records in individuals' personal collections. Ian Chisholm observed, 'we've moved to a much more informal approach... files aren't being passed now, people send notes, they send emails or they send documents which they copy around. So it's assumed that the person in the lead is keeping policy files... but it is more difficult

---

[159] The Public Records Office reflected in 1998 in its Guidelines on the Management and Appraisal of Electronic Records, 'electronic documents are often regarded as informal and personal, especially e-mail...'.
[160] To be sure, the Public Records Office at Kew had devised a system called EROS (Electronic Records in Office Systems) in 1998, in an effort to ensure the storing of important information, but the system did not appear to be known in the Home Office.
[161] Guidelines on the Management and Appraisal of Electronic Records, n. 159 above, p. 9.

with emails ... '. And a colleague in a different part of the Office concurred: 'you've got something like a Bill that goes through, you know, and all the effort that goes into that and papers everywhere, and copies everywhere, and unless you've got somebody at the end of that sweeping up ... '. Paradoxically then, there were significant areas of Drucker's 'information-based organization' which were not information-based at all. Some would argue that such a loss was not wholly inimical to modernization. Richard Sennett, for instance, would maintain that a long institutional memory is occasionally regarded as a barrier to change in the new, flexible organization.[162]

I should not overstate the case. As head of the Justice and Victims Unit, Ian Chisholm maintained an extensive and orderly collection of papers in his office, including hard copies of emails. Had he not done so, this book could never have been written. But there were acknowledged gaps, problems of access, and a want of overall co-ordination across the Office. Even Ian Chisholm's files did not reach back before 1996 (and there were no good practical reasons why they should have done so). In an organization where staff changed position with some, indeed increasing, frequency, where there were the beginnings of 'delayering' and a planned loss of senior management, there could be repercussions for the transmission of experience and knowledge.[163] For example, a junior official who had just joined JVU in 2001 lamented that she had been

---

[162] In a seminar delivered to the Department of Sociology, 15 September 1998. Judy Wajcman pointed out to me that 'it is much debated to what extent the new flexible organisation is a *reality* as opposed to what [the] Harvard Business School *prescribes* for organisational structure.'

[163] In an analogous study, Gerald Cradock approached thirty-five organizations in and about the Government of British Columbia to ascertain their role in the politics of inquiries into child abuse that had punctuated the history of policy-making in the province. The outcome surprised him: 'With the one exception, none of the organizations responding to my letter knew they had made submissions. Indeed, many had never heard of the inquiries at issue ... this means that all memory of the inquiries, and the organizations' submissions to those inquiries, had been more or less erased within ten years. The most usual reason given for this lack of institutional memory was that the persons ... responsible for such submissions were no longer working for the organization.' G. Cradock; *Governing Through Vague Terms: Child Abuse, Community, Government and Group Interests*, Thesis submitted for the degree of Doctor of Philosophy, University of British Columbia, 2003, p. 22.

bequeathed no files to cover her area of work, and she had been obliged to construct her own *de novo*.

One of the most literate groups of men and women had thereby become functionally illiterate and could find it difficult to reconstruct their own history. Indeed, a draft of this book would itself come in time to be the only thorough exposition of what had tran spired in the area of victims' policies at the turn of the century, to be consulted by a new generation of officials.

For want of an organized memory, officials were obliged to return to quite elementary methods of transmitting history. *Faute de mieux*, as Chris Nuttall, then head of RDS, remarked in 1998, 'it's become an oral tradition! I think it's amazing! I think it's stuck in people's heads and then they tell people, they brief them!' If one were senior, it was certainly possible to request a briefing about policies in train from a 'key member of staff'. The woman who became head of JVU in 2001, did precisely that when she asked the 'Grade 7s' to give her a 'written note' about what they were working on and then, later, an oral report. But not all staff were senior enough to secure a briefing, not all key staff would have been in post long enough to provide one,[164] and there were few staff indeed who were capable of remembering the more distant roots of policy decisions. As people moved about the Home Office, retired or became forgetful, so knowledge dissipated, became disorganized or was reworked. Lewis Namier once said that 'one would expect people to remember the past and imagine the future. But in fact, when discoursing or writing about history, they imagine it in terms of their own experience ... they imagine the past and remember the future.'[165] Thomas Hobbes was more succinct: 'memory and imagination are but one thing'. Indeed, I will show how it was possible for a number of policies to evolve precisely because staff were free progressively and liberally to redefine their past and purpose.

In such a world, the practical past and future of policy-making tended to be extrapolations of a present defined by the exigencies of work. Mead once made the more general point quite economically: 'Even in the so-called specious present there is a passage, in which

---

[164] Grade 7s tended to move relatively rapidly, rarely remaining in post for more than 3 years, but JVU was exceptionally staffed by two well-established key officials who were, in effect, its official remembrancers.

[165] In *The Mail on Sunday*, 4 November 2001.

there is succession, and both past and future are there, and the present is only that section in which, from the standpoint of action, both are involved.'[166] Officials were chiefly preoccupied with the pragmatics of what they had to do and were expected to know in order to get on with their jobs. Theirs was a working future that was foreshortened and defined by tasks at hand. After describing a gamut of policies that were occupying him in September 1998, Ian Chisholm remarked 'I don't know where the next big thing is. I mean there's enough there to keep us going a bit.' Very similarly, John Halliday, then Director of Criminal Policy, anticipating the future of policies for victims, talked in October 1998 about developments stemming from *Speaking up for Justice* (an initiative on vulnerable and intimidated witnesses), and from the reorganization of the Criminal Injuries Compensation Scheme, and concluded 'I would have thought that's probably quite a lot'. Current preoccupations were more than enough, in other words, to be getting on with for the time being.

What officials were to get on with reflected their role and accompanying system of relevance within the division of labour. Asked to anticipate what lay ahead for victims, one who worked on the *Victim's Charter* pointed in 2000 to moves to produce a revised, third version of the Charter. One who worked in the Lord Chancellor's Department on policies for witnesses appearing in the courts, also referred in October 1998 to the implementation of *Speaking up for Justice*, 'that's the main task ... It's very difficult to know what's actually beyond that because there's been a lot of concentration on that at the moment.' An official who had lead responsibility for victims' and witnesses' policies in the Crown Prosecution Service talked about a 'growing expectation that a [higher] standard of service will be provided to victims ... and that victims will certainly have a right to be given more information and will be more involved in the consultation perhaps about what the [prosecution] decision is'. An ACPO representative on the Victims Steering Group talked in February 1999 about a future taken up with work on family liaison officers (working with families in homicide cases) in the wake of the report of the Stephen Lawrence Inquiry. For them, the trajectory of future policy was delineated quite precisely by their role and struc-

---

[166] G. Mead; 'The Genesis of the Self and Social Control', *International Journal of Ethics*, April 1925, XXXV, No. 3, p. 273.

tural location: that was where *their* actions and interests would take them. But, predictably perhaps, and again mirroring the division of labour, those at the very apex of the organization, responsible for a broader and more abstract view of policies for victims, talked most confidently, globally, and systematically about possible developments. Charles Clarke, Minister responsible for criminal policy, said:

I think I'd say, I'd be very surprised if there weren't at least formally an ability of victims to make a statement in court, if you're talking ten years down the line say, a statement in court about the impact of the crime upon them and their families. I'd be very surprised if we didn't have a far more structured relationship between victims and in particular the CPS and the police, so that they had a clearer statement of what was taking place. I'd be very surprised if we didn't have a more structured relationship between police, social services and others, about dealing with the consequences for victims and particular crimes that they've had [dealings with]. I think all of those things will certainly happen. If you then go further to a greater stake for victims in the criminal justice system, paying legal expenses and so on, I'm slightly less certain how that will evolve . . . I think another certain thing is we'll have more of the restorative justice type approach around, particularly with young offenders. . . . I think our initial assessment of the restorative justice approach which has been taken has been generally positive . . . And so we'll have to see, but if we're going ten years down the line, I'd be surprised if we didn't have more of that. And I think that generally there will be, seen to be, more of a stake for victims than there is at the moment.

## Conclusion

The Home Office of the turn of the century was in some flux, working simultaneously with older and new administrative systems, and different vocabularies and conceptions of professional identity, role, and responsibility. Its medium was argument carefully formulated for ultimate delivery to Ministers and beyond, moving backwards and forwards between 'key staff' occupying areas of substantive expertise in the Units and those with an even greater power to act who were working with wider and ever more abstract representations of processes and procedures near the 'top of the Office'. Officials characteristically occupied formally delimited roles with attendant systems of relevance and conceptions of time and purpose that lent focus and definition to what they 'knew' for the practical and accountable purposes of getting on with their jobs. As ideas moved up through, and beyond, the hierarchy of responsibility and power, so they were modified to accommodate the interests of others, the 'stakeholders', and became more anonymous and collective in their appearance as they did so. The prime mechanism for moving those ideas was the committee, and it is committees, and the Victims Steering Group, in particular, that will be the centrepiece of the next chapter.

# 3
# Committees

I argued in the last chapter that officials worked inside schemes of relevance and knowledge that became increasingly general and abstract as they ascended the Department's hierarchy. What connected their segmented views was a system-wide architecture of interlocking committees that brought people together regularly and within a common frame. Describing the preparation of the Home Secretary's diary, a personal private secretary remarked in July 1999 that attempts at forward planning over the next six month period could be futile, but, although there would be a number of 'unpredictables', there would also be a number of 'inevitables'. It was those 'inevitables' and the other props of the fixed apparatus of the Department's workings that under-girded policy-making. They sustained the processes that came eventually to deliver proposals for a Victim's Bill of Rights at the end of the first New Labour administration.

Committees were the chief prop of policy-making and they served multiple ends. They were the standard means of taking projects forward. They were a visible proof that problems were being addressed. They gave a timetable—a teleology of goals and deadlines—to the policy process; they were responsible for conveying and collating information across the lines of the criminal justice system; they set and co-ordinated tasks; distributed ownership; conferred structure on what could otherwise be unpredictably contingent and emergent processes; made agencies accountable; and lent a collective authority to decisions. They were made up of the 'stakeholders' from inside and outside the Department who 'led' on victims and witnesses, and they drew people and organizations in, prompted them to act, and developed their ideas. They obliged people to accommodate one another's interests, negotiate outcomes, and make themselves open to discussion. In all this, they outlined who was needed to act, who had to be trusted, who would be acknowledged, and who was to be knowing, and that was a matter of symbolic and practical moment because their composition defined what counted as a problem, who would have a hand in its management and by extension, and important for this history, who were to be recognized as victims. Thus, the important decision taken in June 1999, in the wake of the Stephen Lawrence Inquiry, to expand the Victims Steering Group to add minority ethnic group members led to the inclusion of two women, one of Asian[1] and one of Afro-Caribbean origin, and that, in turn led to a new emphasis on the racialized victim when, for example, it was argued that equality issues should be dealt with in discussions of restorative justice.[2] Beverley Thompson of NACRO, the new Afro-Caribbean member, was to say,

In terms of the Victim Steering Group that I'm on, I've been particularly asked to join that group, not so much from an offender perspective but from a race perspective. Because I think one of my major concerns is that when we talk about victims in its broadest sense, the image always conjured up is of the white elderly woman pensioner. And I think that still with the amount of work that's going on and the very high profile work around victims, that image still remains. And I think that you know, [there is] quite a lot of work to do to shed this image in terms of who victims are in the broader criminal justice system.

It was inevitable that different committees with different terms of reference in the victims' and witnesses' field should have drawn on a common pool of stakeholding experts, 'the representatives of agencies with an interest'.[3] That field was only a minor segment of the criminal justice system, few staff worked in it, and they were to be called on repeatedly to service the web

[1] She was to say that, although she was a District Judge and a member of the Criminal Justice Consultative Committee, 'I don't think I'm on it strictly from the CJCC as such ... it seems to me ... there's nobody from any of the community groups I serve ... so I think it's a combination, because I am very conscious of the ethnic minority aspect of it and at the same time I am in the criminal justice system, in that I am one of the agencies ...'.

[2] Minutes of the Meeting of the Victims Steering Group, 28 April 2000.

[3] Chairman's brief for meeting of the Victims Steering Group, 24 November 1999.

of committees on victims and witnesses.[4] The same people were appointed to lead for the Home Office, the Lord Chancellor's Department, Victim Support, the Crown Prosecution Service, ACPO (the Association of Chief Police Officers), what was then ACOP (the Association of Chiefs of Probation), the Magistrates' Association and the like, and they converged again and again in the Victims Steering Group and its working groups;[5] the Victims Policy Forum (centred in the Prison Service);[6] the Victim Network (centred in the Probation Service); TIG, the Trials Issues Group, and its subgroups;[7] the Steering Group on Child Evidence;[8] RISC, the Racial Incidents Standing Committee;[9] the Working Group on Vulnerable or Intimidated Witnesses; the National Council of Victim Support, and others. It was as if policy-making in England and Wales (and elsewhere[10]) was an elaborate dance with many formal figures but a small, more or less stable, and intimate *troupe* of dancers.

[4] The choreography and composition of the *troupe* could vary. The officials engaged in the routine, working committees tended to be heads of units and 'key staff', the men and women who had the relevant experience to get on with the job. However, protocol demanded that that division of labour should give way where issues were exceptionally managed by Ministers and administrators at the top of the Office. When, for example, the Home Secretary took personal charge and chairmanship of the Lawrence Steering Group, responsible for the implementation of his action plan, itself a response to the report of the Stephen Lawrence Inquiry, his stature required a suitable elevation in the standing of the Group's membership. Unusually, the Group included two Home Office Ministers and the Director of Criminal Policy at the Home Office. And it was no longer enough to second leading policy officials from the pool but the heads of organizations, the Director of Public Prosecutions, and Her Majesty's Inspector of Constabulary, to represent the CPS and police service.

[5] One such body, the Victim's Charter Pilot Projects Working Group, which I shall touch on later in the book, included Helen Reeves of Victim Support, Roger Ford of ACOP, and a long-standing Grade 7 of JVU.

[6] At its first meeting in November 1998 were present Roger Ford, leading for ACOP, Teresa Reynolds of Victim Support, and Ian Chisholm of JVU.

[7] The Witness Care Sub-Group of TIG included Teresa Reynolds of Victim Support, Derek Oakey of the LCD, Pauline Spencer of CPS, and a Grade 7 of JVU.

[8] Containing, in 1997, Helen Reeves of Victim Support, Ian Chisholm, and a Grade 7 of JVU.

[9] Including, in June 2001, a Grade 7 of JVU, Anne Viney of Victim Support and Alan Kirkwood of CPS.

[10] I commented on the same phenomenon in the Federal Government of Canada in the early 1980s. See my *A View from the Shadows: The Ministry of the Solicitor General of Canada and the Justice for Victims of Crime Initiative*, Clarendon Press, Oxford, 1986.

The larger committees such as RISC,[11] the Victims Steering Group,[12] and the National Council of Victim Support,[13] were some twenty to thirty strong to accommodate the numbers of interested stakeholders who had to be included for diplomatic and practical reasons, on the one hand, but which were also limited, on the other, by questions of practicability (the largest committees were at risk of being unwieldy) and by the physical capacity of meeting rooms in the Home Office, Victim Support, and elsewhere to house larger groups. Some met infrequently, like the Victims Steering Group, gathering twice a year, and the National Council of Victim Support, gathering quarterly. Others might meet intensively: the Interdepartmental Working Group on Vulnerable or Intimidated Witnesses met monthly during its relatively brief life, for instance. Their deliberations were prolonged, lasting for two to three hours without respite (the Victims Steering Group, for instance, would start at 11.00am, break at 1.00pm, and then, depending on the volume of business, resume up until 3.30pm). They appeared to be formalized in procedure, lacking much obvious animation and spontaneity. After all, their members were salaried professionals who were expected to act without visible personal passion. And much of the routine stuff of policy-making usually took place outside the rather orderly and public procedures of the grander committees: the more difficult matters of substance, disagreement, and controversy were supposed already to have been forestalled and managed through negotiation by letters, telephone calls and emails or in small meetings, not aired unrehearsed in their raw form before representatives of the criminal justice system at large. A Staff Officer who accompanied an ACPO representative to the Victims Steering Group commented, 'We do a lot of negotiations about *Victim's Charter* Issues out of the Steering Group and then they normally get signed off at the Steering Group ... We discuss these issues in the background and then come up with conclusions without [difficulty] at the Steering Group. But ... not all the discussion is on the day.'

Most members tended briefly to move in and out of the flow of argument, speaking when their department's or agency's interests were affected, and summarizing, when called upon to do so by the chairman or chairwoman, and typically by rote, the actions taken by

---

[11]  20 strong in December 1999.    [12]  26 strong in July 1998.
[13]  20 strong in 1999.

their department or agency since the last meeting Their reports tended to be concise, going to immediate matters of action and resources—usually over the short term—and not to a more discursive or searching exploration of larger or deeper issues of principle. They were occasionally questioned about detail, but that was all: their role was almost wholly to render a formal accounting before their peers and the rest was taken on trust. For the greater part, they were silent, serving chiefly to provide a symbolic audience to ratify the accounting process. Meetings of that size could not have afforded to let members speak on average for more than a total of six or seven minutes, and not all members were of equal importance. Not atypical was a representative on the Victims Steering Group from the Cabinet Office Charter Unit, later Service First, in attendance because of the Group's responsibilities for the *Victim's Charter*, who reflected that 'I simply see what's going on and . . . I have probably only spoken twice. It only meets every six months and I've only spoken a couple of times anyway.'

It may be supposed that it was actually difficult for any of the members, however attentive, to concentrate throughout such a protracted span as two or three hours,[14] or to retain many points in their minds at any one time.[15] For the most part, their attention must have been fitful and their role passive. A senior civil servant reflected that 'a lot of the longer meetings are hopelessly inefficient. People can't and won't concentrate. What they do is focus on the small report or small statement they are to make and then not play much of a role. It is often more agreeable than getting on with a job which is waiting one on one's desk; it takes one out of the office and in the company of one's colleagues; it gives one an opportunity to be funny or clever or have a go at the chairman or appear keen.' 'Meetings of two to two and a half hours should not be allowed', he concluded.

The only members who did play a markedly busier and more vociferous role were representatives of the Justice and Victims Unit, the specialist unit that covered much of the terrain and who often fielded the chairmen, chairwomen, and secretaries who

---

[14] G. Gibbs and T. Habeshaw claim that 'People just can't attend and learn effectively when they are passive for longer than 20 minutes or so.' *Preparing to Teach*, Technical and Educational, Bristol, 1992, p. 42.

[15] See G. Miller; 'The Magical Number Seven, Plus or Minus Two: Some Limits on our Capacity for Processing Information', *The Psychological Review*, March 1956, Vol. 63, No. 2, pp. 81–97.

prepared, orchestrated, and informed discussion; and the representatives of Victim Support who spoke diffusely in the victims' interest and were touched by almost every item reviewed. There were frequent interventions from Dame Helen Reeves, Teresa Reynolds, and Anne Viney, at that time Assistant Director of Victim Support with a special interest in matters of race and 'diversity'. The secretary to the Victims Steering Group said:

> We've had a system whereby other members of the group can suggest items for the agenda, and in my time we've certainly never refused any items that anybody else has suggested, but in practice, it's just been Victim Support, the voluntary organisation, [that's] made all the suggestions for agenda items...We recognise them as the official victims' group, and because we fund them quite substantially and we don't fund, apart from a small sum to Support After Murder and Manslaughter, any other groups at all,...we expect them to provide the victims' perspective to the discussion.

I have been careful to qualify my claim that the membership of the *troupe* was stable because many officials would actually routinely change post,[16] the composition and relations of committees were never fixed, and links were repeatedly being forged, broken, and modified.[17] But there was also a permanent group at the core who did not change during 1997–2001. It was centred *inter alios* on Ian Chisholm and a Grade 7 of the JVU, Derek Oakey of the Lord Chancellor's Department, Alan Kirkwood and Pauline Spencer of the Crown Prosecution Service, and Dame Helen Reeves, Teresa Reynolds, and Anne Viney of Victim Support. Dame Helen Reeves, appointed to administer Victim Support in 1979, having sat on Government committees since the 1980s, one of the co-founders of the Victims Steering Group in 1985, was the longest established member of all. Not unlike Queen Victoria, she had seen the passing of many administrations and many heads of Home Office divisions and units, and she possessed an unparalleled body of knowledge and experience.

---

[16] Particularly from the ACPO Crime Committee. The chair of one committee informed a new ACPO member in September 2001, 'It's good to have another ACPO rep at last. The last one lasted for only one meeting.' There were other problems with ACOP: the ACOP representative to the Victim Support National Council did not attend throughout most of 2000.

[17] Teresa Reynolds of Victim Support said, 'when the officials change there's always going to be a difficult hiatus...when you've been working on an issue with a particular official for some time, and then they go and move on to something else, there is always a hiatus.'

Part of her manifest authority on committees stemmed from her formidable command over history in a world where history was evanescent.

The criminal justice *troupe* was but one of a number working on social problems at the turn of the century, and much depended on how issues were defined and who was assigned to take them forward. After all, no system for classifying social problems is exhaustive, and classifications of victims and witnesses alien to the world of criminal justice could occasionally be employed, calling on quite different casts of stakeholders. It mattered, for instance, whether domestic violence was managed by policy groups based in the Women's Unit in the Cabinet Office, the Department of Health, the Department of Social Security, or the Home Office. Betsy Stanko, once an academic, later working on 'service delivery' in the Cabinet Office, reflected that 'all victims are the same [yet] all victims are not the same. The way in which [they] are located institutionally differs, and that's why racist violence and homophobic violence and domestic violence mean different things to different people...'. Crimes against women defined *as* crimes against women were the responsibility of a distinct network, as were serious crimes defined as serious crimes, much of restorative justice, the victims of 'mentally disordered offenders', and race issues defined as race issues: 'they're all being dealt with by separate people', complained Helen Reeves at a meeting of the Victims Steering Group on 24 November 1999.

The different policy networks were not always fully aware of one another; they were often ill-connected; and they did not necessarily share a common language. The development of a policy to inform the victims of 'mentally disordered offenders' about the release date and plans of 'their' perpetrators offered a fraught and protracted example of what a Minister called 'the problem of offenders falling through gaps between the CJS and the system for dealing with mental disorder': it was riven with problems arising from its association with a policy group interested in problems of mental health defined as health problems, lodged in the Department of Health; beset by issues of patient confidentiality and data protection;[18] and falling quite outside the criminal justice system. An

---

[18] There was an argument, long maintained, that victims were in exactly the same position as any other member of the public unless they were under threat, and that they had no claim in law to encroach on the mentally disordered offender's right to privacy.

official of the Home Office Mental Health Unit reported to a colleague in November 2000 that a woman working in the Department
of Health on the broad area of mentally disordered offenders 'has
been involved with victims for a short while and did not know about
[our] joint working party. DH has therefore neglected the joint
working party discussions and concerns ... [She] knew none of the
early history of the joint HO/DH working party and [felt she had] no
obligation to take its history into account.' Ministers were to comment that treating patients differently from other sentenced prisoners was intellectually and politically indefensible. 'In order to break
the log-jam', said an official of the Home Office to a colleague in the
Department of Health in 2000, 'we should have a workshop which
could inform you more fully about the approach to victims being
taken by the CJS and you could air the difficulties that inhibit your
ability to agree to victims of MDOs [mentally disordered offenders]
being given parity.'

Child protection networks offer another instance. Helen Reeves
said of meetings on child protection:

When we first turned up at this ... all the people sitting around the table,
I knew everyone of them, you know, CPS, the Lord Chancellor's Department, the Chief Constable. I knew all of them but the other people didn't
because they work to Health, the Department of Health. So they have a
different world, a different network ... we were part of the criminal justice
culture who knew the criminal justice agencies but all the other people
came from Health and Welfare and really didn't know people.

## Policy-making as a Social World

The closely choreographed movements and intimacy of the criminal
justice *troupe* had consequences. Meeting regularly, immersed
in common issues, speaking a common language of performance
management,[19] interdependent, needing frequently to communicate,
composed of people who came to know one another well, commit-

---

[19] See I. Loader and A. Mulcahy; 'The Power of Legitimate Naming: Part II', *The
British Journal of Criminology,* Spring 2001, Vol. 41, No. 2: p. 262. Writing about the
impact of the new managerialism on the police, they argue, 'It has also more broadly
served to erode—if not yet entirely erase—some hitherto significant cultural differences between the police and other public and private bureaucracies ... as well as
prompting chief officers to conceive of themselves and their futures as "managers".'

tees became the foundation of a social world[20] ('the usual criminal justice membership'[21]) into which newcomers could speedily became inducted.[22] Members of one committee may have formally reported or sent copies of minutes back and forth to another,[23] but in practice they were usually only speaking to themselves in various guises.[24] They often approached each other unceremoniously, with a measure of confidence and trust, outside the official lines of communication, and often as part of the continuous parallel conversation of emails. Said a member of the Lord Chancellor's Department, 'we have a very simple system here ... We all get copied into each other's submissions, some of it is of little interest to us and we glance at it and that's it. But it all comes round electronically anyway so if we want to know more, we know where to find it ... we're alert to each other's issues.' A constant stream of written, electronic and spoken ideas, news, badinage, and speculation, partly the casual gossip of a professional world, partly practical intelligence-gathering, was then so diffusely to saturate the policy-making process that it became a little difficult to discern quite how things ever arose or became known. Teresa Reynolds of Victim Support said:

On the policy side, I suppose my role is to identify issues that may affect victims. So I would be doing things that are quite difficult to describe, you're doing them all the time, like you listen to the radio and you pick up things that might ... have implications in a year's time ... it's my job

[20] The more common phrases are 'policy community' (see R. King; 'Policy and process in the modern state' in J. Simmie and R. King (eds.); *The State in Action*, Pinter, London, 1990, p. 15) or 'policy network' (S. James; *British Government*, Routledge, London, 1997, p. 11).

[21] Internal Victim Support memorandum about RISC and the work to 'follow up the Stephen Lawrence Inquiry', 7 September 1999.

[22] Helen Reeves said, 'the new person who takes [a] post is having to turn up at so many different places, you very quickly get to know them ... and if we're seeing the same people in a whole series of different meetings, obviously you do get to know each other ...'.

[23] The new draft terms of reference of the Victims Steering Group, devised in November 1997, stipulated that it should, 'where appropriate, ... draw relevant issues to the attention of other groups'. Similarly, the Trial Issues Group's terms of reference laid down that it should 'liaise with other groups and committees and take into account their initiatives, decisions and recommendations ...'.

[24] For example, the Victims Steering Group, attended and often chaired by Ian Chisholm, exchanged papers with the Prison Service's Victims Policy Forum, the Trials Issues Group Witness Care Sub Group, the Vulnerable or Intimidated Witnesses Working Group, and other bodies, also attended by Ian Chisholm.

to ... sense those things that are going on ... a lot of what I do I think is almost *via*, it's not osmosis but it's almost *via* sixth sense ... I go to a lot of conferences. So it's picking up things at conferences, at meetings, one-to-one meetings with people in other agencies, or them coming here. So it's just picking up things and just having the antennae tuned ... it's identifying things, or changes.

I shall show as this book proceeds that the evolution of policy-making on victims and witnesses consisted of an array of histories that originally had quite distinct and scattered antecedents and political objectives. The Stephen Lawrence Report, for instance, had been spurred by a politics of race set within the framework of restoring public confidence in the criminal justice system. The *Speaking up for Justice* report had been initially triggered by a politics of gender. Restorative justice focused on bringing offenders and victims together to reduce crime. What contributed in time to their becoming merged together in a loosely-connected bundle of policies for victims was the continual traffic in ideas between the committees serviced by that common pool of stakeholders. Talking within groups, moving from group to group, officials were to become acquainted with a broad family of policies and it was inevitable that they should diffuse, contrast, compare, and synthesize its constituents. More than once, events occurring at much the same time in different venues were discussed as if they must have a causal and political bearing on one another.[25] Although committees were always conducted in a business-like and focused manner, with an adherence to the agenda and few apparent digressions, it was difficult completely to enforce separations in the imagination between initiatives and themes when the same people talked day after day in different settings about very similar problems. There was to be an abundance of subterranean *ad hoc* syntheses and cross-references that tied developments together.

## Policy-making as Reflexive Work

Consolidation was also encouraged by the recursive properties of policy-making to which I have already alluded in the previous chapter. Officials and politicians were obliged at more or less regular

[25] See E. Husserl; *The Phenomenology of Internal Time Consciousness*, Martinus Nijhoff, The Hague, 1964.

intervals to stand back; make their work problematic and object-like; interpret and describe what they were doing; award it a history and project it into the future.[26] Committees were, in that sense, at once bodies whose procedures required continual navigation, giving rise to the need to take stock; that had to report to others and, in reporting, give an account; and that could themselves be treated and discussed as topics, the objective embodiments of lines of policy development.

Stocktaking was a routine first step in the work of any new committee,[27] and stocktaking would occur at intervals thereafter. There were monthly management meetings to review the progress made by the Criminal Policy Directorate and its units;[28] the Criminal Injuries Compensation Authority had its quinquennial reviews; and the Victims Steering Group its irregular stocktaking meetings. There were Aim 2 'blue skies events' to identify future policies by itemizing 'key aims and issues', and to consider 'new targets and ideas for delivering them'.[29] Officials would brief incoming administrations and new Ministers on developments in substantive areas of policy-making, and in so doing, had to tell a story (thus the Director of Criminal Policy informed heads of units just before the 1997 general election that after the 'stocktake' of 9 April, 'each unit will need to have ready submissions by 1 May 1997': 'Once we have these, we can manage the initial flow and direction of work to best effect. We can reflect on the issues, relating submissions to one another, working out how to present interconnected issues, showing Ministers who is in the lead'). Officials were required to prepare Ministers for parliamentary debates and to draft answers to parliamentary questions (and perhaps draft the questions as well). They might be requested by the European Commission,[30]

---

[26] See P. McHugh; *Defining the Situation,* Bobbs-Merrill, Indianapolis, 1968.

[27] The first meeting of the Vulnerable or Intimidated Witnesses Working Group in August 1997 agreed that it was a 'priority to identify topics to be covered by the review', and its papers included a draft outline of a literature review, and an outline consultation document.

[28] Criminal Policy Directorate: Directorate Statement of Purpose and Practice, March 1997.

[29] Aim 2 SR 2000 Project Plan (Delivery of Justice), 28 October 1999.

[30] As the Home Office responded in December 1999 to the Secretary General of the European Commission on the British treatment of domestic and foreign victims.

parliamentary committees,[31] a Minister or the Prime Minister to supply a briefing, as were the officials who were invited to provide an overview for the Prime Minister's 'Law and Order Stocktake' in October 1998, and for John Birt's review of crime and criminal justice in July 2000. Officials would be asked to write speeches for diverse audiences. They had to describe policy developments in their bids for funding in 'cross-cutting reviews' of the criminal justice system to Ministers and the Treasury.[32] Crises, problems, and political events would provoke reflection and action:[33] after the publication of the Stephen Lawrence Report, for instance, the Director of Criminal Policy met with heads of units to discuss 'what is being done re each of the recommendations, with what timetable and what intended outputs'.[34] Continual analysis fed by retrospective and prospective sense-making was, in sum, a staple feature of the policy official's role.

Very characteristically, what would be produced (and usually produced fast) was a report of the major activities that could at that time be grouped together under a heading of relevant policies bearing on victims and witnesses; tied to the formal aims and objectives of the criminal justice system; laid out in rough chronological order; and sometimes starting with the election manifesto commitments that had not only come first in time but had established a political mandate for what followed. An unusually detailed example of guidance for such a report was provided by a 1999 internal paper, 'Guidance on Trilateral Consultation', that specified that there should be a 'needs rationale and priority for policy consistent with strategic aims and objectives of the CJS; a policy appraisal which specifies objectives and desired outcomes; identifies options; assesses costs, risks and benefits; a plan and a timetable involving consultation with other departments; full specification of the policy which

---

[31] No parliamentary committee discussed victims matters *qua* victims matters between 1997 and 2001, but the Home Secretary was obliged, for example, to appear before the Public Expenditure Committee meeting on the criminal justice system.

[32] Drafts of the Criminal Justice Joint Planning Unit; 2000 SR: SR2000 Cross Cutting Study of the Criminal Justice System, referred to resources demanded by legislation, ministerial announcements, demand-led pressures, and discretionary plans.

[33] See *Report of the Working Party on Recording and Reporting of Racist Incidents*, ACPO, June 1999.

[34] John Halliday to Ian Chisholm and others, 3 June 1999.

says what is to be achieved, when and how measured; at what costs
and to whom; plans and timetables ... '. Very characteristically, too,
the reports were short and succinct, lean inventories of salient committees, initiatives, budgets, actions, and commitments strung together as a list,[35] and their structure and contents could become
stylized, following templates that had evolved to become customary
over time.[36] After all, it was more economical and convenient to
return to set forms of words rather than draft a new description
every time, earlier texts were known already to have been approved,
and much the same text would be used repeatedly on different
occasions. Templates ensured that bodies being briefed or receiving
submissions were given certain stock items of information, and that
reports were standardized and made comparable. In 1999, for instance, a business performance monitoring exercise stipulated that
'Under each aim there is a template for all the ... measures. Returns
for the Management Board require all items identified in the published business plans, manifesto commitments, and additional measures listed ... '.

For reasons of convention and practicality, the reports did not
contain elaborate exposition, explanation,[37] history, or citation.
That was not their function. Reports of the problems faced by
victims were almost never expansive or expressive (although politicians speaking to political audiences might talk more extensively[38]).
These were papers produced internally and in political shorthand for
practical and political ends, cataloguing practical and political

[35] For example, a JVU Grade 7 prepared 'Victims of Crime: Bullet Points—March
2000', which began with the Government's manifesto commitments, moved through
the March 1999 Strategies and Business Plans for the Criminal Justice System, developments in the CPS to introduce direct communication with victims, the work of the
Vulnerable or Intimidated Witnesses Working Group, the Lawrence Inquiry Report,
the Victim Support Witness Service, the Victim's Charter Pilot Projects, changes in the
Criminal Injuries Compensation Scheme, and other items.
[36] See, for example, Chapter 4 of the Annual Report of the Crown Prosecution
Service for April 1998 to March 1999, which dwells on victims and witnesses and
recites the standard list of initiatives.
[37] Although there could be exceptions. Ian Chisholm, for instance, submitted a
paper on Better Services for Victims and Witnesses in July 2000 to the Cabinet Office
which reported, *inter alia*, research on what victims and witnesses 'want from the
criminal justice system'.
[38] The briefing for an adjournment debate in May 1997 contained a draft speech
which talked of the Minister's sympathy for the families of murder victims who often
feel neglected by the criminal justice system.

actions and pressures, taking professional preoccupations and com-
petences for granted, and intended chiefly for knowing, practically-
minded insiders who had little time or inclination to read lengthy
documents, particularly on the relatively minor subject of victims
and witnesses. It was not really the business of policy-makers to
probe or challenge too broadly the mandates and terms of reference
they had been given. Said one member of many committees, 'The
groups I'm in are very task-focused and they just get on with the
task.'

What bound the reports' inventories together during the course of
this history was the common empirical theme of measures for
victims and witnesses as they were defined by practical exigencies
at the moment of stocktaking. Sometimes a marginal item would be
included for no obvious reason other than that it existed nearby at
the time of drafting and could serve a need to bulk out an argument:
thus crime reduction initiatives were represented as projects to
decrease the numbers of victims; and the better preparation of case
files,[39] the Narey reforms to reduce trial delays, efforts to improve
decision-making on bail, and the aborted curbing of the right to trial
by jury[40] were said, without evidence or argument, to be beneficial
to victims. They were neighbouring initiatives in the offing and it
appeared to be reasoned that they might just as well be added to the
list. What may once have started out as a focused response to quite
another problem: the criminal politics of abused children,[41] race or
gender, perhaps, could then be retrospectively appropriated and re-
categorized as part of a portfolio of projects to aid victims, just as
measures for victims could at other times be re-classified and listed
as parts of the politics of children, gender, and race.[42] In his response
to the Stephen Lawrence Inquiry into the investigation of a racist
killing, for example, the Home Secretary pointed to work on what

[39] Key Government Action to Assist Victims/Witnesses January 1999.
[40] See *The Times*, 21 January 2000.
[41] For example, a briefing for a Minister for a Victim Support Fringe Meeting at the
Labour Party Conference of October 1998 contained the only reference I found in all
the files of the JVU to new guidelines to help children abused through prostitution, the
result of an interesting policy reversal in which it was decided that child prostitutes
should no longer be treated as criminals but as victims.
[42] For example, the Lawrence Steering Group was informed in September 2000
about Victim Support, the Victim Support Witness Service and other measures that
had not arisen expressly in a context of responses to the families of victims of racially-
motivated homicide.

was called the 'One Stop Shop', increased financial support for Victim Support and SAMM, Support After Murder and Manslaughter, the Vulnerable or Intimidated Witnesses Working Group and the review of the *Victim's Charter*,[43] all of which could be helpful to bereaved families but none of which had its roots remotely near the politics of race and racist killings.

Little by little then, and with repetition, it became possible to weave a modest, conventional legend around the inventories to suggest that quite disparate efforts were actually cumulative, purposive, and interlinked. I talked about the emergence of templates: the same text could be seen again and again in different documents, adapted perhaps, and absorbing new issues, but becoming with use an established way of portraying and reconciling developments. For example, and like many of its fellows, a 1999 paper on better services for victims, submitted to the Trilateral Ministers Group, referred to the Stephen Lawrence Report, *Speaking up for Justice*, a Victims' Helpline; and a proposed consultation on the *Victim's Charter* as if they were parts of some common enterprise (and indeed, very generously interpreted, so they were).

## Committees as Synthesizers

Committees would strive quite purposefully to synthesize and reconcile different strands inside and around their work. In the case of the more major initiatives, the phrase sometimes used was 'mainstreaming [some issue or policy] into our thinking'.[44] It would not do for policy developments to foul one another, conflicts could create problems (or resources for solutions to problems[45]), and members had continually to keep a weather eye open for what was likely to

[43] *The Stephen Lawrence Inquiry: Home Secretary's Action Plan*, Home Office, London, March 1999.

[44] Employed by the Chairman of the Victims Steering Group in connection with the impact of the new restorative justice measures being introduced in the youth justice system. He added 'Everything we do feeds into the youth justice arena. We've always got to think about youth justice issues.' Meeting of the Victims Steering Group 24 November 1999, my notes.

[45] For instance, Ian Chisholm wondered whether measures in the then new Crime and Disorder Act 1998 to give greater protection to the public could be used as a lever to resolve the problem of patient confidentiality and the disclosure of information to the victims of mentally disordered offenders. Minutes of the meeting of the Victims Steering Group, 21 May 1999.

enter their waters. The Stephen Lawrence Inquiry, in particular, was to carry exceptional political weight, and numerous committees followed its progress for what it might portend for their own work. It was originally envisaged that some of the Inquiry's recommendations might, in the words of the Chairman of the Victims Steering Group, 'be mopped up in *Speaking up for Justice*', but they were more prominent, authoritative, extensive, and certainly more time-consuming than had been originally envisaged. Instead of being 'mopped up', they were themselves commanding enough to mop up other policies, the would-be framed becoming itself a frame. Thus the implementation plans for *Speaking up for Justice* were enlarged in April 1999 to cover 'racial issues [that] needed to be covered in the various projects' following the publication of the Stephen Lawrence Inquiry report two months before. Proposals to change procedures for dealing with the families of murder victims, including the early release of bodies by the Coroner and assistance with travel expenses and accommodation whilst attending trial, received a sudden impetus, and were to be approved in December 1998, in anticipation of the Lawrence recommendations. Considering its strategic plan for 1999–2002 (itself aligned to the Government's Comprehensive Spending Review), the National Council of Victim Support noted that there was a need to take account of the likely impact of the agenda stemming from the Inquiry.[46] Consideration of the Inquiry's recommendations was to be one of the principal reasons given to review the role of the victim in the 'criminal justice system as a whole'[47] at a special Home Office conference in September 1999, and such overviews cannot only synthesize and redefine what is in train but also provide catalysts for new action.[48] There was, in brief, a relentless impulse to reconcile, amalgamate, and exploit adjoining developments—sometimes by making them one. Talking about the reports of the Stephen Lawrence Inquiry and

[46]  Minutes of the meeting of 20 October 1998. In the event, it was to establish a working party, reporting in December 1999, to review its policies and practices in relation to racist crime.

[47]  Minutes of meeting of Victims Steering Group, 21 May 1999.

[48]  Anne Viney, then Assistant Director of Victim Support, dealing with issues of race and victims, noted in a memorandum to the Victim Support Strategic Management Group, 6 April 1999, 'we need to make specific responses to the report of the Inquiry, partly to show that items already in the workplan can be taken up and developed with the Inquiry report as a catalyst'.

the Vulnerable or Intimidated Witnesses Working Group, Ian Chisholm said in February 2000 that 'ideally, all those documents should be read together and be consistent, and ultimately they should be one document'.[49] That would prove to be a far-sighted observation.

I have already remarked that one of the earliest acts of a new committee was to cast around to ascertain what was being done in the area to which it had been assigned.[50] When what was called the Vulnerable Witness Group met for the first time in April 1997, it drew up a list of people and organizations to consult, including VOICE UK (supporting witnesses with learning difficulties), and the Alzheimer's Disease Society and Mind (working 'for a better life everyone with experience of mental distress'). Later, in May 1997, in a submission to Ministers on whether the work of the Group should continue under the New Labour administration, Ian Chisholm pointed to allied developments in ACPO with its interest in witnesses (witness intimidation had been made an operational priority for 1997); TIG with its interest in national standards of witness care; the work of the Law Commission on hearsay evidence and the vulnerable witness; and the Crime and Disorder Bill's proposals on professional witnesses. Ministers replied to the submission, and Ian Chisholm was to be told that the Department of Trade and Industry had announced that it had a limited stake in the issue of vulnerable witnesses because of its interest in the prosecution of white collar criminals; the Minister for Women wished women to be included; the Secretary of State for Health desired that child witnesses be considered; and the Department of Environment wished to include the problem of combating anti-social behaviour on housing estates. Formal incorporation of those priorities was the political price of the Vulnerable Witness Group's continuing existence, and the Group came thereby to absorb a span of new standpoints and policy interests.

The newly re-formed and re-named Interdepartmental Vulnerable or Intimidated Witnesses Working Group decided at *its* first meeting that papers would be required on definitions of the

---

[49] Victim Support Seminar on Stephen Lawrence, 15 February 2000, my notes.

[50] Business planning for implementation of the impending Human Rights Act, for instance, noted that the 'programme took no account of other criminal justice initiatives' and needed to do so. Note of the 2nd Meeting of Human Rights Bill: Business planning exercise, 21 September 1998.

vulnerable witness; crime reporting policies of local authority, social security, and health departments; working arrangements between the police, local authorities, and health authorities; police procedures for dealing with vulnerable witnesses; the uses of professional witnesses, and other matters.[51] Later still, when the Group was about to send outline proposals to Ministers, it was held that a working group would need to be established to cost recommendations against the background of other issues being developed elsewhere.[52] Stakeholding thereby repeatedly made its mark: there was a continual ingestion,[53] fusion, and fission[54] of tasks which I shall discuss at greater length in Chapter 8.

## The Committee as Carrier

Once a committee was in train, therefore, it could attract new business. It was far more expedient and politic to attach new issues as they emerged to a body already established and in motion than to invent a separate organization for each problem. Sue Street, Director of Criminal Policy at one point during the first New Labour administration, observed 'the Macpherson Inquiry and the other elements ... are sort of like iron filings, they're being attracted to something that is already moving forward and so we have to adapt and take into account and see whether it fits comfortably ... '. Fitting comfortably could take the form of modification and re-classification, and it could, in turn, prompt officials and others to re-define the unfamiliar as familiar, to mould the new to make it receptive to old methods. The more substantial committees were to possess a sponge-like capacity to absorb and re-categorize tasks, and it was a result that their focus could waver, their direction shift, and their work swell over time. The way in which that happened, and how it

[51]   Minutes of the first meeting of the Interdepartmental Vulnerable or Intimidated Witnesses Working Group, 1 August 1997.

[52]   Minutes of the fifth meeting of the Interdepartmental Vulnerable or Intimidated Witnesses Working Group, 18 December 1997.

[53]   For example, it was argued at the 16 May 1997 meeting of the Victims Steering Group that its terms of reference were too restrictive and needed to be expanded to encompass new developments in restorative justice, racial harassment, and the like.

[54]   As tasks swelled and became better defined, so they might be consigned to other policy-making bodies at work in the criminal justice system. For example, the Interdepartmental Vulnerable or Intimidated Witnesses Working Group remitted part of its work to the Steering Group on Child Evidence in December 1997.

led eventually to the creation of a somewhat ungainly and unstable mass of policies for victims, will be the theme of much of this book, but the point does need making here, in a preliminary sketch of some of the structural characteristics of policy-making.

The consequences of such a continual process of assimilation were to be profound. Almost by default, they generalized the particular into the general and encompassed larger and larger areas of terrain, and, in so doing, demanded the invocation of *ad hoc* formulae to justify and explain how different categories of victim had thus come to be swollen, reconciled, and aligned. A senior official reflected that 'there are a number of issues which have a fairly specific genesis but which then turn themselves into issues which you might describe as cross-cutting...'. The problems of the few (rape complainants or victims of racially-aggravated violence, for instance) could be met by general political solutions that became extended to the many: the male and female victims of any race.[55] Such assimilation required a repeated re-appraisal, sifting, and re-designation of policies as they expanded and changed. They enforced a kind of entropy. 'Given a degree of similarity between an old and a new activity,' John Van Maanen once argued, 'the new will be approached in much the same way as the old.'[56] And I would hold to that argument. But it should also be noted that each of the histories I shall recount in the following chapters nevertheless seemed to be driven by its own separate logic of growth, and that the different episodes were not mere formal clones of one another but were quite idiosyncratic in their development.

## 'Joined-up Government'

A pivotal phrase in the new managerialism, so far largely neglected, was 'joined-up government'. 'Joined-up government' captured New Labour's quest to fuse and systematize policy-making and 'customer

---

[55] I shall argue when I return to these matters that the campaigners who had originally turned the political gaze towards very special problems of race, gender, or human rights were remarkably generous in welcoming the universalization of the particular. Marc Wadsworth, for instance, an activist in the Anti-Racist Alliance, attached at first to the Lawrence family, said of the impact of the report of the Stephen Lawrence Inquiry, 'I think what we'll see now is a reform of policing which will be good for the whole community'.

[56] J. Van Maanen; 'Doing New Things in Old Ways', unpublished paper, undated, p. 10.

focused'[57] 'service delivery'[58] through the co-ordination of the work of key stakeholders inside and outside the criminal justice system. The aspiration was not wholly new,[59] but its terminology and political force were peculiar to New Labour,[60] and it was to be the *Leitmotiv* of an influential White Paper, *Modernising Government*, Cm. 4310, published in March 1999. The complaint was made that many agencies had had a long history and a tradition of autonomy and independence which inhibited the development of effective co-operation,[61] and the solution was to be the creation or consolidation of bridging institutions and devices to supply a 'clear strategic direction':[62] a 'joint public service agreement' for the criminal justice system[63] with 'cross-cutting criminal justice system performance measures';[64] a harmonization and simplification of the boundaries of the geographical areas covered by the criminal justice agencies; (in 2001) a 'criminal justice reserve fund' to promote 'joined up working' and requiring the joint agreement of the three criminal

[57]   *HOtline*, 13 October 1998.

[58]   For instance, *The Home Office—A Guide, October 2000*, referred to 'how the voluntary sector and the private sector are now partners in delivery, and how with them we have strengthened our capacity for higher standards of service delivery and for social policy formulation' (p. 3).

[59]   See D. Faulkner; *Crime, State and Citizen, op. cit.*, pp. 117–18.

[60]   See E. McLaughlin *et al.*; 'The Permanent Revolution', *Criminal Justice*, August 2001, Vol. 1, No. 3, p. 306.

[61]   *A Guide to the Criminal Justice System in England and Wales*, Home Office, London, 2000, p. 2. Beverley Thompson of NACRO a member of the Victims Steering Group after the publication of the Macpherson Inquiry Report, strongly endorsed that complaint, and particularly in the context of implementing policies on race across the criminal justice system: 'I don't think they feed into each other at all. I think the criminal justice system still passes itself off as a system. It's not a system at all. You know, there are very disparate bits who co-ordinate somewhere in terms of, somewhere in the middle in terms of what happens in the courts. And that's the only point at which they connect. But there is no inter-connection between any of the agencies and that's what the area criminal justice strategy committees were supposed to achieve which was the committee that came out of the Woolf report. Yeah, now that was suppose to achieve you know, a kind of joined up criminal justice system at a very local level. However, it's not really happening . . .'.

[62]   Joint statement by the Home Secretary, Lord Chancellor and Attorney General: 'Criminal Justice Planning Structures', Home Office, ca. July 1998.

[63]   *The Government's Expenditure Plans 1999–2000 to 2001–2002*, Vol. 1, p. 9.

[64]   *Home Office Annual Report, 1999–2000*, Aim 2, p. 26.

justice Ministers;[65] a Trilateral Ministerial Steering Group, chaired
by the Home Secretary, and including the Lord Chancellor, Attorney
General, and Chief Secretary to the Treasury; a Strategic Planning
Group of senior officials from the three main criminal justice departments and the Treasury; a Criminal Justice Joint Planning Unit with
staff from the criminal justice departments and the Treasury;
a Criminal Justice Joint Consultative Council and lesser, local councils, established in the wake of the Woolf Report,[66] to enhance
communication, consultation, and co-ordination; and a range of
sundry other measures.[67] Joined-up government was to permeate
the workings of the criminal justice system[68] and the Home Office.
And one very early prototype of joined-up work in the sphere of
victims and witnesses was the Victims Steering Group. One of its
members, Alan Kirkwood of the Crown Prosecution Service, reflected 'there is a recognition, the importance of all the agencies
recognising... the constraints under which each of them work, and
taking that into account when pushing their own position... Groups
like the Victims Steering Group help to provide that.'

## The Victims Steering Group

The Victims Steering Group had been established in April 1985 as a
joint project by David Faulkner, then Director of Criminal Policy, and
Helen Reeves of Victim Support, and its chief aim was, in Helen
Reeves' words, 'to resolve disputes... about what should be
happening to victims'. In his letter of invitation to ACPO and
ACOP, Faulkner observed that 'in view of the very rapid growth in
both the size and activities of the victim support movement, it was

[65] *CJCC Newsletter*, August 2001.
[66] See H. Woolf; *The Woolf Report: a summary of the main findings and recommendations of the inquiry into prison disturbances*, Prison Reform Trust, London,
1991.
[67] Including, for example, such pieces of *chinoiserie* as the '4 Cs' for the police:
including consultation (how are users involved) and how are views incorporated...
Home Office; *Best Value: Briefing Notes for the Police Service*, undated; and the Trial
Issues Group which 'brings together representatives of all those working in the
Criminal Justice System to iron out inter-agency difficulties and improve the working
of the system generally' ('What is the Trial Issues Group?', September 1998).
[68] It was thought by some to presage the formation of a Ministry of Justice
absorbing the current three trilateral criminal justice ministries (based on my notes
on the Meeting of the Victim Support Trustees, 1 March 2001).

considered helpful if those closely involved with victims of crime could meet to take stock, see how the local schemes were working, in particular, to discuss how all those who came into contact with victims could most effectively work together to achieve their common goals'. The Group met for the first time in July 1985, but it was not until its fifth meeting in early 1988 that the Home Office considered its future role.[69] It was agreed at that meeting that the Group had a useful 'review and stocktaking function' and that it should continue to meet twice yearly. There was no discussion of the Group's terms of reference then or for some long while afterwards, but it was decided that it should not seek to create an independent programme of work, and (rather later) it was agreed that it 'has never... been a policy-making body'. The group was originally supposed to be small and informal, composed principally of representatives of the Home Office, Victim Support (including Helen Reeves and Teresa Reynolds in 1985), ACOP and ACPO, but it was to evolve in *ad hoc* fashion, new 'stake-holders' being invited to become members as their interests were affected: for example, it was agreed that there should be a discussion of the role of the victim in court at the second meeting, and the Lord Chancellor's Department and the CPS joined in September 1986. 'As subjects crept on to the agenda, so the group grew': the Metropolitan Police joined in September 1986 (and remained until 1998 when it came to be represented by ACPO); RSD, the Home Office Research and Statistics Directorate, in April 1987; the Justices' Clerks Society in November 1988; the Criminal Injuries Compensation Authority in October 1990; the Court Service in December 1994; the Charter Unit of the Cabinet Office in December 1995; and so on. It was concluded at the stocktaking review conducted at the time of the May 1997 election that 'VSG is historically the premier "victim group"... By providing a central forum for action through which agencies could encourage others... VSG has made an important contribution to the improvement in the treatment of, and services to, victims over the past ten years.' The Victims Steering Group had by then twenty-six members, and other agencies, including the Magistrates' Association[70] and the Criminal Injuries Compensation

---

[69] Based upon 'Victims Steering Group (VSG)—Evolution', Procedures and Victims Unit, November 1996.

[70] The woman who came eventually to join as the representative of the Magistrates' Association, was to tell me in February 1999 that her association was not actively represented on the VSG and she did not know why that should be so.

Appeals Panel, were applying to join. It was thought to be at risk of becoming 'unwieldy and unmanageable', and a case was developing for it to focus principally on what seemed to have become its key task, the monitoring of the *Victim's Charter* (which will be discussed in a separate chapter) and, by extension, to restrict membership to those who were responsible for implementing the twenty-seven Charter standards. Had that happened, some of the more peripheral members would have been designated 'associates', but there were problems of face. One group about to join was the judiciary, and it was diplomatically impracticable not to offer them a choice of core or associate status, a choice that, in its turn, could set a precedent for the treatment of other applicants. The bifurcation between core and associate members was not to be applied rigorously, and the Group continued to grow. Stakeholding, it was clear, was as much a matter of protocol and, perhaps, of *Realpolitik*, as of strict functionality. As Jordan and Richardson argued some time ago, 'Civil servants and ministers have a working knowledge of who really matters in the consultative process—particularly of those groups who have an ability to exercise some kind of veto...'.[71] It would not do to estrange those with influence.

By the first administration of the New Labour Government, the Victims Steering Group was composed of those who, over time and not particularly reflexively, had become accepted as working within the criminal justice system on problems of victims conventionally defined, including those who could not be expelled or demoted for reasons of protocol. It was, in effect, an instrument through which the Home Office, a body lacking a direct capacity to execute policy, could confer at regular intervals with the agencies which were responsible for implementation,[72] and those agencies, in their turn, could resolve conflicts and difficulties.[73] John Halliday, then Director of Criminal Policy, reflected in October 1998:

[71] A. Jordan and J. Richardson; *British Politics and the Policy Process*, Unwin Hyman, London, 1987, p. 173.

[72] Judge Rodwell, who had been nominated by Lord Auld to represent the judiciary on the Victims Steering Group, said 'As I understood it from Robin Auld, my role was to try and ensure that what is ultimately proposed is practical, that it has the slightest chance of working in the real conditions of a Crown Court'.

[73] Roger Ford, the representative of the Association of Chief Officers of Probation, reflected that 'it provided a very helpful forum for resolving... inter-departmental issues... without it, I think we could be in difficulties'.

... we wouldn't have been able to make progress without a group like that ... It's a very interesting example of the kind of work the Home Office has always felt it necessary to do ... or as a way of working the Home Office has always found it necessary to adopt, because obviously, people sitting in a Whitehall department, who don't actually run many, or hardly any services as such, can only operate with the people who do. So, interestingly, that was an area where quite consistently since it was set up, we've had this kind of open working with the key players ... throughout ... and it increases the chances that outcomes will stick.

Beyond monitoring the *Victim's Charter* and conducting a conversation between the makers and the executors of policy, the Group's role had always been somewhat ill-defined. It had certainly accomplished the central task set by the Home Office and Victim Support in the 1980s of establishing the importance of victims for the politics of criminal justice (Teresa Reynolds of Victim Support reflected in July 1998 that 'in years gone by we were actually saying, you know, "must do this for victims, must do this for victims, this is outrageous", whereas now, quite a few things are being done for victims, so the situation is now quite different, and it's about how we're going collectively to deliver this'). It did exchange general intelligence within the criminal justice system about developments in policies (its Secretary observed in July 1998 that 'it really is taking a helicopter view of things ... and there's no actual work as such that the Committee does as a group'). It provided a mechanism for harmonizing policies that might otherwise have developed in disjointed fashion (Commander Campbell of the Metropolitan Police observed 'the purpose of having the Victims Steering Group was to pull [everything] together, to make sure that these little *ad hoc* groups weren't sailing off down an avenue that was clearly not in the direction of the one we needed to be going ... '). It did bring together in one place and at regular intervals the principals of the criminal justice system and required them to give a formal account of how they had acquitted themselves in complying with a central charter.[74] Present together, in effect confronting one another, being able quite possibly to shame one another, members could exert a measure of collective pressure on each other. Helen Reeves said that 'as long as

[74] Alan Kirkwood said, 'I think it is important there is a group like that which focuses on things like the Victim's Charter ... and monitoring the Victim's Charter, because if there isn't a group like that which focuses upon that, then I think there is a danger that the agencies would not do whatever they're supposed to be doing.'

I can remember,... whichever agency has been told they've got to change, will always be out on a limb against the rest... You generally find that one agency's saying "we can't possibly do that, we haven't got the time, we can't fit the training in, we haven't got the money". And everyone else is saying "but you must!" So, in a sense, that's been the strength, that's really how things have got changed.'

Beyond that, the Group did not have a power to *make* policy (Alan Kirkwood of the Crown Prosecution Service said 'generally the role of the VSG [is] quite remote and just has a sort of co-ordinating overview, it's not very active...'); policy work proper was performed at a remove by its working groups or by other bodies altogether (Ian Chisholm stated that 'it's mainly to review what's going on elsewhere... the policy is really driven forward in smaller groups... all the key players are involved in the smaller groups'); it could not raise revenue or command resources if policy *was* agreed; it did not have the power to enforce agreed policy within its member agencies and departments; it was not even evident whether it was to be considered an expert group; and it was not evident whether it was answerable to, or responsible for advising the new Strategic Board when that was constituted. Meeting only twice a year, concentrating more and more on the *Victim's Charter*, becoming less flexible, discursive and catholic over the years,[75] it had become perhaps a little peripheral to the greater body of active policy work on victims. Helen Reeves reflected in early 1999: 'If you look at the charts [of] all the different committees that are going on, [they're] absolutely massive... And [they don't] all report back to the Steering Group. The Steering Group is almost on the side and has almost been sidelined as being purely a monitoring [body] for implementation of the Charter.'

## The Membership of the Victims Steering Group

It is important to consider the structure and membership of the Group because, as I have already claimed, they disclosed which criminal justice organizations were deemed to have a stake in the

---

[75] Helen Reeves recollected that 'in the earlier years it was much more fluid—you could raise other issues, even in the context of debate you could raise other issues...'.

problems of victims and how victims themselves were to be defined for practical purposes. Victims were clearly seen to be implicated in the work of the civilian police, the prosecuting authorities, the courts in which 'their' trials were mounted, the prisons where 'their' offenders were detained, and the probation service which was responsible for preparing reports about the impact of the crime and for disclosing information about 'their' prisoners' release plans. But the pattern of representation was more than a little haphazard. Like Topsy, the Victims Steering Group had just growed, and there were some groups and agencies that were markedly absent although it might well have been thought that they should have had a role in constituting the politics of victims. It had been agreed in 1997 that the Victims Steering Group was over-large, that an ideal complement might actually be twelve members[76]—less than half its then present number—and that caution should be exercised in enlarging it yet still further, but the omissions are nevertheless striking.

The Bar and Law Society were two such omissions (and for many practical purposes of discussion, victims had little to do with the business of advocacy and forensic examination). The Victims Steering Group was restricted to the criminal justice system, and the Department of Health with its care of 'mentally disordered offenders', accident and emergency departments attended by offenders and victims of violence,[77] and medical and other staff vulnerable to assault, was a third omission. The Department of Education with its responsibility for thefts from schools and for bullied and victimized pupils and staff was a fourth.[78] The Ministry of Defence

[76] Meeting of the Victims Steering Group, 26 November 2001, my notes.

[77] See, for example, J. Shepherd, M. Shapland, C. Scully and I. Leslie; 'Alcohol consumption, intoxication and chronic abuse among victims of violence: an Accident and Emergency Department perspective', *British Journal of Addiction*, 1989, 84, 1045–51; and J. Shepherd; 'Management of victims of assault, *Archives of Emergency Medicine*, 1991, 8, 83–86. The Victim Support response of 23 January 1998 to *The New NHS Modern and Dependable*, White Paper, December 1997, argued that victims of crime were heavy users of the accident and emergency service and acute and primary care. Because many victims did not report their crimes to the police, it was said, medical personnel should be aware of Victim Support and pass on information to victims. Victim Support made allied points in its response of 27 April 1998 to the Green Paper, *Our Healthier Nation*, February 1998.

[78] See S. Anderson *et al.*; *Cautionary Tales: Young People, Crime and Policing in Edinburgh*, Avebury, Aldershot, Hants, 1994.

with its interest in the policing of military bases and the conduct of courts martial was a fifth. The Commission for Racial Equality or other groups concerned with 'diversity issues' were a sixth.[79] The Department of Transport with its responsibility for road crashes was yet another. The victims entering the Steering Group's deliberations were not obviously and distinctively young, or the victims of mentally disordered offenders or of assaults in the playground, roads, barracks, and hospital. Neither were they what has been called 'gendered'.

In a number of other jurisdictions, it was fractions of the women's movement that had galvanized the politics of victims (albeit, perhaps, in the name of 'survivors' rather than 'victims'). In Canada, the United States,[80] Australia,[81] and New Zealand[82] the most visibly iconic victim was a raped or battered woman, and a distinctive politics followed in her train. In Ontario, in 2000, for example, impelled by the 'domestic' murder of Arlene May and a subsequent inquest report,[83] vulnerable women were to be singled out for special attention in a victims' initiative[84] (although there was concern about a threat to the independence of what were called 'gender-based services'). It was otherwise on the Victims Steering Group. Domestic violence, rape, and abuse did occasionally enter its deliberations, but they were never paraded under those titles, and they were very rapidly assimilated through processes of entropy into larger, more 'gender-free' classes of victim. And, as I shall argue, the victims' voice on the committee, Victim Support, represented all victims rather than particular sub-sets of victims. For most practical purposes, the victims of the Victims Steering Group were 'gender-free'.

[79] Although, as I have already pointed out, two minority ethnic members were to be appointed after the publication of the report of the Macpherson Inquiry.
[80] See S. Smith and S. Freinkel; *Adjusting the Balance: Federal Policy and Victim Services*, Greenwood Press, New York, 1988, esp. p. 4.
[81] See New South Wales Law Reform Commission; Discussion Paper 33—Sentencing, Sydney, 1996, Ch. 11.
[82] See A. Church et al.; *Victims Court Assistance: An Evaluation of the Pilot Scheme*, Department of Justice, Wellington, New Zealand, 1995, p. 17.
[83] See Joint Committee on Domestic Violence; *Working Toward a Seamless Community and Justice Response to Domestic Violence: A Five Year Plan for Ontario*, Toronto, August 1999.
[84] Action Plan for Victims of Crime: 7 January 2000—Option 2; and Framework for the support, development and coordination of services for victims of crime in Ontario, Policy Coordination Committee Presentation, 25 March 1999.

## Victim Support

The symbolic ascendancy of the androgynous victim was in part a
mark of the historical failure of special interest groups and of the
success of Victim Support, the sole non-governmental organization
represented on the Victims Steering Group, indeed its co-founder,
which had striven hard since the mid-1970s to win its spurs as a body
with whom criminal justice agencies and Departments of State could
work.[85] The origins of Victim Support lay within the penal reform
organization, NACRO, the National Association for the Care and
Resettlement of Offenders—there had been no other form of non-
governmental institution in the criminal justice system at the time to
give it birth—and its parentage showed. It had not arisen from the
'victims' movement.' It was not composed of 'angry victims' or their
surrogates.[86] It did not represent any specific victim group, or interest. Its formal objects as a charity were to support and give assistance
generally to victims and witnesses at large, their relatives and
friends, and to raise public awareness and recognition of the effects
of crime.[87] It was committed politically not to engage in advocacy, to
attack offenders, or to comment on sentencing policy.[88] It did not
engage in spectacular demonstrations as some women's organizations or bodies campaigning for the families of homicide victims had
done in the past. It did not set out to embarrass the Government
through public confrontation.[89] It was a pragmatic institution. It
was not, declared Helen Reeves, some years ago and at a formative

[85]   I narrated that process at length in *Helping Victims of Crime, op. cit.*

[86]   And, in so doing, it resembled many of the other victim support organizations in
Europe with which it came to be aligned. See M. Groenhuijsen; 'Trends in Victimology
in Europe with Special Reference to the European Forum for Victim Services', 10th
Annual Conference of the Japanese Association of Victimology, Kyoto, 26th June
1999.

[87]   *Victim Support: Report of the Trustees and Financial Statements for year ended
31.3.00*, Victim Support, London, 2000.

[88]   More formally, 'Victim Support does not make statements about the punishment
of offenders... Victims should be free of the burden of decision-making in relation to
the offender.' H. Reeves; 'The Role of the Victim in Criminal Justice', 18 July 2000.

[89]   Peter Hepburn, Assistant Chief Executive Officer of Victim Support, remarked
'We try to hold our independence so that we can say what needs saying. Usually when
we say it in meeting with government, then people listen and we don't have to go
mounting public campaigns and demonstrations in the street and that sort of activity.
And I think the danger is because we don't take part in that sort of activity, we can be
seen as the lackeys of government.'

stage in the organization's development, part of 'a victims movement' and should not be confused with the politics of victims in the United States:[90] a 'campaigning stance... [is] unlikely to find favour in the U.K...'.[91] But it had not muzzled itself. To the contrary: its officials continually egged other agencies and government departments on, reproaching them for simplifying, misunderstanding, and narrowing accounts of victims and victims' needs.[92] They prepared policy papers, some of which were to be exceedingly influential (and Chapter 10 will describe how one such paper fed into the deliberations of the European Commission and became the substance of a Framework Decision). They reported intelligence from their local schemes in England and Wales, their contacts with inter-governmental[93] and non-governmental organizations in North America, principally NOVA, the National Organization for Victim Assistance, and the European Forum for Victims' Services, in which they played a pivotal part. Helen Reeves reflected in a public conversation with Jane Furniss at a seminar in Dublin in October 2002:

Over the years we've been influenced by what the Government of the time is interested in (that's where the funding is). The advantage for the Government in funding us, what the Government gets for its money, is increased victim and witness satisfaction... [it's] very good PR, excellent public relations, and cheap at the price. There's an awareness that there's an increase in public confidence. It gives Government easy access to a group representing victims' interests. [There are] many, many working groups and parties. The Government is able to say that victims were consulted. It is able to adopt policies that we've spent years developing. They adopted

[90] For a description of victims' politics in the United States, see M. Dubber; *Victims in the War on Crime*, New York University Press, New York, 2003.

[91] H. Reeves; 'Towards a British Policy for Victims', December 1984, p. 2.

[92] And, in particular, the probably inevitable and insistent focus on the relations of the victim to the criminal justice system. If, as Victim Support argued, 97% of crime does not lead to the apprehension of an offender, it is only contacts with the police that signify in the vast bulk of cases of victimization: the courts, judiciary, probation service and prison service play little consequential role. Helen Reeves argued, 'The Victim Support agenda should take as its starting point the fact that only a minority of offenders are detected, charged or dealt with in some other way. The most important provisions for victims must therefore be designed to address the rights and needs of victims, whether or not the offender is detected.' 'The Role of the Victim in Criminal Justice', 18 July 2000.

[93] Victim Support had, for instance, consultative status with the United Nations and the Council of Europe. *Victim Support Review of International Work*, 18 March 1997.

them off the shelf. We're an independent organisation so we can challenge the police and judges in a way that Government finds difficult to do. It's quite valuable for Government. The Government gets all of this at a tiny fraction of the normal cost. The advantages for Victim Support are that we get money we couldn't do without. We also get credibility. Other funders recognise we're a professional organisation. That's an enormous help with our service development in, for example, difficulties with court officials. Responsible Government departments were able to help on our behalf. The Home Office has often intervened on our behalf with the police.

For her part, the head of the JVU was able to say:

The relation with Victim Support is a partnership, we do try to work together in it. We realise each of us has skills we can bring. Victim Support is our main—pretty well our only, provider of services to victims and witnesses. Victim Support is still a relatively unusual organisation because it provides a state service on a charitable basis. They are provided better by an NGO. Victim Support can criticise the Government even though it takes the Government's money. Volunteers can represent the community and symbolise society's response to crime. NGOs can be radical, innovative and they can take risks. It is much easier for them to do this than government departments. They try things out and find what works. It's an opportunity to make things work. Independence from the State means that they can criticise Government. It's not always easy but by and large we value that contribution. They are our experts because of their direct contact with victims. We can draw on that expertise. It's a good exercise in public relations, in providing good coverage for the criminal justice system. Victim Support assist us to build public perception and confidence in criminal justice.

Victim Support may have been a Gulliver in the Brobdingnag of the criminal justice system but it was also a Gulliver in the Lilliput of the victims' third sector, and it was continuing to grow fast in the late 1990s and early 2000s, taking on new work under the Government's provisions for vulnerable and intimidated witnesses in the Youth Justice and Criminal Evidence Act 1998, the implementation of the Macpherson Report on the murder of Stephen Lawrence, the growth of restorative justice, the expansion of the Witness Service into the Magistrates' Courts and, possibly, into the Coroner's Court, courts martial and the civil courts, starting to cater for the victims and relatives of the victims of road crashes,[94] and much else. Seventy-

---

[94] Of the 370 local schemes, 139 were taking referrals of families bereaved by road deaths in early 2000, although no specific funding or policy had yet been approved for

two staff worked in its national office on matters of finance, personnel, fundraising and marketing, media and public relations, strategic
policy, training, and field services. There had been a 25 per cent
increase in its national complement of 1,000 paid staff between
1999–2000 alone.[95] Its 370 local schemes and 18,000 volunteers[96]
dealt with over 1,000,000 local referrals annually,[97] offering emo
tional and practical support to victims;[98] and assisting 235,000
witnesses appearing in the Magistrates' Courts and Crown Court
Centres. It was a prime beneficiary of Government financial support,[99] receiving £12.7m. in 1997–8, rising to £19m. in 2001–2, and

the task. It was often thus. Local schemes would informally pioneer work which later
became adopted by Victim Support to become the subject of a specific funding
application to the Home Office.

[95] *Work Plan 2000–2001*, Victim Support, March 2000.

[96] In October 1999 all local Victim Support Schemes were asked to supply information about their volunteers. Information was secured on 7,585 volunteers not
including trainees: 6,971 were volunteer visitors and 614 helped in the office or with
fundraising. Between 1994 and 1999 the number of volunteers declined by 1,500. 1,984
had joined since October 1998 whilst 2,332 had left in same period. 58% of volunteers
had been with Victim Support for over 2 years—26% for 5+ years; 9% for 4–5 years.
There were 5,667 women and 1,918 men: 62% were over 45, 10% were non-white.
*Victim Support Scheme volunteer information—interim results*, May 2000.

[97] Including, in 1999–2000, 762 homicides, 4,145 rapes, 300,387 other violence
(319,694 violent crimes in total); 411,095 burglaries, 125,156 thefts, and 1,126 road
deaths amongst its 1,268,723 referrals. Victim Support, *Annual Report 2000—
1999–2000*. According to M. Maguire and J. Kynch; *Public Perceptions and Victims'
Experiences of Victim Support: findings from the 1998 British Crime Survey*, RSD,
HO, 2000, 40% of all victims expressed a need which did not appear to have been met
from any source. At least 10% of all British Crime Survey incidents reported to the
police resulted eventually in contact between victims and VS. The key factor was the
type of crime, burglary and violent crime being the most common. Contacts tended to
be 'one-off' and by letter only. Victims reported generally that they found the experience helpful, and the likelihood of their being satisfied was increased by face to face
contact with a volunteer.

[98] Victim Support: Performance Indicators Reference Group, meeting held 8 July
1997.

[99] The Home Office repeatedly acknowledged that it could not for practical or
political reasons cease to fund Victim Support, but Victim Support's dependence on
such funding did bring it about that annually, at first, and then triennially, Victim
Support would have to wait with bated breath, expenditure plans in suspense, for
Home Office announcements about funding allocations for the next financial period.
More than once, Helen Reeves was obliged to inform her National Council, as she did
on 20 October 1998, that 'we don't know whether we're going to have cuts or massive
expenditure'.

constituting with SAMM,[100] its *protegé*, the sole recipient of funding through the JVU.[101] It was charged with delivering a number of the Government's aims and objectives,[102] and its achievements were listed in the Home Office's own reports as if they were part of the formal work of the criminal justice system.[103] It was subject to *Victim's Charter* standards[104] as if it were a criminal justice agency.[105] Its work in shaping the contours of victims' policies was officially acknowledged.[106] As we shall see, at one point, in July 2000, it was even on the verge of being recognized by statute as an agency to overcome the difficulties posed by new information disclosure rules under the Data Protection Act and Human Rights Acts of 1998 (the names of victims, it was being maintained, could not be referred 'automatically' by the police to victim support schemes without breaching their right to privacy and only a change in the legal status of Victim Support could rectify the problem).[107]

[100] Support After Murder and Manslaughter, a self-help group. See my *After Homicide, op. cit.*

[101] The Rape Crisis Federation was to receive funding after the elapse of the period covered by this book.

[102] See *The Government's Expenditure Plans 1999–2000 to 2001–2002, Vol. 1*— Home Office aims—1998–9, p. 4.

[103] See, for example, *Digest 4: Information on the criminal justice system in England and Wales*, Home Office, London, 1999, Chapter 2.

[104] The 1996 Charter informed victims that they could expect to be offered emotional and practical support; and that Victim Support would normally send a letter, telephone, or arrange a visit from a volunteer within four working days of the victim reporting the crime.

[105] For a discussion of the consequences of tighter state control over volunteers, see J. Smith; 'Should Volunteers be Managed?', D. Billis and M. Harris (eds.); *Voluntary Agencies*, Macmillan, Basingstoke, 1996, p. 193.

[106] For example, it was to be quoted in Home Office publications and internal papers as part of the formal history of policy-making for victims. One example was the Justice and Victims Unit's 'Victims Charter—draft consultation paper' (ca. August 2000) which cited Victim Support's 1995 *Statement of Victims' Rights* as a constituent of the Home Office's new interest in victims' rights. Another was a Home Office statement made in the Home Office submission on Support for Victims of Crime in the Comprehensive Spending Review of March 1998; the role of victims is likely to remain a key issue for some time, it was argued, 'not least because of the influential role Victim Support plays in policy-making'.

[107] A memorandum from a Minister said 'we should include work on victim support by treating them as an agency of the police so that they can write and get victim's consent'.

Like many other organizations in the voluntary sector at the time, its standing was becoming confused and blurred.[108] On the verge of being a dependent of the State,[109] it was at once inside and outside the criminal justice system; a formal member of almost all the committees touching victims;[110] neither fully subservient nor autonomous, and both a beneficiary of, and somewhat at risk from, the effects of increasing incorporation[111] (one of its imperatives always was to secure more money from private sources to assert its

[108] F. Prochaska wrote, for example, that the 'issue is not that the voluntary sector has become a state within the State, but that so many charities have become *agencies* of the State... In this ambiguous welfare-world, it has become necessary to use the word "independent" before the name of a non-governmental charity, for it is no longer obvious that a charitable institution is not a government body. To believe that there are two distinct sectors, the state sector paid for by taxation, and the voluntary sector, financed by a variety of means, is rather fanciful. The two sectors have become entangled.' 'Let charity begin with charities', *The Times*, 18 December 1997. See also R. King; 'Policy and process in the modern state', in J. Simmie and R. King (eds.); *The State in Action*, Pinter, London, 1990, which talked about contemporary political life being characterized by an apparently messy co-mingling of the public, private and semi-public; and M. Taylor *et al.*; *Encouraging Diversity: Voluntary and Private Organisations in Community Care*, Arena, Aldershot, 1995, which argued that 'The concept of distinct public, private and voluntary sectors is becoming more and more inadequate to describe the range of organisations now operating in the community care field and the relationships between them... a complex territory with hybrid organisational forms...' (p. 59). The increased messiness was a facet of the 'governmentality' which I shall discuss in the next chapter.

[109] George Howarth, then a Home Office Minister, was to tell the Victim Support national conference in July 1999 that 'the difficulty with the hundred per cent funding of an NGO is that it almost becomes an agent of central government, there is a question of independence, as not being seen as a creature of central government'. The Chair of Victim Support's Trustees presaged those forebodings a year earlier when he said that 'I certainly think we're excessively reliant on Home Office funding.'

[110] Including, in 1997, the Victims Steering Group, the Health and Safety Executive, Witness Care Sub-Group of TIG; the Vulnerable or Intimidated Witnesses Working Group, and the Youth Justice Task Force. Victim Support; *report '97*.

[111] As managerialism and 'joined-up government' worked to increase central control through a web of tight regulatory contracts, so the distance between the State and the private sector diminished. In connection with the drafting of the first service level agreement between the Home Office and Victim Support in 1998, for instance, it was observed within JVU that 'with the growing emphasis on value for money and a performance culture, the earlier arrangement which developed from an "arm's length" relationship—is no longer sufficient'. Conversely, a report on risk management prepared for Victim Support in September 2001 flagged the 'danger of victims' interests being hijacked by criminal justice interests'.

independence[112]). It was being coaxed by the Home Office in the 1990s to adapt to a newly re-structured criminal justice system in which probation, prosecutors, and police agencies had been re-aligned within the common boundaries of forty-two 'co-terminous' catchment areas. In short, it faced continual ambiguities in the resolution of a role,[113] constitutional standing[114] and institutional identity.[115] In July 2000, for example, the Board of Trustees of Victim Support discussed their key objectives for the Strategic Plan 2001/2004, and before them was a paper which laid down that a key theme for consideration was 'identity': 'We need to establish clearly Victim Support's independent status:—i.e. our independence from the Home Office; and—address the confusion over perceptions of

[112] For instance, it was deemed necessary to raise £5m. privately 'in order to maintain a proper balance between public and private resources'. *Work Plan 2000–2001*, p. 3. Securing private money had always been problematic. A Fundraising and Marketing Status Report to the Meeting of Victim Support Trustees, 1 March 2001, reported the 'most successful year' ever for Victim Support's fundraising. Money raised outside Government amounted to £917,000 compared with £25m. from the State.

[113] Around the time of the drafting of the first service level agreement in June 1998, there was a sense in Victim Support that it was becoming obliged to serve goals set by others, and particularly to service the criminal justice system, rather than retain and devise an independent conception of its own 'core functions', including supporting the hundreds of thousands of victims who never formally entered the criminal justice system.

[114] It is noteworthy that undated guidance from the Charity Commission (*The Independence of Charities from the State*) stipulated that for a body to be a charity, it must be independent and should not exist for the purpose of implementing Government policy or directions. A charity was not a charity if it were dependent on a Government authority for funding; received funding on terms that enabled the Government authority to make decisions about what services were to be provided and who was to benefit. Trustees, it was stressed, should have a choice about whether or not they accepted funding, take their own legal and financial advice, draw up their own policies and business plan, conduct at arm's length negotiations with Government, retain independence over beneficiaries, and not commit themselves simply to giving effect to the policies and wishes of Government.

[115] The Home Office seemed equally confused. A model proposed in negotiations between the organization, the Home Office, and the Treasury for a grant-in-aid in early 2000 was, declared the Victim Support Broad of Trustees, that of a Non-Departmental Public Body but Victim Support was an independent charity controlled by its trustees, 'Negotiations towards Grant-in-Aid', Paper prepared for the Meeting of the VS Board of Trustees, 14 January 2000.

Victim Support as a criminal justice agency as well as an independent charity.'

The Justice and Victims Unit was in time formally to acknowledge that independence,[116] but doubts persisted. David Faulkner, the first Home Office official significantly to sponsor Victim Support, wondered whether 'Victim Support, which began quite properly as part of civil society (and still is in many respects) is now being conscripted into the service of the State—through public service agreements, performance standards and funding. Of course the situation makes Victim Support very influential, and they use their influence to very good effect, but their position does seem to be becoming ambiguous and I wonder how long they can keep their independence.'[117] Some relations cannot bear too much scrutiny and there were those in the Home Office and Victim Support who wished to conserve for as long as possible the ambiguities of that carefully-negotiated and hitherto unexamined role of insider-outsider. Ben Lyon, a long-standing member of the Victim Support National Council, reflected 'thankfully I think, we are still operating without a clear mandate from the Home Office'.[118] But there were to be difficult changes after the period covered by this book when, in 2003, it was proposed by the Home Office that some Victim Support services be put out to local tender, a confusing instance of the

---

[116] 'JVU', it said, 'recognises that Victim Support is an independent, member based organisation...', Terms and Condition attached to the Justice and Victims' Unit Grant to Victim Support, 23 July 2001. A larger attempt had been made by Government in late 1998 to define the proper relations between the State and voluntary sector under the new managerialism. *Compact: getting it right together. Compact on Relations between Government and the Voluntary and Community Sector in England,* Home Office, November 1998, Cm. 4100, argued that 'In the development and delivery of public policy and services, the Government and the voluntary and community sector have distinct but complementary roles... The Government and the voluntary and community sector have different forms of accountability and are answerable to a different range of stakeholders... [Government undertakes] [t]o recognise and support the independence of the sector, including its right within the law to campaign, to comment on Government policy, and to challenge that policy, irrespective of any funding relationship that may exist, and to determine and manage its own affairs.'

[117] Letter to me, 4 March 2001.

[118] Very similarly, Jeremy Corbett, Chair of the National Council, talked about how Victim Support was 'on the borderline but I think it's probably in a more powerful position because it is on the borderline'.

organization becoming at once closer to, and more distant from, a powerful organizing State.

## The Absence of Women

Victim Support was a founder-member of the Victims Steering Group, and it was ubiquitous wherever policy was being made for victims *qua* victims in Whitehall, an authority[119] representing victims in general as part of what the Home Secretary called a 'seamless and unified service to witnesses and victims'. Dame Helen Reeves said 'there's nobody in the steering group to represent any particular group of victims, and ... the argument is we are non-specific, ... we're not age-specific, sector-specific, crime-specific.' By contrast, the more focused voluntary and campaigning groups, including women's organizations catering for abuse, domestic violence, incest, and rape, were almost wholly absent from the inner policy circles centred on victims.[120] Also absent were the Government institutions that touched on women victims: for instance, anyone standing for the Ministers for Women or the Cabinet Office Women's Unit, newly established in 1997, later transferred to the Home Office, and subsequently at risk of closure,[121] that serviced them; and representatives of the Departments of Health and Housing, the patron departments of the victims of domestic violence and rape. It could have been otherwise. In New South Wales, for in-

[119] Helen Reeves observed in January 1999 that the status of Victim Support had 'been developing really over 10 years and part of it is because victims' issues are definitely on the agenda and because we've actually had years to build up more expertise I think. And the other thing is, if they want to be seen to be consulting victims, we're actually very convenient. But I think quite apart from that, we've delivered. I think that's the important thing really, that the advice that we've given and the information we've given is well thought out and balanced and usually works, you know, in practical ways. Our proposals generally work. We've had a very good track record.'

[120] Crawford and Enterkin observed that 'Despite its status as a non-governmental organization, Victim Support has increasingly come to constitute an appendage to the formal criminal justice system, simultaneously casting other victims' groups and initiatives—such as Rape Crisis Centres, Women's Aid refuges or local racial harassment projects—into the shadows and onto the margins as well as securing itself a place at the centre of government policy' ; *Victim Contact Work and the Probation Service: A Study of Service Delivery and Impact,* Centre for Criminal Justice Studies, University of Leeds, 1999, p. 8.

[121] See *Evening Standard,* 19 April 2001.

stance, a Victims Advisory Council, founded in 1991, contained members from the 'portfolio areas' of the Attorney General, Health, Community Services, Police, and Women.[122] I propose to linger with the specific question of the linkage between representations of victim and gender because it so well illuminates the more general theme of how administrative structures refracted and amplified particular images of victims and shaped policies in the 1990s. Domestic violence, child abuse, incest, and rape had not been discussed as explicit topics by the Victims Steering Group. When they did arise, they would become transformed into the contents of a discussion of victims treated generically, being bleached out as it were, losing their distinctive connection with gender. A draft letter accompanying a proposed consultation on vulnerable and intimidated witnesses—a consultation whose origins lay in the problems of the oppressive treatment of a rape complainant in court—and the terms of reference[123] of the working group, the body intended to take initiatives forward, neglected to refer to victimized women at all.[124] No representatives of women's organizations were included on the Working Group or in its more public deliberations[125] (although they were subsequently approached in the consultation itself).

The absence of women as a topic and force on the Victims Steering Group and other Government committees and bodies focused on victims[126] was somewhat over-determined, having had its roots in a relatively recent past when relations between women's organizations, the State and criminal justice agencies had been marked by a certain *froideur*. There had been a long and diffuse history of resistance by women's organizations to the language of crime and victims and to a close engagement with the State. The very employment of the term 'victim' had been opposed by some who believed it

[122] *New South Wales Law Reform Commission; Discussion Paper 33: Sentencing*, New South Wales Law Reform Commission, Sydney, 1996, p. 416.

[123] Vulnerable or Intimidated Witnesses Working Group: terms of reference, June 1997.

[124] Draft letter on Vulnerable or Intimidated Witnesses consultation, August 1997.

[125] See Women Against Rape; *Speaking up for Women: What the report of the Working Group on Vulnerable or Intimidated Witnesses hasn't dealt with*, undated.

[126] Not wholly uniform. For example, representatives from Women Against Rape and Victim Support were invited to a seminar on 'customer care' organized by the new Criminal Injuries Compensation Appeal Panel on 28 April 1998. It was the first such occasion, reported WAR, that they had been invited.

resonated both a passivity and a loss of power and critical edge.[127] 'Victim' was androgenous, threatening to submerge women victims within a more general and anonymous mass where the distinctively gendered properties of violence and abuse under patriarchy would be forfeit.[128] It was a contested term, and confusion could cloud definition in debates, for example, about whether violent[129] and non-violent[130] women offenders should not more properly be treated as victims themselves, especially when they had struck back at male aggression.[131] There was disquiet about the complicating notion that men could be raped,[132] subject to domestic violence, or associated with projects for the raped and violated.[133] The *study* of victims, 'victimology', was thought to be bedeviled by its association with attributions of 'victim-precipitation', called 'victim-blaming' by some feminists, which a few early victimologists, like Menachem Amir,[134] had invoked to explain how certain women were subject disproportionately to—had even seemed to invite—assault and rape.[135]

---

[127] Dunn argued that '. . . the ways in which initial feminist typifications, like their victimological and popular precursors, construct essentially *unsympathetic* victims, led to new framings of victims as "survivors" . . . '. J. Dunn; 'Identity Work Dilemmas: Social Movements and the Rhetoric of Intimate Violent Victimization', paper presented at the ASC meetings, Chicago, 15 November 2002, p. 26.

[128] There are parallels elsewhere. In Ontario, for instance, arguments were made for retaining the separation of programmes and policies for women victims. Ontario Provincial Services for Victims of Crime: Information Session for Premier's Office and Cabinet Office, 21 January 2000.

[129] See A. Matravers; *Justifying the Unjustifiable: Stories of Women Sex Offenders*, PhD dissertation, Cambridge, 2000.

[130] See P. Carlen; *Women, Crime and Poverty*, Open University Press, Buckingham, 1988.

[131] See S. Westervelt; *Shifting the Blame: How Victimization Became a Criminal Defense*, Rutgers University Press, New Brunswick, 1998.

[132] See N. Naffine; 'Possession: Erotic Love in the Law of Rape', *Modern Law Review*, January 1994, 57:1, 10–37; and J. Gregory and S. Lees; *Policing Sexual Assault*, Routledge, London, 1999.

[133] Thus the membership criteria laid down by the Rape Crisis Federation (undated) stipulated that rape crisis centres were run by women for women and girls. Men could not be members, members of the management committee, counselled, or given ongoing support by the group.

[134] See M. Amir; *Patterns of Forcible Rape*, University of Chicago Press, Chicago, 1971.

[135] See S. Walklate; 'Can there be a feminist victimology?', in P. Davies *et al.* (eds.); *Victimisation: Theory, Research and Policy*, Palgrave Macmillan, Houndmills, Basingstoke, 2003, p. 30.

Indeed, talk about women as victims of male violence was sometimes depicted as presenting them as overly powerless, and there
were arguments advanced to avoid the topic altogether.[136] 'Many
European feminists during the 1980s', asserted van Swaaningen,
'argued against the identification of women as victims. A key focus
on victims reinforces the passive and weak image of "woman", who
needs help from the stronger "man" for her emancipation.'[137]
'Victim', with its connotations of blame and weakness, was dis-
carded and synonyms such as 'survivor' were occasionally preferred
instead.[138]

Uncertainly a matter of victimization, not to be recognized solely
as a matter for the criminal justice system,[139] possessively 'gendered', rape, domestic violence, incest, and child abuse were located
by many feminists within the wider problems of patriarchal society,
identified as a problem for economic, family,[140] and housing policy
as well as for criminal policy and for initiatives centred on the
application of the civil as well as the criminal law.[141] Helen Reeves
observed in the mid-1980s, at a time when a rift was appearing, that
problems of women's victimization were regarded as '"family"

[136] See E. Stanko; 'Safety Talk', *Theoretical Criminology*, November 1997, Vol. 1,
No. 4, 479–99.

[137] R. van Swaaningen; *Critical Criminology*, Sage, London, 1997, p. 223.

[138] Women's Aid remarked that 'It is important to see ourselves as women who *can*
be strong and can take a very *active* part in deciding what to do with our lives.' WAFE;
*Breaking Through! Women Surviving Male Violence*, WAFE, Bristol, 1989. There
may have been a price to pay for that politics of naming. Tamar Pitch has alleged that
'it's only when women are constructed as victims that success [in changing the law] is
obtained'. 'The Legal Construction of Gender, Sex and Sexuality', Paper delivered at
the London School of Economics, 9 March 1999.

[139] Thus, Joyce Quin, a Home Office Minister, reflected in 1998 that, although the
Home Office had a lead role on domestic violence, policy could not be restricted to any
one department. *VESTA: Victims in Europe Surviving through Assistance: A European Project examining the multi-agency partnership approach to tackling the causes
and effects of domestic violence in Europe, Final Report*, no publisher, 1998, pp. 3–4.

[140] See Press Release: Home Office issues *Supporting Families: A Consultation
Document*, 4 November 1998—New Labour, it was claimed, was tackling serious
problems such as domestic violence, truancy, and school-age pregnancy.

[141] See, for instance, the leaflet on the Family Law Act issued by the Lord Chancellor's Department, 1996: the new Act was said to strengthen the civil law and give
better options for those suffering from domestic violence. People could apply for an
order against another person when they are linked by a domestic or family relation.
Orders include non-molestation order, occupation order for the home, injunction, and
so on.

issues with services, campaigning organizations, and a body of knowledge and theory of their own. They have not in Britain been associated either in theory or practice with the development of interest in "victims" of crime. Victims services are generally based only upon incidents occurring outside the family...'.[142]

Campaigning feminists had distanced themselves in the 1980s not only from initiatives for victims at large, but also from many of the bodies superintending victims' initiatives, including the police and Victim Support, and that distancing had been reciprocal.[143] As recently as the late 1990s, a woman working for a campaigning organization centred on rape said:

I mean we've worked very hard to be independent of the police you know and I mean frankly it's a shame that other groups haven't worked as hard as we have to do so. You know and it's not, we very much believe in putting pressure on State agencies to change, but we are not at all going to be co-opted by them, you know, to change what we do or to basically let them off the hook frankly, which is what a lot of the groups have ended up doing. You know the relationship has become far too cosy and it's the same with the Government.

That stance had begun to change in a number of quarters at the end of the 1990s as a new pragmatism came to be driven by a mix of opportunity and need.[144] On the one hand, the imperatives of 'joined-up government' had led to a greater willingness on the part of the Home Office and other bodies to engage with members of the voluntary sector. Some members of the campaigning organizations newly entered into conversations with the criminal justice agencies and departments, including the Criminal Injuries Compensation Appeals Panel, the Home Office (and especially Ian Chisholm, whom they reported finding approachable), Victim Support, and others. On the other hand, there had been the goad of besetting funding crises which had made it difficult for voluntary organizations not only to survive but also to preserve an impeccable distance from possible sources of monetary aid. The Rape Crisis Federation,

---

[142]  H. Reeves; 'Towards a British Policy for Victims', 1984, p. 7.

[143]  See B. Williams; 'The probation service and victims of crime', *Journal of Social Welfare and Law*, 18(4), 1996, pp. 461–74; and B. Williams; 'Probation work with victims of crime', *Criminal Justice Matters*, Spring 1999, No. 35.

[144]  For a parallel discussion of the development of trends of feminism in British policy-making circles, see F. Heidensohn; *Sexual Politics and Social Control*, Open University Press, Buckingham, 2000, Ch. 2.

for instance, reported in 1998 that 'The first half of the year now feels as if it was spent in total panic with little or no concrete funding, the threat of redundancy, moving the office base to save money, worker time and worker exhaustion.'[145] The Federation's financial crisis came eventually to be resolved, first by a grant from the National Lottery, and then by an award of £400,000 a year from the Home Office. *Froideur* and the older antipathies were evaporating. A member of the Federation said:

I think since the sort of development of the Federation and the input that the Federation has had to various Government documents like *Speaking up for Justice* and things like that, we're now beginning to be taken seriously as a movement and as an organization. And I think that probably has added to people wanting to actually, you know, be there as consultants, things like that. So we've been asked, we're on like two or three projects at the Home Office, and we were involved with the *Living Without Fear* document from the Women's Unit... we have far better dialogue with [the police], I worked in Rape Crisis in the 80s, mid-80s, and it was definitely a no-no. I mean you hardly would even go out of Rape Crisis to do police training but in the last 15–20 years, 15 years actually I would think, we've seen a very big change in the police attitude. And maybe the fact that Rape Crisis were willing to go and do some training... we haven't [accepted the word 'victim'] but we've acknowledged that it's used within law. It's not about word cleansing really so hey, if [Ian Chisholm's] got victims and we understand what he means by that, we'll be in there kind of you know, but the only reason, yeah, they're doing this training around working with victims, the reason why we'd say you've got to look at work with survivors is you've got to change the culture of the way you work with people and not just that cleansing the word that you use. So hey, if he's got money for victims, we're going to there you know.

By the turn of the century, however, the divisions laid down in the 1970s and 1980s had become petrified into a taken-for-granted and apparently immutable organization of Government responsibilities.[146] For diffuse semantic, administrative, and ideological

[145] Rape Crisis Federation; *Annual Report, 1997 to 1998*, Nottingham.
[146] £6m. from the Crime Reduction Fund, had for example, been spent on a separate portfolio of projects to tackle violence against women as part of an inter-agency campaign, *Living Without Fear. Home Office Annual Report, 1999–2000.* The Home Office assumed the policy lead on violence against women in July 1999— previously held by the Cabinet Office Women's Unit. One outcome was a new Inter-Departmental Group on Domestic Violence and Violence Against Women, Home Office: The Home Office Agenda on Violence Against Women—December 1999. It

reasons, what was done for and to women 'survivors' or 'victims' was listed as an activity apart. Helen Reeves said 'there are different histories, so . . . different forums get set up, different relationships get established, and you don't necessarily think about changing it . . . Children as victims is one culture. Women as victims is another . . . with a slight gulf between rape and domestic violence . . . They tend to be different people, even though there are quite a lot of overlaps.' So it was that the Labour Party could report that its commitment to victims was also linked with 'Labour's action on domestic violence', [147] as if the two were distinct projects. And even within the Home Office, domestic violence was assigned not to JVU but to another part of the Criminal Policy Directorate. Alan Kirkwood of the Crown Prosecution Service, a member of the Victims Steering Group, observed of the Group in October 1998 that 'I don't think it's in a position to influence policy on domestic violence, which is being handled in a completely different way . . . '.

It is not a matter of moment to this history whether representations of victims in the central forums in and around the Home Office should or should not have been distinctively 'gendered' or otherwise differentiated. It *is* important that what was conveyed by 'victims' in criminal justice policy-making circles at the turn of the century was to be inflected in very special ways, and much of the rest of this book will attempt to demonstrate precisely how, and with what consequences, that work of inflection was to be undertaken. Let me now turn to the ways in which New Labour began, or continued, to construct those representations.

replaced an earlier group, the Inter Departmental Group on Domestic Violence, which had met fitfully at best, and it represented a substantially discrete policy world, being composed of representatives from the Home Office; the Women's Unit; the Department for Education and Employment; the Department of Health; the Department of Social Security; the Department for Culture, Media and Sport; the Health and Safety Executive; the Department of the Environment, Transport and the Regions; the Northern Ireland Office; the National Assembly for Wales; the Lord Chancellor's Department; the Crown Prosecution Service; and the Cabinet Office. Contrast that membership with that of the Victims Steering Group. For a more general treatment of the ossification of styles of management, see K. Scholes and G. Johnson (eds.); *Exploring Public Sector Strategy*, Prentice Hall, New York, 2000.

[147] Labour Party web site July 2000: National Policy Forum Report: Crime and Justice 1999.

# 4

# The Victim as Consumer

## Introduction

A groundwork is now in place to describe how the more significant incarnations of victims developed in the 1990s and early 2000s. Relatively discrete and dispersed at first, welling up from political and administrative preoccupations that had little to do with the direct demands of the larger population of victims and witnesses (there were very few occasions on which those demands were made or could be heard), they came eventually to merge by the end of the first administration. Each of the incarnations I shall discuss would play a distinct role in moulding the politics of victims, some lending content, others form, and others political momentum, and I shall consider their evolution one after another, beginning with the earliest, the representation of the victim as a vaguely 'empowered' consumer of criminal justice services. Sue Street, one-time Director of Criminal Policy at the beginning of the century, an official whose views counted, summarized some of the ingredients of the position I am about to describe:

I think it is all part of increasing the democratization of our services... People want a bigger say. You can trace it back to consumer power. You can trace it back to client-oriented public service. You can certainly [link it] with information technology... So the expectations of people [are] that they will be served and they'll be given the information they need... Any public service exists for the citizen... if you're on the damage end of the health service, if you're ill or uncomfortable or hurt, you want the service that addresses that; if you're at the damage end of the criminal justice system, you're bereaved or you're battered or you've been robbed, then you want the system that takes care of you.

To carry those themes forward, I must return briefly to ground already partly covered. The transformation of the citizen or subject into a consumer of State-provided services was consummated largely in the administrative reforms of the Conservative Government of John Major of 1992–1997. I have already outlined in Chapter 2 the still uncertainly entrenched workings of what the successor New Labour administration of 1997–2001 called 'modernisation', but it might be helpful at this stage to offer a rather more formal model of what was in progress. One way of achieving that would be to turn to a train of sociological analysis, awarded the cumbersome title of 'governmentality', that stemmed from the ideas of Michel Foucault, and align it with allied writings by academic accountants and political scientists on the new performance management. The outcome will be made hybrid and simple for analytic effect, but the diagnoses are remarkably similar, they work well together, and they do throw light on how a number of crucial processes were conceived.

The idea of 'governmentality' and its close relations point to recent and longer lasting mutations of power in and around a late modern State[1] that no longer monopolises control but has become a 'hollowed-out,' 'differentiated polity'[2] in which services and practices which were once its exclusive preserve have become 'self-organising, interorganisational networks'.[3] The wider origins of those changes have been located by some in the emergence of a globalization that eroded the powers and independence of the sovereign State to internationalize and transform consumption, production and politics. David Held, for instance, argued that 'all nation-states . . . [are becoming] enmeshed in and functionally part of a larger pattern of global transformations and global flows . . . [and of] the stretching of political relations across space and time . . .'.[4] Some no longer even talk about the nation-State but about a new market-state built around permeable boundaries and the primacy of

---

[1]   Nikolas Rose has reminded me that there are two discrete but connected strands of thought in the account I give of the transformation of the State: 'the Rhodes governance approach is talking about a recent change—diminishing state power etc.—whereas governmentality points to a longer lasting set of relations and alliances between "political" and non-political authorities'.

[2]   R. Rhodes; *Understanding Governance: Policy Networks, Governance, Reflexivity and Accountability,* Open University Press, Buckingham, 1997, p. 3.

[3]   *Ibid,* p. 53.

[4]   D. Held *et al.; Global Transformations,* Polity Press, Cambridge, 1999, p. 48.

economic transactions.[5] And others more cynical have argued that the weakening of the nation-State is in the manifest interests of business which is substituting its own economic order.[6] What they all flag is a diminishing of State power within the boundaries of the traditional polity and the appearance in its stead of new forms of regulation and relation.

On a smaller and more concrete level in England and Wales, the empirical roots of those mutations lay first with the New Right, and then with the New Centre Left, who identified what they took to be difficulties linked with high taxation and the maintenance of a State that was ineptly managed, professionally dominated, overly interventionist, and lacking in client involvement.[7] The fiscal, social, and economic crises of the 1970s,[8] it was held, prompted a major reexamination of the limits of government; a quest for the new trilogy of economy, effectiveness, and efficiency;[9] a concomitant ideological rejection of the conventionally-conceived modernist State[10] and its professional civil service[11] as repositories of assured answers to political and social problems;[12] and a companion extolling of the

---

[5] See P. Bobbitt; *The Shield of Achilles*, Penguin Books, London, 2003.

[6] See Z. Bauman; *Globalization: The Human Consequences*, Polity, Cambridge, 1998, pp. 67–8.

[7] See N. Rose; *Governing the Soul*, Routledge, London, 1990, p. 226.

[8] See A. Gray *et al.*; 'The Management of Change in Whitehall', *Public Administration*, Vol. 69, Spring 1991, p. 46.

[9] See, for instance, the *Third Report from the Treasury and Civil Service Committee: Efficiency and Effectiveness in the Civil Service*, Report, Session 1981–2, 8.3.82, HC236-1; and 'Efficiency and Effectiveness in the Civil Service, Government Observations on the 3rd Report from the Treasury and Civil Service Committee', Cmnd. 8616. Both papers stress the importance of focusing effort on specified targets, clear measures of performance, maximizing the efficient use of money, information technology and labour, and the like.

[10] In the 1970s, the Conservatives were said to hold that officials were overmighty and needed emasculation. 'How to tackle "the problem of bureaucracy" was the topic of many a seminar discussion'. P. Barberis; 'Whitehall since the Fulton Report', in P. Barberis (ed.); *The Whitehall reader*, Open University Press, Buckingham, 1996, p. 15. When she came to power in 1979, the Prime Minister, Mrs Thatcher, treated the civil service as 'wasteful, inefficient and the true masters of the nation'. K. Dowding; *The Civil Service*, Routledge, London, 1995, p. 64.

[11] Flynn sees that process as part of a much larger withdrawal of authority from the professions that was then current. See N. Flynn (ed.); *Change in the Civil Service*, Public Finance Corporation, London, 1994, p. 2.

[12] Bureaucracy is a bankrupt form of government, claimed D. Osborne and T. Gaebler: 'Hierarchical, centralized bureaucracies designed in the 1930s or 1940s

virtues of an alternative system, the management methods and 'consumerism'[13] of the private sector.[14] Business, it was thought, did things better,[15] and public services were made to seem more business-like through the 'development of quasi-markets, [and the] mimicking [of] market-like mechanisms'[16] in the hope that their reconstruction would lead to a more efficient allocation of resources and choice to consumers[17] and producers.[18] There were attempts simultaneously to check the growth of government, introduce automation into public administration; internationalize public administration; and privatize public administration.[19] The reforms were information-driven, led by what Giddens called a 'concentrated reflexive monitoring'[20] that was tied to the rationalizing,[21]

simply do not function well in the rapidly-changing, information-rich, knowledge-intensive society and economy of the 1990s.'; *Reinventing Government: How the Entrepreneurial Spirit is Transforming the Public Sector*, Plume, New York, 1993, p. 12.

[13] O'Malley has described what he calls 'the triumph of a discourse of "consumers" and "customers" that has begun to displace those of "students", "patients" and "clients", so that public accountability becomes a major concern'. P. O'Malley *et al.*; 'Post-Keynesian Policing', *Economy and Society*, May 1996, Vol. 25, No. 2, p. 141.

[14] Michael Heseltine was reported to have said that 'Efficient management is the key to the [national] revival... And the management ethos must run through our national life—private and public companies, civil service...' in K. McEvoy; *Paramilitary Imprisonment in Northern Ireland*, Oxford University Press, Oxford, 2001, p. 254.

[15] '...the programme represents the continuation of a trend towards tighter management of the public sector on a private sector model. Its significance lies in its redefinition of the citizen as an economic actor—a consumer—and in the extent to which it imports private sector concerns with quality as the touchstone of successful service delivery.' A. Barron and C. Scott; 'Legislation: The Citizen's Charter Programme', *The Modern Law Review*, July 1992, Vol. 55, p. 527.

[16] E. Ferlie *et al.*; *The New Public Management in Action, op. cit.*, p. 57.

[17] In the United States, said Kettl, 'The [National Performance Review's] enthusiasm for customer service builds on the self-evident observation that citizens are truly unhappy with the performance of their government.' D. Kettl; *Reinventing Government: Appraising the National Performance Review*, Center for Public Management, The Brookings Institute, August 1994, p. 34.

[18] See E. Ferlie *et al.*; *The New Public Management in Action*, Oxford University Press, Oxford, 1996, p. 31.

[19] Taken from C. Hood; 'Beyond the Public Bureaucracy State? Public Administration in the 1990s', Extended text of an inaugural lecture delivered on 16 January 1990.

[20] A. Giddens; *Modernity and Self-Identity*, Polity Press, Cambridge, 1991, p. 16.

[21] Thus Miller and O'Leary: '...the affirmation of the possibility of a rationally administered and managed social order, something which was to be undertaken with

data-gathering, and analyzing powers of the new information tech-nology.[22] In this new configuration of governmentality, State author-ity was ceded upwards to international bodies, sideways to commercial organizations, and downwards to private organiza-tions.[23] Within a seemingly shrinking polity, it created a diffuse web of quasi-commercial agreements and contracts[24] which had about it an appearance of self-regulation—a development identified by Hog-wood as a shift 'from hierarchy to contract',[25] by Loughlin and Scott as the rise of 'the regulatory State',[26] by Johnston and Shearing as a move towards 'governance as the property of networks rather than as the product of any single centre of action'[27] and by Rose, in the special context of the criminal justice system, as a growth in the dispersed nature of control practices.[28] The whole thesis has been ably summar-ized by Ericson and his colleagues in their study of insurance:

... the state has three dimensions: it is a country with bounded territory, a nation with a population of citizens, and a sovereign authority with a

the aid of a neutral and objective knowledge'. P. Miller and T. O'Leary; 'Accounting and the Construction of the Governable Person', *Accounting, Organizations and Society*, 1987, Vol. 12, No. 3, p. 246. There was a commitment to ensuring that all dealings with government would be deliverable electronically by 2008. *Modernising Government*, Cm. 4310, March 1999.

[22] Thus Rose and Miller: 'The "representation" of that which is to be governed is an active, technical process. Government has inaugurated a huge labour of enquiry to transform events and phenomena into information ...'. N. Rose and P. Miller; 'Polit-ical power beyond the State: problematics of government', *British Journal of Soci-ology*, June 1992, Vol. 43, No. 2, p. 185.

[23] I. Loader and N. Walker; 'Policing as a Public Good', *Theoretical Criminology* 2001, Vol. 5, No. 1, p. 9.

[24] 'The changes can be ... construed as creating more sensitive service delivery mechanisms, based on a very different set of principles from traditional public bur-eaucracies. Hence disaggregation of structures and devolved managerial responsibil-ities, moves towards contractual rather than hierarchical relationships, and injection of commercial disciplines and extension of consumer choice ...'. C. Painter; 'The Next Steps Reforms and Current Orthodoxies', in B. O'Toole and G. Jordan (eds.); *Next Steps*, Dartmouth, Aldershot, 1995, p. 22.

[25] B. Hogwood; 'The Machinery of Government, 1979–97', *Political Studies*, Vol. 45, No. 4, September 1997, p. 713.

[26] M. Loughlin and C. Scott; 'The Regulatory State', in P. Dunleavy *et al.* (eds.); *Developments in British Politics 5*, Macmillan Press, Basingstoke, 1997.

[27] L. Johnston and C. Shearing; *Governing Security*, Routledge, London, 2003, p. 148.

[28] N. Rose; 'Government and Control', *British Journal of Criminology*, 40, 2, Spring 2000, p. 325.

political regime. The contemporary state is minimalized as it gives ground to, and partners with, private sector institutions on each of these dimensions. It becomes one institution among others, trying to act in the general interest according to principles of public service.[29]

Contrary to some of those theses, and reminiscent of Weber's paradox that the Bolshevik State which sought to wither away would have to gain strength to accomplish the arduous feat of dismantling itself, all that work of shedding, diffusing, and decentralizing power led to increased control being exercised by the centre, for it was at the centre that the apparatus of audit and surveillance, the contracts, standards and inspections, was constructed and applied. There are, it seems, good reasons to question whether the State's role, at least in criminal justice, has indeed been 'hollowed-out' (Nicola Lacey remarked that 'for those of us who have anything to do with criminal justice, it is obvious that the nation-State is alive and well'[30]). It certainly seemed to many practitioners that power was flowing to the centre rather than away from it. Roger Ford, a Chief Probation Officer sitting on the Victims Steering Group, observed:

There's no doubt, I mean I think it's more centralized, you feel more controlled. I can recall earlier days as a Chief or an Assistant Chief Probation Officer where you felt that your, perhaps your accountability was much more local and you got that, you've got much greater accountability centrally. National standards is another example of that. Key performance indicators, tremendous amount of activity by the inspectorate over the last eight to ten years, inspections and reports and documents. It seems to me more accountable. I do think that that trend extends down right throughout the organisation.

Yet, centripetal or centrifugal, the British State was undergoing shifts in the configuration of power. After the 1998 Comprehensive Spending Review, each Government department and executive agency in England and Wales was reported to have a public service agreement or contract in place between itself and the 'tax-paying public', setting out what it should do[31] and how it could determine whether

---

[29] R. Ericson, A. Doyle and D. Barry; *Insurance as Governance*, University of Toronto Press, Toronto, 2003, p. 359.

[30] Research Seminar, London School of Economics, 3 November 1998.

[31] Home Office Issues Performance Indicators Consultation Paper to Police, 24 September 1999. And see the statement by the Chief Secretary to the Treasury, Stephen Byers, in *Sunday Times*, 9 August 1998.

it was achieving it.[32] The criminal justice system was something
of a latecomer to the new performance management,[33] but it
too succumbed in time (it was noted by a trilateral group in
2000 that 'SLAs [service level agreements] and Concordats are a
cardinal feature of the way in which CJ agencies currently work
more closely together'[34]), and, in their turn, many aspects of agencies' dealings with victims and witnesses[35] were covered by a lesser
latticework of agreements, objectives, and performance measures.[36]
It was a latticework that drew Victim Support in as a near-agency
situated on the borders of the formal criminal justice system.
Victim Support entered into a number of 'bilateral protocols' with
separate criminal justice agencies.[37] Its new grant-in-aid from
the Home Office[38] in 1998 was itself regulated by a service
level agreement that laid down a 'new more precisely defined relationship between funder and funded' and, in the process,
transformed what had been a 'grass-roots organisation' into a
'national service, subject to current pressures for accountability in
the public service'[39] and the need to demonstrate 'value for money'.
It is perhaps no surprise that members of Victim Support
came to express uneasiness about the risk of an ensuing loss of

[32] Statement by the Chancellor of the Exchequer on the Comprehensive Spending
Review, 14 July 1998. It became routine to report the performance indicators adopted
by the agencies and to report on success or failure in their attainment. See, for instance,
*The Court Service Annual Report 1997–1998*, HMSO, London, 1998; Crown Prosecution Service Annual Report April 1998–March 1999; and others.
[33] See J. Pratt; 'The Return of the Wheelbarrow Man', *British Journal of Criminology*, Vol. 40, No. 1, pp. 127–45.
[34] Criminal Justice Joint Planning Unit; 2000 SR: SR2000 Cross Cutting Study of
the CJS, 15 June 2000.
[35] See Home Office Circular 41/1996: Witness Care in the Criminal Justice System;
TIG; Statement of National Standards of Witness Care in the Criminal Justice System,
Taking Forward standards of witness care through local Service Level Agreements,
July 1996. Probation Circular: 'The probation service's victim contact work', June
2001, PC62/2001.
[36] See, for instance, *Home Office Annual Report, 1999–2000*—Aim 2, Home
Office, London, 2000, p. 28.
[37] See, for example, Probation Circular 61/1995, 23 August 1995.
[38] Victim Support: Work Plan 2000–2001. For a more general review of that
transformation of the relations between charities and the State at the time, see
*Charities and Contracts*, Charity Commission, London, 1993.
[39] Report to Victim Support Council, October 1998: Implementation of Performance Indicators.

independence.[40] Even the relations between the State and individual citizen were to be recast as a new version of the social contract, entailing what a number of academics awkwardly called 'responsibilization',[41] in which citizens were awarded rights in exchange for the acceptance of a duty to behave properly, protect themselves and render service to the community.[42] Victim Support itself resurrected a Hobbesian version of the social contract in its argument that victims could not be expected to surrender their powers willingly and peacefully to the State unless they received a measure of safety and support in return. Since victims no longer took personal action to obtain redress from the offender, it argued, the State should reciprocate by undertaking tasks on their behalf to provide information, explanation, protection, compensation, respect, and assistance and to relieve them of the 'burden' of criminal justice decisions.[43]

I remarked earlier how the new vocabulary of public administration borrowed directly or indirectly from business school talk about 'efficiency, effectiveness, managerialism and auditing . . . [the] standard neo-liberal justifications drawn from the model of the free economy'.[44] Management was supposed to become more direct and less distant; there was to be a greater emphasis on targets,[45] out-

[40] The document, it was reported to Victim Support's Board of Trustees, was drafted on a model applicable to a government agency rather than an independent charity. It failed to represent the responsibilities and accountability structures of Victim Support, and particularly Victim Support as an independent charity. Board of Trustees—Grant-in-Aid: update on grant in aid, 14 April 2000.

[41] See D. Garland; 'The limits of the sovereign state: Strategies of crime control in contemporary society', *The British Journal of Criminology*, 1996, Vol. 64, No. 4, pp. 445–71; and P. O'Malley and D. Palmer; 'Post-Keynesian Policing', *Economy and Society*, 1996, Vol. 25, No. 2, pp. 137–55.

[42] See Jack Straw; 'Human Rights and Personal Responsibility—New Citizenship for a New Millennium', 2 October 2000. The Australian Human Rights and Equal Opportunities Commission; *Human Rights Explained*, undated, went further and cited Locke and Rousseau. www.gov.au/hr_explained.

[43] Victim Support; *Rights of Victims*, 1995. Fenwick drew another inference. Awarding victims procedural rights, she argued, would entail an unwelcome reversion back towards private justice. H. Fenwick; 'Procedural "Rights" of Victims of Crime', *The Modern Law Review*, Vol. 60, No. 3, May 1997.

[44] R. Sullivan; *Crime, Liberalism and the Autonomous State*, ms, 1999, p. 11 (now *Liberalism and Crime: The British Experience*, Lexington Books, Lanham, Md., 2000) but the statement which appeared in the typescript does not appear in the book).

[45] Targets drive good performance by clarifying the final outcomes on which services ought to focus and encourage the less good to rise to the level of the best,

comes, standards, and indicators, on developing 'levers to drive up standards in public services';[46] and a greater frugality and discipline in the use of resources.[47] One after another, criminal justice agencies started to speak the language of enterprise and the market. Their strategic plans became 'business' plans.[48] The Crown Prosecution Service started to prepare Corporate and Business Plans instead of its earlier 'strategies'.[49] The Home Office Efficiency Consultancy Unit became the Business Performance Unit. The Government itself began issuing *Criminal Justice Business Quarterly Reports*. Police forces became police services. Victim Support produced business plans and started to talk about customer relations,[50] introducing its own notion of responsibilization to determine the proper, quasi-contractual relations between its volunteers and workers, on the one hand, and 'difficult' 'service-users', particularly racist victims, who were obliged to behave well to retain the services of a Victim Support worker, on the other.[51] A new area structure delineated 'units of service delivery and management'.[52] Helen Reeves, once its Director, became its Chief Executive Officer. She said, 'the language is modern management. It's the thing we all have to do.'

Turning to the legitimating rationalities of accountancy practice;[53] pushing 'control further into organizational structures, inscribing it with systems which can then be audited';[54] effectively

said the Chancellor of the Exchequer. HM Treasury; *Spending Review 2000*: New Public Spending Plans, 2001–2004, 28 July 2000—foreword by the Chancellor of the Exchequer.

[46] *Modernising Government*, Cm. 4310, March 1999.

[47] See C. Hood; 'A Public Management for All Seasons?', *Public Administration*, Vol. 69, Spring 1991, p. 4.

[48] In, for example, the Terms and Conditions attached to the Justice and Victims Unit Grant to Victim Support, 23 July 2001.

[49] CPS web site 1998.

[50] Victim Support: Key Objectives for the Strategic Plan 2001/2004.

[51] Meeting of Victim Support National Council, 14 December 1999, Anne Viney: Report of Working Party on Victims of Racist Violence.

[52] Victim Support; Consultation on the future structure of London, 15 March 2000.

[53] Meyer claimed that 'Environments create organizational elements such as accounting and accountants, make it easy and necessary for organizations to use them, and treat organizations that have them as by definition more legitimate than others.' J. Meyer; 'Social Environments and Organizational Accounting', *Accounting, Organizations and Society*, 1986, Vol. 11, No. 4/5, p. 346.

[54] M. Power; *The Audit Society*, Oxford University Press, Oxford, 1997, p. 42.

distrusting the competence, independence, and judgments of its own officials;[55] the Government had reconstituted the civil service so that officials could become more answerable, disciplined, and transparent[56] in their actions; judged not by their claims to be members of a trustworthy, self-regulating, virtually independent and responsible profession but by quantifiable and quantified outcomes; 'calculat[ing] their actions not in the esoteric languages of their own expertise but by translating them into costs and benefits that can be given an accounting value'.[57]

Accounting practices, said Hopwood, are 'now associated with particular ways of seeing and trying to shape organizational processes and actions, with the maintenance of certain forms of organizational segregation, hierarchy and control, and with the furtherance of an economic rationale for action'.[58] We have already seen how the practices of the new performance management modelled[59] the Home Office of the late 1990s into an array of functional divisions, units, and reporting systems ordered by principles of accountability and control.[60] Officials, it was argued, had become more akin to the managers of a market delivering services,[61] and much was changed in the process. It was alleged, for instance, that

[55] See D. Garland; 'The Culture of High Crime Societies', *British Journal of Criminology*, Summer 2000, Vol. 40, No. 3, p. 357. The White Paper, *Modernising Government*, Cm. 4310, March 1999, stated 'We will deliver public services to meet the needs of citizens, not the convenience of service providers.'

[56] 'The targets are challenging and transparent, allowing the public to judge for themselves how performance is improving...' said HM Treasury; Spending Review 2000: Investing in strong public services.

[57] N. Rose; 'The death of the social?', *Economy and Society*, August 1996, Vol. 25, No. 3, p. 351.

[58] A. Hopwood; 'On Trying to Study Accounting in the Contexts in which it operates', *Accounting, Organizations and Society*, 1983, Vol. 8, Nos. 2–3, p. 87.

[59] Meyer also claimed that 'It is now common to see organizations as isomorphic with such available institutional rules as accounting systems. Certain kinds of organizations become easier to construct and legitimate...', J. Meyer; 'Social Environments and Organizational Accounting', *op. cit.*, p. 354.

[60] See A. Hopwood; 'The Organisational and Behavioural Aspects of Budgeting and Control', in J. Arnold *et al.* (eds.); *Topics in Management Accounting*, Philip Allan, 1980, pp. 221–40; and A. Hopwood; "Organisational Contingencies and Accounting Configurations", in B. Fridman and L. Ostman (eds.); *Accounting Development—Some Perspectives—in Honour of Sven-Erik Johansson'*, Stockholm, 1989, pp. 23–44.

[61] A. James and J. Raine; *The New Politics of Criminal Justice*, Longman, London, 1998, p. 23.

issues of justice and morality had been rephrased as questions of efficiency, economy, and added value.[62] In this chapter, and following Miller and O'Leary, I now propose to concentrate on how '... accounting... serve[d] to construct a particular field of visibility',[63] exploring how it was that a particular representation of the victim as consumer was to come into view[64] A senior official, the sometime Deputy Director of the Criminal Policy Directorate, detected just such a change in progress when he returned to the Home Office in September 2000:

One of the big things in my last job was citizens focus, customer focus, and it's, well I was going to say... it's easy to produce the rhetoric and not all that easy just to produce the rhetoric, because you still often find yourself writing White Paper language from a kind of departmental point of view... In terms of what I'm used to in relation to private sector comparisons or areas like tax, say, or maybe the education side, if you look at, for instance, criminal justice web-sites, the organisations that they have, they're not very good, they're not very joined up, they're not very citizen focused. And people are beginning to realise, I think, that there's a... huge amount more to be done there. That then you know, gets you into this difficult area of stop and analyse quite what you mean by the customer, consumer. And again on any view, people will say, well, we think the victims are rather important in that connection.

In the 1990s, the criminal justice system's discourse of 'customer focused services'[65] was starting to complement the emphasis on linking victims' policies to crime reduction (with its argument that contented victims and witnesses would be a better helpmate to prosecutions), with another, intimately connected, emphasis on linking the effectiveness of criminal justice to measures of customer

---

[62] See M. Tuck; 'Community and the Criminal Justice System', *Policy Studies*, Autumn 1991, Vol. 12(3), p. 23.

[63] P. Miller and T. O'Leary; 'Accounting and the Construction of the Governable Person', *Accounting, Organizations and Society*, 1987, Vol. 12, No. 3, p. 239.

[64] 'In part, the refashioning of victims as rational choice customers... has given victims a new standing as consumers of a public service.' A. Crawford and J. Enterkin; *Victim Contact Work and the Probation Service: A Study of Service Delivery and Impact*, Centre for Criminal Justice Studies, University of Leeds, 1999, p. 3. And they came into view, of course, within a much larger process of redefining the public as consumer. See C. Morrison; 'Consumerism—Lessons from Community Work', *Public Administration*, Vol. 66, Summer 1988, pp. 205–13.

[65] Home Office *HOtline*, 13 October 1998, describing the 'New Ways of Working' initiative.

satisfaction (with its argument that contented 'service recipients'[66] point to successful service-delivery by an efficient organization[67]). The 'treatment of victims and witnesses,' it was noted in 1999, 'has been flagged as a key priority because it is a measure of our concern for the quality of service to members of the public involved in the criminal justice system.'[68] The distinction was slight and contingent and may have marked little more than an evolution in the language of policy-making. But it did have a rather different provenance and imagery, the one usage redolent of what used to be called the 'war against crime' with the victim cast as an auxiliary crimefighter; the other, defining criminal justice as a service, rather like any other public service, with the victim cast as the consumer, and it was a difference that was to have some consequences.

It is important to be reminded once more that the Home Office and wider criminal justice system were in flux in the 1990s, that the spread of this form of 'governmentality' and its ideas and practices was uneven, and that what was stirring still elicited very different responses. A Grade 7, working in the Justice and Victims Unit, reflected as late as December 2000 that 'I don't feel we've got that type of function here in terms of looking at [our activity] as service delivery and giving the customer what they want. I don't think we've got that culture really'. Further, in their older, non-utilitarian guise, notions of public service had long been characteristic of a civil service that conceived of itself as a profession.[69] John Halliday, then Director of Criminal Policy, said 'we always were, and we weren't alone in this, of course, a lot of others said it, conscious that the criminal justice system served the wider public, the individual victim, and I think we successfully handled that'. Diverse inter-

---

[66] The White Paper, *Modernising Government*, Cm. 4310, March 1999, observed 'people are becoming more demanding, whether as consumers of goods and services in the market place, as citizens or as businesses', and it concluded, 'In the period ahead, the Government will set milestones to chart our course and success criteria so that the users of public services can judge whether the modernisation programme is working.' A later paper referred to six key targets that include increasing the satisfaction of victims and witnesses: 'they are the ones on which the success of the CJS as a whole is likely to be judged'. Briefing for the PSX meeting on the CJS, 29 April 1999.

[67] See the joint Home Office/Lord Chancellor's Department circular on measuring performance to reduce delays in the criminal justice system, 16 September 1998.

[68] Briefing for the PSX meeting on the CJS, 29 April 1999.

[69] See A. Crawford and J. Goodey (eds.); *Integrating a Victim Perspective Within Criminal Justice: International debates*, Ashgate, Aldershot, 2000, p. 40.

pretations thus vied and co-existed with each another, and a prevalent strain tacitly argued that the new performance management might prove to be a more or less useful tool, a means of focusing the mind and improving methods of planning,[70] but that it was also quite possible to stand back and treat it as a resource or set of metaphors, a *newspeak*, that must be employed under the current regime rather than as an ideology that had to be accepted *tout court*. Charles Clarke, the Minister responsible for victims' policies after Alun Michael, was certainly averse to treating it too literally or exclusively:

I think it's quite fashionable to look at having social institutions as businesses, and so you have customers [and are] profit-driven and all the rest of it, which is all okay, it's a linguistic point, and I think it's good that public sector organisations should be thinking in that sense who are their customers, whether you're the health service or the police. But I wouldn't kind of elevate it, because there is a real sense in which certainly the police, but also other public sector organisations, have a greater community responsibility than simply to their particular customers.

Commercial metaphor could, of course, be awkward.[71] Individual victims were regarded within the criminal justice system neither as the sole nor, indeed, as a wholly legitimate or accepted customer;[72] society or the community abstractly conceived was more commonly accepted by judges and prosecutors as the true, albeit metaphysical victim of crime; and criminal justice agencies and their personnel also required servicing,[73] leading John Halliday to observe, 'there

---

[70] Chris Pulford of the Lord Chancellor's Department certainly found the new methods useful: 'actually it's quite a sophisticated tool and the better you are at it, the better your end product can be. But not everybody's good at it, and not everybody thinks it's a good idea, but the ... better we all become in terms of our skills at articulating what it is we want to do, the more likely it is we know when we've done it or to what extent we've done it and whether it's necessary to change direction.'

[71] See J. Kay; *The Truth about Markets*, Allen Lane, London, 2003.

[72] An official of the Lord Chancellor's Department claimed that, in addition to witnesses (which was his particular, work-based typification of the victim) there were also 'jurors and the defendant and ... all the relatives of defendants and witnesses on behalf of defendants, they're all customers of the court and they must have the same facilities and care'. Those responsible for courts and trials had a scrupulous regard for appearing disinterested in their administration of an adversarial process.

[73] Roger Ford, Chief Probation Officer, and ACOP representative on the Victims Steering Group, said 'we've been saying for some time that the primary customer is the court, the defendant, the magistrates and the judges'.

was [always] a need to recognise the...multiple customers of the criminal justice system [and the]...wider public good'. Victims were not the rational consumers of the economists' models;[74] and they were offered no market in services, no competition, and no prospect of bringing them into being.[75] Consuming services, finally, was not their only relation to the State, and service delivery was not the only task performed by the Home Office (an official of the Business Efficiency Unit remarked 'once we started getting into that [we were] saying this model of customer...doesn't fit a government department very well. Government departments have lots of responsibilities and service delivery might not always be part of them').

Yet it is certain that the new performance management formally, and perhaps sometimes only quite superficially and at the level of public representations, was giving fresh impetus, expression, and definition to the victim. Just as, much more generally, citizens were becoming transformed into consumers,[76] so jurors, witnesses, victims, and others became in the new and inescapable language of management the inhabitants of a landscape of virtual markets[77] in which they could be described as rather special crea-

[74] It was asked at the Victims Steering Group Meeting of 21 May 1999, 'have we gone so far as to publicise these standards to the actual punters? Is there a leaflet laying out charter standards?', and the answer, in one instance, was that 'the Crown Courts advertise how to complain but they don't say what they can complain about'. My notes. In interview, Helen Reeves said in February 1999, 'I think so few witnesses have knowledge of these charters that I don't think it's having a particular effect.'

[75] A. James and J. Raine; *The New Politics of Criminal Justice*, Longman, London, 1998, p. 44. See also J. Chandler (ed.); *The Citizen's Charter*, Dartmouth, Aldershot, 1996, p. 50.

[76] R. Ericson and N. Stehr; *Governing Modern Societies*, University of Toronto Press, Toronto, 2000, p. 112; J. Stewart and K. Walsh; 'Change in the Management of Public Services', *Public Administration*, Vol. 70, Winter 1992, p. 507; D. Faulkner; *Crime, State and Citizen*, Waterside Press, Winchester, 2001, p. 19.

[77] See N. Lacey; 'Government as Manager, Citizen as Consumer: the Case of the Criminal Justice Act 1991', *The Modern Law Review*, Vol. 57, July 1994. Maguire and Kynch reflected that, 'Since 1987...when government funding began to be received by Victim Support on a large scale, the language of "service provision" — and associated concepts such as prioritisation, best practice and performance indicators— had progressively overtaken that of "good neighbourliness".' M. Maguire and J. Kynch; *Public Perceptions and Victims' Experiences of Victim Support: findings from the 1998 British Crime Survey*, RSD, HO, 2000, p. 14.

tures, customers,[78] the targets of action, checks on the work of agencies,[79] suppliers of performance indicators,[80] holders of new forms of quasi-contracts, and a novel kind of practical expert[81] whose judgment[82] was supposed to be matched against the claims of those defined at times as the self-interested producers and providers of services.[83] What Power called 'a technology of mistrust'[84] had, on paper, edged political confidence away from officials and towards a greater confidence in customers,[85] the consumer-victims,[86] and, I and many of the principals in this history (the then officials of the Justice and Victims Unit and Victim Support above all) might add, pleasing victims was no bad thing in its own right.

---

[78] Stewart and Walsh talked, for instance, of a new emphasis in public service on strengthening the position of the public as customer. J. Stewart and K. Walsh; 'Change in the Management of Public Services', *op. cit.*, p. 501. See, too, N. Carter; 'Learning to Measure Performance', *Public Administration*, Vol. 69, Spring 1991, p. 89.

[79] Kettl stated that 'Driving organizations to serve the customers, from the bottom up, can help solve the supervision problems that plague organizations from the top down.' D. Kettl; *Reinventing Government: Appraising the National Performance Review*, Center for Public Management, The Brookings Institute, August 1994, p. 20.

[80] John Halliday was to tell Ian Chisholm in February 1998 that a draft of the very first service level agreement with Victim Support did not 'go far enough': 'there was no information about end users, the recipients of services and their level of satisfaction'.

[81] Service First, the Cabinet Office unit, said 'we want public services that respond to the needs and wishes of people who use them on a daily basis'. Service First web site: Effective Performance Division, November 2000.

[82] The White Paper, *Modernising Government*, Cm. 4310, March 1999, talked about 'making sure that public service users, not providers, are the focus'.

[83] See *The Times*, 16 December 1999. David Omand, the Permanent Under-Secretary, certainly described the Home Office repeatedly in terms of service delivery. He observed in his foreword to the *The Home Office—A Guide*, October 2000, 'We face the challenge of meeting rising expectations of the quality and timeliness of the services we provide to the citizen. We have strengthened our capacity to higher standards of service delivery.'

[84] Power talked about how 'auditing can be regarded as a technology of mistrust in which independent "outsiders" must be summoned to restore that trust. Expert auditing invests heavily in the image of restoring credibility...'; M. Power; 'The audit society', in A. Hopwood and P. Miller (eds.); *Accounting as Social and Institutional Practice*, Cambridge University Press, Cambridge, 1994, p. 301.

[85] See R. Jones; *Modern penality and social theory*, PhD dissertation, University of Cambridge, 1997, pp. 163–4.

[86] Richard Sennett argued, for instance, that under the new welfare state, problems are reduced to fixed sets of tasks or procedures which must be performed and costed, losing sight of the total person with a totality of problems. Sociology Departmental Seminar, London School of Economics, 18 November 1998.

Given the weakness of the metaphor, performance indicators could at times become a kind of surrogate for market choice,[87] and the Home Office,[88] probation service,[89] police,[90] Victim Support,[91] SAMM, and even judges[92] came, by extension, to be appraised by their contributions to victim and witness satisfaction.[93] There was, it was decided in Spring 2000,[94] and without discussion in the Victims Steering Group,[95] to be a target of a 5 per cent increase in victims' and witnesses' satisfaction with their treatment by the criminal justice system by March 2002,[96] and a continuation of that performance thereafter.[97] There were 'baseline data' for victims[98] in the

[87]  See J. Potter; 'Consumerism and the Public Sector: How Well does the Coat Fit?', *Public Administration*, Vol. 66, Summer 1988, p. 152.

[88]  2000 Spending Review: Criminal Justice System Interim Report, 14 March 2000.

[89]  Thus a victim satisfaction survey was built into a thematic inspection of the probation service. *The Victim Perspective*, HM Inspectorate of Probation, Thematic Inspection Report, January 2000, p. 1.

[90]  The Metropolitan Police came to talk about 'our customers, who are the victims and the survivors . . .'; RISC meeting 19 April 2000, my notes; and in Metropolitan Police Service; *Policing Plan 1997/98*, p. 7; about its intention to 'leave our customers with a good impression of the service received'. The Metropolitan Police adopted the language of service-delivery quite early. In the Metropolitan Police, Plumstead Division, Management Report, 1992, for instance it alluded to the 'quality of service to victims of crime' and 'customer satisfaction surveys'.

[91]  In the copious discussion about the first service level agreement between the Home Office and Victim Support, there was to be repeated reference to appropriate indicators, including in February 1998, the need for what the Home Office called 'information about end users—the recipients of services and their level of satisfaction. We need to know more about outputs and outcomes.' Victim Support adopted some of the techniques of quality assurance, defined by Charities Evaluation Services as a 'customer-centred philosophy based on the belief that the quality of the organisation's services must be continuously monitored and that such monitoring should be an integral part of the people doing the job'. Victim Support National Conference 1998, workshop on quality assurance.

[92]  K. Malleson; *The New Judiciary: The Effects of Expansionism and Activism*, Ashgate, Brookfield, Vermont, 1998, p. 43.

[93]  HM Treasury; *Spending Review 2000*: New Public Spending Plans, 2001–2004, 28 July 2000.

[94]  *Criminal Justice System Business Plan 2000–2001*, May 2000.

[95]  Meeting of Victims Steering Group, 26 November 2001, minutes.

[96]  See Home Office Annual Report, 2000–2001—2000 Spending Review, p. 98.

[97]  Home Office Investment Strategy, March 1999, p. 13; HM Treasury; *Spending Review 2000: New Public Spending Plans, 2001–2004*, 28 July 2000.

[98]  HORS; 'Policing and the Public: Findings from the 2000 British Crime Survey', Research Findings, No. 136. Victims were asked about the services they received from the police. 78% said that the local police did a 'good' or 'very good job'.

1998 British Crime Survey but none for witnesses, and the measuring instruments to be applied would be the British Crime Survey, conducted annually instead of biennially after 1999; quite possibly, new regional surveys; and, because so few victims ever became witnesses,[99] and in the absence of a 'base line', there would also be the significantly named 'new customer survey for victims and witnesses'.[100] During late May and early June 2000, the Home Office commissioned that first customer survey of witness satisfaction with criminal justice agencies, the police, Crown Prosecution Service, lawyers, court staff, judiciary, Victim Support and Witness Service: 2,500 witnesses were interviewed, largely by telephone, 90 per cent of whom were prosecution witnesses, and their overall satisfaction was reported to be high at 76 per cent,[101] a 'benchmark figure' that would be so hard to better that it posed difficulties for the agencies thereafter.

The transformation was not complete but it did impart a set of nuances to the official characterization of the victim, and it *was* remarkably well suited to the world of policy-making because it welled up from and lent itself to the performance of practical administrative action that addressed particular, locally-conceived problems. John Dewey once remarked that 'The singular object stands out conspicuously because of its especially focal and crucial position at a given time in determination of some problem of use...'.[102] It was precisely in that sense that the characterization was intertwined with a new working methodology, the one constituting the other. Victims in their novel incarnation were defined by, and defined, the services they consumed.[103] Under 'joined-up' government, their representatives were certainly more frequently consulted. A conference

[99] David Brown and Sheila White; 'Monitoring witness satisfaction through routine surveys', Witness Care Sub-Group, 9/99, 7 July 1999.
[100] 'Briefing for the PSX meeting on the Criminal Justice System, 29 April 1999', 27 April 1999.
[101] Although there was dissatisfaction voiced by victims attending court in cases involving violent and sexual crimes who were especially anxious about seeing their defendant (40% felt some level of intimidation at court, most commonly by defendant and his supporters). *Victim Support News Service*, January 2002, 'What can we learn from the Home Office Witness Satisfaction Survey?'
[102] J. Dewey; *Logic*, Henry Holt, New York, 1938, p. 67.
[103] See A. Crawford and J. Enterkin; 'Victim Contact Work in the Probation Service: Paradigm Shift or Pandora's Box?', *British Journal of Criminology*, Vol. 41, No. 4, Autumn 2001, p. 720.

on the needs of victims of racist crimes, organized under the auspices
of RISC, the Racist Incidents Standing Committee, was intended to
serve as an 'opportunity for practitioners to listen to victims,
and... help more joined-up service delivery'.[104] The Criminal
Injuries Compensation Appeals Panel, CICAP, talked (sometimes
ruefully) about its 'customers'[105] and organized a seminar on
'customer care' in April 1998, to which members of victims' groups,
including, unusually, women from the Rape Crisis Federation, were
invited (as they were later to be invited to a special Home Office
conference on the place of the victim in the criminal justice system
held in September 1999. They had not hitherto been accustomed to
being invited, I was told.). Domestic violence 'survivors' became the
subjects of 'customer care initiatives',[106] and they were polled, because 'service user consultation is now commonplace in many fields
of work... survivors are able to offer essential advice to agencies
on what leaves women and children safe or unsafe'.[107] The
Crown Prosecution Service, following the recommendations of the
Glidewell Committee and the Macpherson Inquiry, attempting to
inform victims about decisions, established 'Customer Service Units'
and adopted what it called 'a customer service model'.[108] The
Courts Service and Crown Court Centres[109] also talked about customer service[110] and also founded 'Customer Service Units' in 1998.
There was discussion generated, pointedly, by a proposal from the
National Consumer Council, that there should be what was called 'a
single point of entry for complaints about the criminal justice
system'.[111] The metamorphosis was clear and, in tracing its impact

[104] Minutes of meeting of RISC, RISC, 15 October 2001; and I. Taylor; 'Crime,
market-liberalism and the European Idea', in V. Ruggiero et al. (eds.); *The New
European Criminology,* Routledge, London, 1998.
[105] *Annual Report, 1996–7,* Criminal Injuries Compensation Appeals Panel, First
Report, Cm. 3840.; and see its Guide to Applicants on the Hearings procedure—The
Standards of Service which Customers can expect to receive from the Panel, undated.
[106] *Living Without Fear,* Women's unit, Cabinet Office and Home Office, undated., p. i.
[107] Policing and Reducing Crime Unit, Briefing Note: A. Mullender and G. Hague;
'Reducing Domestic Violence, What Works? Women Survivors' Views', January 2000.
[108] Victims Steering Group Meeting, 8 December 2000, my notes.
[109] See *Transforming the Crown Court: consultation document: The emerging
proposals,* Court Service, September 1999.
[110] *The Court Service Annual Report 1997–1998,* HMSO, London, 1998, p. 40.
[111] P. Edmundson; 'Single Point of Entry for Complaints in the Criminal Justice
System', 17 March 1998.

on policies for victims, I must dart back and forth between a number of developments that occurred at very much the same time.

## Charters

The most forceful embodiment of that process, bringing the new performance management and consumerism 'into the public arena',[112] was the charter movement. The word 'charter' is elastic enough in meaning to permit a flexibility of application, the principal definition offered by the second *Oxford English Dictionary* being a 'legal document or "deed"... by which grants, cessions, contracts, and other transactions are confirmed and ratified', and the charters of the 1990s, including the *Victim's Charter*,[113] incorporated some of that elasticity. The movement was awarded diffuse antecedents: not the 1838 People's Charter perhaps, but the Cabinet Office had certainly anticipated the themes that would bring about charters in a paper on service to the public in 1988;[114] and York City Council had developed its own prototypical charter in 1989.[115] When New Labour came to power, it could claim ownership of the idea because of that earlier adoption by local authorities administered by members of the party[116] (an official of Service First observed 'a bad idea is always a bastard, a good idea has many fathers, and the Labour government has actually not just adopted this but claims to have fathered it').

The movement's critical achievement in the twentieth century was the omnibus *Citizen's Charter*, launched by John Major, the Prime Minister, in July 1991,[117] as his own 'big idea'[118] and 'personal

[112] N. Flynn (ed.); *Change in the Civil Service*, Public Finance Corporation, London, 1994, p. 1.

[113] J. Shapland; 'Victims and Criminal Justice', in A. Crawford and J. Goodey (eds.); *Integrating a Victim Perspective Within Criminal Justice: International Debates, op. cit.*, p. 152.

[114] *Service to the Public*, Office of the Minister for the Civil Service, HMSO, London, 1988.

[115] J. Chandler (ed.); *The Citizen's Charter*, Dartmouth, Aldershot, 1996, p. 2.

[116] Service First web site: Effective Performance Division, 28 November 2000— Executive Summary.

[117] Although it was presaged in a speech he made to the Conservative Central Council in March 1991.

[118] J. Chandler (ed.); *The Citizen's Charter, op. cit.*, p. 2.

political creation'.[119] It was a 'revolution in choice, in information, in accountability and individual power . . .'.[120] The *Citizen's Charter* brought together 'disparate institutional arrangements for overseeing provisions'[121] in one document, under a single set of principles, very publicly and under powerful sponsorship. It was designed, in the Prime Minister's words, to 'make public services answer better to the wishes of their users, and to raise their quality overall'[122] by advertising the Government's interest,[123] promoting competition, awarding 'chartermarks', establishing explicit standards, 'privatising choice', instituting complaints procedures and methods of obtaining redress—that is, by applying the panoply of new performance measures and the methods of the quasi-market. The *Citizen's Charter* was placed under the *aegis* of a new unit, the Citizen's Charter Unit, later Service First, set down in the Cabinet Office, and the personal scrutiny of the Prime Minister who held meetings with Ministers and Permanent Under-Secretaries to spur progress on.

The *Citizen's Charter* offered to give 'more power to the citizen', but, turning on the vocabulary of 'responsibilised' consumers, it also noted that 'citizenship is about our responsibilities . . . as well as our entitlements'. It was a typical, broad founding document that spanned the public services, including a criminal justice system that served the public at large and the 'many different customers . . . who come across [it] in a particular context': witnesses, jurors, victims, probationers, the accused, and prisoners. *Inter alia*, it promised victims and witnesses enhanced efforts to increase the 'speed of help' from the police and 'familiarisation visits' to courts if they were called to testify as witnesses.

Lesser individual charters were to be drafted by all the public services[124] and presented for inspection to 10 Downing Street (some,

---

[119]    G. Doern; 'The UK Citizen's Charter', *Policy and Politics*, Vol. 21, No. 1, 1993, p. 17.

[120]    J. Major; 'Conservatism in the 1990s: Our Common Purpose', Carlton Club, London, 1993, p. 29.

[121]    C. Scott; 'Regulation inside Government: Re-Badging the Citizen's Charter', undated, p. 4.

[122]    Foreword to *The Citizen's Charter*, Cm. 1599, July 1991.

[123]    See J. Major; *The Autobiography*, HarperCollins, London, 1999, p. 246.

[124]    For example, the charters for the London Underground passenger, *The London Underground Customer Charter*, and the medical patient, *The Patient's Charter*.

like the Prison Service and the Coroners, because of their greater independence, were less eager to do so at first than others). Emanating from what has been called 'consumer citizenship,' employing the terms 'citizen', 'customer', and 'client' interchangeably,[125] they were rooted, some said, not 'in the Rights of Man but in the commercial world of "money back if not absolutely delighted" guarantees'.[126] Barron and Scott remarked that '. . . the programme represents the continuation of a trend towards tighter management of the public sector on a private sector model. Its significance lies in its redefinition of the citizen as an economic actor—a consumer—and in the extent to which it imports private sector concerns with quality as the touchstone of successful service delivery.'[127] The rights conferred by charters were at first more aspirational than justiciable, often vague and unspecific, and tending at first to focus on standards that were easy to measure. But they *were* a public declaration by the State and its agencies that a new form of contract-like relation was in the making, a relation that was supposed to encourage citizen-consumers to formulate new expectations about service, and they certainly talked about the rights of certain groups (whatever 'rights' might mean) for the first time.

## The Victim's Charter

There would eventually be some two hundred national charters and ten thousand local charters; ten charters devised for the criminal justice system alone, including charters for the Coroners' courts[128] and criminal courts;[129] and a charter for victims, the sole charter

---

[125] G. Doern; 'The UK Citizen's Charter', *op. cit.*, p. 20.
[126] J. Kingdom; 'Citizen or State Consumer?', in J. Chandler (ed.); *The Citizen's Charter, op. cit.*, p. 19.
[127] A. Barron and C. Scott; 'Legislation: The Citizen's Charter Programme', *The Modern Law Review*, July 1992, Vol. 55, p. 527.
[128] Home Office Press Release 285/99, 20 September 1999: Charters to take Coroners Service into the 21st Century; Home Office Circular 46/1999: Coroner Service: Model Coroners' Charter, 14 December 1999.
[129] *The Court's Charter*, 1995, aimed at witnesses appearing in the Crown Court, set out the standard of service 'we aim to give you and how you can let us know when you are not happy'; specified standards: 'before the date of your hearing, you can ask to visit a courtroom, and ask us to arrange for seats in the court room (if we can) for anyone who comes to your hearing with you . . . You can speak to our Customer Service Officer. The Witness Service . . . can help to arrange for you to visit the

under the guardianship of the Home Office. The first *Victim's Charter* was actually a maverick, the very first of the new wave, published in February 1990, over a year before the formal launch of the *Citizen's Charter* and lacking a number of its structures and protocols: it was 'slightly post-dated if you look at it historically', said John Halliday. Its wording played loosely with 'rights', 'standards', 'aspects of good practice', and 'expectations', being subtitled a 'statement of the rights of victims of crime', on the one hand, but setting out 'for the first time' how the 'victims of crime should be treated, and what they are entitled to expect', on the other. Under its statement of guiding principles, it declared that victims should be 'treated fairly and without adverse discrimination' and it then proceeded to lay down what they should anticipate in the aftermath of crime. Of their dealings with the police, for instance, it said that officers would respond to complaints of crime 'as promptly as the circumstances require and allow, with courtesy and attention'; and that victims would receive the name, station, and telephone number of the police officer dealing with the case; would be told of significant developments, particularly if a suspect was found, charged, and tried; and where there was an arrest, would be told by the police about prosecution decisions to charge. Similar lists covered transactions with Victim Support; criminal proceedings; attendance at court; and compensation and publicity.

The penultimate section of the Charter mapped what purported to be thirty-five standards of victim care for the criminal justice services, but they did not resemble standards in any familiar sense of the word because they were set out as a scatter of questions or prompts for practitioners rather than as an inventory of yardsticks to be conveyed to victims. For example, the standards for the police service began: 'What is the force policy on responding to reports of crime? Are there quality indicators . . . ? Do victims feel sympathetically treated? Is there a case screening policy? If so, is it explained to the victim? Is the victim told what will happen, and given some idea of the prospects of success?' The remaining standards were couched

---

court . . . You may be able to claim compensation if you have lost money or run up costs because of a mistake by our staff.' 'Witness in Court', Home Office, Citizen's Charter, undated. It promised, for example, that the 'court will aim to make sure you do not have to wait for more than two hours before being called to give evidence'.

in the same style, hardly a set of standards at all but an *aide memoire* for the criminal justice professional.

The first charter was thus a curious document, something of an original, 'written from a service provider perspective' and aimed at 'service providers', rather than at its ostensible audience of victims. David Faulkner, a high official in the Home Office at the time of its drafting, said it was 'a typical document of the period . . . reflecting a rather authoritarian, top-down, statement of what the services think they can deliver rather than an expression of what victims themselves would like to have provided'.[130] The whole was a compilation in one place of what was already on offer without addition or the promise of new provisions, and Nigel Varney, the official who drafted it, would not have represented it as otherwise. Gloria Craig of Service First, the Cabinet Office unit in charge of the Charter programme, commented more generally that 'my impression is that most charters are just that, in that most charters don't break very new ground . . .'. The first Charter contained gaps, and the Prime Minister and others were reported to have complained that it had not gone far enough. Victim Support claimed amongst other charges that it offered no provision for informing victims whose case did not proceed to court; and that it should have been made clear who was responsible for informing victims at each stage of criminal procedure.[131] It was not widely distributed[132] and was little known. It contained no new information; it had no legal standing; it alluded to rights but did not say what they were, actually talking about aspirations rather than enforceable demands;[133] and it offered no guidance about what the victims might do if the so-called rights were breached (they had no more rights in law than any member of the public, Home Office officials were advised). It was neither a commercial contract nor a statement of rights, it was weak and

---

[130] D. Faulkner; *Crime, State and Citizen, op. cit.*, p. 225.

[131] Victim Support; 'The Victims' Charter', response sent to the Home Office, December 1990.

[132] Although it was supposed to be distributed to a number of bodies, including victim support schemes, libraries, police stations, and Citizens' Advice Bureaux.

[133] John Spencer observed, the charter 'conveys no rights or privileges but merely lists what ought to be done'. J. Spencer; 'Improving the Position of the Victim in English Criminal Procedure', paper given at International Conference on the Rights of the Accused, Crime Control, and Protection of Victims, Hebrew University of Jerusalem, 19–23 December 1993.

ambiguous, but it did assemble in a single document under the *imprimatur* of the Home Office a list of obligations touching the victim, and it was treated as having something of a weak force. In the words of Victim Support, 'it confirmed for the first time that there is a problem to be addressed'[134] and the very reference to rights, however obscure, was new and important.[135] Criminal justice agencies cited it as a justification for action;[136] it was monitored, however unmethodically at first, through meetings of the Victims Steering Group and, as Christine Stewart, then head of what was then called the Procedures and Victims Unit, put it, through *ad hoc* contact with criminal justice services with *Victim's Charter* responsibilities and a perusal of publications such as police inspection reports. And, above all, it was a gesture that recognized the symbolic presence of the victim as a more prominent albeit somewhat fuzzy entity in the criminal justice system.

Charters were intended to be periodically reviewed and re-issued, and the second *Victim's Charter* was duly published in 1996, a more solid document, ten pages longer than its predecessor, 'redressing the balance' away from the practitioner and towards the victim; taking forward ideas from the Prime Minister's 1995 seminar on criminal justice and the citizen (which delivered two new standards that will be discussed at length below); and from Victim Support and its *Statement of Rights*.[137] At the insistence of Victim Support and the Victims Steering Group, it had waived the idea that Charter standards should be conditional on the victim behaving in 'responsibilized' fashion (although the idea never did quite disappear[138] and

---

[134] *The rights of victims of crime: A policy paper by Victim Support*, Victim Support, London, 1995, p. 1.

[135] H. Reeves and K. Mulley; 'The new status of victims in the UK: Opportunities and threats', in A. Crawford and J. Goodey (eds.); *Integrating a Victim Perspective Within Criminal Justice: International debates*, Ashgate, Aldershot, 2000, p. 131.

[136] In the case of the police, see *A report of the criminal justice consultative council and area committees*, Conference, 3 March 1995, p. 6. In the case of probation, see National Probation Service; Victim Contact Work, Guidance for Probation Areas, May 2001. See also TIG; 'Statement of National Standards of Witness Care in the Criminal Justice System: Taking forward standards of witness care through Local Service Level Agreements', July 1996.

[137] Victim Support; Victim's Charter Pilot Projects: Information for Volunteers, 12 September 1996; and Victim Support; *report '97*.

[138] One Home Office official said in 1998 'we are getting away from rights and where we have got any kind of feeling that there's a right given by a charter, or some

was certainly present in the thinking of other criminal justice Departments, such as the Lord Chancellor's Department.[139]) It was more detailed, explicit, and substantial in its listing of obligations over the four broad areas charted by officials: providing information, taking victims' views into account, treating victims with respect and sensitivity at court, and providing emotional and practical support. Its obligations were phrased imperatively, stating quite unequivocally what agencies were required to do. Its opening section on the responsibilities of the police now began by reciting how 'The police will respond to your report as quickly as they can', and 'The police will give you the name and phone number of the officer or "crime" desk responsible for your case.' And there was a new section stipulating how victims might complain about criminal justice agencies, and what they were entitled to expect in return (in the case of the police, for instance, victims were told 'You will get an initial response within 10 working days').

There were twenty-seven standards. Victim Support was required to send a letter, 'phone you, or arrange a visit from a volunteer within four working days of you reporting the crime', a slight enough obligation at first glance, but the only standard to be laid on a non-governmental organization, and signifying again the near-agency status of Victim Support as a voluntary body formally tied into the contractual network of the criminal justice system. Two standards, flowing from the Prime Minister's 1995 seminar, were to become especially consequential: the Charter told victims 'you can expect a crime you have reported to be investigated and to receive information about what happens'; and 'the chance to explain how the crime has affected you, and your interests to be taken into account'. I shall

kind of obligation, what we're now trying to do is to bring in some sort of obligation on the person who's being, the Charter's aimed at. So you've got a responsibility, so as with the hospital ones you know, where you say we will see you within a certain time of your appointment but you must turn up.'

[139] An official remarked of the *Courts' Charter*, we would like to expect 'if you do come to court [that you will] co-operate with the system...you help us to help you, you know, be on time, treat our staff with courtesy and respect. And respect the court building you know, please don't gather in a huddle and write graffiti all over the place...what we're, we're trying to remind people that it's a two-way thing.' But the *Courts' Charter* leaflets for witnesses and for defendants actually included none of those stipulations. They dwelt only on what the witness or defendant could expect from the court.

return to the implementation of those two standards below because they implicate major features of the new typification of the victim-consumer as one who has not only an empirically well-founded desire to be informed, but who also needs to give and receive intelligence to conform to the economists' more abstract depiction of what constitutes a rational, effective, and informed consumer.

The twenty-seven standards were more rigorously monitored than their predecessors had been, and ensuring compliance became one of the Home Office's objectives under Aim 2.[140] At a meeting of the Victims Steering Group in May 1997, there were the beginnings of a lengthy process of making standards more specific and measurable, and the work of the Steering Group would thenceforth be dominated by its routine twice-yearly scrutiny of tables of Charter standards prepared by JVU.[141] The British Crime Survey was put to work to measure compliance with Charter standards, its authors submitting special reports to the Victims Steering Group,[142] and focusing particularly at first on how and to what extent victims had received attention from Victim Support, because, as Catriona Mirrlees-Black, one of the RDS researchers who administered the survey, noted in November 1997, there was a 'lack of up to date information on what victims want and need . . . and, for those that had Victim Support contact, the extent to which this meets their needs'. By May 1998, the Victims Steering Group was informed that 'full arrangements for monitoring and publishing results' were in place for fifteen of the twenty-seven standards, and that during the course of 1998 they should have been established for twenty-three standards. There was 'no monitoring or under-monitoring' for three standards only: keeping victims informed, police providing families and victims with special packs of information, and 'taking account of victim's views', and the 1998 British Crime Survey would provide information on two of those standards. From 1997 on, compliance with standards came to be reported publicly and in some detail

---

[140] HO Business Plan 2000–2001—Aim 2—The delivery of justice.

[141] Victims Steering Group Meeting, 8 December 2000, 1996 Victim's Charter.

[142] For example, *Services to Victims: Summary of Findings from the 1996 British Crime Survey*, prepared for the Victims Steering Group. Members of RDS confessed that they were a little disappointed by the apparent lack of interest in their findings displayed by members of the Victims Steering Group.

in the annual reports of criminal justice agencies[143] and the Home Office.[144]

The second Charter retained the tendency of the Home Office to hesitate about the exact character of the entitlements it could proffer.[145] Ian Chisholm reflected that 'it has been a bit, a bit bitty. I mean no doubt this *Victim's Charter* is very much you know, things that were possible to measure really. It wasn't necessarily those that were the most important. In some of them obviously the victims want more information and so on, but it's a bit of what's ideal and desirable and what can be done, what's possible in practice.' Roger Ford, the Chief Probation Officer, said it was 'still stumb[ling] over the word *rights* when we talk of victims'. Stumbling was not very remarkable in the specific environment of the lawyers' and practitioners' aversion to the very idea of rights being bestowed on victims or of victims acquiring a formal role in proceedings, and of the wider environment of a charter movement that treated rights themselves as foreign. Gloria Craig, the official of Service First, recalled in 1998:

We had discussions in a general context about whether you should use the term *rights* at all for charters because there is no legal foundation to any of them ... Some departments felt on legal advice, of course, that you shouldn't use the term *right* at all ... It's a perennial problem with all charters because there isn't any legal backing for it, there's, you know, you can't go to law. In fact, there was a big debate about whether you should make, give a little backing right at the beginning and ..., you know, it's continued all the way through including when we launched the charter last year. And most people's view is that you shouldn't because you don't want to get the thing wrapped up into too much legal technicalities.

Stumbling could also be explained by the financial and allied costs to Government of actually formally recognizing rights at a time of conspicuous austerity in public spending. Talk of rights evoked fears of increasing numbers of applications for monetary redress

[143] For instance, *Crown Prosecution Service, Annual Report for April 1998–March 1999*, Chapters 4 and 5, 2 August 1999.

[144] See, for instance, *Annual Report 1998: The Government's Expenditure Plans 1998–9*, Cm. 3908, Home Office, London, 1998, pp. 68–9.

[145] That hesitation persisted for years. Thus *A Guide to the Criminal Justice System in England and Wales*, Home Office, London, 2000, stated that the *Victim's Charter* informs victims of their rights and that the Victims Steering Group monitors the standards of service set out in the revised edition of the Charter (p. 55).

and compensation (a JVU official observed in an aside in 1999 that 'a lot of Victim's Charter standards are not being met but you can see why the Government is reluctant to meet them fully' and a colleague said 'I would think you'd be daft actually, with the present state of public finances, to give any clear deal like that...').

At the instigation of Louis Blom-Cooper, the draft version of the new Charter thus ceased to be a 'statement of rights' and became instead a 'statement of service standards'. Louis Blom-Cooper, himself a barrister and the then president of Victim Support, argued at a meeting of the Victims Steering Group in 1995 that the word *rights* should be jettisoned because it misled and frustrated victims by unduly elevating their aspirations. A consequence was that the new Charter, in common with its fellows and probably inevitably, still lacked obvious muscle. A Grade 7 of JVU was to email three years later that the Charter 'confers no legally enforceable rights. It simply sets out 27 standards of service which victims of crime can expect of CJ agencies. It explains how victims can complain but does not commit the agencies to make financial or other restitution—although most would offer an apology if they were at fault.' Ian Chisholm was as blunt: 'The 1990 version talked about "rights", but was in practice little more than a description of the kind of services then on offer by the criminal justice agencies. The 1996 version was more precise about the services victims could expect from those agencies, but mention of "rights" was studiously avoided (as is the case with most Charters).' That shunning of rights talk could sometimes rebound on the Home Office. For example, in its dispute with the Department of Health about the competing rights of victims to information and of 'mentally disordered' offenders to confidentiality, a dispute I will return to almost immediately, the Department of Health could claim in 1999 that the *Victim's Charter* was not a legal document and that even the guidance tendered victims where the offender was not mentally ill had no legal foundation. The Home Office had in effect disarmed itself.

*Right* is an indistinct, emotionally charged, and slippery idea required to carry a burden of meaning. *The Oxford English Dictionary* defines it as 'The standard of permitted and forbidden action within a certain sphere; law; a rule or canon', but it also offers other definitions: 'That which is proper for or incumbent on one to do'; 'That which is consonant with equity' ... that which is morally just or due'; 'Just or equitable treatment; fairness in decision; justice';[146] and more. *Black's Law Dictionary*, another lexicon, points to a similar spread of meaning: 'As a noun, and taken in an *abstract* sense, [right] means justice, ethical correctness, or consonance with the rules of law or the principles of morals'.[147] The term can thus refer not only to a justiciable claim but also to one that is moral or just, and it was in those unlike senses that it was being deployed in different quarters as victims underwent transition. It was certainly resisted by many lawyers and judges,[148] and that made outright acceptance impolitic. It was certainly resisted by those who were concerned about its financial implications. And, if arguments about 'governmentality' have any force, the word itself was perhaps in transition, slipping away from the traditional notion of legal rights conferred by the nation-State towards those more redolent of the commercial transactions of the market-State. A member of RDS said somewhat pithily, 'the closest you get to victims' rights is that the victim has a right, say, to be given a leaflet on victims of crime. Therefore (would you please) measure whether that is happening. I mean you *could* see that as a right . . . '. For Victim Support, it was quite simple, said Teresa Reynolds, its policy officer. The organization 'has used that word loosely, as a shorthand if you like, for things that we believe victims should have . . . And that word has been picked up, and analysed, and you know, people have said "you can't talk about rights because what you talk about, you talk about statutory rights, or obligations". And actually, that has never been

---

[146] *Oxford English Dictionary*, Second Edition, Vol. XIII, Clarendon Press, Oxford, 1989.

[147] *Black's Law Dictionary*, Sixth Edition, West Publishing, St. Paul, Minnesota, 1990.

[148] Although Ben Emmerson, the human rights lawyer, made an interesting observation about English legal conceptions of rights. Rights, he said, become much more palatable if they're not regarded as absolute, particularly in the context of the Human Rights Act 1998: 'from my point of view I find the rights-based analysis immensely helpful because the rights, once you accept that they are not absolute, once you accept that they require balance and reasonable interpretation and judgement, and given that they cover everything from an individual's right to property to the right to lie, the gamut [of] the rights that you actually want to protect, it gives you a framework for deciding any legal question by reference to a protection of certain fundamental interests. The problems arise if you talk to, if you equate the concept of a right with something which cannot be interfered with and I think that is a confusion which infects a lot of people who approach this for the first time. And actually there's a . . . difference here.'

defined.' Because of the ambiguities in the word 'right', because of the Charter's own equivocations, hesitations, and ambivalences, it was never to be transparent quite what the new standards represented.[149] It was certainly difficult to differentiate neatly between authorized expectations and rights proper: Alan Baldwin of the Justices' Clerks' Society, and a member of the Victims Steering Group, said 'if you change people's expectations, I suppose you do start shading into rights'.

The Charter itself came to resemble something of a Rorschach blot, open to multiple interpretations, even by the same people over time, and available as a resource to be put to different uses. Helen Reeves could say:

The first *Victim's Charter* was more famous abroad than it was here, I would say. Internationally it would be quoted very often, that the government had a charter on victims, but in this country, I'm not sure that people took a lot of notice of it or even knew about it. And as you know there were no [provisions for] implementation, ... no deadlines, there's no money, nothing really happened very much. They're quite important symbolically. The second one in '96, we only confirmed the basics. It's more or less about information and then there were one or two government hobby horses like One Stop Shop and victim statements.

But elsewhere, she and Kate Mulley of Victim Support described the second Charter's acknowledgement of victims' entitlements as the first substantial improvement in the lot of victims.[150] The Charter Unit called it 'an excellent example of an all-embracing, inter-agency produced thematic document, which other agencies should seek to emulate'.[151] What is undoubtedly true is that the *Victim's Charter* became a formal authority to act. It represented a master document to which people, including victims (in principle),[152] could and would

---

[149] See R. Morgan and A. Sanders; 'the price of protection', *Guardian*, 16 June 1999.

[150] H. Reeves and K. Mulley; 'The new status of victims in the UK: Opportunities and threats', *op. cit.*, p. 131.

[151] Cited in G. Bradshaw's circular letter to members of the Victims Steering Group, 15 December 1997.

[152] Despite the fact that the Charter was launched with some considerable media interest and placed on the web in February 1997, it did lack visibility. The secretary of the Victims Steering Group said in 1998, 'I don't think there's a great awareness of the Charter in the world at large. In my job I sometimes get victims themselves, or their surviving relatives 'phoning up, and I'm surprised at how little knowledge there is, unless they belong to an organization themselves.' A 'Victims of Crime' leaflet,

routinely turn to ascertain the character of obligations formally owed to victims. It was, for example, perused within the Home Office in 1997 to establish whether the victims of stalkers should be notified about their offender's date of release. It became a warrant legitimating probation officers to inform victims about their prisoners' release plans[153] and for officials of the Prison Service to explore their commitments to the victim,[154] including how they might inform victims about parole hearings.[155] It could be cited in 1998 in discussions with a reluctant Department of Health[156] about the right of victims of imprisoned mentally disordered offenders to obtain information about release plans.

The Department of Health had consistently maintained that the demands of medical confidentiality overrode the needs of the victim. The matter was particularly harrowing for an anomalous and distressed group of secondary victims, represented by such organizations as Justice for Victims and The Zito Trust.[157] And there was the

published in 1997 and supposedly given by the police to victims as a matter of course, laid out the provisions contained in the *Victim's Charter*. Issuing the leaflet was one of the Charter's standards, and was itself monitored. The British Crime Survey revealed that only about 15% of the population had heard of it. A. Myhill and L. Sims; 'Victim's Charter Standards—findings from the 2000 BCS', paper prepared for the Victims Steering Group.

[153] See ACOP/Victim Support; Joint Statement; The release of prisoners, July 1996; Home Office: Release of Prisoners: Information for Victims of Serious Sexual or Other Violent Offences, November 1997, a leaflet intended for victims and published in the name of the *Victim's Charter;* and National Probation Service; Victim Contact Work, Guidance for Probation Areas, May 2001.

[154] The Prison Service organized its Victims Policy Forum, convening for the first time in October 1998. The first meeting was told that the Prison Service was committed to the principles of the *Victim's Charter* and to meeting its responsibilities under the Charter. In order to sharpen its focus on victim's issues, it announced, it had committed itself in its 1998–9 business plan to establish a forum which would address those issues.

[155] Sentence Management Group, Prison Service, Review of Parole and Lifer Processes: Victim Issues, October 2000.

[156] Described by a Home Office official in May 1999 as having 'no enthusiasm . . . to tackle this. But not active resistance.'

[157] Victims had no rights under the *Victim's Charter* to information about mentally disordered offenders because of the medical profession's insistence on patient confidentiality. There were other demands from victims' organizations at the time, including a demand for a right to attend mental health tribunals. In the late 1990s, chairs had a discretion to allow victims to submit views, but there was no automatic right to submit views or be a party. Victims or representatives could have access to

question of consistency: it was, thought Home Office Ministers, indefensible, intellectually as well as politically, to treat patients differently from other sentenced prisoners and, they protested, 'our commitment to the rights of victims and protection of public is a matter of public record'. The issue of the mentally disordered offender defined where to 'draw the line about who is a victim' as one official put it.[158] After all, definitions, in the pragmatic and task-oriented world of policy-making, reflect the workings of practical action and legal mandates,[159] in this case, the actions of the probation service as the agency responsible for informing victims about prisoners' release plans, but it transpired that 'there is no clearcut definition of a victim'.[160] The matter was ultimately to be resolved by distinguishing between clinical information, touching on the relation between patient and physician, which would remain confi-

information but in practice the right was not exercised because it would compromise the patient's right to confidentiality. Patients normally had the right to see all information put before a tribunal but victims' representations could be marked 'not for disclosure'.

[158] It is interesting that an agreement between the North London Forensic Service and the Metropolitan Police, 'protocol and procedure for obtaining information about the current whereabouts, and circumstances of victims of mentally disordered offenders', issued 26 January 1999, included the provision that, once victims had been located, there would be a decision taken by social workers, advised by the police, about what action to take, 'including whether victim or relatives should be contacted'. Victims' interests were obviously not paramount as a matter of course. The interests of victims of 'mentally disordered offenders' who had been diverted from confinement were said often to be neglected (see J. Laing; 'Diversion of Mentally Disordered Offenders: Victim and Offender Perspectives', *Criminal Law Review*, 1999, pp. 805–19.) And human rights legislation was applied only to mentally disordered offenders, not their victims, in tribunals and other venues (N. Eastman and J. Peay; *Law Without Enforcement: Integrating Mental Health and Justice*, Hart Publishing, Oxford, 1999, pp. 128–9).

[159] The Human Rights Act 1998 had been consulted on the matter, and it was noted that, although it had nothing to say about victims customarily defined, it did, under Article 8 commit the Government to defend the right to privacy and family life of prisoners, both of which might, rather tangentially, be thought to be at risk if information was ceded to the victim.

[160] The Home Office official then proceeded to say that 'the most comprehensive definition we currently have' is contained in the 1996 Joint Statement by the Association of Chief Officers of Probation and Victim Support, and that recited that a victim was a person against whom an offence was perpetrated; relative of victim who has died; where victim is a child, carer or guardian; probation service will respond positively to any person who considers himself or herself to be a victim.

dential, and 'procedural' information touching on detention and release, which would not.[161] The rights of victims and their families to information, it was decided, should be extended to cover procedural advice about restricted patients who had committed serious violent and sexual offences.[162]

The Charter was a catalyst. It gained influence because it had an objective force and could be quoted in papers and reports as part of the policy environment in which agencies worked.[163] Said an official of the Lord Chancellor's Department. 'I wouldn't like to say it wouldn't happen without the Charter but it does, you know, it puts it in black and white, doesn't it?' It was 'institutionalized', as another official put it, and could thereby formally be cited to commandeer resources ('setting it up institutionalized it, and so [people can say] "we've got that, we've got that document and it's statutory and it's got to go ahead"'). Assembling obligations together in a single document and requiring officials to convene regularly in the Victims Steering Group to report on their compliance, brought about a co-operative thrust, communal attention,[164] and the possibility of collective shaming, often called a 'culture' by officials.[165]

---

[161] See the Green Paper, *Reform of the Mental Health Act 1983: Proposals for Consultation*, Cm. 4480, Department of Health, November 1999, esp. pp. 70–1, and the Criminal Justice White Paper, *Justice for All*, Cm. 5563, July 2002 and the Mental Health Bill, 25 June 2002. Hilary Benn, a Home Office Minister, declared that ' . . . we will introduce new rights for victims of serious offences committed by mentally disordered offenders, bringing them into line with the rights we have already introduced for the victims of other serious crimes'. Department of Health: Press Release 2002/0284. For a wider discussion of the contested reform of the 1983 Mental Health Act, see J. Peay; *Decisions and Dilemmas: Working with Mental Health Law*, Hart Publishing, Oxford, 2003.

[162] See *Criminal Justice: The Way Ahead*, Home Department, Cm. 5074, February 2001, p. 73.

[163] See, for instance, *The Review of the Crown Prosecution Service*, Summary of the Main Report, Chairman Sir Iain Glidewell, June 1998, Cm. 3972, pp. 6, 113.

[164] See A. Crawford and J. Enterkin; *Victim Contact Work and the Probation Service: A Study of Service Delivery and Impact*, Centre for Criminal Justice Studies, University of Leeds, 1999, p. 1.

[165] An official of the Business Performance Unit, said 'Downing Street [and] ministers were very involved [with the Charter] from the very beginning. And so the Permanent Secretary just kept an eye on it. But gradually it became sort of subsumed into the culture of the department and I think that's probably what's happened in most places, it has become part of our culture now to think about customers. The Home Office never thought about customers. It didn't think of itself in that way at all.'

The same Lord Chancellor's Department official reflected: 'I mean what else would we have done, you know, if there hadn't been a Charter idea, what would we have done? You know, how would we have kept it going? So it's kept things together.' And with task and culture came motive. Ian Chisholm could write to a Professor of Law in March 1999 that 'the standards have no foundation in law—if they are not delivered then the victim has no legal redress against the organisation concerned. Nonetheless the organisations do strive hard to meet their commitments.' There was a dialectic in which the Charter articulated and amplified themes bearing on victims just as those selfsame themes drove the Charter on and gave it urgency. Sue Street said 'I think it's very chicken and egg, you know. Was the *Patient's Charter* or the *Victim's Charter* the thing that pushed it forward, or was it the product of a greater drive to articulate the rights? I think probably the latter for me, but it then becomes a virtuous circle, as it were, because you think you need a Charter to acknowledge the rights and then when you've got one, you've actually got to honour it. So I think that's the way it works.' And all the while, victims were acquiring a greater prominence. Helen Reeves observed in January 1999:

Victims have become one of the priorities... For some time the police have had victim issues in their normal routine inspections for about four or five years now... the force will be asked... 'how are you complying with this policy?'... And they are being asked about the *Victim's Charter*, whether they're meeting deadlines or if they work closely with Victim Support and so on. And in Probation, there was a pilot, an earlier pilot inspection about two years ago and we've been having meetings with the [probation] inspectorate for some time. And quite apart from the thematic inspection, the issue is how are you managing the victim contact work, the prisoners... 'have you got leaflets, do you make sure everybody knows about your service, [do] you maintain files as the case goes through the system?' And that's all happening anyway, it's become sort of central. And... it's about status and *kudos* and [other] things.

Citizens' charters may have been John Major's creation, but the New Labour administration's preoccupation with modernization, articulate standards, and active citizenship melded well with his ideology of the consumer-citizen, and the Charter programme was endorsed and boosted by the new Government. A Citizen's Charter Unit seminar held in October 1997 declared that the programme would be re-launched in what a member of JVU described as 'a big way' in the new year. All the forty charters current in 1997 were to be reviewed in the next twelve months and departments were going to be encouraged to 'revise their charters in radical ways'. The *Victim's Charter*, only recently re-issued, came in for 'high praise' but was to be exempt from re-drafting. It was not until 2000 that there was renewed discussion about a third Charter, and that was to be one of the principal motors behind talk about the birth of a Victims' Bill of Rights.

## The Two New Victim's Charter Standards

There is a fit, an absence of conflict, or what some would call an elective affinity, between the nominally distinct typifications of the disorientated, anxious victim[166] and the rational consumer, because both require information to act effectively. The two typifications diverged and converged during the 1990s, and it is difficult on occasion to discern quite what assumptions were actually in play at any one time in the world of policy-makers, or whether, indeed, fully-fleshed images were before them as they formulated plans. I observed that Home Office papers did not embark much on elaborate exposition about root iconography, particularly when that iconography came down from the politicians rather than arose 'spontaneously' from the officials themselves. None the less, and despite a diversity of origins, it was within the ideological

[166] *Services to Victims: Summary of Findings from the 1996 British Crime Survey,* prepared for the Victims Steering Group, May 1997, showed that in only 33% of cases, the victim was informed by the police that a culprit had been identified. In a much smaller survey of just over 200 victims, conducted in conjunction with the pilot project that will be described in this section, 75% said they wanted to know what was happening in their cases or asserted that it was their right to know; 25% cited fear or anxiety about the offender and the criminal justice process, and 69% that they expected information on any verdict; 68% on sentence; 52% on dates of court hearings; 34% on the defendant's plea; and 26% on bail and remand decisions. C. Hoyle *et al.*; 'The Victim's Charter—An Evaluation of Pilot Projects', Home Office; Research Findings No. 107, 1999, p. 2. *zt monitor,* 5, January/February 1999 reported approvingly an article in *The Guardian,* 5 January 1999 which discussed the French *parti civile* system: 'This is a far cry indeed from the way we do things on this side of the Channel. At The Zito Trust we have been contacted countless times by distressed families who have missed the criminal procedures because they weren't told the date, time and place. When asked why they were not kept informed, the agencies responsible often respond by saying something like, "we didn't think you'd want to bother yourself with that sort of thing, luv".'

framework of consumer citizenship and the *Citizen's Charter* programme that victims as service-users principally took shape, acquiring the mark of a number of axioms in and around the Charter movement: the need to provide additional information to consumers to enhance their effectiveness; to introduce or improve complaints and redress mechanisms further to strengthen their position and improve the efficiency of providers;[167] and to utilize the resources of public sector organizations better—in this instance, the police—who were thought politically at the time not to be adequately stretched or effective as service-providers.

'Because the victim of crime has no locus standi in the criminal proceedings' of England and Wales, commented Brienen and Hoegen in their encyclopaedic review of the treatment of victims in European countries, 'there is very little procedural incentive to inform him of the developments in his case, unless he is required to testify as a witness.'[168] To be sure, there had been piecemeal efforts to notify victims well before the twin obligations to inform and be informed had been mooted as new standards for the second *Victim's Charter*. For example, in February 1994 the Criminal Appeals Office, police and other bodies had agreed procedures for notifying victims about impending appeals in cases where there had been a death or serious sexual offence or developments in cases on appeal. The Criminal Appeals Office was supposed to have sent the Crown Prosecution Service notice of appeal, the Crown Prosecution Service were then to have forwarded the information to the police who were in their turn to decide when and how to inform the victim. The procedures had 'not always worked too well', becoming snared in long and complicated lines of communication; there was a failure by the police to use 'proper unique reference numbers' (URNS) that could identify cases, some of which were quite ancient and whose protagonists might well have scattered; and there were difficulties in deciding who should actually assume the responsibility of informing victims.[169] The perceived failings of the system led to a meeting at the Crown Prosecution Service in July 1995 where it was decided to

---

[167] A. Barron and C. Scott; 'Legislation: The Citizen's Charter Programme', *op. cit*, p. 528.
[168] M. Brienen and E. Hoegen; *Victims of Crime in 22 European Criminal Justice Systems*, Wolf Legal Publications, Nijmegen, 2000, p. 285.
[169] See *Evening Telegraph*, 15 March 2000.

'cut out' the Crown Prosecution Service, but the system nevertheless seems to have partially collapsed, and there was reported to have been a 'confusion about subsequent developments'[170] One result was that two years later, Ministers in the New Labour administration still found themselves obliged personally on occasion to enter into protracted correspondence with the bruised relatives of murder victims about the failures of agencies to communicate the dates of appeals.[171]

There had been other difficulties. The Crown Prosecution Service had long maintained that prosecutors were officers of the court, that they acted in the public interest broadly conceived, and that any approach to the victim or prosecution witness would not only compromise their profession of disinterest and impartiality but also risk forfeiting a case because the defence could charge that evidence had been tainted by coaching or improper influence.[172] More informally, prosecutors tended to dislike contact with witnesses in their everyday work in the courts because it involved a dangerous breach of the barriers that separated the supposedly disciplined and calm world of the professional insider from the volatile and uncontrolled world of lay outsiders.[173] Prosecutors tended to insist that informing victims (other than the families of homicide victims) about matters affecting their case was not a duty for them but for the police,[174] but it was the view of politicians that the CPS treated victims and witnesses 'badly' and that the police themselves were not discharging their own role competently.[175] That reluctance of the CPS to engage with witnesses in the mid-1990s was a portent of problems to come at the end of the decade.

[170] Victim's Charter Pilot Projects Working Group—'Keeping Victims Informed of Developments in their Case: the Role of the Criminal Appeals Office', 16 October 1997.

[171] For a report of one such failure, lodged within Home Office files, see *Evening Telegraph*, 15 March 2000.

[172] It is interesting, nevertheless, that Canadian Crown Attorneys and American Public Prosecutors have for some time enjoyed close relations with their witnesses without accusations being successfully levelled that they contaminated evidence or jeopardized their professionalism.

[173] See my *The Social World of an English Crown Court, op. cit.*

[174] The Justice Report on 'The Role of the Victim in the Criminal Justice Process': CPS submission of evidence, undated.

[175] The Justice Report on 'The Role of the Victim in the Criminal Justice Process': Letter from C.J. Stewart, Head of Procedures and Victims Unit, Home Office, to Joanna Shapland, 6 December 1995.

Since August 1995, the probation service had had what was initially the somewhat uncomfortable duty[176] of informing victims about their offenders' release from prison (but not, as we have seen, from special hospitals) in cases of violent and 'serious' sexual offences involving sentences of more than four years' duration, but there were to be similar problems of liaison, and some of the cases, and their accompanying information, also became old and stale, with concomitant difficulties in tracing victims.[177] There were limits on what victims could be told, most especially the offender's address on release, the prisoner's personal details, and the exact release details, mirroring what was thought to be a need to 'balance the safety and peace of mind of victim'[178] with the rights of the offender, and for fear that the victim might exact reprisals.[179]

[176] John Walters, Chief Probation Officer of Middlesex, had written, 'There are indications that the realisation of the harm caused by offenders is in danger of distorting the judgement of probation services and their capacity to work constructively with some categories of offender. A recently published study of racial harassment and violence comments on the probation service's demonisation of racist offenders ... Work with offenders has traditionally been based on condemning the offence, not the offender, and there is a danger that an appreciation of the harm caused by some offences is leading to a failure to hold to the value of recognising the worth of even the most flawed person ... Greater understanding of the effects of crime on victims has reduced sympathy for offenders. A focus on the rights of victims challenges the rights of offenders in the criminal justice process.' J. Walters; 'Victim Perspectives and Implications for Work with Offenders', unpublished, 6 January 1998.

[177] Between 1 January 1998 and 30 June 1998, 1,780 offenders had been so sentenced; the number of victims identified had been 3,095; the number contacted within 2 months of sentence was 788; ; the number of victims seen face to face was 1,150; and the number requesting 'ongoing contact' was 1,034. Letter to me from Roger Ford, 23 November 1998.

[178] Meeting of [Prison] Victims Policy Forum, 12 November 1999.

[179] The matter had become especially salient in late 2000 as a consequence of demands for a so-called Sarah's Law, in imitation of the American Megan's Law, that would make public the names of convicted paedophiles. A young child, Sarah Payne, had disappeared in July 2000; and Roy Whiting, a known paedophile, was arrested that month and then released on bail; was arrested for a second and then a third time; was charged with murder in December 2001 and found guilty and jailed for life. Sarah Payne was beatified, described in a dedicated web site as 'a beautiful princess, living as an angel high above the sky', and her murder evoked considerable public distress, including riots in Portsmouth in August 2000. The tabloid newspaper, *News of the World*, had mobilized a campaign for a Sarah's Law under which any member of the public could have access to the Sex Offenders' Register, and the public pressure was sufficient for one Home Office Minister, Paul Boateng, to say 'The "Sarah's Law" campaign proposals make an important contribution to the debate and demand very

Helen Reeves identified 1995 as a critical turning point in the emergence of policies for victims although quite what that turning-point heralded was not clear at the time:

Victims arrived somewhere around 1995 probably. They'd actually arrived as being something which was thoroughly laudable and everybody believed in, but nobody was quite clear what they were signing up to and all sorts of new things starting coming onto the agenda, or old things started coming back onto the agenda, because they had this new respectability of having a victim tag on them.

Nineteen ninety-five marked the publication of Victim Support's *Statement of Rights,* to which she and others attached importance, and the Prime Minister's special seminar in July,[180] to which she was invited as a 'token victim' and where she led the discussion:

John Major gave that very important meeting at Downing Street . . . and he introduced new things onto the agenda. It was all about victims, I was invited along and I had to . . . do two little inputs, starting off discussion on two different areas . . . And it was my job, in a sense, to be the sort of victim, saying what was wrong and there were various solutions about what was right.

Her own solutions may have stemmed from that selfsame *Statement of Rights* but there were other, formally similar proposals that seemed to have been agreed before ever the seminar met:

serious consideration. This the government will do urgently.' The measure granting public access was resisted, but another, 'multi-agency public protection panels' (MAPPS) to manage high risk offenders in the community, was instituted under the Criminal Justice and Court Services Act, 2000. (Boateng said it was 'Sarah's Law' not 'Megan's Law mark two' (*The Times,* 16 September 2000).) It was, observed an official, 'A clear example of democratic government: done in a rush and off-the-cuff ideas from Ministers.' Subsequent proposals from JVU to 'lower the ceiling' to include the victims of offenders convicted of sexual and violent crimes and sentenced to one or more year's imprisonment in late 2000 confronted resource problems, estimated at £1m. per annum (that sum was submitted as part of the Home Office bid under the Comprehensive Spending Review in 1998), and were to be taken 'slowly and with consultation', eventually to be implemented in 2001, a transparent instance of classes of victims being defined by financial criteria.

[180] I tried to learn more about that meeting but without avail. The Home Office papers did not cover it although there were a few documents in the files of Victim Support. John Major's autobiography makes no mention of it, of victims or of the *Victim's Charter,* and more direct approaches were fruitless. I had instead to rely on interview with two of those who participated.

And of course it was One Stop Shop and the victims statement and those solutions were quite clearly there before the meeting ever started... One was the One Stop Shop, the other one was the victims statement. And I mean I was horrified by this because I was in this very difficult position that... we'd published our Bill of Rights, you know, our victims' rights document, which had really struggled to tease out what was good about these wretched victims statements in North America but what was bad about them, and therefore, how could we design them to make sure that we got the best out of them but not the worst out of them. And there was my Prime Minister, coming from absolutely nowhere, to the best of my know-ledge, 'cause I hadn't heard it anywhere, with an American idea and simply putting it on the table that this is what we're going to do. And he there and then appointed Barbara Mills to act, to set up a working party to develop it because I was on that working party.

The meeting had been convened to discuss the contents of the new *Victim's Charter*, the publication of which had been 'trailed' since the summer of 1995, when it was decided that what was now dismissed as little more than a set of service standards should be developed into a 'proper' Charter. The Prime Minister had expressed a personal interest in victims,[181] and Ministers and the Charter Unit were said to have been keen to publish the new Charter, but there had been unforeseen difficulties. Arrangements for achieving two of the new standards were not in place and 'difficulty' was being experienced in securing agreement from the affected criminal justice agencies. A member of RDS recalled in 1998: 'going back to Charter Two, this was Howard's day [Michael Howard was then Home Secretary]. So Howard didn't have a lot of time for procrastinating on Charter standards and things. So he said, on one-stop shop and victims' statements, that they should come in, um, as of the first of April and it would have been not this year, last year, they should come in... and the heavens fell in. And you know, lots of people got back to him and they started to say "you know nobody's geared up", the police were up in arms about it.' It was partly to resolve those difficulties and accelerate progress that the Prime Minister had

---

[181] In 1996, for instance, he said that 'When I think of crime, I think first about victims. The victims are not always selected by criminals because they are confident, robust, well-heeled individuals who can easily brush aside the trauma of crime or the personal and financial loss involved. Quite the reverse. Most often they are vulnerable, making them easy targets.' J. Major; 'Conservatism in Action: Strengthening the Rule of Law', Conservative Political Centre, London, 1996, p. 6.

convened his seminar on Criminal Justice and the Citizen to discuss how best to keep victims informed and take their interests into account. The Home Office was to be charged with securing agreement on the system to keep victims informed and the Crown Prosecution Service with securing information on victims' needs.

## Victim Impact Statements

'Victim impact statements', the mechanism by which victims informed service providers about their lot, and whose American model had so impressed the Prime Minister, had a slightly longer history. They had been introduced first in Fresno County, California, in 1974[182] and, by 1994, they had been authorized or required by law in forty-eight states in the United States. They were enacted in South Australia in 1988, allowing the victim the right to contribute to sentencing decisions through a statement.[183] They had been recommended by the Canadian Federal/Provincial Task Force on Justice for Victims of Crime in 1983,[184] and the federal government and four provinces had adopted them by 1994. They had been approved in New Zealand in 1989[185] and introduced into Victoria, Australia, in 1994,[186] with the aim of requiring courts in sentencing an offender to have regard to the impact of the crime on the victim.[187] They had been first mooted in the Home Office in 1990,[188] but their precise aims were left undefined and unresolved, largely because of the sensitivity of their implications for criminal

[182] Taken from [Ontario] Attorney General's Program on Victim Impact Statements Pursuant to Section 735 of the Criminal Code of Canada, 1994; and see E. Alexander and J. Lord; 'Impact Statements: A Nation's Responsibility to Listen', 1994, OVC web site.

[183] Based on R. Hardy; 'Victim Impact Statements: Summary of survey findings and the current position in Australia, Canada, New Zealand and the United States', Victim Support Briefing Paper, undated.

[184] See my *A View from the Shadows: The Canadian Ministry of the Solicitor General and the Justice for Victims of Crime Initiative*, Clarendon Press, Oxford, 1986.

[185] Victims Task Force; *Towards Equality in Criminal Justice*, Report to the Minister of Justice, Private Box 180, Wellington, NZ, 1993.

[186] Victoria: Sentencing (Victim Impact Statement) Act 1994, No. 24/1994.

[187] Later, in Ireland, they were to be used in parole hearings. See *Irish Independent*, 18 September 1999.

[188] They had also been introduced informally in a number of courts in England and Wales, for example in Luton Crown Court Centre in 1993.

procedure, and, in particular, their highly contentious relation to sentencing matters and what they signified about the standing of the victim (their 'purpose is usually assumed to be in connection with sentencing'[189] claimed David Faulkner).

Throughout the 1990s and up to very eve of the 2001 general election, politicians certainly considered the possibility of using victim statements as sentencing tools,[190] and, within the Home Office itself, the general usage was 'victim impact statements'.[191] Once in power, the new Ministers were reported to be attracted to a model where victim input was 'possible but not mandatory' and recognized that it would be a major change for victims to be routinely involved in determining sentences.[192] The Home Secretary himself wrote to the editor of a newspaper in 2000, 'In cases where there is a personal victim (as opposed to a corporate victim), it has been suggested that he or she ought to be offered the opportunity to make a statement about how the crime has affected their life. And this statement ought to be considered at every stage of the process, including when the tariff is set in the most serious cases. I am sympathetic to this view and hope to be making a statement shortly.'[193] At one point, indeed, it did seem that victims, broadly

---

[189] Committee on the role of the victim in the criminal justice process, D. Faulkner, 'Victim Impact Statements', 6 February 1995.

[190] As late as the time of the 2001 general election, for instance, the Labour Party's election manifesto stated that 'victims will now be allowed to present their views on the impact of the crime to the court . . . before sentencing'. And the Home Secretary, in his speech to the Labour Party Conference said, 'But the victim's voice should also be heard before sentence. . All criminal justice agencies should know how a crime has affected the life of a victim.'

[191] Papers touching on victims routinely talked about victim impact statements rather than victim statements. Two instances, taken virtually at random, are a 1999 paper on better services for the Ministerial Group; and *CJ2010*: 7 December 2000—Agenda Item 2—Annex A: new ideas. Nevertheless, there were some internal equivocations, David Brown, the RDS researcher responsible for work on victims, corrected a policy official's paper by removing 'impact' from 'victim impact statement' at the same time, December 2000.

[192] They offered, they told the Treasury, 'a potential for victims to influence sentence'. Home Office Comprehensive Spending Review: Support for Victims of Crime, March 1998, p. 51.

[193] Again, Ian Chisholm, speaking at the United Nations Congress on Crime and the Treatment of Offenders in Vienna in April 2000, said 'We are introducing nationally Victim Impact Statements at the time police take a witness statement. They can have an effect on charge, prosecution, and, of course, sentencing.'

defined, might be permitted formally to intervene directly in a sentencing decision after a ruling by the European Court of Human Rights in the case of *T and V v. the UK*,[194] and when the parents of the murdered child, James Bulger were subsequently given leave by the Lord Chief Justice, Lord Woolf, to make representations when he fixed the tariff for 'T and V', Bulger's killers.[195] But, as I shall show in the next chapter, that impression proved to be misleading and there was no simple accord amongst politicians, even within the Home Office itself. Whilst some Ministers linked victim's statements to sentencing decisions during the first New Labour administration, others did not,[196] and irresolution permeated the development of the victim statement.

Defined as a constituent of the sentencing process, victim's impact statements as they had been deployed in North America and Australia,[197] and, quite possibly were about to be deployed in England and Wales, threatened to bring the victim across the general *cordon sanitaire* described in the first chapter, and they were resisted with abhorrence by many lawyers and judges.[198] After all, they could lend victims a more formal role in criminal justice procedure, threaten the balance of power between State and defendant by introducing a disturbing third party; inject emotionality into what was supposed always to be a calm, 'objective' and disciplined process; raise expectations extravagantly high (especially if the North American model was dangled before the victim[199]); and add to the

[194] *T and V v. the United Kingdom*, 16 December 1999. Ian Chisholm said that the Home Secretary had been tempted to give victims a more formal role in response to the Thompson and Venables finding. My notes on the Victim Support Seminar on Stephen Lawrence, 15 February 2000.

[195] See *The Times*, 7 June 2000: 'Woolf to give Bulgers say in killers' sentence'.

[196] See, for instance, C. Clarke; letter to *The Times*, 19 June 2000: 'Courts to Consider Impact on Victims.' Victim statements were not, he said, intended to prescribe sentencing decisions.

[197] And there were Australian doubts too. See New South Wales Law Reform Commission; Discussion Paper 33—Sentencing, Sydney, 1996—Ch. 11: Victims of Crime.

[198] See T. Aldridge; 'No role for victims', *Solicitors Journal*, 28 November 1997. Marc Groenhuijsen noted that victim impact statements had generally been received far less warmly in Europe that in North America: M. Groenhuijsen; 'Trends in Victimology in Europe with Special Reference to the European Forum for Victim Services', 10th Annual Conference of the Japanese Association of Victimology, Kyoto, 26th June 1999.

[199] Comments made at Joint Home Office/IPPR seminar, 18 January 2001 to discuss Victim's Charter Draft Consultation Paper.

costs of criminal justice (the defence was likely to look at victim statements and could question them in court, and, it was thought, there could be 'Newton hearings'[200] that would add to legal aid costs). Academic lawyers such as Andrew Ashworth argued that it would be difficult for courts to know how to test the accuracy of victims' claims, and whether they should take account of 'unforeseen effects' or heed the especially vengeful or forgiving individual.[201] Rod Morgan and Andrew Sanders, the two academic lawyers who would eventually evaluate victim's statements for the Home Office, were as cautious: they acknowledged that there were alleged expressive and instrumental benefits for the victim, and conceded that prosecutors and sentencers would receive better information, but they also voiced doubts about the intrusion of private considerations into public proceedings, the unpredictable reactions of victims who might undermine dispassionate discretion, and the difficulty of separating 'fact' from 'opinion'.[202] Some practitioners were to argue with Louis Blom-Cooper that, in the case of trials for murder and manslaughter, 'the courts have resisted the clamour from some lobbyists to give the victim's family a distinct voice in the courtroom... If expectations should not be aroused, it does not follow that the victim's family is undeserving of consideration. Far from it. But such consideration should be carefully crafted and should avoid spilling over into the judicial process.'[203]

A number of benches had already been experimenting with impact statements in sentencing decisions in the 1990s,[204] and there was limited case law. In Scotland, Lord McCluskey had asked the Crown to ascertain the feelings of a victim before passing sentence,[205] but he had been subject to a successful appeal in 1990

---

[200] In *Newton* (1982) 77 Cr App R 13, it was held that the court should accept the defence's version in matters of substance for the purpose of mitigation, unless it had considered the evidence and concluded that it was sure the defence version was wrong.

[201] A. Ashworth; 'Victims' Rights, Defendants' Rights and Criminal Procedure', paper given at 'Integrating a Victim Perspective within Criminal Justice: An International Conference', York, July 1998, p. 15. And see A. Ashworth; 'Sentencing and the Human Rights Act', *Justice of the Peace*, Vol. 163, 23 January 1999, p. 64.

[202] R. Morgan and A. Sanders; 'the price of protection', *The Guardian*, 16 June 1999.

[203] 'Sympathy and Sentences', *The Guardian*, 6 November 2000.

[204] See P. and J. Cooper; 'Victim Information in Sentencing Reports', *Vista*, September 1995, pp. 2–13.

[205] H.M. *Advocate v. McKenzie* 1990 S.L.T. 28, at p. 31.

by the Lord Advocate on the grounds that a victim had no expertise in sentencing and could not bring a balanced view to bear. In *R v. Hobstaff* CA 22 January 1993, an appeal against sentence, it was determined that assertions of counsel about the impact of crime had to be supported by evidence. There had been a conviction on three counts of indecent assault on children where the appellant had pleaded guilty, and the prosecution had then addressed the court in 'highly emotional terms' about the effect that the assaults had had on the victims. No evidence had been called in support of the statements and there had been no supporting witness statement. It was held that the making of such assertions by counsel without such evidence was quite improper.[206] It was determined more generally that victim statements could influence sentences in two, rather exceptional, circumstances only:[207] where the appropriate sentence would aggravate the victim's distress,[208] and where the victim's forgiveness or unwillingness to press charges was evidence that his or her suffering was 'less than normal'.[209]

---

[206] Later, in *R v. Perks*, Court of Appeal, 19 April 2000, it was ruled that victim statements had to be in proper form and follow guidance. An appeal was allowed against the sentence of a drug addict who had robbed a woman. The woman's husband had sent a strongly worded document to the Crown Prosecution Service to be read out before the court, and the appeal judge said that the court shared the concern that a strongly worded document had not been disclosed to the defence but included in the case papers. The case led to the formulation of a number of principles about the use of victim statements: the sentencer must not make assumptions unsupported by evidence; if an offence had had a particularly damaging or distressing effect, it should be taken into account in sentencing; any evidence of effects on a victim should be in proper form, including the provision of an expert's report, and served on defence; it should be a matter that defence could be expected to investigate; the opinions of the victim on sentence should not be taken into account; and, if the sentence aggravated the victim's distress, it should be moderated. The appeal was allowed and became the basis of a practice direction from the Lord Chief Justice. It is a matter of interest that when the Attorney General appealed against what he claimed were excessively lenient sentences in eleven cases of sexual abuse, the Court of Appeal increased those sentences and ruled on 23 October 2003 that the trial judges had failed to recognize the 'seriousness of the harm caused to the victim'. Sentences that were too lenient could add to the anguish of the victim, it was said (see *The Times*, 24 October 2003).

[207] This is based on a paper by Robert Latham, a barrister and chairman of Victim Support's National Council: R. Latham; 'Victim Personal Statements and Sentencing', 27 November 2000.

[208] *Nunn* [1996] 2 Cr App R(S) 136: a case of death by dangerous driving where the victim and offender were close friends.

[209] *Hutchinson* [1994] 15 Cr App R(S) 134.

Victim Support was as emphatic as the lawyers and judges in resisting an importation of the American model of victim impact statements. It claimed that the genealogy of the two new Charter rights should instead be properly traced to its own policy paper on rights of victims of crime,[210] and tried to talk about victim statements rather than victim impact statements, with all their American associations and the disquieting implication that they were to be a sentencing instrument. It was, it said, 'important to get the terminology right. These are not victim impact statements to be used for sentencing purposes.' Helen Reeves herself said 'In our Statement of Rights ... we include one which is very controversial and not understood by a lot of people which is a right for victims not to have to make decisions regarding the offender ... I am passionately against the American idea of the victim impact statement, which is used in an adversarial context to argue for a heavier penalty.'[211] Impact statements could expose the victim to intimidation ('the more rights they have in the matter, the more vulnerable they become'[212]). They could be challenged, exposing the victim to further distress.[213] They could raise expectations too high. And there was no evidence that victims actually wanted them.[214]

There was to be some subsequent indeterminacy about what exactly the new entity should be called, an indeterminacy described internally as 'a lack of clarity': they were defined by Helen Reeves as victims statements rather than victim impact statements 'because they are not about sentencing';[215] in a JVU briefing to the Chair

[210] Victim's Charter Pilot Projects: Information for Volunteers, 12 September 1996. That position was-reaffirmed by another policy paper originating in Victim Support: European Forum; *The Social Rights of Victims of Crime*, 1998, which asserted that there was a need take victims' views into account and for them to provide information. Indeed, by 2000, Victim Support was to claim that 'all of the 1995 Victim Support report on the Rights of Victims of Crime have been achieved'. Victim Support: 'The role of the victim in criminal justice', 18 July 2000.

[211] P. Fraser; 'Interview with Helen Reeves', *Criminal Justice Matters*, Spring 1999, No. 35, p. 8.

[212] Helen Reeves. Minutes of the sixth meeting of the interdepartmental vulnerable or intimidated witnesses working group, 22 January 1998.

[213] Victim Support; *Rights of Victims*, 1995, p. 11.

[214] Based in part on Helen Reeves' statement in a debate about victim impact statements at the National Conference of Victim Support, Warwick, 1993.

[215] Victim's Charter Pilot Projects, notes of a briefing held at Victim Support National Office, 28 August 1996.

of the Victim Statements Working Group in April 2000 'as victim
impact statements (which is exactly what they are) but Victim Support is likely to remain opposed'; and by the Home Office in
one of its many papers as 'Victim Statements—also known as
Victim Personal Statements or Victim Impact Statements',[216] an
incertitude that amply revealed the open and contested character
of the standard.

Victim Support may have attempted continually to change the
name to victim statements,[217] but even within Victim Support there
was to be a protracted debate about meaning and usage that occupied its National Trustees for over nine months.[218] Teresa Reynolds
told the National Trustees that 'this is the most difficult issue we
have ever had to deal with in years at Victim Support'. It was 'easy to
argue oneself into either position' and 'exceedingly difficult to reach
a conclusion'.[219] After what was described as a 'a long and difficult
process',[220] in which lists of advantages and disadvantages were
drafted and deliberated, the original position of Victim Support
was re-affirmed: statements would be of use to the police and prosecution in deciding whether to continue a case, protect a victim,
provide special measures of support, reduce a charge, or apply for
compensation or bail.[221] Victim Support would endorse the scheme
but it would also retain its reservations about their use in sentencing.[222] It had maintained since 1995 that victims should be
awarded the right to receive and give information about their emotional, physical, and financial position to be given in their
own words at an early stage and personally to the police,
allowing them to be heard, to give information and to enable interests to be taken into account by professionals in the making

---

[216] Invitation to bid for the Victim Personal Statement evaluation survey, 21 May
2001.

[217] Minutes of Working Group on Victim Impact Information, 8 September 1995.

[218] Meeting of Victim Support National Council, 19 June 2001, my notes. The
Trustees at that time included Barbara Mills, the former Director of Public Prosecutions, who had chaired the Prime Minister's working group on victim statements after
the 1995 seminar, and she was in favour of statements being used in sentencing.

[219] Meeting of the Victim Support Board of Trustees, 1 May 2001.

[220] Minutes of Victim Support National Council Meeting, 19 June 2001.

[221] Victim's Charter Pilot Projects, notes of a briefing held at Victim Support
National Office, 28 August 1996.

[222] Victim Support News Service—Information: Victim Personal Statement
scheme, September 2001, p. 4.

of decisions.[223] But it had also adamantly opposed what it called the imposition of the 'burden' of responsibility for decisions about the offender. It was not possible to ascertain the long-term consequences of crime at the point of sentence, and the impact of crime varied with the personal circumstances of, and support received by, the victim.[224] Above all, it was the criminal justice authorities that should remain responsible for the treatment of the offender. And behind Victim Support's opposition was perhaps an older apprehension that the organization would become identified with the retributivism and strident campaigning of its American counterparts and some of the smaller British victims' organizations, contradicting its own core beliefs about the proper relation between State, victim, and defendant, and alienating the State agencies on whose co-operation and goodwill it depended.

Disputes between Victim Support and others, principally Home Office politicians and the Director of Public Prosecutions, about the suitable aims of victim statements would long dog their development, although Victim Support had its allies in Home Office officials, the legal profession, and the judiciary.[225] Thus Helen Reeves would continually remind colleagues on the Victims Steering Group about what she called the 'one main issue, an old hobby horse, the purpose of victim statements'. They should as a group be resolved, she said, that statements were not principally to serve the criminal justice system and the making of decisions about sentence, but rather should focus on the victims' interests throughout the case. The 'danger we've been aware of throughout will be that the criminal justice agencies will see it as a sentencing tool as it is in the USA...'.[226]

It is interesting that the research in the area suggested that the hopes and fears attached to victim statements were both somewhat misplaced. Statements seemed to have very little impact on senten-

[223] Lord Taylor; 'Witnesses, victims and the criminal trial', 12 April 1996: foreword by Helen Reeves, p. iii.
[224] Based on Meeting of Victim Support Trustees, 20 October 2000, 'The Role of the Victim in Criminal Justice', a re-statement of the established position.
[225] For example, the judge on the Working Party appointed by John Major argued that the responsibility for sentence must remain with the sentencer and must not be influenced by the opinion of the victim. Common Sergeant's comments on topic of Victim Impact Information, 26 September 1995.
[226] Meeting of Victims Steering Group, 8 December 2000, my notes.

cing but did afford some minor satisfaction to the victim.[227] And it had been long established that victims were no more punitive than the judges who sentenced offenders.[228] The victim-vigilante has always been more of a demon that haunted the legal imagination than an empirically well-grounded figure.

Let me backtrack. As an immediate product of the July 1995 seminar, John Major had established 'a small, high level, working group to discuss victim impact information'[229] (Helen Reeves added a '?' against the word *impact* in her copy of a letter of invitation). The group's task[230] was to establish the purpose for which the information was required, how it should be taken into account, by whom, at what stage obtained and by whom. Recommendations were to be made by the beginning of October 1995, consultations were thereafter to be held with the judiciary and magistracy, and the group would then report back by the beginning of December in that year.

---

[227] See, for example, M. Fallon; 'Victim Impact Statements: Do They Help or Hinder?', *State-Federal Judicial Observer*, April 1997, No. 14; E. Erez; 'Who's afraid of the big bad victim? VIS as Victim Empowerment *and* Enhancement of Justice, *Criminal Law Review*, 1999; E. Erez; 'Integrating a Victim Perspective in Criminal Justice through Victim Impact Statements', in A. Crawford and J. Goodey (eds.); *Integrating a Victim Perspective Within Criminal Justice: International debates*, Ashgate, Aldershot, 2000; and E. Erez and L. Rogers; 'Victim Impact Statements and Sentencing Outcomes and Processes', *British Journal of Criminology*, Spring 1999, Vol. 39, No. 2, pp. 216–39. On p. 216, they remarked: 'Despite the high hopes of victims rights advocates, and the misgivings of the opponents of victim participation, the inclusion of victim inputs has had little or no effect on the processing or outcomes of criminal cases.' *Justice Research Notes*, Ministry of Justice and Attorney General of Canada, November 1990, Issue 1, Ottawa, reported that, the Ministry of Justice of Canada had initiated six victim impact statement demonstration projects across the country in 1986. Most victims had hoped the victim impact statement would influence sentence, but it did not affect victims' satisfaction, and there were varying degrees of success in influencing the criminal justice system. Very few statements were actually used in court, prosecutors claiming that they contained no new information or were too vague or irrelevant. Victims did not use the victim impact statement as a retributive tool and stated that it did not necessarily lead to greater satisfaction with the criminal justice system.

[228] See *Attitudes to Crime and Criminal Justice: Findings from the 1998 British Crime Survey*, HORS 200, 2000.

[229] Letter of invitation to join the working group from Barbara Mills, 3 August 1995.

[230] Members included Barbara Mills, Helen Reeves, Norman Denison, the Common Sergeant of the Central Criminal Court, John Halliday of the Home Office, Paul Whitehouse of ACPO, Stephen Kay representing the Criminal Bar, and Alison Saunders of the Crown Prosecution Service Policy Group.

And it was chaired by the Director of Public Prosecutions, Barbara Mills, and staffed by officials of the Crown Prosecution Service, leading Victim Support to conclude that victim statements had been appropriated by 'criminal justice interests' in the service of criminal procedure, and was to be more closely tied to issues of prosecution and sentencing than to the interests of Victim Support's own client population, the 97 per cent of victims whose offences never culminate in a prosecution. An authoritative interpretation of the statements' functions, it was thought, was there fixed from the first.

Four principal issues were identified in an *aide memoire* laid before the group. The first was the lack of clarity about the purpose of victim impact statements: was it to affect the severity of the sentence and was it right that the peculiarities of a victim should affect the outcome? It was noted in qualification that 'In the majority of cases, the courts are perfectly capable of assessing the effect the crime would have on an ordinary member of the public. In these cases Victim Impact Statements are of limited benefit' (Helen Reeves added a resounding 'NO!' in the margin of her copy). Secondly, there was the question of what information was required for that purpose: sentencers would need clear, written, and admissible evidence. Where the victim was being treated by a psychiatrist, the material should be made available to court (and Helen Reeves enquired in the margins, 'agreement of victim?'). There was, it was noted, a need for protection against unfounded or excessive allegations by victims. Thirdly, the *aide memoire* asked, who should be responsible for collecting and updating the information? It would not be sufficient merely to collect it at the time the crime was committed. Courts would need current information. Collection was likely to be a police responsibility, and any resulting information should go to the Crown Prosecution Service. Lastly, there was the question of who should present the information to the court. Many organizations, including Victim Support, were opposed to victim impact statements being delivered orally and in person, and there was a risk that vulnerable victims would become more exposed to duress by the defendant and his supporters (Helen Reeves noted that the point was that the victim should not be linked to the sentencing process). The *aide memoire* concluded that the best solution might be for the victim's statement to be written by the victim but produced by the police and Crown Prosecution Service.

A draft report, called simply and possibly significantly, *Victim Statements,* was sent out to consultation in October 1995. Those approached were the Lord Chancellor's Department, and lawyers', magistrates', and judges' professional associations, but, again significantly, not the police or the smaller victims' organizations such as rape crisis centres and campaigning and self-help groups for the bereaved[231] (its place in criminal procedure and the linked notion of 'stakeholders' were there evident). It trod gingerly on the issue of sentencing, and the imprint of Victim Support was visible: information would be 'of use to the courts when deciding and explaining sentences. It must be clear, however, that the effect of the crime upon the victim is only one of many considerations to be taken into account by the courts and the prosecution. Victims should not share the responsibility of the decision-makers.' The drawing of boundaries around acknowledged victims was also evident. They excluded corporate victims; what were assumed to be the more indirect victims of crime (children in households where a burglary had taken place, for instance[232]); and the relatives of murder and manslaughter victims, betraying something of a conception of who the warranted victim was, fears about the costs of victim assistance become over-inflated, and the professional's anxiety about the emotionally undisciplined lay person.[233] Those who would be enabled to make statements were:

[231] Although, of course, the Working Group had included representatives from ACPO and Victim Support.

[232] There were, the Crown Prosecution Service maintained in January 1996, likely to be substantial problems involved in one person supplying information about the effects of crime on another. Many cases would be covered by the hearsay rule. It would be necessary to restrict information to the person making the statement. But further consideration would have to be given to dealing with cases where others affected by crime cannot complete their own statements, for example, children or those suffering mental illness.

[233] Those exclusions would be contested, not only by victims' groups when the pilots were finally announced, but also by the groups consulted. A local branch of the Magistrates' Association replied, for instance, by saying: that it would convey the 'impression that they are not being considered and that they have not been allowed to have their say. Allowing a member of the family to make a statement on behalf of the family might go some way to counter these impressions...'. Patsy Cullinan of SAMM, Support After Murder and Manslaughter, would certainly have wished its members the right to speak: '... it should add to the sentence that the person's going to get. And it should be acknowledged that we are suffering in this dreadful way and that our people are not bodies, the body or the man or the woman.' The proposed

restricted to direct personal victims only... A number of options were considered in cases involving fatalities. It was concluded that it would be inappropriate for a victim's family to make a statement in court after the criminal proceedings had been concluded... This was seen to be divisive because not all cases involving fatalities result in a prosecution and not all prosecutions result in a conviction. Bereaved families in other cases would not... get an opportunity to make such a statement. Equally the point of conviction/sentence is an emotional time for everyone involved in the case and is, therefore, not necessarily conducive to making such statements [but a written statement might be submitted instead].

Victim Support retained its stance that the chief value of victim statements would be to the police in establishing the victims' needs for information, compensation, protection, and the like, although the police had not originally been considered a suitable recipient of any information produced. Victim Support was also successful in changing the title of the working group to incorporate the term 'Victim Statements' (later Victim Personal Statements[234]) rather than 'Victim Impact Statements'.

Those two new standards of informing victims through the police (the 'One Stop Shop') and of 'taking victims' interests into account' ('Victim Statements') were included in the 1996 *Victim's Charter* as a result of the 1995 seminar. The consultation paper had ended with the proposal that any new system would need to be 'tested carefully'[235] in a 'pilot' in five police force areas 'before it was introduced nationally... [allowing] for any unforeseen practical problems to be identified and solved' (although it was also maintained internally by some within the Home Office that the pilots were a stalling technique which was required because the criminal justice agencies responsible for the two new charter standards were not yet in a state of readiness to implement them. The RDS official cited above said, 'they essentially staved [the Home Secretary] off by offering to do these pilots').

It had been agreed in February 1996 that the two pilots should be combined as a single exercise, 'run together and [the] documentation

---

confinement of the scheme to personal victims also led to criticisms that employees of corporations, such as bank cashiers, might well wish to make a statement.

[234]  Minutes of Victim Statement Working Group, 28 April 2000.
[235]  PPWG [Pilot Projects Working Group] 3/97: Victim's Charter: National Roll-Out of One Stop Shop, 6 February 1997.

merged' in trials lasting two years from the end of 1996, but they were actually to be formally severed the very next month (but nevertheless effectively managed as a single project) as a result of doubts raised by the Attorney General's Department, Lord Chancellor's Department, and ACPO about whether the victim impact statement should be introduced at all,[236] and by the Lord Chief Justice whose preferred system of two separate statements taken at different times, one at the point of the witness statement, and one just before court (so that information for sentencing could be fresher), would be piloted in but one Crown Court centre only. The categories to be covered were the personal victims of domestic burglary, domestic violence, grievous bodily harm and sexual assaults, but not the families of victims of murder and homicide; and Rod Morgan, Andrew Sanders, and colleagues at the University of Bristol were appointed in January 1997 to evaluate their experiences.

## The Victim's Charter Pilot Projects and Beyond: The 'One Stop Shop'

The second standard talked about informing the victim, and it would be realized by means of a 'One Stop Shop', a term in general currency in the new politics.[237] In the context of the *Victim's Charter*, it was intended to end confusion and simplify access to information by enabling victims to approach a single point of contact, the allegedly under-utilized police, an agency with the earliest, most frequent and diffuse contacts with victims, about material developments in their case.[238] Gloria Craig had also been present, and she recalled:

[There was] a charter seminar in Number 10, with John Major... It was in 1995 at which we got together, all the, some of the practitioners and the

[236] And the relevant passage of the draft second *Victim's Charter* was diluted and 'bland' in consequence.

[237] See *Modernising Government*, Cm. 4310, March 1999—Ch. 3: Responsive Public Services.

[238] In the beginning of 1997, and at the instigation of JVU, ACPO contacted 39 police forces about the information they provided to victims: 31 replied; 58% provide information to victims with details of the decision to charge or caution; 45% about details of first hearing; 19% with the date of the Crown Court trial; and 87% with details of verdict and sentence.

victims side and, you know, Government departments as well. There were a couple of issues that came out of that. And there have been issues that I've noticed since in dealing with victims stuff. The first thing that is really important to victims is information, how much information they get. In fact, actually it's a key to virtually anything in any public service, you know, if you get stuck on a train, what you want to know is what the hell's going on, how long is it going to take before they sort it out.

The 'One Stop Shop' experiment began in five areas in January 1997 and was evaluated by the Home Office RDS and by Andrew Sanders and his colleagues at Bristol University.[239] There had been delays in mounting the project, interviews with victims were late and rates of 'take-up' were very low. Explained variously by the Narey reforms that were intended to speed the flow of cases through the courts,[240] the criminal justice system's incompatible information technology systems that impeded the flow of cases passed to the police,[241] and what officials and researchers in the Home Office called poor police administration and an inappropriate exercise of discretion, only a small number of cases actually came to the 'One Stop Shop' projects[242] (for their part, the police complained of high rates of officer sickness and the poor initial marketing, design[243] and

---

[239] Sanders proposed to test by telephone and face to face interview the hypotheses that the 'One Stop Shop' would bring about in participating victims a reduction of anxiety and an increase in satisfaction; and a reduction of trauma and of secondary victimization. The scheme, he postulated, would increase understanding but might increase dissatisfaction; and the victims who did not participate were likely to be more dissatisfied than those who did participate. He would examine how different methods of organization affected outcomes. And he proposed to 'put victims' concerns' to the Home Office. A. Sanders; 'Evaluation of the One Stop Shop and Victim Statement Pilot projects', 13 February 1997.

[240] Victim's Charter Pilot Projects Working Group: Chairman's brief for meeting of 27 October 1998.

[241] Victims Charter Pilot Projects, note of a meeting at Scotland Yard, 12 October 1998.

[242] The minutes of the Victim's Charter Pilot Projects Meeting of 4 February 1997, record that there had been 26 referrals in Crawley, 14 of whom had decided to opt-in; no-one had yet opted-in in Winchester; 8 cases fell within the pilot in Chorley, all of whom had opted-in; in Bedford, 95 letters had been sent, and 7 had opted-in; in Merseyside there had been no contact with victims. By May, 271 victims had been approached for the 'One Stop Shop', of whom 103 had 'opted in'.

[243] Commander Campbell of the Metropolitan Police, then a member of the Victims Steering Group, said 'Basically the Home Office letter was of a gobbledy-gook version of what we'd previously had ourselves and generated. And I said "no

funding of the scheme[244]). By February 1997, the numbers of participating victims were described as minute: four in the area with the lowest figure, twenty in the highest, and certainly too low for 'viability'.[245] The team based at Bristol University reported that fewer victims than expected had elected to participate in the scheme, with a 'low take-up rate of 43%', and that it was possible that their appetite for information had been exaggerated.[246] The team was running out of time and requested that their deadline be extend from late February to late April, and that the submission of their report be deferred until July 1998. But the Chairman of the Victim's Charter Pilot Projects Working Group, a dedicated sub-group of the Victims Steering Group, was advised that it would be most unfortunate if the scheme were to 'slip' beyond the spring: after all, the *Victim's Charter* had promised that the projects would be 'up and running by then'. It was, the Chairman was told, 'a very disappointing set of reports at this advanced stage'.[247]

Measures were devised to rescue the evaluation of both projects, the One Stop Shop and the Victim Statement pilots, by extending from April 1997 the range of classes of eligible victims to include all assaults, robberies, cases of criminal damage over £5,000, racially motivated offences, and attempting or conspiring to commit any of these offences; and then to *all* criminal cases by October of that year. Another police area, West Mercia, was added in that selfsame month to increase the population to be sampled.[248]

The Bristol University researchers completed their interviews with victims by February 1998[249] and in May, Rod Morgan, one

sorry, for the purposes of the pilot, never mind we don't think it's as good as ours, we've got to test the pilot so send it out". And of course, the predictable happened, there was little or no response 'cause people didn't understand it . . . it was computer generated. And so the take-up of people who said "yes, we do want to avail ourselves of the One Stop Shop concept" was pretty low, abysmally low.'

[244] Victims Charter Pilot Projects, note of a meeting at Horsham, 29 September 1998.

[245] Victim's Charter Pilot Projects: Draft Information for Volunteers 2, 4 February 1997.

[246] Progress Report 4 on the evaluation of the pilots, 24 October 1997.

[247] Victim's Charter Pilot Projects Working Group—Chairman's brief for the meeting of 28 October 1997.

[248] Victim's Charter Pilot Projects—Recent Developments, 24 March 1998.

[249] Progress report 5 to members of the Victim's Charter Pilot Projects Working Group, 5 February 1998.

of the researchers, advised the Working Group that decisions needed
to be taken about how to prevent victims being left out of contact for
long periods; and about what could be done to improve liaison
between the police and the Crown Prosecution Service in the supply
of information about cases.[250] Doubts were starting to loom within
the Home Office about whether it was worth proceeding with the
project at all.[251] Another interim report, submitted in September
1998, did little to dispel that uncertainty:[252] 564 victims had been
contacted by then, a little under half of whom had agreed to receive
information, although many could not say why they had chosen to
do so. Most thought they would be told about verdict and sentence,
but they had wanted to know more, and many had not received
'even minimal information'. One difficulty was that the Crown
Prosecution Service appeared to be only 'minimally involved' in the
One Stop Shop, and the material it conveyed was couched in 'for-
mulaic terms'. Helen Reeves recollected that 'they decided that
they'd [institute] this One Stop Shop where the police would be
responsible for conveying everybody's information back to the
victim. But there were no systems in place for everyone to get their
information to the police for that purpose . . . '.

Officials decided that the Bristol report had identified several
problems which required resolution: by giving one agency formal
responsibility for informing victims, it had been hoped that victims'
satisfaction would increase and their anxiety decrease, but there had
been difficulty with inter-agency communication; the Crown
Prosecution Service had 'played a minimal role'; and victim discontent had only been amplified by the failure to provide promised
information.

The 'One Stop Shop' was evidently not working as it should. In a
summary report, Ministers were advised that the evaluation's 'positive findings' included the indication that there was an appreciable
demand for information, claimed as a diffuse right; that 'opting-in'
made 'people feel better' and marginally more satisfied with, and
knowledgeable about, the criminal justice system; and that in most

---

[250] Victim's Charter Pilot Projects Working Group: minutes of meeting of 11 May
1998.
[251] Victim's Charter Pilot Projects Working Group: minutes of meeting of 24 July
1998.
[252] C. Hoyle *et al.*; *Draft Report to the Home Office on the Evaluation of the 'One
Stop Shop'*, September 1998.

police areas there was a commitment to inform. But there were also the 'negative findings' that a heightening of expectations engendered dissatisfaction: 10 per cent of those who had opted in declared that they would not do so again; the scheme as it had been applied depressed regard for the police because most victims wanted information that the 'One Stop Shop' could not supply; and there were complaints about the insufficiency and tardiness of information, arising, in part, from 'problems with the CPS'. And that was to become the epitaph on the pilot scheme within the Home Office.[253]

## The One Stop Shop and the Glidewell and Macpherson Reports

By the time the evaluation was released,[254] however, the report of Sir Iain Glidewell into the work of the Crown Prosecution Service had already been published,[255] and the very idea of a police-based 'One Stop Shop' had been made obsolete by the recommendation that a new duty be laid on prosecutors to inform victims. The Chairman of the Pilot Projects Working Group was obliged to advise the group in July 1998 that 'Glidewell completely changes any arrangements for a One Stop Shop run by the police'.[256]

It will be recalled that the Labour Party had earlier recommended in a pre-election policy document that the CPS should take it upon themselves to inform victims about significant decisions in the criminal process,[257] and that proposal had been treated as a political commitment to be entrusted to the review of the CPS chaired by Sir Iain Glidewell. Two parallel developments were then in train, one stemming from the 1995 Downing Street meeting convened by a Conservative Prime Minister and supposedly culminating in a 'national roll-out' of a 'One Stop Shop' run by the police in April 1997

[253] To be reproduced intact, for instance, in an internal memoire: Key Government Action to Assist Victims/Witnesses, January 1999.

[254] C. Hoyle *et al.*; 'The Victim's Charter—An Evaluation of Pilot Projects', Home Office; Research Findings No. 107, 1999, p. 1.

[255] On 1 June 1998.

[256] Victim's Charter Pilot Projects Working Group: meeting of 24 July 1998. Revised chairman's brief.

[257] Labour Party; *The Case for the Prosecution*, 18 April 1997, argued that the local Crown Prosecution Service should be responsible for informing victims about their decisions to discontinue cases or alter charges. It was not the duty of the police to convey information about the work of another agency, it declared.

(but long delayed), the other from the New Labour Government elected in May 1997 and designating the CPS as deliverers of information to victims. It was noted within a month of the 1997 general election that the Victim's Charter Pilot Projects Working Group should consider the Government's plans to 'make a restructured CPS more accountable for decisions and more pro-active in contacting victims',[258] and, eight months later, officials accepted that it was likely to be the CPS that would come, 'post-Glidewell', to assume the role of informing victims about progress. After a period in limbo when 'it was not possible to know the implications for the One Stop Shop',[259] the Glidewell report did indeed recommend that there should be a transfer of responsibility 'for giving information and, where desired, an explanation to complainants/victims... in each CPS Area as soon as the resources of that Area permit'.[260] By the end of 1998, it was evident that the police-based scheme was unlikely to survive.[261] As Ian Chisholm remarked to a meeting of the Victims Steering Group in December 1998, 'that does rather blow a hole in it, doesn't it?' and an official of the CPS replied, 'I feel I ought to say something here, but I don't know what to say. If that Glidewell recommendation is taken on in full, then yes, the CPS would have to take responsibility for the One Stop Shop.'

## The Right to Privacy and Data Protection Measures

The pilot had not worked well: the evaluation of the 'One Stop Shop' had been delayed, its report not being published until late 1998;[262] it had not even been possible to extract 'principles of best practice' from what had been done thus far;[263] and the trial had, in any event,

[258] Victim's Charter Pilot Projects Working Group: Revised Minutes of Meeting, 13 February 1997—note of 24 June 1997.

[259] Minutes of the meeting of the Victim's Charter Pilot Projects Working Group, 28 October 1997.

[260] *The Review of the Crown Prosecution Service,* Summary of the Main Report, Chairman Sir Iain Glidewell, June 1998, Cm. 3972, recommendations 31 and 32.

[261] Home Office Circular 55/1998, 23 December 1998.

[262] Victims Steering Group meeting, 24 November 1999, CPS Communication with Victims; Annex A: Macpherson/Glidewell Recommendations.

[263] Eventually, those principles were to be summarized by JVU, the first version of which was written in May 1999 on the basis of the first draft of the final report of the Bristol research. 1996 Victims Charter Monitoring Standards of Service, VSG 1/99, May 1999.

been superseded by another, more authoritative report. Matters became more complicated still because the release of information by the police to victims was soon to become entangled in legal restrictions flowing from rights conferred by new and impending legislation. Under the Data Protection Act 1998,[264] Article 8 of the Human Rights Act 1998, the repeatedly deferred Freedom of Information Bill and even common law definitions of the proper role of the police, misgivings were being raised about wider police powers and duties of confidentiality in the protection of the suspect's, defendant's, and victim's right to privacy. JVU informed the chairman of the Victims Steering Group in 2000 that there were 'doubts about whether police have powers to take on this role and whether victims are entitled to information about suspects. We have asked for clarifying advice.' The matter was distilled into a series of questions: 'how do we define a victim and what information should he or she be entitled to? ... Can the police release personal details of offenders? Can the details be released for the purpose of civil proceedings?'[265] Officials were advised in late 1999 that under the common law the police could obtain, hold, and disclose information to preserve the peace, prevent and detect crime, and protect persons and property, but that that power was not unlimited and disclosure to the victim of information was lawful only if it was for policing purposes, such as the protection of the victim against a repetition of the crime. Information could be given to a victim because he or she was always potentially a witness and had a legitimate interest in knowing when the case was to be heard and whether a person had been charged, but the personal details of offenders, including their names and addresses, was another matter, and to disclose them for civil matters would be *ultra vires* because that could not be said to be for a police purpose. At this point of legal uncertainty, ACPO declared that it was reluctant to proceed further,[266] and officials of JVU concluded that victims and witnesses would not only become further alienated from the criminal justice system but that they might no longer even know such elementary details as which courtroom they should attend if there was a trial.

[264] The Act implemented the 1995 EC Data Protection Directive.

[265] JVU discussion document on Information Released by Police to Victims and Referrals to Victim Support—confidentiality and data protection issues, 21 July 1999.

[266] Victim's Charter Pilot Projects Working Group: minutes of meeting of 24 July 1998.

## Automatic Referrals

The issue of privacy would surface elsewhere, in other guises[267] and even more critically when the Data Protection Act, the Human Rights Act and common law were thought to prevent the police routinely informing the co-ordinators of victim support schemes about the names of victims who had recently suffered a crime, and reciprocally of victims being informed about developments in their cases by victim support workers and police after referral. It is worth making a slight detour here because the problem was to converge with other difficulties in enforcing the *Victim's Charter* standard to engender a crisis with potentially important ramifications.

'Automatic referrals' had been the practice of most police forces in England and Wales since the mid-1980s, and it was upon them that the very success of Victim Support rested (97 per cent of referrals in 1999–2000 were 'automatic', 2 per cent were by 'direct contact by victims', and 1 per cent stemmed from other agencies[268]). When the victim's right to privacy came to the fore, the practice of automatic referrals was jeopardized, some schemes began to falter,[269] and Victim Support was at risk of becoming in breach of its obligation to comply with the *Victim's Charter* standard to contact a victim within two working days.

The matter had arisen first in 1993,[270] before the New Labour Government had even come to power, but was revived as soon as the various new privacy provisions were announced,[271] and it preoccu-

---

[267] For example, in briefing victims before they decided whether to participate in restorative justice projects. See J. Dignan; *Youth Justice Pilots Evaluation: Interim Report on Reparative Work and Youth Offending Teams*, Home Office, London, 2000, p. 1.

[268] Victim Support, *Annual Report 2000—1999–2000*, p. 9.

[269] There were, for example, reports in Victim Support News Service, September 1997, about difficulties encountered by schemes, and later, in Strathclyde and North Wales, where there had been a reported 75% drop in referrals at the beginning of the century. Draft Minutes of meeting of Victim National Council, 20 June 2000 and *Western Mail*, 22 May 2000. North Wales was especially significant because its Chief Constable was Chair of the ACPO Data Protection Committee.

[270] It fed from a 1993 ruling of a data protection tribunal on an unrelated matter that led police to believe that they could not pass details to victim support schemes unless the victim has given positive consent. That ruling had been clarified in favour of a continuing policy of automatic referral by an ACPO circular centred on the doctrine of implicit consent two years later.

[271] The Data Protection Act 1998 was to come into force on 1 March 2000.

pied Government and Victim Support throughout the period of the first administration.[272] The office of the Data Protection Registrar was at first to adhere to the principle that victims must give their informed consent before their names were forwarded, and expressed its disapproval of automatic referral. The police, it seemed, had exceeded their powers,[273] but to retreat would be to renege on the Government's many-stranded commitment to inform victims.[274] Alun Michael, the Home Office Minister, was moved to write to Chief Constables in 1998 to ascertain what procedures they were adopting and he unearthed disarray: some, like the Chief Constable of Norfolk, still relied on automatic referrals; others, like the Chief Constable of Cheshire, required victims to make a strict objection before refusing to forward their names to co-ordinators; and the Chief Constable of Avon and Somerset adopted a middle position, saying that he did not want to discourage officers from discussing with victims the merits of referral to a scheme. Obtaining the victim's consent, it was thought, would not only be unwieldy administratively and re-introduce a discretionary component to police action, but would also remove any automatic element from automatic referrals. One solution, mooted in 1998, resided in the hope that the Secretary of State was empowered under the Data Protection Act to order certain exclusions from the strictures on the disclosure of sensitive data[275] requiring the subject's consent[276] if they were to further the administration of justice. But that was not to be supported by legal advice. Exclusions applied to the protection of people and prevention of crime and

[272] There were references to it as a problem of some duration in internal Home Office correspondence in March 1998.

[273] It appeared on legal advice that there was no general power for the police to disclose information for collateral purposes and it may be illegal for them to do so. The public interest could not create a power to disclose where there was no such pre-existing power, and the police had to be able to cite a specific authority before disclosing. Discretion could give exceptional authority, for example, the disclosure of information about the whereabouts of offenders to third parties, but the only legitimate purposes of such disclosure were the detection of crime and the bringing of offenders to justice, but not for private law proceedings.

[274] It re-affirmed its position in HO circular 55/1998.

[275] Data Protection web site: Chapter 3: the data protection principles, October 1998.

[276] In the case of racist crimes, see *Code of Practice on Reporting and Recording Racist Crimes*, Home Office, April 2000, pp. 18–19.

it was not possible to represent Victim Support as contributing to either object.

As more papers were written, as more advice was sought and more meetings were held, the apparent ramifications of the restrictions mushroomed. It began to appear in the summer of 1999 that they could also affect information for civil action accident reports, the release of photographs of offenders to the mass media, the preparation of witness statements, the supply of information to the Criminal Injuries Compensation Authority, the implementation of the witness satisfaction survey that was to be conducted in 2000,[277] and the free exchange of information between institutions such as the Customs and Excise and the Inland Revenue within and around the criminal justice system,[278] corroding the working of 'joined-up government'. It was noted by the head of the RDS in late 1999 that 'all our efforts to produce joined-up service delivery depended on data sharing and there are worries at local level'. The new battery of restrictions cramped a number of the Home Secretary's ambitions,[279] and he and his advisers were in a manifest dilemma. On the one hand, the Home Office was informed that he was urging the police to behave unlawfully and in breach of the European Data Protection Directive and domestic legislation, whilst, on the other, Victim Support and the *Victim's Charter* were in jeopardy and, to exacerbate matters, the Government looked as if it was about to flout a key provision on informing victims lodged in a binding European Community Framework Decision on the Standing of Victims to which it was about to become a signatory.[280] The law, especially Article 8 of the Human Rights Act, Ministers argued, was

---

[277] And the advice of the Data Protection Commissioner had first to be sought.

[278] The matter was discussed in the context of information about 'mentally disordered offenders' in the White Paper, *Reforming the Mental Health Act*, 20 December 2000.

[279] Although one official did query whether the Home Secretary should be supporting a measure that would give information about victims against their will. It was, he said, a curious policy for a government that claimed to have the interests of victims at heart.

[280] The European Framework Decision on the Standing of Victims in Criminal Proceedings, adopted by the meeting of the Justice and Home Affairs Ministers on 15 March 2001. The Home Office declared that the Government was already in compliance although there was 'current uncertainty' about the provision of information to victims. Minutes of Victims Steering Group: meeting of 12 June 2001. I discuss the Framework Decision at greater length in Chapter 10.

'about to make everyone an ass' and could be 'catastrophic' for Victim Support and 'damage all that the Government is trying to do for victims'. There was an 'overriding public interest to offer support to victims'.

Legislative amendments were bruited in 2000 to insert a public interest provision in the law on disclosure to outweigh the public interest in the exemptions;[281] to place on the police a statutory duty to inform victims; or formally to identify Victim Support as a criminal justice agency[282] or as an agency of the police involved in the administration of justice.[283] Victim Support might, it was thought, be recognized as working within a new and wider interpretation of overriding public interest. Perplexity was compounded because of the sheer newness of the law, some of which was being discussed only in anticipation. As we shall see in the next chapter, there was, for instance, no domestic case material about the proportionality of victims' rights and offenders' rights under Article 8 of the Human Rights Act, the article that touched on the right to privacy.[284]

Most important from the standpoint of this book, it was also argued by JVU in September 2000 that, in the light of the law officers' view that unless a victim was under threat, he or she was no different from any other member of the public for disclosure purposes, and that it would be unlawful for victims to receive information about the suspect, there might be a case to give the victim some formal legal standing in criminal procedure.[285] If victims are

---

[281] Such steps had been envisaged in the white paper, *Your Right to Know: The Government's proposals for a Freedom of Information Act*, 11 December 1997, Cm. 3818, p. 1; the Public Administration Committee, *Third Report*, 1997–8, 19 May 1998; and the Government Response to the Public Administration Committee Report, *Third Report*, 1997–8, undated—Recommendation 3. The forthcoming Police and Security Industry Bill or a possible fifth session data sharing bill were thought to be possible vehicles for such an amendment.

[282] Meeting of the VS National Council, 21 September 1999, my notes.

[283] Although it was acknowledged by the Home Office that Victim Support was a voluntary organization and turning it into a public body through legislation would 'provoke soul-searching and probably not achieve the desired results'. Helen Reeves' view was that all that would mean is a legislative provision and the implication would be full government funding.

[284] Victims Steering Group Meeting, 8 December 2000, my notes.

[285] Different advice was tendered by the Chief Commissioner, Northern Ireland Human Rights Commission in October 2000 to the effect that crime is a public event in which the victim does not have absolute privacy. Merely disclosing that someone has been the victim of a particular crime is not a breach of privacy.

no more than members of the public, it was wondered, what would be the effect on disclosure rules of placing victims' rights on a statutory basis? Ian Chisholm told the Victims Steering Group that 'it may be that giving victims rights in a Victims' Rights Bill may be enough without any more action... putting victims rights on a statutory basis will resolve the whole thing, but we're still awaiting legal advice'.[286] That possible resolution to the *impasse* seemed at the time to herald a minor revolution in the relations and identities of the criminal justice system. It was such talk about victims becoming legally-ratified principals, talk that had been firmly approved by the Home Secretary, that came in time to contribute not only to the formation of a critical interpretive mass but also to solutions to a vexing problem. And that mass, in its turn, crystallized into proposals for a Victim's Bill of Rights that were presaged in those discussions and are the focus of this history.

In the event, victims and Victim Support were not to be recognized as persons in law for the purpose of mitigating the effects of data protection legislation because a much simpler solution was discovered instead. In 2001, it was agreed that a new victims' leaflet would be issued by the police explaining that victims' details would be passed on to Victim Support unless the victim expressed a contrary wish[287] (except in cases of domestic violence or sexual crime or the families of victims of homicide victims where express consent had always been required). And, on that basis, Victim Support was effectively allowed by the newly renamed Information Commissioner to continue with automatic referrals without the victims' consent so long as it instituted an information security policy.[288]

---

[286] Victims Steering Group: meeting of 12 June 2001, my notes.

[287] The new wording was 'the police will pass information about you to Victim Support so that they can offer help and advice, unless you ask the police not to'. Home Office Circular 44/2001, 3 October 2001.

[288] Meeting of Victim Support National Council, 19 June 2001, my notes. Systems were to be 'inserted' for when victims requested deletion of their data from records and systems of information security. There was a new phrasing for Victim Support's confidentiality guidelines: 'if a victim or witness requests that their personal data no longer be retained by the Service, it is the duty of the service to ensure that all relevant records are destroyed. The victim/witness should be informed, in writing, that their request has been complied with, and that no records remain.' See also *Victim Support Magazine*, No. 80, Autumn 2001.

## The Dropping of the Pilot

The pilot study was deemed to have been 'invalidated' by the Government's proposal that the CPS should contact victims directly.[289] Now that the CPS had been given a role as well as the police, even the use of 'One Stop Shop' as a term had become inappropriate.[290] In retrospect, Ministers concluded in June 1999, it would have been better if the Government had acted immediately on its election commitment to require the CPS to inform victims and witnesses from May 1997 onwards, but it had waited on Sir Iain Glidewell instead, and the One Stop Shop had perforce served as an interim measure. By the end of 1998, the pilot 'One Stop Shops' had ceased to function,[291] they had been 'a bit of an abortion' as Ian Chisholm put it, but the police still retained a caretakers' responsibility for informing victims whose cases did not reach or had not yet reached court and before 'CPS involvement'[292] had started with the new joint police-CPS Criminal Justice Units recommended by Sir Iain.[293]

The Crown Prosecution Service, heir apparent to the One Stop Shop, was itself in the throes of radical reorganization following the Glidewell report and the many other planks of the New Labour

[289] It was thought that the 'OSS had failed to work properly [and since the] police have to deal with information second hand once the case has started, [it would be] best to rely on the decision-makers themselves'.

[290] Minutes of meeting of Victim's Charter Pilot Projects Working Group, 9 February 1998.

[291] Key Government Action to Assist Victims/Witnesses January 1999—Victim's Charter Pilot Projects.

[292] And agencies were again reminded of their duty to convey intelligence to the police so that it could be communicated to the victim: Home Office Circular 55/1998, 23 December 1998: Keeping Victims Informed of Developments in their Case. However, it was noted internally that, under the Data Protection Act 1998, there was not a general power for the police to disclose information for collateral purposes and that it may have been illegal for them to do so.

[293] Under the spur of the Macpherson Inquiry Report, moreover, and the subsequent transformation of racialized victims into the more general category of victims of 'hate crime', they were above all to become charged with providing information rapidly to the victims of racially-aggravated and 'homophobic' crime, and to the victims of sexual offences and domestic violence. *ACPO Guide to Identifying and Combating Hate Crime*, Metropolitan Police, London, December 1999, p. 31. Officers were to ensure that contact was made with the victim within 24 hours, advising them on the progress of the case, establishing what further assistance might be needed, and arranging a personal visit at 'the earliest opportunity'.

Government's modernization agenda. It was required to decentralize, simplify, and flatten its structure; introduce information technology on a larger scale; re-orientate itself to the new criminal justice aims and objectives; and re-align the boundaries of its administrative areas to match those of the police and probation services and, eventually, of Victim Support. The implementation of recommendations touching on the provision of information to victims was thus to be long postponed, the argument being that the 'scale of change elsewhere in CPS precluded earlier action',[294] and projected future action was covered always by the phrase, stemming directly from the Glidewell report, 'as soon as the resources . . . permit'. There was, it was noted, a 'huge change programme that is stretching its resources to the limit. Work with victims must mesh with it. Cannot take place at pace we would desire.' Besides, the Director of Public Prosecutions observed, CPS lawyers were not used to dealing with the public.

If that were not confusion enough, the recommendations of Sir Iain Glidewell and the new Charter standard were joined by the even more powerful impact of the conclusions of the inquiry of Sir William Macpherson into the death of Stephen Lawrence. The Lawrence report, published in February 1999 and adopted as the personal charge of the Home Secretary, also made emphatic recommendations about the duty of the police[295] and CPS to consult with and inform the primary and secondary victims of crime.[296] After early 1999, the recommendations of Glidewell and Macpherson on

[294] Victim's Charter Pilot Projects Working Group: minutes of meeting of 15 June 1999.
[295] When a senior police officer informed a meeting of RISC in September 1999 that he now made it a policy for officers to take CPS staff with them to brief the families of murder victims about possible courses of action, he was informed by a CPS official that issues of confidentiality and the right to a fair trial (under Article 6 of the Human Rights Act) were at stake. The police officer's reply was 'Sir William [Macpherson] did not take that line with us in his questioning and it was made clear to us that we should not raise too many difficulties'.
[296] George Howarth, a Home Office Minister, speaking in *lieu* of Paul Boateng at the Victim Support Conference in July 1999, said 'The Stephen Lawrence case, among other things, brought just how much needed to be done into sharp relief. One of its starkest features was the failure to keep his family informed of developments in the investigation . . . most people *DO* want information. They want to know if someone is caught or charged, whether the charges are downgraded, and the final result of the court case. We also want the CPS to be available to explain decisions for which they have responsibility. We welcome the steps the CPS is taking to assess the feasibility of

the relation between the CPS and victims would be twinned into a single mandate, and the Home Secretary would from time to time intervene personally and forcefully to hasten them along, for example, by 'dressing down' CPS officials openly in committee about their insistence that they were obliged to secure extra resources before acting.

The CPS did come to commit itself to complying with the overlapping *Victim's Charter* standard and Glidewell and Macpherson recommendations on informing victims,[297] but its compliance remained conditional on resources, and it simultaneously embarked on a campaign to obtain money from the Comprehensive Spending Review to fund its new responsibilities. Some within Government wondered why the CPS required extra money for a service that the police had been providing from within their existing budget[298] and they declared that it was unreasonable to expect a transfer of resources from the police to the CPS (which the CPS had requested) because the police had not received extra funds in the first place. The CPS's reply was that the increased volume of work would be substantial, some 100,000 cases *per annum*, that 'just doing what the police did is not enough', and that there would be additional costs in introducing direct communication by the CPS. Not only would new staff be recruited but all staff would have to be trained if they were to deal with victims face to face. Relations between the police, Home Office, and CPS became frayed, and the CPS, which had been portrayed as unhelpful to the police in the mid-1990s and in pioneering the original 'One Stop Shops', was now to be heard belatedly proclaiming that it wished at some expense to take a 'lead role'

this. And we congratulate the police for the efforts they are making to keep victims informed of case progress ahead of the national good practice guidance later this year.'

[297] In October 2001, the CPS issued a new code for Crown Prosecutors with 'A new emphasis on the interests and views of victims': there was a 'new paragraph emphasising the importance of communicating significant changes in a case to victims . . . The review took into account the Glidewell Review and the Macpherson Report. [The paragraphs] require prosecutors to take into account the effects of their decisions on victims, as well as any views expressed by them, when considering whether a prosecution is in the public interest. Victims should also be told about any decision that makes a significant difference to the case in which they are involved.' CPS News Release, 128/00, 1 October 2000: new code published for Crown Prosecutors.

[298] For example in the draft minutes of the 2nd meeting of the Lawrence Steering Group, 27 September 1999.

when, under 'joined-up government', colleagues in other departments averred, there were no leaders but only co-equals.

The repeatedly postponed construction of a new relation between the CPS and victims culminated in what Jane Austen might have called an *éclaircissement*. Under sustained pressure levelled by Ministers, the Attorney General's Department started to talk of 'its enthusiastic welcome to improvement in standard of service to victims', and, in October 2000, it floated three options (bronze, silver, and gold) specifying different levels of service and costing different amounts of money[299] (and yet, it noted still, that 'CPS resources are limited and declining... There will be a bid for additional resources'). An 'options study' would be piloted in six, later seven, different areas, comparing the impact of the different measures, and seeking 'an indication of potential difficulties',[300] under the supervision of a steering committee formed, in usual fashion, of 'representatives of all those agencies with an interest', and absorbing the now defunct Pilot Projects Working Group.

The CPS proposed to explain its decisions to drop or alter charges substantially in all cases with an identifiable victim, including bereaved parents or partners in homicide cases, parents where the primary victim was a child, police officers, and small businesses. Victims would be notified by letter and, in exceptional cases, by telephone; and offered meetings with a 'reviewing lawyer' accompanied by a more senior colleague if a further explanation was required, where there were offences involving a death, child abuse, sexual offence, or a racially aggravated offence, a category of heightened importance after the Macpherson report. There would be a piloting of 'CPS direct communication with victims' between

---

[299] 'Bronze' entailed the direct communication of basic information about prosecution decisions by the decision-maker to the victim with the addition of an offer of a face to face meeting in 'certain serious or sensitive cases'; 'silver', the intermediate option, entailed direct communication with the addition of 'clear full explanations' (so far as the interests of justice permit); face to face meetings to explain key decisions involving Victim Support or any person or agency named by the victim plus work with WS; and under the 'advanced level', gold, the CPS became the 'one stop shop' for victims and witnesses once the case began: any information would be provided, including information from another agency, and there would be customer service units using specially trained individuals equipped with a free telephone information line.
[300] Letter of invitation to join steering group to oversee options on direct CPS communication with victims, 4 February 2000.

November 1999 and March 2000; a 'full scoping/options study' between April 2000 and September 2000; an evaluation between October 2000 and December 2000; planning for national implementation in January 2001; and, three months later, in April 2001, national implementation proper.[301]

JVU officials concluded warily that the professed enthusiasm of the welcome extended by the CPS had not been matched by its proposals. Two years after the New Labour manifesto, all that the CPS had achieved was to accept the *Victim's Charter* recommendation in principle but not to implement it because of resource problems. It would have been preferable if the CPS had made an appropriate bid in the last Comprehensive Spending Review round. Home Office Ministers said they doubted the adequacy of the CPS response.

The new CPS options studies encountered difficulties. A meeting of RISC was informed by a CPS official in April 2000 that his colleagues found meeting victims awkward, they had traditionally adopted a neutral role, but the pilots had required that information be provided direct to victims; and victims, in their turn, had not been eager to meet officials and lawyers.[302] 1,177 letters had been sent, forty-seven follow-up enquiries were received and a mere seven meetings had taken place.[303] Despite an earlier news release declaring that the CPS was 'on target' in implementing the recommendations of the Glidewell Report,[304] the pilots were later announced by the CPS on the eve of the 2001 general election to have failed. The *Evening Standard*, a London newspaper, reported 'The initiative was suspended last year when the CPS admitted pilots were a shambles and said lawyers were too concerned for their own safety to meet victims face-to-face.'[305]

The CPS did manage finally to secure the money it had sought from an innovatory budget measure, the so-called 'unallocated

---

[301] That next step had been made possible by the 2000 Comprehensive Spending Review Settlement: HM Treasury, SR2000/Legal, 18 July 2000.

[302] Later, in January 2001 a CPS official told a joint Home Office-Institute of Public Policy Research that 'as lawyers, we're not very good at communicating with lay people who are quite traumatised and don't want to be victims in the first place. There was a reluctance to be involved with the victim at all.'

[303] Based on Victim Support News Service July 2001.

[304] CPS News Release, 18 July 2000.

[305] [London] *Evening Standard*, 16 May 2001.

reserve' of the 2000 Comprehensive Spending Review settlement.[306] I have already explained how the Treasury and Downing Street had taken it upon themselves 'to lead the drive to more effective cross-cutting approaches',[307] and that the unallocated reserve was just such a mechanism to remedy what were seen to be failings in the trilateral management of an ostensibly joined-up criminal justice system—although the handling of policies for victims and witnesses was not thought to be especially deficient. Ian Chisholm reflected at the time, 'the Treasury, Number 10, are dissatisfied with the way the criminal justice trilateral business works and that was why they put us under pressure to come up with agreed priority bids . . . to try and get the criminal justice departments to operate in a more joined-up way . . . whatever one may think, given the system we have, the co-ordinated machinery in victims issues is quite good, I think. Other areas—it's not really there.' £100m., £200m. and £225m. had been allotted over three successive years for extraordinary expenditure within the criminal justice system, the money to be released after the Home Secretary, Attorney General, and Lord Chancellor had approached the Treasury with agreed joint proposals on its use. Any plans should contribute to the 'overarching objectives and targets' of the criminal justice system; and preferably involve two or more departments, although claims with 'cross-CJS implications' could be funded in one department. Amongst the possible objects of reserve spending suggested by the Treasury was the co-ordinated treatment of victims and witnesses, and there were additional signals from Downing Street that the Prime Minister's office wanted a 'package of joined-up work' in the area. The view of Home Office officials was that it might be best to try for 'a quick win' in an early bid on the reserve for just such a package, and proposals were forwarded in the winter of 2000 for the funding of a comprehensive extension of Victim Support's Witness Service into the Magistrates' Court, the implementation of the victim statement scheme and the *Speaking up for Justice* initiative, and other projects, including the CPS execution of the Glidewell and Macpherson recommendations and *Victim's Charter* standard to communicate directly with victims. In the event, the CPS received half of what it had demanded ('a very good settlement' said the Treasury), allowing the so-called bronze

---

[306] See No. 10 Downing Street Newsroom, 19 July 2000.
[307] Cabinet Office; *Wiring it Up*, January 2000, p. 4.

option for victims to go forward at a cost of just over £3m. a year, and the 'national roll-out' of direct communication took place in April 2001.[308]

## The Victim's Charter Pilot Projects and Beyond: Victim Statements

Let me return to the introduction of victim statements, the other Charter standard. That venture was no less troubled, raising what were called in June 1997 'a number of sensitive issues' centred on the statements' possible use in sentencing, and the prospect of victims being cross-examined on what they said. It too was to be the subject of a linked process of testing by Rod Morgan, Andrew Sanders, and colleagues at Bristol University. And the results were again equivocal.

It proved difficult to secure a sample of victims willing to make statements.[309] The Scottish counterpart of the Victims Steering Group was informed in August 1997 that the number of victims coming forward had been small and that there was a relatively low 'take-up'.[310] Two months later, it was noted that of 1,716 cases in six police areas, only 428, or 25 per cent had 'opted-in' to the scheme.[311] Like its twin, the 'One Stop Shop' pilot scheme, the distribution and completion of victim statements seemed to have been subject to an undue exercise of police discretion in an ostensibly non-discretionary project.[312] Problems were compounded because the researchers were also in time to be charged with interviewing the staff of criminal justice agencies and members of the judiciary to ascertain the uses to which statements were put, and there were inevitable time lags between interviews being conducted with victims and their cases arriving before the courts.

---

[308] CPS News Release, 18 July 2000.

[309] Victim's Charter Pilot Projects Working Group: minutes of meeting, 13 February 1997.

[310] Victims' Statement Group: update on Victim's Charter Pilot Projects—August 1997.

[311] In Southwark, for example, only 5% were reported to have 'opted-in' by February 1998. Victim's Charter Pilot Projects Working Group, 5 February 1998—Progress Report 5.

[312] Victim's Charter Pilot Projects Working Group—minutes of meeting, 28 October 1997.

The Victims Steering Group and its offspring, the Victim's Charter Pilot Projects Working Group, were periodically briefed by the Bristol criminologists about progress, and they received but one reiterated message: victims were discontented because the purposes and uses of victim statements were uncertain. In May 1998, for instance, they were told that 90 per cent of the victims in the project did not know what would happen to their statements, and that there was a gap between taking the statement and the case going to court that engendered a need for statements to be 'updated'.[313] In July, two months later, it was made evident again that the purposes of victim statements remained unresolved and needed clarification. Victims had inflated expectations which had to be depressed.[314] In a proposal approved in July 1998 to explore further the agencies' uses of victim statements, Morgan and Sanders reported that it was not known either to researchers or to victims how or to what extent statements had been used in the pilot areas,[315] and that such a lack of clarity made victims dissatisfied with the way in which they were taken; the uses to which they were put or not put; and the absence of communication from the criminal justice system about what had become of them.

In September 1998, the researchers repeated yet again that, although there was a 'reasonable demand' for the scheme and victims valued it, agencies were still unclear about its purpose. There was still no change four months later, the researchers reporting that it had proved difficult to evaluate the project because there had been little information from the criminal justice system about the uses to which victim statements should and had been put. All the victim statements collected were in Crown Prosecution Service files, and the CPS declared that victim statements rarely provided information relevant to their decisions;

[313] Victims Steering Group meeting: extract from minutes of meeting of 22 May 1998: Victim's Charter Pilot Projects.

[314] It was important, reflected a paper to the Working Group, that they be 'free of the burden of decision-making in matters affecting the offender'; and they should not be allowed to influence the decision on whether to prosecute, what pleas to accept, and what sentence to pass. The uses to which the statement could be put included conveying fears about further victimization, refuting malicious mitigation and better informing judges in sentencing and the awarding of compensation. 'Issues of Concern about Victim Statements', PPWG Paper 2/98, July 1998.

[315] R. Morgan and A. Sanders; Study of Agency Responses to VS Pilot Projects: A proposal, 22 July 1998.

did not influence evidential matters; had a very slight influence on CPS decision-making; affected no bail decisions because they arrived too late; and rarely contained relevant material for the presentation of cases.[316]

And so it went on. Of the third of the sample of victims who had given statements, 60 per cent had done so for 'expressive' reasons, 55 per cent had said that they had wanted to influence the case outcome, and 43 per cent had cited 'procedural' reasons, claiming they had a right to make a statement. A majority had experienced their participation as 'satisfactory', but they still had no good idea why they were completing statements.[317] Some had thought that sentencing would be affected although in practice their statements 'rarely influenced sentencing'[318] and there could be subsequent frustration about the absence of an apparent impact.[319] Neither, it transpired, were statements very effective in supporting an expressive role, and there was a subsequent decline, from 77 per cent to 57 per cent, in the victim's belief that the decision to make a statement had been well advised. Practitioners were described as approving the idea of statements in principle, but they were divided about whether they should affect sentencing decisions, and the information they did receive was largely 'irrelevant, exaggerated or unverifiable'.

Again and again, then, the scheme's purposes were represented as undefined;[320] the statements were said to have no effect on

[316] R. Morgan and A. Sanders; 'Interim Report for the Home Office on the uses to which Victim Statements are put', 26 January 1999.

[317] Victim's Charter Pilot Projects Working Group, 9 February 1998, minutes.

[318] C. Hoyle *et al.*; 'The Victim's Charter—An Evaluation of Pilot Projects', Home Office; Research Findings No. 107, 1999.

[319] Victim's Charter Pilot Projects Working Group, minutes of meeting, 11 May 1998.

[320] R. Morgan and A. Sanders; *The Uses of Victim Statements*, Home Office, December 1999, pp. 1, 2. Richard Thew reported to the Victims Steering Group that one of the confusions of the pilot study had been what the victim statements were *for*. My notes of meeting of the Victims Steering Group, 28 April 2000. Helen Reeves claimed that there 'was a danger of [the statement] being [treated as] . . . a sentencing tool, and it's as clear as day that that's what went wrong with the pilots . . . if there's one message, stop thinking this is about adversarial sentencing, it's about how the crime is presented to the victim. Something needs to be put into the guidelines: "please don't expect the VPS to influence the sentence. The purpose of this is to know about you and how the crime has affected your interests".' Victims Steering Group Meeting, 8 December 2000, my notes.

significant decisions;[321] and many victims came to believe that they had been ignored and were disgruntled as a result. The researchers evaluating the pilot were prompted informally to urge that the Home Office should not proceed with the victim statements programme, recommending instead what they called 'two-way communication between victims, police and prosecutors'. But the programme was the outcrop of a long-standing political commitment lodged in public manifestos and charters, and there could be no retreat.[322] It was, the researchers claimed afterwards, not a good example of 'evidence-based policy-making'.

So complex and unresolved had the business of implementing the Charter standards become[323] that it was determined to expose their difficulties—and other problems arising from the recommendations of the Lawrence Report as well—to a special conference on the place of the victim in the criminal justice system held in Macclesfield in September 1999,[324] before deciding whether to proceed to a formal submission to Ministers. A Grade 7 of JVU emailed a colleague in May 1999:

It has yet to be decided what role if any (other than as witnesses), victims should have within the criminal justice system in this country. That is why we have been conducting pilot studies for the last two years to assess the impact and value of 'victim statements' ... The pilots are coming to an end, and a final evaluation report is due ... This seems likely to be inconclusive, and we are planning a special conference in September to discuss some of

---

[321]  R. Morgan and A. Sanders; *Communications between Victims and Criminal Justice Agencies: Evaluating the Victim's Charter Pilot Projects*, undated, no provenance.

[322]  Victim statements figured, for instance, in a policy statement, 'Building a future for all', laid before the Labour Party Conference at Brighton, 24–28 September 2000.

[323]  Helen Reeves said before the conference, 'There is still, I think, a great deal of confusion about what [victim statements] are for and it was my understanding that the Home Office might have a special conference on these next year..., I personally have great difficulty with the victim statement because I can see, I cannot quite see why one's sentencing should be governed by whether one victim chooses to say how badly he suffered as opposed to the other one who didn't and I think it's putting pressure on victims.'

[324]  At the conference in Macclesfield, it was said by the JVU official leading on the subject that victim statements 'on the line of the pilots are not necessarily the right model. They raised expectations which we have not met.'

the very tricky issues which have emerged. Not the least of these is whether the views of victims should be taken into account by the court...

At the conference, one of the researchers, Rod Morgan, distinguished between the instrumental and expressive dimensions of statements, and proposed that any scheme should incorporate ritual and communicative elements so that victims' expressive needs could be met. He was more circumspect about the instrumental uses of the scheme. There was, he said, 'precious little evidence that victims affect decisions'. Judges wanted current intelligence about the impact of crime, particularly physical injury, 'hard' psychological information and employment and financial information, but they were unable to get it. The material in the victim statement was too stale, and Morgan recommended that the taking of statements be staggered over two stages.

The subsequent meeting of the Victims Steering Group in November 1999 agreed to recommend that victim statements be implemented nationally when the preparations were complete (for there was little political choice in the matter), although the precise detail of the scheme was still unresolved, and, as Teresa Reynolds of Victim Support pointed out, a consensus had still not emerged from the conference about the *purpose* of victim statements. The administration of victim statements would probably be built around two stages, one at the taking of the witness statement immediately after the report of the crime, the other before sentence (and here ambiguities and disagreement lingered, because the ACPO representative on the Victims Steering Group wondered whether the second statement might not be read as a sign that the victim would influence sentencing and Victim Support doubted the need for any such statement at all. Some thought it would not be beneficial to victims, others it would form an important part of the sentencing stage, and there were uncertainties about who would take the statement and at what point.[325]). The Chairman explained to the Group that 'at stage one, you've got information that could inform decisions at every point. At stage two, you've got additional information whose primary purpose is to affect sentencing.' Helen Reeves interjected, 'the issue is, who wants it?' And she was then to be told quite firmly that the 'ultimate issue for me is whether Ministers want it as an act of policy'.

[325] Minutes of the meeting of the Victims Steering Group, 24 November 1999.

Officials proceeded to make a submission to Ministers in December in which it was argued that the pilot's 'patchy take-up' could be explained by an initial lack of clarity that had prevented the police from knowing quite what they were supposed to do; that that problem could well be remedied by training the police; and that victim statements themselves could be regarded as a 'modest way of engaging' victims with the criminal justice system. And Ministers responded by saying that they wanted the scheme to be introduced as soon as possible.[326]

In the matter of victim statements, it was imperative to secure the assent of judges, perhaps the most important, and certainly the most independent stakeholders in the criminal justice system. The Lord Chief Justice, on the one hand, and his senior colleagues acting together under the convenorship of Lord Rose, on the other, declared that they welcomed the proposals,[327] but were concerned about their 'more radical elements', and pointed not only to the risks of

---

[326] Victims Steering Group meeting, 28 April 2000: Victim Statements Progress Report.

[327] He had told a Victim Support reception much earlier in April 1996 that '... the principle remains that the prime object of custodial sentences is to punish wrongdoing, not to compensate for its consequences. This does not mean that the consequences of a crime are irrelevant, nor that the victim's interests should in any sense be left out of account in the way crimes are investigated or criminals prosecuted. On the contrary, the experience and concerns of victims are of considerable importance at many stages in the investigation of a crime ... with some offences the effect the crime has had on the victim does constitute an element in determining its seriousness, and therefore is highly relevant to the question of sentence. The Court of Appeal has long accepted that psychological injury, particularly in considering offences such as rape in which the trauma can be long-lasting and debilitating, although the physical injury may not be obvious. The technical question which arises in these cases is how best to feed such evidence into the process ... Victim Support in particular has worked hard on this subject. It has recognised that to expect victims to submit their own account to the court would not only impose a new burden on them, but would also expose them to the risk of cross-examination if the defendant ... wishes to challenge any of its contents. This has to be the case because of the genuine possibility that some victims may exaggerate the effects of the crime. Others may be stoical to the point of doing themselves an injustice. It has also been recognised that the procedure involving so-called "Victim Impact Statements" in which the victim addresses the court and convicted defendant before sentence would—like minimum sentences—be another importation from the American legal system which some of us feel we can do without. On the other hand, I see no reason why an assessment of the impact of the crime should not form a quite normal and regular part of a police investigation, with the material collected forming part of the file for consideration by the Crown Prosecution Service.'

raising unrealistic expectations[328] but also of placing an additional burden on victims who might have to face cross-examination. If victim statements were to be adopted, the Lord Chief Justice said, they should be applied to all crimes, but confined to the immediate victim, and not relatives or onlookers. The format of the trial should not to be distorted by the proposed innovation: a criminal trial had two parties only, prosecution and defence, and the victim was *not* a party (the hearing was, he said with some emphasis, a substitute for private vengeance, and not an expression of it). There had been references in the proposals to victims or their representatives, but victims had no representatives and it was not appropriate to change that position. It was the prosecution's job, not the victim's, to make sure that the gravity of the offence was made known to the court, and any such statement must be served on the defence, leaving the victim open to questioning. Emotionally charged statements should not be put before the Court[329] and particular difficulties were posed by the prospect of statements that were discursive, heated, and voluble, especially if the statement was rejected. What was required instead was a dispassionate and objective account of the effects of crime, and the scheme could proceed with the Lord Chief Justice's approval only if the police would return to the victim at the point of sentence and prepare a second statement in a professionally-composed manner. The senior judges added that problems were posed by victims becoming parties because they might then be entitled to

It was ironic that some newspapers later represented him as being favourably disposed to Victim Impact Statements. For instance, the *Guardian*, 12 April 1996, reported 'Judge says weigh views of victims'—the Lord Chief Justice 'will call for police assessments of a crime's impact on its victims to be put before the judge as part of the prosecution case at sentencing. The move would be a radical departure for the English criminal justice system.' And for similar reports, see *The Times* and the *Daily Telegraph* ('The impact of crime on victims should become an integral part of prosecution cases, Lord Taylor... said yesterday') of 13 April 1996.

[328] Others also signalled what they perceived to be the same risk. See, for instance, I. Edwards; 'Victim Participation in Sentencing: The Problems of Incoherence', *The Howard Journal*, February 2001, Vol. 40, No. 1.

[329] Other senior judges were to be as concerned. For example, Sir Robin Auld, the author of a major review of criminal procedure (announced in the Criminal Courts Review: Press Notice, 14 December 1999), was anxious lest victim statements became part of an unseemly 'public trading' of allegation and counter-allegation between defendant and victim (R. Auld; 'Rights of Victims of Crime', Indo-British Legal Forum, 25 June–1 July 2000).

disclosure, an especially awkward matter where the victim was also an offender as might well happen in drugs cases.[330] There was the problem too that a proliferation of victims with multiple defendants, all making statements, would make trials unmanageable. The Macclesfield conference, it was concluded, had suggested that 'we treat our victims well and it would be a mistake to implant alien practices developed elsewhere in minor jurisdictions'.[331]

The victim statements scheme did finally become a two-step process,[332] just as the Lord Chief Justice and Rod Morgan had recommended, both parts taking the form of written reports. The first would take place at the evidential statement stage that was organized by the police, and it would deal with matters such as bail, compensation, problems of vulnerability, medical and psychological damage, and the victim's willingness to take part in restorative justice. The police would be allowed to give general advice, but they must 'not lead in a way that might prejudice a trial'. The second statement would be made at a later stage when the long-term impact of an offence might be better known, and it was to be completed in a 'free standing manner' and in whatever form the victim might wish. It was also to be made clear to victims that a statement would constitute only a part of the evidence available; that the court would be unlikely to take into account any opinion about sentence; and that statements would be disclosed to the defence (and thus, possibly, the defendant himself) and other criminal justice agencies, and it was impossible to say what use, if any, would be made of them. Neither could victims be given 'direct feedback' about the effect of what they had said.

There had been an earlier indecision about who would count as a victim for the purposes of the scheme. It had been announced that it would be aimed at what were called 'discernible victims', but proposals now embraced the families of homicide victims,[333] and,

[330]  And, dramatically, in the case of Tony Martin, a man convicted in April 2000 of killing Fred Barras, a burglar with multiple convictions, whose family sought compensation. See Tony Martin Support Group web site. It was reported in September 1999 that travellers had 'placed a £50,000 bounty on Tony Martin's head' (Eastern Daily Press web site). See Chapter 8 for a more detailed discussion of the Tony Martin case.

[331]  The allusion was to the paper given by Brienen and Hoegen which claimed that victims fared relatively well in the English and Welsh criminal justice system.

[332]  Agreed at a meeting of the Victim Statement Working Group, 27 March 2000. What follows is based on Victim Statement Scheme (3rd draft), 14 April 2000.

[333]  Justice for Victims, SAMM, and Victim Support had all decried their initial omission, and their protest had been widely reported in the press.

significantly, they were being tentatively extended towards the victims of road traffic crashes, a marginal category who would repeatedly test the boundaries of recognition. In a paper submitted to what was now called the Victim Personal Statement Scheme Working Group in November 2000, it was noted that many cases of 'road traffic accidents' are victimless, where there is a victim, the consequences can be severe or mild; and being a road traffic accident victim was not same as being a crime victim (although some are crime victims).[334] Yet road crash victims were also to be added in time, perhaps as an indirect result of their increasingly effective representation by organizations such as RoadPeace.[335] The final definition of the eligible victim encompassed 'all practicable categories of offences'[336] (again, just as the Lord Chief Justice had recommended), including:

[any] person subjected to the criminal actions of another, where the crime is an offence for which the prosecuting authority is the Crown Prosecution Service. In the case of road traffic matters...the definition...will be limited to someone involved in an incident resulting in death or serious injury...The term 'victim' includes bereaved relatives or partners in cases of homicide or serious sexual or physical assault. It also incorporates parents, where the primary victim is a child...a victim must be a discernible individual rather than a large company or business. However, it may include a sole proprietor or partners in a small business...[337]

The national launch of the victim statements scheme was long delayed. Originally intended to take place in April 1997, it had not been appreciated how long it would take to start the pilot projects or how few cases they would generate.[338] There had been difficulties of resource (occasioned by an 'unfavourable' settlement in the 2000

---

[334] There had been 564,135 accident victims in 1998; 332,571 cases in Magistrates' Courts; and 600 proceedings for motoring offences causing death or bodily harm.

[335] According to its web site, 'RoadPeace, Britain's charity for all road traffic victims, was set up in 1992 to represent and support this huge neglected victim group.... RoadPeace exists to represent the interests of bereaved and injured road crash victims, to help and support them and work to stop the injustices suffered by them.'

[336] Victim Statement Working Group: Victim Statements: The Next Steps, 17 February 2000.

[337] Annex C: The Victim Personal Statement Scheme, 20 November 2000.

[338] Victim's Charter Pilot Projects Working Group: minutes of meeting, 13 February 1997.

Comprehensive Spending Review[339]) and of allaying the anxieties of the Lord Chancellor's Department, the Attorney General's Department, the Lord Chief Justice, and senior judges. Legal advice had had to be taken about the propriety of informing victims under data protection provisions.[340] But the scheme was inaugurated finally on 1 October 2001, at a cost of £4.6m.[341] and presaged by a practice direction from the Lord Chief Justice.[342] It was described as 'victim led, optional and dependent on what the victim wishes to say'. It was 'not primarily a sentencing tool . . . [or] a victim *impact* statement as understood in some other common law jurisdictions (e.g. the USA). But nonetheless . . . it could prove helpful to magistrates and judges.'[343]

## Conclusions

What lessons can be derived from this opening episode? First, the formal position of victims and witnesses in the criminal justice system had undoubtedly undergone the beginnings of a transformation: they were no longer as shadowy as before, no longer to be described in the language of the victims' movement as the 'forgotten party' of the criminal justice system. As Ian Chisholm observed in June 2000, 'unless they are also witnesses, victims have no formal involvement in court proceedings (although the introduction of victim personal statements from April 2001, might be considered a first step towards changing this)'. Their route to attaining a presence may have been serpentine and unspectacular, but they could no longer be so readily ignored.

Second is the rather laboured point that initiatives for supporting victims may have stemmed from different organizations and ideologies, aimed at alleviating distress as well as reducing crime, but they were also powerfully filtered in this particular episode by a market ideology that had been applied very widely and most certainly not just at the victim. Victims as consumer-citizens were but minor

---

[339] Victims Steering Group meeting, 8 December 2000, Chairman's brief—Victim Statements.
[340] Victims Steering Group: meeting of 12 June 2001.
[341] Home Office News Release, 26 February 2001.
[342] *The Victim Personal Statement Scheme: Guidance Note for Practitioners or those Operating the Scheme*, Home Office, August 2001.
[343] Home Office Circular 35/2001 14 August 2001, emphasis in the original.

figures in a larger mass of citizen-consumers of public services undergoing radical reform in the 1990s and early 2000s. Yet their new colouration did impart certain qualities: it focused on an economistic model, and images of victims became starker and simpler, tinged with the logic of rational choice theory; it emphasized the need to quantify performance, and victims became responsible for supplying units of measurement; it attended to the quality of services, and victims became service-recipients; and it stressed the importance of informing and being informed, and victims were supposedly more knowing and informative in their use of markets abstractly conceived. In all this, the victim was being constructed by the mechanics of performance management rather than emerging spontaneously, as it were, with his or her own unsullied demands.

Third, it is apparent that absolute limits were imposed on the licence extended to would-be reformers and victims. The boundaries of the victim's role and identity were closely patrolled by lawyers, judges, and those responsible for mounting trials who were ever mindful of the precarious equilibrium of the criminal hearing and of their duty to preserve the defendant's rights in particular. 'Joined-up government' housed significant checks and balances that restrained any significant lurches of direction favourable to the victim. If concessions were to be made, it would always be in a context set by notions of 'balance' and an 'equality of arms'. Victims were not permitted to play any part in major decisions affecting the defendant or the conduct of the trial, and they could not influence sentencing, for that was the business of the State, not the private citizen. There was an unqualified ban on the victim speaking in his or her own voice in court lest emotionality, improper considerations and private interest disrupt the decorum and bearing of a courtroom working for what was defined as the public good. The victim's position had been contested throughout, unresolved even when the second *Victim's Charter* was launched in 1996 and its two offspring were announced in 2000 and 2001.[344] Howevermuch Home Office

---

[344] For example, the Prime Minister was quoted as saying in the press release accompanying the launch of victim statements that 'a victim's statement made in open Court... [would] be taken into account by the Judge when sentencing decisions are made'. Home Office Press Release, 293/2000, 26 September 2000. Comments made by Lord Bassam, a Home Office Parliamentary Secretary, on the day of the launch only amplified the impression that victim statements were to be sentencing tools.

Ministers and officials may on occasion have wished otherwise, victims could not be parties in criminal procedure.

Fourth, that denial of formal recognition, particularly in matters concerning the suspect's and defendant's rights to privacy, seemed at one point to threaten the very existence of Victim Support and more than once impeded attempts to inform victims about important developments in the investigation of crime and in criminal proceedings. For a while, it served as such an obstacle that Home Office officials and politicians thought it could be removed only by legislation transforming the victim into a party with enforceable rights. By that time anyway, in 2000, some of those selfsame officials and politicians had come actively to seek ways of endowing victims with more solid rights, their quest emerging dialectically out of their sustained experience of work in the area, and the difficulties posed by privacy could be cited as part of an environment that they themselves were enacting. That they eventually hit upon an easier resolution of the dilemma cannot diminish the significance of the fact that statutory rights for victims had been quite seriously broached within Government. A possible future had been there constructed.

Fifth, time and again, professions of support for the greater emancipation of the victim were not necessarily matched by practical work in the criminal justice system. There was certainly a rhetoric of victims' rights loosely conceived but there was also a protracted failure to act by, say, a Crown Prosecution Service which had long maintained its symbolic and functional distance from victims viewed as volatile, needy, and compromising. There may have been a welter of other reforms with which the CPS had to contend at the time, and structural inertia probably played a part. But so did professional self-preservation. If the staff of the Crown Prosecution Service were to be seen as the disinterested servants of the criminal courts, victims threatened to erode their neutrality and composure. Victims have long tended to be worrying figures in the legal practitioner's imagination,[345] and they were usually best

---

[345] Consider the remarks of Geoffrey Bindman, the prominent solicitor associated with the law and practice of human rights legislation: 'Mr Straw is right to try to improve remedies for victims but, other than as a witness of fact, the victim has no proper voice at the trial of the alleged perpetrator. To give the victim a role in deciding innocence or guilt would flout our notion of impartial and independent justice... Within the criminal process itself the victim or the family may be able to contribute

avoided. Proposals to bring victims and prosecutors into more intimate relation were not wholly welcome.

Sixth, it is clear that who was or was not to be recognized as a victim in the unfolding of the One Stop Shop and victim statements projects was set in considerable measure by an organizational pragmatism. When the evaluation conducted by the group from the University of Bristol was at risk of faltering because of paltry numbers, the categories of eligible victims were expanded. When those who were affected at first or second hand by road crashes were first mooted as candidate victims, it was the availability of resources that was the prime (but not the sole) determinant of their acceptance. Those who were treated as victims were defined in some substantial measure by the practical purposes and financial means of the institutions that had dealings with them. With hindsight, that is not perhaps a very remarkable observation, but it may not always be readily apparent to the outsider who has not examined these things closely.

Seventh, the 'information-based organisations' and 'evidence-based policy-making' of the criminal justice system had to contend with the exigencies of political imperatives that were established well before any research or information was forthcoming. Informing victims and allowing victims to inform criminal justice services are, I would claim, clearly commendable policies, but the pilots did not offer unequivocal support to what was proposed, and there seemed to be little practical way in which they could affect an apparently inexorable political drive to implementation. To be sure, they did provide cautionary material that could guide future action, but they were eclipsed always by commitments that could not be disowned.

Last, it is evident that policy-making is a contingent and emergent process whose strands are ever exposed to possibilities of collision or convergence with other developments that could never originally have been foreseen and may not even have been targeted at victims of crime. Initiatives were liable to veer off in novel directions or be abruptly terminated or reinforced. In a busy political environment, the two new *Victim's Charter* standards were frequently jostled by

something to the sentencing process by providing information which will assist the judge. To this extent, a "victim personal statement" may be of value. Beyond that, sympathy for the victim cannot in modern days detract from the state's responsibility to ensure the independence and impartiality of the justice system.' 'Remedies for the Victim', *Guardian*, 13 September 2000.

legislation affecting rights to privacy and the protection of data; the effort to construct 'joined-up government', the ambition of the New Labour administration to equip the Crown Prosecution Service with new responsibilities, and the massive wash of the politics of race attending the Macpherson Inquiry. In the next chapter, I will turn to a different, albeit wispier, incarnation of the victim that was borne along by one of those other strands, the passage of the Human Rights Act of 1998.

# 5

# The Victim and Human Rights

## Bringing Rights Back Home[1]

On 9 November 1998, the United Kingdom Government belatedly enacted the Human Rights Act, a truncated version of the European Convention on Human Rights that had been promulgated by the Council of Europe. An earlier United Kingdom Government had substantially drafted the Convention and ratified it in 1951, but it had not really been taken by the domestic courts to have much application to England and Wales.[2] The European Convention, in its turn, had been based substantially on the 1948 United Nations Universal Declaration of Human Rights, which the United Kingdom had been the first State to adopt, although again its representatives had not imagined that it would have major repercussions for the internal affairs of their own country, and British judges had tended to treat it as if it were 'an external system like public international law'.[3] Neither had Government officials or members of non-governmental organizations for victims given it much thought. A policy official working in Victim Support declared in July 1998 that 'I have to confess—I mean this is a confession—I tend probably to be

---

[1] A phrase that was part of the currency of New Labour at the time. Jenny Watson, formerly of Liberty and Charter 88, claimed that the slogan, 'bringing rights home', was unfortunate 'because it's made people think that it's something that came from Europe, and that we were then bringing it, you know, bringing it here. Whereas in fact it was the British Civil Service that wrote [the European Convention] and . . . the aim of it was to make sure that what happened in '39 to '45 couldn't happen again because there would be some kind of international mechanism and a court to stop it.'

[2] See L. Scarman; *The Protection of Human Rights in the United Kingdom*, 1976 Cobden Trust Human Rights Day Lecture, Cobden Trust, London, 1977, p. 5.

[3] M. Zander; 'The Human Rights Act 1998: The New Law', mimeo, 1999, p. 8.

parochial in my ambit, I tend not to go beyond these shores a great deal in my focus'.

The Human Rights Act would enable United Kingdom subjects to claim their rights through United Kingdom judges in United Kingdom courts instead of having to exhaust domestic remedies before proceeding to the European Commission of Human Rights and the European Court in Strasbourg. The Act was not to come into effect until late in the period covered by this book, but, throughout the years of the first New Labour administration, its impending but oft deferred implementation impinged directly or indirectly on almost all planning,[4] and it was inevitable that it came obliquely but materially to affect the course of policies for victims.[5] Possibly critical would be Articles 2, affirming the right to life; 3, the prohibition of torture, defined as inhuman or degrading treatment or punishment; 5, the right to liberty and security of the person; 6, the right to due process and a fair trial, relating to those charged, and to matters of defence; and 8, the right to respect for private and family life, the home and correspondence, with exemptions that included the prevention of disorder or crime, or the protection of the rights and freedoms of others.[6] As important, perhaps, the Act was intended by the Government to lend authority to a renewed discourse of rights and citizenship which had hitherto been somewhat alien to the British constitution. It was defined by New Labour as 'a living instrument capable of promoting a culture of human rights to transform public administration'.[7] The Home Secretary, one of the promoters of the Act, said that 'the language of the Convention will be the language in which many of the key debates are settled',[8] and that language would necessarily

---

[4] For example, every Department of State was required to nominate a 'Human Rights contact point' to channel and co-ordinate human rights within and between departments. And ACPO set up a team both to spread information about the new Act and to promote 'best practice' in police forces in England and Wales. Each force was obliged to nominate what was called a 'human rights champion'. *Human Rights News*, July 1999.

[5] See A. Ashworth; 'Sentencing and the Human Rights Act', *Justice of the Peace*, Vol. 163, 23 January 1999, pp. 64–6.

[6] The Human Rights Act 1998, c. 42.

[7] D. Faulkner; *Crime, State and Citizen*, Waterside Press, Winchester, 2001, p. 40.

[8] Jack Straw; 'Building a Human Rights Culture', Address to Civil Service College seminar, 9 December 1999.

embrace the victim of everyday crime as well as others who were more clearly in focus.[9]

As a result of what Kate Malleson called 'an unholy alliance between the Left and the Right',[10] it had taken nearly fifty years for the United Kingdom Government to adopt the Convention domestically, the political Right insisting that common law was the best system imaginable and that 'the convention was something for foreigners' which would only 'fetter' Parliament[11] and politicize the judiciary;[12] and the Left having a faith in its own integrity when in office, and a suspicion of the political inclinations of the judiciary[13] and of the possible domination of the legislation by commercial interests.[14] In the 1960s and 1970s, however, a number of Conservatives began to see in human rights legislation a buttress against what they took to be an overbearing socialist State, just as they were later to be joined by Labour politicians and others who took such an Act to be a buttress against an apparently overweening, radical Conservative Government of unusual longevity.[15] Proposals were to be championed by liberal lawyers such as Anthony Lester,[16] Lord Scarman,[17]

---

[9] John Wadham of Liberty remarked that 'I think the difficulty with the Human Rights Act is that it affects so many different categories of people, so many different subject areas.'

[10] Kate Malleson, speaking at the London School of Economics, 15 March 2000.

[11] See Lord Hailsham in *The Times*, 16 May 1975.

[12] Lord Denning for example argued in 1976 that the reputation of the judiciary would be in jeopardy if they adjudicated on human rights law.

[13] See, for example, J. Griffith; *The Politics of the Judiciary*, Fontana, London, 1977. The book was to go into five editions, the last being published in 1997.

[14] I am grateful to John Wadham of Liberty for two of these points.

[15] Jack Straw said 'Those 18 years of Conservative government were marked by a sustained accumulation of power in Whitehall and its executive arms. Local democracy was systematically undermined ... In recent years, the Democratic Audit has documented this centralising drift in government ... As government in its widest sense became detached and distant, so people's sense of ownership on the services it provided declined. Holding institutions and individuals to account became ever more difficult. It was because of this that we were committed to a profound change [in the way] our country was governed ...'. 'Home Secretary's speaking at Charter 88, 26 November 1998.

[16] See his *Democracy and Individual Rights*, Fabian Tract No. 390, Fabian Society, London, 1968.

[17] Michael Zander claimed it was Lord Scarman's 1974 Hamlyn Lectures, *English Law—The New Dimension*, amplified, because of its focus (on p. 18) on abuses of rights in Northern Ireland, by being relayed in a front page leading story in the *Guardian* newspaper, that revived political interest in an Act, see his *A Bill of Rights?*, *op. cit.*, p. vii. Zander said 'it was his statement that if there had been a bill of rights in

and Michael Zander,[18] whose case seemed to be strengthened by an embarrassing increase in the number of United Kingdom cases being taken to the European Court of Human Rights at Strasbourg for adjudication;[19] a succession of scandals arising from miscarriages of justice in the trials of alleged Irish terrorist defendants[20] and others[21]

Northern Ireland, maybe the IRA would not have felt it necessary to take up terrorism. And that really started the campaign for a Bill of Rights. At that time it was only, I mean what he was talking about was Northern Ireland but it very quickly got translated into the rest of the UK.' Elsewhere, Lord Scarman argued that under the European Communities Act 1972, it might be that the European Convention without further enactment by the British Parliament could become part of the English law. It would, he said, afford a limited opportunity for the individual to seek redress. L. Scarman; *English Law—The New Dimension,* Stevens and Sons, London, 1974, p. 13.

[18] For a more complete account of this history, see M. Zander; *A Bill of Rights?,* Sweet and Maxwell, London, 1997 (4th edition). Parts of this section borrows from that work.

[19] In 1986, Lord Scarman observed, the citizens of the United Kingdom faced grave difficulties in seeking redress: they were obliged first to seek a remedy inside the United Kingdom; if they were unsuccessful, they had to petition the Commission for Human Rights in Strasbourg; and, if they were successful, they might then bring their case before the European Court itself. 205 cases arising within the 13 contracting States were dealt with by the European Court at Strasbourg between 1953 and 1984: 57 violations were established, of which 18, or nearly a third, stemmed from the United Kingdom. By 1996, Malleson reported, the United Kingdom had been found to be in breach 37 times, near the top of offending states. In 1995, the United Nations Human Rights Committee declared that the British legal system did not 'fully ensure that an effective remedy is provided for all violations of the rights contained in the Covenant'. Kate Malleson; 'A British Bill of Rights—Incorporating the European Convention on Human Rights', in Paul Howe and Peter Russell (eds.); *Judicial Power and Canadian Democracy* (McGill Queen's University Press, 1999, p. 3). See also M. Hunt; *Using Human Rights Law in English Courts,* Hart Publishing, London, 1997, App. 1; and A. Smith; 'The Human Rights Act 1998 (1)', *Criminal Law Review,* April 1999, p. 251.

[20] Such as the case of the 'Birmingham Six', the men convicted of bombing offences in August 1975 and released on appeal in 1991, described by the Criminal Cases Review Commission as 'having raised serious issues of concern to all'. Criminal Cases Review Commission web site.

[21] Such as the 'Bridgewater Four' who were convicted in 1978 for murder and then released on appeal 20 years later. Particularly significant had been the convictions obtained by the West Midlands Serious Crime Squad which were systematically overthrown, sometimes decades later, in the 1980s and 1990s. Lord Rose, sitting in the Appeal Court, said in one case (reported in the *Guardian,* 27 October 1999), that it was 'yet another appeal arising from the lamentable history of the now disbanded West Midlands serious crime squad... [during the 1980s] a significant number of police officers in that squad, some of whom rose to very senior rank, behaved outra-

in the 1970s; the appointment of a number of liberal judges, themselves favourable to a Human Rights Act,[22] and whose senior colleagues, particularly in the House of Lords, appeared at times to be the only effective constitutional restraint on an ebullient Conservative Government under Mrs Thatcher;[23] and the centripetal drift of the Labour Party.

There was in the interim to be a scatter of legislation conferring piecemeal rights: anti-discrimination legislation that bestowed positive rights in 1968, 1975, and 1976, for instance; and an acceptance in 1966 of the right of individual petition to the European Convention.[24] In 1975, a Labour Party sub-committee prepared a paper urging the adoption of the European Convention in law as a Charter of Human Rights. In 1988, a non-governmental organization, the Constitutional Reform Centre, re-invented itself as Charter 88 with a principal object of championing a Bill of Rights; and three years later another such organization, Liberty, issued a consultation document, *A People's Charter: Liberty's Bill of Rights,* proposing the incorporation of the European Convention and other human rights covenants and conventions as a first move towards a new regime of positive rights in the United Kingdom.[25] Human rights had become

geously, and in particular extracted confessions by grossly improper means, amounting in some cases to torture . . . During the 1990s it has been the melancholy task of this court to examine the safety of many convictions recorded during that period—and approximately 30 have been quashed.'

[22] See Michael Beloff's foreword to R. Singh; *The Future of Human Rights in the United Kingdom: Essays on Law and Practice,* Hart Publishing, Oxford, 1997. There were those in the criminal justice system in the late 1990s who declared their surprise at the absence of judicial opposition to the Human Rights Act. Zander remarked that 'There was just a mood change as occasionally occurs and it was greatly influenced by the attitude of the senior judiciary which in turn was greatly influenced by the work of a very small number of people of whom, I suppose, Anthony Lester was by far the most important.'

[23] Kate Malleson called them 'one of the few sources of effective opposition to government' in the 1980s. 'Creating a Culture of Human Rights in the UK: The Implications of the Human Rights Act 1998', unpublished, undated, p. 1.

[24] I am grateful to Lord Lester for showing me a proof copy of an unnamed book making this point.

[25] Jenny Watson, who had worked both in Liberty and in Charter 88 during this period, recalled that 'what we did over the last three years was to start saying that bringing the European Convention of Human Rights into British law could be the first step on the road to a fuller bill of rights which might also look at social and economic rights, but certainly for the first half, you know, that convention although it's in some ways a bit outdated, is a good first step'.

222 Constructing Victims' Rights

what Ignatieff nicely called the 'semi-official ideology of the Western world',[26] and New Labour was to be one of its bearers.

In March 1993, John Smith,[27] the new leader of the Labour Party in opposition and a man disposed towards wide constitutional change,[28] delivered a lecture under the *aegis* of Charter 88 on 'A Citizen's Democracy' in which he urged a shift in the balance of power between citizen and State, and claimed that the most ready method of recognizing human rights was to incorporate the European Convention. It was, said Zander, a turning point,[29] committing the Labour Party to act when it came to power, and it was confirmed six months later in *A new agenda for democracy: Labour's proposals for constitutional reform,* and then again in 1995, when the Labour Party formally adopted the principle that it would legislate to import the European Convention.

Tony Blair, John Smith's successor as leader of the opposition, publicly committed himself to retaining that principle in his 1996 John Smith Memorial Lecture and it was subsequently inserted in the party's 1997 election manifesto.[30] Within a few months of entering office, in October 1997, what had been a Labour Party policy paper, *Bringing Rights Home,* produced by Jack Straw

[26] M. Ignatieff; *Empire Lite,* Vintage, London, 2003, p. 20.

[27] John Smith, MP for Monklands East (formerly North Lanarkshire) since 1970, was elected leader of the Labour Party in July 1992 and he died less than two years later, in May 1994, to be succeeded by Tony Blair. He introduced a broad programme of constitutional reform, including Scottish and Welsh devolution and a 'one-man, one-vote' system within the Labour Party.

[28] John Wadham of Liberty, a campaigner at the time for an Act, recollected that the critical event had been the change in the structure of the Labour Party. I mean we nearly persuaded [Roy] Hattersley [caretaker leader of the Party] but once John Smith took over, he had a different approach to the constitution in general and it was much easier for us to persuade... we were the most influential NGO but how influential we were in relation to other... I mean, you know, the Lord Chancellor says he persuaded John Smith on this matter... And we worked very closely, not just then, but we had seminars with the current Lord Chancellor and the Home Secretary and Paul Boateng and others about how it might work... And the reason I know that we had an influence is because you can read the text that Liberty submitted in the '92 policy papers in the Labour Party's own papers in 1996.'

[29] M. Zander; 'The Human Rights Act 1998: The New Law', *op. cit.,* p. 2.

[30] It was highly unlikely, thought John Greenway, a Conservative front bench Member of Parliament in 1999, that the Conservatives would have introduced a Human Rights Act had they been returned to power in 1997. This was one of the instances where the 1997 election had a critical impact on the development of policies for victims.

and Paul Boateng, became the substance of a White Paper, *Rights Brought Home,* Cm. 3782, and legislation was introduced in the House of Lords.

Responsibility for the preparation and implementation of the Act was allotted broadly to the Cabinet Office as part of its responsibility for constitutional matters, and to the Home Office as lead department responsible for legislation.[31] The Home Secretary announced in May 1999 that the Act would come into force on 2 October 2000. After that date, it would be 'illegal to carry out public functions in a way that is incompatible with a Convention right',[32] and all existing and impending legislation,[33] election commitments, criminal procedure,[34] and practical activity[35] were to be scrutinized across the entire criminal justice system[36] and elsewhere[37] for their

[31] And again, some time later, to the Lord Chancellor's Department *The Times,* 19 June 2001. *The Times* observed that it was as if the Lord Chancellor was becoming a Minister of Justice.

[32] Private Sector Public Sector Human Rights for All, The Human Rights Act 1998, Home Office Human Rights web site; and Human Rights Task Force: HRA—Communications Strategy—Public Authorities, HRTF (99) 2, January 1999.

[33] Every new draft Bill was required to be accompanied by a statement of compliance signed by the Secretary of State of the department forwarding it for consideration by Cabinet. Home Office news release, 25 November 1998, 463/98. Paul Boateng was to say about the Crime and Disorder Act 1998 that 'Throughout the consultation and Parliamentary stages . . . the impact of human rights was high on the agenda. We were determined to ensure that the measures we introduced not only complied with the Convention rights set out in the Human Rights Act, but actively supported them.' Draft Speech, 'The Human Rights Act and its Implications for Children', 26 January 1999.

[34] See Criminal Courts Review: Press Notice, 14 December 1999.

[35] See, for example, *ACPO Guide to Identifying and Combating Hate Crime,* Metropolitan Police, London, December 1999; and Home Office HOC 19/2000: Domestic Violence: Revised Circular to the Police, 12 May 2000.

[36] Ian Chisholm, head of a unit responsible for criminal procedure as well as for the treatment of victims, reported in July 2000 that there had been an examination of the likely impact of the implementation of the Act across the whole criminal justice system, with particular relevance of Articles 5, 6 and 7 to criminal procedure and 3, 8 and 9–11 to substantive criminal law. Minutes of the Human Rights Task Force 15th Meeting, 27 July 2000.

[37] The Permanent Under-Secretary at the Home Office wrote to all his counterparts in other departments on 27 November 1998 to say that each department would be obliged to assess the likely impact of the Act on legislation and procedure, identify the public authorities for which they were responsible and alert them to the requirements of the Act, submit an initial report by 31 January 1999, and then report at six-monthly intervals thereafter until the Act was implemented.

compatibility with the new Act.[38] Even the virtually unchallengeable recommendations of the Macpherson Inquiry Report were to be questioned under the Act.[39] Committees were obliged to ensure that any new policy proposals were 'human rights proof' or 'HRA-compliant',[40] and lawyers with a competence in human rights legislation were sometimes drafted to provide guidance (as was Kate Akester of JUSTICE who became a member of the working group founded to superintend plans for what would become the Youth Justice and Criminal Evidence Bill). A Human Rights Task Force was established at the end of 1998 with the object of maintaining 'dialogue between the Government and non-governmental organisations on the readiness of departments, other public authorities and the legal profession for implementation of the Human Rights Act ... provide training opportunities for public authorities outside government [and] to co-operate with other organisations in disseminating awareness ... '.[41]

There was within Government a running reference to the Act and constant modifications of policy proposals in its shadow throughout the 1990s and early 2000s, and the JVU, in turn, scanned all its existing and future commitments. One instance was the Interdepartmental Vulnerable or Intimidated Witnesses Working Group being supplied with a list of European Court judgments that might have a bearing on their work.[42] The Group was reminded, for instance, of

---

[38] *A Guide to the Criminal Justice System in England and Wales*, Home Office, London, 2000, p. 6.

[39] There was, for example, scrutiny, under Article 8, of his recommendation that the use of racist language in private should become a criminal offence. See Labour Party web site July 2000: National Policy Forum Report 1999: Crime and Justice.

[40] For example, Criminal Justice Consultative Council: Race Sub-Group, minutes of meeting of 15 July 1999; the Working Group on Vulnerable or Intimidated Witnesses Provisional Recommendations, December 1997, which explored the bearing of Article 6 on the possibility of holding certain cases *in camera*.

[41] Human Rights Task Force, Terms of reference and method of working, HRTF (99) 1.

[42] Recommendations about the hearsay rules, for instance, were curtailed by the Law Commission in the light of the Act. And there was some debate about whether the group's recommendation prohibiting defendants from personally cross-examining complainants in trials involving certain classes of offence would be a violation of Article 6, the right to a fair trial. The advice of the Criminal Bar Association Working Party Report on Cross-Examination of Rape Victims by the Accused in Person, 1998, citing *X v. Austria, Croissant v. Germany,* and *X v. United Kingdom,* was that that right was not absolute. JUSTICE and Peter Duffy confirmed that opinion, although

the case of *Van Mechelen and others v. Netherlands* 1997 in which it was alleged that there had been a violation of the rights of defendants who had been convicted in 1989 on the evidence of anonymous police officers who had not been heard in the presence of the defence (it was ruled that there had been a breach but that the police were exceptional and that they should be allowed to be anonymous in very special circumstances.) It was reminded too about the similar case of *X v. United Kingdom* that stemmed from the trial of an Irishman convicted of the murder of two British soldiers in Belfast: screens had been used to shield witnesses, and it was submitted that they had interfered with his right to confront his accusers. The European Court found the application ill-founded because it was not necessary that a statement from a witness should always be made in court and in public, and that the applicant had been able to put all the questions he wanted. The use of screens, it declared, had not interfered with his rights.

Eight new High Court judges were appointed in anticipation of a ballooning of court business when the Act came into effect, raising their number to 106, and a major programme of training advocates,[43] officials,[44] and judges[45] was delivered in substantial

---

some senior judges in correspondence with the working party dissented. In the event, the provision was to be challenged in the courts: see *The Scotsman*, 18 February 1999.

[43] JUSTICE annual report for 1998, p. 9.

[44] Keith Vaz, MP, Parliamentary Secretary at the Lord Chancellor's Department, in his presentation to the Human Rights Task Force, 27 July 1999, talked about attendance at seminars on human rights matters run by JUSTICE, Liberty and the Institute for Public Policy Research, for instance. Training for officials was described by *The Times* as the most ambitious ever undertaken (*The Times*, 26 October 1998). 4,000 Home Office staff alone were trained (Home Office *Annual Report*, 2000–2001, p. 60). Ministers of the Lord Chancellor's Department made a progress through the Magistrates' Courts between September and November 2000 to broadcast the significance of the Act. There were 'walk throughs' and 'dry runs' organized by the Lord Chancellor's Department in the Magistrates' Courts and the Crown Court to rehearse possible difficulties and discuss hypothetical cases.

[45] It was said in 1999 to be the largest training programme in the history of the Judicial Studies Board, 3,000 judges attending a one-day training seminar at a cost of some £6m. 32,000 magistrates also received training at the same time. Magistrates had been a little slow to respond to the Act. The Magistrates' Courts were not courts of record and they were waiting for a steer in training guidelines from the Judicial Studies Board and from appeal cases. When new legislation is passed, observed Brenda Large of the Association, there is often a flurry of new cases to determine the significance of the Act.

measure by the lawyers who had had an interest and competence in what used to be called civil liberties and were now called human rights, the more radical lawyers to be found in JUSTICE,[46] Liberty (the former National Council for Civil Liberties), and the Doughty Street Chambers of such barristers as Ben Emmerson. Quite new ways of conceiving law and judging[47] were to be instilled.[48] Emmerson reflected:

The funny thing about this is that it's not really training in that way you would have with most legislation ... this is much more conceptual and it's about leaving some of your common law baggage behind ... It's difficult for all criminal lawyers. They're very much inclined to say 'well, it doesn't say this in the text of the Convention, where do you get that from?' I mean, for example, this whole doctrine of positive obligations requires a conceptual understanding of the object of the Convention which is to seek a practical and effective protection of people's rights in a way which regards a text as the starting point rather than as the finishing point. And so you do find common lawyers of really quite a great deal of experience and seniority are [perusing] it as if it were a statute. In other words reading it and seeing what the rights say, whereas in fact the only rule you can say with any certainty about the Convention is that the rights don't mean what they say.

Politicians and officials had some feeling of wonderment at the scale and implications of what they were doing: it was a reform of very considerable importance symbolically, constitutionally, and procedurally;[49] a 'move from form to a concern with substance';[50] 'a cornerstone of our work to modernise the constitution ... one of the most important pieces of constitutional legislation ... a major step change in the creation of a culture of rights and responsibilities

[46] JUSTICE *annual report for 1998*, p. 5.

[47] See K. Malleson; *The New Judiciary: The Effects of Expansionism and Activism*, Ashgate, Brookfield, Vermont, 1998, p. 3.

[48] Lord Browne-Wilkinson talked about 'a very, very big change ... Up until now, English law has been a wholly unprincipled operation. You look for a case and ask has this been done before and what were the reasons for it ... Now for the first time we are having to move to having a wide statement of principles and having to work from that.' *The Times*, 18 October 1999.

[49] The Human Rights Task Force called it 'one of the most significant pieces of constitutional legislation ever enacted in the United Kingdom.' Draft Core Guidance for Public Authorities, April 1999.

[50] Attributed to the Lord Chancellor, JUSTICE *annual report for 1998*, p. 4.

in our society';[51] and, reflected the Home Secretary, the most important piece of legislation enacted since the Bill of Rights three hundred years ago.[52] It would install for the first time a 'more explicitly moral approach'[53] and a conception of positive rights. Advocacy and judging would no longer be case-driven but affected by interpretations of the original intent of the lawgiver and a moving political and social context, no longer a static but a contingent process. Sir Quentin Thomas, then head of the Constitution Secretariat at the Cabinet Office, stated 'this Act will initiate a process...which cannot be fully foreseen in its nature. It will be evolutionary...'. And Ben Emmerson remarked 'the notion of human rights law, and what makes it such a vibrant area in which to work, is that it is what they call a living instrument, a moving body of water as they sometimes describe it, which is susceptible to the currents and changing times of public opinion and so, as standards change in society, so does the interpretation, which gives them a terribly flexible approach'.

So important were the politics of human rights taken to be by the incoming administration that they were the topic chosen by New Labour's Home Affairs Team for a training weekend in Oxford prior to the 1997 general election. Alun Michael recalled 'like other teams we were asked to choose one element of our programme and to spend time during that period, beforehand and [at] that weekend, actually looking at implementation which we did with the ex-civil servants and other experts. And the Home Office Team's choice was the incorporation of the European Convention on Human Rights.'

There could be no assurance about the future ramifications of the Act when it was at last applied, but they would undoubtedly be deep and diffuse (an official of the Lord Chancellor's Department observed at the September 1999 Home Office conference on the standing of the victim in criminal proceedings 'I seem to be obsessed with the Human Rights Act. I would be reluctant to change the current system [of the victim] without a steer from the decisions coming out of the Human Rights Act post-October 2000.'). *The Times*

[51] The words are attributed to the Home Secretary. *Human Rights News*, July 1999.
[52] Foreword by Jack Straw to J. Wadham and H. Mountfield; *Blackstone's Guide to the Human Rights Act 1998*, Blackstone Press, London, 1999, p. ix.
[53] Lord Irvine, 'The Development of Human Rights in Britain under an Incorporated Convention on Human Rights', *Public Law*, Summer 1998, p. 236.

conjectured that 'the vast majority of relevant institutions have no idea about what is likely to hit them' and that there would be '[a]n explosion of litigation at all levels'.[54] Writing to Ian Chisholm, an official of the Home Office-based Human Rights Task Force remarked of Ben Emmerson's proof chapter on the Act in a forth-coming edition of *Archbold*, the advocates' manual, 'The evidence and procedure stuff is rather alarming.'

There was accompanying trepidation within the Home Office, a Department that had had in the past 'comparatively large exposure to Strasbourg'. 'We face', reflected John Halliday at the time, 'a situation of considerable uncertainty.' British judges had begun ruling in anticipation of the Act before its formal implementation,[55] and the very first case brought even before it had formally come into effect was disconcerting, stirring premonitions about possible diffi-culties to come. In *Kebilene and others*,[56] the detention of four Algerians summarily detained in 1999 under the Prevention of Ter-rorism Act was declared unlawful under Article 6 which prescribed rights to a fair trial with its constitutive presumption of innocence. One issue was whether the Act could be applied retroactively before October 2000, but Lord Steyn ruled that trial and appeal were parts of a single process. Officials were advised that there were *dicta* in *Kebilene* that appeared to assume that the Human Rights Act would have full retrospective effect. In any trial taking place before 2 October 2000 and appealed after that date, the accused could never-theless bring proceedings based on a breach of his convention rights which occurred before 2 October 2000. There was said to be 'con-siderable and overwhelming Home Office concern about the impli-cations of *Kebilene* for the Human Rights Act'. 'The floodgates might be opened.'

The direst predictions,[57] based chiefly on officials' reading of the Canadian experience of the introduction of the 1982 Charter of

---

[54] *The Times*, 26 October 1998.

[55] R. Auld; 'Investigation and Surveillance', The Human Rights Act and the Crim-inal Justice and Regulatory Process, University of Cambridge, 9–10 January 1999.

[56] *R v. Director of Public Prosecutions, Ex parte Kebilene*, 28 October 1999.

[57] An official of JVU talked in June 2000 not only about the Human Rights Act, but also about the complementary rights vested in the promised Freedom of Information Act and the Data Protection Act. There are 'all sorts of conflicting issues which we're having, which are actually maybe mutually reconcilable, well, at least, well they can't because you've got to make 'em, you've got to reconcile them somehow. But *prima*

Rights and Freedoms[58] (the 'worst case scenario' it was called in February 1998), suggested at different times and somewhat inconsistently that there would be a curtailment of police powers (including their powers of covert surveillance) that would bring about a decline in successful prosecutions; a dramatic increase in the number of cases[59] (the Court Services were preparing for a 15 per cent increase in business because lawyers were expected to invoke the Convention wherever possible) and the effects of the Narey reforms on speeding up justice would thereby be compromised;[60] the problem that more appeals and pending cases under the 'fast-tracking procedure' might lead to indefinite adjournments and cases 'stacking-up';[61] extra police costs entailed by additional escort duties;[62] a lengthening of cases; a substantial rise in the legal aid bill;[63] more successful applications for bail, even from defendants

*facie* they're mutually reconcilable... we are no longer the arbiter or the final word on all these things, whereas we may have been before we passed the Human Rights Act.'

[58] Enacted as Schedule B to the *Canada Act 1982* (UK) 1982, c. 11, which came into force on April 17, 1982. 'If the Canadian experience is anything to go by, the only people likely to gain from the Human Rights Act will be lawyers and the judiciary. Judy Fudge, Associate Professor of Law at York University in Toronto, says the main effect of the 1982 Canadian Charter has been a massive transfer of power to judges and a substantial increase in work for lawyers.' A. Clarke; 'Lawyers and judges gain from the Act', *The Times,* 3 October 2000. Amanda Finlay of the Lord Chancellor's Department was reported to have said that the New Zealand and Canadian experience suggested that in the first two years of implementation there would be a considerable increase in the number of appeals and challenges in criminal cases, and cases would take more time because of arguments on rights. Much work would be needed for implementation (*TIG Update* 9, August 1998).

[59] Centred, it was thought, on such matters as the disclosure regime, admissibility of hearsay evidence, the right to silence, bail provisions (under the right to liberty), invasions of privacy, restrictions on right to bail, and possible failures to protect life or the welfare of children. Also see *Transforming the Crown Court: consultation document: The emerging proposals,* Court Service, September 1999, p. 9.

[60] The Government, reflected an official in September 1998, seemed to have been involved in three incompatible enterprises: speedier justice, the prompt implementation of the Human Rights Act which might clog up the courts; and tight Comprehensive Spending Review expenditure constraints.

[61] Minutes of Human Rights Act second Trilateral meeting, 7 March 2000.

[62] Human Rights Bill: Business Planning Exercise, Notes of 1st meeting of Steering Group, 4 August 1998.

[63] It was said that, following the precedents set in New Zealand and Canada, the most expensive and obvious impact of new human rights legislation would be felt in the first five years after the Act came into effect. Report of the Interdepartmental

charged with serious offences;[64] a congestion of the prisons as delays mounted (an additional 2,000 prisoners were predicted); submissions from prisoners about their conditions of confinement;[65] and successful challenges that might 'paralyse' legislation and procedures. October 2000 itself would offer a 'field day for crackpots, a pain in the neck for judges and a gold mine for lawyers',[66] predicted Lord McCluskey, the Scottish appeal court judge.[67] The 'courts will become overrun once lawyers start advising people to make claims which fly in the face of commonsense' said Ann Widdecombe, the Shadow Home Secretary, in 2000.[68] Foreseeing a vast increase in litigation and consequent expense, based in part on figures of appeals, legal aid applications, and prison population projections supplied by other departments, one Home Office official wrote to a colleague in early 1998 that it was 'all pretty appalling, and [there was a need to] propose a range of options for containing the cost as much as possible'. Her senior colleagues were more inclined to scepticism and suggested that such alarm should be taken with a 'pinch of salt': if the figures were accepted, they said, it was difficult to see how the policies could be afforded, but other departments had run similar 'scare stories' in the past about the cost of new ventures centred on the Home Office and they had been proved wrong. After all, the Convention had been observed in England and Wales for fifty years and major changes were unlikely.[69]

Working Group—Human Rights Bill: Cost Implications for the Criminal Justice System, January 1998.

[64]  *The Times*, 14 December 1999.

[65]  BBC News On-Line, 12 September 2000 reported that 'The Prison Reform Trust pressure group claims the Prison Service is likely to face "hundreds" of court battles under the Human Rights Act which becomes law in England and Wales from 2 October...'.

[66]  'How Euro Law will Change your Life', *Sunday Times*, 6 August 2000. David Pannick QC, adviser to the Home Office, retorted 'the Court of Appeal has made it very clear that it will take a tough line with litigants, and lawyers, who take unrealistic points... All the rights guaranteed under the Convention are a familiar part of the common law. And potential victims have long been entitled to bring a claim before the [ECHR] in Strasbourg. With rare exceptions, English law has withstood the scrutiny of the European Court' (*The Times*, 3 October 2000).

[67]  Lord McCluskey served as Solicitor General from 1974 to 1979. He was Chairman of the John Smith Memorial Trust, a patron of the Scottish Refugee Council, and vice-chairman of the Human Rights Institute of the International Bar Association.

[68]  Conservative Party Conference 2000, October web site.

[69]  Home Office; Human Rights Act: Preparing for Implementation, 29 June 2000.

There were delays in implementation flowing from the gargantuan labour of training officials and judges; scrutinizing existing and forthcoming legislation, election commitments, policies, and procedures; and, it was alleged, the Prime Minister's own ambivalence about an Act he had inherited from his predecessor. But there were also political pressures to implement the legislation rapidly, particularly in Northern Ireland, where it could play a part in the 'peace process' after the Good Friday settlement of April 1998, and thus, by extension to the rest of the United Kingdom for consistency's sake. No special financial provision had been made for implementation, costed vaguely at £150m. over three years, and officials cast about them for ways of saving money, including curtailing legal aid and a new Mode of Trial Bill[70] that would restrict the right to a jury trial in 'triable either way' cases ('the only initiative with the potential to produce significant savings against which to offset the costs of the HRA').

In the event, instead of '[t]he surge of new cases [that] will begin within weeks of the introduction of the controversial [legislation]',[71] the Human Rights Act made only a modest impact on its introduction.[72] The absolute number of cases coming before the Crown Court actually declined.[73] Francesca Klug observed that '[a]lthough voices in some quarters predicted that the Act would cause chaos in UK courts, no such result in fact materialized. Indeed, it appears that the Act has been successfully pleaded much less often than was anticipated in the months before its coming into effect.'[74] In the first three months after implementation, there were 168 occasions on which human rights issues were raised in the Crown Court, less than 0.5 per cent of all Crown Court cases; and in the Court of Appeal Criminal Division, 277 out of 2,491 cases, or 11 per

---

[70] In the event, the Bill was rejected decisively by the House of Lords, and was not revived during the period covered by this history. See *Evening Standard*, 21 November 2000, and *The Times*, 21 January 2000.

[71] *Sunday Times*, 1 October 2000.

[72] Victim Support Information October 2001: Human Rights Act: update 2, remarked that the Act's implementation in October 2000 had not led to the disruption of court processes that had been anticipated. 167 cases were decided in the higher courts but most would probably have gone to court without the Act.

[73] *Evening Standard*, 22 January 2001.

[74] F. Klug *et al.*; 'Briefing: Year One of the Human Rights Act 1998', HRA Research Project, undated.

cent, contained human rights points.[75] Four cases involving victims were reported to have arisen in the first year: in *R v. A* (which I shall discuss in Chapter 8), the House of Lords emphasized that the rights of victims of rape were to be balanced against the alleged perpetrator's right to a fair trial; in a case centred on the use of closed circuit television links in the youth courts, victims of crime and witnesses were held to possess the right to give evidence in the least stressful way possible, so long as the rights of the accused were respected; in a case involving the Shipman inquiry,[76] originally intended by the Department of Health to be held *in camera*, the decision was that it must be heard in public, because closed proceedings would have breached the victims' families' rights to freedom of expression and their right to receive information;[77] and Duwayne Brooks, the friend of Stephen Lawrence and witness to his death was given leave by the Court of Appeal, citing *Osman*, to sue the police for the way in which he had been treated.

## Human Rights and the Commonplace Victim

The European Convention's conception of victims had been framed in the immediate aftermath of the Second World War, 'when memories of Nazi oppression and inhumanity were fresh',[78] and it was designed expressly to protect European populations from the crimes against humanity of the kind inflicted by totalitarian States in the 1930s and 1940s.[79] It was, said *The Economist*, 'a generation old, Hitler aftermath definition of civil liberties'.[80] The perpetrator of

[75] Lord Chancellor's Department; Human Rights: Impact on the Courts, Human Rights Act 1998: a statistical update, http://www.lcd.gov.uk/humanrights/hrimpact.htm.

[76] Victim Support News Service, October 2000, Human Rights Act: update 1. Harold Shipman, a lone general practitioner, was convicted on 31 January 2000 of 15 murders, and of forging a will. The subsequent judicial inquiry, to which the families of his patients and victims were at first denied access, determined at the end of July 2002 that he had murdered 215 of his patients, and could have killed 250.

[77] F. Klug *et al.*; 'Briefing: Year One of the Human Rights Act 1998', HRA Research Project, undated, p. 3.

[78] L. Scarman; *Human Rights: Can they be protected without a written constitution?*, Eileen Illtyd David Lecture, University College of Swansea, 6 March 1986, p. 1.

[79] See Lord Irvine, 'The Development of Human Rights in Britain under an Incorporated Convention on Human Rights', *Public Law*, Summer 1998, pp. 221–36.

[80] *The Economist*, 21 February 1976.

abuse was the State,[81] the victim a man or woman abused by the State[82] and, in what the Convention regarded as the relatively peripheral context of criminal procedure,[83] he or she was the defendant. John Wadham of Liberty explained in September 1999 that that emphasis flowed not only from the Convention's original framing of the State as perpetrator, but there was also a presumption in legal doctrine that the victim proper needed no Convention rights because protection was already axiomatically built into 'the substance of the heart of the State' as the policing and prosecuting authority. It was the defendant who was vulnerable to the improper use of power: 'the Convention is generally seen to be an issue for defendants' rights in the criminal justice system. In relation to victims, it's a kind of secondary thing . . . it is directed for, towards, defendants in general.'

In common with a number of other similar human rights instruments,[84] then, the Convention and the Act had not been framed directly to protect the rights of the victims of everyday offences, the robberies, burglaries, thefts, and assaults committed by citizen on citizen, other than as citizens at large. Textbooks on human rights law often omitted any reference to them.[85] Michael Zander, a considerable authority on criminal procedure who later trained solicitors and others on the new Act,[86] told me flatly in May 1999:

---

[81] Thus the question asked by Lord Scarman of human rights legislation was how can we use our constitution to establish legal safeguards which will protect basic rights and freedoms against an irresponsible, negligent or tyrannical legislature? L. Scarman; *Human Rights: Can they be protected without a written constitution?*, Eileen Illtyd David Lecture, University College of Swansea, 6 March 1986.

[82] Rather tautologically, a victim was defined under the Act by the Home Office as 'A victim is a person whose case could be heard by the Strasbourg Court. This includes companies as well as individuals and it may also include relatives of the victim where a complaint is made about the death of the victim.' The Human Rights Act 1998: Guidance for Departments, Home Office, 1999.

[83] Andrew Ashworth argued that the Convention had not been drafted with criminal proceedings in mind. See his *The Criminal Process: an evaluative study*. Second edition, Oxford University Press, 1998, p. 49.

[84] In Canada, for instance, where no reference is made to mundane victims of crime in the news releases and other publications associated with the Canadian Human Rights Commission and the Charter of Rights and Freedoms, 1982.

[85] For example, P. Sieghart (ed.); *Human Rights in the United Kingdom*, Pinter Publishers, London, 1988; J. Wadham and H. Mountfield; *Blackstone's Guide to the Human Rights Act 1998*, Blackstone Press, London, 1999.

[86] He conducted for, instance, a Human Rights Training Course, in March 1999, organized by the Legal Workshop in association with 'regional and local law societies'.

I've never seen any discussion of the question of victims of crime...
I haven't thought about the problem of victims and whether there's anything in the Bill of Rights, in the Human Rights Act, for victims and if so,
what... Victims will have difficulty in establishing any basis on which they
can proceed... you've got to be a victim of a breach of the Convention in
order to bring a proceedings, of course, but... you're not a victim of a
breach of the Convention by virtue of being a victim of crime unless the
crime is committed by the State or someone in the State... Is there any
potential interest for victims of crime? I would say at this point, no one's
probably even thought about it or virtually never even thought about it,
I would guess.

When, in July 1998, there were discussions about establishing a
task force to 'look at ECHR implementation', the Home Secretary
decided that non-governmental organizations should be included,
but no organizations representing mundane victims were invited
to join.[87] And other commentaries and papers tended to follow
suit and elided the victim.[88] Thus a report by the Human Rights
Task Force on the 'very wide' repercussions of Article 6, the right to a
fair trial, made no mention of victims at all.[89] An inventory of initial
departmental responses on the implementation of the Act requested
by the Home Office Permanent Secretary in November 1998 included an entry from the Home Office itself, but there was no
reference in its long list to commonplace victims other than elliptical

---

[87] The membership consisted, *inter alia*, of Ministers from the Home Office,
Lord Chancellor's Department and Solicitor General; members of the Bar; officials
from the Home Office (but not JVU), the Cabinet Office, Lord Chancellor's Department and Crown Prosecution Service; the Local Government Association; and non-
governmental organizations such as JUSTICE, Liberty, the Institute of Public Policy
Research, the 1990 Trust (founded in 1990 'to promote good race relations by
endeavouring to eliminate discrimination on the grounds of race and encouraging
equality of opportunity between persons of different racial groups'), and the Human
Rights Incorporation Project (established by King's College, University of London, in
1997, and including Francesca Klug, to 'provide research on an appropriate model for
incorporating the European Convention on Human Rights into UK law'). (Minutes of
the meeting of 28 January 1999.)

[88] See, for instance, C. Dyer; 'Bringing home the basics', *Guardian*, 12 November
1998. It was argued in a paper on human rights presented to the Auld review by
Professor John Jackson that there had hitherto been two themes, the protection of the
victim against ill-treatment at the hands of law enforcement authorities and
the protection of individuals against arbitrary arrest, detention, trial, or punishment.
John Jackson; 'Human Rights Issues for the Auld review', 26 June 2000.

[89] *Human Rights News*, Issue 2, November 1999.

allusions to 'mental health review tribunals, mentally disordered offenders... [and] anonymous witnesses'.[90] There were fears in Victim Support that, in Teresa Reynold's words of September 1999, 'Most people are looking at it from the offender's stance, no one from the victim's stance.'

'How can we have got it so wrong that people believe that human rights law extends only to defendants and prisoners and not to victims of crime?' asked Francesca Klug. Yet the victim and witness in criminal proceedings had not been entirely forgotten. A Grade 7 of JVU did remind the Victims Steering Group in April 2000 that the Act 'affects everything we do'. And Home Office officials and politicians sometimes made studied references to victims lest it be thought that the new Act was unbalanced and would benefit only defendants and offenders,[91] an impression that was not politically to be encouraged. Perhaps with the parallel progress of policy-making for vulnerable and intimidated witnesses in mind,[92] seeking to avoid appearing to favour malefactors only, and anxious to emphasize the notion of proportionality which was key to the politics of the responsibilized citizen,[93] the Home Secretary told *The Times* on 12 September 2000 that the Act would not merely be a charter for prisoners and defendants: 'It is about the rights of victims and the wider community.' An official of JVU subsequently commented that Jack Straw had not been briefed on the matter and had been wrong to say that there were clear victims' rights in the Human Rights Act, but the Home Secretary had felt obliged to 'counterbalance the talk

[90] Human Rights Task Force; Preparing for Implementation: Initial Departmental Responses, HRTF (99) 6.

[91] For example, a policy paper noted that the 'HRA... is seen to benefit the offender'. JVU; 'Review of the Victim's Charter/Victims' Rights', September 2000.

[92] The Criminal Policy Group presentation to the Human Rights Task Force, 27 July 2000, made one reference to victims and witnesses in its review of the impact of the Act on criminal procedure, and that was to Article 3 and the personal cross-examination by defendants of witnesses.

[93] In a speech delivered at the Capita Conference on Human Rights in September 1999, Mike O'Brien, a Home Office Minister, said '...the Human Rights Act... is very much about balancing rights against each other.... That thread runs right through the Convention. Nearly all the individual rights come with a detailed statement of the rights of the state which may limit the exercise of the individual right... What we are looking at here is rights and responsibilities going together, hand in hand.'

about offenders' and prisoners' rights' which was then current.[94] And that was to be significant indeed.[95] Not only had the deliberations about the provision of information to the victim under the *Victim's Charter* standards made it appear that Article 8 protected the offender's interests against those of the victim, a problem which, as we have already seen, triggered speculation about the need to legislate for compensating victims' rights, but it was disquieting that a lack of victims' rights was also seemingly at stake in the Human Rights Act considered much more generally. Without those rights, JVU was beginning to argue in the wake of the Home Secretary's pronouncement in Autumn 2000, the standing of victims was uncertain indeed. Victims' rights were beginning to acquire animation and form.

## Speculation About the Impact of the Human Rights Act

Kate Malleson said that the Act had been 'very cleverly drafted' to allay the fears of those who would defend parliamentary sovereignty against the judges.[96] A unique solution had been propounded: the courts would be obliged to interpret legislation as far as possible in the context of the European Convention and require all public authorities, including the courts[97] (and, by extension, the courts' conduct of trials) to act compatibly with convention rights; and, if they could not do so, they would issue what was called a declaration of incompatibility in the expectation that Government would amend it. Five steps were to be involved in making such a declaration: was a convention right at issue; had there been an interference with that

[94] See, for instance, *The Times*, 12 September 2000, which predicted that 'Prisoners will make a battery of legal demands under the Human Rights Act ... A report today by the Prison Reform Trust warns the Prison Service that it is in danger of violating every right under the new legislation.'

[95] As was the very similar comment that the Act 'gives a greater role for victims rights' made in a speech by Ross Cranston, then Solicitor General, at the Victim Support Annual General Meeting in November 2000.

[96] Lord Lester wrote to *The Times* of 21 August 2000 to argue that the Act did not empower the courts to strike down incompatible legislation but left it to the Government to decide.

[97] Courts and tribunals at every level would be affected by the Act, not just the Court of Appeal but also the Magistrates' Courts and County Courts. Moreover they would be subject to the HRA not only as adjudicating but also as public authorities. (Keith Vaz, MP, Parliamentary Secretary at the Lord Chancellor's Department, presentation to the Human Rights Task Force, 27 July 1999).

right; if there had been an interference, was it lawful; was it for a legitimate aim; and was it proportionate?[98] 'You only lose those rights which are necessary for the preservation of others in the community', observed Francesca Klug.[99]

That last step was vital to the politics of victims, because the proportionality test applied to defendants was one of the few portals through which commonplace victims' interests could enter.[100] Government departments, it was said in August 1998, would need to be familiar with ideas touching on the equality of arms[101] and proportionality. A number of the core rights vested in the European Convention were not absolute[102] but balanced the rights of individual against other public interests, including those of other parties affected by a ruling.[103] John Wadham of Liberty put it that proportionality permitted 'victims . . . in relation to Article 6 and the

[98] Based on Dianne Luping (Liberty); The Human Rights Act: 'Rights of Victims of Crime', Victim Support Conference, 6 July 2000.

[99] Delivering a seminar at the London School of Economics, 17 May 2001.

[100] It is important that, in response to criticism that the new Act would give greater licence to offenders, the Home Secretary announced 'But we shall also be getting across that rights always flow from responsibilities, a human rights culture is a one-way street—victims' rights as well as defendants, for example.' Home Office news release, 9 November 1998, 444/98. Jenny Watson of Victim Support, and once of Liberty and Charter 88, remarked of Jack Straw's position, 'the whole point of human rights legislation is that it's a balancing act. And so it's right that you should be able to put human rights, put victims of crime, put the case of victims of crime within the human rights framework because . . . there are two sides to it. And I think that's really what he was saying that you know it enables you to have a sense of balance.'

[101] The idea was introduced in *Neumeister v Austria* (1968) and it required that there be a fair balance between the opportunities afforded the parties involved in litigation. A defence witness should be examined under the same conditions as a witness for the prosecution. J. Wadham and H. Mountfield; *Blackstone's Guide to the Human Rights Act 1998*, Blackstone Press, London, 1999, p. 79.

[102] 'Absolute rights cannot be derogated from. They are the right to life, to protection from torture, inhuman and degrading treatment and punishment . . . and protection from retrospective criminal penalties. Other rights, such as the right to liberty and right to a fair trial, can be limited under explicit and finite circumstances defined in the Convention itself. Qualified rights include the right to respect for private and family life, the right to freedom of expression, religion and association, the right to the peaceful possession of property . . . ' (The Human Rights Act 1998: Guidance for Departments, Home Office, 1999). An official of the Home Office Human Rights Unit said that the 'case law will establish how things develop. The Act will emerge with court decisions. One right does not have precedence over another, it's a question of checks and balances.'

[103] *Rights Brought Home: The Human Rights Bill*, Cm. 3782, October 1997, p. 5.

Convention and the right of defendants, [to] have a kind of collateral attack . . . it's not that the text of the European Convention is enough to help you make those decisions, it's actually what do the judges think'. But for all the flexibility of interpretation, the doctrine of proportionality and the possibility of collateral attack, victims of mundane crime could enter the Convention's orbit only with some difficulty: not expressly covered by the legislation, certainly ceded few absolute rights,[104] they were not even empowered to submit a counterpart of an American class action to contest their position.[105] Despite remonstrations from Helen Reeves (and others) to the Home Secretary[106] and the Victims Steering Group,[107] it was only the immediate personal victim of a breach who had the right to petition,[108] and everyday victims had no such direct rights because they were not thus personally affected, were not parties to proceedings and had no *locus standi*.[109] Victim Support's own role was to be

---

[104] That would have been expensive to attempt and impossible to deliver. No State has the capacity to guarantee the protection of its citizens against crime. Robert Latham, a member of the Doughty Street Chambers, and Chairman of the Victim Support National Council, commented 'it would be quite inappropriate to suggest that the State has an unqualified duty either to protect victims of crime or to compensate them when it fails in that duty. The answer is that an absolute duty cannot be imposed upon the State.' Comments on a draft paper on victims' rights written by myself.

[105] Although some organizations were mobilizing themselves to take an interventionist stance there was, for instance, JUSTICE's Third Party Intervention Project which was, in the words of Kate Akester, going to 'alert us to anything they think we may be interested in to intervene in and then we'll be taking a sort of human rights perspective'.

[106] In May 1998, particularly, when the Bill was being drafted. The matter, officials declared, had been debated, and amendments were defeated in the House of Lords by 71 to 46. The Home Office case rested on an isomorphism between the new Act and the Strasbourg procedures which had been incorporated. Victim Support would be able to provide assistance through *amicus* briefs.

[107] She protested 'there isn't a remedy at all in this country!' Ian Chisholm replied, 'It all comes down to the problem that the victim has no status in the proceedings.' Meeting of the Victims Steering Group, 12 June 2001, my notes.

[108] Cases could be brought only by victims of a breach. Interest groups were unable to bring actions direct unless they met the victims test, but they would be able to assist those who are direct victims. Home Office: Human Rights Act: Frequently Asked Questions, 9 October 2000. Organizations such as Victim Support, Liberty, and JUSTICE were thus obliged to play only an ancillary role in any action touching on victims of crime.

[109] J. Wadham and J. Arkinstall; 'Rights of victims of crime', *New Law Journal*, Vol. 150, 6944, 14 July 2000, p. 1084. Many conventional victims were unlikely,

confined solely to acting in judicial review proceedings or as an adviser from the wings,[110] and it was moved to recommend a closer link between victim and the Crown Prosecution Service, representing the State as one such party, in consequence.[111]

The Act incorporated most of the provisions of the European Convention apart from Article 13, which conferred a right to an effective remedy (and that had been excluded because the Act was itself deemed to be a remedy[112]). And no Human Rights Commission[113] was envisaged although many other jurisdictions, including those studied in drafting the new legislation, incorporated a Commission to police abuses, review progress, and advise

it was thought by officers of Victim Support, to litigate even if they did have standing, and Victim Support itself, as we have seen, had not in the past fought cases on behalf of victims. Rowan Hardy of Victim Support reflected, 'I think we were concerned that people who were or had been victims of crime might be particularly vulnerable and not able to take an action on their own, in which case it would be helpful if organisations, not just Victim Support, but other organisations could bring actions. But given our situation, I think in reality we certainly haven't got the money to bring actions at the moment, and whether we ever would have enough money...'.

[110] Jenny Watson reflected that 'the voluntary sector hasn't been given standing within the Bill to take a case. So, whereas with judicial review, we would have standing to take a case on behalf of a group of victims, we don't have within the Human Rights Act. And that was one of the things that...we were trying to get overturned. We only have standing if we are supporting an individual victim as an individual party to a case...So I'm sure that there will be a time when we will be looking at it and saying "well, how does the human rights impact on for example on privacy and certainly now it's there". When we argue for the rights of victims and witnesses we will use human rights arguments where they are applicable. I think there's no doubt about that. I think it's probably a little early to say whether it'll be a springboard to lots of other things at the moment.'

[111] Victim Support: 'The role of the victim in criminal justice', 18 July 2000. Andrew Ashworth argued that 'Whereas it will be for the accused's legal representatives to question the compatibility of offence definitions with the Convention, it will fall to the prosecution to draw attention to respects in which the interests of victims or potential victims ought to receive protection from the court (e.g. the right to life, the right not to be subjected to inhuman or degrading treatment, etc.).' A. Ashworth; 'The European Convention and Criminal Law', The Human Rights Act and the Criminal Justice and Regulatory Process, University of Cambridge, 9–10 January 1999.

[112] J. Wadham and H. Mountfield; *Blackstone's Guide to the Human Rights Act 1998*, Blackstone Press, London, 1999, p. xiv.

[113] In 2003, however, the founding of an omnibus rights commission was announced that would cover responsibility for the Human Rights Act.

Government.[114] The Government may have claimed that 'everyone will ... be able to claim their rights' when the Act came into force,[115] but the victims of conventional crime seemed singularly disadvantaged.[116] It would take time before any gains became evident, and they could arrive only in oblique fashion. Sir Louis Blom-Cooper, the barrister and former President of Victim Support, reflected in May 1999:

What I would simply say is that in the long term and indirectly, I think, there will be a very marked impact. But if you're saying that in the year 2000, in the first year of the next millennium, we're going to see the impact of the Human Rights Act on victims' rights, I think the answer's 'no, we won't'. They'll be much more indirect and they'll be much more long term ... when the courts start dealing with the question of fair trial, I think the victim may very well play a role in there. I mean it may be the courts will start saying that the fairness is not only to the accused, it's fairness to the prosecution and it's fairness to the wider community and particularly those who are, who have been, hurt by the criminal act.

At the outset, as a JVU official observed, there was 'an awful lot going on and it [was] very difficult to keep on top of it'[117] The date of the Act's implementation remained unsettled for some time.[118] There could not as yet be United Kingdom case law to guide practitioners and policy-makers,[119] the meaning of the law was still 'emerging' and the critical doctrine of proportionality would be refined anew (although it was not itself new[120]) with the application

---

[114] See Charter 88: Parliamentary Briefing: Incorporation of the European Convention on Human Rights, undated.

[115] Home Office news release: Government to 'bring rights home', 12 July 2000.

[116] See J. Wadham and J. Arkinstall; 'Rights of victims of crime', *New Law Journal*, Vol. 150, 6944, 14 July 2000, p. 1084.

[117] Victim Support Conference: My notes on workshop on human rights, 6 July 2000.

[118] The absence of a firm date at the beginning occasioned what was called 'serious concern' amongst members of the Human Rights Task Force (minutes of third meeting, 20 April 1999).

[119] Victims Steering Group Meeting, 8 December 2000, my notes.

[120] Lord Williams, the Home Office Minister responsible for human rights during the first administration, reminded me that weighing the interests of victim and offender had long been practised: 'that's not a new balancing difficulty. I mean we have to do that when we let people out on license who are doing mandatory life sentences. You know ... every submission that comes in has a paragraph that says, Victim Support, *Victim's Charter* issues. And so before people are let out on mandatory life sentences, the victims are contacted.'

of local criteria in the English and Welsh courts;[121] there was not even a clear definition in the Act of a public authority;[122] and some would argue that the institution that was critical to the Act, the State, and its constitutive founding charters and practices, was itself hazy and problematic in the law of the United Kingdom.[123]

In the midst of so much doubt, JVU decided just before the Act came into force that its 'line... [might be] to wait and see'.[124] Human Rights litigation centred on victims was, in John Wadham's phrase, 'a potential green field site for... imaginative and creative human rights lawyers', but, he added, 'I don't think anybody has sat down and said "let's look for cases to improve the position".' Indeed, the Minister, Charles Clarke, invited Victim Support to sponsor test cases to impart greater clarity to the area of victims' rights under the Act.[125] In practice, as we have seen, that organization was not equipped or allowed to litigate, and it had refrained from funding litigation in individual cases on principle in the past,[126] but a number of its staff were beginning to waver as the Act began to loom. Rowan Hardy, who had prepared a paper on human rights as a policy officer within Victim Support, said in 1999: 'I don't think our policy is that developed as yet. We're sort of, we haven't got that far as deciding, yes, that's what we would do. I mean I'm sure that we would want to

---

[121] 'Given the weight accorded to national procedures in the Strasbourg jurisprudence, and the acknowledged relativism of much of the ECHR, it seems that an English court should properly decide the issue of fairness [under Article 6] for itself.' Lord Justice Buxton; 'The Convention and the English Law of Criminal Evidence', The Human Rights Act and the Criminal Justice and Regulatory Process, University of Cambridge, 9–10 January 1999.

[122] *Conventional Behaviour: Questions about the Human Rights Act*, HRTF (99) 5 revised.

[123] Sunkin and Payne argued that 'England is unusual within western Europe in forming a "stateless society", a society which lacks a State tradition... The fact [is] that there has been no permanent rupture which has brought us the paraphernalia of modern settlements—written constitutions, documents proclaiming the fundamental principles of the political order and the like...', M. Sunkin and S. Payne; *The Nature of the Crown: A Legal and Political Analysis*, Oxford University Press, 1999, p. 43.

[124] Working Group Meeting—Likely Issues, September 2000.

[125] *VSM*, Victim Support Magazine, No. 76, Autumn 2000, p. 5.

[126] A position to be challenged by the solicitor, Robin Makin, in December 1999 who sought assistance in litigating in the case of *T and V v. United Kingdom*, a case I discuss at the end of the chapter. The position of Victim Support was that it neither gave financial help in individual court cases nor supported the right of victims to state an opinion about mode of trial or sentence.

enter, support cases, testing out the boundaries [to see] what protection would be for victims and witnesses, but how much of an active role we can take in that at the moment, is very much dependent on resources and time and money.'

A meeting was held in April 1999 between Victim Support officers and Jonathan Cooper, a human rights lawyer based in JUSTICE, to probe some of those opportunities. The officers sought guidance about what kind of resource the new Act might be and how it would bear on matters such as disclosure to victims and the right to protection, but it was advised only equivocally and tentatively that 'some say that its implications are going to be very wide-ranging and broad, and then I've heard other people say that it's actually going to have little effect. I think it's impossible to know... there has to be some way that you can get, at least [to] challenge a court decision, I mean to be able to pursue an action in the courts...'.[127] The future was indeterminate indeed.

All that uncertainty about the possible shape of the impact (if any) of the Act on victims of crime,[128] induced a number of organizations such as the Criminal Injuries Appeal Panel[129] and Victim Support[130] first to ask questions and take stock and then closely to inspect the workings of the Act over time[131] (including the Act's implications for their own practices as public authorities[132]). But there had been

[127] Transcript of my tape recording of the meeting.

[128] Kate Akester of JUSTICE reflected in May 1999 that 'we don't know how it's going to work out. I mean there are certain areas which you can put a pretty strong bet on there's going to be areas of activity and I certainly think that lifers is going to be one of them and all their problems. It doesn't affect victims so much maybe.'

[129] Its Chairman wrote to Ian Chisholm in October 1999 soliciting advice about the safety of its procedures under Article 6.

[130] Victim Support 1999 *Annual Report*, p. 8. Victim Support called upon its members to relay information to National Office about any developments they encountered, including the indirect consequences of challenges, in the implementation of the Act (Victim Support Information June 2000: The Human Rights Act 1998).

[131] Victim Support: Work Plan 2000–2001—strategic policy unit—key objectives. Victim Support sensed that the Act might comprehensively open up possibilities of rights for victims (minutes of Victim Support annual general meeting, 10 November 1999).

[132] Meeting of Victim Support Trustees, 20 October 2000, New Victim Policies. Those Articles conceived to be most promising were summarized for its members, including the application of Articles 2, 3, 5, 6, and 8 which offered the right to life and security, protection from oppressive treatment in the courts, benefits for victims under

almost no domestic cases, many of the European cases were quite recent[133] and unfamiliar, they had not hitherto been aggregated and considered together as instances of human rights law (because they had not been salient *as* human rights law),[134] and they had certainly never before been exposed to such scrutiny in the United Kingdom (Jonathan Cooper of JUSTICE told Victim Support at that meeting in April 1999 that 'it was never argued, you could never enforce it domestically, and so none of these arguments were ever put'). It was certainly the recollection of Sir Louis Blom-Cooper that no thought had been given to human rights matters in Victim Support in the mid-1990s. All that changed. An explosive burst of exploration at the turn of the century brought the European Court's judgments affecting victims and witnesses into a new and sharper relief, and the legal character of victims acquired bolder outlines.

the umbrella doctrine of the equality of arms, and rights to privacy. Under Article 5, ensuring the right to liberty, authorities might consider whether refusing bail was justified because people's lives might be put at risk. Alison Paterson, Victim Support Scotland; 'European Convention on Human Rights: Potential implications for victims of crime and victim policy', May 1999, p. 2.

[133] The European Court had started to develop principles about the rights of victims and witnesses at the turn of the century. Andrew Ashworth observed to me in an email in January 2001 that 'The way in which the Strasbourg Court is starting to develop Article 6 to protect some rights of victims and witnesses is important.' Ben Emmerson's own comment in March 1999 was that 'one of the things that you see in the Convention case law is a much greater emphasis on the rights of victims and witnesses within the Criminal Justice System. So far we've been looking at their right vis-à-vis the State's protection. But there is now an increasing recognition that even in cases where defendants are claiming rights, those rights must be balanced against the rights of the victim or the witness. So for example, the right of the defendant to confront his or her accuser in criminal proceedings, to cross-examine, which is an aspect of the right to a fair trial. In the past the Court tended to take a terribly strict view of the obligation to confront. In other words that they were very uncomfortable with witness anonymity arrangements or with any procedure which if you like which diverged from the classic concept of adversarial justice. In recent years, particularly the last three or four years, the Court has begun to recognise that it is essential to consider the rights of the victim as well or the witness. Now obviously the interesting thing there is that it goes in parallel with this development of positive obligations 'cause the Court must actively protect victims' rights too.'

[134] Helen Reeves said in October 1999, for instance, that 'when I started going into it, I realised that a lot of those cases in Europe, I already knew about, I'd already been quoting [them] in my own material. I just hadn't really put the tag of human rights on it. I know it sounds silly but . . . I knew about some of those Dutch witness cases and child abuse cases for example.'

Not only were the Government's legal advisers, committees,[135] and task forces[136] engaged in the enterprise, but non-governmental organizations such as Liberty,[137] JUSTICE, and Victim Support[138] individually and collaboratively, scanned the case law for its bearings on legislation and procedure after an 'NGO coordination meeting' convened in November 1997,[139] a month after the publication of the White Paper. Rowan Hardy of Victim Support said in January 1999: 'it's not entirely clear from the Convention what implications there might be for victims and witnesses... We took that up with

[135] For example, the Interdepartmental Vulnerable or Intimidated Witnesses Working Group sought advice at the beginning of 1998 on the application of Article 6 to the rights of a defendant personally to cross-examine a complainant in rape cases, and was told that, under *Croissant v. Germany* 1993, a national law compelling a defendant to be legally represented for court proceedings did not breach Article 6, and, in *Philis v. Greece* 1991, in certain circumstances it would not be a breach for the defendant to be refused the right to represent himself. Article 6 rights, it was declared, are not absolute. The matter was to be debated extensively in the House of Lords in March 1999.

[136] For example, the Human Rights Task Force, Minutes of 6th Meeting, 22 September 1999.

[137] John Wadham of Liberty told Victim Support at its annual conference in July 1998, 'there is a way forward to creating a criminal justice system that ensures that everyone gets a fair deal and the victim doesn't get victimised twice. The balance will be carefully constructed. I hope that Liberty will work with Victim Support to ensure that that is possible.' Liberty maintained always a disinterested approach to the Act, and remained as committed to the protection of defendants' rights. Indeed, it raised a number of difficulties with the proposed Youth Justice and Criminal Evidence Bill which sought to curtail the defendant's rights in trials for rape and other serious sexual offences, arguing, 'We are concerned that these proposals taken in full undermined the defendants [sic] right to a fair trial and therefore the Governments [sic] commitment to human rights' (Liberty briefing on the Youth Justice and Criminal Evidence Bill, 6 January 1998).

[138] Victim Support is what Liberty defined as a 'single-issue pressure group', it is not an organization of lawyers, and it does not engage in advocacy. It was not therefore part of the new Human Rights Development Network or the Human Rights Coalition, but it was aligned with them from the wings. Rowan Hardy, one of its officers said that Victim Support had a 'sort of a watching brief with the Human Rights Development Network that was set up by Charter 88 and JUSTICE and Liberty. We weren't able to take an active role in the group because of other work commitments but we received all their mailings and we wrote to the Home Secretary when the Bill was going through Parliament, asking for standings to be changed so that groups such as Victim Support could take actions under the Act as well as individual victims or would be victims.'

[139] See, for instance, C. Harlow; 'Public Law and Popular Justice', *Modern Law Review*, Vol. 65, No. 1, 2002, p. 1.

Liberty. We actually went through the convention trying to identify where there might be implications... [140] the response we had from Liberty was sort of mixed. Mostly it was referring to ... equality of arms, so that defendants have rights, but the European Court had to recognise that victims and witnesses have rights, and so yes, it would be a question of balance. But where the balance will actually lie...'.[141]

Liberty produced during that period what were probably the most comprehensive analyses[142] of the bearing of the Act on victims and witnesses, and it foretold major consequences: the Convention, it said, would oblige the State to have in place measures to protect the right to life and security of the person, prohibit inhuman and degrading treatment, and the right to family and private life. Under Article 3, there was provision for the protection from

[140] She wrote to Liberty in February 1998 with an inventory of questions troubling Victim Support at the time: 'You suggested I think about the issues affecting victims and the Convention and then send a list to you for discussion. I have now consulted colleagues and would be grateful for views on the following issues: Article 3—Would victims/witnesses experiencing excessive cross-examination (e.g. intrusive questioning about previous sexual history...) be able to claim that this was inhuman and degrading treatment?...Article 6...Would victims and witnesses in criminal cases be classed as "parties" to the case...so that protection of their private lives would be a justifiable reason for excluding the press and public from part of the trial? Are victims included in the definition of the "public" so that they may be excluded from the trial?...Article 8...Would victims be protected from any media coverage by public broadcasters?' Liberty replied, having referred the questions to Peter Duffy, who was taking the case of Julia Mason to Strasbourg under Articles 3, 8, and 13 (to which the Registry had added Article 14). Duffy was said to be optimistic about an outcome although the case was eventually settled out of court and in expectation of the Youth Justice and Criminal Evidence Act. Under Article 6, Hardy was advised, victims were not considered parties to the case, and under Article 8, it was unlikely that their privacy would be defended against the mass media.

[141] For his part, Liberty's John Wadham reflected: 'We would not have had any contact with them ten years ago...Now Liberty's position is that we see...the European Convention and other international human rights instruments as our kind of mandate. So...we're always looking for cases where...whether it's on the behalf of victims or defendants or whatever. And...we've developed the beginnings of some contacts with Victim Support over the last few years.' For the genesis of that relation, see my *After Homicide, op. cit.*

[142] For example, J. Wadham and J. Arkinstall; 'Rights of victims of crime—1', *New Law Journal*, Vol. 150, 6943, 7 July 2000, and 'Rights of victims and the Human Rights Act', June 2000.

assault of certain victims.[143] Under Article 8, the Act would require the prosecution more formally to consider the interests of the victim when it made decisions about prosecution. In its review of cases, Liberty referred to *McCourt v. the United Kingdom* 1993, in which the mother of a murder victim was denied the right to contribute to sentencing; *Doorson v. the Netherlands* 1996, which afforded protection to witnesses testifying in court;[144] *Z v. Finland* 1997 and its ruling that a victim's confidential medical records (in this instance on HIV status) could be admissible under Article 8; *McCann v. UK* 1995 under Article 2 and the right to life, which touched on the unlawful killing of an IRA suspect in Gibraltar; and *Osman v. UK* 1999 in which the immunity of the police and other public bodies to suits for negligence was declared unlawful and where the Court found that, under certain circumstances, there was a 'positive obligation on the authorities to take preventive operational measures to protect an individual whose life is at risk from the criminal acts of another'.[145] It invoked *Whiteside v. UK* in which the

[143] JUSTICE cited *A v. UK* 1999 in which a child complained to the Court that the State had failed to protect him from ill-treatment in violation of Article 3 following the acquittal of his stepfather on a charge of causing actual bodily harm. The jury had acquitted the stepfather, accepting a plea of reasonable chastisement, but the European Court accepted that a violation of Article 3 had occurred.

[144] The issue in *Doorson* had dwelt on how the balance should be struck between the public interest in prosecuting dangerous and violent offenders and the rights of the accused to challenge evidence brought against him. The European Court had found that it was justifiable to protect the rights of witnesses to life, liberty, and security of the person by preserving their anonymity.

[145] The Court declared that 'Article 2 § 1 enjoins the State not only to refrain from the intentional and unlawful taking of life, but also to take appropriate steps to safeguard the lives of those within its jurisdiction... such an obligation must be interpreted in a way which does not impose an impossible or disproportionate burden on the authorities... The Court does not accept the Government's view that the failure to perceive the risk to life in the circumstances known at the time or to take preventative measures to avoid that risk must be tantamount to gross negligence or wilful disregard of the duty to protect life. Such a rigid standard must be considered to be incompatible with the requirements of Article 1...' (ECHR case of *Osman v. The UK*, 87/1997/871/1083, Judgment, Strasbourg, 24 September 1998). See also 'Osman v. United Kingdom, 28 October 1998', *Criminal Law Review*, 1999, pp. 82–3. Ben Emmerson had fought the case at Strasbourg, and his observations were that 'the Government was prepared to accept that it had structural, what they called structural obligations under Article 2. In other words a positive obligation to provide a law prohibiting homicide, a police force to enforce the law and if you like a basic system of justice. Beyond that, the Government was prepared to accept that in certain very

appellant claimed that she had been subject to sustained harassment by her former co-habitee, and alleged that the Government had failed to provide the means to protect her (the European Court held that she had failed to exhaust the domestic remedies available although the State did have a positive duty to protect her). It turned to *X and Y v. Netherlands* 1986 in which Y had been sexually abused by the son-in-law of the owner of a home for the mentally disabled. She could not file a rape complaint because of her disability, and her father could not do so because she was too old, and the outcome was that she had been left without a remedy. The European Court held that the State did in this instance have positive obligations to uphold respect and family life. And under *Aydin v. Turkey* 1998, where the applicant had been raped and assaulted by the police, the Court maintained that the authorities had not conducted a proper inquiry although the State had a positive duty to investigate crime.

JUSTICE also set to work on the human rights of victims in 1998,[146] and it too found itself embarking on a new liaison with Victim Support: Kate Akester commented, 'Well I think the landscape generally is changing in all sorts of ways and because we're moving away from case work and we're moving away from

limited circumstances, there might be an operational obligation. In other words, "structural" they accepted. As far as operational obligations were concerned, they were prepared to concede only an obligation where the police had, if you like, accepted responsibility to protect somebody and then had failed to discharge that responsibility. None of which really dealt with, if you like, the paradigm situation of a police officer who stands by while one individual shoots and kills another. In the end, the Court held after some argument with the Commission in the case that the obligation on the State is to do all that can be reasonably required of it in the circumstances, taking account of all of the factors in the case, including the age and vulnerability of the victim and the potential threat and the duration and the extent of the threat. Now, again, on the fact the Court managed to hold that there was no breach of Article 2, but that was because they found on certain of the factual disputes for the State, rather than for the individual. Had they found for the individual in all the factual disputes the result would have inevitably been different. But really that's beside the point for the purposes of the development of the law on that ground, because they had established . . . a very high test which puts in an obligation in international law and, obviously, once the Human Rights Law comes into effect, in national law, they're enforceable at the suit of the individual, an obligation on the State and the police effectively to prevent crime and do all that can be reasonably required of it in the circumstances to prevent crime. And that's a pretty high obligation where somebody's died.'

[146] JUSTICE *annual report* for 1998, p. 9.

miscarriages of justice, you know, we're looking at the new situation, and it's quite difficult even to ask the question as to what, how it's going, how criminal justice is going to emerge ... Victims' interests, if you like, are things that are taken into account now. Maybe not as much as they should, I'm sure victims would say not as much as they should be, but it's certainly, don't you think, an ingredient in everybody's [thought].'

JUSTICE sought the opinion of a leading human rights barrister, Peter Duffy, on proposals embedded in *Speaking up for Justice* to prohibit the exploration in court of a complainant's previous sexual history and to prevent a defendant charged with rape or other serious sexual offences personally cross-examining his complainant,[147] and he advised that they did indeed comply with the Convention and the Act (I shall return to those issues in Chapter 8). And at much the same time, other advocates with a human rights competence briefed their colleagues, the Government, and the committees and agencies of the criminal justice system with summary reviews of the provisions of the Act and its likely effects on the legal standing and practical treatment of victims and witnesses.[148] Most illuminating

---

[147] JUSTICE opinion on the White Paper 'Speaking up for Justice', by Peter Duffy, 11 June 1998. In the event, on 17 May 2001, the House of Lords did lay down guidelines under which rape victims could be questioned in court about their previous sexual history. The 1999 Act was not declared incompatible with the Human Rights Act. Lord Steyn said that due regard had to be paid to 'protect the complainant from indignity and from humiliating questions'. Consent might be given by one who had recently had sex with the defendant. See *The Times*, 18 May 2001, and *VSM: Victim Support Magazine*, No. 79, Summer 2001, p. 12.

[148] Ben Emmerson, for example, also pointed to the State's duty to take reasonable steps to protect a citizen from violation of his or her convention rights by others, to prevent inhuman and degrading treatment under Article 3, and to offer reasonable protection in specified circumstances following the *Osman* decision of 1998 which removed the immunity of the police from negligence suits. 'The Human Rights Bill: its effect on Criminal Proceedings (Part II)', *Archbold News*, Issue 3, 9 April 1998, p. 5. And John Jackson of Queen's University, Belfast, declared that victims should not be allowed to take decisions about what happened to offenders or how the case had progressed or whether there should be a prosecution. There was, he said, a distinction between information and explanation, on the one hand, and consultation on the other. Information and explanation should be fact-based and straightforward, but consultation was more problematic. There was a risk that victims' views might unduly influence decision-makers, inflate expectations and prejudice the legal process. But, wherever possible, victims should be informed and consulted. On balance, he concluded, there should be consultation. John Jackson; 'Human Rights Issues for the Auld review', 26 June 2000.

perhaps was Ben Emmerson[149] who treated victims' rights as if they were dialectical, a set of negative rights to be defined in counterpoint to the defendant's positive rights:

I think there's a general conception amongst people who are coming to European Convention law for the first time that its application in criminal proceedings is essentially as a sort of charter of villains' rights. And one of the things that I'm trying to impress upon all of my audiences, which [include] judicial training for the judges, is that that's not right and that there really is a sort of burgeoning body of victims' rights case law. And that's actually helpful from a number of points of view. It's obviously helpful in terms of persuading judges to be friendly to the Convention because it gives them a sense of balance in the process and gives them a recognition that actually, you know, their instinctive sense that the rights of the defendant and the rights of the victim need to be balanced the one against the other, actually finds reflection in the Convention. And I find . . . it says the dual purpose of reinforcing the judges' duty to recognise victims' rights and at the same time familiarising them, if you like, in making them more Convention friendly. So the starting point is really that the Convention has traditionally been regarded as imposing what are called negative obligations on the State.

In its own internal reviews of the likely impact of the Act on criminal legislation and procedure conducted at diverse points in 1998, the Home Office at first made few references to the victims of commonplace crime, citing the right to freedom from oppressive treatment under Article 3[150] (including the cross-examination of certain victims);[151] *Doorson* under Article 6 ('where no action is necessary'[152]);

---

[149] One of the Lord Chancellor's Department officials servicing the Human Rights Task Force remarked in September 1998 that 'Emmerson offered to help in future and he has clearly thought deeply about the likely impact of the Bill on criminal law and procedure.' Emmerson did indeed come to present some of the Crown Court 'dry runs'.

[150] 'We in the Home Office have been thinking about the impact the Act is likely to have on criminal cases . . . it is not only defendants who have rights. A careful balance will need to be struck between Article 3 . . . and Article 6 . . . so it might require advocates to adjust their treatment of witnesses and victims to ensure that their rights are protected.' Speech for Lord Williams, College of Law, 28 January 1999, The Human Rights Act 1998.

[151] 'Building a Human Rights Culture', Address to Civil Service College seminar, 9 December 1999.

[152] *Doorson*, it was held, would not require legislation because practice derived from common law and judges would have to take it into account in any event without need for further legislation.

and the Article 8 right to privacy which was not said to be especially problematic ('It raises no HRA issues whatsoever'[153]), although, as I have shown, it was actually a matter receiving quite anxious attention elsewhere. Ian Chisholm, who had commandeered the reviews commented during that period, in mid-1998: 'Well the Human Rights Act could have a number of implications for criminal policy but I haven't got in the forefront of my mind any big implications for victims or witnesses.' And his more junior colleague, the secretary of the Victims Steering Group, said at the same time, '[human rights] certainly hasn't surfaced on the victim side. It may well have done on the other side of our unit's interest which is to do with court procedures. But they're kept separate from the Victims Steering Group.'

That position was to change. Over time, more cases were unearthed, more advice was tendered, more problems were encountered, and more cases were taken to Strasbourg (and particularly the cases of *T and V v. The United Kingdom* and of Julia Mason), and the department's stance became more schematic, analytical and expansive. By 2000, the Home Office Minister responsible for implementing the Act, Lord Williams, was able to write that there were five broad areas where victims would be affected: the duty to protect victims in the criminal justice system; the possibility of an increased role for victim statements in the sentencing process; the requirement on the State to provide adequate deterrents in criminal law; a duty to protect where there is a known risk to an individual or group; and a duty to carry out a thorough and impartial investigation.[154]

## *T and V v. The United Kingdom 1999*

Two Strasbourg cases did for a while promise very prominently to test particular aspects of the victim's legal *persona*: one, that of Julia Mason, was settled before it went before the Court, and it will be discussed in Chapter 8; and the other, *T and V v. The United Kingdom*, secured less than some had at first expected, but it is worth examining because of the light it sheds on themes central to this book. *T and V v. The United Kingdom* stemmed from the trial of an

---

[153] The impact of HRA on Home Office Manifesto Commitments—Keeping Victims Informed, 22 February 1999. There had, of course, been difficulties that were still being resolved at the time.

[154] *Victim Support Magazine*, Summer 2000, p. 5.

extraordinarily harrowing murder case that had galvanized media and popular sentiment in Britain and overseas, pitted idealized typifications of good and evil against one another,[155] and invited prolonged reflection on the moral and social condition of England.[156]

On 14 February 1993, two young boys, Thompson and Venables, the T and V of the Strasbourg case, kidnapped a two year-old child, James Bulger, in a shopping centre in Liverpool, subjected him to numerous indignities and injuries as he was taken to a railway line, and then killed and abandoned him. The image of the kidnapping was vividly poignant because it had been preserved by a close circuit television camera and was replayed and relayed in the mass media continually thereafter. Liverpool had already been the centre of major displays of public grief after the Heysel football riot of May 1985 and the deaths of ninety-six Liverpool football supporters at the Hillsborough stadium four years later, and it was the centre of a vigorous politics of the victim exemplified by Joan Jonkers' Victims of Violence,[157] the Hillsborough Justice Campaign, and the large and activist homicide survivors' group, Merseyside Support after Murder and Manslaughter.

Thompson and Venables, both aged 11, were tried and convicted at Preston Crown Court in November 1993, having been described by the sentencing judge as guilty of an act of 'unparalleled evil and barbarity'. Thereafter, they were to be the targets of massive public execration[158] as the murderers of an innocent and tiny child,[159] on

---

[155] Melanie Phillips and Martin Kettle wrote in the *Guardian* two days afterwards, 'The crime touches very raw nerves indeed. The violation of innocence by violence is as disturbing as anything can be: the pictures of the two boys, themselves still only children, taking the two-year-old fills us with special fear… The lost child who wanders off only to be "rescued" by evil forces is an image straight out of the nightmare fairy-tales of the Brothers Grimm.'

[156] I was myself questioned by French, American, and Canadian television reporters about the case's significance for the decline of Britain.

[157] See J. Jonker; *Victims of Violence*, Fontana, London, 1986.

[158] 278,300 people signed a petition saying that the boys should never be released. On the newspaper reporting of the murder and its aftermath, see B. Franklin and J. Petley; 'Killing the Age of Innocence: newspaper reporting of the death of James Bulger', in J. Pilcher and S. Wagg (eds.); *Thatcher's Children*, Falmer, London, 1996.

[159] One of the police officers who had interviewed Thompson and Venables, Sergeant Roberts, said 'These two were freaks who just found each other. You should not compare these boys with other boys—they were evil.' *Guardian*, 25 November 1993.

the one hand, and, on the other, of unease about the application of what were in effect adult criminal procedures to very young defendants, and those issues touched on the provisions of the European Convention.[160]

The impact of their crime, the conduct of their trial and the terms of their sentencing were referred under Articles 3 and 6, first to the European Human Rights Commission in Strasbourg in March 1999, and thence to the Court, and applications having been received in May 1999,[161] the President of the Court granted leave to JUSTICE and to James Bulger's parents, Ralph Bulger and Denise Fergus, to submit written comments in connection with the case.[162] Three months later, it further granted leave to the victim's parents to attend the hearing in person and make oral submissions to the Court.[163]

---

[160] Most recently in 2001 when Judge Butler-Sloss awarded Thompson and Venables lifelong anonymity under Article 2 of the Human Rights Act. *The Times,* 9 January 2001.

[161] Robin Makin wrote to the Court's Registrar on 14 May 1999 that he considered that it would be in the interests of the proper administration of justice for him to intervene so that the Court can consider material and representations relating to 'victims interests'. 'From the tragedy which Mr Bulger has suffered and continues to suffer he hopes to achieve something useful and constructive by ensuring that the system of administration of justice in the United Kingdom (which will emerge as a result of the decisions in these cases) will have had proper regard to the position of victims.' He also asked for the right to make representations orally: 'Victims have already been excluded from the fact-finding process conducted by the European Commission of Human Rights. Not all the relevant factual points were made. Some of the judges might wish to make points about victims' interests and it would be appropriate to have an opportunity to respond.'

[162] Those representations were to be joint written comments, limited to 10 pages, not taking the form of pleadings in the cases, and describing 'in general terms, the extent to which the views of the victims of serious crimes can and should effect [*sic*] the trial and sentencing of suspected perpetrators, together with comparative law material addressing the same issue.' ECHR, Grand Chamber, *T v. the United Kingdom, V v. the United Kingdom,* Joint Written Comments of the Parents of James Bulger tendered by Rex Makin, 16 July 1999. Victims themselves were defined as including 'the families of a person who has been criminally killed, victims of specific crimes and victims (or potential) victims of crimes generally'.

[163] Denise Fergus and Ralph Bulger would be permitted to attend throughout the hearing on understanding that proceedings were held in private and would be allowed to address joint submissions to the Court, during ten minutes in total, following the submissions of the two applicants and before those of the Government. Deputy Registrar, European Court of Human Rights, to Rex Makin, 6 September 1999.

It was the very first time that an individual third party had been thus allowed to put his or her case to the Court.[164] Robin Makin, the solicitor representing Ralph Bulger, said 'This ruling is very important: it is highly unusual for a third party in a case to be allowed the right to intervene unless they are an organisation such as Liberty.'[165] The United Kingdom Government had known about the Bulger application, which had not been entered with a complaint but as an attachment to the Government's own submission, and it had not opposed it. The Home Secretary himself agreed that the Government would support Ralph Bulger's proposed intervention 'to the point of principle but would not get enmeshed in the content of that principle', although there were officials who demurred because, they said, it had yet to be decided what role if any (other than as witnesses) victims should have within the criminal justice system. There had already been some exploration of the matter in connection with victim impact statements, but the issues were 'very tricky' and the 'results inconclusive'. The fact that the Home Secretary had decided to support Ralph Bulger's case should not, it was thought, be seen as pre-empting decisions about what might happen domestically. Ian Chisholm remarked: 'we didn't object, put it that way'. And that was an interesting and politically pregnant stance to adopt, because the Government, in effect, had there ceded victims the right to be a party in a tribunal in Strasbourg but had not yet done so in the courts of the United Kingdom. Before the judgment, the Home Office was obliged to consider 'contingencies' about the 'rights of defendants, victims and witnesses . . . in the light of the Thompson and Venables case'. A Grade 7 of JVU said in June 2000, 'we're having to sort of wrestle with at the moment [the question of] giving victims a more formal role in the criminal justice process . . . a very open question. We were very conscious of that, that we were allowing them to do in Europe what they would not be able to do in a domestic court.'

[164] *The Times*, 16 September 1999. Rule 61 of the European Court did allow for third party intervention: under 'Article 36 § 2 of the Convention, the President of the Chamber may, in the interests of the proper administration of justice, invite or grant leave to any Contracting State which is not a party to the proceedings, or any person concerned who is not the applicant, to submit written comments or, in exceptional cases, to take part in a hearing. Requests for leave for this purpose must be duly reasoned and submitted in one of the official languages, within a reasonable time after the fixing of the written procedure.'
[165] *The Times*, 13 September 1999.

Denise Fergus attended in the hope that her participation would be more than 'just a symbolic act but will assist in establishing actual rights for victims'. She told the Court through her own solicitor at the hearing on 15 September 1999 that there had been a violation of her son's right to life and his right not to be subjected to torture. She wished to tell the court how she felt about Thompson and Venables: how their crime had affected her physical and mental health, her marriage and her family; and what punishment she felt was appropriate for youths who had concealed her son's body and abandoned him on a railway line. No mechanisms were in place for her views to be heard in the courts of the United Kingdom,[166] and it was a 'magnificent gesture' that she and her former husband had been allowed to intervene in Strasbourg, a gesture that recognized the importance of establishing the rights victims should have in the judicial process—the right to be consulted by a prosecutor about a plea of guilty to a lesser charge; and the right to tell a sentencing tribunal about the effects of a crime on them and their families. For his part, Ralph Bulger said through Robin Makin, his solicitor, that the victim's interests should be given priority over those of the offender, especially in the area of sentencing, and that if a victim wished to participate in the trial process or wished to become involved in the sentencing process, then he or she should not be prevented from doing so. There was, Bulger claimed, a case for sentencing as retribution. Robin Makin himself recollected:

The thrust of my argument [was] that when you're talking about retribution and deterrence, the deterrent side of it, I think is minimal... So the real part is what is retribution, and retribution really basically boils down to vengeance, and has got deep historical and religious reasons... Sentencing for retribution... [is] not really so much on society's point of view, [but] from the point of view of making sure the victims are satisfied. Because if the victims aren't really satisfied then there's disrepute in the law...

The Court ruled that, although there had been no breach of Articles 3 or 5, there had been other breaches of the European Convention: it

---

[166] The Government position at the time, it will be recalled, was that it was still testing victim statements. As for the Crown Prosecution Service, it was committed to considering evidential and public interest tests, acting, it said, in the public interest, and not just that of any individual, but it had always to think about the interests of the victim when deciding where the public interest lies. The CPS could take into account the victim's views where 'appropriate and practicable', but those views were only one of a number of factors and could not determine any outcome.

rejected the Government's contention that the applicants had not exhausted domestic remedies in the United Kingdom,[167] and determined that they had been denied a fair trial and effective participation under Article 6 because of the 'severely intimidatory' character of the proceedings for juvenile defendants;[168] and it had been improper for the Home Secretary, who was not an 'independent and impartial tribunal', to fix the terms of their sentence under the 'tariff' for life sentences. Denise Fergus was said to be 'upset and devastated'[169] at the outcome. 'The decision has "sickened" the Bulger family, and one of their solicitors described the ruling as a another turn of the knife in a case that would not go away. Rex Makin [sic][170] ... said there had to be justice for everyone—including the murdered child's parents.'[171]

Most of the accompanying internal discussion within the Home Office at the time inevitably dwelt on the implications for the management of trials for vulnerable young offenders, and on a possible need to reconsider the Youth Justice and Criminal Evidence Act, only recently passed into law. But the role and treatment of James Bulger's parents as 'secondary victims' did surface as well, raised in part by David Pannick, who appeared before the European Court on behalf of the Government, and by the JVU which had tendered advice for the preparation of the United Kingdom's memorandum. That advice did little more than recite the standard provisions available for victims in the United Kingdom, noting that 'comparatively few victims' "rights" are enforceable at law', and it said nothing about the victims' standing in criminal procedure.

In late May 1999, an official of the Home Office's Lifer Review Unit told me that he did not attach undue importance to the submissions made on the parents' behalf: that if the Court had not admitted the parents it would have been embarrassed because they would have waited outside the door and the BBC and other media would have made much of their plight. Although the Court had admitted representations from the parents, they were 'too late in the day' to have an

---

[167] Judgments delivered in cases of *T & V v. UK*, 16 December 1999: Press release issued by the Registrar of the European Court.

[168] Criminal procedure was subsequently transformed. See the report of the trial of two young boys in Liverpool in June 2000. *Evening Standard*, 20 June 2000.

[169] *The Times*, 17 December 1999.

[170] Rex Makin was the practice of which Robin Makin was a partner.

[171] BBC News On-Line, 15 March 1999.

effect and no impact could be discerned in its judgment. He certainly could see no recognition of the idea that victims' vengeance should play a part in sentencing. To the contrary. (Robin Makin himself conceded that the judges were 'saying... vengeance is not a form of justice and in particular vengeance against children in civilised society should be completely excluded'). And the official concluded that Robin Makin had probably made too much of the significance of what had happened, although he did admit that the Bulger parents had 'secured a foot in the door' and, having done so, the door might never close again.

David Pannick, who had appeared for the Government took a different view. It was not the substance of the judgment but the form of the procedure which had been at issue:

I haven't looked at the judgement myself for a couple of months, but I can't remember any paragraph that specifically addresses the rights of victims, but the most significant aspect is not the substance of the judgment but rather the procedure. Now the procedure was that we had the oral hearing in, I think, September, and the victim's families asked the court if they could be heard and make representations. And the Court, surprisingly to many people, said 'yes'. I mean, normally, their procedure would be simply to hear the Government, it would hear the applicants' lawyers... But this was significant in that the victims' interests were formally recognised and they were allowed to make oral representations through their lawyers... I'm not aware of any earlier case in Strasbourg where the victims have sought the right to be heard. I'm certainly not aware of any case in this country where that's happened, and I think that's very significant. The court may not have appreciated the significance of formally recognising that the victims have a separate and distinct interest to that of the State which is responsible for prosecuting crime and defending the integrity of the judgements of its own courts. Now, it may well be, and I suspect probably is, that in this case the European Court... had taken a view on a matter of principle but... the court was well aware, it could hardly have been otherwise, that this was a matter of enormous sensitivity, and really as a matter of public relations, it would look very unsatisfactory to refuse such a request from the victims.

Liberty concluded that some would read into the decision that the European Court was moving away from the position earlier established in *McCourt*,[172] although it did not set a precedent

[172] Liberty; 'Rights of Victims and the Human Rights Act', June 2000; J. Wadham and J. Arkinstall; 'Rights of victims of crime', *New Law Journal*, Vol. 150, 6944, 14 July 2000, p. 1084; and Dianne Luping, Liberty; 'Rights of Victims of Crime'. Victim Support Conference, 6 July 2000.

for the courts of the United Kingdom, and David Pannick concurred:

I would think, if after the 2nd of October you have a murder trial in this
country and the victim says through his lawyer, 'I'd like to be heard please.
It's all very well the State prosecuting, but I'd like to make submissions to
the jury', I don't think an English judge would have much difficulty in
saying, 'well', you know, 'you can make your points to the prosecution,
they're more than willing to listen to you. I'm not going to listen to you as
well.'

But David Pannick did suggest that I should ask Robin Makin about
whether he intended to make representations to the Lord Chief
Justice when the tariff was fixed, and 'the Lord Chief Justice will
then have to determine whether he takes them into account. And
I personally would be very surprised if he ignored them (he may not
find that they add very much).' We shall see that those representations were indeed made.

On 13 March 2000, the Home Secretary's response to the judgment was to announce that the tariff for defendants aged under 18
would in future be set by a judge in open court and that, in the
interim, the sentences of existing detainees would be reviewed by the
newly appointed Lord Chief Justice, Lord Woolf. Lord Woolf, in his
turn, issued a practice statement in July 2000, announcing that he
would invite written representations from the detainees' legal advisers and the Director of Public Prosecutions,[173] who could include
representations made on behalf of the victims' families,[174] although
those representations must be limited to the effects of the crime upon
the victim's family and were not to indicate the family's views about
what they regarded as the appropriate tariff.[175] He had appeared to

[173] The Director of Public Prosecutions was awarded the role of intermediary
between the Home Office and the Lord Chief Justice in resolving the tariff in the
Bulger case.

[174] A very senior judge concluded in private that Lord Woolf obviously intended to
'make a signal in talking about T & V'. He was, it was thought, much more interested
in victims' matters than Tom Bingham, his predecessor.

[175] It was the view of some that Michael Howard, the previous Home Secretary,
had given the Bulger family the impression that they would have an impact on the
sentence, and Jack Straw had done the same, 'and the DPP was stuck in the middle'.
Michael Howard subsequently accused the Lord Chief Justice of putting criminals
before victims in his approach to releasing the killers of James Bulger. It should be
politicians, not judges, who set the minimum term to be served (*The Times*, 26
October 2000).

indicate, in effect, that after the judgment of the European Court, he would accord James Bulger's parents a new role.[176] And that statement, and the manner in which it was publicly reported,[177] suggested at the time that there had been a critical transformation of the victim's standing, to the chagrin of Victim Support,[178] many lawyers and at least one Minister.[179] Under the headline, 'Woolf to give Bulgers say in killers' sentence', *The Times,* for instance, stated:

The family of James Bulger are to be given a say in the fate of his killers in an unprecedented move by Britain's most senior judge to ensure that victims' voices are heard... [He] pledged to take the views of the murdered boy's parents into account... 'I think it is very important that all those involved [in the Bulger case] should have an opportunity of making an impact on the process.'... Robin Makin, the solicitor who represents Ralph Bulger, said that he was not surprised by Lord Woolf's announce-

[176] He said: 'I think it is very important that all those involved should have an opportunity of making an input into the process... the director of public prosecutions... is going, with the encouragement of the court and the encouragement of my predecessor, to take the views of the victims, and in a case where somebody is killed, that means the victim's family, and present those to the court.... In that judgment, I will make it clear... that I have taken into account the views of the victims... I have not yet received the representations, so I do not know precisely what form they take— my understanding is that the family are going to express their views to the Director and the Director is going to be the method of communication to the court of their views... when I receive the representations... it is only right that those who represent the two young men have an opportunity to comment on those... it is an innovation but we are in a new situation.' Transcription of Lord Chief Justice, Press Conference, 6 June 2000.
[177] Thus the BBC 5pm Radio News of 6 June 2000 proclaimed 'And the new Lord Chief Justice of England and Wales says James Bulger's parents will be consulted about the length of his killers' sentence.'
[178] A senior figure in Victim Support stated in a letter to me that. 'The political dynamic also highlights the danger that "victims rights" can be hijacked for a quite different agenda, namely the punishment of offenders (e.g. the press response to the sentencing of Thompson and Venables and the involvement of the Bulger family).' And a colleague reflected at a seminar about 'the Bulger case where the parents have become more and more discontented... The Bulger family did not get what they need, did not get support, activists and lawyers moved in and made it a criminal justice issue. They should have attention to their own needs.'
[179] A Minister told me that the Bulger parents' intervention in the release decision had been improper and Woolf had been weak to allow them to speak. The Strasbourg decision was not a precedent at all. The idea of a victim impact statement was anathema and should not have been allowed. And Louis Blom-Cooper reflected that he could 'not think what Woolf was doing allowing the Bulgers to talk to him. He was only raising their expectations but wouldn't alter the tariff date.'

ment that he would consult the family. 'This is something that we have
been working quietly behind the scenes on...We were aware that we
would be able to make representations. I don't think it would be helpful
to comment publicly as to what the representations will be.'[180]

Robin Makin reflected as he prepared his case in early September
2000 that 'things are changing on a daily basis. We've got until 25
September to make our representations to the DPP...it's a question
of reworking what we did in the Strasbourg materials. I've two
weeks at the most but it's difficult to get source materials and put
in a neat form to the Lord Chief Justice all the competing arguments.... How do you decide when [a sentence] is proportionate,
to take into account the loss suffered and retribution, deterrence and
what they mean. Whilst vengeance has a nasty overtone, when you
boil it down, retribution is really vengeance. It's pretty synonymous.'

Representations were made first by James Bulger's mother and
then by his father, and three months later Lord Woolf announced his
recommendation that the tariff for Thompson and Venables should
be eight years,[181] before they had become eligible for transfer to the
adult prison system, and it would be up to the Parole Board to
consider their cases at the end of that time. Declaring herself 'disgusted and shocked', Denise Fergus proclaimed that she would
proceed to seek a judicial review of the decision.[182] Robin Makin's
judgment was that judicially to review a ruling by the Lord Chief
Justice was 'not the easiest thing to do', although there were
grounds: speaking 'before hearing representations'; creating 'legitimate expectation that he would take things into consideration but
he didn't'; 'we put in detailed written representations, we got the
transcripts, took into account all the aggravating features—he didn't
take any of that into account—and there was sexual abuse that
wasn't take into account'. 'Ralph Bulger had been so incensed that
he went on television, although he had not wanted to say anything
before.'

In the ensuing action in the Court of Appeal in February 2001,
Ralph Bulger raised the issue of whether he had the standing to

[180] *The Times*, 7 June 2000.
[181] And the views of James Bulger's parents would also eventually form part of the
written reports considered by the parole hearings on Thompson and Venables. *The
Times*, 31 October 2000.
[182] See *The Times*, 27 October 2000; *Sunday Times*, 7 January 2001.

challenge the tariff fixed by the Lord Chief Justice,[183] and it was determined that his views and those of Denise Fergus were not a sound basis for re-assessing a sentence. The Crown and defendant, it was said, were the traditional, invariable and only proper parties to criminal proceedings, and there was neither the need nor justification for a third party to intervene to uphold the law. If the family of the victim could become a party, why not the family of the defendant, or organizations representing victims? The victim's family could have no standing to seek judicial review of any tariff set in murder.[184]

What is material to the theme of this book in the case of *T and V v. The United Kingdom*, then, was the double-barrelled attempt by Ralph Bulger and Denise Fergus, the parents of James Bulger, to be recognized as parties with a right to make representations to courts and judges in the fixing of sentences. It was a practical extension and propellant of the debates rehearsed about victim impact statements,[185] and its outcome was to be the same as that of those debates. The Home Office determined, in the words of Ian Chisholm, that the lessons of the Thompson and Venables case were, first, that victim statements had been awarded legitimacy: 'the judgement in European jurisprudence on Thompson and Venables, we clearly have to allow the parents to make representations. And while we're doing that internationally, well domestically, with the victim statement, the Court of Appeal have ruled it's alright. I don't

---

[183] *Bulger v Secretary of State for the Home Department and Lord Chief Justice of England and Wales*, 16 February 2001.

[184] *The Times*, 7 March 2001.

[185] And it was cited in December 1999 when arguments were prepared within the Home Office about the possible development of such statements, and became a catalyst to the Home Secretary deciding publicly about their future when he made a statement to the House of Commons about the ECHR judgment in *T and V*. Having agreed at the beginning of 2000 to the national implementation of victim statements, he was to say 'I also plan to ensure that the views of the victims and their relatives are better taken into account. I shall announce our proposals in due course . . . The murder of young James Bulger was horrific. It is seared into the memory, not just of his family but of the public as a whole. What I have sought to do is ensure that the binding decisions of the European Court of Human Rights are implemented in a way that secures that young people who commit dreadful crimes are properly brought to justice in an environment that is as open as possible, and that the interests of victims and their families are properly taken into account.' (Debate in the House of Commons on the European Court of Human Rights judgment on Thompson and Venables, 13 March 2000). His comments received support from his counterparts in the Conservative Party and the Liberal Democrats.

think we can [resist it], whatever the views are'; and, second, that it was necessary to 'draw a distinction between representations about the effects of the crime on the victim and direct representations about what the length of the tariff should be. Because I think the first is okay, but the second, we don't want to get into clearly. But it's a fine distinction.'

If the Bulger parents' attempt to achieve standing as a party had been successful, it would indeed have reconstituted the legal and political identity of victims. Robin Makin reflected:

It's a very complicated issue and what tends to happen is you just have mob rule. I mean one thing I've been trying to do is to sort of untangle what the real victims' interests are, where they actually come from and how they're pursued, you know, in a sensible and constructive way... We say is that there are two victims' interests. One's the victim impact, and then the other one is victim participation, having a say on the sentence... That's what the judges don't want, but that is what the real battleground is, because the thrust of this is it's a very vengeful society in this country, for various historical and religious, for all sorts of reasons. So the real part is, what is retribution, and retribution really basically boils down to vengeance, and has got deep historical and religious reasons, and that's what you're pandering towards. And the judges don't really like to say that, but if you're actually exacting vengeance, who are you exacting it for?

## Conclusions

The European Convention and the Human Rights Act were never explicitly intended for the victims of commonplace crime. Their impact could not but be tangential and dialectical, established negatively and somewhat haphazardly as positive rights were secured for defendants. But they began to redefine United Kingdom citizens as rights-bearers, and victims were swept along with them, in part as a product of the new coalitions being formed between Victim Support and the older civil liberties groups, the Act creating the very social formations by which it was interpreted. Their elision of the victim in the political balancing work of a State newly engaged with victims' issues, and their apparent favouring of the defendant and suspect, prompted the Home Secretary to emphasize the existence of victims' rights under the Act, however premature his declaration may have been. The Convention and the Act thus again encouraged the emergence of a rights talk in which those involved in circles making policies for victims began to participate. When that talk was to be deployed in the context of revisions to the *Victim's Charter* before the 2001 general election, it no longer seemed to some to be quite as strange or untoward, although, it was concluded, the manifest distress of the parents of James Bulger underscored the hazards of unduly raising victims' expectations about anything that might be attempted.[186] And, finally, what the protracted history of *T and V v The United Kingdom* demonstrated once more was the clear and strenuously policed limits set by the judiciary on any such rights: victims were not and were unlikely ever to be parties to criminal procedure.

---

[186] Based on observations made by a JVU official at the Victims Steering Group Meeting, 8 December 2000.

# 6

# The Victim and Compensation

This brief chapter on criminal injuries compensation is little more than a minor episode, and it is intended to contribute four principal ideas. The first is the introduction of the *caveat* that some policy developments centred on the victim of crime were in effect somewhat more semi-detached or loose-coupled than others, and that the critical mass that was to emerge at the end of the first New Labour administration was unevenly shaped by the ingredients that had passed through the crucible of the Victims Steering Group and the JVU. To be sure, there were linkages and commonalities because the Criminal Injuries Compensation Scheme had been exposed to the same legal regulation and management ideology as any other institution in the criminal justice system of the 1990s. The procedures instituted to receive applications and handle appeals against awards had to be refined to become compliant with the Human Rights Act, for instance. In step with all other State agencies, the Criminal Injuries Compensation Authority and its associated bodies[1] adopted the practices and discourse of the new performance management, defining its work as service-delivery, its applicants and appellants as consumers[2] entitled to standards of care[3] under the *Citizen's Charter*, and attempting to secure a 'better relationship

---

[1] See, for instance, *Annual Report, 1996–7*, Criminal Injuries Compensation Appeals Panel, First Report, Cm. 3840, London, February 1998, in which the standard array of targets, aims, objectives, and key performance indicators was mapped out.

[2] The Criminal Injuries Compensation Appeals Panel ran a seminar on customer care in 1998, to which lawyers representing the employees of the police and fire services and members of the Rape Crisis Federation were invited.

[3] See 'CICA: A guide to the criminal injuries compensation scheme, (effective from 1 April 1996)' and 'CICAP—A Guide to Applicants on the Hearings procedure—The Standards of Service which Customers can expect to receive from the Panel'.

to benefit those we serve, the victims of crime'.[4] Michael Lewer, a lawyer and the Chairman of CICAP, the Criminal Injuries Appeals Panel, was appointed by the Home Office in 1996 with a brief precisely to consider the implications for the appeals procedure of the new *Citizen's Charter* and second *Victim's Charter*.

The second idea is that the typifications of victims found in the neighbourhood of criminal injuries compensation retained their original emphasis on moral desert, and that that quality once again reflected the contingent and practical character of policy-making. If the new performance management generated the victim-consumer, and the importation of human rights the victim as an oblique and embryonic rights-bearer, the distinctive representation of criminal injuries compensation was the blameless victim, and it is important to put it firmly in place, if only for completeness' sake.

The third idea is intended to register that the major impact of the criminal injuries compensation scheme flowed from its character as a demand-led enterprise whose appetite for resources could affect the money left available to other initiatives, including, for example, the expansion of the Victim Support Witness Service into the Magistrates' Courts, the two *Victim's Charter* standards projects, and the implementation of the vulnerable or intimidated witnesses programme, costing some £9m., which I shall discuss in Chapter 8 below. And the final idea is that, whilst criminal injuries compensation may not have attained the status of a firm justiciable claim in law, by 1995 its legal standing, and the identity of victims which followed in its tow, was to undergo an appreciable and interesting change which did introduce a combination of entitlements fringing on near-rights.

Criminal injuries compensation was conceived after the Second World War not only as an inferior substitute for restorative justice (it was thought by its author, Margery Fry, that offenders were usually too poor to make direct reparation to their victim, and that the State should act as a proxy offender for purposes of compensation); but also as a kind of *Danegeld* to buy off what were imagined to be the angry victims of criminal violence and their allies who could obstruct the introduction of a mass of liberal policies planned

[4] Howard Webber; 'First Impressions', October 1999 intended for *VS Magazine*.

by penal reformers.[5] I narrated at some length the history of those and subsequent developments in *Helping Victims of Crime*, and, although I have annexed a few quotations from that earlier book, it is unnecessary to repeat its argument here. What should here be noted is that an enduring legacy of problems was bestowed by a scheme that was established in 1964 and which came into effect a year later. There was the difficulty posed by the tacit assumption injected into policy-making for victims from the start that the needs of victims had in effect been substantially and generously met,[6] and that was an assumption that took time to shake off. Compensation was conceived at a time when recorded levels of criminal violence were low, and could be supported, it was thought, by an *ex gratia* scheme based on common law awards that were initially costed by the then Government statistician, Leslie Wilkins, at £150,000 *per annum*. But the volume of money awarded grew so appreciably that, although policies and programmes for victims in England and Wales might seem to be receiving very large sums by international standards, their budget was almost entirely consumed by compensation. In its first year of operation, the scheme paid £400,000 to 1,164 victims; but by 1980 it paid £21,000,000 to 20,000 victims; by 1990–91, £109,000,000 to 35,000 victims; and by 1997–8, over £200,000,000 to over 45,000 victims.[7] Howard Webber, the Chief Executive of the Criminal Injuries Compensation Authority, remarked in August 2000, 'it is by far the largest element of Government spending on victims. It dwarfs anything else.' In 1999, compensation absorbed 92 per cent of the Comprehensive Spending Review's allocation of money for victims. The Treasury and others

---

[5] Nigel Walker, a member of the JUSTICE Committee that sponsored compensation in the very early 1960s said that he could 'recollect Louis Blom-Cooper [a fellow member] making the point very forcibly that the public would be less severe in its demands for punishment of violent offenders if they felt that victims were getting compensated. This was one of the heads of steam behind the reformist lobby, that it would strengthen the hands of the Howard League, in trying to reduce the severity of punishment... [This was] one of the strong arguments for doing something about victims of violence, that the public would be less punitive if they felt that victims were being compensated.'

[6] In 1984, for instance, the Home Office's evidence to the Home Affairs Committee stated that 'a great deal is already done for the victims of crime. The Government's principal contribution is the Criminal Injuries Compensation Scheme...'.

[7] Figures taken from *Compensation for Victims of Violent Crime*: Home Office Consultation Paper, April 1999, p. 4.

might argue that victims did not fare ill in Government budgets, but there was little enough left for other purposes.

Quite characteristically, compensation had been an initiative dreamed up by penal reformers pursuing goals that were only incidental to the victims' interests, no victims themselves had actually been consulted about what they actually wanted,[8] and the victim of violence constructed by the scheme was an extrusion of the practical purposes of those who wished to soften punishment, and the exercise of corporal punishment in prison above all. It was never certain that monetary compensation was what victims of violent crime would have preferred above other choices (Tom Sargant of JUSTICE, one of the prime movers of compensation in the early 1960s, remarked 'it wasn't a thing that occurred to us. We took it for granted that they wanted compensation'). Neither was it certain that victims of violence were the angry vigilantes that the reformers feared (indeed the very first British Crime Survey of 1982 was to reveal them to be quite otherwise). Once the scheme was in place, however, it was difficult politically to dismantle it or reduce the sum of individual payments, and it became an albatross. Understood by victims, victims' organizations and the scheme's administrators[9] to be as much a symbol of recognition and 'respect' as material assistance,[10] any attempts to alter its provisions could appear to belittle victims, their importance and their suffering. The United Kingdom, it was noted, was paying out 'more to victims than all the other countries of Europe combined',[11] but, the Chairman of the Victims Steering Group wondered in 2000, 'even within the victims envelope there can be discussion about whether inflating criminal injuries compensation is the best way of spending money'.

[8] And it had been just so in Germany. See H. Jung; 'The Renaissance of the Victim in Policy Making', in L. Zedner and A. Ashworth (eds.); *The Criminological Foundations of Penal Policy,* Oxford University Press, Oxford, 2003, p. 452.

[9] The Chairman of the Criminal Injuries Compensation Appeals Panel reflected, for instance, that 'we aren't just compensating people because they've been injured because it would cost millions. With a dog bite it would bankrupt the scheme.'

[10] See J. Shapland; 'Victims, The Criminal Justice System and Compensation', *British Journal of Criminology,* 1984, Vol. 24, No. 2, pp. 131–49. The purpose of the scheme was to express sympathy, not to provide finely tuned compensation, said the Grade 7 in charge of criminal injuries compensation at a meeting of the Victims Steering Group in December 1998.

[11] G. Bradshaw; Article 36 Committee, Agenda Item 13, protection of victims in the European Judicial Area, undated.

The Criminal Injuries Compensation Board had been constituted in 1964 under the Royal Prerogative as a 'non-departmental public board' that received light direction from a predecessor of the Justice and Victims Unit of the Home Office. The very first major initiative for victims in England and Wales, financially over-shadowing every other initiative, pursuing its own focused and clearly demarcated role, functionally and institutionally independent of much of the rest of the work of the criminal justice system, it had tended to develop apart from the larger political environment of victims. The Chief Executive of the Criminal Injuries Compensation Authority said in 2000 that he had little contact with fellow agencies and departments represented on the Victims Steering Group 'apart from the Home Office [and] Victim Support [which] is the organisation we probably feel most related to. [The others] don't have very much interest in us.' Some time later, he was to email the JVU lamenting the neglect of the Authority in its draft plans for a national strategy for victims and witnesses: 'The Home Office may well be concerned at the amount of money which is spent on criminal injuries compensation . . . But given that so much is spent—by far the largest slab of spending directly for the benefit of victims, the largest such programme in the world and so on—couldn't the strategy make something positive of it? . . . The only direct reference at present is the gnomic "CIC— improvements" in para 15.' Criminal injuries compensation had taken its own distinct evolutionary path.

It took a long while to place the scheme on a statutory basis because it was feared that doing so might signify that the State had formally assumed both an obligation in law to protect its subjects against harm, and a companion liability to compensate them should that protection fail,[12] not only against crimes of violence perhaps, but also, in time and by extension, against theft, burglary, robbery, and other offences.[13] Yet it was difficult to pretend that compensation had not attained the standing of a virtual entitlement, and

[12] Thus Ian Chisholm was to emphasize in internal discussions within the Home Office in October 1999 that the criminal injuries compensation was the most generous in the world. It was intended to provide expression of public sympathy but the State, he said, is not liable for injuries. An internal paper noted that the 'State is not liable for injuries caused to people by acts of others' (Key Government Action to Assist Victims/ Witnesses January 1999).

[13] D. Miers; *State Compensation for Criminal Injuries*, Blackstone Press, London, 1997, p. 4.

especially so after 1970 when the scheme's decisions became subject to judicial review. There was continual talk about reforming such an expensive and uncontrolled programme, perhaps through legislation, and the re-constitution of criminal injuries compensation on a statutory footing was indeed presaged in the Criminal Justice Act 1988 c. 33. The scheme was to be revised in 1990 but the Conservative Government still havered about committing itself to the formal and symbolic act of granting a statutory status to compensation. At last, driven by financial imperatives and the politics of austerity, and with the blessing of Victim Support,[14] the Government, in Lucia Zedner's words, resorted in 1993 'to mak[ing] radical changes to the scheme without recourse to legislation'.[15] In place of the old common law system, and against the judgment of the Criminal Injuries Compensation Board itself,[16] a tariff scheme was introduced 'to control the rapidly escalating compensation bill'. It did not thrive, having been ruled unlawful by the House of Lords in an action brought by trades unions and others in 1995,[17] the older common law damages scheme was re-instated, and the Government was obliged at last to legislate for a tariff scheme and a new administrative structure, including an appeals procedure,[18] in the Criminal Injuries Compensation Act 1995.[19] The Labour Party was then in

[14] H. Reeves and K. Mulley; 'The new status of victims in the UK: Opportunities and threats', in A. Crawford and J. Goodey (eds.); *Integrating a Victim Perspective Within Criminal Justice: International debates,* Ashgate, Aldershot, 2000, p. 131. See UK and Ireland Forum Compensation Working Group; *Compensation—a human right,* Victim Support, October 1999, in which the tariff scheme was praised for its transparency, certainty and equality.

[15] L. Zedner; 'Victims', in M. Maguire *et al.* (eds.); *The Oxford Handbook of Criminology,* second edition, Oxford University Press, Oxford, 1997, p. 604.

[16] Their judgment was that the new tariff scheme would not be fair or cheaper and could 'not be run by civil servants'. When the outstanding cases left under the old scheme had been substantially cleared up, the Board itself would be dissolved, and that came eventually to pass in the Spring of 2000.

[17] R v. Secretary of State for the Home Department, Ex parte Fire Brigades Union and others [1995] All ER 244 (HL).

[18] CICAP came into existence on 1 April 1996 when the new Act came into effect. The first appeal it received was in July 1996 and the first oral hearing in January 1997.

[19] And Victim Support began to talk about it within the newly supplied framework of human rights. UK and Ireland Forum Compensation Working Group; *Compensation—a human right,* Victim Support, October 1999. The Human Rights Act did not, of course, establish that right (see J. Wadham and J. Arkinstall; 'Rights of victims of crime', *New Law Journal,* Vol. 150, 6944, 1 April 2000, p. 1084) but it is interest-

opposition and it accepted in guarded fashion[20] the introduction of a tariff during the passage of the Act, but it made no commitment to restore the earlier system, only saying cautiously that any Government it formed would have to keep within prevailing expenditure limits. Officials of the Justice and Victims Unit themselves had originally expressed reservations about the tariff model, noting that the total amount of money available for distribution had been cut, but by the time of the new Labour administration in 1997 they had come to acknowledge that it was a simpler and administratively more straightforward system that speeded payments to the victim.

The 1995 tariff laid out in minute detail 380 categories of injury and twenty five levels of compensation from '1' (£1,000 for, say, a 'deviated nasal septum') to '25' (£250,000 for, say, the paralysis of all four limbs); procedures for allocating additional proportions of the tariff amounts where there were several injuries, and for the application of 'multipliers' where a loss of earnings was likely to continue over a period of time. The new scheme was not amended for five years, but the reversal of the unlawful 1993 scheme (described by the Labour Party-supporting *Daily Mirror* as a 'Tory bungle'[21]) and the return to the 1990 common law system had left a number of unadjudicated cases in limbo[22] (including, most poignantly, some 200 cases affecting the families of

---

ing, in the light of the previous chapter, that Victim Support was interested in developing a rights discourse in that fashion.

[20] Citing the approval of Victim Support, Alun Michael said in debate in the House of Commons in December 1995 that 'We welcome the introduction of a tariff system to simplify the process of decision making and to speed it up. Many victims have wanted a decision quickly and not to have reminders of their suffering over an extended period...'. But he then proceeded to list a number of reservations, including, for instance, the depletion of the sums to be awarded, and the lack of provision for inflation over time, and he concluded 'It is rather sad that the Home Secretary's approach to the issue is an attempt to save money at the expense of victims of crime. Many victims will suffer as a result, although there will be benefits from the tariff scheme. In some ways the Government are making victims of the most horrific and damaging injuries pay for the Government's failure to stem the increase in crime and particularly in violent crime.'

[21] *Daily Mirror*, 14 September 1998.

[22] By June 1997, just after the election, 72,000 applications had been received under the 1994 scheme. Those who had been offered an award were allowed to keep it. Some 55 fatal cases were decided under the 1994 scheme, and another 1,200 had been lodged but not determined.

murder victims,[23] where a possible £2.5m. was at stake), and the two schemes were to run in parallel for a while until the residue was settled by the Board.[24] At the start of the 1997 financial year, a little over 44,000 applications to the old 1990 scheme were still unresolved. 21,730 cases were settled during 1997–8, leaving 22,854 outstanding at 31 March 1998.[25] A year later, there were over 12,500 cases outstanding.[26] In 1998–9, £195m. was paid to 46,000 successful applicants, of which £81m. was allotted to claimants still eligible under the pre-1996 scheme.

It was thought quite wrong from the start to recompense a morally-undeserving or morally-complicit victim from public funds.[27]

---

[23] They were ineligible for certain amounts of compensation because of the withdrawal of the original, 1993, version of the tariff. There cases had been subject to review but the Government had 'decided not to do anything' because it could not make an exception for one class of applicants alone. Under the tariff scheme the eligibility criteria for dependants and relatives of murder victims had been widened to include unmarried but long-term partners, the fathers of illegitimate murdered children, the parents of adult victims, and the adult children of such victims. Those who had been assessed under the withdrawn scheme received compensation, those whose cases were still pending did not. Under the new tariff, a fixed payment of £5,000 was payable to each qualifying relative, £10,000 if only one ('Information for Families of Homicide Victims'—second edition, September 1998: The Criminal Injuries Compensation Scheme). Those cases were to be the subject of media interest and copious correspondence between the bereaved, Members of Parliament, and Alun Michael.

[24] *The Government's Expenditure Plans 1999–2000 to 2001–2000*, p. 24. The Criminal Injuries Compensation Scheme Departmental Committee Meeting of 12 January 2000, noted that the average award for the 1996 scheme appeared to be stabilizing but that for the 1990 scheme was 'rising beyond expectations'. The backlog was cleared eventually and the Criminal Injuries Compensation Board was wound up at the end of March 2000.

[25] Victim Support News Service, February 1999: *February News*.

[26] All applications received before 1 April 1996 would be dealt with according to the 'provisions of the non-statutory Scheme which came into operation on 1 February 1990'. *The Criminal Injuries Compensation Scheme*, Home Office, December 1995, p. 17.

[27] The House of Commons debate on the 1964 White Paper on compensation made that quite evident. The Member of Parliament for Croydon stated, for example, that he was a 'very strong advocate of compensation being paid to innocent—and I stress "innocent"—victims of crimes of violence'. And Alan Brown, the Member for Tottenham talked about how compensation would become 'a happy hunting ground for a highly undesirable type of young criminal who is prone to carry a knife or razor... I cannot accept the view that the public should pay for such things as that. If public money is to be used, it should be used solely to compensate innocent people.' There was no record of any dissent from that stance.

The proper recipient of compensation was a 'blameless' victim of violence.[28] Perhaps it was a conception that reflected the rather different constellations of crime and victimization that were publicly visible in the 1950s when recorded rates of offending were low and victims of violence were thought to be relatively uncommon.[29] It was redolent too of a more innocent period before victimology and the crime surveys[30] disclosed how bystanders, victims, and offenders of violence tend to compose a complex grey mass of gradated and overlapping populations.[31] But it was also held inappropriate and repugnant to reward those who had brought suffering on their own heads; who had themselves been responsible for the suffering of others; whose conduct before, during or after the incident was deemed morally questionable; or who had not assisted the criminal

---

[28] 'Blameless' and innocent tended to be used interchangeably. Thus '[B]lameless victims of violent crime committed in Great Britain can receive compensation from the state ...'. Home Office Annual Report 1998–9—Chapter 10: Victims of Crime. The Criminal Injuries Appeal Panel declared that its purpose was to assist the Government's 'aim of providing a tangible measure of sympathy for the blameless victims of violent crime.' Annual Report, 1996–7, Criminal Injuries Compensation Appeals Panel, First Report, Cm. 3840, London, February 1998, p. 3. 'CICA: A guide to the criminal injuries compensation scheme, (effective from 1 April 1996)'; 'the scheme is intended to be an expression of public sympathy and support for innocent victims'. And see S. Walklate; Victimology: The victim and the criminal justice process, Unwin Hyman, London, 1989, p. 130.

[29] See J. Young; 'Crime and Social Exclusion', in M. Maguire et al. (eds.); The Oxford Handbook of Criminology, Third Edition, Oxford University Press, Oxford, 2002.

[30] Terence Morris said of Margery Fry, the scheme's progenitor: if she had had 'in her hands the British Crime Survey, I think she would have been staggered to discover that victims and assailants are well known to each other. They seem to be young men, heavy drinking at weekends ... She still held to this stereotypical image of the victim of violent crime as an essentially gentle, absolutely innocent, unsuspecting person ... the dear little old lady sitting in her cottage with wire-rimmed spectacles like the lady on the Mazawattee tea box ... In fact the victims of violent crime aren't like that at all.'

[31] Antilla remarked that 'Generally, one can say that the earlier stereotypes of "black and white" have been exchanged for "grey versus grey" ... the stereotype of the innocent and unsuspecting victim has proved to be false ... ' I. Antilla; 'Victimology—A New Territory in Criminology', Scandinavian Studies in Criminology, Vol. 5, Martin Robertson, London, 1974; and see S. Singer; 'Homogeneous Victim-Offender Populations—a Review and Some Research Implications', in J. Dahman and J. Sasfy (eds.); Victimology Research Agenda Development, 1980, Vol. 1. Cretney and Davis observe that the relation between criminal offending and susceptibility to assault 'is quite striking'. A. Cretney and G. Davis; Punishing Violence, Routledge, London, 1995, p. 32.

justice system in bringing offenders to heel (so that, for instance, a guide to the scheme made it evident that, unless there were 'good reasons', the claimant should have reported the incident personally to the police as soon as possible after it had happened).

Applications were considered on evidence submitted by the claimant, police, medical experts, witnesses, and others, and, in 1998–9, 34,000 or 58 per cent of the 59,000 claims were successful; 13,000 proceeded to review within the Authority; and a further 3,000 to appeal, of which 37 per cent were successful.[32] Most of the appeals against the adverse findings of the Criminal Injuries Compensation Scheme were, said a member of the Appeals Panel, 'about the eligibility of young men involved in brawls who are turned down'. A claim to compensation could be rejected under the scheme because of a lack of co-operation in bringing an assailant to justice; because conduct during or after the incident made it inappropriate; or because the victim had precipitated the offence or was in collusion with the offender. 'We have to take character into account because we can't ignore it. Parliament has made that clear,' said Peter Spurgeon, Chief Executive of the Criminal Injuries Compensation Authority in 1998. Offenders should not benefit from awards[33] (and until October 1979, victims of domestic violence were excluded lest the offender gain or be in collusion with the victim). Victim provocation or participation invalidated applications.[34] So did excessive risk-taking. Prostitutes who had been raped, for instance, might expect a lesser award[35] because they

---

[32] *Third Report: Accounts for the year ended 31 March 1999*, Criminal Injuries Compensation Authority, HC 353, 2000.

[33] The Criminal Injuries Compensation Scheme, 12 December 1995, p. 5.

[34] 'CICA: A guide to the criminal injuries compensation scheme, (effective from 1 April 1996)', p. 14 laid down that an award could be reduced or withheld if 'your injury was caused in a fight in which you had voluntarily agreed to take part ... If you invited someone "outside" for a fist-fight ... If without reasonable cause you struck the first blow ... If the incident in which you were injured formed part of a pattern of violence ... Where you were injured whilst attempting to obtain revenge ... If you used offensive language or behaved in an aggressive or threatening manner...'. The Chair of a meeting of the Criminal Injuries Compensation Appeal Panel in May 1998 determined, for instance, that an application was suspect because 'you don't know if he wasn't winding the guy up in the pub—you can slip very easily into the hard man sphere [and] the genuine victim will usually go to the police straightaway'.

[35] Thus the Chair of the Criminal Injuries Compensation Authority wrote in December 1998 to an organization supporting rape victims that 'we make no moral

were deemed knowingly to have exposed themselves to hazard in their work, and a woman who had been drinking[36] or taking drugs[37] could have her award cut by 50 per cent. Classes of people were thereby systematically delineated and rewarded on moral grounds. 'What they are doing is making a moralistic judgement' said WAR, Women Against Rape.[38]

Repeatedly, those who appealed the decisions of the Authority were reminded about the moral foundations of the scheme. An unsuccessful applicant who had appealed against a decision of the Criminal Injuries Compensation Authority was told on appeal to the Criminal Injuries Appeals Panel that 'we aren't satisfied that your injuries weren't caused by your own conduct. An applicant has to satisfy the board that they were the *innocent* victim, and we think it would be inappropriate for you to have an award from public funds.'[39] 'In our view it's not appropriate to make an award when you've been in so much trouble' another applicant was told after he had disclosed four convictions for driving offences.

'Blamelessness' was not absolute but the apex of a hierarchy of desert,[40] the assessment of moral character having been partially mitigated by the introduction of an apparently objective scheme of penalty points for 'unspent' criminal convictions, 'even if the convictions are totally unrelated to the incident which led to the claim'.[41] Thus ten points were awarded for a biography that included a period of imprisonment of more than thirty months and one point was given for a community service order; and an ensuing calculus was used to compute percentage reductions in the award

judgements but where any claimant was involved in unlawful activity, that is inevitably a factor in determining the size of an award'. And see *Legal Action: Monthly Journal of Legal Action Group*, June 1996, p. 22, and a report of the same case in the *Guardian*, 19 April 1996.

[36] The award would be cut if it was decided that the drinking had led her to act aggressively.

[37] Howard Webber said that 'We would have to take account of the consumption of (illicit) drugs ... because this constitutes an illegal act.'

[38] *Independent on Sunday*, 20 December 1992.

[39] Meeting of CICAP, 8 May 1998, my notes.

[40] And such ranking made it possible for organizations such as Women Against Rape to complain that there was discrimination against those who were devalued by such other criteria as race, gender and class not 'to fit the moral code' of the Authority. WAR; 'Who Counts and Who Pays?', 15 December 1993.

[41] CICAP—A Guide to Applicants on the Hearings Procedure, p. 2.

(ten or more points would culminate in a total loss of award, for example). Peter Spurgeon of the Criminal Injuries Authority observed that 'the points system was to try to reduce the value-judgement laden character of the award... The idea of the penalty points system is to take out of the judgement some of the bias and prejudice about the awards.'[42]

As applications and costs mounted in the 1990s, so pressures collided. On the one hand, resources were held to be strained under the first New Labour Government, new and potentially expensive initiatives were being mooted for victims, and the Treasury prevailed on the Home Office to reduce the costs of an unchecked system described repeatedly in Homeric terms as the 'most generous criminal injuries compensation scheme in the world'. The Criminal Injuries Compensation Scheme was held up as a prime candidate for financial cuts.[43]

On the other hand, it was very difficult to deny the moral and political claims of the blameless victim of criminal violence (the Chief Executive of the Criminal Injuries Compensation Authority observed in October 1998 that public and political sentiment bestowed on victims of crime a very special sympathy: 'it is... largely emotion which is the driving force in our jurisdiction, setting compensation above, and apart from, general welfare provision'). Any action to reduce awards could and would be interpreted as a gratuitous form of secondary victimization inflicted by a callous State at a time when there was a growing and consequential fear of crime and crime itself was politically contentious. Furthermore, and to the dismay of the founders of the Scheme from the first, a number of those claiming compensation proved not to be individual victims of violence but groups of employees in hazardous occupations, such as the police and fire services, who were professionally and forcefully represented by trades unions and specialist lawyers, and who were unlikely to accept casually any erosion of their entitlements. Indeed, it was the Fire Brigades Union who had won the pivotal case overturning the first attempt at a tariff scheme in 1995.

---

[42]  CICAP seminar on customer care, 28 April 1998, my notes.
[43]  In the event, there was actually an 'underspend' of £20m. towards the end of the Comprehensive Spending Review three-year cycle. Criminal Injuries Compensation Scheme Departmental Committee, minutes of meeting of 12 January 2000.

Ancillary demands exacerbated the dilemma: organizations such as Women Against Rape and Victim Support came increasingly to challenge the presumption that only the morally deserving should be compensated, arguing that criminal history should be disregarded; there were demands for a more flexible tariff; a re-calibration of awards to take account of the starker inequities and omissions of the original scheme;[44] the introduction of a provision for inflation (the real value of the awards was said to have declined by some 8 per cent since the tariff had first been fixed); additional payments for loss of earnings and bereavement; the abolition of the maximum 'cap'; and calls for a right to an oral hearing in appeals under Article 6 of the Human Rights Act. Bereaved families petitioned and newspapers campaigned about what were claimed to be the inequitable awards for homicide, most particularly in the cases of the Russell and Nickell families[45] (Ministers noted the 'waves of media interest in what are thought to be perverse decisions'), and the fire fighters and police demanded more generous compensation because of the exceptional risks they confronted.

Yet all this occurred at the very time that the Home Office was obliged to claim in its submission to the 1998 Comprehensive Spending Review that significant overspends were forecast for 1998–2000 as the more expensive cases under the old system continued to travel through the system,[46] and that there were no ways of containing expenditure on compensation other than by reducing eligibility to the scheme. Radical proposals began to circulate: expenditure could be lessened by raising the lower threshold from £1,000 to £2,000; £10m. could be saved by removing injuries

---

[44] For example, the incurring of sexually transmitted disease, including HIV and AIDS, as a result of sexual assault; and the case of rape resulting in pregnancy.

[45] Lyn Russell and her daughter Megan were killed on 9 July 1996, and Rachel Nickell was killed in 1992.

[46] In Home Office Comprehensive Spending Review: Support for Victims of Crime, March 1998. The cases were to be made even more expensive by what was described as a landmark ruling in a case in the House of Lords which held that personal injuries compensation would no longer be based on the assumption that it would be invested in equities and gilts but in Government securities. See *Independent*, 17 July 1998. The outcome, it was thought, would affect future loss settlements by the Criminal Injuries Compensation Board under the 1990 scheme, adding £24–26m. to the 'compensation spend' by 31 March 2000. No provision had been made for this sum. The Home Office would not, however, have to follow suit with the 1996 scheme which had deliberately broken the link with common law damages.

in public house related injuries where elements of risk, moral hazard, and victim precipitation were present (known colloquially as 'cutting out drunks'); and by transferring responsibility for compensation to employers for those injured at work, and particularly for the police and fire services (although it was noted not only that there would be vehement opposition to a complete shift from the Police Federation and the Fire Brigades Union,[47] but that the workings of the existing scheme depended on police co-operation). In the event, the 1998 Comprehensive Spending Review settlement[48] allocated an extra £20m. to the scheme, the actual sums being £228m., £217m., and £217m. *per annum*, chiefly to accommodate the as-yet-to-be determined rump of cases inherited from 1993–6,[49] but no allowance was made for 'reflating the tariff bands'. It 'is not enough' decided the Chief Executive of the Criminal Injuries Compensation Authority and officials of JVU concurred.

After the financial settlement, it was thought evident that the internal structures and categorizations of the scheme would have to be reviewed and revised.[50] There could be no return to the old common law system. Neither at this stage could there be a major review that asked big and expensive questions. Change would have to be modest and constrained by the tight resources set for 1999–2002. All that seemed open to intervention were 'changes in amounts on the tariff and whether things should

[47] Although, interestingly, the Fire Brigades Union made no response to the 1999 consultation on criminal injuries compensation.

[48] The Home Office received an extra £2.8bn. *in toto*, mostly for crime prevention (see No. 10 web site: Money for Modernisation: the Comprehensive Spending Review, 14 July 1998). There was no mention of victims as the object of a dedicated budget, but there was reference to extra support for victims of crime, including victims and witnesses, and funding for Victim Support increased by 50%. *The Government's Expenditure Plans 1999–2000 to 2001–2002, Vol. 1*, p. 2.

[49] After 1999–2000, the Chief Executive of the Criminal Injuries Compensation Authority believed in 1998, the allotment should be adequate.

[50] George Howarth, Parliamentary Under-Secretary of State, told the July 1999 Conference of Victim Support 'The [Spending] review recommended no changes to the basic structure of the current scheme, but in the subsequent financial settlement more money was made available. We want to see these extra resources used as effectively as possible for the benefit of victims and taxpayers alike. And so we have held a public consultation exercise inviting views on how the scheme might be refined or improved within the parameters of the present tariff-based arrangements and the financial provision set for the next 3 years.'

be moved up or down' and 'the question [of] whether the relativities are appropriate'.[51]

In September 1998, the Home Secretary himself announced spontaneously[52] in what an official called 'a throwaway remark that was misinterpreted'[53] that there were inequities which demanded attention: in particular, the paucity of awards to rape victims and the families of murder victims,[54] and a preliminary draft consultation document on the scheme was then almost immediately distributed within the Home Office in October. The tariff was the right structure, it was said, but the scheme should probably be more comprehensive and consistent, and there might be other changes in priorities so that extra money could be given to the more seriously injured victim. There were outstanding questions about whether the 'tariff bands should be reflated', how any changes should be paid for, and whether there were other ways of saving money. Ministers approved the draft, proposed that the threshold should be increased, and agreed to proceed with the consultation. During those deliberations, Alun Michael queried whether it might not be possible to go even further and not reflate the tariff figures: if payment was symbolic, he ventured, there was no need to reflate. There was uncertainty about whether compensation was really a matter for criminal justice or for the welfare system under the care of the Department of Social Security. There was musing about whether employee injury should not be the responsibility of employers, and a proposal was floated to hold an early prior meeting with Victim Support and the Police Federation so that they would

---

[51] Meeting of Victims Steering Group, 4 December 1998, my notes.

[52] And particularly in a lobby briefing to *The Sun* newspaper in response to widespread criticism of the tariff award of £10,000 to the father of a daughter who had been kidnapped, raped, and murdered. The matter was complicated because it had not then been referred to Cabinet or to the Treasury. In October 1998, Teresa Reynolds asked the Secretary of the Victims Steering Group about a report of the Home Secretary's remark in *The Times*, 17 September 1998 and requested that it be added to the agenda of a forthcoming meeting.

[53] Meeting of Victims Steering Group, 4 December 1998, my notes.

[54] Speaking at the annual conference of the Police Superintendents Association and reported in *The Times*, 17 September 1998. It was the view of the Chief Executive of the Criminal Injuries Compensation Authority, Howard Webber, in August 2000 that the apparent discrepancies between awards to primary and secondary victims were explicable because 'our job is primarily to provide compensation to victims, not however tragic, to the families of victims'.

'not feel bounced and critical'.[55] There was also caution: given the financial restrictions under which the scheme would labour, it would not be appropriate to open up a debate about the more fundamental options for reform because that might only raise expectations about strategic change that could not reasonably be addressed in the short term and which would require legislation. Any consultation exercise should in the immediate future focus on changes within the existing framework, but 'if we do not [ask searching questions] others will', and it was concluded that it might be best for the consultation document to 'trail the possibility of a more fundamental review' when more money might be forthcoming under the next Comprehensive Spending Review.

In January 1999, the Home Office sought Cabinet approval for the issue of a consultation document on the 'Criminal Injuries Compensation Scheme within the financial provision of the Comprehensive Spending Review'. An invitation would be made to take note of any more radical suggestions that could be borne in mind for the next Comprehensive Spending Review (that, it was thought, 'might placate some of the fiercer critics'). Other departments voiced no objections to the consultation although it was thought that critics of the scheme 'will take advantage of the opportunity to lobby for more fundamental change'.

So it was that an announcement was made in March 1999[56] that some 200 organizations would be approached to elicit their views about possible changes in 'injury descriptions and thresholds',[57] in cases particularly of child abuse and sexual assault which had been seen as relatively disadvantaged under the original tariff;[58] the pay-

---

[55] A meeting between the Criminal Injuries Compensation Authority, JVU and Paul Boateng, a Minister, in November 1998 agreed eventually that it would not be a good idea to transfer responsibility for compensation on to employers: that step would require primary legislation and 'open up everything to debate'. The Police Federation might, for instance, regard such a measure as a way of saving the money of injured police officers. But Paul Boateng did not preclude the matter being considered internally within the Department.

[56] Criminal Injuries Compensation: Giving Victims a Say, Press Release, 25 March 1999; Home Office Press Release, 104/99, 25 March 1999.

[57] Although the Chief Executive of the Criminal Injuries Compensation Authority reflected in 1998 that only 140 of the 18,000 claims submitted could 'not be resolved' under the tariff.

[58] See Parliamentary All Party Penal Affairs Group; *Increasing the Rights of Victims of Crime*, July 1996, p. 8. (The Group had been chaired by Alun Michael

ment of compensation to the same sex partners of homicide; adjustments for inflation; and whether injuries suffered as a result of drugs and drink should be taken into account: 'with continuing pressures on public spending, and with demand on the scheme continuing to rise, the Government is anxious that the money now provided should be used to the best effect... while still reflecting society's sense of responsibility for and sympathy with the blameless victims of crimes of violence... '.[59]

Victim Support's reply to the consultation re-affirmed its endorsement of a tariff-based scheme because it was speedier, more certain, more open and accessible.[60] But several changes were thought necessary. *Inter alia*, the overall level of funding should be raised because the number of claims and the severity of injuries could not be predicted at a time when levels of violent crime were rising and the numbers of firearms were growing. The tariff should be 'uprated' in line with inflation and the minimum level of award should be abolished. Awards for rape and child abuse should be increased, and same sex partners should become eligible for awards. Awards should not affect entitlement to income-related benefits. Neither should they be reduced or refused because of an applicant's previous convictions: a criminal history was irrelevant to the harm suffered by a victim. The eligibility of the scheme should be extended to those suffering psychological injury as a result of other offences, and racial harassment was cited (and that was part of the massive backwash of the Macpherson Inquiry[61]). Victim Support would not exclude drunks or proscribe drug users from eligibility.

who then, it will be recalled, became Minister responsible, *inter alia*, for victims in the new Government). The then Conservative Government had replied that it might well review the tariff (David Maclean's reply to Alun Michael and comments on PAPPAG; *Increasing the Rights of Victims of Crime*, 22 October 1996). The disadvantages suffered by those groups were said to have arisen because awards to women and children had not been as influenced by common law damages arising from civil litigation and were therefore lower (*Compensation for Victims of Violent Crime*: Home Office Consultation Paper, April 1999, p. 9).

[59] *Compensation for Victims of Violent Crime*: Home Office Consultation Paper, April 1999, p. 3.

[60] *Compensation for Victims of Violent Crime*, Home Office Consultation Paper April 1999, A response by Victim Support, 18 June 1999.

[61] Reviewing the submissions, JVU noted that 'In light of Macpherson, probably worth pursuing'.

In its summary analysis[62] of the fifty-two replies received, JVU reported that most respondents were averse to cutting the lower bands to raise the eligibility threshold (only one of the twenty-six replies that touched on the question was in favour, but JVU concluded that those replies combined opposition with an unwillingness to face the issue of costs). Very small numbers had commented on the discount for criminal convictions (four out of six responses were in support of relaxing the discount rule[63]). There was opposition to 'excluding drink/drug abusers' ('cutting out drunks' had generated a 'fair amount of comment', seven replies being in favour, and nineteen against. There did seem to be a risk of excluding the 'blameless victim', JVU admitted, and consideration might have to be given in the making of awards to assessing whether alcohol or drugs could have contributed to the victim's involvement in the crime.). Three respondents reported that they felt that the scheme was unfriendly to victims of 'intra-family' violence and other abuse, and Victim Support was concerned about applications being turned down where victims continued to live with the assailant. Whilst one can appreciate the point in principle, JVU observed, there was the problem of how to stop compensation falling into the hands of the assailant. There was support for the extension of the eligibility for compensation to the same sex partners of homicide cases (and Ministers, it was noted, had urged some such move at the time of the Admiral Duncan bomb that killed and injured several people a mere month after the consultation paper was issued[64]). There was strong support

Criminal Injuries Compensation Scheme Consultation Exercise, Analysis of Responses, 4 October 1999.

Sheffield University was said to have suggested that taking account of long past or unrelated convictions was contrary to the 1983 Council of Europe Convention on Criminal Injuries Compensation.

Shortly after 6.30pm on Friday 30th April 1999, the Admiral Duncan, a homosexual bar in Soho, was the target of a bomb. Three people died, and at least 79 were injured. The man eventually convicted of the offence, David Copeland, had previously attacked street markets in Brixton and Brick Lane, areas of London heavily populated by minority ethnic groups. Jack Straw, the Home Secretary, observed on the day: 'This is a terrible outrage committed by people with no humanity. I know that the police are devoting huge efforts to find the perpetrators. Our hearts go out to those injured, their families and friends. This awful crime reinforces the need for all of us to be vigilant. We are dealing with people who have warped minds, right-wing extremists who are obviously racist and homophobic. That we know. I know too that the British people will not be intimidated by this outrage, nor will the harmony between different

too for the relaxation of the 'exceptional risk rule', reflating the tariff bands, increasing awards for child abuse and for rape (a number of campaigning organizations had replied, conflating child abuse and rape, and, in JVU's judgment, contributing little to substantive argument: the increased levels of award had been justified 'only very loosely') Overall, JVU concluded, the responses had 'not added to the debate' because they had not heeded the problem of financial constraint, but consideration might be given to some relaxation of the rules.

Ian Chisholm, the head of JVU, then took stock of the consultation and its possible aftermath in October 1999, remarking that the issue of compensation would need an early response, in part because Charles Clarke, the Minister, wanted to announce his intentions before the end of the year. The main 'pressure points for change' were that there should be a general increase in tariff bands to allow for inflation; that tariff awards for child abuse and rape should be increased; and 'fatal' awards should be extended to partners of the same sex. There was the difficulty that, although the 'spillover' of the 1990 common law cases into 1999 had made the scheme more expensive than had been anticipated, and there was 'no financial headroom', the consultation had revealed 'virtually no support for any of the money-saving recommendations'. Indeed, many of the respondents on the level of tariff for child abuse and rape were 'single issue pressure groups' that had tended to gloss over the difficulties. In the main, he said, the responses had not added to the debate on the issue. There would have to be some degree of reflation, and consideration should be given to how that could be accomplished. The inclusion of same sex partners in homicide cases had met with Ministerial sympathy although it could lead to a wider extension of demands for gay rights with implications for other branches of Government.

His colleague, the Grade 7 with special responsibility for compensation matters in JVU, proposed in November 1999 that he should

minorities be disturbed by it' (BBC News On-Line, 30 April 1999). The Admiral Duncan bomb was to have other repercussions, most notably to encourage the Metropolitan Police to cluster a number of crimes together as hate crimes and apply the category in the implementation of the Macpherson Inquiry report. The view of John Grieve, one of the senior officers responsible, was that if misogynist and anti-homosexual crimes were not so clumped with racist crime, there would have been less political momentum behind their repression.

work up 'a package of recommendations' with Howard Webber, the Chief Executive of the Criminal Injuries Compensation Authority, and Michael Lewer, the Chairman of the Criminal Injuries Compensation Appeals Panel, so that an announcement about future intentions could be made early in the new year. There could be two sets of changes: the 'noncontentious and cost-neutral', and those that were 'more complicated with significant cost implications'. The first category could include changes to tariff awards to improve their consistency and transparency. Ministers were 'keen on extending eligibility to same sex partners' but they would need to 'clear lines' with other departments. The second category would include reflating the tariff bands, and changing awards for child abuse and rape.

The consultation and review of the scheme were eventually considered by Ministers at the end of 2000, after the Spending Review announced in July of that year had made no greater immediate financial provision to the Home Office for victims and witnesses in the first year and had created 'shortfalls' in the succeeding two years. Any new money for victims had been 'parked in the unallocated reserve' of £500m. to await agreed joint proposals from the three Departments of State administering the criminal justice system, the Treasury manoeuvre to foster joined-up government which I already described in Chapter 2. Casting about them, Ministers eyed the prospect of 'cutting the baseline provision of the criminal injuries compensation scheme' to support a number of initiatives waiting in the slips, including the introduction of victim statements, extra measures for vulnerable and intimidated witnesses, and the expansion of the Magistrates' Court Witness Service. Whether that move would have been feasible is not clear,[65] but simultaneously, *deus ex machina*, JVU also revisited its estimates of expenditure on compensation, and discovered that the pre-1996 cases would probably prove less expensive than feared, with possible savings of £5m., £46m., and £47m. over the forthcoming three year period of the Spending Review. There would, it was thought, be 'no headroom in 2001–2' but the

---

[65] Particularly since the National Audit Office had just published a review of the workings of the Criminal Injuries Compensation Scheme and recommended that it be made more accessible and widely known. *Compensating Victims of Violent Crime*, Report by the Comptroller and Auditor General, Stationery Office, London, 2000, esp. p. 12.

position would be more certain thereafter, and there were savings that could be used to fund the mooted changes in the Scheme, the 'uprating for inflation', increasing of awards for sexual assault and child abuse, and the provision of fatal awards for same sex partners.[66]

The greater portion of that surplus, some £25m, was indeed to be diverted to 'meet the shortfall in funding' for the other projects for victims and witnesses, but £16m. still remained for a newly revised scheme that was approved in March 2001 and which came finally into effect on 1 April 2001 with 'presentational changes and changes of substance to the tariff of awards',[67] including compensation to same sex partners in homicide cases,[68] and the payment of larger sums to victims of rape (minimum awards were increased from £7,500 to £11,000), sexual assault, child abuse, and serious multiple injuries, increasing the tariff bands between 7 and 23 by 10 per cent.[69]

## Conclusions

I suggested at the beginning of this chapter a number of themes that might emerge from an analysis of the evolution of the criminal injuries scheme in the 1990s. Let me re-emphasize two here. The 1988 and 1995 Acts appeared scrupulously to have avoided the word *right* (and, indeed, *victim*) except that the latter granted an express right of appeal to the newly established Criminal Injuries Compensation Appeals Panel under Sec. 5(a). Note the rather careful phrasing of the opening section of the 1995 Act: 'The Secretary of State shall make arrangements for the payment of compensation to, or in respect of, persons who have sustained one or more criminal injuries . . . Any such arrangements shall include the making of a scheme providing, in particular, for (a) the circumstances in which awards may be made; and (b) the categories of person to whom awards may be made.' No mention is there made of rights under what remained a discretionary

---

[66] Email, 3 October 2000.

[67] Charles Clarke, statement to the House of Commons, 1 April 2001.

[68] Strategic Board: Delivering an Improved Service to Victims and Witnesses, 9 October 2001.

[69] Criminal Justice: *The Way Ahead*, Home Department, Cm. 5074, February 2001, p. 69.

scheme,[70] and the repeated general qualification was that compensation 'was introduced to provide an acknowledgement of society's sympathy for... victims' and was not an admission of failure or liability by the State. Yet note also that in its very first annual report, and after the passing of the Act, the Criminal Injuries Compensation Appeals Panel talked about how, under the new scheme, 'payments, which were formerly made on an ex gratia basis, are now made as of right...'.[71] In a formulation suggested to me by my colleague, the lawyer, Nicola Lacey, compensation might best be described as a legitimate expectation or quasi-right with a peripheral right attached. But the development of criminal injuries compensation *had* evidently begun to edge victims closer to attaining a standing of a sort in law, and its administration had been entrusted to a body whose semi-detached relation to the criminal justice system and the State symbolized something of its tentativeness. It is not perhaps remarkable that it should have had so little impact on the other main currents of victims policy in the twentieth century.

Secondly, this episode demonstrates very clearly how the boundaries of classes of morally-deserving victims were defined by the economic imperatives of a demand-led compensation scheme operating within financial constraints, on the one hand, and, on the other, by countervailing political pressures emanating from lobbies and victims' organizations (some of whom were discounted precisely because they were interested parties) and Ministers who had been moved by a mix of specific, highly dramatic events and more general policy considerations. Some quite radical shifts in moral taxonomy were effected without undue fuss, and chiefly the recognition of the same sex partners of homicide victims as legitimate claimants. But it was impossible to afford every claim, and the victims who were recognized were those worthy applicants whose needs could be

---

[70] Officials and agencies with an interest in victims' policies point to the Criminal Justice and Court Services Act 2000 as the legislation which did come finally to establish a statutory right for victims. That Act created a national probation service whose aims included 'ensuring offenders' awareness of the effects of crime on the victims of crime and the public' (Criminal Justice and Court Services Act 2000, 2000 Chapter 43). Victim Support stated that it 'puts victims' rights into statute for the first time in the UK'. Victim Support; The probation service's victim contact work: Guidance for Victim Support Schemes and Witness Schemes, June 2001, p. 5.

[71] Criminal Injuries Compensation Appeals Panel; *Annual Report 1996–1997*, Cm. 3840, Home Office, London, 1998, p. 25.

afforded within budgetary limits. The moral and the deserving were, in that sense, emanations of quite pragmatic criteria of affordability.

And finally, the sheer scale and urgency of the activity centred on the reform of criminal injuries compensation added to the appearance of busyness attending the politics of victims. There was, admittedly, much else being transacted in the Home Office that did not involve victims, and victims remained a dwarf of the political world, but the area was clearly stamped as a site of policy importance, and that was to contribute both rhetorically and impressionistically to the construction of a sense of the critical mass that required political reorganization in 2001.

# 7

# The Victim and Reparation

## Introduction

Perhaps the most widely employed definition of restorative justice was devised by Tony Marshall,[1] at first a Home Office research officer with a training in social anthropology and subsequently a moral entrepreneur working in the mediation and reparative justice movement.[2] Restorative justice, said Marshall, is 'a process whereby all the parties with a stake in a specific offence come together to resolve collectively how to deal with the aftermath of the offence and its implications for the future'.[3] That is an eclectic and vague description embracing a large cast of people, including the victim, in many possible relations,[4] and it extends to a correspondingly broad span of activities, amongst them victim-offender mediation (originating in its modern phase in Canada and where victims and offenders are

---

[1] See P. McCold; 'Restorative Justice—Variations on a Theme', in W. Lode (ed.); *Restorative Justice for Juveniles,* University of Leuven Press, Leuven, 1998. His definition was adopted, for example, by the Working Party on Restorative Justice established by the United Nations Alliance of Non Government Organisations on Crime Prevention and Criminal Justice. (D. Van Ness; 'Proposed UN Basic Principles on Restorative Justice', undated, no place of publication.)

[2] He was, for instance, Director of FIRM, the Forum for Initiatives in Reparation and Mediation, now called Mediation UK, in the early 1990s.

[3] T. Marshall; 'Seeking the Whole Justice', Paper delivered at ISTD conference, 1997 and *Restorative Justice: An Overview,* Home Office, London, 1999.

[4] See *Sentencing and Corrections: Issues for the 21st Century,* US Dept of Justice, September 1999, which noted that even sex-offender notification laws, and the right of relatives of murder victims to be present at executions were deemed restorative by some. It is not perhaps remarkable that Home Office officials attending the 2000 UN Congress on Crime and the Treatment of Offenders, a Congress replete with enthusiasm for restorative justice, should have been a little guarded in their response, claiming that the new ideology was still muddled and ill-defined.

brought together to reconcile their disputes); family group conferences (which I shall discuss at greater length below); sentencing
circles (based on Canadian aboriginal practices in which all affected
parties contribute to a resolution that is intended to reintegrate the
offender); restorative cautioning (aimed at eliciting an apology or
reparation and enabling protagonists to discuss the offence); and
regulatory cautioning (involving negotiated control between parties
in order to secure greater future compliance with rules).[5] Sticking to
the theme of this book, it is largely upon the victim's role in those
processes that I shall dwell.

The motives and meanings of restorative justice have been as
diverse as its forms.[6] There were the strains within the North American penology of the 1970s that saw in reparation an opportunity not
only to soften or bypass[7] punishment[8] but also to resolve the fiscal
and social crises of prison crowding[9] by decanting economic and
administrative responsibilities for control into the community.[10]

[5] Taken largely from A. Ashworth; 'Is Restorative Justice the Way Forward for
Criminal Justice', typescript, undated, pp. 5–6.

[6] Faget observed that restorative justice 'is the conjunction of three movements of
thinking which are ideologically heterogeneous. The first denounces the devastating
effects of the repressive system on delinquents' future paths; the second emphasises the
absolute necessity to give back conflicts to the victims, conflicts which have been
confiscated from them by the State and the professionals; the third movement notes
that the great majority of offences opposes people from the same community and
therefore considers it logical to deprofessionalise their treatment.' J. Faget; 'Mediation, Criminal Justice and Community Involvement. A European Perspective',
European Forum for Victim-Offender Mediation and Restorative Justice (ed.);
*Victim-Offender Mediation in Europe: Making Restorative Justice Work,* Leuven
University Press, Leuven, 2000, p. 39.

[7] Although there are those, like Dignan, who would argue that restorative justice is
probably inexorably implicated in punishment. See J. Dignan; 'Towards a Systemic
Model of Restorative Justice', in A. von Hirsch *et al.* (eds.); *Restorative Justice and
Criminal Justice,* Hart Publishing, Oxford, 2002.

[8] See R. Hofrichter; 'Techniques of Victim Involvement in Restitution', in
J. Hudson and B. Galaway (eds.); *Victims, Offenders, and Alternative Sanctions,*
Lexington Books, Lexington, Mass., 1980; and A. Scull; *Decarceration: Community
Treatment and the Deviant: A Radical View,* Prentice-Hall, Englewood Cliffs, 1977.

[9] The 1999 Annual Report of Penal Reform International talked about 'A new
agenda for penal reform' including restorative justice, because it could restore a
balance between victim, offender, and community and was likely to lead to a reduction
in imprisonment.

[10] See A. Daniels; 'Future for Alternatives', *Correctional Options,* Fall 1981, Vol. 1,
No. 1.

There were pressures within American jurisprudence both to transcend the alienating and harmful oppositions of the adversarial system and to void the courts of so-called petty 'junk cases'[11] that clogged civil and criminal proceedings.[12] There was the religious mission of North American and other Christian groups, such as the Mennonites and Quakers, to reconcile people in conflict.[13] Dispute resolution and reparation in the United States and elsewhere were intended to prevent discord and heal communities by bringing together those in dispute: shopper and shopkeeper, landlord and tenant, pupil and teacher, and neighbour and neighbour.[14] Restorative justice could act as an agent of crime reduction by neutralizing, as NACRO put it, the rationalizations of an 'excuse culture', mobilize shame and oblige offenders to confront the consequences of their acts. It could reduce the fear of crime by 'demystifying' offenders and making them less terrifying.[15] Restorative justice was developed in Australasia, South Africa[16] and Canada[17] where it was

---

[11] See C. Blew and R. Rosenblum; *An Exemplary Project: The Community Arbitration Project, Anne Arundel County,* US Department of Justice, Washington, DC, 1979.

[12] Implemented in England and Wales, it was also defined by some as a diversion programme. *The Times,* 25 November 1998, for instance, spoke of 'thousands of young offenders [who] will escape sentencing by the courts under government plans to reform the youth justice system ... [Panels] will issue a contract under which the youngster will apologise to the victim, do community service and take part in meetings to tackle offending behaviour and other problems.'

[13] *Victim-Offender Reconciliation Program,* Probation and Parole, Cambridge, Ontario, 1980.

[14] See *Mediating Social Conflict,* Ford Foundation, New York, 1978.

[15] See J. Hogarth; *Studies on Diversion: East York Community Law Reform Project,* Information Canada, Ottawa, 1975.

[16] Where it blended the Christian idea of reconciliation with the Xhosa concept of *Ubuntu* as personally mediated relations (I borrowed this idea from Claire Moon).

[17] RCMP, Restorative Justice: A Fresh Approach, no date, called restorative justice a more satisfying system of justice that is needed in place of the formal justice system. The RCMP, it noted, was championing community justice forums. My notes on a talk with the Canadian delegation at the UN Congress on the Prevention of Crime and the Treatment of Offenders, Vienna, 2000 recalled that they had been in touch with the Alliance of Non Governmental Organisations on Crime Prevention and Criminal Justice, and had been approached as a delegation to propose an amendment to the UN Declaration, the so-called Vienna Declaration, that the non-governmental organizations had drafted. They were 'very supportive' of the restorative justice movement because it had strong links with aboriginal justice. Canada sought to add the following paragraphs to the Declaration 'We commit ourselves to formulating restorative justice

implicated in a sometimes apologetic recognition by the State that it had in the past ridden roughshod over aboriginal practices and that correction, amends, and, indeed, emulation might be due.[18]

In all this, it is once again clear that the revival of restorative justice had little directly to do with the interests or wishes of the victim clearly expressed or conventionally defined.[19] It was a creature of different impulses. There had been no swelling of demand for reparation or mediation from victims or from the organizations that represented them,[20] although the occasional victim might have sought to meet an offender, such as a murderer, better to understand his action.[21] It was simply taken for granted that victims would or should somehow wish to play their part in doing good to the offender. When restorative justice first began to spread across England and Wales in the 1980s, Victim Support reflected that 'No-one actually knows what victims of crime think about the idea of reparation by offenders . . . Reparation has, however, been presented as a course of action which would be in the victims' best interests . . . '.[22]

---

legislation, policies, procedures and programmes, that are respectful of the rights, needs and interests of victims . . . , offenders, communities and all other parties and that promote a culture favourable to mediation and other RJ processes . . . '. 'We invite the Commission on Crime Prevention and Criminal Justice to formulate UN basic principles and standards to guide States in the fair and effective use of mediation and other restorative justice processes.' Versions of those statements did indeed eventually enter what was called the 'whereases' at the beginning of Declaration. The Conference was peripherally involved with the rights of victims and offenders, more centrally with transnational crime.

[18] See, for example, the report of the Task Force on the Criminal Justice System and its Impact on the Indian and *Métis* People of Alberta; *Justice on Trial*, Government of Alberta, Edmonton, 1991. It states at 1.1 and 1.7, 'We believe that to achieve harmony between the justice system and the Aboriginal people, they must be fully involved in any policy development, program planning and implementation and service delivery with respect to the criminal justice system . . . It is our position that numerous changes can be made relatively quickly to the existing criminal justice system to make it more sensitive to the needs of Aboriginal people. The first step in this process is the "indigenization" of the criminal justice system . . . [which] can, in fact, go a long way toward meeting the wishes of some Aboriginal people.' pp. 1.1, 1.7.

[19] Criminal Justice Consultative Council, meeting of 14 April 1998, minutes, p. i.

[20] It may be revealing that a poster for the 3rd International Forum on International Family Group Conferences, 4–6 April 2000, listed a number of representatives of organizations who were to speak, but none was from a victims' group.

[21] See, for example, L. Moreland; *An Ordinary Murder*, Aurum Press, London, 2001.

[22] 'The Victim and Reparation', NAVSS, London, 1984, p. 1.

And, twenty years later, Susan Herman of the American National Center for Victims of Crime claimed that restorative justice in the United States was not led by the practitioners or by victims' groups but by penal reform groups, offender groups, and academics who were persuaded that offenders had been mistreated. In restorative justice as elsewhere, victims remained the pragmatic construction of others.[23]

Restorative justice had always been as much an ideology, a theory, and a social movement as a utilitarian practice (one of its champions told an audience 'I was involved in this RJ movement or theory or action from the beginning.'[24]). And it was perhaps for that reason that it seems to have taken on trust the benefits it would confer on its participants, including the victim. After all, it promised a civilized alternative to the brutalities of a retributive and conflict-laden system of trial and punishment; it could assuage the guilt of colonial or post-colonial powers; it resonated religious themes of peace-making;[25] it claimed very diffuse spiritual roots;[26] it had about it

[23] In its evidence for the preparation of the JUSTICE Report on 'The Role of the Victim in the Criminal Justice Process', NACRO, for instance, declared in November 1995 that 'Fundamental to our contribution has been the belief that traditional approaches based on punishment—taking it out on the offender—are of generally limited value to the victim and that the system should strive to promote reconciliation and restoration wherever possible ... The development of mediation, reconciliation and reparation schemes ... can provide therapeutic benefits for both victims and offenders more effectively than the criminal justice process.'

[24] L. Walgrave; 'Regulating Coercion in Restorative Justice', American Society of Criminology meetings, Chicago, 13 November 2002, my notes.

[25] Thus the New Zealand judge, Fred McElrea, wrote in 'Restorative Justice: a Christian Approach to Conflict Resolution', 'By rejecting legalism and formalism in favour of personal encounter and the engagement of those directly affected, restorative justice has a distinctly "New Testament" flavour. Because it is based outside the courts (even where courts have a supervisory role) restorative justice is free from the rituals of the courtroom and the formalism of the Pharisees. If a lawyer is present it is not as advocate, but as advisor and supporter. Professionals do not run or own the process ... it occurred to me that it was often God's grace at work in restorative justice. In such a context an expression of forgiveness cannot be something expected of victims—it is theirs to give if they feel it appropriate at the time, and they sometimes do. More often, though, there is a place for grace, that unearned generosity of spirit, and its transforming power.' On the *Reality* web site.

[26] See M. Hadley (ed.); *The Spiritual Roots of Restorative Justice*, State University of New York Press, Albany, New York, 2001, esp. p. 23, where it was said that 'The writers of this volume ... have engaged in discovering spiritual truths which political powers and structures have purloined and distorted—or merely forgotten.'

something of the iconography of the noble savage; it healed hurts[27] and repaired communities; it had been celebrated in truth commissions and linked with the charismatic authority of Nelson Mandela; and, at times, it acquired an almost eschatalogical tone.[28] It seemed irresistible. Carolyn Hoyle remarked that 'Conferences on the theme of restorative justice tend towards uncritical celebrations of its merit, with delegates happily assuming the role of evangelists.'[29]

In its most romantic guise, restorative justice could be traced back to a Golden Age of the Victim[30] before the State grew overmighty and usurped the place occupied by the individual victim in the folk moot or in the simpler and more direct justice devised by a Hamurabi, Moses, or Solon. In England and Wales, it was said, the Normans had initiated a long process of centralizing and consolidating power under the Crown that came in time utterly to dispossess the personal victim,[31] culminating in the Prosecution of Offences Act 1879, and giving rise to the two parties now alone recognized in the adversarial system, the defendant and a State that personified the community or society metaphysically conceived.[32] Victims and offenders had by then been stripped of all control over conflict to become alienated from their own disputes, from justice, and each other.[33]

[27] D. Van Ness said 'Restorative Justice is a growing international movement within the fields of juvenile and criminal justice. It is different from conventional justice processes in that it views crime primarily as injury... and the purpose of justice as healing...'; 'Restorative Justice: International Trends', paper given at Victoria University, Wellington, New Zealand, 7 October 1998.

[28] Heather Strang concluded *Repair or Revenge: Victims and Restorative Justice*, (Clarendon Press, Oxford, 2002) by declaring that the momentum of the restorative justice movement 'has given rise to some extravagant claims for its superiority to formal justice processes in dealing with crime', p. 192.

[29] '"Restorative Justice" and other new Penal Patterns', unpublished paper, 2000.

[30] See S. Schafer; *The Victim and His Criminal*, Random House, New York, 1968.

[31] See J. Jeudwine; *Tort, Crime, and Police in Mediæval Britain: a review of some early law and custom*, Williams and Norgate, London, 1917.

[32] Perhaps the classic definition of crime is that of William Blackstone: 'public wrongs, or crimes and misdemeanours, are a breach and violation of the public rights and duties due to the whole community, in its social aggregate capacity... since besides the wrong done to the individual, they strike at the very being of society'. *Commentaries on the Laws of England*, Oxford, 1778, Book IV, p. 5.

[33] N. Christie; 'Conflicts as Property', *British Journal of Criminology*, 1978, Vol. 17, No. 1.

But what had been lost in Europe was still held to be evident
elsewhere in the reports of colonial administrators, criminologists,
lawyers,[34] social anthropologists, and judges seconded to aboriginal
areas.[35] Set against the adversarial system with its distorting and
harmful polarities and its silencing of the victim, were the restorative
practices of pre-literate societies, the Maori,[36] the Bushmen, the
Australian and Canadian[37] Aborigines, and the inhabitants of
the Gold Coast[38] and Uganda,[39] which penal reformers sought to
retrieve, adapt, and apply to their own domestic criminal justice
systems. Thus the Australian sociologist, John Braithwaite, wrote
that his own model of restorative justice, reintegrative shaming, was
shaped by two challenges: 'Helping indigenous communities to learn
from the virtues of liberal statism—procedural fairness, rights, protecting the vulnerable from domination. [And] [h]elping liberal state
justice to learn from indigenous community justice—learning the
restorative community alternatives to individualism.'[40]

Mediation and reparation had a first flowering in England and
Wales[41] in the 1980s under the patronage principally of a probation
service[42] that regarded them as a mechanism for rehabilitating the

[34] See M. Boldt and J. Long (eds.); *The Quest for Justice: Aboriginal Peoples and
Aboriginal Rights*, University of Toronto Press, Toronto, 1985.

[35] See, for instance, the decision of Judge Barry Stuart of the Yukon Territorial
Court to re-institute sentencing circles in *Philip Moses v. The Queen* (1992).

[36] W. Tallack; *Howard Letters and Memories*, Methuen, London, 1905, p. 35.

[37] Bonta and his colleagues remark 'approaches originating in Aboriginal communities such as sentencing circles and family case conferencing have found their way
into the mainstream North American criminal justice system', J. Bonta *et al.*; *Restorative Justice: An Evaluation of the Restorative Resolutions Project*, Solicitor General
Canada, Ottawa, 1998, p. 2.

[38] See M. Fry; *Arms of the Law*, Gollancz, London, 1951.

[39] See E. Jones; *Margery Fry: The Essential Amateur*, Oxford University Press,
London, 1966, p. 232.

[40] J. Braithwaite; 'Conferencing and Plurality', *British Journal of Criminology*,
Autumn 1997, Vol. 37, No. 4, p. 505.

[41] And in the separate criminal justice system of Scotland which had adopted some
restorative elements in its Children's Hearings System that were later to be borrowed
in the Youth Justice and Criminal Evidence Act 1998. See A. Crawford and T. Newburn; 'Recent Developments in Restorative Justice for Young People in England and
Wales', *British Journal of Criminology*, Summer 2002, Vol. 42, No. 3, p. 479.

[42] Playing a principal role was John Harding, some time Deputy Chief Probation
Officer of the West Midlands and later Chief Probation Officer, Inner London Proba-
tion Service. See his *Victims and Offenders: Needs and Responsibilities*, Bedford
Square Press, London, 1982.

offender and emptying the prisons (but with perhaps fewer benefits for a barely-considered victim[43]). A survey of schemes conducted for the Home Office by Tony Marshall and Martin Walpole at that time counted seven community dispute-settlement projects; three police-based mediation schemes; six police juvenile panel reparation schemes; five schemes that were described as 'reparation within intermediate treatment', 'twelve probation-run court-based reparation schemes', two 'other court-based reparation projects', and two 'indirect reparation projects'.[44] None, it will be observed, had been established by victims or victims' organizations. Helen Reeves herself called the schemes a 'new distraction',[45] a way of invoking victims without meeting their needs.

For a while, the British Conservative Government of the 1980s itself considered sponsoring reparation as a cheap alternative to the fine and imprisonment in a criminal justice system that was processing ever larger numbers of unemployed and indigent defendants, and it funded four demonstration projects, only to discover that it was actually an expensive and complex procedure which raised delicate problems of timing, equity, enforcement, and administration.[46] To the frustration of its proponents,[47] it then receded politically in England and Wales for more than ten years,[48] being expunged almost entirely from the corporate memory of the Home Office,[49]

[43] See, T. Marshall and M. Walpole; *Bringing People Together: Mediation and Reparation Projects in Great Britain*, Home Office, London, 1985, p. 4: 'Prominent among the reasons given for facilitating reparation is the help it may provide to victims, but it is apparent from the context within which it is being developed that it is being employed first of all as a means of helping or rehabilitating the offender or of providing alternative disposals for the criminal justice process.' David Mellor, a Home Office Minister at the time, was reported to have said that 'the victim may feel the system is primarily concerned with the offender'. *The Times*, 17 September 1985.

[44] T. Marshall and M. Walpole; *Bringing People Together: Mediation and Reparation Projects in Great Britain, op. cit.*

[45] H. Reeves; 'Victims Support Schemes and Reparation', NAVSS, London, 1982.

[46] See *Reparation: A Discussion Document*, Home Office, London, 1986.

[47] See Prison Reform Trust; *Restorative Justice from Margins to Mainstream*, 2000.

[48] See *The Victim Perspective*, HM Inspectorate of Probation, Thematic Inspection Report, January 2000, p. 97. The Essex Probation Service noted in 1995 that restorative justice had 'come and gone' in the last 25 years. Essex Probation Service, briefing for Justice Working Party on the Role of the Victim in the Criminal Justice Process.

[49] None of those officials I spoke to recollected that earlier phase of restorative justice, although some had known Tony Marshall as a research officer in the Home

despite the labours of organizations like Mediation UK,[50] the Restorative Justice Consortium[51] and NACRO,[52] and of individuals like Martin Wright, John Harding, and Tony Marshall,[53] who strove to keep it afire as a vision of different possibilities before politicians and criminal justice agencies.

That was to change by the end of the century,[54] at first overseas (Miers talked in 2001 about a remarkable and substantial international growth in restorative justice[55]) and then domestically. The brief sputtering at home in the mid-1980s, and the larger developments abroad,[56] had had only a slight impact upon Conservative

Office or in his newer incarnation as organizer of Mediation UK, a voluntary body external to the Home Office.

[50] Originally founded in 1984 as FIRM, the Forum for Initiatives in Reparation and Mediation. It changed its name in 1991 and claimed to represent some 300 mediation services by the beginning of the 21st Century.

[51] Formed in 1997, it appointed its first Director in 2001, and sought to promote restorative justice in the criminal justice system, prisons, schools, the workplace, and elsewhere.

[52] See 'Family Group Conferencing—a Draft Briefing paper', NACRO, London, May 1995.

[53] See M. Wright; *Making Good: Prisons, Punishment and Beyond*, Burnett Books, London, 1982; M. Wright; *Restoring Respect for Justice*, Waterside Press, Winchester, 1999; M. Wright; *Justice for Victims and Offenders: A Restorative Approach to Crime*, Waterside Press, Winchester, 1996; T. Marshall; *Restorative Justice: An Overview*, Home Office, London, 1999; T. Marshall and S. Merry; *Crime and Accountability: Victim-Offender Mediation in Practice*, HMSO, London, 1990.

[54] See Prison Reform Trust; *Restorative Justice from Margins to Mainstream*, 2000.

[55] D. Miers; *An International Review of Restorative Justice*, Home Office, 2001, p. 5.

[56] Restorative justice had become the energetic pursuit of foreign non-governmental organizations (such as the Alliance of NGOs on Crime Prevention and Criminal Justice and Prison Fellowship International. See *Prison Service Journal*, May 1999, No. 123.) and of sympathetic States. See, for example, the Council of Europe: Committee of Ministers recommendation No. R(85)11 of the Committee of Ministers to Member States on the Position of the Victim in the Framework of Criminal Law and Procedure, 28 June 1985; and recommendation No. R(87)21 of the Committee of Ministers to Member States on Assistance to Victims and the Prevention of Victimisation, 17 September 1987. The *Real Justice Forum* reported in its Issue 9, p. 2: 'Restorative justice received significant attention at the 10th UN Crime Congress in Vienna, Austria, during April, 2000, thanks to the work of the Alliance of NGOs on Crime Prevention and Criminal Justice, who have been working for the past five years to place restorative justice on the Congress's agenda. Paul McCold, director of research for the International Institute for Restorative Practices reports "The congress

Government policy in the 1980s and 1990s. John Halliday, Director of Criminal Policy in the Home Office, commented in 2000, 'there's a long history of these ideas in the UK but they didn't take off and nobody seemed to hear'. What was to make a difference, and what did lead people to hear, was the personal engagement of new Ministers who came to transform it into one of the Government's 'big ideas' in the criminal justice policy of the first New Labour administration,[57] and the lineage of their engagement is clear.

## The Rebirth of Restorative Justice in England and Wales

Those who mediated restorative justice to British criminologists and criminal justice activists in the renaissance of the 1990s were chiefly Martin Wright, Roger Graef, Tony Marshall, and Charles Pollard in England; Nils Christie, the Norwegian, with his ideas of conflict as property, the not-so-bad offender,[58] and the morally-compromised victim;[59] and, above all, John Braithwaite, the sociologist working

was great. We managed to get the UN delegates from all over the world talking about restorative justice. Restorative justice had a high profile in official sessions...".'
When I spoke on restorative justice at a session of that Congress I noted that the delegates' arguments about restorative justice were not empirical but a prioristic. There was no criticism of restorative justice in an abstract and rights-driven talk. Any references to traditional penal process took it as axiomatic that restorative justice was a newer, more just and efficacious model. Restorative justice was to be embodied in international instruments and declarations, and it required a response from the Government of the United Kingdom. For example, the United Kingdom response of 4 May 2001 to the United Nations *note verbale* on restorative justice, in which the Government declared, *inter alia*, that it recognized the 'potential' of restorative justice to offer a constructive response to crime, had recognized it in the statutory system, noted a growing interest in restorative justice in United Kingdom, and would be carrying out further research into the effectiveness of restorative justice for older offenders.

[57] The engagement of officials was a little less sure. Even in 2000, I was told by a senior Home Office official that the Department's position was more cautious, partly because 'all sorts of things were branded together' and it did not quite know what restorative justice was.

[58] N. Christie; 'Roots of a Perspective', in S. Holdaway and P. Rock (eds.); *Thinking About Criminology*, UCL Press, London, 1998.

[59] See his 'The Ideal Victim', in E. Fattah (ed.); *From Crime Policy to Victim Policy*, Macmillan, Basingstoke, 1986.

at the Australian National University, who championed restorative justice as a form of regulation that actually worked.

Braithwaite was born in 1951, took two degrees at the University of Queensland, and worked broadly and actively in the field of regulation and control, concentrating on the study of globalization, the regulation of corporations (and of the pharmaceutical industry in particular), restorative justice, crime and inequality, and consumer protection; and on the practice of police education, restorative justice programmes, law reform, the monitoring of drug use, business regulation, health and safety at work, and much else. In his involvement with restorative justice, he married the scholarly with the practical, being a member in the 1990s of the Council of the International Institute for Restorative Justice and of the Working Party on Restorative Justice of the NGO Alliance. And it was his *Crime, Shame and Reintegration*, published in 1989,[60] and awarded prizes by the Society for the Study of Social Problems in 1990 and by the American Society of Criminology in 1991, that galvanized policy and politics by delivering an intellectual authority and a practicable methodology to restorative justice. He claimed that 'The theory of reintegrative shaming has been offered as a way of achieving two major aims. First, to recast criminological findings in a more coherent and productive fashion. Secondly, to offer a practical basis for a principled reform of criminal justice practices.'[61]

Braithwaite's framework and emphases were elastic and evolving. He defined restorative justice in catholic fashion as 'healing, moral learning, community participation and community caring, respectful dialogue, forgiveness, responsibility, apology and making amends'.[62] In 1996, it was shaming he emphasized: 'reintegrative

---

[60] J. Braithwaite; *Crime, Shame and Reintegration,* Cambridge University Press, Cambridge, 1989. Some 40,000 copies had been sold by early 2000. He was to publish other books on restorative justice: (with others) *Shame Management Through Reintegration,* Cambridge University Press, Melbourne, 2001; and *Restorative Justice and Responsive Regulation,* Oxford University Press, New York, 2002; and editing (with H. Strang) *Restorative Justice: Philosophy to Practice,* Dartmouth, Aldershot, 2000; (with H. Strang) *Restorative Justice and Civil Society,* Cambridge University Press, Melbourne, 2001; and (with H. Strang) *Restorative Justice and Family Violence,* Cambridge University Press, Melbourne, 2002.

[61] J. Braithwaite and S. Mugford; 'Conditions of Successful Reintegration Ceremonies', *British Journal of Criminology,* Spring 1994, Vol. 34, No. 2, p. 140.

[62] J. Braithwaite; 'Restorative Justice: Assessing Optimistic and Pessimistic accounts', *Crime and Justice: A Review of Research,* Vol. 25, 1999, p. 6.

shaming is shaming followed by efforts to reintegrate the offender back into the community of law-abiding or respectable citizens through words or gestures of forgiveness or ceremonies to decertify the offender as deviant'.[63] In April 2000, it was healing: 'Healing is relational, healing for the offender is healing for the victim and vice versa.'[64] In October 2000, he returned to Tony Marshall's definition of restorative justice as a collective process,[65] but he preferred more generally to contrast his own 'values conception' with the 'process conception' of Marshall, saying that 'Restorative justice is about healing (restoration) rather than hurting.'[66] In 2001, he talked about one of the values of restorative justice being to 'enrich democracy, to implement participatory deliberation...'.[67] In 2002, he talked about 'contextual justice': 'if you achieve the maximum of justice for offenders, you damage the interests of victims; if you maximise the interests of victims, you damage the interests of the offender'.[68] Throughout, he stressed the processual character of a balanced procedure that was intended to repair the breach between those who harm and those who are harmed, awaken informal control, and restore errant members of the community.

*Crime, Shame and Reintegration* melded reports about techniques of dispute settlement in Japan[69] and elsewhere with a body of propositions derived from the sociology of crime, deviance, and control. Its principal theme was that informal social control is more efficacious than formal social control; that informal control can be mobilized most effectively by shaming the offender; and that those

---

[63] J. Braithwaite; 'Crime, Shame, and Reintegration', in P. Cordella and L. Siegel (eds.) *Readings in Contemporary Criminological Theory*, Northeastern University Press, Boston, 1996, p. 35.

[64] Speaking at the Tenth United Nations Congress on the Prevention of Crime and the Treatment of Offenders: Crime and Justice: Meeting the Challenges of the Twenty-first Century, Vienna, Austria, 16 April 2000.

[65] J. Braithwaite, seminar given at the London School of Economics, 10 October 2000.

[66] J. Braithwaite and H. Strang; 'Introduction: Restorative Justice and Civil Society', in J. Braithwaite and H. Strang (eds.); *Restorative Justice and Civil Society*, Cambridge University Press, Cambridge, 2001, p. 1.

[67] *Ibid*, pp. 11–12.

[68] J. Braithwaite; 'In Search of Restorative Jurisprudence', Meetings of the American Society of Criminology, 13 November 2002.

[69] See J. Braithwaite; 'Applying Some Lessons from Japanese and Maori Culture to the Reintegrative Shaming of Criminal Offenders', *Japanese Journal of Criminal Psychology*, 1994, Vol. 32, pp. 181–96.

best equipped to induce shame are the people whose judgments matter most to him, the intimate social circle of family and others whom he cannot readily discount or dismiss. Shaming, 'according to theory, is more likely to be reintegrative and more likely to be effective in conditions of high interdependency between the disapprover and the disapproved'.[70] Lest shame might lead to social exclusion with all its risks of estrangement, antagonism, and secondary deviance,[71] restorative rituals must also incorporate strategies of reintegration that will enable offenders to return to the moral community: 'Reintegrative shaming actually has symbolic advantages over stigmatisation because ceremonies of repentance have even more integrative potential than degradation ceremonies.'[72] The prototype of reintegrative shaming was the family conference practised in New Zealand, a gathering of a police representative, offender, and victim with their families and supporters under the supervision of a 'facilitator', designed to elicit a public accounting of what happened, an appreciation of its impact on those whom it affected, an apology, an offer of reparation, and a measure of reconciliation. In New Zealand,[73] the family conference was employed to confront all offences except murder. And it would proceed through a prayer and a blessing; a welcome and introduction; a statement of the purpose of the meeting; a police summary of the offence; the offender being asked if he agreed with the police account; the victim describing the impact of the offence; a wider discussion of the circumstances of the offence; a private adjournment to consider possible outcomes; a resumption of the meeting and, perhaps, the tendering of an apology; an offer to undertake community work or reparation; the recording of an agreement; a formal conclusion, and the sharing of food. At the least, reintegrative shaming was intended to bring about a better understanding of the history, circumstances,

[70] T. Makkai and J. Braithwaite; 'Reintegrative Shaming and Compliance with Regulatory Standards', *Criminology*, August 1994, Vol. 32, No. 3, p. 362.

[71] According to Allison Morris, it was deemed important in Canberra to trace a distinction between being *a*shamed and being shamed. Those who are merely shamed tend to re-offend more frequently.

[72] *Crime, Shame and Reintegration, op. cit.*, p. 156.

[73] This account is based on a paper presented by Allison Morris at the International Conference on Integrating a Victim Perspective within Criminal Justice , York, 18 July 1998. My notes. See also G. Maxwell and A. Morris; 'The New Zealand model of family group conferences', in C. Alder and J. Wundersitz (eds.); *Family Conferencing in Juvenile Justice*, Australian Institute of Criminology, Canberra, 1994.

and consequences of an offence. At most, it could lead to what Braithwaite would call 'healing'. And at the instigation of John MacDonald, then the staff officer to the New South Wales Police Commissioner in 1991, a man knowledgeable about what was afoot in New Zealand, it was applied for the first time in Australia[74] to youth justice in Wagga Wagga, New South Wales, a town then of some 41,000 people. It was applied innocent of theory by MacDonald's friend, a police sergeant, Terry O'Connell:

Because I had been appointed to establish a community police-based unit, I saw it as a wonderful opportunity to focus on the issues and problems in the community. And what we did was, we were aware of what was happening in New Zealand, the police youth advisor had been part of the working group and gone over there and we had this vague notion of conferencing. Now without any details, I thought about it in the context of how we delivered cautions, and said look, of course it makes sense so I just started running conferences.

MacDonald had read *Crime, Shame and Reintegration*, and he told John Braithwaite about what was afoot in Wagga Wagga.[75] O'Connell continued:

John MacDonald had located John Braithwaite and invited ... [him] to come across from Canberra and the first time John had even known about what those conferences would look like was sitting in on what we were doing[76] ... he didn't have an awareness of those developments

Braithwaite's version of restorative justice was imported into England and Wales through many channels in the 1990s, but only one is of importance to this book. Heather Strang was first a student of and then a collaborator with, John Braithwaite, later to be the director of the Centre for Restorative Justice at the Australian National University, where she had received her doctorate for a

[74] F. Spencer and G. McIvor; 'Conferencing as a Response to Youth Crime', Paper delivered at the British Criminology Conference, July 1999, and published in Volume 3 of the Selected Proceedings, edited by G. Mair and R. Tarling, June 2000.

[75] I am grateful to Heather Strang for this account.

[76] Declan Roche, a student of John Braithwaite, pointed out to me that Braithwaite wrote *Crime, Shame and Reintegration* without 'knowing about restorative justice' (although the term had not then been devised). See J. Braithwaite; *Restorative Justice and Responsive Regulation*, Oxford University Press, Oxford, 2002, esp. p. 24; and D. Roche; 'Gluttons for restorative justice', *Economy and Society*, November 2003, Vol. 32, No. 4, p. 634.

study of victims and restorative justice.[77] She had met Charles Pollard,[78] the newly appointed Chief Constable of the Thames Valley Police[79] at a Ditchley Park conference in 1992:[80] 'I was supposed to say something interesting and novel and I said to John [Braithwaite] "this is an interesting idea, would you mind if I borrowed it?" It was a wonderful event and it made an impact because no one had heard of restorative justice.' It was her recollection that 'that was the first time [Charles Pollard himself] had heard of restorative justice and he appeared very enthusiastic'. Charles Pollard himself recalled in September 1999:

You know they fly people in from all over the world for a weekend. And I met there, in a Ditchley Conference on Youth Crime back in '92, someone called Heather Strang who is working in Australia. She works directly with

[77] H. Strang; *Repair or Revenge: op. cit.* In a randomly controlled trial in Canberra, Australia, she found that restorative justice could offer victims restoration, 'especially emotional restoration', for the harm they had suffered. In her conclusions, she claimed that restorative justice was generally benign for victims: 'twice as many of the court-assigned property victims and five times as many of the violence victims believed the offender would repeat the offence on them, compared with their conference-assigned counterparts'. 'Conference victims reported that their feelings of fear, anger and anxiety fell markedly after the conference while feelings of sympathy and security rose ... '. 'Conference victims reported that their treatment most often had a beneficial effect on feelings of dignity, self-respect and self-confidence. Two-thirds of them reported that the conference experience had given them a sense of closure about the offence ... '. 'Almost every victim, regardless of the offence they had suffered or their treatment assignment, believed that their offender should have apologised to them. Six times as many conference-assigned as court-assigned victims actually received an apology.' 'Most striking of all were the responses of violence victims about feelings of vengefulness and unresolved anger towards their offenders: more than half of the court-assigned said they would harm their offender if they had the chance, compared with only eight per cent of the conference-assigned ... '.

[78] Charles Pollard was Chief Constable of the Thames Valley Police from 1991 to 2002 following service in London and Sussex. He was later to join the Youth Justice Board and became the chair of its Youth Crime Prevention Committee and Restorative Justice Subcommittee.

[79] The Thames Valley Police is responsible for policing the counties of Berkshire, Buckinghamshire and Oxfordshire with a population of 2m. and a geographical area of over 2,000 square miles. In September 1998, the force had a strength of some 3,700 full-time, 86 part-time officers and 556 special constables (*Thames Valley Police: Primary Inspection,* Her Majesty's Inspectorate of Constabulary, 1998).

[80] The Conferences were run by the Ditchley Foundation whose aims were 'to promote, carry out or advance any charitable objects, and in particular any branches or aspects of education, likely to be for the common benefit of British subjects on the one hand and citizens of the United States of America on the other'.

John Braithwaite. For the last four years she's working directly with John Braithwaite running this big, the world's biggest evaluation of restorative justice in Canberra... And I kept in touch with Heather... and then she gets in touch with me to say would we see an Australian police officer called Terry O'Connell... a sergeant in New South Wales police, like a lot of good innovative police officers fed up with the old ways that don't seem to achieve anything. And goes to the town of Wagga Wagga and without any knowledge of restorative justice, sets up a community policing scheme which leads into... offenders and victims and... conferencing. [He] then learns about John Braithwaite and they meet up and so that develops. Terry has got that idea from New Zealand as well. He then wins a scholarship to travel the world for a year... and he calls on us where we're already doing it at Milton Keynes involving victims and he's very keen to move into the conferencing... We get him back about a few months later and he trains some people up... And then we tried to start a conferencing programme at Aylesbury and... that was a botch in the sense that we didn't, we didn't do it in the way we might have done,... so we again then get Terry O'Connell... to train people properly and... we set up a Restorative Justice Consultancy... And once we're satisfied to our level of satisfaction [that] the model in Aylesbury is pretty good. I mean it's not perfect, it's got wrinkles but it's pretty good. And sufficient to say this is something we should be doing across the force, we then roll it out across the force.

And O'Connell said:

I guess it was July of 1994, at that point I was actually on a twelve week research fellowship [from the] Winston Churchill Trust, looking at victim-offender mediation in United Kingdom, North America and South Africa. I became aware of Charles Pollard at Thames Valley because... Heather Strang is also here. My connection with Heather came out of the fact that when I first started developing conferencing processes, she was working with John Braithwaite, and John Braithwaite subsequently got involved and anyhow, when I was awarded this fellowship, Heather actually said look, 'I know a chief constable who would be interested, he's a sort of strident critic of criminal justice and its unresponsiveness in terms of victims, etc.' So anyhow I factored that in and I ended up actually running a workshop. I think I got a large group, there were about... 110 people in [it], as one of the sessions in the three days that I was visiting and I met Charles and spoke with him and then made this presentation. He was very excited about it because I think what I was on about represented to him, the bit that was missing... the concept wasn't new [to him] but the practical application and the operationalising of it was certainly new, and I guess the way I described it was in very simple terms, as an unexceptional police process, one that you know, with a little bit of insight, skill...

Terry O'Connell talked about Charles Pollard's receptiveness:
'I can recall vividly when I went to meet him and he was a pretty
busy guy and you know, in some respects I thought he was paying me
a courtesy, being pleasant etc., but as I started to talk about my work,
its developments, the impacts it was having, he became animated
and he asked me [to] slow down. Now for me to be asked to slow
down, you know, I knew he was ... and the reason was he wanted to
write a whole lot of things down. [He seemed to] like the simplicity
of it, the sensibility of it, the fact that it actually addressed the whole
crime equation, the fact that I developed some true protocols that
made it, you know, very practical.'

Charles Pollard became an *aficianado* of restorative justice,
saying in September 1999: 'I did a major speech at the conference
at ANU [the Australian National University], [I had] another four
weeks actually working with John Braithwaite ... I've been to New
Zealand ... to Minnesota where they do a lot, and I've also been to
Saskatchewan and I've also spent time with the Royal Canadian
Mounted Police on restorative justice. So ... at a senior level [I]
probably know more than anyone else in the world or as much as
anyone else in the world about the schemes.'

Viewed in a police context, restorative justice not only possessed a
capacity to enhance the relation between police and victim;[81] but
also appeared to have an eminently serviceable potential to reduce
youthful crime, it 'fit[ted] our problem-oriented style',[82] and 'the bit
we control of the system [is] young offenders before they go to
court'; and the ideas of John Braithwaite were accordingly adopted,
adapted, and implemented by Charles Pollard and his colleagues.[83]
Its first application was the Milton Keynes Retail Theft Initiative of
May 1994, and that was designed to confront shopkeepers and
young shoplifters in order to bring about a reduction in the level of

[81] See C. Hoyle and R. Young; 'Restorative justice, victims and the police', in
T. Newburn (ed.); *Handbook of Policing*, Willan Publishing, Cullompton, 2003,
p. 689.

[82] Thames Valley Police; 'Restorative Justice: A Balanced Approach', undated,
1999.

[83] 'The Australian criminologist John Braithwaite's work on "Crime, Shame and
Reintegration" provides the theoretical underpinnings for Conferencing ...
Braithwaite's theory was incorporated into the model of conferencing developed by
the New South Wales Police at Wagga Wagga and adapted in this country by Thames
Valley Police.' Anon; 'Restorative Justice' (July 1999), paper in Charles Pollard's files.

re-offending for those arrested for shop theft and related offences[84]
It led to what was claimed to be a significant drop in re-convictions
from 35 per cent to 3 per cent.[85] Charles Pollard stated:

I've always had a concern frankly as a police officer and as a chief constable... [that] our officers are on the front line trying to sort out problems
and they feel, with some justification, that the way the laws are made, the
way the directives come, the way the system is run, just does not take
account of the real world, and therefore they're under, they're really under
huge pressure to try and make things work. And I've always felt very
strongly about that and being clear that as police officers... we can't just
sit there and not say anything, as a chief constable you have a role in the
way criminal justice works as a whole, to say what needs to be done. Now,
having sort of got involved in that, up in Milton Keynes we had a very
innovative police area commander... she was concerned as a police area
commander on the ground, in Milton Keynes, about the utter frustration of
everyone in dealing with what we used to call the million pound burglars... the spree offenders... young offenders, usually youngsters from
the age of about 13–14, who go completely out of control and will be
doing 20–30 crimes a day... Caroline got together all the agencies, they
formed this, this is long before Partnership was a regular thing, tried to
brainstorm what's at the heart of all this if we share what we've got.
And... then they focused on the problem of young shop offenders in
Milton Keynes... a huge shopping centre, I mean years ago this was one
of the biggest three in the country, large shop thefts, we're getting loads of
people arrested by store detectives. The shop managers are pretty fed up
with the police. They say that, you know, nothing happens to these people
anyway, the whole thing's a waste of time, arresting them and they get
cautioned and what we want to see is police officers on patrol and all this
sort of stuff. And... so we said well let's get around the table and really sort
this out. What is the real issue? And so out of that came something called
the Retail Theft Initiative... all the agencies come together to create a way

[84] R. Willcock; 'Retail Theft Initiative: Does it Really Work?', K2 Management
Development Ltd., 1999.
[85] Although there was some scepticism about those figures in the Research Development and Statistics Directorate of the Home Office where it was observed in 1997
that practices in the Thames Valley were variable and new and there was little evidence
about victim satisfaction. The numbers were small and the offenders were carefully
selected. Re-offending it was said, is 'a blunt tool' and the situation of conferencing
likely to remain experimental for some time. However, an undated Home Office
Police Research Group Briefing Note, 'Shop Theft: Improving the Police Response'
by H. McCulloch, argued that the 'evidence from this study is that the scheme is
having a real impact on reoffending rates for first time offenders'.

of dealing with the youngsters where they are really confronted with the impact they've had on other people, including the impact on the victim which is the shops. And so, every Wednesday at Milton Keynes, you'll find 40 or 50 youngsters turn up for... a sausage machine of a process... And part of that process is that they meet the shopkeeper, the people who own the shops, they have a sort of rota and store managers come... it's quite sophisticated the way they confront the youngsters with the impact of their crime on other people. So we've got a completely different way of dealing with the young offenders and we're actually involving victims, albeit it's corporate victims.

Its second application was a pilot scheme in Aylesbury where a form of conferencing was practised in 1995 and then, by 1998, was being 'implemented across the Force'[86] as a 'restorative cautioning initiative'. Every individual cautioned for an offence would be invited by the police openly to examine his or her behaviour and the harm it had caused. In appropriate cases, and with the consent of the participants, a caution could take the form of a conference where offenders would be asked by the police to reflect on their behaviour by considering its impact on their victims and their own social circle; victims were encouraged to explain how they had been affected by the crime and to put questions to the offender; and apologies and reparation could follow. The theory and practice of restorative justice in the Thames Valley rapidly moved beyond simple restorative cautioning for delinquency to encompass bullying, truancy, and other forms of youthful conflict. In March 1997, for instance, two young men on a 'drinking spree' broke into a village hall and caused damage. A restorative conference was called and the men were told about how they had rendered the hall unusable. 'They looked even more ashamed when their parents said how appalled they were by their sons' behaviour. When asked what they thought they could do to make amends, the young men offered to pay damage and help by painting and decorating the hall.'[87] Two years later, adolescents who had broken into schools were brought into confrontation with teachers and governors in the presence of their parents. A police sergeant who had attended the conference was reported to have said 'It was the first time I have been involved in this process, and I found it a very powerful, and moving experience. Three of the four lads

---

[86] *Thames Valley Police: Primary Inspection, op. cit.,* para. 13.

[87] Thames Valley Police web site.

were in tears ... '.[88] Between 1998 and 2001, some 2,000 restorative conferences had taken place with victims present, and the views of victims were conveyed *in absentia* in a further 12,000 restorative cautions. It was reported that the offenders, victims and their supporters were generally satisfied with the fairness and results of the procedure, believing that the meetings induced in offenders feelings of shame and a better understanding of the effects of what they had done. Restorative practices also appeared in an evaluation to reduce by half the rate of re-offending within a year of the conference,[89] although as its authors, Hoyle and Wilson, would concede, theirs was a very small, selected sample of some fifty young offenders who had not committed serious crimes and

---

[88] *Oxford Mail,* 21 October 1999.

[89] 'An evaluation of the implementation and effectiveness of an initiative in restorative cautioning', *Findings,* Joseph Rowntree Foundation, York, May 2002. An earlier, interim report recorded that the average attendance at conference was four, a small and relatively ineffective number. The majority of victims and their supporters found restorative justice 'easy', but the majority of offenders did not because it was difficult to accept shaming. All offenders and victims felt they were fairly treated, and there had been a general satisfaction with the process. Victims and supporters stated that they had been well prepared initially, and believed that the police gave authority and solemnity to the proceedings. Most offenders felt they had no choice about participation; but most victims felt they had had a choice. Much preparation was not face-to-face because of the cost. It was conducted instead by telephone or letter. Victims received more preparation, but they would nevertheless have liked more information about who would be present, whether they could talk directly to the offender, and what they could expect by way of reparation. C. Hoyle and R. Young; 'Restorative Justice as Practised by the Thames Valley Police: Some early research findings', All Souls College, Oxford, 26 May 1999. See also R. Young and C. Hoyle; *Restorative Cautioning: Strengthening Communities in the Thames Valley, Preliminary Findings from the Interim Study,* Centre for Criminological Research, Oxford, October 1999, in which it was concluded that victims benefited from restorative justice: 'They appreciate having some involvement in the handling of "their" case, and gaining an opportunity to meet the offender... Some report being surprised at how "ordinary" the offender turned out to be, others feel satisfaction at having vented their emotions and confronted the offender with the harm caused. Institutional victims are most likely to take part out of a sense of public duty... The more a cautioning session was run on restorative lines, the more satisfied victims tended to be. But even when cautioning sessions had been "de-railed", as where offenders were not asked by facilitators to take responsibility for the offence, victims were still glad they had participated.' One difficulty of any evaluation of recidivism and restorative justice is that the participants tend to be highly selected. See G. Johnstone; *Restorative Justice,* Willan Publishing, Cullompten, 2002, p. 22.

were chosen precisely because they were likely to benefit from restorative work.[90]

Victims had been given a greater prominence in the Thames Valley than in the earlier wave of English restorative projects of the 1980s,[91] and Charles Pollard began to speculate that they might in future be awarded a more substantial role, and cross a major frontier, by becoming a party to proceedings who would be able to affect punishment as participants in sentencing circles.[92] And restorative justice might then be allowed to progress yet further to become the sovereign mode of justice, 'restorative policing', that would turn the country's 'outmoded approach to crime'[93] upside down. Charles Pollard remarked: 'we've always been very keen to try and give a victim focus . . . I think restorative justice is the way of the future, to involve victims in the criminal justice system. I mean my vision of criminal justice in 10 years or 15 years time will be that the whole system is based on the restorative model . . . the system needs to give victims a stake in the system.' Involving victims in restorative justice would then supersede every other remedy and mode of support for victims:

Restorative justice is a very high priority. I can't think of any offence where somewhere in the world they aren't actually doing something [restorative]

---

[90] See J. Braithwaite and H. Strang; 'Introduction: Restorative Justice and Civil Society', *op. cit.*, p. 4.

[91] Charles Pollard was reminded that restorative justice referred to that form of dispute resolution which had been practised in Western Europe before the twelfth century 'when superseded by the justice of a centralizing monarchy . . . Until colonial times [it] was the norm in non-western cultures in New Zealand, Southern Africa, and North America where, today, it is enjoying a renaissance . . .', Anon; 'Restorative Justice' (July 1999), paper in Charles Pollard's files. He was also reminded in the same paper that 'The 1980's reparation movement foundered because it failed to recognise the needs and interests of victims, being dominated instead by a vision of "reparation for the sake of diversion". Restorative justice differs in recognising that the restoration of the victim's dignity, material losses and sense of security are integral to a "satisfactory" outcome for victim and community and essential to promoting public confidence in the rule of law and justice.' 'We believe that tackling the causes of crime is better than dealing with its consequences. We are committed to responding to the needs and rights of victims at all stages of the criminal justice process' said a joint statement by the Crown Prosecution, Police, Prison and Probation Services in September 1998. 'Restorative Justice in the Thames Valley: Joint Statement', Thames Valley Police, 1998.

[92] *Oxford Mail*, 23 December 1999.

[93] *Oxford Mail*, 29 March 2001.

with it and finding a way of doing it. Because the whole rationale of victim support was to try and find these rights of victims and help victims. But if we'd had restorative justice from the start, that would do it. I mean it would actually involve victims, the culture of the system would be such that the victims are so much part of the system and their cares need to be taken seriously, that we wouldn't have needed a Victim Support scheme at all. So you could argue that once we move into restorative justice and it's been done really professionally and well, the victims' needs will be so well looked after.

So great was the confidence that the victim and the victim's interests were properly accommodated in what was being done, that local representatives of Victim Support claimed that there had been no earlier consultation when the restorative justice projects were under construction in the Thames Valley (Chris George, just such a local representative, working for the Thames Valley Association of Victim Support Schemes on behalf of victims in restorative justice, recalled in September 1999 'Well we just had to push our faces in really, quite forcefully... We were seen as ... making objections, you know, being troublesome, and yet if this was such a good thing for victims, why weren't we, why were we so concerned about it? We have excellent relationships with them. I mean we do. I mean Thames Valley Police even pay my salary to do my work. So it wasn't as if, it wasn't that they didn't want to talk to us, 'cause they were talking to us about all sorts of other issues but the approach that they'd got from Australia was that Terry O'Connell did everything on his own. You know they never consulted the other partners.'). Her claim was contested: Judith Johnson, one of the police officers responsible for running re- storative justice in the Thames Valley said: 'we have from the begin- ning involved [Victim Support] in actually putting together... the model that we now use. And indeed recognising the need for victim awareness of facilitators as being crucial to really underpin subse- quent training... I mean the work that Chris George has done in relation to victim awareness forms a crucial part of our training programme.' And it could be argued that Victim Support had had at first a very limited knowledge of victims' experiences of restora- tive justice, but Chris George's observation nevertheless reveals an interesting perception of the police service's self-confidence at the time.

Restorative justice as a project to reduce crime and support victims[94] became integral to the strategic planning of the Thames Valley force.[95] It not only spread but began to attain celebrity[96] and permanence.[97] Charles Pollard observed:

What is fascinating is the rate at which Restorative Conferencing is being accepted by Thames Valley police officers. Once they realise its potential, most see it as a viable alternative to their dog-eared law books; their enthusiasm fires colleagues; then other officers get to hear of Conferencing through the grapevine and they too want to use it in their daily routine. Conferencing is now used not just formally in Youth Justice for delivering police cautions in a very impactful way...: it has also evolved naturally as a vital tool for dealing with nuisance and minor disorder on the streets; for resolving difficult neighbour and community disputes; for dealing with

[94] Young and Hoyle noted from a preliminary survey of some 23 cases between January and April 1999 that facilitators tended to give disproportionate emphasis to what offenders had done and thought at the time of the offence and the issues of who were affected—particularly the victim—were given relatively little attention. Facilitators also often forgot to ask offenders to say in what ways people had been affected by the offence. Only half of the 27 offenders observed apologised to anyone present. It was also reported that none of the victim supporters showed any interest in material reparation. What was important was symbolic reparation. R. Young and C. Hoyle; *Restorative Cautioning: Strengthening Communities in the Thames Valley, Preliminary Findings from the Interim Study*, Centre for Criminological Research, Oxford, October 1999, pp. 43, 53, 105, 127, 186.

[95] Thames Valley Police long-term plan 1996–2002, Year 4—long-term priorities towards 2002: Aim 3: 'to help communities reduce crime and to support victims:... We will seek to unlock and harness community energy more effectively, for example by broadening the application of restorative justice principles to our policing activities...'.

[96] Indeed, Declan Roche would maintain that some other practitioners were a little piqued at the disproportionate attention it received. Personal comment.

[97] An officer in charge of the implementation and practice of restorative justice in the Thames Valley area remarked, 'one thing is the fact that it's the realisation that what we're doing in Thames Valley is of international interest, that it isn't another little fad within the police service, it's something which is being practised throughout the world in different forms. So I think that's the first point. And the fact that we're being independently evaluated is pretty important to that too. But and also, the other thing is we had a strategic partnership with two other police forces, Nottinghamshire and Surrey, and indeed we are directly influencing other police services through an ACPO Working Group on Restorative Justice and very soon there will be a paper out whereby the processes we're using will be seen as best practice across the whole, the whole country.'

school exclusion, bullying and truancy; and, internally, for resolving disputes and grievances.[98]

Charles Pollard and the Thames Valley Police were said to have been 'very effective at marketing restorative justice to the public, media and government . . . '.[99] And they marketed it to Jack Straw, the new Home Secretary, a man searching for new ideas, in September 1997,[100] just after the general election:[101]

He became very supportive . . . I know Jack Straw reasonably well from various things, [and he] was invited to come and sit in on a conference. And he'd been to a youth court in the morning and was appalled, and in the afternoon he came and sat in the conference [at Aylesbury] and said, 'well this is incredible. I've just seen two opposites in terms of the way you do things and the latter is clearly the way we have to deal with youth crime.' . . . and that's why all the youth justice legislation is framed around this because he came to sit in this conference and saw it.

---

[98]   C. Pollard; 'If your only tool is a hammer, all your problems will look like nails', paper given to the Australian National University, Research School of Social Sciences, Law Program, 16 February 1999. The paper was later published in a revised version in J. Braithwaite and H. Strang (eds.); *Restorative Justice and Civil Society, op. cit.*

[99]   M. Liebmann and G. Masters; 'Victim-Offender Mediation in the UK', in European Forum for Victim-Offender Mediation and Restorative Justice (ed.); *Victim-Offender Mediation in Europe: Making Restorative Justice Work*, Leuven University Press, Leuven, 2000, p. 341. Chris George reflected that 'they developed a very good mechanism and machinery for publicizing it and showing it to all kinds of people, . . . people within the UK and people all over the world. Including the Home Secretary, the Lord Chancellor, the people in the Home Office, you know, every single person has got access to this and the access was very open and they were very proud of it.'

[100]   See R. Young and B. Goold; 'Restorative Police Cautioning in Aylesbury', *Criminal Law Review*, February 1999, p. 127, and BBC News On-Line, 29 October 1997 in which it was reported that he had been 'impressed with the success of the ground breaking project run by Thames Valley Police in Aylesbury which has borrowed Maori concepts of justice to achieve a cut in the reoffending rate from 30% to 4%.'

[101]   Richard Young showed me a note made shortly afterwards by an officer of the Thames Valley Police in which it was said that 'Jack Straw did sit in on a Conference at Aylesbury . . . Prior to sitting in on the Conference, he had visited a Youth Court . . . where he had watched a young person go through the traditional system just confirming his name. Jack Straw had then spoken to the young man outside the courtroom and discovered all sorts of background to the case by talking to him that there would never have been an opportunity to discuss or disclose in the existing system. The Conference therefore had quite an impact on him.'

An official of the Juvenile Offenders Unit, chiefly responsible within the Home Office for the introduction of restorative justice in the youth justice system (and thus the criminal justice system itself) of England and Wales, endorsed that account of Jack Straw's epiphany:

I think in very specific terms it is as pragmatic as Jack Straw visiting Charles Pollard in Thames Valley... I think that is at the root of it and he was impressed with what he saw and felt that there was a place for it. It all came together at the right time because youth justice reform was quite clearly, even when this Government was in opposition, a very key plank of their manifesto commitment. And trying to find something new to do, and with the Crime and Disorder Act refocusing on preventing offending, getting away from punishment for punishment's sake, and trying to find a rather more effective and positive intervention. That all came together at the time that he was seeing what was going on in Thames Valley and I think felt that would have a reasonable place within the scheme of things... He harked back to it quite a lot and without us writing it into his speeches or whatever, he will often say when he's talking in the House or addressing a conference about restorative justice, he will often hark back to Thames Valley and how what he saw inspired him.

Partly in response to an Audit Commission report on youth justice,[102] the New Labour Party in opposition had defined delinquency and the youth justice system as major policy problems to be confronted when it entered office.[103] It argued that, despite contrary appearances, there had actually been a significant increase in youth crime in the 1980s and 1990s, particularly involving car theft and

[102] *Misspent Youth: Young People and Crime*, Audit Commission, 21 November 1996. The report claimed that prosecution through the courts was slow, little was done to 'address offending behaviour', there was a lack of co-ordination between the agencies working in youth justice, and little preventative work was undertaken. They argued that the apparent fall in youthful offending could be explained by demographic change, a reclassification of offences, an increased use of warnings, and a fall in the percentage of defendants found guilty at trial. Their conclusions were to be criticized by Denis Jones some considerable time afterwards in ' "Misjudged Youth": A Critique of the Audit Commission's Reports on Youth Justice', *British Journal of Criminology*, Vol. 41, 2001, pp. 362–80. But Jones recognized that the Commission's work was 'often taken as the final word on the topic' (p. 362).

[103] Geoff Hoon, a Minister in the Lord Chancellor's Department, was to say that the 'Government is strongly committed to tackling youth crime, and it is their highest law and order priority'. Juvenile Offenders Unit; Information on Demonstration Projects: Demonstration project seminar, 17 February 1999.

burglary,[104] and that the youth courts were ineffectual and plagued by problems of delay, multiple adjournments, and a failure to make offenders confront the consequences of their actions.[105] And it saw in restorative justice a vista of a radical new approach that 'worked'. Jack Straw remarked that 'Crime is an act of great selfishness with people thinking about themselves only. So getting these youngsters to recognise that the victim isn't them, it's the old lady they've robbed, it's the school mate who they've bullied, it's the community whose walls they've defaced. Getting them to recognise that is stage one and getting them out of re-offending.'[106] Restorative justice was perhaps the one promising project in a world where nothing else seemed to 'work', 'one of the most promising counter-trends to both the politics of punitiveness and criminologists' despair'.[107]

Jack Straw and Alun Michael proposed the introduction of reparation to enable 'young offenders to understand the harm done to victims and communities... In Australia and New Zealand family group conferences appear to have had considerable success in confronting young offenders and their families with offending behaviour and securing change.'[108] Indeed, before the general election, and explicitly citing work in the Thames Valley, Jack Straw declared himself enthusiastic about restorative justice as a mechanism for reforming the youth justice system.[109] No explicit proposals to

[104] That analysis was challenged, for example, by David Downes in 'Crime and Social Policy: Four Years of New Labour', undated.

[105] Jack Straw told the Home Affairs Committee on 26 October 1999, 'What we inherited was an absolutely shambolic set of arrangements for dealing with young offenders which could not be described even as a system. The Audit Commission pointed out in a report which they published in November 1996 that this set of arrangements was costing £1bn. a year for very little effect.' Home Affairs Committee, Minutes of Evidence.

[106] Jack Straw, in interview on 5pm Radio News, BBC 4, 1 June 2000.

[107] D. Roche, 'Gluttons for Restorative Justice', review article, *Economy and Society*, November 2003, Vol. 32, No. 3, p. 631.

[108] J. Straw and A. Michael; *Tackling Youth Crime: Reforming Youth Justice: A consultation paper on an agenda for change*, Labour Party, London, May 1996, p. 12.

[109] News from Labour: Labour outlines plans for Radical Reform of Youth Justice System, speech by Jack Straw at the annual general meeting of NACRO, 20 November 1996: We are, he said, 'very interested in looking at the lessons to be learned from the experience of other countries, and in particular the family group conferencing approach pioneered in New Zealand. And here at home from the very imaginative schemes in the Thames Valley and Hampshire police force areas.' Those statements, Ministers were told, were read as encouragement by Mediation UK and other cham-

introduce reparation orders were included in what was a small section of a slim election manifesto, but there was a reiteration of the claim that youth crime and disorder had risen, and the election commitments to introduce Youth Offender Teams and to 'streamline the system of youth courts' *were* to be invoked retrospectively to lend added authority to restorative justice.

Soon after his visit to Aylesbury, Jack Straw moved to the theme of restorative cautioning and conferencing in the Thames Valley: 'I want to see far more emphasis put on ensuring that young offenders understand the effects that their actions inflict on victims and the community... The Aylesbury project has shown the value of getting young offenders to face their victim, in person... it is undoubtedly an extremely effective way of communicating the distress and hurt which young offenders can cause. Young offenders should be confronted with their behaviour not excused from it.'[110] Replying to a question in the House of Commons in July 1997, Alun Michael said: 'The operation of caution plus schemes in a number of areas has demonstrated the value of early, positive intervention with young offenders. I have been impressed by a number of initiatives such as the Retail Theft Initiative in Milton Keynes which show the value of the police working with local authorities and the community—including the business community—to tackle crime and to "nip things in the bud". We are studying "best practice" in the Thames Valley and elsewhere in working towards implementation of our proposed final warning for young offenders and the intervention which will be associated with it. Our first consideration is how best to see "what works" in order to prevent crime and reduce reoffending.' The 'key now', he remarked in January 1998, 'was to make changes in the system and to make people take mediation on. The Thames Valley project was an example of success in this respect as there had been an attempt by the police to ensure a more radical shift in the way one approaches offenders.' In effect, restorative justice had become a project personally associated with the incoming Home Secretary and his Ministers. It was their 'big idea'.

Observe that from the first, despite Charles Pollard's own emphases, and although victims were perfunctorily mentioned, it was

pions of restorative justice, and Ministers themselves concurred that that was how they should be interpreted.

[110] Home Office News Release 298/97, 29 October 1997.

upon offenders, crime reduction, and the reform of the youth justice system that the new Government's political stress was placed.[111] Restorative justice was seen in lopsided fashion as a mechanism to confront crime, not to alleviate the distress of victims ('inevitably perhaps', thought Heather Strang. 'At best, restorative justice can assist the 3 per cent of victims whose offences are prosecuted.'). Helen Reeves reflected about that imbalance in October 1999:

It's had a life of its own completely. But the issue of restorative justice is again 'what are we going to do that's constructive about young offenders?' And... there's the prison problem, the prison budgets and all that sort of thing. And... I'd be the first to say that as far as the young offenders are concerned, it's a very, very positive constructive idea. The problem for us is that there genuinely hasn't been sufficient thought about what it means to victims or why victims would want to be involved or even the fact that asking the first question is involving them... And we're trying to be positive and constructive about it but it's always been our concern.

## Youth Justice and Reparation

In November 1997, the Home Office issued a consultation paper, *No More Excuses—A New Approach to Tackling Youth Crime in England and Wales*,[112] in which it was argued, in the words of the Home Secretary, that young offenders had protected themselves with an excuse culture and that 'rarely are they confronted with their behaviour and helped to take more responsibility for their actions'. Reparation orders would be introduced under the overarching imperative of crime reduction and as part of a new armoury to 'stop offending behaviour', although, to be sure, it was noted that 'not all victims want reparation. The Government's proposals ensure that the victim's views will be sought before an order is made.'[113] Victim Support's reply to the paper was cautious, echoing its hesitations of the 1980s, saying that it welcomed restorative justice but that misguided assumptions about what was best for victims could lead to dissatisfaction. It insisted on the importance of consulting victims before any form of intervention from the offender was

---

[111] See, for example, Labour Party press release, 'Labour Unveils Plans to Tackle Youth Crime and Reform Criminal Justice', 20 May 1996, which talked only of cutting offending.

[112] Cm. 3809, November 1997.

[113] *Ibid*, p. 14.

considered (an unsolicited apology could add to the victim's distress); and it stressed that it was vital to ask whether victims wished to participate in restorative practices, and to afford them adequate time for preparation[114] (and that was an issue becoming fraught under the spell of another Government reform being pursued at the same time, the so-called 'fast-tracking' procedures in youth justice,[115] which sought to accelerate criminal proceedings and were being piloted in the first few months of 1999).

The consultation evolved into twin pieces of legislation. There was the omnibus Crime and Disorder Act 1998 which came into force in the summer of 1998[116] with sections 67 and 68 representing the 'first attempt to introduce elements of a "restorative justice" approach into English criminal justice procedure'.[117] The Act was designed expressly to 'prevent[ . . . ] offending by children and young people' *inter alia*[118] by 'encouraging reparation by young offenders to their victims'.[119] And, second, there was the Youth Justice and Criminal Evidence Act 1999,[120] which provided for referral to a

---

[114] Victim Support response to *Tackling Youth Crime* consultation paper, September 1997. See also J. Dignan; *Youth Justice Pilots Evaluation: Interim Report on Reparative Work and Youth Offending Teams,* Home Office, London, 2000, pp. 3, 14. Although it must be said that there was so little experience of victims passing through restorative conferences that there was scant evidence about what victims needed or demanded. Heather Strang observed of her work in 2003 on testing the extension of restorative justice to the adult criminal justice system, involving follow-up interviews with some 250 victims, that 'I've never heard of a victim being distressed by an unsolicited apology.'

[115] Under *Review of Delay in the Criminal Justice System: A Report,* February 1997 (chaired by Martin Narey known as 'The Narey Report'). Pressure was being put on the courts to speed cases through. See Home Office Circular 24/1998—Reducing Delays: Addressing the Reasons for Non-Compliance with the Pre-Trial Issues Group Time Guidelines. 27 May 1998. The Government had made it a 'first priority' to reduce delay in youth proceedings and halve the average time of 142 days from arrest to sentence. See *The Government's Expenditure Plans 1999–2000 to 2001–2002.* By February 2000, the delay had been reduced to 110 days: *TIG Update,* February 2000.

[116] Home Office Circular, 38/1998, July 1998.

[117] J. Dignan; *Youth Justice Pilots Evaluation: Interim Report on Reparative Work and Youth Offending Teams, op. cit.,* p. 7.

[118] There were also, for instance, provisions for parenting orders and curfews. See *Supporting Families: A Consultation Document,* 4 November 1998.

[119] *A Guide to the Criminal Justice System in England and Wales,* Home Office, London, 2000, p. 47.

[120] Later consolidated in the Powers of the Criminal Courts (Sentencing) Act 2000.

youth offender panel of all young offenders pleading guilty and convicted for the first time who might then be subject to a referral order.

In the beginning, restorative justice was tested in eleven pilot projects for young offenders across the country[121] and then, after evaluation,[122] it came into force nationally in 155 schemes[123] in April 2000.[124] Where there was a first, minor offence[125] admitted by the offender, and judged not to warrant a prosecution in the public interest, the case should proceed to a youth offender panel[126] composed of the representatives of 'appropriate organisations'[127] for an assessment and the preparation of a 'rehabilitation programme to tackle the reasons for the offending and prevent further offending'. The young offender, his family, and the panel members would review the offence and its consequences, either with the participation of the victim or with the victim's views being represented, and a contract

---

[121] Delivering the Aim—News from the Youth Justice Pilots Issue 2 May 1999—advance information before the implementation of the Crime and Disorder Act.

[122] Young offenders were said generally to have been happy with their experience of attending an initial panel meeting; over 2/3 said they felt they had a clearer idea of how the offence had affected people after the meeting; the majority of their parents believed that victims should be present; the involvement of victims was lower than had been expected and lower than in other projects elsewhere in the world. The victim attended in only 13% of cases; in a number of cases the victim made other representation than a personal appearance; and 78% of victims who attended said expression of feelings was very important to them. In 95% of cases there was no victim representation. In most cases, victims wanted only to be informed of progress. T. Newburn *et al.*; *The Introduction of Referral Orders into the Criminal Justice System: Final Report*, Home Office, London, 2002.

[123] Home Office Press Release 32/2000, 22 February 2000.

[124] Home Office, Department of Health, Welsh Office, DfEE; Interdepartmental Circular: Establishing Youth Offending Teams, 22 December 1998.

[125] The seriousness of the offence was assessed chiefly by the impact of the offence on the victim (The Crime and Disorder Act, Final Warning scheme, Draft, September 1998).

[126] 'Youth offender panels should operate on the restorative justice principles of responsibility, reparation and reintegration.' *Referral Orders and Youth Offender Panels, Guidance for Courts, Youth Offending Teams and Youth Offender Panels*, Home Office/Lord Chancellor's Department/Youth Justice Board, February 2002, p. 5.

[127] Victim Support was not listed explicitly as such a suitable organization other than, presumably, one of a group of 'other agencies and organisations where this is considered appropriate'. *Crime and Disorder Act 1998, Introductory Guide*, Home Office, London, 1998, p. 10.

would be agreed which could include a reparation order:[128] 'a new disposal requiring a young offender to make reparation to the victim or to the community at large'.[129] The order would, it was said, help young offenders understand and face up to the consequences of their actions and offer some practical recompense to victims.

There were interesting ambiguities and lacunae in official conceptions of restorative justice in the late 1990s, just when they seemed suddenly and massively to have infiltrated great swathes of the Home Office. Still working in RDS, Tony Marshall distributed a circular letter to officials in October 1997 stating that 'RJ is an issue that a good many separate parts of the HO have suddenly found themselves having to address, although there is little substantive knowledge. As a result, many parts of the HO are duplicating similar ground, often unknown to each another, and usually have to generate proposals with partial or imperfect knowledge of the topic.' Colleagues did not necessarily warm to that description of their grasp of restorative justice, but one centrally placed man's description of the scale, indefiniteness, and spread of restorative justice in the Department is worth reporting.

Restorative justice could indeed be put to many uses.[130] Thus, in a letter to the director of one of the organizations promoting restorative justice, Alun Michael wished it to be said in November 1997 that the Home Office was exploring different aspects of restorative justice, including services for victims, the proposed youth courts, the reparation order, the work of the probation service, making offenders more responsible, and 'as alternatives to some of the less efficient of our current practices'. An official of the Juvenile Offenders Unit told me in August 1999:

I think to be perfectly honest, the idea of restorative justice in its widest form is what has been embraced by the government, and by that I mean Ministers and officials. But I don't know that anybody's really got a very

---

[128] *Referral Orders and Youth Offender Panels, Guidance for Courts, Youth Offending Teams and Youth Offender Panels*, Home Office/Lord Chancellor's Department/Youth Justice Board, February 2002, p. 5.

[129] *Crime and Disorder Act 1998, Introductory Guide*, p. 8.

[130] And not only inside the Home Office. It was noted in June 1998, for instance, that the Department of the Environment, Transport and the Regions was involved in mediation in the housing field; the Department of Health had an interest in family mediation; the Lord Chancellor's Department in civil law interests; and the Department for Education and Employment in parent-school relations.

clear idea about what model they're really talking about. And I include myself in that. You know, I've just broken off now to talk to you from the first draft of the guidance to youth offending teams about implementing reparation orders you know, which is based on, the concept is based clearly on restorative justice ideas. But when you come to write the guidance you realise that you don't really know quite what model it is that we're talking about. I don't necessarily see that as a particular weakness because, you know, professionals have got very different... ideas about what restorative justice actually means... One can interpret [it] in a wide variety of ways. I mean, I know Charles Pollard doesn't believe that restorative justice exists without a victim being present. There are others who will say you can do quite a lot of work without a victim actually being present... And I think the youth justice pilots that are looking at the action plan order or reparation order, final warning scheme, may go a little way to establishing what it is we mean.

Reparation evidently at first offered a large and diverse assortment of sometimes ill-defined approaches to crime, victims, and criminal procedure. It acted as a kind of *tabula rasa* on to which different aspirations and objectives could be inscribed, any one of which could be given primacy in different policy frames. At one pole, it could be construed as a new community penalty, what a Minister called 'a radical shift in the treatment of offenders', and the more succinct the description, and the closer its authors were to implementing the central politics of crime control, the more insignificant the victim seemed to be become, sometimes to be relegated to the occupancy of a mere auxiliary role in support of a new form of punishment (offenders were being monitored in the pilot projects, for example, but victims were not[131]). Thus in a speech to a conference organized by the Youth Justice Board and Channel 4, the Home Secretary portrayed the 'bigger picture' within which the youth justice reforms were to be set as the Government's crime reduction programme, the agenda of parenting and family support, the effort to tackle truancy and school exclusion, and the Government's strategy for tackling drug misuse[132] but not victims and victim support (although it must be acknowledged that in other places he had given emphasis to the place of the victim in restorative justice. Different inflections were imparted in different settings.) As close as anyone could be to that central politics, Liz Lloyd, the Prime Minister's

---

[131]   Meeting of Victim Steering Group, 28 April 2000, my notes.
[132]   Home Secretary's Speech to YJB/Channel 4 Conference, 8 March 1999.

policy adviser on home affairs, observed quite emphatically in early 2000 that youth justice reforms were the Government's 'big idea', that restorative justice was being pursued as what was then the most fundamental reform of the criminal justice system, and that victims themselves were seen simply as beneficiaries of those wider reforms, and certainly not as policy targets in their own right.[133] Perhaps that is why there were only two references to victims in the Youth Justice and Criminal Evidence Act,[134] and an annual report on the work of Government during 1998, published on the No. 10 Downing Street web site, talking about the provisions of the Crime and Disorder Bill under the heading of 'cracking down on juvenile crime and anti-social behaviour' made no reference to victims as beneficiaries or participants at all.

There was no cavilling about the prime 'purpose of the youth justice system [being] to cut offending',[135] reparation was one weapon in a battery of what were tellingly called 'community punishments',[136] and, at best in this phrasing, victims were its instrument:[137] Chris George of Victim Support said warily 'Currently the criminal justice system only tends to want to deal with victims so they can do something with the offender. If an agency's main motivation for developing restorative justice is to prevent offending, there is a real danger that the victim will be used as a tool to rehabilitate the offender.'[138] It is certainly revealing that a major Home Office-sponsored evaluation of restorative justice schemes, published in its Crime Reduction Series, was conducted with the twin aims of 'identify[ing] which elements, or which combination of elements, in

[133] Again, an internal briefing prepared within the Home Office in 1997 reflected that restorative justice fitted current Government policy well because it tackled the causes of crime, community involvement, the accountability of offenders and social exclusion. It is revealing that a section on initiatives for victims contained in an official guide to the Home Office omitted any reference to restorative justice. *The Home Office—A Guide, October 2000*, Home Office, London, 2000, pp. 8–9.

[134] One reference was to the referral order and the other to the need for the victim's consent. The explanatory notes accompanying the Act stated that its primary aim was to improve the effectiveness of the youth court in preventing offending.

[135] *Crime and Disorder Act 1998, Introductory Guide*, p. 1.

[136] *CJCC Newsletter*, May 1998.

[137] Home Office: The Crime and Disorder Act: Draft Guidance Document: Reparation Orders.

[138] C. George; 'Victim Support's Perspective on Restorative Justice', *Prison Service Journal*, May 1999, No. 123, p. 13.

[the]... schemes are most effective in reducing crime and at what cost... [and] provid[ing] recommendations on the content of, and best practice for, schemes to be mainstreamed'.[139]

Managerially, the Crime and Disorder Act and the Youth Justice and Criminal Evidence Act were defined as a part of the assault on youth crime and the reform of the youth justice system, and the locus of their co-ordination within the Home Office was not the Justice and Victims Unit, with its administrative concentration on victims, but the Juvenile Offenders Unit,[140] whose interest was youth justice.[141] Victims, Victim Support and the victims' experts on the Victims Steering Group were not perhaps initially awarded as much attention in the framing of restorative projects and programmes as they might otherwise have received. An official of the Juvenile Offenders Unit said in 1999:

I think we have to think very carefully about how we use the victim. As soon as you start using that terminology, you realise, you know, you

[139] D. Miers et al.; An Exploratory Evaluation of Restorative Justice Schemes, Crime Reduction Series Paper 9, Home Office, London, 2001, p. 1. There is, said David Moxon, the Head of the Crime and Criminal Justice Unit in RSD, in his foreword, 'insufficient robust research evidence... on the effects restorative justice has in practice, particularly on reoffending', p. iii. It should be noted that there were also interviews with 23 victims who were reported to be 'in general well-disposed towards the aims of restorative justice', p. vii.

[140] The Home Office web site recites that 'The Juvenile Offenders Unit (JOU) deals with youth justice policy, law, processes and organisation covering 10 to 17 year olds in England and Wales. Its key task is oversight of the youth justice reform programme including remands, the final warning scheme, court sentences, pre-court and court procedures and national and local youth justice structures. JOU sponsors the Youth Justice Board (YJB) for England and Wales, a separate body responsible for the national co-ordination of the youth justice system.' An official remarked that 'the draft national standards [on reparation orders]... said, victims will never be approached to be involved in anything which is primarily for the benefit of the offender... I questioned that and said, you know, is this really honest because everything that we're doing on the Crime and Disorder Act and Youth Justice Criminal Evidence Act is primarily for the offender.' On one occasion, for example, PVU (later JVU) was asked to draft a speech on restorative justice for a Minister who was about to visit a self-help project for victims of violence established by a local victim support scheme. An official of PVU wrote 'surely this is not a PVU matter—[the Minister's private secretary] saw the magic words victim support and thought of us. The lead lies elsewhere.'

[141] JOU represented the pilot projects as a test of the proposals contained in No More Excuses for action to change the culture of the youth courts. JOU; 'Information on Demonstration Projects', undated.

realise . . . the danger that you're in really. I mean I work quite closely with Teresa [Reynolds of Victim Support] and . . . I was very interested. Victims is not my business essentially you know, young offenders is my business. Victims is Ian's business and Ian's staff's business. But I mean I was very anxious that I should understand the victim side of it . . . and I talk to Teresa about, you know, professionally what she thinks is good practice and what she thinks is bad practice. And I've been very up front with Teresa and with others in the victim world that what I am doing is primarily with the aim of helping young offenders and helping offenders to change the course of their lives and to prevent offending. But . . . I will not do that if it adversely affects victims and I would positively like to do it in a way that it helps victims. And both Teresa and I agree that we should be able to do that. I mean she recognises my agenda, she recognises that what I'm doing is primarily to prevent offending. And of course that is something that is important to victims, too. I've stuck my neck out a little bit here. I don't think all my colleagues on the offenders side have been quite so open to considering the position of victims . . .

It took time to develop a countering position and shift the centre of gravity, and two principal parties were involved, both of whom were placed professionally to attend to victims' issues. One was the Justice and Victims Unit, which certainly defined reparation as a vehicle that might advance victims when the issue came before it, although it was never a prime mover in the crafting and implementation of restorative justice. In the text which the JVU prepared on 'Support for Victims of Crime' for the Home Office Comprehensive Spending Review in March 1998, for instance, it noted that 'Victims are *not* obliged to report a crime to the police . . . Once victims have reported a crime . . . [they] have little further control over events . . . Restorative models can give some power back to the victim . . . Interest has grown recently in restorative justice . . . A primary aim . . . is to materially, psychologically and socially restore the victim as far as possible.' 'Victim-empowerment' was a reading quite different from those tendered by other Units within the Department. Indeed, Ian Chisholm told the Victims Steering Group that he regretted that witnesses and victims had not been included in the title of the Youth Justice and Criminal Evidence Bill[142] (although he was almost certainly thinking about that bifurcated Bill's concentration on the protection of vulnerable and intimidated witnesses).

---

[142] Meeting of Victims Steering Group, 4 December 1998, my notes.

The second body was Victim Support, and it was at first kept distant from what seemed to be a managerially *laissez-faire* and decentralized mass of local pilot projects. It had been decided by the Home Office that it would be a matter for the pilot areas to take forward work with victims in the manner they considered most appropriate, and they were awarded devolved authority to decide on the role of the Youth Offending Team and the involvement of voluntary organizations. Teresa Reynolds felt impelled to ask the Secretary of the Victims Steering Group to place the matter of what was then the victims' and Victim Support's murky and difficult role in restorative justice on the agenda of its meeting of 4 December 1998. She and Roger Ford of ACOP wished to know 'whether there is any Home Office co-ordination of the pilot areas; whether links are being forged with Victim Support in the pilot areas; whether the victim elements within the Final Warning, Referral Order and Action Plan Order are being co-ordinated across the pilot areas; which agency or agencies is involved with the victim elements, and are they different in different areas; what training is provided to those involved with the victim elements ...?'.[143] In the Chairman's briefing for that meeting, advice on the matter was tendered in the form of a series of questions and answers, the answers having been supplied by the Juvenile Offenders Unit: it began 'Is there Home Office co-ordination of the pilot areas?' and the reply was 'The Home Office Juvenile Offenders Unit is managing the overall piloting process, but each pilot is a distinct project and ... it is for each area to develop and operate the pilot as they consider most appropriate.' The second question asked whether links were being forged with Victim Support in the pilot areas, and the answer was 'The extent to which the pilot areas forge links with Victim Support ... will be a matter for local decision.' The third asked whether victim elements within the orders were being co-ordinated across the pilot areas, and the answer was 'Within the guidance ... it will be a matter for the pilot areas to take forward work with victims as they consider most appropriate'. The fourth asked about links with Victim Support ('a matter for local decision'), and about training about 'victim elements' ('Again, a matter for local decision'). When the time came to speak to the matter at the meeting, Teresa Reynolds remarked that reparation would inevitably form a topic central to

[143] Letter, 26 October 1998.

the Group, particularly given the copious discretion that attended it. The interests of victims should demand proper recognition and room in the new pilot projects.[144] She complained again to the Group's next meeting: 'where does victim policy fit in this area? Where does the victim bit fit in? Policy is developing in an *ad hoc* way.'[145] And she and Roger Ford told a joint meeting between ACOP and Victim Support that they were anxious about whether 'victims' concerns were being sufficiently addressed' within the pilots. Reflecting that agencies often had only a limited experience of working with victims, they wondered 'whose needs were being addressed by reparation orders and what was the purpose of contact with victims?'.[146]

Yet the victim and Victim Support nevertheless discovered that they *were* being 'fitted in' *faute de mieux*. At an early point, in the Autumn of 1999, all Victim Support regions reported that their constituent schemes had had some involvement in local restorative justice initiatives[147] and that they had received a stream of invitations to collaborate with what was afoot. Typical was an overture from a senior police officer in Powys, Wales, who wrote to Teresa Reynolds about the need for a 'balanced approach between the victim, community and the offender, by providing the opportunity for each one to become involved. This in practice requires that the victim, community and the offender should receive equal consideration...The success of our initiative will be very dependent on the support, the encouragement and the involvement of our local Victim Support Groups...'.[148] In Reading, Berkshire, part of the Thames Valley Police area, an *ad hoc* agreement had already been concluded to regulate the relations and role of the local victim support scheme in restorative justice, it having been laid down that the victim and the local victim support scheme would have no part to play in the sentencing or punishment of offenders; that the scheme would support and provide personal feedback to the co-ordinator of the Youth Offending Team and train a small group of volunteers to support victims in restorative conferencing; and that the Victim

---

[144] Meeting of Victims Steering Group, 4 December 1998, my notes.
[145] Meeting of Victims Steering Group: 12 June 2001, my notes.
[146] Notes of a meeting of the ACOP/VS Practice Advisory Group, 23 July 1999.
[147] Summary of feedback on the substantive agenda items from the Autumn 1999 Council Consultative meetings, Report to National Council. Restorative Justice.
[148] Chief Inspector Thomas, Powys Police, to TR, VS, 13 May 1998.

Support scheme co-ordinator would be available for consultative work with the restorative justice team.[149] Given the appearance of such a growing, largely unregulated and haphazard involvement in restorative justice, there were substantial pressures upon Victim Support to produce national guidelines and policies about how victim support schemes should conduct themselves.[150]

Victim Support was initially both divided[151] and a little reluctant to become involved in a new region of work and training which might 'stretch it quite far'. It was difficult to gauge the size of the task and the resources required;[152] it had no desire to act as mediator or negotiator for other criminal justice agencies in discussions about a victim's participation in reparation;[153] and any such commitment could require decisions to be made about whether it was indeed proper for Victim Support to bargain about what was, in effect, diversion from the criminal justice system.[154] Victim Support cer-

[149] Restorative Justice: Victim Support Involvement in the Process, Agreed proposals, Reading and District, 17 April 1998.

[150] Teresa Reynolds wrote to the co-ordinator of the Reading scheme in June 1998: 'you asked for comments. As there are no national guidelines for Victim Support involvement in restorative justice as yet I cannot give an "official" response.' That was a pattern that had been repeated again and again in the development of Victim Support: local schemes would innovate and advance into new terrain, and Victim Support, ever mindful of the need to maintain consistency and standards, would labour hard in their wake to devise national standards of practice and training. It had happened before in the supporting of prosecution witnesses in the courts. It was also happening in the support of the families of victims of road crashes.

[151] Teresa Reynolds said in July 1998, 'I think with this issue there are differences of opinion throughout the organization, throughout this office and throughout the membership. I think what's, what's happening around the country is that our local groups are being asked to become involved—and there's quite a lot of positive feedback coming from those people. There's also a lot of confusion about Victim Support's role, which is something I need to remedy and if I had more time I would be sitting down and writing those guidelines and getting them out, but there's this constant [tension] between responding to what's coming at us and actually sitting down and doing that kind of stuff.'

[152] Meeting of Victim Support National Council, 19 January 1999, draft minutes.

[153] Teresa Reynolds said that it was not appropriate for Victim Support to act as a liaison for victims in restorative justice because he or she should be trusted by both parties. Speaking on 'Restoring Victims', Victim Support national conference, 5 July 1999, my notes.

[154] Helen Reeves at the meeting of Victim Support National Council, 19 January 1998, my notes. It was eventually agreed, in the words of Robert Latham, the Chair, that it was a 'primary principle that we should do work only if it is to support the victim . . . we should say we can provide this training and service in the interests of

tainly thought it was obliged to provide support to victims; and almost certainly to advise and protect them in any decision they might take about participating in conferences (although, again, there was little enough empirical evidence from any quarter about what victims actually did want); but there were those who were unsure about whether the organization should be involved in the conferences themselves. It was not, after all, itself a party[155] and there was no provision for '*ex officio*' participation in restorative work.

Yet Victim Support was unwilling to stand aside. It sensed it was losing control over important terrain and it had to protect its own (Helen Reeves told its members in the summer of 1998: 'victim support is no longer *our* issue. The trend started with the last Government... an enormous amount is happening. Restorative justice has really gained currency and brought the victim into the centre. What is our role? Do we support victims in mediation? I hope victims will be allowed to choose whether they want to go into restorative justice and we will support them if they decide not to do so'[156]).

Restorative justice was too massive a political and practical fact to be ignored. Helen Reeves said in October 1999: 'it's not going to go away. Victims are going to be involved and so the best thing that we can do is to get in not only on policy-making but training. And to try to make sure that people who are dealing with victims... are properly sensitized and... they've worked out where their responsibilities need to be.' There were early indications that liaison with

---

victims, but not take in work that is outside our normal remit.' In later draft guidelines, it was said that there was a need to explore whether the victim wishes to attend the initial meeting of the Youth Offending Panel and receive direct reparation. Victims should be referred to Victim Support Schemes to discuss their decision. Home Office, *Implementation of Referral Orders—Draft Guidance for Youth Offending Teams*, 24 January 2000.

[155] Chris George said 'I wrote a set of guidelines... about the role of Victim Support in the conferences. When I first got involved with restorative justice, I thought that Victim Support should be in every conference, you know guarding the victim's interests. The more work I've done, and the more research I've done and the more training courses I've been on, both here and in other places, made me think that really that's not our role... I believe it's not our role because we're not affected by the offence and for the conference to really have a meaning for people, you need the people that are affected that have a stake in the offence to participate.'

[156] Helen Reeves speaking at the Victim Support Annual Conference, July 1998.

victims could be 'contracted out' to other bodies with the 'danger of limited quality control and training' and it was probably incumbent on Victim Support to intervene to ensure that adequate standards were upheld in the victims' interests. And this time, in its new phase, it was perhaps possible that things would be different and restorative justice could work on behalf of the victim: Helen Reeves said in July 1999 that 'in the 1980s I think we were rather difficult and said that victims were being used. Now in youth crime at least, victims will at least be consulted. [There's a] possibility of victims understanding something more about their crime.'[157]

Most significantly of all, there was a need to mobilize a defence of the victims who were being drawn into restorative justice[158] (Helen Reeves said 'Victim Support ought to take a very strong role to protect the victim.'[159]). Victims could be vulnerable, ill-prepared and liable to exploitation; those organizing the new system were not always alert to their interests; and the response to victims in the pilot projects could sometimes be less than exemplary.[160] Take the candid observations of a woman working in the victim-offender conference office of a London Youth Offending Team in July 1999:

We're not contacting the victim direct and people are busy writing the pre-sentence reports, not getting the information to us. We don't get the information at the stage we are supposed to get it, we often don't get it until a week before the court. So there's no chance of us seeing the victim before the court hearing, so that's the first problem... the difficulty is that the victim needs time for preparation... I think they are not getting proper

---

[157] And there was some evidence that that was so. *Attitudes to Crime and Criminal Justice: Findings from the 1998 British Crime Survey*, HORS 200, 2000, reported on pp. 41–4 that 41% of victims said they would have liked to take part in restorative justice, 56% would not have liked to do so, and 3% unsure. The circumstances of crime had little impact on decision. Many victims would have accepted restorative justice as an alternative to more conventional criminal justice procedures. Elsewhere, Helen Reeves continued to voice her caution about the capacity of restorative justice to be a distraction. See H. Reeves and K. Mulley; 'The new status of victims in the UK: Opportunities and threats', in A. Crawford and J. Goodey (eds.); *Integrating a Victim Perspective Within Criminal Justice: International debates*, Ashgate, Aldershot, 2000, pp. 138–9.

[158] There was a 'consensus that Victim Support must be involved to protect victims' interests'. Draft minutes of the meeting of Victim Support National Council, 24 March 1998.

[159] Meeting of the VS National Trustees, 19 October 1999, my notes.

[160] See J. Dignan; *Youth Justice Pilots Evaluation: Interim Report on Reparative Work and Youth Offending Teams*, Home Office, London, 2000.

time for preparation. Because really they need, in terms of the Act, to make up their minds before court...they may get a 'phone call and be given a weekend to think about it and then get another 'phone call. I don't consider that sufficient at all. I think that's terrible what's happening. It's what's happening, but it's terrible. Every victim should be offered a visit...my fear is...we work with Victim Support and keep them informed...and victims will be going to them and saying things like 'do I have to do it?'... I think there's a real fear that Victim Support might turn round at some point and say this is not beneficial to victims at all. I don't think [Victim Support are involved at all]. That's a very good question actually. As far as I know they're not.[161]

Little by little, then, and sometimes reticently, Victim Support became implicated in the work of the two Acts.[162] It thought it had to be involved in supporting victims in and around conferences and mediation,[163] and other, equally compelling roles were being constructed for it, including contacting victims, establishing their views, preparing them,[164] and speaking on behalf of those who did not wish to attend.[165] It was becoming engaged in the preparation of crime audits.[166] It might well find itself selecting and helping to train members of Youth Offender Panels and Youth Offending Teams in 'victim awareness'.[167] It was actively preparing guidance

---

[161] Interview conducted by Katie Gould for an MSc dissertation at the London School of Economics. I am grateful to her for allowing me to quote from it.

[162] The Victim Support 1999 Annual Report recorded that the policy and information team had co-ordinated and developed Victim Support's response to restorative justice and the implications of the Crime and Disorder Act and the Youth Justice and Criminal Evidence Act.

[163] In his interim evaluation of the pilot projects, Jim Dignan observed that there was a need to provide information and support to victims, and that Victim Support might be able to provide such support. *Youth Justice Pilots Evaluation: Interim Report on Reparative Work and Youth Offending Teams*, Home Office, London, 2000, p. 23.

[164] Work preparing victims for reparation was being contracted out: 'it's all up for grabs' said Teresa Reynolds, and Victim Support would probably tender (Meeting of National Council of Victim Support, 19 January 1998, my notes).

[165] Crime Concern had won a contract to prepare guidance and consultancy for local authorities in submitting their bids for youth justice funding. Victim Support News Service—Referral Orders and Youth Offender Panels, Revised September 2001.

[166] Victim Support News Service, November 1998: November News.

[167] 'Proposal from VS to Youth Justice Board proposing that VS work with YOT staff, 30.11.99—reparation is an integral part of the new Crime and Disorder Act and Youth Justice and Criminal Evidence Act—all require some form of reparation to victims to be considered. For the first time those charged with preventing and addressing the behaviour of young offenders will also have a responsibility for victims. It will

for its own members.[168] As important as any undertaking, however, was the securing of formal safeguards for the victim in restorative justice. After all, as Peter Hepburn, the Deputy Chief Executive of Victim Support, said in January 1998, 'we are the only agency that gives absolute priority to the interests of victims'.[169]

A new procedure and a novel cluster of risks had thereby given rise to what Victim Support read as a need to confirm victims' procedural rights in restorative justice, and the organization busied itself in late 1998 and early 1999 in tendering advice about appropriate protection to Crime Concern,[170] the Youth Justice Board,[171] and the Home Office Juvenile Offenders Unit.[172] Helen Reeves remarked, 'one of our priorities is to prevent secondary victimization in the youth justice process. It's a balance that we need to retain from the very beginning: work with victims has a value in its own right.'[173] Victim Support asked Crime Concern to prevail on the

require skill to reconcile the demands and interests of the two groups. Most YOTs members will not have experience of dealing with victims. VS is increasingly being asked by YOTs to provide advice and training. We want to participate but are hampered by lack of resources. Victim Support eventually secured a training contract as part of a consortium with Mediation UK and the Thames Valley Police for £145,000 with the Youth Justice Board for 20 courses of training in victim awareness for 500 YOTs to run from October 2000 to March 2001.' (Victim Support Regional Meetings Spring 2001: Papers).

[168] Victim Support, News Service, September 1998.

[169] Meeting of Victim Support National Council, my notes, 19 January 1998.

[170] Victim Support had itself been invited to tender for a contract but National Office thought this was an inappropriate role for it to play. Draft Minutes of a Meeting of the Victim Support National Council, 23 March 1999. Crime Concern described itself as 'a national crime reduction organisation and registered charity that . . . provides advice and help to a wide range of professional and voluntary agencies to support their work in reducing crime and the fear of crime within local communities . . . [It] also run[s] over 50 projects across England and Wales, many of which are youth and neighbourhood-focused.'

[171] Restorative Justice and Victim Support, Report to the National Council, 19 March 1999.

[172] Minutes of meeting of Victims Steering Group, 4 December 1998.

[173] Victims Steering Group: meeting of 12 June 2001, my notes. Deborah Singer of Victim Support remarked at the launch of the report evaluating restorative work by the Thames Valley Police, 'one of the main concerns is that it shouldn't just be to prevent re-offending. It is not sufficient to involve the victim. The approach needs to be victim-centred and beneficial to them.' Launch of C. Hoyle and R. Young, 'Proceed with Caution: An evaluation of police-led restorative justice', London, 10 May 2002; my notes.

Youth Justice Board to include 'a victim perspective' in its guidance, and by that it meant that representatives of the local victim support scheme should be invited to join the management committee of any mediation, reparation, or conferencing project; a 'protocol' should be agreed for referring victims between a victim support scheme and a Youth Offending Team, the local victim support scheme should provide support to victims before, during, and after any major procedure; and Victim Support itself as a national body should be involved in shaping training strategies. Victim Support urged that 'victims must feel free to decline reparation if they so wish. Where reparation is chosen, this must be supervised at all times ... [and] victims must be involved in the consultation leading up to the court's judgement on what kind of reparation is appropriate ... [I]n order to preserve their independence ... Victim Support workers should not be required to mediate in such consultations.'[174] And, for her part, an official of the Juvenile Offenders Unit said of Teresa Reynolds of Victim Support, 'if she came to me and said what you're proposing in that guidance is potentially very damaging for victims, ... I would think very hard about doing something about it.'

The final guidance eventually issued for the implementation of reparation orders in 2002 did indeed contain provisions for the protection of victims,[175] most having been formulated by Victim Support,[176] and a formal balance between offenders and victims was thereby installed. The Chair of Victim Support's National Council, himself an Assistant Chief Probation Officer, was encouraged to observe in June 2000 that restorative justice was 'different from the last time because it did not merely treat the victim as an instrument

[174] *VSM Victim Support Magazine,* Winter 1998, No. 69, p. 5.

[175] Parallel professional guidelines issued by the Restorative Justice Consortium placed equal stress on balancing the interests of the parties involved and on refraining from subordinating restorative justice to 'single over-riding ends such as diversion or punishment limitation'. They also stipulated that participation must be voluntary; needs (vindication, compensation, relief of suffering, and general welfare) should be fully recognized; victims should be given adequate time to decide whether to participate; personal victims should be given priority; victims' needs should have priority over offender rehabilitation; agreements should be complied with; no victim should be obliged to accept an offer of reparation; and programmes should be designed in consultation with victims' representatives, who should be involved in their management and oversight. Restorative Justice Consortium; *Standards for Restorative Justice,* London, undated.

[176] Minutes of meeting of Victims Steering Group, 4 December 1998.

to help the offender'. *Inter alia*, that official guidance insisted that victims must be approached sensitively and with an appreciation of their potential vulnerability, and those who contacted them 'must be trained and skilled in victim awareness'; victims' involvement must be entirely voluntary and based on clear information and informed consent; their views must be 'respected', including the decision to withdraw from participation, and no pressure must be exerted on them to form a decision; they must be fully consulted about the time and place of any meeting, and have its structure, relations, roles and functions properly explained; they should be able to bring a supporter of their own choosing, including a victim support volunteer; and be informed about the contents of the contract and the young person's progress in completing it.[177] How those provisions were to be monitored was not clear. What would happen if they were breached was not specified. And once again they could not be represented as justiciable rights (Ian Chisholm remarked that 'We have rather avoided the issue of rights because it raises problems of enforceability'[178]), but victims had acquired a growing[179] and rather more securely guarded position in one small area of criminal procedure. And that they had done so moved them a little further towards the standing of a recognized party with an influence on procedure and sentencing.[180]

---

[177] *Referral Orders and Youth Offender Panels, Guidance for Courts, Youth Offending Teams and Youth Offender Panels*, Home Office/Lord Chancellor's Department/Youth Justice Board, February 2002, p. 23.

[178] Joint Home Office/IPPR seminar, 18 January 2001, to discuss Victim's Charter Draft Consultation Paper, my notes.

[179] The Government's stance towards the role of victims in restorative justice had become even more robust some time after the expiration of the period covered by this book. There are, for instance, numerous solicitous references to the victim in a consultation document, *Restorative justice: the Government's strategy*, Home Office, July 2003.

[180] And that was not necessarily well-regarded by legal scholars. Andrew Ashworth claimed, for instance, that it encroached on Article 6 rights to a fair trial before an impartial tribunal. 'Is Restorative Justice the Way Forward for Criminal Justice', typescript, undated, p. 18.

# 8

# The Vulnerable or Intimidated Victim

## Introduction

The developments I have described so far formed a series of loose-coupled, parallel histories which attained definition through the resolution of problems that never flowed expressly from victims proper. They were carried along, as it were, by other tides, bearing the negative imprint of other groups' preoccupations and problems, and serving practical purposes that were not the victims' own. In the two episodes that will be discussed in this and the next chapter, however, policies were turned directly upon the plight of a particular groups of victims, but they did so chiefly because they once again refracted larger or more pressing political designs that not only seemed on occasion to have little to do with the larger body of victims proper but sometimes complicated the way in which those victims were defined and treated.

Being the victim of many forms of crime is an unstructured and fleeting experience for the most part, unaccompanied by any publicly acknowledged identity, script, and role.[1] How is one supposed to *be*, say, a victim of burglary over any period of time? There are, to be sure, a number of possible existential consequences of being a burglary victim, and they may be severe, including anger, a sense of defilement, a loss of control, anxiety, mistrust, and the fear of crime,[2] but they do not constitute the materials of a stable, performable, and well-rounded public *persona*. Neither do they provide much of a foundation for a social movement in any conventional

---

[1] See my 'On Becoming a Victim', in C. Hoyle and R. Wilson (eds.); *New Visions of Crime Victims*, Hart Publishing, Oxford, 2002.

[2] See M. Maguire and T. Bennett; *Burglary in a Dwelling*, Heinemann, London, 1982.

sense.[3] Burglary victims are too diverse, too little different from the mass of the population, too ephemeral in their occupancy of the victim role, to constitute a self-conscious group with clear aspirations. They are what might be called victims *an sich*. Yet where a crime *is* particularly acute and prolonged in its impact, the identity it provides may well not be that of *victim*, with its weak or non-existent script and its unwelcome connotations of passivity, pain, defeat, misfortune,[4] and blame,[5] but that of the ever-more frequently employed *survivor* with its images of fortitude and adversity overcome.[6] There has even been resistance to the term *victim* amongst the members of Victim Support itself, some of whom called it 'unhelpful' and championed the alternative in its place.[7]

Some survivors of what is called serious crime, the victims at first- or second-hand of rape, domestic violence, incest, racial assaults, and

---

[3] One classic definition of a social movement is that of Turner and Killian: 'a collectivity acting with some continuity to promote or resist a change in the society or group of which it is a part' (R. Turner and L. Killian; Collective behaviour (second edition). Prentice-Hall, Englewood Cliffs, New Jersey, 1972, p. 223). Victims of volume crime are not a collectivity acting together with continuity. Another stock definition is that of Smelser who talks about a number of prerequisites including generalized belief, the mobilization of participants, and mechanisms of social control (N. Smelser; *Theory of Collective Behaviour*, Routledge & Kegan Paul, London, 1962). Victims of volume crime share no generalized belief, they are not mobilized, and they are not controlled.

[4] *The New Shorter Oxford English Dictionary* defines victim as a sacrifice, 'A person killed or tortured by another; a person subjected to cruelty, oppression, or other harsh or unfair treatment or suffering death, injury, ruin, etc., as a result of impersonal agency... A person who is taken advantage of; a dupe.' None of those attributes is particularly desirable.

[5] See L. Montada and M. Lerner; *Responses to Victimizations and Belief in a Just World*, Plenum Press, New York, 1998.

[6] Although, as Plummer argues in his *Telling Sexual Stories*, the insistence on new narratives and new terms for victimization may be experienced as oppressive by those who feel under compulsion to accept them. One rape victim publicly objected to the word survivor, claiming that 'it came in with the crop of PC language that veils over true experience. There's nothing to be ashamed of in being a rape victim. It's an experience that you have, not a definition of who you are. Hiding things with little words makes me mad.' A. Sebold; 'Don't call me a Survivor: I am a Victim', *The Times*, 4 June 2003.

[7] The term was discussed at a plenary meeting of the 2001 Victim Support Conference. One member remarked, '[the word *victim*] has a strong 1970s feel to it, like Electricity Board and Gas Board'.

homicide, *have* formed reflective campaigning and self-help groups *für sich* that proffer distinct social identities[8] manufactured and rehearsed in campaigns and public testimony.[9] The impact of such crimes may well be percussive and enduring, coaxing strong emotions and reactions; an urgent attempt to restore proper balance through some combination of public acknowledgement, reparation, remedy, and punishment; an effort to re-moralize a world that appears to have lost meaning; the search for others who have also undergone and grasped the experience and are able to commiserate; and the emergence of a catechism of binary oppositions that divide the good from the bad, the friend from the enemy, and the enlightened from the unenlightened. Claims to authority and support tend to be vested in the intense, harrowing, and extraordinary character of what they have been through, often portrayed as a kind of transformative moral passage, which confers existential legitimacy and an incommunicable understanding. Victims may take themselves to be set apart from others who have not been so afflicted and who cannot and should not claim to comprehend or represent them—set apart, indeed, from the survivors of other crimes that might also be identified as devastating in their consequences. The outcome has been that there is no one unified social or political world of the crime survivor but a series of symbolic fault-lines that have been constructed, elaborated, and put to competitive use in what Gouldner once called a 'conflictual validation of the self', identities being forged through separation, contrast, and negation. Thus, women rape victims may be encouraged to see themselves not as victims but as gendered survivors under patriarchy, sharing little in common with male victims of rape, and even less with the victims of theft, robbery, and burglary. The families of homicide victims distance themselves from the victims of volume crime. They tend to distance themselves from the families of people who have committed suicide or of children who have suffered 'cot deaths'. Black, Asian, or Jewish victims may argue that no crime can, or should be, compared with a racist attack. Gay victims may say that homophobic attacks are uniquely deplorable. It is in this fashion that competitive claims have been traded in the enactment of what the Americans have called

---

[8] The history of some of those organizations was traced in my *After Homicide, op. cit.*

[9] See K. Plummer; *Telling Sexual Stories*, Routledge, New York, 1994.

'identity politics': 'According to the logic of identity politics, it is strategically advantageous to be recognised as disadvantaged and victimized. The greater a group's victimization, the stronger its moral claim on the larger society.'[10]

The one politically substantial organization for victims in England and Wales, Victim Support, was actually dwarfed by the other official and quasi-official institutions of the criminal justice system, its funding but a tiny fraction of the system's budget (of a total of £12.1bn., £0.2bn. was spent by the Government on victims in 1999–2000, of which 95 per cent was absorbed by criminal injuries compensation[11]), and its status as the monopoly supplier of services to victims sporadically questioned within the Home Office. Its public style was the politics of restraint. Although, as we have seen, it could be robust and effective enough in committees and small private meetings, and it had been successful in winning concessions for victims in restorative justice, data protection, the *Victim's Charter*, and elsewhere, it had quite deliberately refrained from mobilizing victims for political ends or from participating in debates about the treatment of offenders, sentencing, and punishment (and others, such as Norman Brennan, the representative of a comparatively obscure organization, the Victims of Crime Trust,[12] described inside and outside the Home Office as a 'one man band', were often allowed by the mass media to become the public face of victims in its stead[13]). It mustered none of the big guns of the criminal justice system, being bolstered chiefly by the personal authority and long experience of its chief executive officer, Helen

[10]   J. Jacobs and K. Potter; *Hate Crimes: Criminal Law & Identity Politics*, Oxford University Press, New York, 1998, p. 5.

[11]   *Digest 4: Information on the Criminal Justice System in England and Wales*, Home Office, London, 1999, p. 70.

[12]   The Victims of Crime Trust describes itself as having been 'established in 1994 to support victims of crime throughout the UK and to represent their interests. From this wide base of victims concerns it has narrowed its area of activity in 1996 and has developed specific expertise in providing help to those who are the secondary victims of homicide. Victims of Crime Trust's mission now is to support any individuals bereaved through murder and manslaughter by ensuring they receive appropriate personal help at their time of need. The objective being that they can have as much normality as possible returned to their lives as soon as possible.'

[13]   He was, for instance, the only victims' representative to be quoted, and quoted at length, in *The Times*' report of the decision by Nottingham Crown Court to allow Brendon Fearon to sue Tony Martin for damages, an episode I discuss at some length below.

Reeves, and by its record of providing an established, comprehensive, proven, and inexpensive service For a long while a voice crying out in the wilderness, still certain that others had not quite accepted its representation of the victim as one whose crimes are rarely prosecuted and whose needs lie largely outside the criminal justice system,[14] Victim Support was often over-shadowed by the central institutions of police, judges, prosecutors, politicians, and policy-makers. The successor to Ian Chisholm as head of JVU stated baldly in October 2002: 'Victim Support has less status than the police or the CPS, but they're strongly affected by the decisions those bodies take. Victim Support can't require action of others—it can make a lot of noise—but at the end of the day, they can't say "you will, you must". Their funding is insecure.[15] They have amateur status. They may be seen as having a weak voice and a limited influence. They can challenge the State but they can't make us listen. Problem: are we giving victims a lesser status because they are not catered for by a State institution?'[16]

To compound its problems, Victim Support discovered that the political parties had begun to vie with one another and largely over its head to devise policies for victims around the turn of the century: an official of JVU mused in January 2000 that 'Victim Support used to make the agenda, but now the parties are running away with it [and it] is a bit concerned about losing control'. And the once barren

[14] Victim Support reported to itself that there was a 'danger of victims' interests being hijacked by criminal justice interests. The risk is closely related to the fact that the government is the main funder of Victim Support. It has become very evident that the government's main interest is in the smooth running of the criminal justice process and the effective management of offenders. Victims become more important when they are acting as witnesses in a criminal trial or taking part in restorative justice programmes. The risk is that the interests of victims whose offenders are not identified will be ignored and that resources will gradually be diverted towards the 3% who will become involved in the criminal justice system.' Victim Support; SORP 2000: risk management briefing, News Service September 2001.

[15] Although in practice it was secure enough in the period covered by this history. In discussing the move towards a service level agreement in 1998, a Grade 7 of JVU observed 'Change can only be brought about by consensus. We have been trying to move to a closer relation, but based on persuasion and slow. Our only sanction is withdrawing funds which would not be practicable or politically feasible.' That was to change in 2003 when a new Home Secretary and a new Minister, following the market logic of the new performance management, talked about placing victims' services out to tender to local Criminal Justice Consultative Committees.

[16] At the Phare Workshop, Dublin, 2–4 October 2002.

landscape about it had begun to teem in the 1990s and 2000s with Youth Offender Teams, probation liaison officers, special police units, police family liaison officers, restorative justice projects, and other formal and voluntary groups supporting victims, many of whom made a loud noise. Victim Support reflected to itself in January 2000 that 'One issue which will need to be addressed is the increasingly competitive situation in which Victim Support is now placed. With the growth of interest in victims' issues many other agencies, both statutory and voluntary are currently identifying new roles in relation to both victims and witnesses.'[17] To be sure, and as I have shown, Victim Support was formally included on the numerous committees that supervised all that new activity,[18] it tendered advice,[19] it was consulted,[20] and it was heeded, but the ownership of victims as a policy issue was becoming more dispersed and confused, and there was a 'real danger that, in the rush for change, the needs of victims and witnesses [would] be subordinated in the debate over how best to deal with offenders and offending behaviour'.[21]

The outcome was that the generality of victims in England and Wales did not compose the makings of an independent, self-propelled, and consequential political force. They were more

[17] Meeting of the VS Board of Trustees, 14 January 2000, Introduction to the 2000–2001 National Workplan. The introduction went on to say 'Victim Support has always enjoyed productive partnerships with other agencies and has attempted not to duplicate services which are provided adequately by other agencies. A difficult but necessary aspect of the review will be to determine which tasks are most appropriate to Victim Support and which can be safely left to others.'

[18] In 2000, it reported, for example, that it was a member of Government working parties on victims, witness care, vulnerable and intimidated witnesses, racially motivated crime, HM inspections of probation, and the review of the sexual offences legislation. Victim Support: National Office Performance 1999–2000: Strategic Policy Unit, 14 April 2000.

[19] For example, it responded in 1998 to such diverse White Papers and consultation papers as 'Working Together to Safeguard Children'; 'Our Healthier Nation'; on access to justice with conditional fees; the Criminal Cases Review Commission's consultation paper on priority-ranking applications; on the reform of Offences Against the Person Act, 1861; the British Society of Criminology's Draft Code on Taste & Decency; 'The New NHS Modern and Dependable'; 'Opening Up Youth Court Proceedings'; and 'Claims for Wrongful Death'.

[20] Thus Helen Reeves was appointed a consultant to Sir Robin Auld's review of the criminal courts. Draft minutes of meeting of VS Trustees, 14 April 2000.

[21] Meeting of Victim Support Trustees, 20 October 2000, Strategic Plan 2001–2004.

defined than defining, politically subdued, and lacking a distinct mass movement, and it was not their preoccupations that necessarily shaped their public identity. When quotidian victims did acquire a significant political character, it was almost invariably because it had been bestowed by others more powerful, coherent, vociferous, or organized than themselves. We have already seen how that shaping process had unfolded in different sequences of policy-making at the turn of the century, developing quietly and by default in performance management, human rights legislation and criminal injuries compensation, attracting little public attention, and unremarked by all except those who had been close to the events themselves.

But policy-making was not always driven by the sober, unobtrusive, and sustained work of routine policy-making. It could be propelled by what the former Prime Minister, Harold Macmillan, once called 'events'. Home Secretaries, said Jack Straw, 'are driven by events. Some literally fall from the sky.'[22] Ministers confronted untoward incidents, sometimes called 'shocks to the system' by officials; that could be made more dramatic still by gusts of political and popular interest; mediated, constructed, and amplified[23] by the press, radio, and television;[24] borne up by campaigning organizations—the groups of politicized victims *für sich*, on the one hand, or the campaigning groups representing larger vulnerable populations, some of whom were victims and witnesses, on the other—who were waiting in the wings for the opportune moment; sometimes engendering or re-vitalizing those very campaigning organizations; and seeming always to demand a political response.

A crisis could powerfully distil and signify complex political problems. It could indeed be *made* to distil and signify complex political problems by those who had an interest in moving matters forward by enacting an environment of causes and representations,

---

[22] Interview with the Home Secretary, *Sunday Times*, 9 July 2000.

[23] See E. Sutherland; 'The Diffusion of Sexual Psychopath Laws,' *Journal of Criminal Law and* Criminology, 1950, 40.

[24] Alistair Campbell, the Prime Minister's Director of Communications, was reported to have said 'Sometimes we gave a sense that we were more worried about what kind of press we were getting than what a policy was going to do over time.' *The Times*, 9 May 2002.

as Weick would put it,[25] and seizing an incident and its associated victims as a vehicle to carry policies through to a conclusion they might not otherwise have attained.[26] After all, the phenomena of crime and criminal justice are constituted critically by issues of morality, boundaries, and transgression;[27] the dramatic incident iconically condenses or defines social and political problems;[28] and part of its iconography may well reduce issues symbolically to special representations of the *persona* of the victim or victims at its core. Depictions of victims could become a forceful strand in any account. Such an iconography could be especially potent if the victims' suffering was not only extraordinary, poignant, and undeserved,[29] but also amenable to presentation as a key to important truths about the condition of England. It was as if bellwether victims could be clustered into *tableaux vivants* at strategic moments to exemplify cautionary lessons[30] about the parlous state

---

[25] See K. Weick; *The Social Psychology of Organizing*, Addison-Wesley, Reading, Ma., 1969.

[26] So it was with the first, and expensive, British Crime Survey of 1982, which was presented to, and accepted by the then Home Secretary, William Whitelaw, as a way of 'doing something' quickly and impressively in response to the Brixton riots of 1981.

[27] See J. Douglas (ed.); *Deviance and Respectability*, Basic Books, New York, 1970.

[28] Kai Erikson argued 'It may well be that without this ongoing drama [between deviants and control agents] at the outer edges of group space, the community would have no inner sense of identity and cohesion, no sense of the contrasts which set it off as a special place in the world.' K. Erikson; 'Notes on the Sociology of Deviance', in H. Becker (ed.); *The Other Side*, Free Press, New York, 1964, p. 15.

[29] Best claimed that 'Claims about new crimes lean heavily upon melodramatic imagery. The key figures in melodrama are the villain and the victim. In melodrama, the victim is good, innocent, vulnerable, powerless.... In contrast, melodrama's villains are not just bad, but threatening: they are evil, depraved, cruel, powerful, vicious predators... Defining social problems in terms of villains and victims makes it easy to understand these issues... In contrast, effective social policy tends to be boring... We aren't much interested in these mundane policies, and we usually don't hear much about them.' J. Best; *Random Violence: How We Talk about New Crimes and New Victims*, University of California Press, Berkeley, 1999, pp. 89, 158.

[30] Murray Edelman says: 'Problems come into discourse and therefore into existence as reinforcements of ideologies, not simply because they are there or because they are important for well-being. They signify who are virtuous and useful and who are dangerous or inadequate, which actions will be rewarded and which penalized.' M. Edelman; *Constructing the Political Spectacle*, University of Chicago Press, Chicago, 1988, p. 12.

of childhood,[31] gender, age, race, and other symptoms of a current problem that cried out for redress.[32]

There is evidence that victims have increasingly been used for central narrative purposes in the fiction and mass media reporting[33] of crime and crisis. In a world where, it is said, many truths seem less sure, where authority is less certain, and a moral pluralism prevails, the personal victim's palpable suffering can come by default to serve as an alternative validation of a moral theme.[34] With some little exaggeration perhaps, Boutellier claimed that 'the only thing that counts in a secular, liberal society is that people are vulnerable to humiliation and cruelty, pain and suffering; the extent to which we show ourselves to be sensitive to other people's experiences of this kind determines the morality of our culture... Victimhood serves... as an active and dynamic focal point for a secularized morality.'[35]

But representations of victimhood accomplish more. They act as a graphic shorthand or metonym for complicated groupings of moral and political problems that are not otherwise easily depicted, grasped, or managed. Politicians and their advisers give order to their sense of priorities by speaking about *issues*, issues tend to be attached symbolically to incidents, and it is to incidents that they have often to respond, and be seen to respond,[36] quickly, publicly,

[31] See Jack Straw's speech to Labour Party Conference, 24 September 2000.

[32] See R. Ericson, P. Baranek and J. Chan; *Representing Order: Crime, Law and Justice in the News Media*, University of Toronto Press, Toronto, 1991, esp. pp. 4–5.

[33] See the report about news agencies 'ambulance chasing' victims of crime as a new phenomenon. *The Times*, 29 June 2001. Reiner and his colleagues state: 'Probably the clearest and most significant changes we have found are in the representation of victims. Victims have moved from a shadowy and purely functional role to a pivotal position. Their suffering increasingly constitutes the subject position or the *raison d'etre* of the story.' R. Reiner, S. Livingstone and J. Allen; 'Casino culture: media and crime in a winner-loser society', in K. Stenson *et al.* (eds.); *Crime, Risk and Justice*, Willan Publishing, Cullompton, 2000, p. 187.

[34] See J. Allen, S. Livingstone and R. Reiner; 'True Lies', *European Journal of Communication*, 1998, Vol. 13, No. 1, pp. 53–75.

[35] H. Boutellier; *Crime and Morality: The Significance of Criminal Justice in Postmodern Culture*, Kluwer, Dordrecht, 2000, pp. 15, 17.

[36] Waddington has talked about how, in policing, the demand that the police 'do something' can lead to incident-driven policy making. P. Waddington; *The Strong Arm of the Law*, Clarendon Press, Oxford, 1991, p. 264. Also see M. Edelman; *Politics as Symbolic Action*, Markham Publishing Company, Chicago, 1971.

and effectively.[37] So it was that Alun Michael said in 1999: 'I think that we were certainly affected by events that came thick and fast. There were the pressures which arose out of the Stephen Lawrence murder. There were the sort of individual cases of sex abuse or individuals coming out of prison which justified Harold Macmillan's old statement when he was asked, "events, dear boy, events". So certainly all of that was there.' And Justin Russell, Jack Straw's political adviser, said in February 2001 that there had been 'the Paynes last summer. I'm trying to think if there's been anything since the Paynes as important for driving things; Michael Stone [the murderer of Lyn and Megan Russell]; and Lawrence, [and the] Tony Martin shooting [which I discuss below]. I mean they've been the sort of four, five . . . '. Pragmatically, it was those events[38] 'driving things' to which politicians were obliged to turn in their mapping and planning of key developments.

The idiographic impulse was strong, particularly in those who were lawyers by training and who were thus inclined professionally to think in terms of cases. Consider the content of two speeches made by Jack Straw, himself a former barrister. In talking to the 1998 Labour Party Conference, he said 'From today racist violence and racial harassment are now specific crimes. One particular act of racial savagery, which touched us all, was the killing of Stephen Lawrence. The judicial inquiry I set up into his death is still continuing. And I look forward to receiving its findings and learning the lessons from this appalling case.'[39] In talking to the same Conference two years later, he said 'I am proud to have been the Labour Minister responsible for setting up the inquiry into the murder of Stephen Lawrence. We were all moved by the words of Neville Lawrence

[37] Downes and Morgan put the matter thus: there is 'the unpredictable realm of scandal and concern. For all their pretensions, both Parliamentary and extra-Parliamentary groupings can be utterly outpaced by events which explode in such a way that unusual responses are called for by "public opinion"—a phenomenon for which media attention is often taken to be the proxy.' D. Downes and R. Morgan; 'The Skeletons in the Cupboard', in M. Maguire et al. (eds.); The Oxford Handbook of Criminology, Oxford University Press, Oxford, 2002, p. 310.

[38] One instance involved an adjournment debate in May 1997 about the question of tariff-setting raised by Hugh Bayley, the Member of Parliament for the City of York, in whose constituency the family of a murder victim, Peter Windass, lived. Ministers are required publicly to offer a public defence of the treatment of particular cases in such situations.

[39] Speech by Jack Straw at Labour Party Conference, 1 October 1998.

[Stephen Lawrence's father] at last year's conference. We must never, ever, forget the lessons of what happened...'. And then, after a while, he continued: 'Of all the dreadful consequences of crime, nothing is worse than when it involves a child; and worst of all the murder of a child, a child like Sarah Payne. I've met Sarah's parents. Their courage is remarkable.'[40]

## Tony Martin

The politics of the critical event was not, of course, simply a matter of the galvanic response. There was always scope for interpretive and political latitude (Gewirth once reminded us that there is no sociological law that someone, somewhere, may not choose to break) and politicians and policy-makers may decide that what has been presented as a crisis need not be so treated, and that they do not propose to react or react in what might be considered a predictable or obvious way. One example was provided by the case of Tony Martin that unwound during the life of the first New Labour administration.

Tony Martin was a Norfolk farmer convicted in November 1999 of the murder[41] of Fred Barras, a sixteen year old who had burgled Martin's home four months before, and, according to the Eastern Daily Press Web Site, his was a case that 'created worldwide interest' and popular agitation for Martin and Barras alike.[42] It was reported that Barras had previously appeared in court eighteen times and had twenty-nine criminal convictions.[43] His companions, Bark and Fearon, had amassed eighty-five previous convictions between them. There was some resulting confusion about who could and should be represented as the victim in the telling of the offence: Fearon could claim to be the victim of an injury inflicted by Martin; Barras and his family the victim and 'survivors' of murder; and Tony

---

[40] Jack Straw's speech to Labour Party Conference, 24 September 2000.

[41] Later reduced on appeal to manslaughter in October 2001 and sentenced to 5 years.

[42] Supporters demonstrated vociferously outside the Magistrates' Court when Martin was arraigned in September 1999, and police and politicians were 'shouted down' at a public meeting at Tony Martin's local village hall the next day. But 'hundreds' were reported to have attended Fred Barras's funeral. (Based on Eastern Daily Press web site.)

[43] Tony Martin Support Group web site.

Martin the victim of a burglary and a 'secondary victim' of the criminal justice system. Those who supported Martin (and they were many[44]) depicted him as '... a man with a previously unblemished record [who]... is in jail for life, a political prisoner... Tony Martin may have fired the fatal shot but it was Fred Barras Jnr's "family" who killed him.'[45] There were allegations about the intimidation of jurors in Martin's trial[46] and, it was said, the prosecution itself had been ill-advised and Martin was a casualty of the criminal justice system: 'Over the coming months, politicians, commentators and public opinion turned the Norfolk farmer into something approaching a folk hero.'[47] Fearon, as victim, was reported to have been told that he was entitled to be consulted about Martin's possible release from prison under the *Victim's Charter*, and he was said to be contemplating suing Martin for £15,000 for loss of earnings because of injuries to his leg from Martin's shotgun, his concern about his 'long-term sexual functioning', and his distress at watching films in which people died. Much later, he did indeed obtain leave to sue (and there was anger in the press about the decision[48]). But he was certainly not an 'ideal victim', having been an accomplice to a burglary, a man with a long criminal record, and

[44] He was said, for example, to have received 7,500 Christmas cards in prison. *Daily Telegraph*, 2 January 2003.

[45] R. Littlejohn in *The Sun*, 15 June 2001.

[46] *The Times*, 20 June 2000.

[47] *Guardian*, 30 October 2001.

[48] Ananova web site. He was eventually allowed to sue under Article 6 of the Human Rights Act by Nottingham County Court on 13 June 2003, the judge stating that 'it would be wrong, subject to other considerations, to deprive the claimant from airing his claim and having a full trial'. (*The Times*, 14 June 2003). Tony Martin's supporters were said to have been 'outraged' by the decision (*ibid*). And a number of newspapers fulminated. The *Daily Mail*, 14 June 2003, reported the story on an entire page under the heading 'Thief can sue Martin (because, of course, a heroin-dealing career criminal's human rights MUST be respected.' It commented 'Yet again, British justice is blind to decency, morality and ordinary common sense. In the name of "human rights", hardworking taxpayers have funded the legal bills of a leech on society who hasn't done an honest day's work in his life....'. *The Sun*, 14 June 2003, reported the story under 'PURE INSANITY Fury at burglar's OK to sue Tony Martin.' And the *Daily Express* made it front page news on the same day, with the headline 'BURGLAR TO SUE HIS VICTIM And YOU pick up the Bill.' It continued inside under the heading, 'Our crazy courts protect burglars.' In the event, Tony Martin threatened to counter-sue, and both claims were withdrawn in September 2003.

with fresh convictions for drug-dealing after the burglary at Martin's home.[49]

What made Martin's case interesting was the multiple ambiguities of his and the others' moral status and the problem of the politician's response. Martin was not the first man to have been convicted for assaulting a burglar, and the limits to a householder's right to protect property and person were being actively contested.[50] At a time of local government elections in early May 2000, where political claim and counter-claim were being traded, the Leader of the Conservative Party in Opposition, William Hague, championed Martin as a 'victim who hit back', and promised a reform of the criminal law 'so that there is a "strong presumption" that the State will side with home-owners rather than criminals'.[51] But *The Times* newspaper predicted that 'Mr Hague's approach is likely to prompt accusations that he is encouraging people to take the law into their own hands...'[52] and, indeed, he was to be discomfited by criticisms from the Bar's public relations committee, the secretary of the Law Society's criminal law committee, ACPO, and members of the judiciary. He was widely reported to have been barracked in public by a seventy-seven year old woman who said 'Why do you hitch your wagon to the star of a man found guilty of murdering a 16 year old boy by shooting him in the back?'[53] His arguments were spurned by Jack Straw[54] and by Charles Kennedy, the Leader of the Liberal Democrats, who called them 'the worst kind of immature saloon-bar politics'.[55] And he was obliged to retreat a little in April 2000 ('Nothing I have said has suggested that more people should have guns or they should have their houses surrounded by lethal electric fences...'[56]) although the retreat was minor and short-lived (and the matter of Tony Martin continued to influence the Conservative Party's thinking, being fed into its election manifesto in 2001 as we

---

[49] He was, for instance, convicted and imprisoned on separate drugs charges some time after the burglary.

[50] See, for example, an anticipation of the Court of Appeal case in which the limits of Tony Martin's right to self-defence would be clarified. *The Times*, 27 April 2000.

[51] *The Times*, 26 April 2000.

[52] *Ibid.*

[53] *The Times*, 27 April 2000.

[54] Justin Russell, Jack Straw's political adviser, nevertheless observed 'he made some good running on it for maybe a week or so'.

[55] *The Times*, 27 April 2000.

[56] *Evening Standard*, 27 April 2000.

shall see in Chapter 10). Within a few days, an unbowed William Hague returned to the case of Tony Martin to deliver a message about the proper balance between criminal and victim:

... of course, there was Tony Martin. The details of the particular case are best left to the courts, but politicians and the police have a duty to understand why it generated such an explosive public reaction. The fact is that the law-abiding majority are fed up with a system that allowed the three burglars who broke into Mr Martin's home to collect 114 convictions between them without any of them serving more than a few months in prison and a couple of dozen hours community service. We believe it is time to overhaul the law in this area so that we are on the side of the person defending their home and their family against the criminal, and not the other way around.[57]

The established institutions of the criminal justice system turned against William Hague, the *Guardian* newspaper reporting that 'Crispian Strachan, chief constable of Northumbria police, warned that Mr Hague's proposal would lead to a "serious increase in violent crime" similar to levels in the US', and that Colin Langham-Fitt, the acting Assistant Chief Constable of Norfolk, the county in which the murder had taken place, had said that 'There's nothing in the Martin trial or its verdict that takes away from people the right to defend themselves. I can't see how you could practically change the law without risking all sorts of miserable sad effects and uninvited consequences.'[58] In retrospect, long after the initial *furore* had subsided, the Chairman of the Parole Board, before whom Martin had appeared, concluded that 'Some newspapers decided very early on that Mr Martin was a victim of the criminal justice system ... I don't believe that to be true ... Mr Martin was a very dangerous man. He shot a 16-year-old boy and killed him—shot him in the back at the range of about 4ft.'[59]

For Home Office politicians in the first New Labour administration, delaying their response because of their inability properly to comment on a case coming before the courts, having seen what had in the mean time befallen William Hague, the Tony Martin incident was evidence, in the words of Justin Russell, the Home Secretary's

---

[57] William Hague addressing the Police Federation Annual Conference, Conservative Party News, 19 May 2000.
[58] *Guardian*, 27 April 2000.
[59] *The Times*, 27 May 2003.

political adviser, that not only that 'we felt, you know, you have to draw a line somewhere' but that an unconsidered populist response could well be politically hazardous. Officials believed that it had at first been attractive to Labour politicians because William Hague had seized the agenda, but he had been 'rubbished' in the press, and his 'mauling' was regarded as salutary. Jack Straw and his colleagues had elected not to align themselves with Martin, although they could well have done so (and it was reported that the Prime Minister had wavered about whether to intercede[60]). The Leader of the Opposition may have prepared a political rhetoric to attach to the Tony Martin crisis but the Government had chosen not to accept it.[61] (And perhaps it was a crisis which the Government would never have felt comfortable owning. A Labour Party officer working on home affairs, reflected 'Tony Martin was an issue which was particularly seized upon by the Conservatives as also fitting in with their wider arguments about rural issues and the countryside and you know, Labour doesn't understand the countryside.')

A similar capacity to negotiate the possible political impact of an incident was illustrated by the campaign for Sarah's Law,[62] and it

[60] See *Guardian*, 30 October 2001.

[61] Such things happen against the will of the principals. Kumar has supplied an example of a social movement about rape that was conducted in the name of a woman who had no desire to be associated with it. R. Kumar; *The History of Doing: An Illustrated Account of Movements for Women's Rights and Feminism in India 1800–1990*, Kali for Women, New Delhi, 1993.

[62] Sarah Payne was the iconic focus of a campaign for legislation to allow the concerned public a right of access to information about convicted sex offenders, and it followed upon another campaign with another iconic victim at its core. In the United States, after what the Klaas Kids Foundation called 'the brutal 1994 rape and murder of seven-year old Megan Kanka', the New Jersey State legislature enacted the Registration and Community Notification Laws, known as 'Megan's Law'. The Act had been passed in October 1994 'In response to the public's demand for greater information regarding the identity and whereabouts of previously convicted sex offenders who might prove a threat to the safety of those in the community... [and it] provides for the creation of a state registry of sex offenders and a community notification procedure...' (Attorney General Guidelines for Law Enforcement for the Implementation of Sex Offender Registration and Community Notification Laws, State of New Jersey, March 2000, p. 1). In 1996, Megan's Law became binding on all 50 states. There was to be a shadow of Megan's Law in England and Wales, known informally in the Home Office (for example, in the Practice Guidance SubGroup: Terms of Reference, 20 September 2000) and elsewhere as 'Sarah's Law' to memorialize Sarah Payne. Sarah Payne, an 8 year old, had been reported missing on 1 July 2000 and was found dead 16 days later. In December 2001, Roy Whiting, a man with a previous

will be illustrated yet again in the next chapter where it will become clear that there need never have been a judicial inquiry into the investigation of the death of Stephen Lawrence, and that all the apparently imperative nature[63] of the recommendations of the Macpherson report was quite freely willed.

## Julia Mason

An official working in the Juvenile Offenders Unit, reflected:

(*n. 62 contd.*) conviction for a sexual offence against a child, was found guilty of abducting and murdering Sarah Payne and was imprisoned for life. A vigorous campaign was waged by the press, and especially by the *News of the World*, for an English version of Megan's Law, that would provide, *inter alia*, for every parent to have the right to controlled access to information about individuals in their neighbourhood, including convicted child sex offenders who may pose a risk to their child. In appropriate cases this access would also have been given to members of the public who had a responsibility for the care of children (*For Sarah*: The *News of the World* campaign to protect children from sex offenders, web site). On 17 September 2000, the *News of the World* published a critical piece arguing that Jack Straw was ignoring the general will and should resign: 'A mighty coalition of professional bodies—including the NSPCC, the probation service and ACPO—backed our FULL Sarah's Law proposals.' The names of a number of alleged offenders were published in the newspaper in July 2000, and there was vigilante action against some of those so identified (BBC News On-Line, 25 July 2000). A Minister was moved to warn privately against complacency and declare that the Home Office would need to take account of public pressures on matters such as paedophiles. Yet there was also a hostile response to the campaign. The BBC reported that ' the government swiftly drew back from the central demand after the Association of Chief Police Officers, probation officers and criminologists warned that it would be impossible to control access, and the risk of vigilante attacks would push the offenders underground' (BBC News On-Line, 13 December 2001). The result was a compromise, the Criminal Justice and Court Services Act, 2000, which was described by Victim Support as the first recognition of victim's rights in statute. The relevant clause which was added as a direct result of the Sarah Payne campaign put a duty on probation services to contact the victims of sexual or violent offences where the offender was sentenced for a year or more, to find whether they wished to be informed of any conditions of release and whether they wished to make representations (Victim Support: 'The probation service's victim contact work', June 2001). It was, said a senior official in September 2000, 'a clear example of democratic government: done in a rush and off-the-cuff ideas from Ministers'.

[63] ACPO, for instance, wrote about how 'Recent events, in particular the Stephen Lawrence Inquiry, have raised the profile of issues of racism. There is now a political and social will, greater than ever before, to confront and tackle racial prejudice and discrimination throughout society. Public awareness has never been higher and sensitivity to these issues has never been greater.' ACPO *Guide to Identifying and Combating Hate Crime*, Metropolitan Police, London, December 1999.

you generally find that what happens is that [there is] some shock to the system . . . Stephen Lawrence needed to be as huge as it was and I think the rape victim [Julia Mason] also. There's so much that needs doing that you then fasten on one particular prompt which dramatises it. I can see the dangers of that, but my general approach is that we have to listen to . . . what can be described as high trauma, high social trauma crimes, and Sarah Payne was another, Megan Russell[64] . . . it is just a fact but I think about most of these *cause célèbres* in terms of the victim and many others do.

It was the dramaturgy of the victimization of two of those people, Julia Mason and Stephen Lawrence, that drove two leading and prolonged episodes of policy-making for victims,[65] and it gave victims a political edge, because it was embroiled from the outset by the potent and organized campaigning politics of gender and race, the salient identity politics of the time. It is with them I shall remain in this and the next chapter, and so diffuse and intense was the activity they generated that I can select only a few themes for analysis.[66]

[64] It will be recalled that the claim of Josie Russell, the young daughter of Lyn Russell and the sister of Megan Russell who had been viciously killed in July 1996, had been cited in arguments for the revision of payments made by the criminal injuries compensation scheme to the families of murder victims.

[65] The difficulty with the idiographic approach is, as Smith and Frenkel argue, that policies may be based on 'definitions that . . . represented the extremes in a given victims' problem. Ambiguities [are] excluded or submerged. Focusing on the extremes skews policy away from the "gray" situations, in which . . . a large portion of victimization occurs.' S. Smith and S. Frenkel; *Adjusting the Balance: Federal Policy and Victim Services*, Greenwood Press, New York, 1988, p. 172.

[66] For example, much of the lobbying about the Youth Justice and Criminal Evidence Bill that stemmed from the developments I shall outline focused on restrictions on press reporting of crimes and criminal proceedings, particularly under Clause 43, but I have chosen not to discuss it for reasons of parsimony. It should be noted, however, that the press were powerful enough to make their will felt, and they secured a major modification of the proposed legislation. Paul Boateng announced that 'We are persuaded of the need to provide protection for children who might be harmed by publicity in relation to a crime. It is only sensible, when crimes and criminal investigations are reported, to ensure that attention is paid to the welfare of children and the possible consequences of their being identified in the media . . . But we are also clear that there is a proper balance in the public interest to be struck and that Parliament should not without good reason bring into effect restrictions on responsible and legitimate reporting of the news. We have had discussions with media representatives throughout the passage of this Bill. We are pleased that the industry and the Press Complaints Commission are now considering strengthening the Code of Practice

Julia Mason, a thirty-four year old woman, was the iconic figure at the core of what became known as the vulnerable or intimidated witnesses initiative,[67] although her place in its pedigree could be sporadically over-shadowed. On 9 December 1995, she was abducted at a bus stop by Ralston Edwards, and was taken to his home, where she was subjected to a savage and prolonged rape. Edwards was arrested three days later, and his case, turning on the issue of the victim's consent, went to trial at the Central Criminal Court in August 1996. Only Julia Mason's evidence could establish that her consent was lacking, and her examination-in-chief and cross-examination assumed a pivotal importance. In July 1996, and again at pre-trial review in early August, the Crown Prosecution Service was notified that Edwards had dismissed his solicitors and would be representing himself. On two occasions, before trial and before cross-examination, the judge asked him to reconsider his decision, but he was adamant that he would waive his rights to legal representation. Evidence-in-chief was delivered on the 6 August and cross-examination began in the afternoon of the following day. Before he began, the judge explained to Edwards that he would have to seek leave if he wished to cross-examine about Julia Mason's previous sexual experience: Edwards submitted seven questions on the matter, and the judge disallowed all but one. Cross-examination itself lasted six days until the 14 August, but was broken up into short sessions, and, before every resumption and during cross-examination itself, Edwards was warned about the need to be relevant.

Edwards was dressed in the clothes he had worn at the time of the rape, and many of the questions he asked were prurient, repetitive, and distressing. Julia Mason subsequently observed that:

He was reliving the rape moment by moment... What made it worse was that Edwards was defending himself. At least when a barrister is asking questions he is doing it to get to the truth. When a rapist is asking the questions he knows what he's done and he's furthering the act. From the

better to protect children...'; Youth Justice and Criminal Evidence Bill—New Amendments, Home Office press release 180/99, 16 June 1999.

[67] Her trial was to be given in internal Home Office papers as one of the events that had precipitated the vulnerable and intimidated witnesses initiative. For example, in Criminal Justice Conference: Vulnerable or Intimidated Witnesses, Training Issues, 17–19 November 1998: Gillian Harrison; Summary of Proceedings.

moment he opened his mouth the filth and degradation of my ordeal was replayed in violent and vivid detail.[68]

Edwards was eventually convicted of two counts of rape on a majority verdict and was awarded two life sentences in early October. His trial and its aftermath were avidly reported[69] and they generated a campaigning response, orchestrated in part by Julia Mason herself, who had sacrificed the anonymity to which she was entitled in law. She said 'To male politicians, I would urge them to change the law. For God's sake and women's sake, may this never happen again... I feel like I have been raped twice, once in his filthy den and once in front of a judge.'[70] Julia Mason pursued her complaint to the European Commission of Human Rights in Strasbourg, alleging breaches of Articles 3, 8, and 13 of the Convention,[71] to which the Registry added Article 14,[72] but she eventually withdrew, having settled with the Home Office and being aware of the passage of the Youth Justice and Criminal Evidence Act that would prohibit cross-examination in person by defendants in rape and allied trials (the Home Office observed to itself at the time that the Act would remove the source of the complaint). A new composite organization, the Campaign to End Rape,[73] was created with the argument that 'In 1996 a woman was cross-examined in court over 6 days by her rapist. The facts... are a shocking indictment of the failure of British justice for women and children who have

[68] *Daily Telegraph*, 18 May 2001.
[69] See N. Fyfe and H. McKay; 'Desperately Seeking Safety: Witnesses' Experiences of Intimidation, Protection and Relocation', *British Journal of Criminology*, 2000, Vol. 40, p. 672.
[70] *Daily Telegraph*, 10 October 1996.
[71] Article 3 covered the prohibition of torture ('no one shall be subjected to torture or to inhuman or degrading treatment or punishment'); Article 8, the right to respect for private and family life ('everyone has the right to respect for his private and family life, his home and his correspondence'); and Article 13, the right to a remedy ('everyone whose rights and freedoms as set forth in this Convention are violated shall have an effective remedy before a national authority notwithstanding that the violation has been committed by persons acting in an official capacity').
[72] Article 14 covered the prohibition of discrimination ('The enjoyment of the rights and freedoms set forth in this Convention shall be secured without discrimination on any ground such as sex, race, colour, language, religion, political or other opinion, national or social origin, association with a national minority, property, birth or other status.').
[73] It was jointly sponsored by Justice for Women, the Rape Crisis Federation, and Action Against Child Sexual Abuse.

been raped... For the minority of cases which do get to court women talk of the experience as being "like a second rape"... The Campaign to End Rape says that the current legal framework amounts to a rapists' charter.' Chris Pulford of the Lord Chancellor's Department, and a member of the Interdepartmental Working Group on Vulnerable or Intimidated Witnesses, remarked in October 1999 about the political environment that had thus been created:

There's no doubt, you know, that various pressure groups in terms of representing particular interests have nudged us all along. So there's quite a strong witness lobby, if you see what I mean, and rape victims are represented by various organizations. They've grown up in relatively small pockets but quite a lot of them are now sort of banding together, as it were.

The trial had been noted by officials of the then Procedures and Victims Unit, becoming described in Government as a *cause célèbre*. It had been noted by Ian Chisholm[74] who floated the idea of a radical change in the conduct of cross-examination to the Home Secretary in September 1996. It had been noted in the Lord Chancellor's Department (an official reflected that 'defendants directly cross-examining rape complainants is seen to be something that wasn't conducive to giving best evidence'). At a time when ideas were being framed for a forthcoming general election, manifestos were being drafted, and political responses had an overtly campaigning complexion, it had been noted by Members of Parliament,[75] by the Home Secretary, the Leader of the Opposition,[76] and Jack Straw, the Shadow Home Secretary, who wrote to the Home Secretary about the matter.

[74] He himself later looked back on it as a 'political *cause célèbre* issue—there's been a lot of froth and media hype about that'. Speaking at Victim Support National Conference, 5 July 1999, my notes.

[75] More than 100 MPs were reported to have petitioned Jack Straw to reform the law on rape law when New Labour came to power. *The Times*, 14 June 1997.

[76] 'On his visit to Worcester in June, the Prime Minister [Tony Blair] mentioned the case of Julia Mason who was cross-examined by her assailant for several days and undertook to look closely at what can be done to stop that kind of cross-examination.' Working Group on Vulnerable or Intimidated Witnesses: Discussion Paper 2: Prohibition on Unrepresented Defendants Personally Conducting Cross-Examination, VIW 97/11.

In short, the case of Julia Mason had attained the power symbol-ically to define and illuminate a stark problem[77] (although, like many such iconic and stark issues, it was actually an instance of a very rare occurrence[78]). Michael Howard, the then Home Secretary, observed trenchantly, 'That woman was made a victim twice over    No woman should ever be put through an ordeal like that. It's completely wrong. It's got to stop. And I'm determined to make sure it does.'[79] In the trial's wake,[80] he declared that 'I fully sympa-thise with victims who have had to endure further distress by being cross-examined by their alleged attacker... I think it is right that the courts should have the discretion to protect such vulnerable victims', and he established at the beginning of October 1996 what was called at first, and rather clumsily, a 'Working Group on the Cross-examination of "Rape" Victims by Unrepresented Defendants', a group composed of officials representing the Law Officers, the Home Office, the Lord Chancellor's Department, the Crown Pros-ecution Service, the Northern Ireland Office, ACPO, the Scottish

[77] On 30 November 1997, Alun Michael told the Magistrates' Association, 'We have recently seen the terrible case of a rapist who cross-examined his victims for several days, subjecting them to trauma and distress. I am appalled by this further victimization, and I am determined that vulnerable witnesses should not have to go through this type of experience.' Again, speaking at the Victim Support Annual General Meeting, 22 November 2000, for instance, Ross Cranston, the Solicitor General, talked about how in '1996 reports of the Ralston Edwards rape trial high-lighted the plight of rape victims'.

[78] Only two other examples of personal cross-examination of rape complainants were reported to the Home Office during the first New Labour administration, and, as I shall argue, the judiciary would claim that the problem was neither acute nor out of control. Julie Barnard of the Rape Crisis Federation concurred in October 1999: 'It's not the defendant in the majority of cases. The defendant never hardly takes the option of representing himself or cross-examining the [survivor].' Ian Chisholm himself remarked that 'The cross-examination, in one case by the defendant himself, of rape victims had attracted considerable criticism... [and raised] concerns about the par-ticular distress caused to victims when being cross-examined personally by the de-fendant.' The Criminal Bar Association also noted in 1998 that there had been two highly publicized cases but no evidence of a growing trend for defendants to dispense with legal representation so as to further torment their witnesses (CBA Working Party Report on Cross-Examination of Rape Victims by the Accused in Person, 1998).

[79] 'Protecting the Public from Crime', *Politics Today,* Conservative Research De-partment, No. 1, 31 January 1997, p. 16.

[80] The Government had stated its intention of dealing with the issue of personal cross-examination by the defendant in rape cases as early as October 1996. See Victim Support; *Women, rape and the criminal justice system,* London, October 1996.

Lord Advocate's department, and others (but not Victim Support or any other voluntary body or any organization specifically representing women), that was to move gingerly and slowly into an area riddled with risk[81] (and note the caution with which the word *rape* was used). The Home Office Minister, David Maclean, put it that, 'If we propose taking away the right of defendants to represent themselves, we have to be careful how we do it, in what cases we do it and where we draw the line. It could be a slippery slope towards removing the rights of defendants to represent themselves in quite the wrong cases.'[82]

## The Witness with Learning Disabilities

I argued in Chapter 3 that once a Government committee or working group has been established, it acquires a sponge-like capacity to absorb new tasks. So it was with the Working Group on the Cross-examination of 'Rape' Victims by Unrepresented Defendants. Once the committee had been jolted into activity, and was available for lading, it picked up an ever-growing baggage of extra work. The first enlargement was prompted by the need to deal with the impending publication in late 1996 of a report of research on witnesses with learning disabilities by Andrew Sanders,[83] commissioned by the Home Office to explore the recommendation of the Pigot report about the extension of provisions for children to adult vulnerable witnesses;[84] and prompted by a practical concern about the failure of cases involving such witnesses to reach the courts. Andrew Sanders had 'wanted to do something on victims and that was a way in. It was remarkably well funded. It only occurred to me later', he said, 'that it was part of a broader strategy on vulnerable victims. We did agree that [we] shouldn't fix [our] eyes on learning disability

---

[81] The Criminal Justice Consultative Council recorded that the Home Office was 'considering what steps might be taken to limit the chances of victims of rape or stalking, being questioned in court by the defendant in person'. *Summary of activities 1996–97*, Home Office, 1997, p. 5.

[82] Speaking in the House of Commons, 18 December 1996.

[83] A. Sanders *et al.*; *Witnesses with Learning Disabilities*, Research Findings No. 44, HORS, December 1996.

[84] See *Speaking up for Justice*, Report of the Interdepartmental Working Group on the treatment of Vulnerable or Intimidated Witnesses in the Criminal Justice System, Home Office, London, 1998, p. 1.

alone.' And he professed himself later surprised at the scale of the consequences of what he had done when he discovered that the Home Office had developed a 'broader agenda to level the playing field'.

An important part of the Sanders' research 'was to talk to witnesses who hadn't been listened to' and it unearthed a substantial array of problems: it was reported that people with learning difficulties do not form a homogeneous population and require individual assessment; only in cases involving sexual offences did specialist police interview witnesses with learning difficulties; the police and prosecutors in a case rarely consulted experts with a knowledge of disability; only a few special measures, such as the use of video-taped statements as evidence, were employed in such cases; carers were unclear about whether counselling could be given before the witnesses' appearance at court;[85] and there was ample scope for offering more support to them in their role as witnesses. Sanders' conclusions and recommendations were lodged in a report that had been commissioned by the Home Office and they would require a formal Home Office response. They were likely to encourage watchful voluntary bodies such as VOICE UK and Mencap to place pressure on the Government to act. And the Government came under further duress when it learned that the Scottish Lord Advocate proposed to add an amendment to the Crime and Punishment (Scotland) Bill to relax the rules of evidence for learning disabled witnesses.

Not only did the Home Office Bills before Parliament at the beginning of 1997 not include matters touching on criminal procedure but the Sanders report was thought to raise 'varied and complex issues' about witnesses with learning disabilities. It was decided that it would be sensible for the Home Office formally to accept the report's recommendations and then assign them to the new Group for further development. David Maclean was reported to have said that 'This work is a natural extension to that currently being undertaken by the interdepartmental group looking at the issue of rape and other vulnerable victims and their cross-examination.'[86] Witnesses

[85] There was always the hazard that witnesses could be accused in cross-examination at trial of having previously been 'coached' and that their testimony was no longer an unspoilt recollection of events.
[86] See Home Office Press Release 012/97, 23 January 1997.

with learning disabilities were accordingly added to its terms of reference. At the same time, there was to be yet another extension encompassing 'other vulnerable witnesses', including those with a mental illness and, possibly, child witnesses. The interdepartmental group's name was changed to the 'Vulnerable Witness Group' and it met for the first time under that title in April 1997, immediately before the general election,[87] to discuss its new terms of reference and to listen to Andrew Sanders.

The Group was, in effect, being re-constituted in a political limbo, its continuing survival depending on the will of whichever Government might be returned to power in May (although the Group noted that both major parties had signalled their interest in vulnerable witnesses in their manifestos and that any such decision was likely to be favourable). But, during its brief existence, it had come to agree that the recommendations of the 1989 Pigot report[88] on the protection of child witnesses[89] should be extended to adult vulnerable witnesses (as the original report and the later Sanders report had urged), and Ministers had accepted the principle of a discretionary scheme prohibiting in appropriate cases the cross-examination of rape and other victims by unrepresented defendants.[90]

Three virtually independent currents there converged: the aftermath of the Julia Mason case and the issue of the cross-examination of complainants by unrepresented defendants; the earlier, unfinished work and recommendations on the treatment of child witnesses embodied in the Pigot report; and the extension of that work and

---

[87] It is interesting that a parallel Scottish working group also changed its title at much the same time from the Working Group in Cross-Examination by Unrepresented Defendants at the end of 1996 to the Vulnerable Witness Group at the beginning of 1997 and the Vulnerable and Intimidated Witnesses Working Group at the beginning of 1998.

[88] T. Pigot et al.; Report of the Advisory Group on Video-Recorded Evidence, HMSO, London, 1989.

[89] The report recommended that video-recorded interviews with children, conducted by a police officer or social worker, should be admitted as a substitute for live examination-in-chief in criminal cases.

[90] See Home Office Press Release 090/97, 14 March 1997. Michael Howard was reported to have said that 'I fully sympathise with victims who have had to endure further distress by being cross-examined by their alleged attacker. I think it is right that the courts should have the discretion, where necessary, to protect such vulnerable victims.'

those recommendations to vulnerable adults.[91] Campaigning organizations were waiting in attendance to make representations about the groups of victims and witnesses who had been flagged in the committee's terms of reference,[92] and, in what was clearly a politically propitious moment, Mencap,[93] VOICE UK,[94] Mind,[95] RESPOND,[96] and *Community Care*[97] stirred themselves into action. There was a new flurry of lobbying activity, and the originating politics of the rape survivor would from time to time be eclipsed in the re-telling of history and the re-interpretation of events.

Both main political parties included the provision of protection for vulnerable witnesses in their manifestos for the May 1997 general election: the Conservative Manifesto, 'A Safe and Civil Society', promising 'We will also allow a judge to stop a defendant personally cross-examining in rape cases'; and the Labour Party manifesto promising, 'Greater protection will be provided for victims in rape

[91] Andrew Sanders, the source of one current, reflected that he had not known at the time of Warwick Maynard's work on intimidated witnesses and that he had not 'seen the connection with rape'.

[92] There had, for instance, been a critical and sometimes angry report issued by the Rowntree Foundation: C. Williams; *Invisible Victims: crime and abuse against people with learning disabilities*, Jessica Kingsley, London, 1995. On p. 31, Williams observed that 'The subject of police victimization against minority groups is usually considered in relation to race, but people with learning difficulties occasionally suffer similar injustices.' On p. 75, it was reported that few 'cases concerning people with learning disabilities reach the courts. Some, it appears, are inappropriately blocked by the police or CPS on the basis of a stereotyped view of the abilities of people with learning disabilities.'

[93] See the report in the *Independent*, 7 January 1998, in which Mencap complained about the failure of the Criminal Justice System to support witnesses with learning disabilities. Mencap later published *Living in Fear: The need to combat bullying of people with a learning disability*, in June 1999, with recommendations for the police but not for the treatment of people with learning disabilities as witnesses in court.

[94] See *Competent to Tell the Truth*, A Report of a VOICE UK Working Party, 1998. Alun Michael would eventually talk to VOICE UK about vulnerable witnesses and *Speaking up for Justice* at the VOICE UK All Party Subject Group, 20 July 1998.

[95] Mind ran a survey on access to the criminal justice system in September 1998.

[96] RESPOND described itself as providing 'a range of services to victims and perpetrators of sexual abuse who have learning disabilities, and training and support to those working with them'.

[97] See the answer by Home Office Minister, Joyce Quin, to a parliamentary question about plans for equal treatment for people with communication or learning difficulties in the criminal justice system, 24 November 1997.

and serious sexual offence trials and for those subject to intimidation, including witnesses.'[98]

The outrage engendered by the Julia Mason case had led to a broad political support for change:[99] John Greenway, a Conservative Home Affairs spokesman in the late 1990s, recalled, 'the special arrangements for victims, victim witnesses particularly, to give evidence in rape trials, sexual abuse trials, trauma of that sort generally, the scandal was breaking at the time of the election, we were all in favour, we actually tried to amend the ... Crime and Disorder Bill, in the first session of this Parliament to see whether ... and in fact at one point, Jack Straw got quite stroppy with us because he wanted time to get it right'.

Immediately after the election, and in the routine *tour d'horizon* offered the new Ministers by officials, Ian Chisholm was able to claim that the newly founded Interdepartmental Working Group on Vulnerable Witnesses was well placed to promote the Labour Party's manifesto commitment to protect witnesses, and he sought approval for it to continue as a 'priority submission' in the manifesto's name. Thenceforth the work of the group was allowed to proceed with 'a wide-ranging remit', having become appropriated politically as a fulfilment of the Government's commitment to provide greater protection for vulnerable witnesses 'including those in rape and other serious sexual offences'. It was a decision that directly reflected the wishes of the new Home Secretary. Alun Michael told me that 'a lot of the impulse on vulnerable victims had come from Jack Straw, he had wanted to get things moving, and', he added, 'I want to have the role of ministers acknowledged in the analysis of policy processes.'

It must be noted, however, that the proposal to protect vulnerable witnesses in criminal procedure was not without its difficulties from the first, affecting as it did the continuously and vigilantly defended principle of balance in criminal procedure,[100] and the problematic notion of victims' rights, and the extent and detail of the manifesto commitment were to be actively contested. It met a guarded response

[98] Ian Chisholm noted those two manifestos and told members of the new group that considerable political importance was attached to vulnerable witness issues and that there was a likelihood of political support after election.

[99] More than 100 MPs were reported to have signed a House of Commons motion in June 1997 calling for sweeping changes to court procedures in rape cases. *The Times*, 14 June 1997.

[100] Although defence witnesses were to be subject to the new provisions as well.

akin to that being meted out to the like propositions that victims
might become a party in criminal proceedings or affect sentencing
that were being floated at much the same time. The opening encounter took place in November 1997 when the Lord Chancellor took
exception to a report in the *Daily Telegraph* in which Alun Michael
had declared his intention to legislate to protect the vulnerable
witness.[101] That observation, said the Lord Chancellor, would feed
public expectations. Cross-examination by rape defendants was 'not
a big problem' as alleged by the Home Office: the answer lay instead
with tighter case management by judges[102] and not legislation, and,

---

[101] The report stated that curbs on the rights of alleged attackers to question their
victims in court were to be urgently considered by Ministers after two women were
forced to undergo days of humiliating and intimate cross-examination by their assailant. It was prompted by a case at Knightsbridge Crown Court in which a rapist who
had dismissed three sets of lawyers had cross-examined two complainants at length.
One of the victims had asked the judge 'Do I have to put up with this? I have never been
so humiliated in my life.' Alun Michael was reported to have said that he was
'extremely concerned by a number of recent cases where it appears that the right of
cross-examination has been abused . . . We want to protect vulnerable witnesses and
introduce new laws as quickly as possible. But this has got to be done in such a way as
not to undermine the legitimate interests of the defence.' *Daily Telegraph,* 6 November 1997.

[102] Senior judges had argued, quite properly, that cases involving personal cross-
examination by a rape defendant were extremely rare. They concurred that the matter
was problematic, but contended that it had been resolved by a practice direction in *R v.
Milton Anthony Brown,* Judgment, 6 June 1998, an appeal against conviction which
claimed that the trial judge had been wrong not to sever counts in the indictment. The
practice direction stated that the trial judge had noted in sentencing that Brown was
mercurial and unpredictable, and had directed his unstable temperament, *inter alia,* at
the complainants in merciless fashion with an intention to intimidate and humiliate.
The judge's response to Brown's waiving counsel had not been part of the application,
and he handled the trial with fairness and judgment, trying to minimize the complainant's ordeal, but 'the law as it stands permits a situation where an unrepresented
defendant in a sexual assault case has a virtually unfettered right personally to
question his victim in . . . needlessly extended and agonising detail for the obvious
purposes of intimidation and humiliation'. The Lord Chief Justice offered help to
any trial judge who might face a similar difficulty in future with problems of self-
representation and the defendant's lack of knowledge of the form and content of
procedure. The trial judge must ensure that the defendant has a fair trial but must
also have regard for the interests of other parties. It was unfair if the defendant gained
the advantage, and there was no licence to 'have his head to ask what he wishes'. If he
did not comply, the judge should stop further questioning or take over questioning
himself. And, if the defendant was intimidating in any way, there should be use made
of a screen to shield the complainant. The Lord Chief Justice and Lord Justice Judge

in any event, legislation was an issue that should have been settled in Government first.

There was to follow a succession of running skirmishes and negotiations[103] between the judiciary and the Lord Chancellor, on the one hand, and the Home Office and Downing Street,[104] on the other, throughout the history of the Interdepartmental Working Group.[105] It was a debate that was built into the very division of labour within Whitehall and the criminal justice system (and endemic to criminal justice systems across the world[106]). If the Home Office and its associates were charged con-

had been quoted in the media as opposing the working group's recommendations to prohibit defendants personally cross-examining complainants in rape and serious sexual offence trials. They believed that the interests of defendants had not properly been taken into account. They also had doubts about video-recorded pre-trial cross-examination. The Home Office view was that the judgment in Milton Brown would be helpful but that it could not allay wide public fears. Legislation was still needed. Moreover, if the cross-examination of rape victims was as simple a matter as the judges suggested, why had it taken massive public outrage to get them to take action? Ministers were acting in pursuit of an election promise and did not have to apologise. At the launch of *Speaking up for Justice* in June 1998, Jack Straw took pains to emphasize that he was 'determined to ensure that the victims of crime receive the highest standards of justice' but that there was need for balance between the rights of the victim and the defendant. It was, he said, a 'substantial and considered report', retaining the rights of the defendant to a fair trial and 'that is of considerable importance. If we don't make trials fair, we won't get convictions.'

[103] The Home Office held that judges were concerned about encroachment on their authority and there were meetings between Ministers and the Lord Chief Justice 'to explain the Government's position and see whether any minor adjustments might be made'.

[104] See, for example, the No. 10 web site: Report on Government's Strategy, 30 July 1998. 'What we will do next: ... Victims and witnesses: We will strengthen support for the victims of crime and provide better protection for vulnerable witnesses particularly those in rape and serious sexual offence cases.' It is noteworthy that Cherie Blair (and Hillary Clinton) both spoke powerfully for the better protection of child witnesses at a Child Line Conference in May 1999, just at the time that the Youth Justice and Criminal Evidence Bill was before Parliament.

[105] As we shall see, the matter eventually went to the House of Lords under Article 6 of the Human Rights Act 1998 after the passing and implementation of legislation, the Youth Justice and Criminal Evidence Act 1999, that embodied the recommendations of the Working Group.

[106] Scottish Executive Central Research Unit, Crime and Criminal Justice research findings No. 60: *Vulnerable and Intimidated Witnesses: Review of Provisions in Other Jurisdictions*, 19 July 2002.

stitutionally through the Victims Steering Group, the Justice and Victims Unit, and its management of the police[107] with the care of victims and prosecution witnesses (as well as with procedural fairness), the judiciary,[108] Lord Chancellor's Department[109] (acting in part as the political voice of the judiciary[110]), and, to a modest degree, the Law Society, were quite centrally occupied with balance and the safeguarding of defendants' and defence witnesses' rights. The Bar, representing both the defence and the prosecution, did not fit neatly on either side of the divide, and its members were split[111]

---

[107] It is interesting that in the statement of Home Office Counting Rules for Recording Crime, issued in April 2003, the police service is divided into the British Transport Police and 'Home Office Forces'.

[108] Robert Latham, Chair of Victim Support's Trustees, himself a barrister (but not at the criminal bar) noted that 'I do think there is a significant shift in judicial attitude as to when it is appropriate to intervene. And again the judicial arm is going to be strengthened by the Convention. I think the difficulty is this, it is only too easy in the Julia Mason case to say that this case went too far and was out of control of the judge. But for a judge to know at the time when do you intervene ... ?'

[109] A somewhat more floridly political description of the structural alignments in the first New Labour administration was offered later by the columnist, Anthony Howard. His was an *ad hominem* description of the politics of individuals. The Lord Chancellor, he said, 'has done his best in difficult circumstances to uphold the independence of the judiciary, and has acted as an effective counterweight to the more authoritarian, populist tendencies of his colleagues, particularly... Jack Straw...'. *The Times*, 10 June 2003. And there were other threads added by other commentators. The Lord Chancellor had been the Prime Minister's pupil master in chambers. In his memoirs, the former Foreign Secretary, Robin Cook, talked about how the Lord Chancellor would refer to the Prime Minister as 'young Blair', and the Prime Minister called the Lord Chancellor 'my old pupil master' but, he noted, 'In the power relationship between them it was always the prime minister who had the upper hand.' (*The Sunday Times*, 12 October 2003). It is evident that more was at stake than the impersonal, embedded perspectives of a structured division of labour, but the perspectives I have reported were certainly consistent with administrative responsibilities and the Prime Minister did not have the 'upper hand'.

[110] In 2003, after the period covered by this book, and at a time when there were proposals to abolish the office of Lord Chancellor, the Lord Chief Justice, Lord Woolf, protested that the role of Lord Chancellor had always been to 'speak up for the judiciary'. *The Times*, 10 July 2003.

[111] The Bar was divided on some of the issues. The human rights lawyer, Peter Duffy, for example, came to the view in June 1998 that the right of a defendant to represent himself in person was not absolute under the European Convention. He argued that the White Paper was plainly compatible with the European Convention and that failure to act would lead to breaches of the Convention for failure to regard

—even the more libertarian and radical members of the Bar were split.[112]

(*n. 111 contd.*) the convention rights of victims. The proposals in *Speaking up for Justice* did not infringe the defendant's rights but they did take into account victims' rights and interests ('Speaking up for Justice: Response to Consultation', undated). Kate Akester of JUSTICE, which had asked Duffy to give an opinion, reflected that 'we asked him to advise on this question of the abolition of the defendant's right to cross-examine and in the context of ECHR jurisprudence, he was quite clear that it was fine that with these other cases like *Doorson* and *Croissant* and so on, that actually the ECHR is not going to be a defendant's charter if you like. It's going to be something which is a sort of traditional balancing act but which very much is pushing forward the rights of victims and witnesses now. So you know we get a changing landscape'. In January 1998, the Criminal Bar Association accepted the proposal that there should be a prohibition on the right of defendants personally to cross-examine rape complainants. As a matter of principle, it said, it was highly desirable that a defendant's case should be put to the complainant, but the Association did recognize a need to protect as far as possible a rape victim from direct confrontation with the defendant. The Association favoured prohibiting defendants cross-examining adults in person where the defendant had wilfully refused legal representation without reasonable cause, provided there was the safeguard that the trial judge could allow cross-examination by an *amicus* (CBA Working Party Report on Cross-Examination of Rape Victims by the Accused in Person, 1998). JUSTICE claimed that the law on previous sexual history was based on 'outdated, stereotypical ideas of women' and reported that it had held a meeting with members of the Bar who expressed different views on the 'vexed question of sexual history evidence'. JUSTICE's response to the White Paper 'Speaking up for Justice', July 1998. In Scotland, similar proposals to those contained in the Youth Justice and Criminal Evidence Act were abandoned on the grounds that they would be in breach of Article 6 of the Human Rights Act. See *Sunday Times*, 13 February 2000.

[112]   At a session on 'Victim-Friendly Justice', part of a conference sponsored by the now defunct *Living Marxism,* it was argued by John Holbrooke, a representative of Freedom and the Law, a libertarian lawyers' organization, that there should be no incursion on the defendant's rights and, in particular, on the right of the defendant to be seen by the witness as testimony was given, and no withdrawal of the right of the defendant to cross-examine in person (*LM Magazine*: 'Culture Wars—Dumbing Down, Wising Up', 6 March 1999, my notes). Others spoke in like mode. Rajiv Menon, who had represented Duwayne Brookes at the Macpherson Inquiry, similarly declared his opposition to the curtailment of sexual evidence or the right of cross-examination in person. See too Holbrooke's letter to *The Times*, 25 January 1999, in riposte to an earlier letter from Helen Reeves on the matter of vulnerable witnesses: 'Much of the clamour for litigation on this issue stems from Julia Mason's lengthy cross-examination by the man who raped her... In the two and a half years since that celebrated trial hardly any instances of witness intimidation have reached a victim-friendly media. By contrast, the media have been full of cases where witnesses have either lied or been mistaken. Today you report the conviction of a jealous woman who made false rape allegations against six men . . . '. And there was a companion series of

Home Office Ministers remained steadfast in their championing of the Interdepartmental Working Group and the principle that certain vulnerable witnesses required protection under the law. Their 'overriding concern,' they claimed, was 'not to revictimise victims whilst also ensuring that the defendant's rights [were] protected'. The Home Secretary, for example, took the view that Alun Michael had been entirely justified in what he had said: there was a clear expectation of legislation and very great public concern. After all, the Lord Chancellor was detached, but as elected politicians, Home Office Ministers had to take note of popular sentiment, and there was a need for a wide-ranging criminal bill to ensure delivery of the Government's manifesto commitments. Unbowed by the reproof issued by the Lord Chancellor,[113] and within days, Alun Michael returned to his theme:

We have recently seen the terrible case of a rapist who cross-examined his victims for several days, subjecting them to trauma and distress. I am appalled by this further victimisation, and I am determined that vulnerable witnesses should not have to go through this type of experience. In June we set up an urgent review to identify ways to improve the situation of all vulnerable witnesses, including people with physical, mental or learning difficulties. There are many issues to be addressed, including how we can balance the needs of the vulnerable witness and their right not to be intimidated, whilst maintaining the right of the defendant to a fair trial.[114]

The Lord Chancellor continued to voice his reservations for some little time, claiming still that Alun Michael should not have said what he said, and that there ought to have been a collective decision before legislation. After all, he maintained, there was a problem of scarce legislative time, some expectations of legislation would

articles in *LM Living Marxism* by a woman lawyer representing a group calling itself Feminists for Justice, which argued that the new proposals would be a new form of lynch law: 'they would remove the right to a defence; restrict the evidence open to defendants; remove defendants' ability to see the witnesses against them; convict on less evidence; take the victims' views into account when sentencing—a step backwards to the retributive justice of the vendetta . . . ' (S. Hinchcliffe 'Ending rape "by any means necessary?"' *LM Magazine*, 16 June 1997). There were similar articles on the same theme published by her. See, for instance, 'Rape: a special case?', *LM*, issue 95, November 1996.

[113] The Department came to acquiesce in November 1998, reluctantly accepting proposals and bowing to the 'weight of opinion'.

[114] Speech to the Magistrates' Association, 30 November 1997.

necessarily be disappointed, and the making of what were called 'pre-emptive strikes' contradicted settled policies. Any allegations about detachment and electoral responsiveness only damaged good inter-collegial relations.

On 20 May 1998, the Home Secretary told the Police Federation that:

recent cases where victims of crime have been cross-examined by their attackers in court have produced widespread revulsion and dismay. I share those feelings. I warmly welcome the guidelines issued recently by the Lord Chief Justice on this issue. They will go a long way to helping victims in court... But I think we may need to go further. That is why the report next month will include the proposal that unrepresented defendants should be prohibited from personally cross-examining victims in rape and other serious sexual assault cases. Of course, there must be safeguards...

Two days afterwards, the Lord Chancellor yet again declared that he had been disappointed not to have been consulted about the speech: policy of that kind should not be announced until clearance had been given, and the principle of cross-cutting reviews suggested that departments should have been working closely together so that surprises of this sort should not happen.

None the less, and little by little, the initiative moved on under the chairmanship of Ian Chisholm, a Home Office official, and was to be located ever more squarely within the evolving frameworks and objectives of New Labour policy as they were being developed within the Home Office in the late 1990s. It lost some of its memory of ancestry as it did so, and the received past of the initiative became unstable and contingent, reflecting in part the loss of formal records and their supplanting by a shifting oral history. Ian Chisholm himself commented that 'people forget, the last Government, in January '97 announced a working group to look at vulnerable witnesses'.

The lineage that had stemmed from the Working Group on the Cross-examination of 'Rape' Victims by Unrepresented Defendants had been transparent enough at first and it was certainly still invoked from time to time: in 1997, for example, the initiative's 'impulse' was described by a JVU official sitting on the Working Group as coming 'from cases of defendants cross-examining victims in rape cases and [the ensuing] manifesto commitment about the same'.[115] It was

---

[115] Speaking at the Criminal Justice Conference: Vulnerable or Intimidated Witnesses, 1 December 1997. My notes.

flagged again in the press pack accompanying the launch of *Speaking up for Justice* in June 1998. And it was underscored by Jack Straw when he addressed the 1998 Labour Party Conference:

But conference, there is a particular group of victims who cry out for our help. Over the last twenty years the number of rapes reported to the police has increased six fold. Yet the number of people punished for this dreadful crime has in fact fallen. All too often the prospect of intrusive and unnecessary cross-examination in court is too much for many women. Cases are dropped and men walk free. Conference, women who have been raped need our protection under the law. So cross-examination of victims by defendants in person will be stopped. And courts will be given greater powers to halt irrelevant questioning about a victim's previous sexual history.

In April 1998, too, Ian Chisholm, speaking in lieu of Alun Michael, told the National Police Conference that the 'impetus' for the working group had flowed from the Ralston Edwards case and the Pigot Report's recommendation of an extension of provisions to adult vulnerable witnesses.

At the end of that year, however, the initiative had almost inevitably begun to take its colouring from more recent events, and Ian Chisholm described how 'one [source was] the emphasis given in the Labour Party manifesto to the needs of vulnerable and intimidated witnesses. This had continued in a number of ways, including the decision arising out of the Comprehensive Spending Review that one of the key overarching objectives of the criminal justice system was the requirement to satisfy the needs of victims and witnesses.'[116] Yet a year later, the ingredients had been sifted again: Ian Chisholm spoke to the 1999 Victim Support Conference on the evolution of the initiative and recalled how its origins could be traced to the Labour Party manifesto and to the Pigot Report recommendation that the system for children should be extended to vulnerable adults, a recommendation that had in its turn led to the Sanders report on the learning disabled who were not only heavily victimized but relatively neglected because they were not regarded as credible witnesses. The outcome was a more general concern with what could be done to help witnesses to give best evidence, the obtaining of ministerial agreement to review the issue, and the establishment of a

---

[116] Ian Chisholm speaking at the Criminal Justice Conference on Vulnerable or Intimidated Witness Training Issues, Darlington, 17 November 1998.

working group whose object was to encourage witnesses to give evidence so that there were more trials and more convictions. The group, he said, had also had a look 'because of the manifesto commitment' at victims of rape and serious sexual assault and the Labour paper on crime and disorder.[117]

There was to be a requisition of themes introduced earlier by the Conservative administration. When in November 1997 a parliamentary question was put to Joyce Quin, a Home Office Minister, about plans for the equal treatment of people with learning or communication difficulties, she could answer that the Government had announced in June 'an urgent, wide-ranging review of the way in which vulnerable and intimidated witnesses, including those with communication or learning difficulties, are treated by the criminal justice system'. The treatment of rape complainants as the prime precipitating event thereafter waxed and waned in importance, never completely disappearing, sometimes obscured and sometimes coming to the fore, and not always evident to those who had been less than intimately involved with the whole span of the group's work.[118] So it was that an official of the Lord Chancellor's Department, representing the interests of child witnesses on the Group, was prompted pragmatically to mark the centrality of children and the Pigot report:

That process was started, if you like, in relation to child witnesses and victims and those measures were introduced, implemented, amended, added to and it's been a sort of learning process if you like, for all those concerned in the system as to how to ensure that children can give their best evidence and of course the *Speaking Up For Justice* report [that was to be issued by the working group] has taken that further, both in relation to child witnesses but also the recognition that vulnerable or intimidated witnesses may need similar measures in order to help them give their evidence.

In all this change, and given the predominance of oral history over the written file, it is evident that the symbolic environment of policies on the move will itself move, bringing about a continual rereading of the past, present, and future, and invoking new and more

---

[117] Victim Support National Conference, 5 July 1999, my notes.
[118] From a distance, origins could be quite opaque. A CPS official involved with victims' policy issues, and a member of the Victims Steering Group but not of the Interdepartmental Working Group, said in October 1998 'I'm not quite sure what the origins of the work on the vulnerable and intimidated witnesses were. I'm not sure whether that was a specific government commitment.'

appropriate sources of legitimacy as they present themselves. The authority of a decision made by a Conservative Home Secretary under the old regime could not but be slight compared with the force of an election commitment given more recently by a successor who was actually in power. More, and as I shall argue below, symbolic environments are perhaps best regarded as rhetorical resources available for continual adaptation and use as the shifting needs of the policy process themselves warrant. In the history of the Interdepartmental Working Group, they certainly changed to accommodate new demands and new crises as they arose.

The Working Group continued to acquire (and seek) policy strands, one of its very first acts in August 1997 being to open a succession of consultations with others in and around the criminal justice system, not only to ascertain how they construed its task but also to construct 'stake-holders', it being a 'good idea to consult others early not only to learn but also to involve others'. The group's terms of reference having been given,[119] the review was described as 'wide-ranging' in its invitation for comments, and, instead of specific questions being put, 'the views of interested organisations and individuals [were solicited] both on the problems which they believe need addressing and suggested solutions'. The list of those first consulted was itself revealing: catholic,[120] it was tacitly defined by broad assumptions about who was vulnerable and who would have a professional interest in the vulnerable witness. Included were police domestic violence units, the British Council of Disabled People, the Commission for Racial Equality, JUSTICE, Liberty, the British Deaf Association, Disability People International, Women Against Rape, VOICE UK, the Alzheimer's Disease Society, MENCAP, RESPOND, and Age Concern. But the views of organizations such as the NSPCC, Childline, or gay men and women were not then sought and, it may be presumed, they were not initially regarded

---

[119] '[T]o identify measures at all states of the criminal justice process which will improve the treatment of vulnerable victims, including those likely to be subject to intimidation; to encourage such witnesses to give evidence of crime and enabling them to give best evidence at court; to consider which witnesses should be classified as vulnerable; to identify effective procedures for applying appropriate measures in individual cases; and make costed recommendations.'

[120] The Home Secretary had observed that the group had started with the manifesto commitment about rape and serious sexual offences but that its terms of reference were 'very wide'.

as constitutive of vulnerability as it should be understood by the Group.

This was a working group operating at speed,[121] meeting monthly with a tight deadline in quite new terrain (Helen Reeves told Victim Support in July 1999 that 'the vulnerable witnesses initiative is a recognition of victims who would never have been recognised ten years ago'[122]), and the definition of who composed the universe of proper 'stakeholders' would grow as the politics of the process evolved, largely in response to those who elected to put themselves forward. Vulnerability was allowed to remain a contingent matter that could expand and change as events unfolded and as organizations mobilized, made themselves known, submitted representations, and impressed their case on the working group.[123] There was no evidence of groups actually being denied recognition. To the contrary, the question of vulnerability seemed in the middle and later phases to have been resolved almost wholly by self-recruitment.[124]

The consultation letter circulated and was channelled from group to group through organizational networks to those who may not have been originally targeted, a reply being received, for instance, from the Rape Crisis Federation and eight replies from rape crisis centres. There were five responses from organizations representing those with learning difficulties; three from organizations for those with physical disabilities; five from professional associations in the criminal justice system; three from women's organizations; one from NACRO; one from a religious organization; and five from academics. The rape crisis centres concentrated on matters affecting rape,

[121] The working group's recommendations were to be ready for incorporation in a Bill in the 1998–9 session of Parliament.
[122] Plenary session of Victim Support National Conference, 5 July 1999, my notes.
[123] For instance, raped asylum-seekers were championed by the Black Women's Rape Action Project in May 1999.
[124] The parallel histories of other initiatives for vulnerable and intimidated witnesses are instructive. A Scottish review examined developments in England and Wales, Australia, New Zealand, Canada, and the USA, and observed that children were the witnesses most widely recognized in legislations where special measures were provided. There was, it was said, less focus on other groups such as the physically impaired and considerable variations in the definitions of who was vulnerable. The balance between the rights of offenders and victims was controversial in all the jurisdictions. Scottish Executive Central Research Unit, Crime and Criminal Justice research findings No. 60: *Vulnerable and Intimidated Witnesses: Review of Provisions in Other Jurisdictions*, 19 July 2002.

and in particular, the questions of evidence of previous sexual history, cross-examination by the defendant, the curtailment of multiple cross-examination where there was more than one defendant; the requirement that women police officers should interview rape victims, and the need to refer victims or survivors to rape crisis centres rather than to victim support schemes. The Commission for Racial Equality talked about equality of treatment between ethnic groups and the need for improved facilities for interpretation and translation; disability organizations about 'disability equality', training in disability equality, and the disabled not being treated as a homogeneous group; and other bodies tended to be more general in their replies.

The Working Group simultaneously commissioned Robin Elliott of the Home Office Research and Statistics Directorate to compile a literature review that was eventually to be completed in November 1997. Elliott flagged the difficulty of defining vulnerability and the paucity of material in the area, but, proceeding at a level of some abstraction rather than composing an empirical typology of witnesses of specific offences,[125] she produced a multiplex definition based on formal properties of the witness, the offender, and the relations that obtained between them.[126] Her classification was adopted by the Interdepartmental Working Group: the vulnerability of a witness, they said, was to be identified by properties of the person (age, ethnic background, or relationship to any party to the proceedings); the offence; the dangerousness of the defendant in relation to the witness; and 'any other relevant factor', that would satisfy a court that the person would be likely to suffer severe emotional trauma, or would be likely to be so intimidated or stressed as to be unable to give evidence.[127]

Towards the end of its life, when a number of the definitional problems had been resolved, the working group consulted further by organizing two special conferences in November and December

---

[125] The idea of an empirical typology of vulnerable witnesses had been aired in April 1997 when it was suggested that objective criteria might be used to define vulnerable witnesses. If so, the group wondered, what should they be: learning disability or a wider definition including people with a mental handicap or an offence-based definition?

[126] *Vulnerable and Intimidated Witnesses: A Review of the Literature*, 12 November 1997.

[127] Draft definition of vulnerable witness, October 1997.

1997 on practical operational matters 'as part of the...process... to review procedures for dealing with vulnerable or intimidated witnesses'. The conferences' programme was organized quite deliberately around a focused, procedural, and pragmatically driven agenda, where Elliott's definition of a vulnerable witness was disseminated unchanged,[128] and larger definitional problems were left largely untouched.[129] For instance, groups were invited in one section to discuss the advantages and disadvantages of a blanket prohibition on defendant cross-examination in rape cases; of a presumption that the defendant could not personally cross-examine a witness unless the witness agreed; or of allowing the judge to have discretion to determine whether defendants should be allowed to cross-examine. There were similar batteries of questions in the same section about the use of video pre-trial cross-examination; the admission of written statements instead of oral evidence; the utility of questioning by an intermediary; the occasions on which it would be proper and necessary to clear the courtroom; the extent to which witnesses should be afforded anonymity; the desirability of changes in the admissibility of evidence of previous sexual history in rape trials and so on.[130]

## The Intimidated Witness

The inventory of vulnerable witnesses continued to grow. Before the 1997 general election, there had been episodic political and policy

[128] Apart from the addition of clauses stipulating that there should be a rebuttable presumption that a victim who is a witness in prosecutions for offences of rape and other serious sexual offences should be regarded as a special witness and that there should be regard to witnesses' views about being declared a 'special witness'.

[129] Participating in the November conference were representatives from the criminal justice agencies and Departments of State; magistrates and Circuit Judges; members of the Law Society, the Witness Support Service; and Mencap. Attending the December conference were, again, representatives of the criminal justice agencies and Government departments; JUSTICE, the National Council of Women, the Commission for Racial Equality, NACRO, Age Concern, Victim Support, the National Institute for Social Work; and academics. On this occasion, there were members of the Women's Aid Federation and Rape Crisis but no representation of organizations for gay men and women or of charities catering for children.

[130] Ian Chisholm later reported that there was a 'remarkable degree of agreement at Chester conference on difficult issues, videotaping pre-trial cross-examination, greater use of written statements, and extent to which rape victims should be cross-examined on previous sexual history'.

interest in the problem of witness intimidation that had arisen out of 'a concern that relations between police and public were being hampered'. In response to what were called anecdotal accounts, Warwick Maynard of the Home Office Police Research Group had been asked to undertake a survey[131] between August 1993 and February 1994 on the prevalence of witness intimidation. He concluded that the problem was not widespread but that it was undoubtedly intense on certain high crime housing estates where 13 per cent of crimes reported by victims and 9 per cent reported by witnesses led to intimidation, and 6 per cent of crimes not reported by victims and 22 per cent not reported by witnesses were unreported because of fear of intimidation.[132] A small inner core of individuals were said to be in need of high levels of protection; about them there was a middle ring subject to 'non-life threatening' harassment; and an outer ring who feared intimidation. One consequence was the inclusion of a new offence of witness intimidation in the 1994 Criminal Justice Act, c. 33, s. 51; and another was the creation of guidance for the treatment of intimidated witnesses in 1996.[133]

Witness intimidation had been the subject of a Labour Party policy paper, *A Quiet Life*, issued in 1995, in which it was alleged that 'Time and again, criminal elements avoid sanction by the court through intimidating victims and witnesses',[134] and that new legislation was required[135] (although, as a Home Office official commented in the paper's margin, 'we already have the offence of witness intimidation'). And intimidation continued to be a pronounced but loosely defined[136] theme in Government

---

[131] 1,100 respondents on housing estates were interviewed personally, and 4,000 postal questionnaires were sent out.

[132] W. Maynard; *Witness Intimidation: Strategies for prevention*, Police Research Group, Home Office, 1994, p. v. His work was on all fours with other work at the time. See, for example, A. Cretney and G. Davis; *Punishing Violence*, Routledge, London, 1995, p. 61.

[133] TIG; *Statement of National Standards of Witness Care in the Criminal Justice System*, July 1996.

[134] Labour; *A Quiet Life*, Tough action on criminal neighbours, 19 June 1995.

[135] News from Labour; 'Labour proposes tough new measures to tackle criminal anti-social neighbours', 19 June 1995.

[136] A senior Home Office official commented, 'there was a Labour policy document on that as well which is really sort of Crime and Disorder Bill strategy and it doesn't really say much again when you look at it. It only mentions professional witnesses which is really not you know, not terribly major... So I think... this is

thought.[137] It entered the Labour Party election manifesto ('Greater protection will be provided for victims in rape and serious sexual offence trials and *for those subject to intimidation, including witnesses*' [my emphasis]) to be perused by officials seeking a steer for future policy. Indeed, it will be recalled that Helen Reeves had claimed at the beginning of 1999 that the stress on protection was the one element that distinguished the new Government's stance towards victims and witnesses from that of the old. It was certainly singled out by Charles Clarke in his own reflections about New Labour policy:

I think there are two policy driven things which are fantastically important. The first is the desire to ensure that there is protection within the criminal justice system for victims and witnesses because that would be a way, too, of getting convictions and there's a policy view about that which is strong and...we don't do as much as we need to. We're doing more. We've funding for Victim Support, for witness support, and so on [which] is important but we're not doing enough. Secondly, the whole question of active communities as I put it, to the extent that communities are not prepared to be oppressed by criminals, particularly housing estates, particularly in urban areas where you often have a group or a family which dominates in a particular area and people are frightened, which means that there's no process out of the situation.

Intimidation had evidently come to take some of its meaning from the wider political preoccupation with what was called crime and disorder, the issue that engendered the 1998 Act bearing that name, although the Group's deliberations had not by then advanced far enough to be covered by the legislation.

Almost immediately after the election, witness intimidation became a political event in the sense intended by Harold Macmillan. Ministers were disturbed by reports of intimidation, first in the London newspaper, the *Evening Standard*, in mid-May 1997,

the more major area, the witness intimidation thing, and we're now, there's quite a lot of recommendations and in the *Speaking up for Justice* where we have of course picked up the way Labour saw it as part of their strategy on crime and disorder and the local authority police having this remit now to do an audit problems.'

[137] In November 1997, for instance, Alun Michael told the Magistrates' Association that delays mean that witnesses can forget details, extend the period during which witnesses and victims are vulnerable to the growing scourge of intimidation, and prevent victims from getting on with their lives.

and then in the *Sunday Times* of 7 December 1997,[138] recording how Islington Council in London had refused to find acceptable accommodation for the frightened witnesses of a murder seeking shelter under police protection. The *Evening Standard* report recited that the witnesses 'claim their lives became a "nightmare of harassment", they were attacked and their children were threatened after they gave statements to detectives investigating the killing'. Ministers declared that the story was 'atrocious' and sought a 'line to be taken' should there be oral parliamentary questions, and the line readily to hand was a reference to the 'proposed review on vulnerable and intimidated witnesses'.[139] And it was during just that period, in May 1997, when the new Government was taking stock and decisions were being taken about what work initiated by the old regime should be allowed to continue, that Ministers agreed, first to proceed with the review of vulnerable witnesses begun by their predecessors, and then, at the end of the month, that the review's terms of reference should be enlarged to include a reference to the 'improve[ment of] the treatment of vulnerable witnesses, including those subject to intimidation'.[140] The continuing pursuit of the matter of vulnerable or intimidated witnesses went to Cabinet and was approved, and the Interdepartmental Working Group was re-launched once again with the announcement that 'Jack Straw has begun an urgent review to improve the way in which victims and vulnerable witnesses are treated by the Criminal Justice System'. In talking about the review, he alluded to the Julia Mason case ('Everyone was disgusted when a rape victim had to face lengthy cross-examination by her attacker... I am determined that we will stop putting victims through this traumatising experience') but he also turned to the principle that 'Witnesses should feel free to come

---

[138] The newspaper contained an extended piece on a witness to a murder on the Marquess Estate in London who had had to be given witness protection. She would have liked to have been rehoused in a 'decent' house, but Islington Council was reported not to have been helpful and offered her blatantly unsuitable housing instead.

[139] Letter from Ian Chisholm, 4 June 1997.

[140] It was also suggested that the Working Group could ingest other work then in progress, for example, an inquiry by ACPO on witnesses, the Trials Issues Group's work on national standards of witness care (see Home Office Circular 41/1996: Witness Care in the Criminal Justice System), and the Law Commission's work on hearsay evidence (see the Law Commission Annual Report, 1997).

forward to the police without being intimidated by bullies and thugs trying to pervert the course of justice.'[141]

After June 1997, the newly re-born Vulnerable Witnesses Working Group changed its name once more to be called the Vulnerable or Intimidated Witnesses Working Group, meeting for the first time under that title on 1 August with an expectation that it would report by the end of the year. It housed representatives from the main agencies, and Warwick Maynard and Helen Reeves were now added to its membership, but there was no member from the Cabinet Office Women's Unit or from the voluntary organizations representing women. Neither were there representatives of other groups potentially eligible for definition as vulnerable. Indeed, when its re-establishment was announced by the Prime Minister, the group was awarded a history that harked back to the problem of tackling intimidation that had begun with Warwick Maynard's research on high crime estates,[142] only to be revived by events in Islington. And it is noteworthy that, when the time came, all the anticipatory reports appearing in the press represented *Speaking up for Justice* as a measure to deal with intimidation, with no reference at all to Julia Mason or rape.[143]

## Physical Disability

Physical disability was added to the definition of vulnerability after a prosecution that had aborted in the Crown Court in Birmingham in August 1997 was brought to the Working Group's notice. In *R v. Vasdev S. Sond*,[144] a charge of indecent assault was abandoned against the carer of a woman so severely ill with multiple sclerosis that she was unable physically to attend court. Her witness statement was a compilation of others' readings of what she had wished to say, as was a video-recording of her being questioned, and they were ruled by the judge as 'highly objectionable' under the rules of evidence: 'it involved a lot of hearsay and so on'. The judge held that

---

[141] Home Office News Release 142/97, 13 June 1997, *Stopping Witnesses being Scared into Silence.*

[142] See *The Times*, 13 June 1997.

[143] See, for example, *Mail on Sunday, Sunday Business, News of the World, Sunday Times, Sunday Express, Sunday Mirror*, all on 7 June 1998, and *Guardian* and *The Times*, 8 June 1998.

[144] T970879, 8 August 1997.

he could not 'permit this evidence to stand as her evidence in this case. A fair trial would have been impossible.' The witness was deemed incompetent to give evidence and a not guilty verdict was ordered. The case was discussed 'at some length' at the Working Group's third meeting in October 1997, and thereafter references to the physically disabled crept into the papers constituting the initiative.[145]

In diverse ways, then, the matter of witnesses was undergoing expansion, redefinition, generalization, and absorption back into the mainstream of criminal justice policy-making. Witnesses were becoming a group that was larger and more undifferentiated[146] than the quite specific category of rape complainants that had catalysed policy-work at the first,[147] reflecting perhaps something of the 'ungendered' and generalist proclivities of the Victims Steering Group and its associated committees in their management of victims matters. Victims were characteristically discussed on those committees as a generic group, the victimization of women *qua* women being managed elsewhere in the Office (in the Domestic Violence Unit, for instance) and beyond by Units, such as the Cabinet Office Women's Unit, with special responsibilities in the area.[148] An official

---

[145] For example, the Home Office Comprehensive Spending Review submission on support for victims of crime of March 1998 talked explicitly about how vulnerable witnesses included the mentally ill and those with mental and physical disabilities. VIWIMP SG11/99: Evaluation of Provisions in the Youth Justice and Criminal Evidence Bill: Discussion Paper, stated that the aim of the Act was to help young, disabled, vulnerable, or intimidated witnesses to give best evidence in criminal proceedings. And see R. Elliott; *Vulnerable and Intimidated Witnesses: A Review of the Literature*, 12 November 1997, p. 2.

[146] For example, Lord Williams said in the debate on the Youth Justice and Criminal Evidence Bill and *Speaking up for Justice* in the House of Lords on 22 June 1998 that the report cast 'its net very wide and deals with vulnerable or intimidated witnesses of all sorts'.

[147] Although Ministers and officials were periodically to be reminded of the issue. For instance, the 1997 annual conference of the Police Superintendents Association informed the Home Secretary that it had passed an 'overwhelming' vote in favour of giving the victims of rape a fair deal. Points from the debate were said to include the need for the use of screens; the admissibility of evidence of similar fact in case of defendants; victim impact statements to give victims the right to tell their story and assist judges in sentencing; the need for training of lawyers and judges; video links; restraints on intimidation, especially when the victim's address is disclosed in court; and restrictions on revelation of previous sexual history.

[148] Although the Women's Unit had no policy-making powers.

## 374 Constructing Victims' Rights

of the Domestic Violence Unit said 'it's been seen as distinct...
domestic violence has always sat in this particular [box]. We used
to be what was C1 whereas victims were somewhere else [C4] and
are still somewhere else [JVU].' At the very outset, Helen Reeves and
an official from the Department of Social Security were moved to
declare that they were 'concerned... to ensure that women's interests and experience were properly covered...'.[149]

What perhaps was also in play was the systematic application of
bureaucratic rationality, the extraction of abstract and rule-like
principles or forms from the multiple and diverse empirical contents
of an emerging policy to enable their methodical implementation
across a broad area.[150] It was a process redolent of Simmel's distinction between content and form. 'Form' is, he said, 'from the point of
view of the function it exercises, the unification of material: it
overcomes the isolated separateness of its parts.'[151] And the varied
and detailed content of a bullied rape victim, witnesses with learning
difficulties, frightened witnesses in Islington, a victim with multiple
sclerosis, and the rest were being ordered by the more inclusive and
abstract bureaucratic typification of the witness as an object of
equitable and routine policy-making.

The ends of the Working Group were also undergoing progressive
re-definition and generalization. Under the new and imperious hierarchy of criminal justice system-wide aims and objectives, the outer
descriptive cladding of policies veered always towards crime reduction.[152] It was said, for example, at the Interdepartmental Working
Group's second meeting in September 1997 that:

---

[149] Minutes of the First Meeting of the Interdepartmental Working Group on
Vulnerable or Intimidated Witnesses, 1 August 1997.

[150] One of the constitutive features of a much older version of bureaucratic management, Weber once argued, was the following of 'general rules, which are more or
less stable, more or less exhaustive... the authority to order certain matters by
decree... does not entitle the bureau to regulate the matter by commands given for
each case, but only to regulate the matter more abstractly'. Taken from H. Gerth and
C. Wright Mills; *From Max Weber: Essays in Sociology*, Routledge and Kegan Paul,
London, 1961, p. 198.

[151] From G. Simmel; *Kant*, Duncker and Humboldt, Munich, 1924, p. 64.

[152] 'Putting the public's protection first also means putting the needs of victims first.
Offenders cannot be brought to justice unless victims and witnesses report crimes to the
police and are willing, if necessary, to give evidence in court. Yet the criminal justice
system has been too slow in recognising its responsibilities towards victims and witnesses.' Government's Crime Reduction Strategy, Home Office, 29 November 1999.

Many people will see the purpose of the... Review as being to provide better treatment for victims and witnesses for their own sake, but the Working Group has to recognise that its terms of reference give rise to other concerns, notably the public interest in witnesses giving best evidence so as to secure the conviction of the guilty—which may from time to time be in tension with the interests of the victim/witness—and also fairness to the defendant and to defence witnesses.[153]

Witnesses could be represented in that guise chiefly as an instrument of reporting crimes, giving evidence in court, and securing convictions: the greater their willingness to testify and the better their evidence, the more effective would the criminal justice system be. The estimates supplied to the Working Group were that 6–22 per cent of crimes were not reported because of attrition each year in the later 1990s; and that some 200,000 witnesses were involved in trials, of whom perhaps 5–7 per cent were vulnerable and 2–3 per cent intimidated.[154] And the repeated phrase was that 'offenders cannot be brought to justice unless victims and witnesses report crimes to the police and are willing, if necessary, to give evidence in court'. The Victims Steering Group was to be told in time that there was 'a real challenge about the way we treat witnesses because if we don't [meet it] we'll not improve our ability to get convictions'.[155] The central proposals to prohibit personal cross-examination and restrict evidence of sexual history in rape cases were defended in the name of combating attrition in rape cases, a matter that had become of concern in and around the discussions about the Julia Mason case.[156] The most notorious case, one discussion paper on banning defendants from conducting personal cross-examination noted, was that of 'Ralston Edwards/Julia Mason in which Edwards, who was unrepresented, cross-examined his victim for six days... The main purpose of providing this protection in the form of a ban on personal cross-examination... would be to minimise the trauma experienced

---

[153] Minutes of the Second Meeting of the Interdepartmental Working Group on Vulnerable or Intimidated Witnesses, 29 September 1997.

[154] Official, RSD, to Ian Chisholm, 4 December 1997.

[155] My notes on meeting of Victims Steering Group, 26 November 2001.

[156] Linked particularly with the arguments and research of Sue Lees that were produced at much that time. Sue Lees was one of those consulted by the Working Group. See her *Carnal Knowledge: Rape on Trial*, Hamish Hamilton, London, 1996; and her edited collection, *Ruling Passions: Sexual Violence, Reputation, and the Law*, Open University Press, Philadelphia, Pa., 1996.

by the witness when giving evidence and hence to enable them to give better evidence, which would clearly be in the interests of justice.[157]

I was careful to use the phrase the 'outer descriptive cladding of policies' because one must ever be mindful about the diversity of views that prevail in complex organizations, the differences between private belief and public utterance, the artful uses of language, the need to deploy arguments to best effect before different audiences in different settings at different times, and the political requirement that policy-making should invoke the mandates currently flowing from the dominant aims and objectives of the criminal justice system. A transparent election manifesto commitment to protect witnesses was on occasion evidently a less substantial warrant to proceed than the more recent strategic plan for the system and, in centripetal fashion, criminal justice policy-making was driven ever inwards towards its central (and perfectly laudable) objects of increasing rates of reporting,[158] securing more successful prosecutions and reducing crime.[159] Confronted with such a rhetoric, Victim Support's trepidations about the manner in which victims were regarded as the servants of criminal procedure appeared not without justification.

Yet the arguments of policy-making were dependent always, there were other aims and objectives to which appeals were made on other occasions, including those set by the new performance management, and it is perfectly possible to conjecture that measures were being developed for victims and witnesses for reasons that were not wholly and invariably unambiguous or instrumental.[160] Consider the revealing contention later made by JVU in one internal paper that

---

[157] Working Group on Vulnerable or Intimidated Witnesses Discussion Paper 2: Prohibition on Unrepresented Defendants Personally Conducting Cross-Examination, VIW 97/11.

[158] See *Criminal Justice: The Way Ahead*, Home Department, Cm. 5074, February 2001, where it was reported that the Government wanted a greater proportion of those who committed crime to be brought to justice, and that that aim depended on victims and witnesses reporting and giving evidence.

[159] The papers are replete with the sentiment that witnesses who are well treated will deliver better evidence and secure more convictions. See, for instance, Alun Michael's praise for Victim Support and its work with victims and witnesses. Home Office Press Release, 9 July 1998.

[160] S. Kelman; 'Why Public Ideas Matter' and P. Heymann; 'How Government Expresses Public Ideas', in R. Reich (ed.); *The Power of Public Ideas*, Harvard University Press, Cambridge, 1990.

the recommendations of the Interdepartmental Working Group were 'not expected to contribute to crime reduction' but were 'expected to bring about a 5% increase in victim/witness satisfaction'[161] and, in another paper, that they would increase confidence in the criminal justice system, reduce fear amongst vulnerable persons, and afford greater protection for vulnerable or intimidated witnesses. Crime reduction could be sovereign in one place and time, but not in another, and rhetorical effectiveness clearly played its part in establishing how measures should be portrayed. Underlying it all, it may be supposed, were also the procedures of officials who spoke the public language of bureaucracy to attain more private aspirations not wholly subordinate to crime reduction or performance management.

## Children

Children, the archetypal vulnerable victims and witnesses, the direct focus of the Pigot report, and indirectly implicated in the commissioning of the Sanders report, were another strand that came to swell the Group's work, although that had not been envisaged at first.[162] Before the election, Victim Support,[163]

[161] No. 10 Crime Project—standard form for completion. JVU submission. Action for Justice—implementation of the speaking up for justice report, September 2000.

[162] In his submission of May 1997 proposing the continuation of the Working Group, Ian Chisholm had observed that 'I do not envisage that this particular group would be primarily concerned with the treatment of child witnesses, although there may well be consequences for their treatment . . . I do not propose that any reference to child witnesses should be included in the terms of reference. The most appropriate forum for the consideration of child witness issues is the Steering Group on Child Evidence, an interderpartmental group which I chair.'

[163] See J. Plotnikoff and R. Wilson; *Children in Court: Evaluation of Witness Service support for child witnesses*, Victim Support, London, 1996. In her foreword, Helen Reeves argued that many child witnesses were profoundly distressed by the experience. The report recommended that all children should be prepared for court after early identification; the length of time during which children were kept waiting should be reduced to a minimum; children using closed-circuit television should be provided with the same level of support as other witnesses; the needs of child witnesses should be communicated to the authorities; and cross-examination should be appropriate to age and ability. In due course, and in parallel with the interdepartmental working group, the Victim Support Witness Service prepared to support children more fully (Witness Service: Working with Child Witnesses, Implementation of a National Comprehensive Witness Service for Children Attending Court, 20 January 1998). It

officials[164] and the home affairs team in the Labour Party[165] had made it known that they were interested in what was called colloquially 'implementing the full Pigot'[166] and, indeed, Jack Straw, the Home Secretary in waiting, and Janet Anderson, the Shadow Minister for Women, had been the joint authors of a paper citing criticisms by the NSPCC, the National Society for the Prevention of Cruelty to Children, about the management of child abuse cases by the criminal justice system.[167] Their report, *Protecting our Children,* had also drawn on a 1994 paper by the Department of Health, *The Child, the Court, and the Video,* which claimed that very few videos were actually in use in the courtroom, that very few convictions had resulted from cases where video evidence was employed, and that

was to do so occasionally in conjunction with the NSPCC (Court Issues Meeting, minutes of meeting of 26 March 1998).

[164] Plans anticipating reforms in the treatment of child witnesses, funded privately by the Nuffield Foundation, were already in train in 1996. A feasibility study had been supported by the Nuffield Foundation and conducted between March and June 1995. The video proposal, Ian Chisholm was told in 1996, 'had quite a long history'. In 1993, Joyce Plotnikoff had approached various organizations previously involved in the production of a Child Witness Pack about producing a video to demonstrate good practice for judges and lawyers when children are witnesses and designed to ensure that those elements of the judicial process which cause undue distress to children are minimized without prejudicing the rights of the defendant. The issues included live television links and screens, and arrangements for children to see a video-taped interview before it was produced as evidence. The video was intended to demonstrate good practice to judges and lawyers when children appear in court as witnesses. Although there had been 'considerable improvement in recent years in the treatment of children' in the criminal justice system, this had tended to be undermined when cases reached court. Often this had resulted from a lack of awareness on the part of judges and counsel of the need to treat children in a more sympathetic and appropriate manner, a need which the video was designed to address. Minutes of meeting of advisory group on making a video demonstrating good practice for judges and lawyers when children are witnesses, 4 March 1996.

[165] Indeed, the Prime Minister's wife, Cherie Booth, a barrister, was herself in time to become involved publicly with a campaign to better the lot of children appearing in court, and she commended the work of the NSPCC and Victim Support, writing about 'frightened children in the witness box... we have to help [a] child to give the best evidence she can in court'. *Sunday Times,* 7 June 1998.

[166] The only major Pigot recommendation on the treatment of children not to have been implemented was the proposal that pre-trial cross-examination should be video-recorded.

[167] J. Straw and J. Anderson; *Protecting Our Children: Labour's proposals for dealing with paedophiles,* September 1996.

the defence persisted in trying hard to discredit children. It referred too to another (apparently unpublished and untraceable) 1996 report by the Home Office Police Research Group that judges were reluctant to allow video recordings to be used in court. Children were additionally to be sponsored by the incoming Minister, Alun Michael, charged with responsibility for victims in the new administration, who had chaired the Parliamentary All Party Penal Affairs Group committee when it issued *Increasing the Rights of Victims of Crime* in July 1996. That committee had also recommended the use of a television link for the delivery of evidence by child victims of violent and sexual offences, a point expressly taken up by officials in their briefing to the new administration,[168] and Alun Michael worked to promote 'the full Pigot' when in office.[169]

I noted that no groups of witnesses had been mentioned by name in the proposed terms of reference of the latest incarnation of the Interdepartmental Working Group. All that had been suggested at the outset was that the group should 'consider which witnesses should be classified as vulnerable'. Representations from the Department of Health on 12 June 1997[170] may have proposed that children be listed in the Group's terms of reference,[171] but the terms remained general as before, and there was to be no change (they were not negotiable, Ian Chisholm told the first meeting of the Group[172]). Still, the prompt cannot have been ignored, and some members of the working group did take it that they had been formally charged by their own departments with promoting the interests of children (for example, the representatives from the Department of Health and the

---

[168] Election Briefs—Volume 5, Victims and Witnesses, 2 April 1997.

[169] At the plenary session of the Victim Support Conference, 9 July 1998, he flagged the particularly acute plight of vulnerable witnesses, especially children, which could lead to the abandonment of cases or not even starting cases. 'The most obvious way is to change the way evidence is given.' Pigot had recommended that child witnesses should be spared from giving evidence in chief by means of a live television link from outside the courtroom. (My notes.)

[170] The letter of 12 June 1997 said that 'I realise the primary focus for the group will be vulnerable adult witnesses, however, I think it would benefit from an awareness of child witness issues.'

[171] An undated outline of a Consultation Document paper prepared for the Group asked, under the heading of arrangements for child witnesses, whether changes for vulnerable witnesses apply to children if they do not already do so.

[172] Minutes of the First Meeting of the Interdepartmental Vulnerable or Intimidated Witnesses Working Group, 1 August 1997.

Lord Chancellor's Department[173] who saw the group primarily as a body taking forward the Pigot Report's policies for children[174]). Papers on the protection of child witnesses certainly came before the Group. At the instigation of an official of the PVU, for instance, a research report on the use of screens and of closed-circuit television for child witnesses in Western Australia was considered at its second meeting in September 1997.[175] And Ian Chisholm alerted the group[176] to the fact that the Utting report on child abuse, due in mid-November, would probably endorse acceptance of the 'full Pigot'.[177] Implementation was regarded internally on the Working Party as being as much an expressive as a pragmatic matter, a gesture to the voluntary organizations, and a recognition of strong political interest (the 'political problem is that it was one of the Pigot recommendations', it was observed, and 'doing the full Pigot was an election commitment eagerly awaited by child protection groups'). There were discussions about its possible practicability,[178] and the difficulties of organization, delays, and expense it might incur. In

[173] The Department was represented on the interdepartmental group because of its existing membership of the inter-departmental Steering Group on Child Evidence, and Chris Pulford of the Lord Chancellor's Department was responsible for children's evidence and child witnesses.

[174] Chris Pulford said 'that process was started, if you like, in relation to child witnesses and victims and those measures were introduced, implemented, amended, added to and it's been a sort of learning process if you like, for all those concerned in the system as to how to ensure that children can give their best evidence and of course the *Speaking Up For Justice* report has taken that further, both in relation to child witnesses but also the recognition that vulnerable or intimidated witnesses may need similar measures in order to help them give their evidence'.

[175] C. O'Grady; *Child witnesses and jury trials: An evaluation of the use of closed circuit television and removable screens in Western Australia*, Ministry of Justice, January 1996. The papers of the group also contained a copy of K. Müller; 'The Child Witness in the South African Law of Procedure', *Expert Evidence*, 4(2), 1995, pp. 52–5.

[176] Minutes of the third meeting of the Interdepartmental Vulnerable or Intimidated Witnesses Working Group, 29 October 1997.

[177] Sir William Utting; 'People Like Us, The Report of The Review of The Safeguards for Children Living away from Home', Department of Health, The Stationery Office, London, November 1997. Recommendation 20 was that 'Government should implement the remaining recommendations of the Advisory Group on Video Evidence (The Pigot Report), and undertake a comprehensive review of arrangements for prosecuting sexual offenders against children.'

[178] *Practical implications of the legislative recommendations in Speaking up for Justice: Issues to Discuss* on 13 October 1998. To be sure this was not the only issue to be discussed. Others included how barristers might be found to put questions in lieu of

October 1998 it was noted that the 'arguments of expense and delay are presently winning', but, commented Ian Chisholm, it was 'very difficult to back down now. The reason we came down in favour was strong political support and the symbolism of the measure.'

As with the other episodes involving witnesses with learning difficulties and rape survivors, a parallel stream of activity was sustained by voluntary organizations in the field of child protection and targeted at the work of the Group. The NSPCC were consulted and made representations. ChildLine[179] ran a seminar in November 1997 and invited Alun Michael to speak.[180] Asking a Minister to speak before the members of an organization promoting children's interests at a time when vulnerable witnesses were being discussed in Government could well produce a statement or commitment that could subsequently be turned back on its author and put to political advantage.[181] After Alun Michael had spoken to the November seminar, he was invited by ChildLine to clarify the Government's intentions, and he did say two months later that he was 'determined to ensure that children and vulnerable witnesses can give best evidence with the minimum of distress, and that our court practices should be adapted wherever necessary and appropriate to improve their effectiveness and afford greater protection for children'. Such

counsel who had been dismissed by defendants in rape and allied cases; applications to introduce previous sexual history should be pre-trial and in writing; and reporting restrictions on the identity of witnesses. The senior judiciary claimed that cross-examination pre-trial would almost certainly be followed by later cross-examination so that the benefits of pre-recorded cross-examination would be slight. It was affirmed in correspondence attending debates on the passage of the Youth Justice and Criminal Evidence Bill in the House of Lords that there should be judicial control throughout and that recordings would be introduced only when it was in the interests of justice to do so, there would be a power to excise portions unduly prejudicial to the accused; and cross-examination would be controlled by the judge at all stages.

[179] ChildLine was a charity launched in 1986 that offered a free, 24-hour helpline for children and young people in the United Kingdom.

[180] The reference to the seminar was found in Home Office papers. Copious searches conducted by ChildLine itself in 2003 failed to unearth any further details about the seminar, its purpose, or theme.

[181] Valerie Howarth, the Chief Executive of ChildLine, was later to write about the Youth Justice and Criminal Evidence Bill: 'I do not claim that ChildLine is responsible for this progress, nor that our task is now over. If we have helped to add to the clamour for change . . . then we have achieved the task that we set out to do.' *Hearing Children's Voices: Conference Report*, 13 May 1999, ChildLine, London, undated, p. 20.

an announcement might have lacked detail but it nevertheless conveyed a strong commitment willingly extracted.

When the Working Group's report, *Speaking up for Justice,* was published in June 1998, its aim was described as improving access to justice for vulnerable or intimidated witnesses, 'including children', it was welcomed by the NSPCC, and one of the speakers and symbolic supporters at its formal launch[182] was the NSPCC's director who talked about how testifying could be a terrifying experience for children, as bad if not worse than the original abuse, an experience that left them hurt and insecure, and confirmed their very worst fears.[183] Although children had been partially protected before under the Pigot reforms, they were added to rape complainants in the Youth Justice and Criminal Evidence Bill as a category of vulnerable witness expressly eligible for special measures and exempt from cross-examination by unrepresented defendants in cases of sex, violence, kidnapping, cruelty, and neglect.[184] Later, indeed, and partly under urging from the NSPCC,[185] the Government promised

[182]  Three women from WAR, Women Against Rape, were also present, but they did not speak.

[183]  The Launch of *Speaking up for Justice,* 10 June 1998: my notes.

[184]  See Home Office Press Release: Youth Justice and Criminal Evidence Bill receives Royal Assent, 28 July 1999, which talked about fulfilling commitments to provide greater assistance to rape complainants, children, and other vulnerable and intimidated witnesses. A supplementary pre-trial checklist for cases involving child witnesses was issued for special Plea and Directions Hearings in which it was laid down that judges will need to have seen videoed evidence in advance of the Plea and Directions Hearings so that decisions could be made about the admissibility of the videotape. A videotape would often be used to refresh the child's memory. There was, it was said, a benefit for the child to see both prosecutor and defence before trial providing there is no discussion of evidence. For an evaluation of new provisions for children, see G. Davis *et al.*; 'The Admissibility and Sufficiency of Evidence in Child Abuse Prosecutions', Research Findings, No. 100, Home Office, London, 1999. It was reported that the initial video-taped interview with the child actually served multiple and sometimes contradictory purposes; that police officers were given insufficient legal training to implement some of the new provisions; that prosecutors and police were deterred from bringing cases that relied solely on a child's unclear testimony; that the reforms were working quite well in some areas but technical problems remained; and that practice in other countries merited study. See also G. Davies *et al.*; *Child Abuse: Training Investigating Officers*, Police Research Series, Home Office, August 1998. Both reports were later said by the Home Office to have provided a foundation for improving practice. See Home Office news release 308/99, 7 October 1999: Improving the Quality of Evidence in Child Abuse Cases.

[185]  NSPCC: Briefing on the Youth Justice and Criminal Evidence Bill, 18 January 1999.

that all the recommendations of the Pigot report would be implemented and children would not be required to appear in court, unless it was imperative that they do so.[186]

## Race

The witnesses and victims of racial assaults became defined as a special category of vulnerable and intimidated[187] people to be considered with others in the Working Group's deliberations after the murder of Stephen Lawrence had been awarded overriding political importance by the new Government.[188] Ethnic origin became one of the formal criteria for defining vulnerability ('but should not automatically be a trigger for special measures'[189]) and there was to be much exchange and conferring between the cognate committees that worked in and around the politics of race and criminal justice. In its consultation in August 1997, the Interdepartmental Working Group had gone to the Commission for Racial Equality. In its evidence to Sir William Macpherson,[190] the Home Office had solicited the Lawrence Inquiry's views about the proper treatment of vulnerable and intimidated witnesses (and enclosed as an annex information about the work of the Interdepartmental Group); and the ensuing recommendations of the Lawrence Report that touched on the matter were referred back by the Home Office to the Interdepartmental Group for consideration and development.[191] The Lawrence Report was

---

[186] See the report in *The Times*, 17 June 1999, about a ChildLine conference at which Cherie Booth, the Prime Minister's wife spoke. It was said that, as a result of representations from Cherie Booth and the NSPCC, children's evidence would be pre-recorded so that they would no longer be questioned in court, and Paul Boateng, the Home Office Minister, had announced that eventually children would no longer have to appear in court.

[187] There was, for instance, a report in Ian Chisholm's files (Chisholm being the chair of the Interdepartmental Working Group) about the collapse of a case of racist violence because of witness intimidation, *Eastern Eye*, 8 August 1997.

[188] The newspaper centrally implicated in the politics of the Stephen Lawrence murder, the *Daily Mail*, 4 June 1997, reported that the proposals would reflect a concern about intimidated witnesses in the Stephen Lawrence inquiry.

[189] Minutes of the second meeting of the Interdepartmental Vulnerable or Intimidated Witnesses Working Group, 29 September 1997.

[190] Sir William Macpherson's Inquiry, evidence submitted by the Home Office to the second part of the Inquiry, 1999.

[191] *The Stephen Lawrence Inquiry: Home Secretary's Action Plan*, Home Office, London, March 1999.

384 Constructing Victims' Rights

published in February 1999, and, in its train, only a month later, it was agreed at a meeting of the steering group superintending the implementation of *Speaking up for Justice* that racial issues should be covered in the various projects executing the recommendations (it was agreed, for example, that there was a need to identify witnesses from minority ethnic communities who might be intimidated[192]). After early 1999,[193] then, it was assumed almost axiomatically that vulnerable and intimidated witnesses included members of minority ethnic groups[194] and that '*Speaking up for Justice* [was] taking account of these issues'.[195] Conversely, members of the Victims Steering Group were reminded of their obligation to represent victims' and witnesses' interests in the proliferating committees and working groups that had arisen to implement the recommendations of the Lawrence Report.[196]

## Women

A raped woman's ordeal had been the symbolically charged event that had precipitated the founding of the first incarnation of the Interdepartmental Working Group, and other women victims were also to be tacked on to its growing catalogue of the vulnerable and the intimidated. The victims of domestic violence, for instance, were to be so defined after consultations in 1998,[197] and, through cross-

[192] Implementation of Speaking up for Justice: Implications for victims of racist incidents and for witnesses from ethnic minority communities: Discussion paper. VIWIMP SG15/99, April 1999.

[193] And, indeed, some time before. *Daily Mail*, 4 June 1997, reporting the re-formation of the Working Group after the general election, claimed that it reflected concern about witnesses to the Stephen Lawrence inquiry.

[194] In, for example, the 'Discussion Paper for the Meeting of the *Ad Hoc* sub group of the Victims Steering Group to consider the implementation of the recommendations of the Stephen Lawrence Report', JVU, February 2000.

[195] CPG Lawrence Action Plan, May 1999. Looking back at the *Speaking up for Justice* report, Ian Chisholm told members of Victim Support that it included recommendations for vulnerable and intimidated witnesses, and 'that obviously includes victims of racist crime'. My notes on the Victim Support Seminar on Stephen Lawrence, 15 February 2000.

[196] Victims Steering Group Meeting, 21 May 1999, my notes.

[197] Welsh Women's Aid, for example, impressed on the group that victims of domestic violence were also vulnerable (*Speaking up for Justice*: Response from Welsh Women's Aid, undated). The Home Office's Multi-Agency Guidance for Addressing Domestic Violence (undated) talked about new provisions for vulnerable and

fertilization from committee to committee, they were to be cited in the Working Group's deliberations as examples of witnesses peculiarly exposed to intimidation.[198] The Cabinet Office and specialist Units of the Home Office[199] came publicly to represent *Speaking up for Justice* as a vehicle of the Government's work to tackle domestic violence.[200] And the implementation group established to oversee the execution of the report's recommendations was joined in March 1999 by an official from the Domestic Violence Unit because of his formal responsibility within the Home Office for violence against women.[201]

By January 1999, Helen Reeves was to protest that the original target group of victims was at risk of being eclipsed altogether: 'the specific interests of victims of rape and sexual offences might be overlooked in both the vulnerable and intimidation projects...'.[202] It was, said Betsy Stanko of the ensuing Act, 'the most amazing transformation of a piece of legislation I've ever seen'.

## The Report

The Interdepartmental Working Group worked fast. Provisional recommendations were formulated by December 1997 and pitched

intimidated witnesses that included the victims of rape, sexual assault, and domestic violence.

[198] Helen Reeves, for instance, reported the conclusion of a working party on domestic violence which said that it was unfair to imprison a witness if no effort was made to protect her. Minutes of the third meeting of the Interdepartmental Vulnerable or Intimidated Witnesses Working Group, 29 October 1997. Similarly, a member of the working group, Pauline Barrett, head of the women's unit at the Department of Social Security, reminded the group at its meeting in July 1997 that the next meeting of the Cabinet sub-committee on violence against women would be in November and that she would mention the meeting to her Secretary of State.

[199] See, for instance, *VESTA: Victims in Europe Surviving Through Assistance: A European Project examining the multi-agency partnership approach to tackling the causes and effects of domestic violence in Europe, Final Report*, no page number, 1998.

[200] Cabinet Office: Fact Sheet—Violence against Women, undated; and *Living Without Fear*, Women's unit, undated.

[201] Vulnerable or Intimidated Witnesses: Implementation Steering Group, chairman's brief for meeting No. 5, 10 March 1999.

[202] Minutes of the Steering Group on Vulnerable or Intimidated Witnesses, 25 January 1999.

against case law from the European Court of Human Rights.[203] The
definition of a vulnerable witness had by then been changed to
embrace two broad categories, those who were vulnerable as a result
of 'their innate characteristics, such as mental or physical disability,
or illness', and those who were vulnerable because of circumstantial
factors 'such as the nature of the crime, for example, rape, domestic
violence, racist attacks, the witness' relationship with the defendant,
the dangerousness of the defendant etc.'[204] Witnesses, it was said,
were expected to give a good account, but they required special
assistance to give their best evidence, and there should be a portfolio
of measures available to all vulnerable and intimidated defence or
prosecution witnesses. Fifty-three provisional proposals were
offered, amongst them that the Pigot report's recommendations
should be extended to vulnerable adult witnesses; provision should
be made for video-recorded interviews and live closed circuit television links; the possibility of questioning by an intermediary; the use
of screens to shield the vulnerable witness (they had been subject to
contention in the past but the Working Group held, following the
human rights case law, that it was not necessary for the defendant to
see the witness, only the judge and jury); judges should have a power
to restrain unnecessary, improper, or oppressive questions; there
should be restraints on cross-examination in multi-defendant
cases; and there should be a blanket prohibition on unrepresented
defendants personally cross-examining victims in rape cases, serious
sexual assault ('we may need to define this more clearly' it was
noted), and stalking.

A preliminary meeting attended by Home Office Ministers of
State concluded in December 1997 that the work of the defence
was to try always to discredit the vulnerable witness, that there
was a concomitant need to change the culture and practice of the
courtroom, and that that would require legislation. The report was
submitted formally to Ministers in January 1998, and was then

[203] The review of the pertinent human rights legislation had been undertaken by the
CPS member of the working group, and the working group was referred in particular
to the bearing of *Van Mechelen and others v. Netherlands* 1997 (the case where
applicants had been convicted on the evidence of anonymous police officers not
heard in the presence of the defence) and *X v. United Kingdom* 1999 (involving the
issue of Article 6, the right to a fair trial, and the use of anonymous witnesses).

[204] Working Group on Vulnerable or Intimidated Witnesses Provisional Recommendations, 19 December 1997.

published as a consultation document,[205] *Speaking up for Justice*, with seventy-eight recommendations, twenty-six requiring legislation, and no prospect of any commitment to spend money until after the March Comprehensive Spending Review.[206] The report's broad themes were represented as the requirement that witnesses should be compelled to attend only if it were essential for justice; that efforts should be made to arrange trial dates that were convenient to witnesses; witnesses should be given as much notice of a hearing as possible; special measures should be made available for the vulnerable or intimidated witness; all witnesses should be treated sensitively; and witnesses should be given timely information about their cases.[207]

Some 140 responses to *Speaking up for Justice* were received by the Home Office, mostly clustered about the controversial proposals to disallow personal cross-examination and restrict evidence of sexual history in rape cases.[208] Two principal camps were reported internally to have emerged around the vexed issue of cross-examination in person:[209] those who supported the recommendations were said to have taken the view that the fear of many complainants offered 'a sufficient threat to be taken seriously despite the fact that personal cross-examination is uncommon'; whilst the second camp, 'in which the judges [were] well represented', believed that the provision was unnecessary because the abuse was rare, judges could prevent it happening, and pre-trial fear was not a

[205] The Home Secretary observed at its launch 'these recommendations... have my broad support but the report must go to consultation'.
[206] In the event, the implementation of *Speaking up for Justice* was to be very protracted because, as I have reported, the 2000 Comprehensive Spending Review allotted the bulk of funds that might be used for the purpose to the 'unallocated reserve' where it was to be the subject of agreed, trilateral bids. Victims Steering Group meeting, 8 December 2000, Chair's brief.
[207] Launch of *Speaking up for Justice*, 10 June 1998, Press Pack.
[208] For example, the NSPCC asserted that the recommendations 'contain many very important proposals for significant improvements in our current system of justice', and supported the curtailment of severing indictments; the amendment of the law on previous sexual history the use of intermediaries, the extension of the prohibition on the cross-examination in person of children to cases of false imprisonment, kidnapping, and child abduction; and 'wholeheartedly welcome the recommendation that video-recorded pre-trial cross-examination should be available for child witnesses'. NSPCC Response to the Home Office Report 'Speaking up for Justice', London, August 1998.
[209] Steering Group on Vulnerable or Intimidated Witnesses, VIWIMP SG3/98.

sufficient reason.[210] And three camps were said to have grouped themselves around the almost equally vexed question of admitting evidence of sexual history: those who did not accept that there was a problem needing attention, arguing that judges had become more watchful about protecting complainants; those who thought that all sexual history was irrelevant; and those who argued for clearer lines within which relevance would be determined. Many correspondents were reported to have criticized the current statutory definition of consent, whilst others favoured a 'tit for tat' rule.[211]

The judiciary, particularly the Lords of Appeal in Ordinary, the 'Law Lords', formed the most substantial critics of the new proposals and there were to be prolonged discussions in meetings and by correspondence about the tenability of the proposed new legislation. The Law Lords counted: they had the power to speak and vote during the passage of any legislation in the House of Lords; their rulings would affect the progress of cases and appeals under any laws that were passed; and they constituted an authoritative, outspoken, and independent arm of the criminal justice system. Over the period of the consultation and during the passage of the Bill, they concentrated on four problematic areas: restrictions of evidence of sexual experience (it was, they said, important that the Home Secretary did not impose a strait jacket on judges[212]); the prohibition on cross-examination of a complainant by a defendant in person (the judges declared that they did not wish to compromise their neutrality by acceding to the proposal that they should cross-examine the com-

---

[210] The dissent became quite public, the Lord Chief Justice telling the Bar Conference that the proposed ban on defendants personally cross-examining victims could lead to guilty men walking free and innocent ones being convicted. There had only been two relevant cases, he said, and the Court of Appeal had already issued guidelines. The Chair of the Bar's Public Affairs Committee concurred: 'we share the concern of the Lord Chief Justice about making special rules ... that limit a defendant's usual rights'. *The Times,* 5 October 1998. And see *The Times* and the *Evening Standard,* both of 29 July 1998, where the same points were made, to be met by Alun Michael's insistence that vulnerable witnesses do need more protection.

[211] An established rule in the courts whereby the criminal history of a party may be admitted if that party has already raised such a history in questioning his or her adversary.

[212] There were a number of areas where sexual history might be pertinent, the judges claimed, where, for instance, it was contemporaneous to the rape and the complainant had had intercourse with the same person during the one day. If justice was to be done, it was very important to retain the judge's discretion.

plainant themselves in lieu of the defendant or counsel); the use of video-recorded cross-examination (there were concerns about 'open justice' and the probability that pre-trial video-recorded cross-examination would not vitiate the need for the vulnerable witness to return to court to be cross-examined in person[213]); and the apparent neglect of the defendant in the new measures.[214] They dwelt on the need to maintain the balance and fairness of criminal procedure, and on the adequacy of the existing provisions, particularly under the judgment on Brown (which 'should enable judges to prevent the abuse'), for the judicial management of proceedings. The measures were said to be unworkable, unfair to defendants whose interests had not been taken properly into account and which also needed protection, and were possibly in breach of Article 6 of the European Convention on Human Rights: (a senior judge declared that he had 'reservations about *Croissant*, it is not permissible under Article 6 to deprive the defendant of the right to represent himself'); they were unnecessary because they could effectively be provided under the Brown judgment; they assumed *ab initio* that rape complainants were victims, although the rape was no more than an allegation until a verdict had been returned (the Lord Chief Justice later said in debate in the House of Lords that 'the trial cannot be conducted on the assumption that [a defendant] is a rapist and the complainant a victim, since the whole purpose of the proceeding is to establish whether that is so or not'); and they might lull prosecution witnesses into thinking that testifying would be easier than it proved to be. Moreover, trials of the kind represented by the Julia Mason case did

---

[213] Lord Justice Kay later told a meeting to launch a phase of the *Speaking up for Justice* provisions that he had become aware of the problem when he had presided over an eight-month long child abuse trial in which children had given pre-recorded evidence and were then thrown straight into cross-examination and resented coming to court only to be told they were liars. Launch of *Speaking up for Justice*, 24 January 2002, my notes.

[214] Not only the senior judiciary but the Bar objected to the measures not being available to defendants and it was also acknowledged that there was a presentational problem that young defendants would be defined as vulnerable precisely when the Government was trying to make them responsible for their actions. Minutes of the Steering Group on Vulnerable and Intimidated Witnesses, 18 September 1998. Note also an academic lawyer's dissenting voice in a section of a chapter titled 'Sacrificing the Defendant's Rights?', J. McEwan; 'Special Measures for Witnesses and Victims', in M. McConville and G. Wilson (eds.); *The Criminal Justice Process*, Oxford University Press, 2002, pp. 250–1.

not involve rational people: defendants in such cases refused representation and legal aid, and were prone to be obsessive and 'substandard mentally'[215] It was simply not feasible to expect a member of the Bar to represent them because they would not be briefed, and there was an ensuing risk of a man being acquitted because the jury might think he had not had a fair trial. The judges held that if the Milton Brown ruling proved inadequate, there could be a need for new law, but there had been only two cases since, and that was a slender base for legislation. There was a real prospect of unjust acquittals and unjust convictions and the *Speaking up for Justice* proposals did not meet the problem.

The Home Office's countering view was that, in the matter of evidence of sexual history, sexual mores had changed and sexual experience, no longer signifying what it had done in the past, should be admitted only if it was relevant and not to discredit the complainant. Moreover, the Home Office wished to extend the provision on such evidence: the existing law referred only to sexual behaviour with people other than the defendant but there was a desire to exclude irrelevant evidence of the complainant's sexual behaviour with the defendant as well; and judges had to admit evidence if it would be unfair to the defendant not to do so. The new Bill would replace that provision with the need to consider whether excluding evidence would lead a jury to reach an unsafe conclusion on an issue in the case. It would also prohibit sexual behaviour evidence from being used to impugn a complainant's credibility. And the fact that the complainant had consented in the past did not mean that she had consented on a current occasion.

The Home Office further accepted that trial judges could do much and had done much in the Brown judgment, and that cases of personal cross-examination were rare, but the Ralston Edwards case had engendered fears and the Government needed not only to deal with the wider public perceptions of trial but also to remove obstructions to women continuing their complaints. Examination in person was a key deterrent to reporting and testifying in cases of rape and the Home Office had satisfied itself that there would be no breach of Article 6: *Croissant* had confirmed that defendants could be required to appoint a lawyer and there was no absolute right

---

[215] A Home Office official noted that that was 'all the more reason they should be represented'.

under the Convention to conduct one's own defence or personally to cross-examine witnesses. Moreover, and with Julia Mason's possible hearing at the European Court in Strasbourg in mind, the Department argued that aggressive, humiliating, and unnecessarily prurient questioning of a complainant by an accused in person might raise other Human Rights issues bearing on victims and witnesses under Articles 3 and 8. Judges certainly had powers to control cross-examination, but that would not be enough to prevent witnesses from being distressed by the very fact that a person whom they alleged had raped or abused them was asking questions about that rape or abuse. Neither would it prevent a defendant asking inappropriate or distressing questions, and there would still remain the risk of unjust acquittals because people did not pursue their case.

The Home Office did however concede that it could legislate but wait before bringing the proposals into force to see how the Milton Brown direction 'worked out'. The defendants' rights had certainly to be protected, it argued, but defendants already enjoyed the benefits of PACE, the Police and Criminal Evidence Act,[216] and the right to legal representation, and they could decline to give evidence.[217] *Speaking up for Justice* had been directed at what other, relatively unprotected witnesses might need. But the matter of defendants' rights could be examined again.[218]

---

[216] The long title of the Police and Criminal Evidence Act 1984 was 'An Act to make further provision in relation to the powers and duties of the police, persons in police detention, criminal evidence, police discipline and complaints against the police; to provide for arrangements for obtaining the views of the community on policing and for a rank of deputy chief constable; to amend the law relating to the Police Federations and Police Forces and Police Cadets in Scotland; and for connected purposes.' The Act regulated the circumstances under which police interviews with suspects were conducted, and led to the exclusion of such evidence if it was obtained unfairly or if a confession was made 'under oppression'. PACE led to the introduction of the police taping interviews at first by audio and then by video-recorder.

[217] And that was a point accepted by ACPO, the CPS, the Lord Chancellor's Department and the Criminal Bar Association in its representations about *Speaking up for Justice*. The Criminal Bar Association did, however, argue that it should not apply to child defendants, and particularly after the recent case of *T & V v. the United Kingdom*. The Director of Criminal Policy commented that the Commission was likely to force the Home Secretary's hand and that some of the findings went 'with the grain of the youth justice reforms'. The easiest course, it was concluded, would simply be to apply the recommendations to all child witnesses.

[218] Helen Reeves was certainly persuaded that the Bill would not adversely affect the defendant. She wrote to *The Times* of 18 January 1999 arguing that the

Twenty-nine legislative proposals in *Speaking up for Justice* were eventually incorporated in a Bill 'after taking into account comments received during the consultation period and with other departments'. It was decided to retain the requirement for the court to appoint a legal representative where the defendant had declined to appoint one. A court-appointed barrister would receive access to all prosecution papers and would 'test the evidence in the interests of the accused', although it was anticipated that the Law Society,[219] Bar, and judiciary[220] would strongly oppose the proposal ('they think it is unrealistic but the alternative is to let defendant stew'). But there were three modifications 'where minor variation had proved necessary' and which had elicited what was called reluctant approval from the Attorney General's department and the Lord Chancellor's Department: automatic legal aid without means testing would not be reserved for recalcitrant defendants who chose to represent themselves ('otherwise [there would be a] perverse incentive to play the system'); in the matter of admitting evidence of previous sexual behaviour, proposals now incorporated 'the best practice' in Scottish, Canadian, and New South Wales law, excluding what was deemed to be irrelevant evidence whilst complying with Article 6 of the Human Rights Act (sexual evidence would now be admitted only when it was contemporaneous with the assault or

defendant had a right to a fair trial but none of the measures would diminish that right. The Bill ensured that the rights of the witness were balanced against those of the defendant. Elsewhere she wrote that 'We have long campaigned for better protection for children, rape victims and witnesses with physical and mental difficulties. This Bill is the major landmark that we have been waiting for.' *Victim Support Magazine*, No. 70, Spring 1999, p. 3. The Steering Group established to implement the Act's provisions did indeed eventually reconsider the defendant's position and reiterated that the defendant enjoys the safeguards of the presumption of innocence, the burden of proof being placed on the prosecution, the high standard of proof that insisted that a jury must be sure, and the defendant not being a compellable witness. Vulnerable or Intimidated Witnesses Steering Group: 'The rights and protections afforded to defendants in criminal proceedings in England and Wales', November 1998.

[219] The Law Society would have preferred the judge to ask questions but judges were reluctant to become involved in questioning.

[220] Their view was that counsel could not cross-examine without instructions. He or she would need to know the defendant's case which was not part of the papers. There was special training for judges in rape cases who were authorized to preside by the Lord Chief Justice on the recommendation of presiding judges. The system, it was thought, 'works very well'.

'goes to issue of honest belief'[221]); and there was to be a presumption of competence by which witnesses could give evidence so long as they could understand and answer questions put in a way that the court itself could understand.

What was at that stage still called the Youth Sentencing and Witnesses Bill was declared 'HRA-compliant'[222] and approved by Cabinet for inclusion in the 1998–9 legislative session, and an implementation steering group was founded in May in expectation of

[221] Evidence would be admitted only by leave of the court; it had to be relevant to the issue at hand or to the issue of consent, and the alleged behaviour must have taken place within 24 hours of the alleged offence. It was, considered the Home Office, an appropriate balance between allowing the defendant to put his case and protecting the complainant. The material issues could be whether sex had taken place, whether the complainant had consented, and whether the defendant had believed that the complainant consented. Past sexual behaviour itself was not relevant to the issue of consent. The compromise was not welcomed by some women's groups, for example Women Against Rape who argued in a leaflet in late April 1999 that there was 'widespread sexism' in the criminal justice system, allowing victims to be trashed in court. Realizing it cannot ignore 'women's heartfelt demands', WAR asserted, the Government included limits on sexual history evidence, but the Bill still had loopholes: there was no distinction traced between sex with the defendant and with other men, and evidence could still be introduced if the man believed the complainant had consented (see also a *Daily Express* report on WAR's campaign of opposition to the Bill, 10 December 1998). The Cabinet Office Women's Unit made substantially the same point about the problem of the plea of honest belief and the admission of evidence of sexual history (see *The Times*, 1 March 1999). The Home Office riposte was that it had concluded that such a ban would be unfair to the defendant. There were issues in rape trials about whether the intercourse took place between the complainant and accused on the occasion in question; whether the complainant consented; and whether the accused believed that the complainant consented. The sexual experience of the complainant could be relevant, the Home Office concluded. Concerned with issues of class and race as well as with gender, WAR also complained that the prohibition on cross-examination in person was a breach of the defendant's civil rights.

[222] Section 19 of the Human Rights Act was by then in force, and all new Bills had to be accompanied by a statement from the Minister in charge that in his or her view the Bill was compatible with the Convention. It was nevertheless recognized that there might be a challenge on the grounds that some of the Bill was unfair to defendants under Article 6, the right to a fair trial, and Article 10, which might cover reporting restrictions. *À propos* Article 6, it was argued that the defendant had a right to a legal representative of his own choosing, where there were court-appointed representatives not of the defendant's choosing, the appointment was made only when the defendant had refused to appoint his own choice. Under Article 10, press restrictions could be imposed in the interests of justice.

the Bill becoming law.[223] The main measures, it was noted, were intended 'to help vulnerable and intimidated witnesses to give evidence in criminal trials': there would be a presumption of vulnerability in sexual cases; and other witnesses would be eligible for support if they were under seventeen or if they suffered from mental disorder physical disability, or physical disorder, but were still capable of testifying coherently and accurately. In assessing vulnerability, the court would have to take into account the views of the witness,[224] the age of the witness and the nature of the offence; his or her social, cultural, and ethnic background; domestic and employment circumstances; religious and political beliefs; and the behaviour displayed towards the witness by the accused or members of his family. If a court did determine that a victim was vulnerable or intimidated, it would then have to decide whether special measures would improve the quality of evidence, including the use of screens; live links; exclusion from the court of particular people; dispensing with the wearing of wigs or gowns; the admission of video-recording as evidence in chief; permission to examine through an intermediary; the protection of witnesses from cross-examination by the accused in person; and, in cases where the charge was a sexual offence, indecency with children, or kidnapping, the court could appoint a person who was legally qualified to represent the interests of the accused. There was, in addition, a provision for broad reporting restrictions that Ian Chisholm described as one of the most controversial sections of the Bill, controversial because they curbed the work of the most vocal and well-guarded of all institutions,[225] the mass media, and the mass media did indeed remonstrate abundantly in private and in public throughout the evolution of the policy.

---

[223] There were some private forebodings about what might ensue if they were successful. One estimate offered in the papers accompanying the preparation of legislation was that some 10,000 to 20,000 extra cases a year could cost between £50 m. and £150 m. in the long term and there were doubts about the capacity of the criminal justice system to cope with all the new work. The actual figures secured to fund the initiative were much more modest. Some £7 m. of the £9 m. Home Office bid for implementation had actually been approved by the Treasury in the Comprehensive Review Settlement. The rest would have had to be funded out of the existing allocation to the police. Later the costing was put at £6.3 m. *per annum*.

[224] And Victim Support was nervous about that provision because, it argued, bestowing such a right on the witness would open him or her to the possibility of further intimidation.

[225] Speaking at the Victim Support National Conference, 5 July 1999, my notes.

The new composite legislation was announced in the Queen's Speech in November as the Youth Justice and Witnesses Bill, later to be renamed the Youth Justice and Criminal Evidence Bill. Part I of the Act introduced the apparatus of restorative justice described in the previous chapter, laying out the mechanics of contracts, panels and Youth Offender Panels. Part II, quite different and by far the more substantial, flowed from *Speaking up for Justice*: Chapter 1 marked the criteria for identifying vulnerability and the special measures that could be mustered to protect the vulnerable witness; Chapter 2, the prohibition of cross-examination in person in certain cases, and the provisions for alternative representation; Chapter 3, the tighter regulation of evidence of sexual history in rape cases; Chapter 4, the imposition of reporting restrictions; and Chapter 5, the new presumption of competence. There was broad support from Members of Parliament[226] but some objections were still expected to emanate from the senior judiciary in relation to the provisions for preventing cross-examination in Chapter 2. The passage through the House of Lords, it was thought, would be 'difficult' and, indeed, the senior judiciary, including the Lord Chief Justice, did express concern at the second reading and in committee about the need for those provisions, and whether a ban should be mandatory, and also about Clauses 40–42 of Chapter 3, which touched on evidence about sexual history.[227] The debate was active, detailed, and prolonged, divided broadly on functional or occupational rather than political lines, and I can give but a sample of its argument.

There was support from the Opposition. Baroness Byford, a Conservative peeress, opened by citing Victim Support, claiming that there was a 'lot wrong with the present system', and that the recommendations were 'all condensed, common sense'. She was, she

---

[226] For example, John Greenway, a Conservative Party Home Affairs spokesman, said in committee that 'Now considering what kinds of questions can be asked: many leading practitioners in Committee in the Lords "are not convinced that a change is necessary... There is, however, a general sense among those of us who are not legal practitioners... that aspects of rape victims" personal lives and sexual histories have been trawled through the courts on too many occasions. This has been done in a way that shocks us all and which we find wholly deplorable.' Youth Justice and Criminal Evidence Act—Standing Committee E, 24 June 1999.

[227] Lord Williams as the peer representing the Home Office in the House of Lords, was to engage in extensive and prolonged correspondence with every member of the House who had made points about the provisions of the new Bill.

said, appalled by the manner in which rape was treated. Baroness Kennedy, a Labour peeress and barrister, stated that judges like Lord Ackner would say they could prevent humiliating cross-examination but in the case of some defendants that was impossible. It was not, she held, fitting for the system to witness the kinds of exchanges that would inevitably occur if judges alone had to prevent invasive cross-examination but she suspected that 'colleagues from the Bar speaking after me will err on the side of conservatism'.

Lord Ackner, a Lord of Appeal, did indeed have reservations. It was a pity, he observed, that the authors of *Speaking up for Justice* had not consulted the judiciary.[228] The very use of the term 'victims of rape' was unfortunate because it prejudged whether a case has been proved: there were, he said, no victims but complainants, and complainants were not all alike. *Speaking up for Justice* was flawed because it did not distinguish between 'date rape' and 'stranger rape', and defendants in the former class should not be debarred from personal cross-examination. And he proposed an amendment that judges should be entitled to give leave for personal cross-examination in rape cases. But Lord Williams, leading for the Government, refused to accede: 'there is already a prohibition on the right to cross-examine in cases involving the incestuous rape of one's own daughter or any other sexual offences against one's daughter... If the Milton Brown and Ralston Edwards cases were never to occur again, there would still be that significant fear that women would be subjected to a cruel and degrading experience that is forbidden by the European Convention. On behalf of the Government I do not accept the amendment.' Lord Ackner's *riposte* was that such a refusal could compromise trials:

It is very easy to see how the guilty person can be convicted because no judge can stop the defendant in his final speech indicating how unfairly he has been treated by his inability to cross-examine, although every other stage of the defence was conducted by him personally. It is very easy to make out a situation of unfairness, the little man being faced by the heavier personalities of the prosecution.

Baroness Mallalieu, another Labour peeress and a barrister, complained that she detected the understated assumption in the report

---

[228] Four members of the judiciary had attended the special conferences on *Speaking up for Justice* and, maintained the Home Office, their views had been taken into account.

that vulnerable and intimidated witnesses were truthful. Children could make false accusations, and no changes should be made which might prevent the truth emerging. She would defend the use of video cross-examination and screens—witnesses should not be bullied—but the judges already had a power to stop oppressive cross-examination and unnecessary or irrelevant cross-examination on sexual history was not allowed. And so it went on. Frequently invoked was the Human Rights Act, and Article 6 above all. A Law Lord, Lord Lowry, for instance, declared that the proposal to prohibit personal cross-examination by a defendant was a mistaken response to the 'deplorable proceedings of two years ago'. He was not persuaded that Article 6 of the European Convention would not be infringed. The German precedent of *Croissant* was not one 'he admired in the context of the United Kingdom', and any proposal to act on it would reduce minimum rights under Article 6.

In the event, the Government accepted without dispute 108 of the 346 proposed amendments, and lost only one vote, and the Bill received Royal assent in July 1999. 'Everyone is now competent to give evidence,' announced the Home Office, 'as long as they understand the questions and can give intelligible answers.'[229]

The law's symbolic owners were signalled at different phases of the report's history: three women from Women Against Rape having been present but mute at the launch of *Speaking up for Justice* (although they were actually more than critical, regarding themselves not so much as an audience but as a spurned lobby[230]), and

---

[229] Home Office Press Release: Youth Justice and Criminal Evidence Bill receives Royal Assent, 28 July 1999.

[230] The women considered themselves to be a lobby rather than guests, and they demanded that Home Office officials should meet the WAR delegation. They complained about the venue (a bar-restaurant in St Martin's Lane, central London); being excluded from the consultations; the failure to remove judicial discretion in matters touching on previous sexual history (judges had not exercised their discretion since 1976, they claimed); the removal of the right to personal defence because it would disadvantage poor, working-class defendants and set a dangerous precedent applying only to a few cases. WAR press release on *Speaking up for Justice*, 9 June 1998. They were indignant that they had not been invited to the November and December 1997 conferences, declaring in Women Against Rape; *Speaking up for Women: What the report of the Working Group on Vulnerable or Intimidated Witnesses hasn't dealt with*, undated. 'We gave written evidence to the working group . . . in November 1997. We have direct contact with raped women, but were excluded from both conferences of the working group's consultation process in November and December 1997.'

the speakers having been drawn from the Home Office, Victim Support, VOICE UK, and the NSPCC. Measures to support and protect witnesses were subsequently introduced progressively as monies allowed,[231] technical equipment was installed in courtrooms, and training was undertaken.[232] When a new stage of implementation was formally celebrated in January 2002, those in attendance included sixteen representatives from the CPS; nineteen from the police service and police authorities; twenty one from the Home Office; two from the Lord Chancellor's Department; fifteen from non-governmental organizations for the disabled; seven from non-governmental organizations for children; four independent consultants; six judges; one official from local government; three independent consultants; two people representing the Criminal Injuries Compensation Appeals Panel and the Criminal Injuries Compensation Board; one from the Magistrates' Association; two from Victim Support; three officials from the Department of Health; five academics; four Ministers and Members of Parliament; one member of the Law Society; one person from the Scottish Executive; one Law Officer; two Justices' Clerks; five barristers and members of the Bar Council; two representatives of the probation service; two members of the social services; two members of the Court Services; one hospital consultant; one member of NACRO; one member of the Institute of Public Policy Research;

---

[231] Because of financial restrictions and competition for resources from the so-called 'unallocated reserve', implementation was staggered. For example, the allocation from the reserve to the vulnerable or intimidated witnesses measures was cut from £30m. to £12m. in November 2000.

[232] See Home Office Press Release, 361/99, 18 November 1999, which promised the introduction of pagers for witnesses by the end of 1999; escorts to and from court by the end of Spring 2000; the use of video-recorded evidence, live CCTV links, screens and communication aids by the end of 2000 in the Crown Court; the clearing of the public gallery in certain circumstances by the end of 2000 in the Crown Court. Home Office news release 247/2000, 7 August 2000, announced that the prohibition on the personal cross-examination of victims of rape and other sexual offences would come into effect in September 2000 and the prevention of cross-examination on previous sexual history unless it is absolutely relevant to the case in early December 2000. A small number of harrowing cases resembling that of Julia Mason were reported to have taken place between the passing and implementation of the Act: see, for instance, the report of the humiliating personal cross-examination of a complainant in a rape trial in *The Times*, 29 March 2000. A full discussion of the application of the Act's provisions would occupy a chapter in its own right in a book that cannot embrace issues of practical implementation.

and no one at all from gay, minority ethnic, or women's or old people's organizations. Witnesses at large had been awarded greater protection, and rape victims in particular had been shielded, but the progressive enlargement and transformation of the cast of perceived beneficiaries of the initiative were intriguing.[233]

## *R v. A*

We have seen that there had been a continual dispute about the possible compatibility of key sections of the provisions of the new Youth Justice and Criminal Evidence Act with the Human Rights Act, and especially Article 6 of the Act, and it was anticipated from the outset that there would probably be a challenge. The Working Party had certainly deliberated at length about whether the provisions were 'HRA-compatible' (and not all the members had at first been satisfied that that was the case). Between September and November 1997, it had consulted the law officers and independent counsel. It had finally come to the judgment, endorsed by Ministers, that rape was special and deserved to be made an exception in law,[234] and the Cabinet had accepted the Home Secretary's assertion that the legislation was compliant. The Act passed. But it did still embody critical contentions about the proper status and relations of defendants, complainants, witnesses, and prosecution—about what the Lord of Appeal, Lord Steyn, would later come to call 'the familiar triangulation of interests of the accused, the victim and society'[235]—and it was still contested.

When a test case did present itself in the Central Criminal Court in early December 2001, only days after Section 41 of the Youth Justice and Criminal Evidence Act had come into effect, it was seized on

---

[233] There might be some merit in one limited sphere to Van Swaaningen's radical complaint that 'Feminists have quite specific reasons for opposing the way in which criminal justice officials have taken feminist claims "seriously". The actual way in which concern for the victim is given shape has forgotten about the initial feminist, or indeed any power-critical, meaning.' R. Van Swaaningen; *Critical Criminology*, Sage, London, 1997, p. 222.

[234] Minutes of the second Meeting of the Interdepartmental Vulnerable or Intimidated Witnesses Working Group, 29 September 1997.

[235] *R v. A* [2001] UKHL 25, 17 May 2001.

with alacrity. It revolved around the so-called 'rape-shield' provisions[236] and the allegation that the defendant would not be permitted to put his evidence in cross-examination on previous sexual history before a jury at trial. There was an issue of consent based on a previous sexual relationship, and the Crown Court Judge was said to have allowed the appeal at a preparatory hearing on 8 December 'with enthusiasm': it 'certainly *prima facie* offends Article 6', he said, and 'this problem is likely to arise in many, many cases before the Crown Court'.[237]

In an interlocutory appeal that was 'fast-tracked' to the Court of Appeal hearing a month later, it was held that it was 'not myth but common sense' that a person who had consented to sexual relations with another recently was more likely to have consented to them on the occasion in question. The Court under Lord Rose indicated that it considered evidence of a relationship between the complainant and defendant was relevant for the purposes of establishing actual consent and that to prevent this evidence going before the jury for that purpose might distort the trial process.[238] However, it also concluded that it was premature to consider the question of fairness in advance of the trial, in circumstances in which it could not be considered 'in the context of the proceedings as a whole'. Any declaration was therefore likely to focus on the scope for unfairness where section 41 of the Youth Justice and Criminal Evidence Act restricted evidence or questioning to sexual behaviour with the defendant himself. The Court certified that a point of law of general

---

[236] Based on a Canadian case, section 41 was based, in the words of the House of Lords' judgment, 'on the decision of the Supreme Court of Canada in *R v. Seaboyer* 1991 83 DLR (4th) 193. In that case a first attempt to introduce "rape-shield" provisions directed against the admissibility of sexual history evidence in rape cases was held to be invalid under section 7 of the Canadian Charter of Rights and Freedoms.'

[237] *The Times*, 12 December 2000.

[238] In the House of Lords' judgment, it was said that 'Rose LJ concluded that the effect of the Act is that the alleged previous sexual relationship is inadmissible on the issue of consent. On this supposition Rose LJ further stated that the Crown accepted that the trial judge will, in due course, have to direct the jury that the evidence of the complainant's consensual activity with the defendant during the period before the alleged rape is solely relevant to the question of the defendant's belief as to consent and is not relevant to the question of whether the complainant in fact consented. However, Rose LJ was of the view that such a direction might lead to an unfair trial because a previous sexual relationship may be relevant to the issue of consent as well as belief in consent.'

public importance was involved under Article 6 of the Human Rights Act, namely 'May a sexual relationship between a defendant and complainant be relevant to the issue of consent so as to render its exclusion under section 41 of the Youth Justice and Criminal Evidence Act 1999 a contravention of the defendant's right to a fair trial?' and, after an intervention in the appeal by the Home Office under Section 5 of the Human Rights Act,[239] the issue was allowed to go before the Lords of Appeal meeting as the Appellate Committee of the House of Lords in January.

The appeal in *R v. A* was brought to the House of Lords on 26 March 2001, the focus of the challenge and the focus of questioning during the appeal being related to the relevance of, and therefore the fairness of excluding, evidence of sexual behaviour between the complainant and the defendant. The burden of the Home Office case was that section 41 had been based on Canadian experience where amendments to 'rape-shield' provisions contained in the Criminal Code of Canada had been introduced and found lawful after an earlier adverse Supreme Court judgment in *R v. Seaboyer* brought under section 7[240] of the Canadian counterpart of the Human Rights Act, the Charter of Rights and Freedoms.[241]

---

[239] Section 5 touches on the right of the Crown to intervene and be joined as a party to proceedings where a declaration of incompatibility is at stake.

[240] 'Everyone has the right to life, liberty and security of the person and the right not to be deprived thereof except in accordance with the principles of fundamental justice.'

[241] The amended text of article 276 of the Criminal Code reads: '[E]vidence that the complainant has engaged in sexual activity, whether with the accused or with any other person, is not admissible to support an inference that, by reason of the sexual nature of that activity, the complainant (a) is more likely to have consented to the sexual activity that forms the subject-matter of the charge; or (b) is less worthy of belief. (2) In proceedings in respect of an offence referred to in subsection (1), no evidence shall be adduced by or on behalf of the accused that the complainant has engaged in sexual activity other than the sexual activity that forms the subject-matter of the charge, whether with the accused or with any other person, unless the judge, provincial court judge or justice determines, in accordance with the procedures set out in sections 276.1 and 276.2, that the evidence (a) is of specific instances of sexual activity; (b) is relevant to an issue at trial; and (c) has significant probative value that is not substantially outweighed by the danger of prejudice to the proper administration of justice. (3) In determining whether evidence is admissible under subsection (2), the judge, provincial court judge or justice shall take into account (a) the interests of justice, including the right of the accused to make a full answer and defence; (b) society's interest in encouraging the reporting of sexual assault offences; (c) whether

The Home Office was a little guarded about the likely outcome of the appeal: it accepted that section 41 was controversial, it had 'received a rough ride from senior members of the Bar and judiciary during its passage through Parliament', and the Court of Appeal had already given a clear steer that it considered that the provision would create unfairness. Moreover, it was apparent from questions put to counsel during the appeal that the Law Lords would need to be persuaded of the appeal case and there was 'a real risk that they [would not] be with the appeal on this issue'. JVU noted that 'the questioning [had] indicated that they had some difficulty with the Crown's position, although they gave no formal indication of what the outcome will be'.

It was recognized by the Home Office that it was not itself empowered to appeal against a further adverse judgment to the European Court of Human Rights at Strasbourg and that the only outcome would be a declaration of incompatibility and amending legislation. It would be the first such declaration in a criminal matter and therefore especially 'sensitive', because it 'might set an unhelpful precedent', although the Human Rights Act did 'preserve parliamentary sovereignty in respect of declarations of incompatibility and that the final decision in amending the legislation therefore remain[ed] with Parliament'. Draft letters were prepared to pave the way for responding to the consequences of such a declaration should it be made.

Lord Slynn of Hadley introduced the judgment on 17 May with the statement that 'in recent years it has become plain that women who allege that they have been raped should not in court be harassed unfairly by questions about their previous sexual experiences. To allow such harassment is very unjust to the woman; it is also bad for society in that women will be afraid to complain and as a result men who ought to be prosecuted will escape.' But, he continued,

---

(*n. 241 contd.*) there is a reasonable prospect that the evidence will assist in arriving at a just determination in the case; (*d*) the need to remove from the fact-finding process any discriminatory belief or bias; (*e*) the risk that the evidence may unduly arouse sentiments of prejudice, sympathy or hostility in the jury; (*f*) the potential prejudice to the complainant's personal dignity and right of privacy; (*g*) the right of the complainant and of every individual to personal security and to the full protection and benefit of the law; and (*h*) any other factor that the judge, provincial court judge or justice considers relevant.'

the accused is entitled to a fair trial and there is an obvious conflict between the interests of protecting the woman and of ensuring such fair trial. Such conflict is more acute since the Human Rights Act 1998 came into force. The question is whether one of these interests should prevail or whether there must be a balance so that fairness to each must be accommodated and if so whether it has been achieved in current legislation. That is essentially the question which arises in this case.

A prior consensual sexual relationship between a complainant alleging a sexual offence and defendant might, it was held, in some circumstances be relevant to the issue of consent and the absence of evidential material adduced on it could infringe Article 6 of the Human Rights Act. Under section 41 of the Youth Justice and Criminal Evidence Act,[242] there had been a virtually wholesale exclusion of evidence and that constituted an 'excessive inroad into the absolute right to a fair trial'. The test should be whether that exclusion of sexual history would endanger the fairness of the trial. He ruled that section 41 was significantly more restrictive than article 276 of the Canadian Criminal Code and that it compromised the principle of proportionality under Article 6, that the defence of belief in consent would be unavailable in practice, and that the judge's direction to the jury 'would always have to be to the effect that the past experience between the complainant and the accused is

---

[242] The actual section in question should be quoted at length: '(1) If at a trial a person is charged with a sexual offence, then, except with the leave of the court—(a) no evidence may be adduced, and (b) no question may be asked in cross-examination, by or on behalf of any accused at the trial, about any sexual behaviour of the complainant... (3) This subsection applies if the evidence or question relates to a relevant issue in the case and either... (c) it is an issue of consent and the sexual behaviour of the complainant to which the evidence or question relates is alleged to have been, in any respect, so similar—(i) to any sexual behaviour of the complainant which (according to evidence adduced or to be adduced by or on behalf of the accused) took place as part of the event which is the subject matter of the charge against the accused, or (ii) to any other sexual behaviour of the complainant which (according to such evidence) took place at or about the same time as that event, that the similarity cannot reasonably be explained as a coincidence. (4) For the purposes of subsection (3) no evidence or question shall be regarded as relating to a relevant issue in the case if it appears to the court to be reasonable to assume that the purpose (or main purpose) for which it would be adduced or asked is to establish or elicit material for impugning the credibility of the complainant as a witness...' I am no lawyer but the section would not seem to be an absolute but a discretionary ban that permitted evidence on sexual history under specific conditions.

irrelevant to the issue of consent'. And he rejected the submissions of counsel for the Home Secretary on that point. Section 41 amounted to a 'blanket exclusion of potentially relevant evidence' but, assuming that the legislature would not have wished to 'deny the right to an accused to put forward a full and complete defence by advancing truly probative material', section 41 could and should be interpreted as consistent with Article 6 of the Human Rights Act, and that 'the result of such a reading would be that sometimes logically relevant sexual experiences between a complainant and an accused may be admitted under Section 41 . . . '. He therefore 'decline[d] to make the rulings sought by the Director of Public Prosecutions and the Secretary of State. Given the terms of this speech it is unnecessary to answer the certified question.' And he dismissed the appeal. The effect was to place the interpretation of the intent and application of Section 41 of the Youth Justice and Criminal Evidence Act under the control of the Human Rights Act.

Lord Hutton concurred:

pursuant to the obligation . . . that section 41 must be read and given effect in a way which is compatible with article 6, I consider that section 41(3)(c) should be read as including evidence of such previous behaviour by the complainant because the defendant claims that her sexual behaviour on previous occasions was similar, and the similarity was not a coincidence because there was a causal connection which was her affection for, and feelings of attraction towards, the defendant . . . the matter should be remitted to the trial judge in the Crown Court to consider if the evidence which the defendant wishes to give (as amplified by him if he wishes to do so) is admissible . . .

The Home Secretary's appeal was dismissed, but, signally, section 41 of the 1999 Act was not declared incompatible with the Human Rights Act.[243] It was a little confusing. Whilst Baroness Kennedy concluded that 'You cannot purchase justice for women at the expense of justice for men. There are circumstances in which previous sexual history may be relevant,'[244] other lawyers inside and outside

[243] See the report in the *Sunday Times*, 20 May 2001, which did not do much to clarify matters. The report argued that there was a general assumption that women were the victims of predatory men and that complainants always told the truth. That was an abuse of power which the Human Rights Act was supposed to offset. But the Law Lords had said there was compatibility, and they had done so by reversing the implications of the law.
[244] Quoted in *The Times*, 12 March 2001.

the universities were bemused. Kate Malleson of the London School of Economics, a human rights lawyer, observed that the judgment had laid down that the Act had to be interpreted with discretion, but that she did not know how an absolute prohibition on the disclosure of sexual history could be treated in that way. Neither she nor Andrew Ashworth of Oxford University understood it. Ashworth said that he was 'puzzled at the use of the judges' interpretive power in this way ([under] s.3 Human Rights Act 1998); in substance they found s.41 incompatible with the defendant's Convention rights . . . but did not have the courage to issue a declaration of incompatibility. Thus the decision in A. stands as probably the furthest-reaching use of the power of interpretation.'[245] Jenny Temkin, a feminist law professor and an expert on the law on rape, believed that the judges had expanded the small area of discretion about disclosure of sexual conduct to undo the effects of the Act and to take matters back to 1977.[246] It was, she believed, a deliberate attempt to undo the law.

## Conclusions

The vulnerable or intimidated witnesses initiative probably conforms best to the outsider's view of the policy-making process as a succession of sensational events so erupting in the environment of criminal justice, so illuminating and amplifying the plight of particular groups, that politicians were impelled to act, or at least impelled to deliberate about whether to act. The ensuing initiative was to become public property, too conspicuous and politically valuable, too imbued with human interest, not to be grasped by politicians, the mass media, and members of the voluntary sector, and the mark they imposed was to be highly visible. The episode shows that groups organized around the poignant politics of, say, gender, race, or childhood may on occasion be needed to instigate and spur policies for victims on, even if those policies did eventually come to benefit all victims, including those who were not so affecting. But who had actually come into focus was contingent on time and place. Other vulnerable groups, such as 'trafficked women', illegal immigrants,[247] and asylum-seekers, the elderly, and gay men and women, had not

[245] Email, 23 July 2003.
[246] She was alluding to the Sexual Offences (Amendment) Act 1976.
[247] The bodies of 58 Chinese immigrants were found in a sealed lorry in Dover in September 2000, for instance.

influenced what transpired, though their claims might well have weighed if they had been dramatized in an appropriate way and at an opportune moment.[248]

In the event, vulnerability became such a swollen and omnibus category that those groups' apparent omission was to have little practical significance, and vulnerable witnesses other than rape claimants and children did not anyway have to be listed on a pre-scribed register. The particular became the general as it was trans-formed into the material of a Government committee functioning in routine fashion, became exposed to universalistic principles and styles of work, and accommodated the claims of an ever-growing multitude of claimants. Of quite another setting, Molotch talked about how the style of things produced imparts uniformity: 'Style provides stability in that individual items are not free to change willy-nilly on their own; they have to work within a larger context of how things are done and get recognized.'[249] It was just so with the labours of the Working Group as it processed a succession of different cat-egories of witness. Disparate categories had to be subordinated to the way in which 'things were done' and became the ingredients of recognizable policy. Ian Chisholm came to reflect of the general consequences of the Julia Mason case that 'I don't think the origin does actually affect the outcome'.

It must be noted, second, that the structural divisions, ideologies, and commitments of the criminal justice system brought it about that the judiciary and the Lord Chancellor, their political represen-tative, continued to police the strategic frontiers of criminal proced-ure, reluctant often to concede that victims could be acknowledged *as* victims until a verdict had been delivered, and, more important, unwilling to compromise engrained jurisprudential principles of fairness and the balance of power in the relation between State and defendant. The episode underscores the authority of the judges, and why it was that the Home Office was obliged to be conciliatory in broaching any changes to the standing of victims.[250] It conveys the

---

[248]  Again, the bombing of the Admiral Duncan, a gay public house, occurred on 30 April 1999, rather too late for the Working Party, although, as I shall show in the next chapter, it did affect RISC, the Racist Incidents Standing Committee, which began to add new categories of hate crime to the initial definition of a racist incident.

[249]  H. Molotch; *Where Stuff Comes From*, Routledge, New York, 2003, p. 95.

[250]  At the time when the Youth Justice and Criminal Evidence Bill was passing through Parliament, for instance, Jack Straw felt obliged to remind his audience at a

tenacity of Ministers driven by the imperative to reduce crime, confront the electorate, and respond fittingly to the dramatic and dramatized pathos of individual victims. And yet perplexingly, and perhaps because those powers and principles were so very evenly matched, it also documents how there was to be no neat and immediate resolution in the House of Lords of an apparent contradiction between Article 6 of the Human Rights Act and section 41 of the Youth Justice and Criminal Evidence Act. The outcome was a stalemate. There were still effectively defended limits to change in the victim's status, and some of the recommendations of *Speaking up for Justice* had been altered or remained unsettled in consequence, but the lot of the witness and victim had certainly been ameliorated.

Last, the environment of policy-making for victims was becoming ever-more crowded. Not only did it now more noticeably include witnesses,[251] but a mass of new policy relations, transformations, and combinations was in the making as *Speaking up for Justice* came to overlap, intersect, and interact at various points with other ventures and pieces of legislation, most especially the Human Rights Act, the new performance management[252] (the implementation of

ChildLine Conference that 'A person is only guilty when they are convicted in court and it is essential to have a system which ensures effective rights for the accused because the prosecution system cannot be perfect . . . It is important that we balance the interests of the victim, the witnesses . . . and of the accused.' *Hearing Children's Voices: Conference Report*, May 13 1999, ChildLine, London, undated, p. 2.

[251] And the Justice and Victims Unit became after 2001 the Justice, Victims and Witnesses Unit and then again, after June 2003—and more witness-oriented still—two separate units: the Victims Unit and the Justice and Witnesses Unit. It was, I was told, a reflection both of the ever-growing emphasis on witnesses and 'a matter of resources'. A bifurcated unit could command more funding than a single entity. The change accompanied the publication of a strategy paper, appearing under the names of the new trilateral Ministers, on victims and witnesses, with a markedly greater emphasis on witnesses: *A new deal for victims and witnesses: National strategy to deliver improved services*, Home Office, London, 2003. I shall return to that paper briefly in Chapter 10.

[252] I have already stated that improving victim and witness satisfaction could compete with crime reduction as an objective for the initiative. As important, perhaps, was the management of the implementation of the initiative as a test bed for new management techniques. The Home Office Business Performance Unit decided in September 1998 to try out 'new project management techniques as part of New Ways of Working on [its] implementation'. *Speaking up for Justice* would be 'a template for modernising the programme of work based on the Modernisation Programme and its key characteristics' (New Ways of Working: Outline for Session at Speaking-Up for Justice Steering Group Meeting, 13 November 1998). The Steering

*Speaking up for Justice* was treated as an opportunity to test new ways of managing projects under the Home Office's 'banner of New Ways of Working'[253]), and the emergent and powerful politics of race that accompanied the Macpherson Inquiry. It is with those politics that I shall deal in the next chapter.

Group was invited to consider such questions as 'is there a buy-in for the programme management template? If not, why not and what could be used instead?' And it was encouraged to adopt the new techniques laid out in, say, F. Smith; *Project Management—Keeping out of trouble*, Home Office Modernisation Unit, 14 July 1998, which talked about avoiding the serious risks of time slippage, cost over-run and project failure occasioned by 'not identifying/confronting problems; lack of proactive risk management', 'identifying and classifying risks', 'not confronting the problem when it is identified, hoping it will work out' and the like. The solutions, it was argued, were to tackle all problems resolutely, plan properly, and track progress by means of a baseline and 'progress tracking'; the use of early milestones; structured project plans, 'no compromise project management', 'independent verification, [and] good quality assurance'; the collation of information the preparation of a 'programme risk register', and the like.

[253] Home Office *HOtline*, 13 October 1998. The newsletter reported that PVU were applying project management techniques to the implementation of the *Speaking up for Justice* report and quoted Sue Street, then Director, Fire and Emergency Planning, as saying that 'there should be little mystique about New Ways of Working... a project-based approach simply means knowing what you are trying to do, how you do it in the most effective manner, and knowing when it has been done' (After directing the Fire and Emergency Planning Unit, she became Director of Criminal Justice Policy in 1999 before leaving to become Permanent Secretary of Culture, Media and Sport). And Ian Chisholm was reported to have said, the 'Procedures and Victims Unit work is all about *joined-up government* and working with groups in the community, such as Victim Support and the NSPCC. I see Project management and team-working as crucial in making these partnerships effective.'

# 9

# The Victim and Race

It is significant . . . as former Home Secretary Jack Straw pointed out, that the *cause célèbre* that prompted shifts in criminal justice in the 1990s, was not the overzealous pursuit of an offender or a wrongful conviction, as in the 1970s and 1980s, but the failure to convict the murderers of African/Caribbean teenager, Stephen Lawrence.[1]

## Introduction

The death of Stephen Lawrence was to have a delayed but galvanic impact on the criminal justice system, touching the recruitment,[2] deployment, and working methods of the police;[3] sentencing practices;[4] the employment and promotion of staff in the Home Office,[5] and other Departments of State;[6] the work of the courts,

---

[1] C. Phillips and B. Bowling; 'Racism, Ethnicity, Crime, and Criminal Justice', in M. Maguire *et al.* (eds.); *The Oxford Handbook of Criminology*, Third Edition, Oxford University Press, Oxford, 2002, p. 582.

[2] See N. Bland *et al.*; 'Career progression of Ethnic Minority Police Officers', Policing and Reducing Crime Briefing Note: Police Research Series paper 107, April 1999, which opened 'The position of ethnic minority police officers has come under ever increasing public scrutiny.'

[3] As a minor illustration, the police began to take benchmarks from the Macpherson Report and incorporate them into their code of practice. RISC meeting, 19 April 2000, my notes.

[4] Sentencing Advisory Panel, Advice to the Court of Appeal: Racially Aggravated Offences, July 2000.

[5] See *Race Equality*, foreword by the Home Secretary, Home Office, London, 2000.

[6] For example, the Lord Chancellor's Department; 'Race Issues and the Lord Chancellor's Department, Actions taken by the Lord Chancellor's Department to implement the recommendations of the Stephen Lawrence Inquiry', undated. The report dealt with employment matters; policy-making and 'customer service'; the lay magistracy; the professional judiciary; judicial discipline; promoting race awareness in the judiciary; and sentencing and bail decisions.

prisons,[7] and prosecutors; and much else,[8] including the character of information collected and presented to the criminal justice system[9] and the treatment of victims.[10] There have been other accounts of the police investigation into Lawrence's death,[11] the coroner's inquest, the failed public and private prosecutions, and the Macpherson Inquiry, and most of those events will be only lightly sketched here. In this chapter, I propose to view the repercussions of his death solely through the narrow aperture defined by the task of this book, and explore how they affected Government policies for victims in and around the turn of the century.

[7] The Prison Service stated in February 2000, for instance, that it proposed to add racially-aggravated offences to prison rules, and it set itself a target of the number of such offences falling after 2004. Minutes of RISC meeting, 9 February 2000.

[8] Patricia MacFarlane of the Operational Policing Policy Unit, Chair of RISC (the Racist Incidents Standing Committee) and later secretary to the Steering Committee on the Macpherson Report, told a Victim Support Seminar on Stephen Lawrence held on 15 February 2000 that 'this is a police investigation that went wrong, but [the recommendations of the Macpherson Report are] incumbent on all institutions'. That sentiment became conventional. For instance, the executive summary of *Winning the Race: Policing Plural Communities: HMIC Thematic Inspection Report on Police Community and Race Relations 1996–7* observed that 'it must be recognised that racial discrimination, both direct and indirect, is endemic in society and the police service is no exception'.

[9] For example, after 1999, the British Crime Surveys and Witness Satisfaction Surveys would have 'ethnic booster' samples and 'ethnic monitoring' was to be introduced into a number of data bases in the criminal justice system. See C. Mirrlees-Black; 'Confidence in the Criminal Justice System: Findings from the 2000 British Crime Survey', HO Research Findings No. 137, 2001, which compared black and white responses to criminal justice. See also *The Home Office—A Guide*, Home Office, London, October 2000, p. 9.

[10] Including, of course, the work of Victim Support itself. At a meeting of its National Council in June 2000, it was agreed to give a high priority to victims of racist crimes, to mount a specialist training programme, to inject an awareness of issues of cultural diversity in training more generally, and to change the organization's code of practice. Victim Support also issued a 'Good Practice Guidance on Tackling Racist Harassment' in June 2001. The Stephen Lawrence Inquiry, it was minuted, would be 'a regular item to check that recommendations were being implemented'. A volunteer recruitment campaign targeting Blacks and Asians took place in February 1999 (*Victim Support News Service*, December 1999). By 1999–2000, Victim Support was to be represented on three separate Government committees pursuing the implementation of the recommendations of the Macpherson Committee (Victim Support: Report of the Trustees and Financial Statements for year ended 31 March 2000).

[11] Above all, of course, the *The Stephen Lawrence Inquiry*: Cm. 4262-I, published on 24 February 1999.

## The Framing of the Murder

Stephen Lawrence, an eighteen-year old black man, was pursued and murdered in an unprovoked attack by a marauding group of young white men shouting 'what, what nigger!' in Eltham, South London, on 22 April 1993. He had been with a friend, another young black man, Duwayne Brooks, who was left traumatized and incoherent as the witness of his stabbing and death.[12] Lawrence was an A-level

---

[12] The submission by SIA, the National Development Agency for the Black Voluntary Sector, to the Macpherson Inquiry remarked that Brooks' 'treatment by the police at the time was read as evidence of racism. On arrival at the scene of Stephen's murder the police did not acknowledge Duwayne Brooks as a traumatised victim of a racist attack but rather as someone who was hostile and a potential suspect. Fundamental to this point is the police perception of black people as aggressive and as the perpetrators of crimes rather than the victims.' There is, of course, a semantic problem here. The police responding to a murder scene tend to be suspicious of everyone they encounter for practical professional reasons, and there is always a concomitant risk that they will alienate those who may become witnesses at a later stage. Until they have reasons to suppose otherwise, the police suspect parents when a baby has been killed and partners when a woman has been killed, and they have good actuarial grounds for so doing. They do not therefore immediately assign those on the murder scene to the status of innocent bystander. The Metropolitan Police Service's own submission commented that 'When attending scenes of violent crime, officers are frequently faced with both a victim and an assailant. It is reasonable for officers to consider their own safety in these circumstances and to act with appropriate caution throughout such an encounter.' Mark Simmons, then a Chief Inspector, reflected: 'The Inquiry took a different thing. They've seen, Duwayne Brooks, Stephen's friend with him . . . a witness to the murder certainly, no questions, highly excited at the scene, swearing, jumping up and down, called an ambulance, didn't want the police, very abusive towards both . . . One of the first questions he gets asked by the officer who speaks to him is have you got a knife? And there's an imprint there that there's a stereotype of a young black male at play in that. The inspector who turns up at the scene from the territorial support group in his actions and his evidence, there's an inference that . . . , one of the . . . first things he considered was had this been a fight as opposed to an unprovoked attack. While I would say yes, you would consider that as an option . . . It's either within the family or a close associate and that the murderer is often either present at the scene or returns shortly afterwards there when police arrive.' Similarly, Assistant Commissioner Ian Johnston of the Metropolitan Police remarked, 'Duwayne Brooks' there, our people turn up and [gave] Duwayne Brooks what in his terms is a bit of a hard time. I think that would have happened to a white boy because, by and large if you turn up to an event where one of a group of young men is lying on the ground injured, by and large it's the product of a fight of some description . . . '. More generally, see Martin Innes who quotes a detective as saying: 'When you are dealing with a victim's family you are in actuality subject to a number of potentially contradictory considerations . . . in the back of your mind you always have

student hoping to become an architect. He was church-going, middle-class, and law-abiding.[13] His alleged attackers, by contrast, were demonstrably racist,[14] swaggering, violent young men,[15] one of whom stemmed from a notorious criminal family,[16] whose public demeanour continually flaunted their defiance. It was reported, for instance, that their 'faces [were] contorted with hatred as they lashed

that lurking suspicion that they might be involved in the case.' M. Innes; 'The Symbolism of the Murder Investigation', American Society of Criminology meetings, Toronto, 1999. See also his M. Innes; 'Beyond the Macpherson Report: Managing Murder Inquiries in Context', *Sociological Research Online,* Vol. 4, No. 1, 1999, p. 3. Peter Waddington, in an unpublished review of Innes' book, *Investigating Murder,* said that his 'work produces ample justification for the relevance of academic criminology, for observing a single case in isolation can prove misleading and perhaps in some respects Macpherson was misled. Viewed in this wider perspective we find that many of the supposed flaws of the Lawrence investigation are both routine and perfectly justified features of murder inquiries. For instance, Macpherson complained about how Duwayne Brooks had not been treated as a victim, but Innes tells us that detectives habitually regard *everyone,* especially those nearest and dearest to the victim, as suspects, for the very good reason that amongst that number the killer is often to be found. It would have been an abdication of investigative rigour to accept uncritically Brooks's description of how Stephen Lawrence met his death. Macpherson was savagely critical about those police witnesses who refused to accept that Stephen's murder was racially–motivated, yet Innes tells us that any investigation is replete with hypotheses that are not accepted until tested . . .'.

[13] Neither he nor Duwayne Brooks had criminal convictions. Marc Wadsworth of the Anti-Racist Alliance said 'this was the fourth racist murder in that area . . . And also it fitted the, a profile to be blunt with you, that chimed with the news media . . . Clean record, church-going, law-abiding, church-going family, you know, it fitted. This was a suburban victim really.'

[14] Made particularly manifest in the Transcript of Compilation Video IC/3, the result of the police audio-visual surveillance of the suspects conducted in December 1994, which contained copious racist abuse and simulated violence. One complicating feature was that the alleged murderers had been linked to attacks on others in the area, including a white youth, Stacey Benefield, in May 1992. The five suspects seemed to have a penchant for violence which was not exclusively directed at racist targets.

[15] Although, again, despite a number of allegations of serious assaults, their official criminal records were that one had had two police cautions and none had a criminal conviction. One of the suspects had been excluded from school for uncontrollable, violent behaviour.

[16] See the *Daily Mail,* 14 February 1997. It was those family connections, and the possibility of police complicity in protecting a member of a family containing a powerful informant, that led to repeated allegations of corruption as an explanation of the failure of the police investigation. See *The Mercury,* 13 August 1998; P. Foot; 'Tiptoeing by the truth', *Guardian,* 19 May 1998; *Daily Mail* 20 February 1999.

out at anybody within reach . . . '[17] when they quit the Macpherson Inquiry in 1998. Their angry gestures were captured on film and were frozen thereafter to become their defining image. The one was an ideal approximation to the blameless victim,[18] the others to the quintessentially evil perpetrator; the one eligible for beatification, the others for demonization;[19] and there was much about the subsequent portrayal and impact of Stephen Lawrence's death that was Manichaean, a stark confrontation between good and evil[20] (Commander John Grieve, later deeply involved in implementing the Metropolitan Police's anti-racist strategy that was a response to the death, remarked that there was 'Something about Stephen himself, something about the Lawrences. If you can recognise evil, you can recognise good. There's something about Neville [Stephen Lawrence's father]. There's something about the campaign that was run . . . something about Stephen and the events of that night which touched a lot of people.'[21]). And the symbolic confrontation between the innocent victim and his wicked assailants was delineated almost from the first by the volatile politics of race, policing, and criminal justice in South East London in the 1990s, an area described by Brian Cathcart as 'riddled by an unapologetic racism'.[22]

[17] *Daily Mail*, 1 July 1998.
[18] And yet, said Ben Bowling the criminologist, 'even though Stephen Lawrence was in many ways an ideal victim, what made him less than an ideal victim was the fact that he was black, which meant that by the colour of his skin, he was not an unimpeachable victim'. And see D. Brooks; *steve and me: My friendship with Stephen Lawrence and the search for justice*, Abacus, London, 2003, esp. Ch. 6, which gives a less unblemished picture of Lawrence and his family.
[19] Some time after the murder and just after the publication of the report of the Inquiry into its investigation, Paul Condon, the Commissioner of the Metropolitan Police was able to say 'I want those scum to feel they are hunted' (*Daily Mail*, 25 February 1999). For the most senior police officer in the country to call suspects 'scum' is demonization indeed.
[20] Brian Cathcart, the author of a detailed and authoritative book on the murder and its aftermath, concluded, 'The murder had about it a terrible purity: the victim was a young man of impeccable character, the attack was unprovoked; the racial motive was, or should have been, beyond question. It was impossible for anyone to take refuge in the idea that the victim was to blame. The character and judgement of Stephen's parents were all-important.' B. Cathcart; *The Case of Stephen Lawrence*, Viking, London, 1999, p. 417. See also B. Bowling and C. Phillips; *Racism, Crime and Justice*, Longman, London, 2002, p. 15.
[21] 11th Eve Savile lecture, King's College, London, 27 June 2000, my notes.
[22] B. Cathcart; 'The Story that Wouldn't Die', *Night and Day: The Mail on Sunday Review*, 12 October 1997.

The reactions of families and friends to murder can lend themselves to urgent and radical attempts to re-moralize a universe that
seems to have been thrown abruptly and bewilderingly into chaos; to
turbulent emotions centred often on angry accusations targeting
particular hurts; to an insatiable quest for knowledge that might, it
is hoped, enable the bereaved to restore control over a life thrown
out of control; to the ensuing formation and maintenance of strong
binary oppositions in which good and evil, truth and falsehood,
innocence and depravity, friend and enemy are repeatedly set against
one another in a new master logic that erects a shield against disorder; to the commemoration of the dead so that their memory may
be reconstituted and retained; and occasionally, and as a synthesis of
a sort, to campaigning as a conduit for the disturbing feelings that
might otherwise play havoc with the mourner, that allows names to
be remembered, hurts to be remedied, and good to appear out of
tragedy in a restoration of meaning and morality to an otherwise
meaningless, amoral, and wasteful act.[23] Anger can halt time so that
it does not move beyond the moment of injury. Mourning can
become a public identity that, if foregone, might seem like an equally
public betrayal of the dead. Campaigning can be a way of testifying
for those who can no longer speak. It possesses a special moral
authority conferred by harrowing experience. It is a way of being
in truth that cannot be denied. And the outcome is that the activist
survivor of murder (or 'victim' as members of Justice for Victims, the
North of England Victims Association, Victim's Voice, and other
organizations of the bereaved would prefer it) may be long fixed and
adamantine in role. Such reactions are not uncommon. They abound
in the world of homicide survivors, and we have already encountered
the campaigns conducted by parents in the names of Polly Klaas,
Megan Kanka, Sarah Payne, and James Bulger. The responses to the
death of Stephen Lawrence came to be attended by just those polarities, that campaigning, and that unremitting and sometimes diffuse
anger,[24] and Lawrence himself, and his grieving parents, Neville and

---

[23] I deal with the phenomenology of traumatic bereavement at length in my *After
Homicide, op. cit.*

[24] Many (but not all) of the families of homicide victims I met in the course of work
for what would become *After Homicide* were quite understandably angry people
whose distress was directed not only against the world at large but also against specific
incidents that seemed to encapsulate the murders which had so appalled them: the
problem of measures then in place that prevented the police from taking intimate

Doreen, became idealized, just as other murder victims and their families have been idealized in the polar oppositions of intense grief, and particularly after the Lawrence family had been publicly endorsed by the most influential black man of all, Nelson Mandela, the first politician of any prominence to speak to them, less than a month after Stephen Lawrence's death.[25] Following a twenty minutes' meeting in central London on 5 May 1993, organized by Marc Wadsworth of the Anti-Racist Alliance,[26] Mandela said 'the Lawrences' tragedy is our tragedy. I am deeply touched by the brutality of the murder, brutality that we are all used to in South Africa, where black lives are cheap.'[27] Thereafter, the Lawrences and their campaign seemed to be beyond reproach, having borrowed some of Mandela's own moral and political authority.[28] Matthew Seward, a Labour Party official working as a home affairs expert, remarked long after, in October 2000:

The Stephen Lawrence thing: there was the whole issue, I mean, that did sort of roll on in terms of greater prominence and people like Nelson Mandela becoming involved and it became such a, such a big issue... I think [the intervention of Nelson Mandela] was probably a big influence ... these particular events have, you know, political symbolism [in terms of] the wider situation in terms of minorities in London and how it's perceived.

samples from suspects; the problem of the poor supervision of psychiatric patients under 'community care'; the problem of multiple post-mortems being conducted by experts commissioned by the defence, and so on. It is interesting that the anger of Doreen Lawrence was never set in such a context by those who wrote about the events surrounding the murder of her son.

[25] In its evidence to the Macpherson Inquiry, the Commission for Racial Equality talked about the 'international importance of the part played by Nelson Mandela'.

[26] He recalled, without 'the likes of Marc Wadsworth and the Anti-Racist lads [the death] wouldn't have been as influential, had you not had the Anti-Racist Alliance there, then you'd have had no movement, no action at all, had you not had Nelson Mandela coming over and me being able to introduce him to Doreen and Neville, the big publicity...'.

[27] He was to meet them again in July 1997 where he was reported to have said 'we regret such a tragedy. We would like this family to keep strong and remain full of hope', and agreed to be a patron of the Trust established in Stephen Lawrence's name (*The Voice*, 14 July 1997).

[28] A BBC journalist, Nick Higham, commented 'remarkably, Nelson Mandela was pictured meeting Stephen's parents, and some of Mandela's own qualities were transferred in the coverage to the couple themselves, who were soon being routinely described as the "stoical," "dignified" and "deeply religious" parents of a "hardworking," "bright" and "ambitious" son.' BBC News On-Line, 19 February 1999.

A set narrative emerged which could be recited again and again. In the absence of a national newspaper report the day after Stephen Lawrence's murder, Doreen Lawrence contacted *The Independent* newspaper. Brian Cathcart, the author of a book on the death and its aftermath, wrote how *The Independent* journalist, Nick Schoon, then interviewed Stephen Lawrence's father:

Schoon talked mainly to Neville, who went over a story he was to repeat at the press conference and many times after that in the days that followed. Stephen, he said, was a popular young man with high hopes of becoming an architect; he had never been in trouble; the family was law-abiding and unpolitical and had nothing to do with gangs or race matters. In short, neither Stephen nor his parents had ever done anything to deserve this.[29]

Stephen Lawrence's death was to take its chief significance from its place in a structured sequence. It was one of a succession of attacks[30]

[29] B. Cathcart; *The Case of Stephen Lawrence, op. cit.*, p. 107.

[30] There had been several quite discrepant counts of racial incidents during the early 1990s, but they may convey both something of the size of the problem and of the many attempts to measure it. According to the annual report of the local police division, there had been 101 reports of racial assaults, of which 10 were not substantiated, 16 were 'no crimed' and 15 arrests were made in 1991–2. The Metropolitan Police; Greenwich and Plumstead Community Safety Unit produced an undated Briefing Note in which 531 incidents were recorded for 1992; 544 for 1993; and 622 for 1994. Other figures compiled in the Greenwich Borough Joint Council/Police Racial Incident Unit 1996/7 Annual Report recorded 376 reports of racial incidents in 1992, 367 in 1993 and 400 in 1994 (*incidents* are of course a more elastic category than *assaults*). The Greenwich and Plumstead Divisions of the Metropolitan Police had monitored the incidence of racial incidents since the 1970s, and had reported a growth in the level of attacks during the early 1990s. According to the Greenwich Housing Department there had been 115 reported cases of racial violence and harassment in 1990–91, 120 in 1992, and 184 in 1993. (Taken from Re Lawrence Inquiry—Submission by Greenwich Council, 2 April 1998.) The Metropolitan Police counted 258 racial incidents in 1992, and 236 in 1993, representing over 7.6% of all such incidents in the whole area covered by the Metropolitan Police Service. According to the police, part of the scale of reports could be explained by the monitoring of racial incidents that began in Plumstead in 1988 and the subsequent establishment of a Racial Incidents Unit in 1990, at first staffed by a single officer, later by two officers, and by concomitant campaigns to encourage people to report racial incidents, including a campaign mounted by the Commission for Racial Equality in 1993 (Metropolitan Police: Strategic Analysis Unit: Environmental Scan for the London Borough of Greenwich (1992/93), November 1997).

and murders[31] targeted at black and Asian victims[32] in and around the London Borough of Greenwich,[33] it was thought to be part of a clear pattern[34] (he was, declared a local newspaper, 'Killed—just for being black'[35]), and it was read in the context of an upsurge of racist violence lent even greater political urgency and definition for some by the establishment in 1988 of the headquarter offices of a neo-Fascist organization in Welling, in the adjoining London Borough of Bexley in Kent.[36] Those, like the

---

[31] To be sure, homicide remains a relatively uncommon event in England and Wales and it can still command attention. There had been 623 offences recorded as murders and manslaughters in 1991; 581 in 1992; and 565 in 1993, of whom 110 were young men between 16 and 30, and 122 were male victims stabbed as Stephen Lawrence had been (*Criminal Statistics England and Wales 2000*, Cm. 5312, Home Office, London, 2001). There were 166 cases of homicide in the Metropolitan Police district between April 1993 and March 1994, of which 143, or 86% were 'cleared up' (*Report of the Commissioner of Police of the Metropolis 1993/94*, July 1994).

[32] Lawrence's murder was presented by the Anti-Racist Alliance in a leaflet as 'the fourth killing of a young black male in the area in the space of two years'. Between 1991 and April 1993, when Stephen Lawrence was killed, the murders that were connected politically as a patterned series including the killing of 15-year old Rolan Adams in Greenwich, South London in February 1991; Rohit Duggal in July 1992 in Eltham, South London; and Ruhullah Aramesh in Thornton Heath, South London, in July 1992. Between April 1993 and February 1999, when the Macpherson Inquiry reported, there was the murder of Michael Menson in January 1997 in Edmonton; and the alleged murder of Ricky Reel in Kingston, Surrey, in October 1997.

[33] In 1991, the last Census year before the death of Stephen Lawrence, 12.7% of the Borough's population was classified as belonging to Black and minority ethnic groups.

[34] For an analogous case of reading pattern into serial killings see P. Jenkins; 'Catch Me Before I Kill More: Seriality as Modern Monstrosity', *Cultural Analysis*, Vol. 3, 2002.

[35] *Greenwich and Eltham Mercury*, 29 April 1993.

[36] Thus 7,000 people at a demonstration on the first anniversary of Rolan Adams' death protested at the racial attacks and demanded the closure of the BNP office in Welling. The Anti-Racist Alliance claimed in one of its leaflets that 'Since the British National Party opened its headquarters in Bexley, this part of London has become known as the race hate capital of Britain.' In the case of the murder of Stephen Lawrence, the connection may have been a little tenuous, no more than a matter of an elective affinity. The Transcript of Compilation Video IC/3 contains a passage in which the suspects show some contempt of the BNP and its followers: 'They're thick as shit coz they're getting all the fucking skinheads and all that to stand out and be all their armed guards and all that and hows anyone gonna wanna vote for them, perhaps like you know all these straight bods they wanna vote for them mate but they see all these fucking yobbo fucking skinheads and they think who wants to vote for them. . .'. For its part, the BNP denied that the suspects were members (*Daily Mail* 17 February

Anti-Nazi League,[37] protesting at the foothold acquired by the British National Party[38] (or BNP), found it easy by syllogism to link the palpable presence of racist politics with a growth in racist assaults.[39] Both the attacks and the headquarters had excited political agitation outside and inside Parliament,[40] in local

1997). Of course, membership is not a necessary prerequisite of an influence being exerted by an organization on individuals.

[37] For the Anti-Racist Alliance, the focus on neo-Nazism obscured the importance of the politics of racism. Marc Wadsworth of the ARA commented 'You know I coined a phrase that Greenwich was the racist murder capital of Britain. I coined a phrase that you know, we were trying to close down a Nazi bunker which the anti-Nazi League latched onto 'cause that was their obsession. They weren't particularly concerned about racist attacks, it supported their thesis about the rise in Nazism. That was a complication, that was a difficulty. And it did muddy the waters, it did make things more complicated in dealing with this particular family.'

[38] The BNP was founded in 1982. According to its web site, 'Membership of the British National Party is open to those of British or kindred European ethnic descent. While we welcome contact and co-operation with nationalists and patriots of other races, and with the many non-whites who also oppose enforced multi-racialism, we ask them to respect our right to an organisation of our own, for our own, as we respect and applaud their measures to organise themselves in like fashion.' The BNP has policies on a plethora of areas. On immigration, for instance, its position is that 'On current demographic trends, we, the native British people, will be an ethnic minority in our own country within sixty years. To ensure that this does not happen, and that the British people retain their homeland and identity, we call for an immediate halt to all further immigration, the immediate deportation of criminal and illegal immigrants, and the introduction of a system of voluntary resettlement whereby those immigrants who are legally here will be afforded the opportunity to return to their lands of ethnic origin assisted by a generous financial incentives both for individuals and for the countries in question.'

[39] For example, in 'The danger of Nazi BNP vote' by Helen Shooter, it was argued that 'The BNP may want to appear as a respectable party, but when they hold an election leaflet in one hand they hold a baseball bat in the other. Racist attacks in the area shot up after the BNP set up its headquarters in Welling, near Bexley, in 1989.' *Socialist Worker*, No. 1706, 22 July 2000. The link between the BNP and racial violence in the area had also been discerned by the Commission for Racial Equality, whose Chair, Herman Ouseley, wrote to Peter Bottomley, MP, on 27 April 1993: 'racial attacks are often perceived as attacks on individuals and frequently the role played by extremist organisations is ignored. It is with this in mind that I am concerned about the proximity of the British National Party's headquarters in the area where the stabbing [of Stephen Lawrence] took place.'

[40] For example, the Hillsborough Survivors and Relatives and Supporters for Justice Campaign who wrote to the Lawrences to say that 'Whilst our group doesn't have to deal directly with the cancer of racism and facism, we have found out that the police and law care little for ordinary people, and it's up to us all to act on our own

councils[41] and on the streets. The local police reported that 1992, the year preceding the murder, had 'been a busy and difficult one . . . Following two separate murders in Thamesmead and subsequent protest marches, racial tension was high.' And, the report continued:

The murder of Rolan Adams has remained an issue throughout the past year. Feelings in the area were fuelled by the subsequent though unconnected killing of Orville Blair, a British National Party (BNP) march in May and the presence of the BNP bookshop in the neighbouring Borough of Bexley. A principal cause of minority ethnic anger and concern were particular groupings of youths ('gang' lends an unjustified credence to them)—mainly white whose anti-social activities included racial harassment.[42]

That pre-existing anger, concern, and protest could readily and rapidly be extended to envelop and confer meaning on the death of Stephen Lawrence as part of a seemingly logical progression[43] (a placard for the Stephen Lawrence Family Campaign bore the legend: 'No more Racist Killings. Remember Stephen Lawrence. Close the BNP', and a draft declaration by the Greenwich Council for Racial Equality read 'The plague of racism has taken the life of yet another innocent child, Stephen Lawrence. . . . We call for justice for Stephen Lawrence and the victims of all racist murders . . . We ask all responsible authorities to take action against racist activities . . . We call for the headquarters of the British National Party in Welling to be closed. In order for evil to triumph, it is enough for good people to do nothing').

initiatives whilst gathering the support of the people.' Undated. Union branches, such as Swansea UNISON, also expressed support.

[41] Immediately after the murder of Stephen Lawrence, the Leader of Greenwich Council wrote to the Leader of the London Borough of Bexley on the 27 April 1993, describing the murders of Adams, Duggal, and Lawrence, arguing that the existence of the BNP 'Centre in Welling is [not] unconnected with these appalling acts of violence upon law-abiding citizens of Greenwich' and asking him to review the position of the BNP Centre.

[42] J. Philpott; foreword to Metropolitan Police, Plumstead Division, *Management Report 1992*, no page numbers.

[43] Best argued that 'few criminal acts lack the potential to be defined as instances of some larger crime problem. In addition to generalizing from particular cases, claims about crime waves imply changing levels . . . ' J. Best; *Random Violence: How We Talk about New Crimes and New Victims*, University of California Press, Berkeley, 1999, p. 36.

Practical and symbolic connections were to be endorsed and amplified by a retinue of political groups who attached themselves within days to the Lawrence family. The Anti-Nazi League[44](or ANL), Panther UK, the Anti-Racist Alliance[45] (or ARA), and others, including churches, trades union branches (and particularly members of UNISON ('the union for people delivering public services')), and the local council,[46] supported at a distance by Members of Parliament, were already joined in conflict with the BNP and

[44] The ANL was founded in 1970 as a response to the National Front, a racialist organization of the time, and was re-launched in January 1992 in response to the growth of 'Euro-Nazis'. It describes itself on its web site as 'a broad based, mass organisation. Anyone who wants to stop the Nazis can join, regardless of political belief, religion or creed. We have one single aim, to stop the Nazis reaching a wider audience and growing. This is done by pinning the label of NAZI clearly on the likes of the BNP and NF. They have the same aim as Hitler's Nazis. Far from believing the Holocaust never took place, they wish to repeat it. We fight them in many ways, by use of propaganda, demonstrations and counter-mobilisations.'

[45] The Anti-Racist Alliance was a predominantly Black organization that, according to the web site of its youth wing (no adult web site was found), believed 'that as a collective, we can combat the evil injustice of racism in our society by initiating pro-active solutions'. The web site then proceeded approvingly to quote Malcolm X: 'We believe that our fight is just, we believe that our grievances are just, we believe that the evil practices against Black people in this society are criminal and those who engage in such criminal practices are to be looked upon as nothing but criminals, and we believe that we are within our rights to fight those criminals by any means necessary.' It campaigned against racism, and especially what it deemed to be the racism of the police and politicians. Marc Wadsworth, at the time the National Secretary of the ARA, summarizing the conclusions of a national conference, observed that 'What we are witnessing is race-hate, whipped up by unscrupulous politicians, feeding off the economic recession... On 22nd April 1993, Stephen Lawrence... was brutally murdered in Eltham, sparking widespread protests. The ARA was contacted by the family to give help and advice. Since the tragedy, the ARA has organised several events with the Lawrence family aimed at highlighting the murder, so that Stephen's killers are caught and severely punished.' At a Workshop on Racist Attacks and the Police, the *rapporteur*, Lee Jasper, said 'It is important to identify the police as one of the main perpetrators of racist attacks and thereby set out an agenda to respond to this.' The general conclusion was that: 'Throughout the conference there were repeated calls for unity within the Black communities and for mass mobilisation around the issues of racism.' (*Outlaw racial harassment*, A report on the Anti-Racist Alliance national conference in Greenwich, June 1993).

[46] For one representative action by Greenwich Council at an event commemorating the death of Rolan Adams, see *Greenwich and Eltham Mercury*, 10 September 1992.

protesting about racist attacks,[47] and they saw in what had happened yet another incident in a series, one more manifestation of the cruelty of race and racism in British society and its institutions,[48] and in the British police in particular,[49] and another opportunity to deplore the victimized status of the Black population[50] and to mount an anti-racist politics. The *Woolwich and Plumstead News Shopper*, a local newspaper, reported that 'The racially-motivated murder of Stephen Lawrence has re-kindled anger at the rising number of racist attacks in the borough . . .'. Hardev Dhillion of the Greenwich Council for Racial Equality, warned: 'The community is angry about what's happening in the borough. I think the young have been very patient, but something has to be done to remove the BNP from Welling.'[51] The newspaper then solicited and reproduced the responses of a number of local political figures, including the local Member of Parliament, the local police Chief Superintendent, the leader of Greenwich Council, and the Anti-Racist Alliance, much in the manner described by Hall and his colleagues in *Policing the Crisis*,[52] to create a powerful representation of united

[47] Which tended to be seen rather exclusively as a process involving black victims and white perpetrators. For a protest against the local police Racial Incidents Unit treating black assaults on white victims as racist, see *The Voice*, 25 February 1992.

[48] Linda Bellos, a radical Black activist in South London, and former leader of Lambeth Council, declared that 'I could go on naming black people who have died in dreadful circumstances and for whose deaths no one was brought to justice. In the black community we can all recite their names by heart; after all we are a relatively small community.' *Daily Mail*, 19 February 1997.

[49] And that was part of a wider and engrained pattern of mistrust. Peter Waddington reflected that black-police interaction in the United Kingdom is governed by mutually hostile stereotyping. 'Discretion, "Respectability" and Institutional Police Racism', *Sociological Research Online*, Vol. 4, No. 1, 1999, p. 8.

[50] Betsy Stanko remarked that ' . . . women's advocates, minority campaign groups, children's rights, and homophile organisations [have] harnessed the political message of the fear of crime for their own campaigning purposes'. E. Stanko; 'Victims R US: the life history of 'fear of crime' and the politicization of violence', unpublished, undated, p. 2. See also her 'Re-thinking violence, re-thinking social policy', in G. Lewis *et al.*; *Rethinking Social Policy*, Sage, London, 2000, esp. p. 10; and J. Jacobs and K. Potter; *Hate Crimes: Criminal Law & Identity Politics*, Oxford University Press, New York, 1998.

[51] *Woolwich and Plumstead News Shopper*, 28 April 1993.

[52] S. Hall *et al.*; *Policing the Crisis: Mugging, the State and Law and Order*, Macmillan, London, 1978.

political outrage and the beginnings of what some would call a moral panic.[53]

In this manner, a mass of individuals and organizations, little and large, established and yet to be established, cohered around the issue and sought symbolic and political sustenance from it, imparting a distinctive symbolism and politics in their turn. Within two days of the murder, the ARA held a torchlight vigil and wreath-laying ceremony.[54] Marc Wadsworth of the ARA reflected that the families of the victims 'had no locus in the legal system. So they had no right to representation, no legal aid . . . So we pioneered a new model because we'd learned a great deal from the Rolan Adams case actually. (This is a picture of the demonstration that we helped to organise it and see our banner's there . . . ) As an anti-racist campaign we were concerned about black families and the huge rise in racist attacks.' There were demonstrations linking Stephen Lawrence's death to the larger spate of racist killings (Stephen Lawrence 'was murdered for no other reason than that he was Black. The racists who killed him did so for the same reason they murdered Rolan Adams, Orville Black and Rohit Duggal—because of the colour of their skin,' claimed an ARA leaflet advertising a 'Human Chain for Justice, on 16 May 1993). A Youth Against Racism in Europe demonstration against the BNP headquarters was held in Plumstead on 8 May, and the speakers included the radical Labour Member of Parliament, Tony Benn, Neville Lawrence, and the family of Rohit Duggal.[55] The Indian Workers Association organized a meeting on 22 May to

[53] See S. Cohen; *Folk Devils and Moral Panics*, Paladin, London, 1973. In a preface to a third edition of his book, published by Routledge in 2002, Stan Cohen, one of the authors of the term, explicitly exempted the Lawrence case from identification as a moral panic. It lacked, he said, three ingredients: a suitable enemy (although I would contend that the alleged assailants and the police were certainly vilified on a wide scale); a suitable victim (but I would argue that it would be difficult to conceive a more suitable victim than Stephen Lawrence); and, third, a consensus that the beliefs or actions denounced were not 'insulated entities' (but universal institutional racism must surely represent just such a candidate entity). Perhaps there is a political awkwardness in applying such a term to an issue where so compelling a consensus appeared to exist.

[54] *News Shopper*, 23 April 1993.

[55] Its leaflet recited 'Stephen Lawrence, only 18 with his whole life ahead of him, was murdered by a group of Nazi thugs. He is the fourth young person to lose his life in this way. This racist violence and murder is the direct result of the Nazi British National Party...We are marching against racist murders and violence. SHUT DOWN the BNP HQ.'

protest at the 'racist murder of Stephen Lawrence'. A National Black Caucus pronounced that Lawrence was a 'symbolic son and brother to all of us' and organized a benefit night for him and Rolan Adams on 31 May. The ARA mounted a national march against racist murders on the 12 June in the names of Ruhullah Aramesh and Stephen Lawrence. The ARA picketed Plumstead Police Station in August demanding extra resources for the investigation of the murder of Stephen Lawrence.[56] A Black Unity and Freedom Party condemned 'the continual white British racist power structure to put down those Lynch mobs... As Black people assert themselves throughout the world, the white backlash is rarely far away. THE BLACK UNITY AND FREEDOM PARTY, respects, and share the grief of the Lawrence family, and gladly, will give whatever support we can.'

What was markedly missing from that retinue were the established (or indeed the fringe) victims' groups that would have drawn attention to the death as the murder of a *crime* victim and to the Lawrences as the 'secondary victims' of a murder.[57] Victim Support had sent a volunteer who had retired when it became evident that the family was already attended by a large group of supporters. Support After Murder and Manslaughter, Justice for Victims, Mothers Against Murder and Aggression, and the rest were absent. From the first, Stephen Lawrence's murder was construed as an issue in the organized politics of race, not the organized politics of murder.

Assistant Commissioner Ian Johnston, a senior police officer at Scotland Yard, later deeply involved with the events, reflected that the scale of Stephen Lawrence's posthumous influence was due to the 'timing around it. You know it's at a moment in time. He was a nice, Stephen was a very nice boy. They were a very nice family. So they were good clients if you like for the cause.' And Rajiv Menon, the barrister who represented Duwayne Brooks at the Macpherson Inquiry, said 'I think [the murder and its aftermath formed] a particular moment in the anti-racist movement's history... Just before the murder of Stephen Lawrence the Anti-Racist Alliance had been formed and for a brief period of time it did offer something new because it brought together a lot of people. (In the end it was a disaster because vested interests took over... )'

[56] *Greenwich and Eltham Mercury,* 5 August 1993.
[57] I am grateful to Janet Foster for reminding me of this point.

The death was a political issue that was injected directly into Parliament,[58] and particularly by the Lawrences' own constituency Member, Peter Bottomley, then the Conservative Member of Parliament for Eltham. Within six days of the murder, on the 28 April 1993, he asked five questions in the House of Commons about racial attacks, stabbings, and the British National Party.[59] On the same day, he wrote to the head teachers of all the secondary schools in his constituency seeking witnesses to assist the police in their investigation of the murder: 'There is a particular responsibility of the white community. Murderous attacks have been made by white youths on black youths locally... There is an obligation to fight racism whether organised or not, it has no place in our community or our nation.' And a number of the head teachers in their turn urged Peter Bottomley to do his utmost to bring about the closure of the BNP office. It would, said one, 'be seen as a very important sign that public institutions are not prepared to tolerate the presence of such an obviously racist focus'. Peter Bottomley developed working links with the Anti-Racist Alliance and the Commission for Racial Equality. He sought the introduction of a separate offence of racial violence, telling Herman Ouseley, the Chair of the Commission, that it would 'demonstrate unambiguously the abhorrence by Parliament

---

[58] And that was part of a continuing pattern. For example, on 31 March 1993, just before the murder of Stephen Lawrence, a motion was moved in the House of Commons by Bernie Grant, a radical Black MP, John Austin-Walker, a local MP, and five other members, to mark the second anniversary of the death of Rolan Adams, to commend his parents 'for their stalwart support for the Anti-Racist Alliance in its struggle to combat racial terror; and welcome[d] the proposal to establish a Rolan Adams Memorial Fund to aid victims of racial violence'. Another motion headed 'Racial Violence and the British National Party', put on 26 April 1993, immediately after the death of Stephen Lawrence, and supported, this time by forty-seven MPs (including Paul Boateng, the future Home Office Minister), stated 'this House shares the sense of outrage... following the brutal racist killing of Stephen Lawrence... recognises the state of shock in the area in view of the previous murders of Rolan Adams and Rohit Duggal; believes that the presence and activity of the British National Party in the area incites racial hatred and contributes to the level of racial violence...'.

[59] His questions were addressed to the Home Secretary and they touched on the number of incidents of racial abuse in South East London the membership and activities of the British National Party; the number of proceedings taken against racist organizations; and how many black and how many white youths had died from stabbings in South East London, London proper, and England, how many of the killers were black and how many white.

and government of this kind of crime'.[60] He appealed to the murderers of Stephen Lawrence to surrender themselves, saying 'It's better not to try to hide. Come forward and talk to the police.'[61] He wrote supportive letters and donated money to the Stephen Lawrence Family Campaign. He offered his home as a refuge to the family.

It is common after the violent death of a young person that copious symbolic work, often following its own vernacular conventions, will be done to refashion and preserve memory. So it was with Stephen Lawrence. He was buried in Jamaica, not in London, and that was a potent statement.[62] Poems were written in his honour.[63] There were annual memorial services on the anniversary of his death.[64] A plaque was laid at the place where he had died. A Memorial Trust was established with support from Caribbean High Commissioners, the Chairman of the London Stock Exchange, Cliff Richard, and Peter Bottomley. Neville and Doreen Lawrence took part in a People's Tribunal on Racial Violence and Justice in April 1994, extending protest beyond the direct criminal victimization of minority ethnic people to include those who were held to have been wrongly convicted or harshly treated by the criminal justice system (and that reflected an inbuilt ambiguity of the politics of black victimization[65] to which I shall return). Brought together

[60] Letter to Chair of Commission for Racial Equality, 30 April 1993.

[61] In unidentified press cutting in Peter Bottomley's files.

[62] I am grateful to Coretta Phillips for this point.

[63] One, for instance, was composed by Alison Moore. The concluding stanza read:
'Your life has shown so many people of every race colour and creed.
That inflicting pain because of colour, for this there is no need.
I know you're up in heaven, building all the things you dreamed.
And here on earth we're trying to build, a place of love and peace.'
Such poems, informal and formal shrines (there was an inscribed memorial stone laid at the spot where Stephen Lawrence was killed), candle-bearing ceremonies, and the like are stock ways in which people try to restore meaning to murder.

[64] For example, a Song for Stephen in support of the Lawrence family was held at the Greenwich Seventh-day Adventist Church on 21 June 1997; and a vigil was conducted at the site of his murder on 22 April 1998.

[65] Recall the period of Black Power in the United States where black inmates claimed that they were political prisoners. That legacy survives in, say, the International Concerned Family & Friends Of Mumia Abu-Jamal (ICFFMAJ), and, in the United Kingdom, in an organization called Prisoners of War which argues that 'We believe all prisoners are inside for inherently political reasons, as both the concept and the reality of justice and punishment are political and central to the functioning of this system.' *Do or Die* Issue 7.

were those who spoke about Rolan Adams; Joy Gardner (who had died in July 1993, after being gagged and restrained with a body belt at her home, whilst being served with a deportation order); Quddus Ali (a 17 year-old victim of an assault by a group of older white people in September 1993 in Tower Hamlets); Ruhullah Aramesh; 'the M25 Three' (convicted of a murder, assaults, and robbery that took place in December 1988); Winston Silcott (found guilty and subsequently acquitted on appeal of killing Police Constable Keith Blakelock during the Broadwater Farm riot in Tottenham, North London, in 1985); Satpal Ran (convicted and subsequently acquitted on appeal of a killing that took place in Birmingham in 1986), and others. Doreen Lawrence observed, 'I want people to see that Stephen's death is not an isolated incident. Racially motivated violence takes place as regularly as you blink an eyelid and we need to take a stand.'[66] A Stephen Lawrence Family Campaign was inaugurated and ribbons were sold in its aid in April 1996. There was a proposal to found Stephen Lawrence Memorial Traineeships in Architecture in early 1999.

Neville and Doreen Lawrence themselves became public figures[67] associated with (and lending weight to) a plethora of human rights and anti-racist campaigns.[68] They were placed on the *Sunday Times* Power List 1999 and named Media Personalities of the Year by the Commission for Racial Equality in the same year, the first time the award was made (the editor of *The Mirror*, making the award, said 'it has been the sheer force of their own personalities that has

---

[66] *Caribbean Times*, 19 April 1994.

[67] They were both eventually to be awarded the Order of the British Empire in 2002.

[68] Neville Lawrence was asked, for example, to endorse a training pack on racial harassment (letter from Leeds Racial Harassment Project, 27 July 1998). He attended a lunch as part of the Freedom for Ismail Besikei: Peace in Kurdistan Campaign in Scotland, in July 1998; with his wife, he was invited to be Guests of Honour at the African and Caribbean Finance Forum Charity Winter Ball in November 1998; they were recipients of the RADAR (Royal Association for Disability and Rehabilitation) Abbey National People of the Year Awards in 1998; they were invited frequently to appear on radio and television (for example in a debate about race relations in the United Kingdom on LWT in September 1998); to speak at the NUS Black Students Conference in November 1998; the annual general meeting of the National Assembly Against Racism in the same month; the Greenbelt Festival organized by the Church of England Archbishops' Council in July 1999; and so on.

shaken this country into confronting the ongoing cancer of racism that seeps through our society'[69]).

In short, Stephen Lawrence had become the centrepiece of an epic tragedy and an epic campaign played out before the public gaze,[70] an iconic public figure who animated and personified very general questions about race and racism in criminal justice,[71] and much of what was done for and to him was phrased on a plane of symbolic politics that moved far beyond the particular circumstances of one sad death on a suburban street.[72] Consider the closing remarks of Azim Hajee, a member of the Stephen Lawrence Family Campaign, in his address to the Trades Union Congress Black Workers Conference on 27 April 1996:

... let us remember Stephen—a promising Architect student, who had everything to live for, before his life was taken away callously, efficiently, and brutally. We will always remember Stephen—in the words of Doreen, his spirit burns bright, burns torrid orange in our hearts. Conference, let us do something more. Let us commit our unconditional solidarity to the parents—that we will ensure that our unions and the TUC will continue to remain 100% behind the parents and their exemplary quest for justice and truth.

Consider too the black criminologist Ben Bowling's preface to the revised second edition of his *Violent Racism: Victimization, Policing and Social Context*:

For reasons which I have yet to fathom, I felt unable to describe the details of this brutal and untimely death. I felt I could not do justice to the horror of the stabbing, to the pain of the families and friends, or the disbelief and incredulity at the ineptitude and arrogance of the police. This extraordinary tale of terror, error and misjudgement which can never be compensated ... the murder of Stephen Lawrence symbolizes not only the scores of

---

[69] CRE News Release, 23 April 1999.

[70] The Campaign Against Racism and Fascism talked on its web site about how 'The heroic struggle waged on behalf of Stephen Lawrence has spurred a nation-wide hunger for a movement for racial justice ...'.

[71] David Downes and Rod Morgan observed that 'the murder of Stephen Lawrence ... came to symbolise both the character of violent racism and the inadequacy of policies to address it'. 'The Skeletons in the Cupboard: The Politics of Law and Order at the Turn of the Millennium', in M. Maguire *et al.* (eds.); *The Oxford Handbook of Criminology*, Third edition, Oxford University Press, Oxford, 2002, p. 311.

[72] For example, a memorial stone that was laid at the place where he was killed was vandalized more than once. See *New Shopper*, 10 June 1998.

black and Asian people who have been murdered by racists in Britain, but also the thousands who, day-in, day-out, are intimidated, abused, and assaulted because of the colour of their skin.[73]

Stephen Lawrence had been promoted to such a position of importance, such a pressing preoccupation in the lives of those who were campaigning for convictions, that his mother expressed surprise when she was told by her Member of Parliament, Peter Bottomley, that the then Prime Minister, John Major, had not heard of him ('That said a lot', she said[74]). Neither, she complained, had she received any communication from the Home Secretary,[75] the Queen, or the Leader of the Opposition.[76] She was reported to have been distressed that the detonation of an IRA lorry bomb at Bishopsgate in the City of London[77] just after the murder had displaced reporting of her son's death from the front pages of newspapers.[78]

## The Stephen Lawrence Family Campaign

Victims of yet another outrage, part of a sequence already mustering a developed political response[79] and a pattern of expectancy, the

[73] B. Bowling; *Violent Racism: Victimization, Policing and Social Context*, Oxford University Press, Oxford, 1998 pp. xii, xiii.

[74] J. Moorehead; 'Mrs Lawrence', *Guardian*, 20 January 1997.

[75] A Home Office Minister, Peter Lloyd was to retort that there had been no neglect by the Government. He had himself seen a delegation of Members of Parliament and members of the Lawrence family soon after his murder. 'I also visited Mr and Mrs Lawrence at their home. I have been in the Home Office for some five years now, and this was the first time I had visited or written to the family of anyone who had been murdered. I continue to take a close interest in the developments in this case.' Letter to the editor, *Caribbean Times*, 30 June 1994.

[76] *Caribbean Times*, 19 April 1994.

[77] The explosion on 24 April 1993 caused over £300 m. worth of damage, killed one person and injured over 50 others.

[78] J. Upton, review of Macpherson Report and B. Cathcart; *The Case of Stephen Lawrence*, London Review of Books, 1 July 1999, Vol. 21, No. 13. John Upton describes himself as a lawyer who lives in London.

[79] Marc Wadsworth wrote 'Just a few months after the Anti-Racist Alliance held its Racial Harassment conference at Greenwich, Stephen Lawrence became the fourth Black youth to be murdered in the area since the nazi British National Party moved in ... What we are witnessing is race-hate, whipped up by unscrupulous politicians, feeding off the economic recession ...'. Foreword to *Outlaw racial harassment*, A report on the Anti-Racist Alliance national conference in Greenwich, June 1993, p. 5.

Lawrences attracted almost instant support. The day after the murder, the Lawrence family were visited by Ros Howells[80] of the Greenwich Council for Racial Equality, who became a close adviser: 'And my first thing was one of support, to find out what they needed, is there anything we can do. That's part of my culture but it's also well a bit of my role. And you have to understand in Greenwich we had two other murders, three murders really before that. That was quite serious and it was all taking of a black man's life you know, by the knife . . . So we were all on red alert. I met the Lawrences then. And I have to say that all I did at that time was listen to them and tried to be supportive and see if I could assist them in anyway.' I shall return to Ros Howells below because she was to play a major role as a *confidante* and political intermediary.

Four days after the murder, and on the recommendation of the Black Lawyers' Society who had been approached by Palma Black of the Anti-Racist Alliance, a solicitor, Imran Khan, became attached to the Lawrence family *pro bono publico*. It is most uncommon for bereaved families to be so legally represented (after all, as we have seen, they had no legal standing as parties) and certainly at such an early stage in an investigation (although some campaigning groups of homicide survivors like Justice for Victims would wish it were otherwise) and it lent a formality, consequence, and occasional *froideur*[81] to encounters between the Lawrences and others that

---

[80] According to the National Black Womens Network on-line, 'Baroness Howells of St David, OBE was the first black woman to sit on the GLC's [Greater London Council's] Training Board; the first female member of the Court of Governors of the University of Greenwich; and was the Vice Chair at the London Voluntary Services Council. She had an impressive career in grassroot organizations before making her mark at the Greenwich Council for Racial Equality. She has worked tirelessly in the area of race relations and community services. It was during this time that she was able to use her influence on behalf of the New Cross Fire victims, Roland Adams, and the Stephen Lawrence Family Campaign. It was her contribution to the development of racial equality policies in Britain, and her personal involvement in community projects to enhance opportunities for Black people, that led to her being given the ordinary officer status of the Civil Division of Her Majesty's most Excellent Order of the British Empire (OBE) in December 1993. In 1999, Baroness Howells was appointed by Prime Minister Tony Blair, as one of 22 new Labour Life Peers.'

[81] For example, the Metropolitan Police Service solicitors department effectively told Imran Khan in March 1994 to cease busying himself in aspects of the case: '. . . your letter is disturbing. No information has been ignored by the police. On the contrary, it is you who have been ignoring communications from the investigating team . . . It would be altogether better if . . . any matters relevant to the investigation of

was equally uncommon. (Simon Holdaway, the criminologist and adviser to the Commission for Racial Equality, claimed that relations with the police broke down rapidly as a result.[82]) But it was not uncommon in the racial politics of crime and victimization in London in the early 1990s. Imran Khan remarked:

It wasn't unusual for me back in the '93 and the reason... is that my involvement is from the anti-racist way. And I think rather than from a crime perspective in terms of general crime, if I can put it that way, the experience of black people in particular has been that there is no voice for them. And there is, white victims of crime tend to be able to get access to justice in a better way... So what I was involved in, particularly in West London and Southall... was advising families who weren't getting justice. So they would be for example, attacked, perpetrator next door or down the road, police arrive and the victim's arrested. That's one way of getting involved. And so you would then make representations on behalf, you'd represent the victim, and then subsequently if there's an acquittal or the police accept that in fact the victim, the person is in fact the victim, then you would want to ensure that there was justice done by prosecution. So I was already, not in such a grand scale as the Lawrence case, but already representing victims in that way. So it's wasn't unusual.

His role was to play the advocate and counsellor across a broad front:

... most victims that you would represent, there was a plethora of things that they will want you to deal with as a lawyer, the inquest, dealing with coroner's office, return of the body, and those sorts of things. Then they'll want to ensure that the police are doing the job properly, advice as to what happens, and dealing with outside agencies. And in a sense you become a buffer and you know, the police complained about that as being a barrier but in a proper sense, it's the buffer, it's to avoid all the hassles the family get.

There was much for the Lawrences, Imran Khan, Suresh Grover, Ros Howells,[83] the Family Campaign, and its satellite organizations to

Stephen's murder could please be handled where both the objectivity and expertise lie, namely, by Detective Superintendent Brian Weeden and his team.' The report of the Kent Police inquiry into the investigation claimed that the relations between the Lawrence family and the police had collapsed by May 1993, very soon indeed after the murder.

[82]  S. Holdaway; 'Statement to Inquiry into the Police Investigation of the murder of Stephen Lawrence', 23 April 1998.

[83]  Cathcart said that after the *putsch* of 1994, Howells and Khan became the Lawrences' most trusted advisers. B. Cathcart; *The Case of Stephen Lawrence, op. cit.*, p. 176.

criticize and investigate. There had been a flawed police investigation which had led to an aborted public prosecution of three of the suspects in the summer of 1993;[84] a re-launched, vigorous, but ultimately barren 'second' police investigation after August 1993; an internal review of the investigation conducted between August and November 1993 which was later dismissed in an evaluation by the Kent Police as misleading in its 'positive flavour'; an announcement by the CPS in November 1993 that they could not take a case to court for want of evidence and the mounting of an unsuccessful private prosecution by the Lawrence family in lieu of the CPS[85] in April 1996[86] (and rumours of a second private prosecution in July 1997;[87]) requests to the Home Secretary and the Chief Crown Prosecutor in November 1993 for public explanations of 'the handling of the case by the police' and the decision to drop charges; a preliminary coroner's inquest in December 1993 that was adjourned, as such inquests are, pending the outcome of police inquiries, and then resumed in February 1997;[88] allegations, accusations, and invitations to sue levelled against the suspects by the *Daily Mail* newspaper straight on the heels of the second inquest;[89] talk at the same time about the possibility of a civil suit for compensation from those selfsame suspects;[90] an outside assessment of the performance of the Metropolitan Police by the Kent Police in March 1997 that had been triggered by a letter from Doreen Lawrence to the Commissioner the month before; and yet no conviction.

[84] Neil Acourt was charged on 13 May 1993 and Luke Knight on 23 July 1993. Both were discharged on 27 July 1993 after the Crown Prosecution Service announced that 'there is insufficient evidence to proceed'.

[85] The Director of Public Prosecutions wrote to Peter Bottomley on 10 October 1995, 'the private prosecutors have not asked the Crown Prosecution Service to take over the prosecution. However, if they were to make such a request, the Crown Prosecution Service would only be able to take over the prosecution to pursue, if the tests met the tests set out in the Code for Crown Prosecutors ... '.

[86] The funds of which were nevertheless paid for out of public funds, see *Daily Mail*, 26 April 1996.

[87] Minutes and Agenda of Stephen Lawrence Family Campaign, 28 July 1997.

[88] The coroner, Montagu Levine, said 'a group of youths killed a young man in cold blood and for no other reason than that the colour of his skin was black'. *Daily Mail*, 16 February 1997.

[89] See the *Daily Mail*, 14 February 1997. The newspaper named the alleged killers and invited them to sue, claiming there is 'still no justice for Stephen Lawrence. The case threatens to damage race relations and the reputation of British justice.'

[90] *New Nation*, 17 February 1997.

Doreen Lawrence had protested to Sir Paul that the police had failed to administer first aid to Stephen Lawrence (they had not wished to be sullied by black blood, she said); that a proper record had not been kept of the details of the people who had attended the crime scene; that there had been no adequate management of the crime scene and no agreement about which officer was in charge; that there had been a failure properly to communicate to the Lawrence family news about their son's condition[91] and a failure thereafter of the Family Liaison Officer to provide 'adequate support and information'; and that there had been a more general failure rigorously and objectively to manage, direct, supervise, and review the investigation.[92] Sir Paul's answer was to refer her letter to the Police Complaints Authority which commissioned a report by the Kent Police, and that report came in its turn before Parliament in December 1997. The Kent Police report did substantiate many of the complaints made about the investigation, and particularly the initial investigation, talking, *inter alia*, about a 'careless approach'; the failure to take seriously a number of assertions made by informants and to pursue other anonymous callers who had identified the alleged suspects and to conduct 'analytical work... to identify some of these callers'; a failure to collate information; a failure to conduct interviews methodically and with preparation; a failure to adopt a consistent approach to eliminating suspects, allowing some credible suspects to be rejected on spurious grounds; a failure to treat seriously a letter making allegations or to examine it forensically; a failure to investigate other attacks alleged against the suspects which 'may have provided supporting and corroborating evidence for the investigation of Stephen Lawrence's murder' and, in particular, a failure to make an early arrest of two of the alleged suspects in connection with an assault on Stacey Benefield in April 1993, the month when Stephen Lawrence was killed, based on an apparent ignorance of the law by the officers concerned, and a concomitant missed opportunity to search the suspects' homes; a failure to subject tissue samples found at the crime

[91] Mark Simmons, the Chief Inspector engaged in preparing evidence for the Commissioner's appearance at the Macpherson Inquiry, reflected 'it was the first contact at the hospital, the gross insensitivity that was shown to Mr and Mrs Lawrence by the acting inspector who was there, in terms of the way he dealt with them'.
[92] Based on the report of the Kent Police into complaints against police made by Doreen Lawrence.

scene and on Stephen Lawrence's person to forensic examination; and a misbegotten surveillance operation on 26 April 1993 which 'lacked clear direction and proper guidance', was out of communication with other officers elsewhere, and which failed, in particular, to bring about the interception of a suspect leaving his home with a black bin liner possibly containing contaminated clothing.

More generally, the Kent Police report stated not only that the Lawrence family had lost confidence in the police officers in the case from an early stage, but there was also no evidence that the Metropolitan Police Service had been enterprising in trying to overcome those problems of estrangement and distrust once they had arisen. But it also declared that the 'Kent Police have found no evidence to support the allegation of racist conduct by any metropolitan police officer involved in the investigation . . . '[93] and it concluded that the Metropolitan Police investigation had been 'well organised and effective and that there was no evidence of racist conduct by police officers . . . however, there were significant weaknesses, omissions and opportunities lost during the murder investigation'.[94] (Against the statement that there was no evidence of racist conduct, Ros Howells wrote 'What was the criteria used to judge the racist conduct.') The response of the Commissioner of the Metropolitan Police was that his service 'deeply regrets that the racist murder of Stephen Lawrence was not followed by the successful prosecution of his killers . . . the investigation has not found any evidence to support allegations of racist conduct by police officer. However, the Kent investigation found significant weaknesses, omissions and lost opportunities . . . with hindsight it is possible to see how the first murder investigation could, and should, have been carried out

---

[93] And that was a conclusion dismissed by the Commission for Racial Equality: 'The Commission's view at the outset was, and still is, that the approach taken to issues of race by the Kent Police was wholly inadequate in that in their investigation of the Lawrence family's complaint of racism they focused solely on the acts and belief systems of individual officers. The Commission submits that that approach excluded any examination of the values and norms of the culture within which individual officers operate, and to that extent the findings of Kent cannot and should not be relied upon.' J. Yearwood and M. Sikand; 'The Inquiry into the Matters Arising from the Death of Stephen Lawrence, Closing Submissions', Commission for Racial Equality, 18 September 1998, p. 1.

[94] Written answer by the Home Secretary in the House of Commons, 15 December 1997.

more systematically and effectively.'[95] But the Campaign was not appeased. Those weaknesses and omissions and that failure to secure a conviction were in time held to require a public accounting in a context set by the alleged racism of police and prosecutors.

The Lawrences and their immediate followers waged an indefatigable campaign. They wanted convictions[96] (although within a year they were beginning to despair that convictions would ever be secured[97]). It was an 'outrage', they said, 'that the murder of an innocent young man at the beginning of his life in an area we once called our home should not go unpunished'.[98] They wanted a reckoning. And they wanted more and better information and, by implication, more control over the details and *sequelae* of their son's death.[99] Such a craving for knowledge is endemic to many bereaved families. It constitutes part of the quest for the restoration of order in

---

[95] 'Met Comments on Initial PCA Report of Stephen Lawrence Case', News Release, Metropolitan Police Service News Release, 15 December 1997.

[96] Their Christmas message for 1996 was that 'The CPS and the police may be able to rest comfortably on this catalogue of error and complacency, but for us, and many other families left behind after brutal racist attacks, there is only one thing that will make us rest: when Stephen's murderers and the hidden perpetrators of all racist attacks are brought to justice.'

[97] Neville and Doreen Lawrence wrote in a circular letter to their supporters on 8 April 1994, near the first anniversary of the death, 'A full year of loss and a full year of no justice, where we have seen two youths arrested and then released because of "insufficient evidence".' Ros Howells reported that the '[likelihood] of anyone being charged appears to be a romantic dream now. As the anniversary looms, the family grow more despondent...'.

[98] Statement from Doreen and Neville Lawrence, November 1993.

[99] Ros Howells said: 'There are two things. Mrs Lawrence wanted to know what happened in the last hour of her son's life. Every mother, every father, waits for the doorbell to ring or a movement of the key knowing that your child has come in... So they wanted to know. Mrs Lawrence wanted to know, this was her son. Everybody in the world wants a first son, you know, it's very nice to have a daughter but the son is the thing isn't it? If you go throughout the world, the son, this is her firstborn son and a young man, gone through the society, you've brought him up with all the Methodist principles of living, you know, he's supposed to come home or at worst, at worst, he's been involved in a scuffle and he's had a cut you know, he's knocked down by a bus. But not, not six people attacked him in a bus stop for no obvious reason. So they wanted to know that. They wanted to know the hour by hour. They wanted to know the minute by minute, what did the police do? Why didn't they call them straightaway? Why did a neighbour have to tell them and the police never ever actually came to tell them? Do you see? Now by the time the Lawrences got to the station... to the hospital—if there wasn't a senior officer there... One should have been there by the time they'd heard this news... [And] if you'd lost your son, right, what you're looking

a world turned upside down.[100] Yet when Peter Bottomley and others asked the Metropolitan Police Commissioner why the police could not share with the Lawrences information about what had transpired; and what limits were imposed on the information that could be given to the family, it appeared that very little indeed could and would be given. The police replied they had been advised by their solicitors that the Lawrences could only be offered information that was already in the public domain.[101]

The Lawrences were to behave with relative restraint and propriety. They were manifestly ill at ease with the coterie of radical organizations that had camped out in and around the issues of the death and the investigation; and they came within a few months to distance themselves from a number of the groups,[102] their

for is the murderer. If you've never been a campaigner, yeah, it's difficult to understand the great strides we've made and this is not to underestimate these people, I think they now know, they've learned, but at the end of the day what they want is some justice for this child, okay?'

[100] It is not remarkable that one of the very first cases brought under the Human Rights Act was against the decision of the Department of Health to hold the inquiry into the murders committed by Dr Harold Shipman *in camera*. Harold Shipman was a general practitioner convicted of murdering 14 patients and alleged to have killed nearly 200 more. The Independent Public Inquiry into the issues arising from the case of Harold Shipman under the chairmanship of Dame Janet Smith opened in May 2001. The Inquiry web site reported that 'On 1 February 2000, the Secretary of State for Health announced that an independent private inquiry would take place to establish what changes to current systems should be made in order to safeguard patients in the future. Although it would be held in private its report would be made public. Many of the families and sections of the British media sought a Judicial Review in the High Court, which found in their favour and recommended that the Secretary of State for Health reconsider his decision that the Inquiry should be held in private. In September 2000, the Secretary of State for Health announced that the Inquiry would be held in public under the terms of the Tribunals of Inquiry (Evidence) Act 1921. Both Houses of Parliament ratified this decision in January 2001.'

[101] Letter from Detective Chief Superintendent Bill Ilsley to Len Duval, Leader of the Council, London Borough of Greenwich, 14 October 1993.

[102] Imran Khan said: 'I think the family were feeling that these were other people's agendas and not their own. And that they weren't the main force in it and plus it wasn't a family, this was a family that wanted everybody involved.' See too the report in *The Times*, 14 September 1993, in which it was stated that the Lawrences had written to the Anti-Racist Alliance that their son's name was 'too precious to be used in a cynical way'. After initially welcoming the group's support, they said, 'to our dismay we found that the political agendas and rivalries of different organisations began to take over'.

politics,[103] and their more aggressive methods of demonstrating[104] (just as the groups tended to distance themselves noisily from one another,[105] quarrelling particularly over the importance of the BNP, and described by Marc Wadsworth as 'all sorts of hyenas coming to the door and wanting a part of the carcass'). Doreen Lawrence was reported to have said that she had felt under siege: first there had been Palma Black of the ARA ('but how she got to my place I do not know'); then came the ANL and the Black Panthers ('When the Black Panthers came I found it really frightening. They were in hoods with dark glasses. I could not understand why they had come'). Of the ARA, she said 'I did not know them or anything about them.'[106]

The Lawrences also tended in the main to distance themselves from any exclusive identification with the politics of a single ethnic group.[107] Theirs was a campaign waged to right a particular wrong, expose the partiality of the criminal justice system and illuminate the plight of vulnerable young blacks abroad on the streets of London, and it was not to be subordinated to the larger ambitions of what were sometimes seen to be exploitative radical groups. The Anti-Racist Alliance, the Anti-Nazi League, and others were expelled

---

[103] See *Caribbean Times*, 19 April 1994; and *The Voice*, 2 May 1995 in which she claimed that racist and anti-racist groups alike were treating the death as a 'political football'.

[104] The local newspaper, the *Greenwich and Eltham Mercury*, 13 May 1993, reported a plea by shopkeepers and others to halt an ANL march on BNP HQ. During the last march, there had been 10 arrests and 19 people injured.

[105] The Report of Kent Police into complaint made by Mr and Mrs Lawrence stated on p. 147 that GACARA (the Greenwich Action Committee Against Racial Attacks) had complained that the ARA had set up camp in the Lawrence home and controlled communication.

[106] *Daily Mail*, 26 March 1998.

[107] For example, the Stephen Lawrence Family Campaign's briefing notes for speakers at the memorial service for Stephen Lawrence in April 1996—coinciding with the trial of two of the suspects—stipulated that they should 'celebrate the huge support from such a wide range of people who have been touched by the Lawrences' courage and the determination of black people and white people, christians, sikhs, muslims ... trade unionists, civil servants, community activists... [In order not to prejudice the trial] The family want no presence, or picket or demonstration outside the Old bailey...'. The Lawrences themselves received copious letters from white people, many of whom enclosed donations and professed their shame at the conduct of the white suspects. One wrote, for instance, 'I am a white old age pensioner and I feel ashamed of my race.'

from the Lawrences' immediate circle in 1994 (although the chaotic political penumbra of the Campaign never did seem to disappear altogether[108]) and, in their stead, Imran Khan brought in Suresh Grover, a solicitor who worked for the Southall Monitoring Group,[109] and who became closely associated with the Family Campaign. Grover himself recalled 'the early stages when national anti-racist groups attempted to take control. The needs of the family [had subsequently] been prioritised over those of individuals and organisations with their own personal and political agendas.'[110] And Rajiv Menon, also linked with the Southall Monitoring Group, said 'they were using them and abusing them... like a political football really for their own ends to win support within the black community and to marginalise others who were far better qualified than them to do that kind of work'. At Imran Khan's instigation, the campaign was then re-launched with 'all parties involved... fully

[108] Thus Suresh Grover complained about the disorderliness of one meeting held as late as July 1998: 'the evening meeting ended in shambles. There were motions by various organisations for the campaign to consider... and there were comments about the campaign being too "Indian orientated". However, the biggest upset was caused during the distribution of invites for the social. At this stage King's Cross Women's Centre, movement for justice and a number of individuals began to shout abuse when invites were not given to them. In my view the representatives from the King's Cross Women's Centre, especially, were out of order.' Report by Suresh Grover, 28 July 1998. (The King's Cross Women's Centre, now called the Crossroads Women's Centre, describes itself as existing 'To provide support, advice and survival information on a wide range of issues including anti-racism, disability rights, health and ecology, immigration, lesbian and gay rights, prostitution laws, welfare'.)

[109] The Group, now describing itself on its web site as 'The Monitoring Group Ltd.' is a 'charitable organisation providing assistance and support to victims of racial harassment, and domestic violence. Its history dates back to April 23, 1979 when a protest by the local community in Southall, West London against the National Front led to over 700 arrests, hundreds of injuries and the murder of Blair Peach. The campaign into the death of Blair Peach focused local people to examine racial attacks on local estates, for example the Golf Links Estate, in the London Borough of Ealing. This led to the formation of the "Golf Links Racial Attacks Groups", and later the "Southall Monitoring Group". The Southall Monitoring Group evolved to become the leading agency in the West London area providing a range of services to victims of racial harassment and domestic violence. As it evolved it began to help people from across London and later from different parts of the United Kingdom. In 1996 the management committee decided to change the name of the group to The Monitoring Group to reflect the changing nature of the work. It is a registered charity and receives funding mainly from different trusts and charities.'

[110] S. Grover; 'Stephen Lawrence Inquiry: A Turning Point?', in programme of *The Colour of Justice*, Tricycle Theatre, undated, no page numbers.

co-operat[ing] to achieve the prosecution and conviction of Stephen's killers'. Thus began what Khan called the second phase: 'The first was dominated by the national anti-racist organisations, who moved quickly to assist the family after Stephen's murder... and this period ended up in bickering... The second period was marked by the assistance given by the then Southall Monitoring Group, to which the family turned to.'[111]

To be sure, the Family Campaign's own stance could be quite robust, and particularly after the coroner's inquest of February 1997 where the behaviour of the alleged suspects in refusing to testify at all was so insouciant[112] that Doreen Lawrence was prompted to say: 'In my opinion, the judicial system is making a clear statement—saying to the black community that their lives are worth nothing, and the justice system will support anyone, any white person, who wishes to commit any crime or even murder against a black person...'.[113] She was to talk about a looming black Holocaust and apartheid in Britain.[114] She had, it was said, 'a talent for the controversial sound-bite and a willingness to use the language of racial struggle in order to be sure of the media's attention....'.[115]

The conduct of the principals at the inquest had also been noted by the *Daily Mail* newspaper[116] which began vigorously to support the Lawrences and their campaign.[117] It accused the five suspects of murder and challenged them to sue: 'It is no light matter when a national newspaper condemns as murderers five men who have never been convicted in court. But when the judicial system failed so lamentably to deal with the killers of Stephen Lawrence, extraordinary measures are demanded.'[118] Another, rival newspaper, the

[111] *London Monitor*, Issue 1, Spring 1998.

[112] See B. Cathcart; 'The long, hard fight for justice', *The Runnymede Bulletin*, November 1997.

[113] *Greenwich Mercury*, 13 February 1997.

[114] *Guardian*, 19 February 1997. The world, black and white, is full of tales of conspiracy. It is interesting that very similar apocalyptic stories about AIDS, drugs, and genocide were told by Duneier's otherwise sober and sensible black subjects in his study of Chicago. See M. Duneier; *Slim's Table*, University of Chicago Press, Chicago, 1992, p. 75.

[115] J. Upton, review of Macpherson Report and B. Cathcart; *The Case of Stephen Lawrence*, London Review of Books, op. cit.

[116] Neville Lawrence had worked as a painter for the editor of the *Daily Mail*.

[117] See *Guardian*, 15 February 1997.

[118] *Daily Mail*, 14 February 1997.

*Guardian*, noted what it called 'a very belated conversion by the Mail. Until yesterday, the Mail's coverage of the shameful killing had been somewhat peripheral.' But, it commented, 'yesterday's edition was a powerful and bold stroke . . . When the Mail is ready to have a go at racists, it is time to cheer.'[119] Thereafter, and for some while, the *Daily Mail* devoted itself to the Family Campaign, amplifying its voice and transforming it into an organization of national consequence.

## The Racialization of the Politics of the Victim

I have made so much of the framing[120] of the death of Stephen Lawrence for five principal reasons: I wished to establish why it was that the murder attained political importance when so many other campaigns energetically waged by the bereaved fail to attract interest or attain their object;[121] how the political momentum achieved by the campaign was almost (but not quite) irresistible, seemingly capable of sweeping all before it; how the failure to secure convictions was regarded increasingly as a quite inexcusable lapse by the criminal justice system ('It was now heresy to suggest that there should have been anything other than a trial and conviction of the Eltham Five'[122] said Upton); how the Campaign achieved importance in a context so saturated by the politics of race and racism[123] that the death, the police investigation, and assumptions of racism could not readily be severed in any dissection of what had happened;[124] and how, in consequence, the 'racialisation' of the victim in the politics of Stephen Lawrence had for some while a tenacity which had not been displayed, say, by the 'gendered' politics flowing from the cross-examination of Julia Mason.

---

[119] *Guardian*, 15 February 1997.
[120] For a larger discussion of the politics of framing, see B. Klandermans; *The Social Psychology of Protest*, Blackwell, Oxford, 1997.
[121] I cover some of those less than successful campaigns in my *After Homicide, op. cit.*
[122] J. Upton, review of Macpherson Report and B. Cathcart; *The Case of Stephen Lawrence, London Review of Books, op. cit.*
[123] Whether or not racism played a part in the investigation is not the point I wish to establish. I am interested only in reconstructing the significance that the death and the police inquiry came to assume.
[124] For example, the submission to the Macpherson Inquiry by the National Assembly Against Racism and the 1990 Trust remarked that 'The relationship

It was as a result difficult indeed for any examination of the police role in the investigation of the murder not to have been powerfully mediated by the politics of race and racism.[125] And that last observation was to take an interesting and doubly self-validating turn. Simon Holdaway, a former police officer and later a criminologist, specializing in studies of the police and racism in England and Canada, an adviser to the Commission for Racial Equality in its submissions to the Macpherson Inquiry, argued that the Metropolitan Police was racist first and precisely because it had *failed* during the troubled year of 1993 to apply the 'widest possible definition of racial incident' to 'racialise' the Stephen Lawrence murder, leading to the 'absence of police work that took account of "race" as a central feature of an investigation ...'.[126] And second, the inability to bring about a conviction was 'a combination of cock-up and racism', the racism inhering, he said, in the poor police handling of the Lawrence family and their interpretation of the significance of what they conceived to be their marginalization by the police: 'If it cannot be shown that they acted in an openly racially discriminatory manner, it can without doubt be demonstrated that their actions had a negative effect on relationships between the Lawrence family and the police ...'.[127] That principle was real to the family and real in its consequences, not only leading the Inquiry to make an inference of racism but also encouraging the formulation of Sir William Macpherson's definition of a racist incident, subsequently adopted by ACPO, as 'any incident which is perceived to be racist by the victim, or by any other person'.[128] ('This definition', Sir William added,

between black communities are currently at an all time low. The perception of black communities in general terms is that the Police are racist, aggressive and increasingly corrupt ... The submitting organisations all agree that the metropolitan police is an institutionally racist organisation.'

[125] Ben Bowling observed 'Now what I think happened was that Lawrence became a touchstone for or symbolic of all the other racist murders and also the failure of the police to respond to racist crime in general and also the treatment of the black community as suspect ... Lawrence has been framed in the context of race because it was, it was a campaign around full racial justice.'

[126] S. Holdaway; 'Statement to Inquiry', *op. cit.*, p. 18.

[127] *Ibid*, p. 17.

[128] Actually, that definition was quite similar to its predecessor, laid out in the Metropolitan Police Service Crime Desk Manual of 23 November 1990, and following the guidance of the Home Affairs Select Committee and Home Office Circular 42/1991: 'A racial incident is any incident in which it appears to the reporting

'should be universally adopted by the Police, local government and other relevant agencies.'[129])

The repercussions of the murder had thus taken their own distinct semantic route. Imran Khan reflected in November 1999 of his own experience of working with victim-clients:

I think victims can go in two different directions. One is the political understanding of the situation, of criminal justice system and the way they've been treated. And if you're black it tends to be that way because you tend to see it from that particular perspective. There's another direction in which you can go which is that you become [involved in issues of] law and order... the first thing that Neville said when he went on for the appeal, and a lot of families do, is that they go there with the police and he said, I want [justice], or I want the people who did this to be hanged. Now if you ask him that question now or indeed you asked him that question two years afterwards, it would have been, he would have realised that the community that would have been at risk would have been the black community because he was meeting people within the black community and was talking to them about, you're not getting justice because black people don't get justice. It's the race aspect which is causing you difficulty. So there's a realisation. And I know what the police certainly said as far as I was concerned, that because I was political that I was somehow... manipulating the family. And... and people have said to me; 'why don't you tell the Lawrences this [and that]' and I said, 'it's not for me, they've got to find out for themselves.' And I was very, very careful that my perception of the criminal justice system wasn't forced upon the Lawrences and that they had to find it out for themselves.

or investigating officer that the complaint involves an element of racial motivation, or any incident which includes an allegation of racial motivation made by any person.' (But, Coretta Phillips pointed out, 'this part of the definition was never acknowledged, recognised or acted upon'. The new definition stemming from the Inquiry was a deliberate challenge to police practice.) There was some demur about its possible application. The Lord Chancellor was uncertain, for instance, about the principle that a judge must impose a heavier sentence on an offence because, despite evidence to the contrary, it was asserted only by the victim to be a racist incident. And another Minister said that 'we should not allow the police to redefine racist incidents as nonracist, neither should we accept frivolous representations from people other than the victim that a crime is racist'.

[129] *The Stephen Lawrence Inquiry: Report of an Inquiry by Sir William Macpherson of Cluny, op. cit.* That definition did create problems for some agencies. For example, ACPO ruled that it could not stand as proof positive that an incident had been racist, and the Lord Chancellor made it known that it must be objectively assessed 'otherwise false perception would shut out the truth'.

So it was that a single preferred reading came to be sustained although the murder and its investigation were themselves multivocal. Suggestions that the murder of Stephen Lawrence could have been the result of what John Grieve, a liberal Commander of Metropolitan Police,[130] called 'general thuggery' were scotched: 'Some police officers got extremely badly beaten up for making exactly that point at the Stephen Lawrence Inquiry', he said. Suggestions that the police investigation of the murder was marred significantly by anything other than institutional racism[131] were also scotched. 'Racism', said Duwayne Brooks, 'killed my best friend Stephen. Racism also rubbished our chances of convicting the killers of Stephen Lawrence. Racism has also shattered my life.'[132] 'This was an issue about race', Imran Khan said, 'and we shouldn't muddy the waters . . .'.

It could have been otherwise. The Macpherson Inquiry unearthed no egregious racist utterance or action by police officers and turned instead to the more elusive and perhaps more sociologically sophisticated notion of institutional racism[133] that embraces

---

[130] He was to say in October 2000 that all that kept him in the police service was the hope of convicting Stephen Lawrence's killers. See the *Evening Standard*, 24 October 2000.

[131] Suggestions that were made, *inter alia*, by the Commissioner of the Metropolitan Police Service who initially resisted the term with some vehemence in, for instance, his lecture, P. Condon; 'Working together towards an Anti-Racist Police Service', 18 December 1998. Deployment of the phrase 'institutional racism', he said, polarized views rather than promoted reform. To say most officers were racist did not do them justice. It was instead 'simplistic and pejorative labelling'. The CPS was to be similarly unhappy about the term: see CPS news release 137/99, 14 October 1999.

[132] *The Voice*, 1 March 1999.

[133] Imran Khan himself commented, 'I couldn't point you to one particular thing. I don't think I could and I think it'd be wrong if you did that. I mean in the beginning there was a sense of this was because of racism on the part of the police. There's no doubt that there's some incompetence there. There's no doubt about it. You can't have every single officer from you know, the PC at the, you know, ground level up to the senior officer all being you know, in sort of cohesion and going in one particular direction. There's a level of incompetence. But I always look at it this way and this is my perception, this is the way that we approached it in the Inquiry, is that although there is some level of incompetence, you have to wonder why the incompetence is there. Why are people bad when it's, the victim is black? . . . Do you explain it by way of incompetence? I think it is incompetence but what is, what is driving that incompetence is the institutional racism that we talked about. The assumption that this is not important, the assumption that Duwayne might be in some way involved in the attack. Those all I think influence the level of incompetence or you know, and so you can't explain it simply in that way . . . [There was a] lack of urgency, lack of motivation, all

the inadvertent practices embedded in an organization that have the unintended consequence of producing racist outcomes. It is a definition that permits by ellipsis a charge to be sustained even in the absence of explicit proof. Michael Ignatieff protested that 'What is most dismaying, looking back on Lawrence, is that it became a story about just one thing—race. But the central issue was not race, it was justice. Why were we talking about institution-alised racism when the issue was institutionalised incompetence? Why were we talking about "race awareness" when the issue was equal justice before the law?'[134] And, indeed, there are criminologists expert in the study of policing who would argue with him[135] that organized incompetence[136] (or possibly corruption) were no less compelling candidates for explaining why the police investigation into Stephen Lawrence's death proved fruitless.[137] Martin

there because you know, to use that very hackneyed phrase you know, that Nelson Mandela used, black lives are cheap. Seeing a black victim, is it somehow important?...this is perhaps too you know, too exaggerated but if you've seen a dog that's died on the street, you know, it doesn't give you that same sense of loss and all the rest of it. Now perhaps that's the institutionalized racism which you're talking about.' And that was to be the case put by Michael Mansfield at the Macpherson Inquiry. Mark Simmons, then a Chief Inspector at New Scotland Yard, and the author of the Commissioner's submission to the Inquiry, stated: 'Mansfield's case on behalf of the Lawrences was always it is incompetence, it's clearly incompetence, but it's incompetence at such a scale that it must have some wider explanation and that is either in corruption and/or it's in racism. That's been the prosecution case if you like.'

[134] M. Ignatieff; 'Less Race, Please', *Prospect*, April 1999, p. 10.

[135] But see M. Punch; 'Rotten Orchards: "Pestilence", Police Misconduct and System Failure', *Policing and Society*, 2003, Vol. 13, No. 2, p. 173.

[136] Brought about in part because of the institutional practice at the time of rotating police officers between different roles lest patterns of corruption develop, leading to the demise of traditions of skilled homicide investigation. Ben Bowling commented 'detectives no longer have [the practice of] the person who becomes a detective with three years' service and does the remaining twenty seven years as a detective. They're moved on quickly... So you'd do... three, four years as a detective. But the old guard... the old regime detectives moved on, taking their craft skills away with them to other posts or to leaving the service altogether.'

[137] Ray and his colleagues observed that the behaviour of the police in the Lawrence case was compatible with institutional racism, the finding of the Macpherson Inquiry, but it was also compatible with ineptness, incompetence, and irrelevance. L. Ray et al.; 'The Macpherson Report: A View from Greater Manchester', *Sociological Research Online*, Vol. 4, No. 1, 1999, p. 6.

Innes, the only British criminologist who has so far[138] conducted an intensive study of murder inquiries,[139] was one. Innes remarked that the major part of the attention in discussions of the Lawrence case focused on issues of police racism, but they had thereby ignored an important theme, systemic problems in the situation in which murder inquiries are conducted, rather than difficulties unique to the Lawrence investigation.[140] Peter Waddington, another former police officer turned criminologist, echoed Simon Holdaway when he called the investigation 'policing as usual—cock-up', and he said 'The accusation of racism did not arise from the manifold deficiencies of the murder investigation. It could not have done, for there are many reasons for such incompetence from personal ineptitude to managerial failings. It arose from the aura that surrounded the inquiry.'[141] And there were those inside and outside the police with an intimate knowledge of the case who agreed with that diagnosis of 'policing as usual'. Rajiv Menon, the counsel who represented Duwayne Brooks at the Macpherson Inquiry, said 'I don't think that this investigation was particularly [more] incompetent or racially tarnished than others. I mean I think there are clearly some things about it which are quite unique, and we've now discovered in light of the Inquiry, but I don't think at the time anybody really, I mean, realised this... I don't want to downplay race, because

---

[138] As I write, Janet Foster is undertaking a study of murder inquiries in the Metropolitan Police 'after Lawrence'. Conversation with her suggests that she would support Innes' and Waddington's contention that the situated moral identity of a homicide victim massively transcends the lesser particulars of class, race, age, and gender.

[139] M. Innes; *Investigating Murder : Detective Work And The Police Response To Criminal Homicide*, Oxford University Press, Oxford, 2003.

[140] M. Innes; 'Beyond the Macpherson Report: Managing Murder Inquiries in Context', *Sociological Research Online*, Vol. 4, No. 1, 1999.

[141] P. Waddington; untitled typescript article for *Police Review*, undated. In an email to me he was to add 'What struck me about Macpherson is how little the inquiry actually revealed. Almost everything that was damaging came straight out of the Kent PCA [Police Complaints Authority] inquiry. Save, that is, for the fact that Kent selected a comparative case, the murder of a white lad called Everett in circumstances very similar to those that occurred with Stephen Lawrence. They found that the Met cocked both up equally. The HMIC [Her Majesty's Inspector of Constabulary] report on murder investigation in the Met was equally damning. I think this adds weight to your (already very weighty) conclusion that Macpherson was conducted within the parameters of an inquiry into RACE rather than the treatment of victims and their families.'

clearly race is the major achievement and success of this Inquiry. I think there's no doubt about it, its stereotyping infected this investigation at many levels, and that has institutional dimensions to it that clearly cannot be ignored. But I have no doubt in my mind that there was corruption at some stage of this investigation.' And Assistant Commissioner Ian Johnston, who, in April 1994, assumed charge of the police area in which the investigation was still taking place; who, together with the Commissioner for Metropolitan Police, Paul Condon, agreed to meet the Lawrences as police officers for the first time; and who subsequently put the inquiry on a new and more vigorous footing,[142] said:

You know we've seen worse, we've seen better. They didn't have a lot of luck. There were some things to do with how the investigation was handed over two to three days into it, it was handed over because the guy who picked it up had a major murder trial starting at the Old Bailey and on the Monday the guy coming back to it was coming back off sick, a week into the investigation his mother-in-law gets killed outside of church and he's time off looking after his wife who'd stressed up about it. So there were some things in the very early stages about the management ... but I wouldn't have said it was inordinately different from what was around at that time. Now what they've done is subjected it to a clinical analysis,

[142] He said 'On taking up appointment, had a chat with the Commissioner about a range of things, one of them was the Lawrence case which was starting to bubble at that time and in discussion with the Commissioner decided to see what we could do by way of a second investigation. And set up the second investigation, put this covert work into operation, had a re-look at the material that was available to the first investigation but the main thrust was a sort of forward look to see whether, well in essence what we were trying to do was take out people who were potentially protecting them. So old man Norris [the father of one of the suspects] who was on the run for a drugs job, we eventually tracked down and arrested him in possession of a load of firearms. We tried to infiltrate the team, tried to put somebody into the, an undercover officer in ... We tried to identify the weakest link and negotiate with him over culpability issues ... We mounted a surveillance operation to see if we could get them for something else as a lever ... We found out where their weakest link lived, put surveillance equipment into the flat, monitored all of that. We saw again all of the key witnesses, we did a lot of, we did a lot of things which in my mind took us a little bit further forward but not very far forward.' 2,600 people were interviewed, 500 statements were taken and 10,000 appeal notices issued. Ian Johnston stated 'I can understand Mrs Lawrence's distress, but I do want to get across to the black community that we take crime against them just as seriously as we do any others. When someone is murdered, we do not think of the colour of their skin.' Statement by Assistant Commissioner Ian Johnston following the inquest into the murder of Stephen Lawrence, 13 February 1997.

the likes of which no criminal investigation has ever been subject before, and through it, have exposed you know what are undeniably a massive range of flaws. Now that has led to the police service nationally looking at how it investigates murders . . . This coincided with a look under Operation Enigma at linked, potentially linked murders over the last decade . . . And what that did nationally was, it didn't actually show that we'd missed any links, but what it did show was that some of the standards in investigation were pretty poor. Now as a result of that we have a new murder investigation process 'cause it would surprise the world to know that we didn't have a system. It was intuitive, experienced based, [that] SIOs [senior investigating officers] took from one case to another. I mean my analysis of it was it was incompetence of a nature which was not I think absent from all cases at that time. Now that is no satisfaction to the Lawrence family, no satisfaction for the police service. But it was not something that we had put under the microscope and it having been put under the microscope, it's up to us to get our act together.

More generally, Martin Innes makes the ancillary point, remarked upon elsewhere,[143] that in major police inquiries, the victim's status as victim tends usually to eclipse all other characteristics, including race.[144] What counts for practical policing purposes is that a person has been killed: 'the fact that [a person] had been killed was identified as more significant than any more mundane, normative status considerations'.[145] Yet the frame of race had been used forcefully to describe the problem posed both by Stephen Lawrence's murder and by its subsequent investigation, it had lent velocity and stature to the demands levelled by the Campaign, and it was to be carried intact through the Stephen Lawrence Inquiry and some way beyond.

[143] For example, P. Moskos; 'Black and White in Blue: Racial Distinctions within a Common Police Identity', paper presented at the American Society of Criminology meetings, Chicago, 15 November 2002.

[144] His actual words were ' . . . in respect of particularly serious crimes, the fact of victimisation often appears to be of more significance to the police than the social status of the individual who has been victimised . . . Following on from this, it appears that any moral equivocation that officers might usually feel in respect of the behaviour of the victim, is at least temporarily suspended in the hunt for the killer.' M. Innes; 'Somebody's brother, somebody's son.' Police Culture, Morality and Constructing the Role of the Victim in Homicide Investigations', unpublished, 1999, p. 4.

[145] M. Innes; 'Organizational Communication and the Symbolic Construction of Police Murder Investigations', unpublished paper, p. 9. And that was the contested, police case. Cathcart stated that 'The officers contended that their feelings and opinions . . . were of no importance. A murder was always a very serious crime, whoever the victim, and they gave their all to solve it. Barristers for the "prosecution" teams [in the Macpherson Inquiry] did not accept this . . . '.

## The Inquiry

Michael Howard, the Conservative Home Secretary until May 1997, had refused to meet the Lawrence family and had not acceded to the Stephen Lawrence Family Campaign's request for a judicial inquiry.[146] The request had not been supported by the Lawrences' Member of Parliament, Peter Bottomley.[147] It had not been supported by the Conservative home affairs front bench team. An inquiry, it was thought, would simply offer another pretext to attack the police and complicate their task.[148] John Greenway, a member of that team, said in November 1999:

It was resisted and resisted and I doubt, I doubt that we'd probably would have [an Inquiry]...what you're going to have is the position, the Lawrence Inquiry conclusion gives the impression that somehow or other if you made the police responsible, I don't think that's quite the right word, but if the police were bound by race relations legislation somehow this would solve the difficulty. But what I think you'll discover is, over time, is that it makes an already bad situation worse for the great majority, which is the police...The minute that they think that there's some potential racist element to this, and likely criticism of senior officers, then they, their natural inclination is to deal with the matter, not to get out the, necessarily, the ultimate truth and natural justice for everybody but to make sure that they cover their own back.

What might otherwise have been portrayed as the seemingly inexorable drive of the Family Campaign was, in other words, quite resistible, the influence it exerted a form of soft determinism, and all the authoritative constraints that flowed from the Inquiry Report need never have been imposed. I have already argued that the New Labour administration was from time to time to enact or construct

---

[146] Although there were contrary rumours. See *Greenwich Mercury*, 20 February 1997.

[147] He wrote to a constituent in March 1997, 'I am not sure that a public inquiry would be enormously useful which is why I have not called for it but I have tried to make a number of the other issues very plain as you might have noticed if you have been able to listen and watch...TV and radio programmes.'

[148] That was a line to be pursued throughout the episode. William Hague, the leader of the Conservative Party, was reported to have said when the report of the Macpherson Inquiry was published that 'What must not happen...is for this report to act as a trigger for a backlash against the police service as a whole. We still have one of the best police services in the world, this must be forgotten' [*sic*]. *Conservative Party News*, 22 February 1999.

its own environment, willing the causes that would oblige it to act and, in part, signalling what kind of Government it proposed to be. Assistant Commissioner Ian Johnston of the Metropolitan Police said, 'race issues in any event have grown into problems. We had a change in Government half-way through [the campaigning] so a promise is made, loose or otherwise, in opposition when it has to be played out in the real world of Government... It becomes a very useful political tool in the sense of [the] Conservatives try to suppress, Labour [being] open.' The Inquiry could be read as part of the new Government's human rights agenda, affording a remedy to those vulnerable to abuses of State power; together with the proposed Freedom of Information Bill, it could be read as a part of a shift towards greater transparency; with the new performance management, as part of a new discipline imposed on the providers of services by those who were their recipients; and, much more simply, as a response to a good family that had striven hard to right a wrong and learn the truth about their murdered son. And it was New Labour, not the Conservative Party, that won the general election in May 1997 and agreed to submit to the recommendations of the Inquiry it had established.

After the much publicized inquest of February 1997, on the eve of the general election, and through the intercession of Ros Howells, the Lawrences did meet Jack Straw, the Shadow Home Secretary, who had already heeded the finding of the coroner's court, saying 'The verdict leaves the Lawrence family in a dreadful situation. It is a matter of huge sorrow and regret that no individuals have been convicted of the appalling, unprovoked murder of Stephen Lawrence. I am arranging to see the family as soon as possible. Meanwhile I am keeping an open mind on whether there are any further avenues of investigation or of inquiry which could be pursued.'[149]

Ros Howells had noted from the first that what was distinctive about the Lawrences and the Stephen Lawrence Family Campaign was their abjuring of the clamorous street demonstrations[150] that had defined the politics of anti-racism in South East London:[151]

[149]   *The Voice*, 17 February 1997.
[150]   If it had not been for the Lawrences, Peter Bottomley told Sir Paul Condon in a letter, 'there might have been major disruptions in London'.
[151]   The iconography of Stephen Lawrence and his family was, moreover, perfectly reassuring to a centre left political party. Coretta Phillips observed that the 'ingredients were all there for a non-threatening political response from New Labour'.

For me, the break came through when there was a march planned for, the community has already responded to what they see as police inaction on their part by marches. And for me, the break came when the Lawrence family wrote a letter to community groups saying that they didn't want to head up a march, they didn't want to be part of a march. We don't have to go down the streets and turn cars over and you know, march and shout and scream and scream for justice. The police ought to give us justice. They can't be inactive, do you understand? And that line has guided me through whatever I've done with them. I don't want to take away anything from the strength of that family and what they have achieved. But I had another role that I could use. I'm saying to you why it became prominent was the family did not want to march. So we had to find another way. So the Campaign was kind of stymied in a funny way and therefore we had to move on in another way, I, in my job, and not me as a person, have contacts, knew how to pull those strings.

Ros Howells was politically well connected. As a member of a forum advising the then Home Secretary, she had arranged for the visit to the Lawrence family of Peter Lloyd, the Home Office Minister in the Conservative administration that was voted out of office in 1997:

I just want you to know that I did have a role, where the solicitors and so on couldn't get to the Home Secretary, as a community official, I can get to the Home Secretary. I took it to Peter Lloyd, he came down, he couldn't do anything. So we then went to see Jack Straw before he became Home Secretary. We went to see him, Mr and Mrs Lawrence, their solicitor and their lawyer, myself, Bernie [Grant] and Diane Abbott [two black Labour Members of Parliament]. And Jack Straw turned up with Paul Boateng, yeah? So like two camps. And the Lawrences explained to Jack how they felt, things had not gone right and they couldn't accept that the police could not find a murderer. I mean six people, it's not one man who disappears into the bushes. It's not a Jill Dando incident[152] ... It must be much more difficult to find a needle in a haystack than it is to find six needles in a confined space like Eltham. Do you understand? So what was interesting is that Jack Straw was touched by the unassuming sincerity and the human need to find out well what happened to their son. And equally he was appalled that the family felt that the police force had let them down. This was the Met, do you understand? So when he came into office, we went

---

[152] Jill Dando, a BBC presenter, was killed on 26 April 1999 and had been subject to a substantial murder investigation involving 45 officers who had interviewed 4,000 people and identified some 140 people with what they called 'an unhealthy obsession' with her. An arrest was made finally in May 2000.

back, and by then, the family was convinced that the need to ask for a judicial enquiry was important... They asked for a judicial enquiry and I'm sure that he, he didn't say yes. He sort of studied it... and looked at the case and whatever. But anyway he was minded to do this right? And he was content to do it because he felt it was important.

There was a lobbying of both major parties before the general election. There was frequent lobbying of the new Home Secretary and his Ministers at first and second hand[153] after the general election.[154] There were discussions between members of the Campaign and Ministers. Imran Khan reported to the Stephen Lawrence Family Campaign on 17 June 1997 that 'Various meetings were held with Condon and Straw... It was agreed that the key issue was the call for the judicial enquiry.'[155] And the Minister, Alun Michael, privy to deliberations within the Labour Party, recollected:

I was involved in those discussions [within the Labour Party]. At the end of the day it was Jack Straw's decision. I mean he was both courageous and right to say, we cannot live with a boil simply about to burst. It has to be lanced and to personally intervene, to listen to what Mr and Mrs Lawrence have to say in order to get an inquiry that was on the basis that was acceptable to them and to others who were genuinely concerned, to get the truth out. There were people who wanted to use the whole issue but there were others that wanted the truth out. And as I say, I mean I think that was a personal decision that took some courage to make and it was absolutely right... It was the fact that there were questions that needed to be answered... I think one thing that Jack always said, and I believe it's what made him a great Home Secretary, is that you must start off by deciding what's right, and then deciding how to handle it. And the fact that there were unanswered questions that needed to be answered, was the starting point. The fact that the parents needed answers and that many other people supporting them needed answers, justified making sure that answers could be given... right at the heart of the Lawrence inquiry and the decision to have one, was the fact that there were questions to be answered.

[153] For example, John Austin MP asked by Parliamentary Question on the 22 May 1997 what recent representations Alun Michael had received about the murder of Stephen Lawrence, and what plans he had to establish a public inquiry.
[154] Nineteen Members of Parliament and the Commission for Racial Equality eventually came to ask for an independent judicial inquiry. See *The Voice*, 23 June 1997.
[155] Minutes of Meeting of Stephen Lawrence Family Campaign, 17 June 1997.

On 24 June 1997, Imran Khan returned again to the Home Office with the Lawrences and two Labour Members of Parliament. One, John Austin, the Member for Erith and Thamesmead, recalled 'The fact that [the Home Secretary] had assembled the whole of his ministerial team indicated the seriousness with which he viewed the situation. After the meeting, and after having had a discussion with Neville and Doreen Lawrence, the Home Secretary was deeply moved...'.[156] The Home Secretary was himself reported to have said that 'I recognise that a strong case has been made by Mrs Lawrence for some form of inquiry and I am actively considering what she put to me', and rumours and leaks about an imminent announcement about a 'race inquiry'[157] began to spread.[158] (Ros Howell's copy of the agenda of a meeting of the Stephen Lawrence Family Campaign on 1 July 1997 contained the pencilled comment 'amazing—public enquiry led by judge e.g. Scott Enquiry'[159] against the entry 'Report of Straw Meeting'.) Finally, and in response to arranged Parliamentary Questions from Clive Efford, the new MP for Eltham, and John Austin, the Home Secretary announced on 31 July 1997 that there would be an inquiry under section 49 of the Police Act 1996[160] 'into the matters arising from the death of Stephen Lawrence on 22 April 1993 to date, in order particularly to identify the lessons to be learned for the investigation and prosecution of racially motivated crimes'.[161]

Amongst the issues the Inquiry were to examine were the workings of family liaison; the management of the initial contact with Duwayne Brooks; and 'issues of race', including 'The effect, or

---

[156] House of Commons debate on Stephen Lawrence Inquiry 29 March 1999. The Home Secretary himself said to the House of Commons in his statement of 24 February 1999 on the Stephen Lawrence Inquiry: 'I first met the family in early 1997, and saw both parents again shortly after becoming Home Secretary in May that year. They persuaded me of the case for a thorough, independent scrutiny of the investigation of their son's murder.'

[157] See *Guardian*, 25 July 1997.

[158] See *Guardian*, 29 May 1997.

[159] The Scott Inquiry was a judicial enquiry set up in 1992 under Lord Justice Scott by the Prime Minister following the collapse of the prosecution in the Matrix Churchill case that had centred on the sale of arms to Iraq.

[160] That power enabled the Home Secretary to order a local inquiry into the policing of any area.

[161] Letter from Head of Race Equality to Leader of Greenwich Council, 31 January 1994.

452 Constructing Victims' Rights

otherwise, either consciously or subconsciously, of the race of the victim on the conduct of police in the investigation', 'The effect, or otherwise, either consciously or subconsciously, of the race of the Lawrence family on the conduct of police in the investigation', 'The awareness and/or experience of individual officers of apparently racially motivated crimes', 'Any express evidence of racism', 'Any inferences of racism', and 'The effect, or otherwise, of issues of race on all or any of the issues listed in the schedule.'[162] The second part of the Inquiry, pointed at the 'lessons to be learned', invited submissions but also reminded those who might write[163] that it would 'necessarily concern itself only with the matters which relate directly to racially motivated crime'.[164] And the opening comments by Edmund Lawson, Counsel to the Inquiry, on the very first day, framed the project of the Inquiry squarely in a context of questions about race and racism:

No pre-judgment (Inquiry impartial): but it makes no sense for us to ignore the indications already available from the hundreds of statements & thousands of documents available: it appears that in a number of material respects the police conduct of the investigations did go badly wrong ... Is there evidence or an explanation to contradict the impression that things went badly wrong? If not, why did things go so wrong? Were any errors due to 'simple' incompetence? Or were they—as some have vociferously asserted and as police have vociferously denied—attributable or contributed to directly or indirectly by racism? Those = the main issues.

Preliminary matters were dealt with on 8 October 1997 and the Inquiry proper opened on 24 March the next year. The culmination of a fervid and often angry campaign, infused with the polarities of a polemical politics, conceived to be a potential turning point in the evolution of criminal justice,[165] it was in some manner taken to be

---

[162] Media Pack: Public Hearings: Schedule of Issues, 23 March 1998.

[163] And it was in response to that letter that the Home Office made a submission in which it stated that it 'would welcome the Inquiry's views on the recommendations for measures to protect vulnerable or intimidated witnesses ... in the report of the Working Group on Vulnerable or Intimidated Witnesses ... which recognises that a witness may be vulnerable or intimidated because of his or her cultural or ethnic background'. Evidence submitted by the Home Office to the Second Part of the Inquiry, undated, p. 10.

[164] Letter from Secretary to the Inquiry, 18 May 1998.

[165] See *Victim Support News Service*, February 1999: 'The Report of the Stephen Lawrence Inquiry'.

tantamount to an English Truth Commission on race[166] and criminal justice[167] and it carried a burden of expectation and passion. It was an accounting[168] and an atonement[169] that attracted many of those critical of the police service and its relations with minority ethnic groups.[170] It offered an opportunity, in Duwayne Brooks's words, 'to bring the police under the race-relations laws'.[171] It was an apex of the Lawrence family's ambitions, and to mark it, the Stephen Lawrence Family Campaign was re-launched again to 'mobilis[e] supporters and people to attend the inquiry; writ[e] and publish[ed] a booklet from the campaign informing the public of the families

[166] There was, for example, a letter of protest on 27 March 1998 to Sir William from Babubhai Master, the general secretary of the Asian Congress on Local Affairs, about the absence of Asian representation on the tribunal.

[167] 'The Lawrences' campaign had constructed a conjunctural space within which: the murder of their son and the failure to convict his killers was being successfully transformed from a private tragedy into a matter of urgent public importance; previous campaigns for justice, forgotten by the media and ignored by the authorities, could assert their rights to be heard.' The Macpherson Inquiry, he said, was being 'forced to operate as a *de facto* Truth Commission in which the concerns of black communities could be publicly articulated and acknowledged'. E. McLaughlin; 'The search for truth and justice', *Criminal Justice Matters*, Spring 1999, No. 35, p. 14.

[168] Herman Ouseley, the Chairman of the Commission for Racial Equality, wrote to tell Sir William Macpherson, the Chairman of the Inquiry, on 31 July 1998: 'The political leadership in Britain since 1981 has encouraged the police to feel that they are on some higher moral ground, that they are untouchable when it comes to any disciplinary action involving ethnic minorities or allegations of racism. They have felt few constraints in treating Black people as more likely to be criminals than victims of crime, even though the facts show this is not the case. They regularly buy off litigants without apology or admission of liability. The police have been able to operate in these ways because of the weakness of police authorities to whom they report, and the failure by political leaders to demand change.'

[169] Sir William Macpherson said in his opening statement on 24 March 1998, 'Our hope is that at the end of the day we will establish what happened, and what may have gone wrong over these last years...To Mr & Mrs Lawrence these years must have been dreadful. We hope sincerely that, while nothing can alleviate the pain and loss which they have suffered, they may accept that all of us have done our best to establish what was done or not done, so that the future may not see the repetition of any errors which may be uncovered during our hearings.'

[170] For example, attracting the presence of Alex Owolade, who called himself a Black civil rights leader and trades union steward, of The Movement for Justice By Any Means, and a dramatic (or melodramatic) incursion by the Nation of Islam and subsequent violence. The Lawrences were condemnatory, demanding 'don't wreck our crusade' by trying to make political capital out of murder. *Daily Mail*, 30 June 1998.

[171] D. Brooks; *steve and me, op. cit.*, p. 163.

view of the Inquiry and what it expects of it; [and] endeavour[ing] to publicise the "race issue" in a high profile manner'.[172] And the Inquiry and its chairman were both watched closely lest they betrayed the ambitions of the Family Campaign.[173] (Imran Khan said[174] 'we put Macpherson on notice. I think simply put, we were saying "look, we, we're going to look carefully at what you're going to be doing". And Macpherson will say to us, which was what was troubling throughout the period leading up to the beginning of the enquiry, "I'm going to let you do whatever you want, I'm going to give you whatever you want but you may not necessarily agree with my conclusions" .')

In the manner of other such inquiries, the Macpherson Inquiry was inquisitorial rather than adversarial.[175] It was 'reasonably

---

[172] S. Grover; 'Stephen Lawrence Family Campaign; Campaign Working Group Terms of Reference', 7 April 1998. The Macpherson Inquiry was held to 'offer a victims family the rare opportunity to almost forensically examine on a hourly basis the nature and competence of police investigation of racially motivated murder. It allows the family to cross examine state decisions in a case that has enormous policy and practical implications for the black and asian communities.' (Stephen Lawrence Family Campaign Some Notes on a Short Term Press Strategy, 8 April 1998.)

[173] The announcement that Sir William would chair the Inquiry was, for instance, immediately attacked by Neville Lawrence on the grounds that he was not equipped to take a proper stance on issues of race, racism, and criminal justice. Lawrence asked him to stand down. See *Observer*, 15 March 1998. The Home Office was unmoved (see Home Office press release, 17 March 1998).

[174] Imran Khan said more generally: 'I mean the stuff with Macpherson was, we had reservations about Macpherson as soon as he was appointed. As soon as he was appointed, my 'phone just went bananas with people saying "you have got an awful, awful judge". And we had to make a decision as to whether we do, and I think the decision we took at the time was if we criticise him now, simply on the basis of rumours, we're just simply [alienate him]. So we thought we'd wait and wait and wait and see what happened. Finally the *Observer* article came out [in which Neville Lawrence had castigated Sir William as being personally unqualified to conduct the Inquiry]. We thought we have to do something now because if we don't, if the report that we get isn't what we want, then people will say "well why didn't you raise the objections". So we had to raise it at that point in time. Having raised it, the position then was, Straw having sort of given us assurances that this was the right person, not that we were necessarily [persuaded] by [him], but the point was that Straw had given assurance that we could say "look, you're the one who appointed him", plus Macpherson himself had been given notice of our intention that we were looking at him very carefully. And so that coupled with the fact that the advisors, such as John Sentamu had some sort of credibility within the people of the black communities, the minority communities, meant that there was you know, a safety valve.'

[175] Chairman's Opening Statement for Preliminary Hearing on 8 October 1997.

informal . . . the stricter rules of procedure and evidence do not apply
to us in our search for the truth'.[176] It did not pretend to be emotionally disengaged,[177] tending to give the Lawrence family[178] and their
cause the special moral standing so often associated with the campaigning families of the murdered dead.[179] It was imbued with a
sense of occasion, being staffed by some seventeen lawyers representing the family, Duwayne Brooks, the Commission for Racial
Equality, the London Borough of Greenwich, the Crown Prosecution Service, and different combinations of police officers. It was a
public event that came in time[180] to be enlivened by the vigorous
involvement of its spectators: McLaughlin and Murji wrote about
how 'Anyone who attended the inquiry . . . soon realised that something quite extraordinary and unprecedented was happening. Observers in the public gallery were active participants, talking to
each other, reading the various leaflets handed out by various

---

[176] Chairman's Opening Statement, The Inquiry into the Matters Arising from the
Death of Stephen Lawrence, 24 March 1998.

[177] And Sir William was obliged subsequently to respond to harsh criticisms by
some (*The Times* of 1 April 1999 talked about accusations of his 'pandering to black
opinion' and that 'some of his ideas were naive, or simply unworkable'.). He was to
reply that 'My shoulders are broad enough. I did not hold back and never would . . .
People have become alive to the fact that there is a problem.'

[178] Thus Doreen Lawrence was reported to have reacted with some indignation at
being cross-examined by the counsel for the Commissioner of the Metropolitan Police
Service; 'From the time of my son's murder', she said, 'I have not been treated as a
victim. I can only tell you or put in my statements what I know. For me to be
questioned in this way, I don't appreciate it.' Cross-examination then ended at the
instigation of the Chairman. Neville Lawrence subsequently commented 'I was
expecting an apology from the Metropolitan Police for the way they have behaved
over the last five years. Instead I saw the representative of the Metropolitan Police
attack my wife as if she were on trial . . . ' *Daily Mail*, undated.

[179] A statement read at the outset by the Reverend John Sentamu, adviser to the
Inquiry, recited how 'I have nothing but admiration for the Lawrence's tenacity and
perseverance,' and he concluded 'Throughout this Inquiry the name of Stephen
Lawrence will be used again and again. May I ask you all please to stand in silence
to honour his memory and to remember him, now and always. **Rest eternal grant unto
Stephen Lawrence, O Lord. And let light perpetual shine upon him and may he rise in
glory.**' (Emboldened text in the original.) John Sentamu invited a number of the
principals to a memorial vigil for Stephen Lawrence on the anniversary of his death
on 22 April 1998.

[180] Although the public was reported at first to be preponderantly white. Marc
Wadsworth was said to have commented that 'activism is not there'. See *New Nation*,
23 March 1998.

campaigning groups and voicing their incredulity at the multiple organisational failures of the Metropolitan Police.'[181] It focused on the exposure of error, omission, and failure.[182] For members of the Stephen Lawrence Family Campaign it was a theatrical *dénouement*, a moment of realization: Ros Howells said:

It was, I mean a Hollywood drama has nothing on that, on it, okay? That's one. But from the first...this was a judge highly respected...but he couldn't at one time believe what he was hearing. You know, you almost saw him feeling 'hang on a minute'. And almost, you can think him thinking, 'how many times have I sat in judgement when these people [the police] have been lying to me?' Do you see? Because they were not even lying in a covering up way. They were lying as though we all belonged to the same society...But it took all of Mansfield's[183] skills to bring them to the attention that this was serious.

For the police, on the other hand, it was a Calvary. The Inquiry was, in short, highly charged and often confrontational, veering between what Upton called 'saccharine sentiment and naked adversarial aggression',[184] and some witnesses, like the Commissioner of the Metropolitan Police, were jeered when they testified.[185] The effect on the police was disturbing and constraining. Ian Johnston remembered, it was 'dreadful and the impact on what you say, what you don't say, you know that you are, you know you're going to be shouted down so do you say it and wind them up or do you not say

---

[181] J. McLaughlin and K. Murji; 'After the Stephen Lawrence Report', *Critical Social Policy*, August 1999, Vol. 19, No. 3, p. 371.

[182] Sir William recalled that 'It was the hardest thing I ever had to do. It was not at all an easy case to conduct. Many people would have failed to conduct it at all. I had to cope with extreme views from all directions.' *New Statesman*, 21 February 2000.

[183] Michael Mansfield QC, acting for the Lawrence family is, one of the doughtiest counsel in the United Kingdom. Variously described in the mass media as 'flamboyant' and 'colourful', and by the *Guardian*, 19 January 2003, as 'A law unto himself [a man who] has made his name fighting cases no one else would touch.' BBC On-line of 2 July 2001 observed that 'If Michael Mansfield QC worked in the United States his profile would probably be on a par with OJ Simpson's flamboyant lawyer, Johnny Cochran.'

[184] Ian Johnston remembered that 'you'd hear error after error after error after error after error. Did they do nothing right? Of course they did nothing right because you never heard about the things that went right. They're only hearing about the things that went wrong.'

[185] BBC News On-Line, 19 February 1999. One of the officers involved in the 'first investigation' reported that 'From the time we walked in we were abused, jeered at, laughed at—and I felt the chairman allowed [it to] happen.' *The Times*, 25 February 1999.

it and ... ? ... It blows you mentally. I was exhausted. ... I found it
the worst experience.' Brian Cathcart reported that the Inquiry:

remained tense and ill-tempered throughout. The 'prosecution' teams were
in varying degrees sceptical about the whole inquiry process and one
lawyer went so far as to remark that it had been 'set up to fail'. The
'defence' teams, representing the police and the CPS, accumulated their
own grievances, both against the 'prosecution' teams and against the
inquiry itself, while the inquiry staff—counsel, secretariat and panel—felt
themselves to be caught in the middle and unfairly criticized.[186]

## The Report

Race is back on the agenda in Britain. ... The new interest in racial issues is
directly traceable to a single event—the inquiry into the murder of Stephen
Lawrence.[187]

I have already anticipated some of the findings of the Inquiry report
that was to be published in February 1999, and I propose to confine
myself largely to their bearing on the treatment of victims of crime.
The Inquiry had lasted for sixty-nine days, was held in four cities,
heard eighty-eight witnesses in its first stage, and received one
hundred thousand pages of evidence.[188] I could find no sign in any
of that evidence of submissions made by groups supporting[189] and
campaigning for those bereaved by homicide: the voices of Justice
for Victims, SAMM (Support After Murder and Manslaughter),
Victim's Voice, the North of England Victims Association, the Suzy
Lamplugh Trust, the Zito Trust, and others were silent. It was not
their occasion[190] (Patsy Cullinan, then co-ordinator of SAMM, told

---

[186]   B. Cathcart; *The Case of Stephen Lawrence*, *op. cit.*, p. 315.

[187]   'Stephen Lawrence's Legacy', *The Economist*, 30 January 1999.

[188]   Home Secretary: Statement to House of Commons about report on Stephen
Lawrence Inquiry, 24 February 1999.

[189]   Other than the generalist Victim Support.

[190]   Interestingly, the converse was also to be true. A Grade 7 of JVU told the Racist
Incidents Standing Committee in October 2001 that there had not been a single reply
from the 25 minority ethnic groups that had been approached in the consultation on
the review of the *Victim's Charter*. If organizations for the secondary victims of
homicide did not take the Macpherson Inquiry to be their concern, minority ethnic
groups did not seem to take policies for victims to be theirs, such was the compart-
mentalization and racialization of the effects of the murder of Stephen Lawrence.

me simply in October 1999 'I've not read up on it . . . I don't think we were involved in it. I really don't.').

Instead, many of the principals observing and participating in the Inquiry, including the social anthropologist, Robin Oakley, who specialized in matters of race and who was one of those who came to propose the notion of 'institutional racism'[191] as an explanation

[191] He was to submit to the Inquiry on 18 April 1998 a note on 'Institutional Racism and Police Service Delivery' in which he argued, *inter alia*, that there is a 'well-recognised potential [amongst the police] for producing negative stereotypes of particular groups. Such stereotypes become the common currency of the police occupational culture . . . Failure to address them is liable to result in a generalised tendency . . . whereby minorities may receive different and less favourable treatment than the majority. Such differential treatment need be neither conscious nor intentional, and it may be practised routinely by officers whose professionalism is exemplary in all other respects . . . There is great danger in focussing on overt acts of personal racism by individual officers may deflect attention away from the much greater institutional challenge that has been identified above. This challenge potentially manifests itself in the daily activity of each member of staff. It was potentially— though not necessarily actually—manifest in the actions of every officer involved in the events following Stephen Lawrence's murder . . . institutional racism in this sense is . . . pervasive throughout the culture and institutions of the whole of British society, and is in no way specific to the police service . . . There is a need . . . to present the challenge in the clearest and most forthright terms possible, and a need also to demonstrate how a more subtle form of "racist conduct" may manifest itself at the level of service delivery on the street. The nature of the Stephen Lawrence Murder Inquiry provides a unique opportunity for these two needs to be met.' The Inquiry's report subsequently stated at 6.35: 'As Dr Oakely points out, the disease cannot be attacked by the organisation involved in isolation. If such racism infests the police its elimination can only be achieved "by means of a fully developed partnership approach in which the police service works jointly with the minority ethnic communities. How else can mutual confidence and trust be reached?".' There were others who laid claim to having suggested the term to the Inquiry. One was Herman Ouseley, the Chair of the Commission for Racial Equality, in his Annual Greenwich Lecture: 'Racism: Facing the Challenge, Making the Change', 16 November 1998. In his turn, Herman Ouseley had been advised by the sociologist Simon Holdaway, who recalled that 'The Commission for Racial Equality had asked me to write their evidence for Part 1 of the Lawrence Inquiry, which was about the police investigation. The dominant idea in the minds of the counsel representing various parties was one of individual police officers who were racists, of policies that were deliberately discriminatory, and so on. This was understandably getting them nowhere, and the Commission needed to fathom how they could move beyond that individualistic analysis of officers as racists which was dominating the Inquiry. My view was that counsel has to tease-out the ways in which officers of all ranks neglected to take "race" into account during their routine work and, when they did account for it, how it was mediated in discriminatory ways through the occupational culture.' S. Holdaway; 'Sociologists in the News: A Sociologist's involvement in the Lawrence Inquiry', *BSA Network*, October 1999, p. 11.

of police conduct, had focused almost wholly on issues of race as they arose.[192] The report was 'expected to be a devastating criticism of racial attitudes in the Metropolitan Police'.[193] And the police themselves awaited it with trepidation (Commander Campbell of the Metropolitan Police said a few days before its publication: 'we're going to get hammered over Lawrence, there's no doubt about it.'). So did Government departments: an official of the Court Service Agency recollected, 'you know there'd been mad letters going around to all Government departments asking them to certify themselves as being institutional racism-free zones which as we hadn't had the report and didn't have a clue what "institutional racism" meant put us in rather a difficult position. But needless to say we, like the judges, are absolutely certain that they're not institutional racists. How could I possibly be?'

I have said that, with perhaps one very marginal exception,[194] the Inquiry had not found evidence of explicit racism[195] and

---

[192] For instance, his notes after attending the Inquiry in the morning of 8 April 1998 read in part: 'Asked whether he considered the possibility of an unprovoked stabbing of a black youth by a group of whites being racially motivated, Mr J [the former Detective Inspector Jeynes] agreed that he did not do this until he heard of the evidence from Duwayne Brooks, who stated that one of the attackers shouted "Nigger, Nigger". This is indicative of a low level of awareness of the possibility of racial motivation in such incidents among officers, and a low priority being given to this aspect of crime. It may also be indicative of the presence of diversionary stereotypical assumptions about young black people (e.g. involvement in drugs/gangs) among officers.'

[193] *Daily Mail*, 24 February 1999.

[194] That was the use by Ian Johnston of the word 'coloured' instead of a more correct term. 'Mr Johnston had the unfortunate experience of allowing himself to use the word "coloured" when describing people from various ethnic backgrounds. The word plainly slipped out wholly unexpectedly and mistakenly. We accept his explanation in this respect and believe that Mr Johnston would not otherwise use such an expression, which is now anathema, and that he would reprimand anybody who did use this word, which is notoriously offensive to black people.' (*Report*, 30.13).

[195] Cathcart observed 'As the inquiry moved towards its close it was still the case that no evidence had been produced of a single act of deliberate, malicious racism by a single officer. Nor had it been shown that racism in any form had been the primary cause, or even one of several primary causes, of the failure of the Stephen Lawrence investigation. But this did not mean that the Met had won the argument, for the chairman still had the power to "infer" racism...', p. 357. Waddington wondered 'whether or not the inquiry was logically entitled to infer the existence of institutional racism from a single case... [yet] the inescapably *political* fact is that the routine activities of police officers have been authoritatively branded as racist'.

propounded instead the quite widely endorsed[196] thesis that what
had marred the investigation of the death and the treatment of the
Lawrence family was 'institutional racism',[197] a Black Power idea
flowing from the 1960s,[198] defined in the report as 'The collective
failure of an organisation to provide an appropriate and professional
service to people because of their colour, culture or ethnic origin.
It can be seen or detected in processes, attitudes and behaviour
which amount to discrimination through unwitting prejudice, ignorance, thoughtlessness or racist stereotyping which disadvantage
ethnic people.'[199] 'We put it that way,' said Sir William, 'because
we wanted to get across the distinction between the "bad apples" of

P. Waddington; 'Discretion, 'Respectability' and Institutional Police Racism', *Sociological Research Online*, Vol. 4, No. 1, 1999, p. 1. Much of the debate about institutional racism is redolent of another, more or less contemporary academic debate
about the existence of embedded racism in British education. An article asserting that
there were no racist practices in a school studied was itself defined *ipso facto* as racist.
See M. Hammersley; 'Research and "anti-racism": the case of Peter Foster and his
critics', *British Journal of Sociology*, September 1993, Vol. 44, No. 3, pp. 430–48.

[196] For example, the submission by National Assembly Against Racism and the
1990 Trust argued 'The perception of black communities in general terms is that the
Police are racist, aggressive and increasingly corrupt... The submitting organisations
all agree that the metropolitan police is an institutionally racist organisation.'
[197] Some academic commentators, including Peter Waddington, would hold that
the concept of 'institutional racism' was supported as a consolation to the Lawrences
in the absence of compelling evidence of individual racism.
[198] And particularly S. Carmichael and C. Hamilton; *Black Power: The Politics of
Liberation*, Penguin, Harmondsworth, 1968.
[199] And, phrased thus, it was not necessarily acceptable to a number of activists
who would have had the Inquiry address issues of police accountability. Institutional
racism, some claimed, finessed those issues. Marc Wadsworth of the ARA said: 'there's
a real danger I think that you know, all the way through the report you show the
reference to institutional racism but you also, rather alarmingly, see this definition of
unintentional racism of individuals. So in other words, the institution is racist but no
one, no one in the institution is responsible for that racism.' Rajiv Menon, who had
appeared at the Inquiry as counsel, had other reservations: 'this is the real difficulty
with this report. Because I mean, on the one hand, it's wonderful that we've reached
this position that the arguments that have been raised by, you know activists, for so
many years have now gotten this sort of platform, this sort of credibility. On the other
hand, there's a real danger that it's just going to be completely wasted and you
know... unwitting racism... institutional racism, does have an element of so-called
unwitting unconscious racism, but to say that that's it... I mean effectively we become
thought police... I've never been in favour of creating new offences of racist violence.
The problem is not that we don't have sufficient laws. We've got more than enough
laws. The problem is laws aren't being properly used and implemented. So creating

Scarman[200]—the few individual overtly racist officers—and those who support a culture within an organisation such as the police force without intending to do so. I believe we have made it crystal clear that, because we call the Metropolitan Police institutionally racist, not every policeman is a racist.'[201]

In common with other public inquiries, the report of the Macpherson Inquiry read rather like a judicial summing-up of the evidence instead of a structured or historically informed analysis,[202] but it was none the less condemnatory of the Metropolitan police, describing them as riddled with 'racism, professional incompetence and bad leadership'. Written in what The Times called 'graphic and unequivocal language',[203] it ruled that there had been a lack of adequate police documentation; a neglect of Duwayne Brooks' evidence; a lack of proper searches; a lack of arrests when names were received; an unwitting racism at work; and incompetently conducted surveillance. The Lawrences had been treated badly: 'From the first contact with police officers at the hospital and thereafter, Mr and Mrs Lawrence were treated with insensitivity and lack of sympathy. One of the saddest and most deplorable aspects of the case concerns the failure of the family liaison. Mr and Mrs Lawrence were not dealt with or treated as they should have been. They were patronised. They were never given information about the investigation to which they were entitled.' There had been a 'deplorable failure' of family liaison. There had been a failure to treat Duwayne Brooks as a 'primary victim'.

And seventy recommendations were made, ten of which bore directly on the treatment of victims, and eight of which were to be

additional burdens to prove mental motive and mental elements of racism is just making it more difficult.'

[200] The Brixton Disorders, 10–12 April 1981: report of an inquiry chaired by Lord Scarman. Cmnd. 8427, HMSO, London, 1981.

[201] The Times, 1 April 1999.

[202] Ben Bowling said that 'the Lawrence Inquiry lacks a coherent analysis of the problem of violent racism and the failures of the state response to it.' Violent Racism: Victimization, Policing and Social Context, op. cit., p. xvii.

[203] The Times, 25 February 1999. Ian Johnston agreed: 'it gives no attention or scant attention to social context. There isn't a proper historical perspective. I just think it's a real shame ... although we, many of our people regard it as unfair and the like, I think it was very cathartic, invaluable, you know, horrible but it was definitely motivational. And I think faced now with just the report, I think it is, it doesn't crystallise the issues in the way that Scarman did.'

entrusted, *inter alia*, to the Victims Steering Group: recommendation 9 reciting that the Freedom of Information Act[204] should be
open to all aspects of policing; recommendation 12 that a racist
incident should henceforth be an incident so defined by a victim or

[204] The introduction of freedom of information was part of New Labour's modernizing, constitutional reform and human rights projects, and it was designed to
make Government and public authorities more transparent. It was presaged in the
1979 election manifesto; and appeared as a white paper in December 1997 (*Your
Right to Know: The Government's proposals for a Freedom of Information Act*, 11
December 1997, Cm. 3818). Responsibility for freedom of information was assumed
by the Home Office in Summer 1998 to be developed alongside other constitutional
measures such as the Human Rights Acts and data protection (that critical matter of
the 'balance between the right to know and the right to privacy' had been noted by
Public Administration Committee Reports, *Third Report*, 1997–8, *Access to Information and the Right to Privacy*, p. 1). The House of Commons was told in a debate on
the Macpherson report and freedom of information on 29 March 1999 that the
Government proposed to exclude two classes of information: information about
investigations or prosecutions, and information about informants. A draft Bill was
then published in May 1999, and it was obliged to be consistent with the contradictory
European data protection directive and the Data Protection Act which overrode it (the
white paper noted that protection in the area of law enforcement is common to all
freedom of information legislation). It included special exemptions flowing from the
Data Protection Act that would have blocked the demands of the Lawrence family for
information about the course of the police investigation, including information held
for the purpose of a criminal investigation and criminal proceedings (under section
28); (section 29) the prevention or detection of crime, apprehension or prosecution of
offenders, the administration of justice; and (section 30) court records and papers laid
before a court in proceedings. Legal advisers at the Home Office, considering the
recommendation of the Macpherson report, argued initially that the Bill contained a
class exemption. There was, they said, no need to show any harm. The power to
disclose information to a third party was governed by the complicated relations
between the Data Protection Act and the Freedom of Information Act, and no greater
power was likely to be conferred in practice. The Freedom of Information Act created
no right of information held by the police or other criminal justice agencies about the
conduct of a particular case. Officials and politicians then began to have doubts,
observing that the public interest in disclosure might outweigh the narrow restriction
on disclosure for policing purposes. A consultation paper had stated that 'There will
be a requirement on police forces to give out information about the conduct of
inquiries (provided it does not prejudice law enforcement)' (Freedom of Information
Consultation on Draft Legislation, Cm. 4355, May 1999) and the Home Secretary
had declared that 'A careful balance has to be struck between extending access to
information and preserving confidentiality where disclosure would be against the
public interest... the scales [are] weighted decisively in favour of openness' (Home
Office press release 161/99, 24 May 1999). There was to be a new criterion of the
public interest, and debate hinged on what was meant by harm, substantial harm, and
prejudice. But, in the event, the line was held and the public interest in policing was

'any other person'; 23, that trained family liaison officers[205] should be available at local level; 25, that family liaison officers should treat victims' families 'with respect'; 26, that investigating and family liaison officers should keep families informed; 29, that there should be new guidelines for the handling of victims and witnesses of racist incidents, and that the *Victim's Charter* should be 'reviewed in this context'; 30, that the police and Victim Support should ensure the 'pro-active use of local contacts within minority ethnic communities' to assist Victim Support; 35, that the CPS should consult the victim or family if there was a proposal to discontinue proceedings; 36, that the CPS should notify the victim and family personally if a case was to be discontinued; 41, that victims or their families could become 'civil parties' to criminal proceedings; and 44, that the police and courts should help to prevent the intimidation of victims and witnesses by imposing bail.

Such was the moral and political authority of the report that it could not lightly be disregarded or criticized (although Doreen Lawrence was reported to have said that it had 'only scratched the surface and has not gone to the heart of the problem';[206] Imran Khan, a solicitor more usually representing defendants, voiced the conventional lawyerly anxiety that it might upset the proper

---

defined as before as matters affecting the prevention or detection of crime, the protection of informants, the apprehension or prosecution of offenders, and the administration of justice. The police in the 1990s began seeking Home Office guidance on how they should proceed and were told that procedures would not secure the rights of victims in the way envisaged when the report was prepared, although rights could be safeguarded by the preparation of guidance to the police on liaison with victims and their families and by the CPS communicating directly with victims when charges are dropped or downgraded. Yet there was a small element of discretion creeping in so that the meeting of the Lawrence Steering Group was told in June 2000 that the Government had published its Freedom of Information Bill in November 1999, that it covered 'all aspects of policing apart from two exemptions', and that, even when those exemptions applied, discretionary disclosure provisions would enable information to be disclosed where it is in the public interest. There were repeated delays in enacting the Bill. The Act was passed finally in 2001, but the Lord Chancellor stated that it was unlikely to come into effect before 2005 (*The Times*, 13 November 2001).

[205] A police role, established originally at the instigation of Victim Support, and attached only to the families of murder victims, that would relay intelligence from the family to the investigating officers, and provide support and intelligence to the family in return.

[206] *The Voice*, 1 March 1999.

relations between defence and prosecution;[207] the Police Federation, representing junior officers, rejected the finding of institutional racism;[208] and some Conservative Members of Parliament dismissed the report as an unwarranted and dangerous attack on the police[209]). The prime target, the Commissioner of the Metropolitan Police, Sir Paul Condon, accepted the report and its conclusions and declared that he had come to feel ashamed of the police investigation and the way in which his officers had failed the family. He was repeatedly to say thereafter 'we have learned some very public and painful lessons',[210] but recriminations lingered. There was a spate of calls for his resignation (which Jack Straw dismissed). And

[207] 'For me, there's got to be a balance that's got to be struck between the victim's rights and defendant's rights and my worry is that this Government will, there will be a sense of imbalance and what Lawrence and every other case, in terms of miscarriage on victim's points of view, is going to allow the Government to introduce far greater draconian legislation against defendants. And I think that that's wrong.' Duwayne Brooks' counsel, Rajiv Menon, echoed his concern: 'I am opposed' he said, 'to any measure that encroaches on the rights of defendants ... Against any [and] any new law professing to be more victim friendly but [which] actually gives more powers to the police and authorities' (Speaking at a session on 'Victim-Friendly Justice' at a conference organized by *LM Magazine* on 'Culture Wars—Dumbing Down, Wising Up, 6 March 1999, my notes). The magazine devoted a major portion of one of its issues to the Report, and was largely condemnatory of the proposal to award victims greater rights. See especially J. Fitzpatrick; 'The Macpherson Report in the Dock', *LM*, 119, April 1999, pp. 19–20.

[208] They were broadly supportive of the report's recommendations but argued that many mistakes had stemmed from bad management decisions and not necessarily because of inherent racism by individual officers. Police Federation's response to the Macpherson Report.

[209] Gerald Howarth MP remarked in a House of Commons debate on the report on 29 March 1999 that 'every allowance is shown towards the Lawrences—quite understandable in the circumstances—but little latitude is afforded to the police, who are subject throughout to the precision weapon of 20:20 hindsight. That is rich, coming from a committee of inquiry that was so incompetent that it overlooked the publication of the names and address of vulnerable witnesses.' William Hague, the Leader of the Opposition, then told the Police Federation Annual Conference in May 2000: 'I well understand your resentment of the charge of "institutional racism". No one, and I suspect least of all you, would deny that there are many things we need to improve in our police service, and many things we need to improve in society at large—but the slogan of "institutional racism" has been lifted out of context from the Macpherson Report and used by some to brand tens of thousands of decent, unprejudiced police officers as racists.' The Shadow Home Secretary, Ann Widdecombe, promised on re-election to return to a '"colour-blind" approach to policing.' (*Evening Standard*, 27 September 2000).

[210] In, for example, 'Protect and Respect: The Met's Diversity strategy', undated.

Sir William was to say of Sir Paul's description of his force as grieving: 'The Lawrences grieve and they will never stop grieving...A police force does not grieve. The police have been castigated. They have taken a blow. They have got to get over it.'[211]

In his statement to the House of Commons on the day the report was published, the Home Secretary also talked both of Sir Paul's shame and his own shame at the conduct of the criminal justice system. The Government had decided, he said, to accept the findings and conclusions of the first part of the Inquiry. It accepted the report's finding of the central part played by racism and its definition of institutional racism ('The central and most important issue for the inquiry was racism...The inquiry addresses that matter with care and sensitivity'). He welcomed the recommendations, and promised to lay before the House a detailed response and action plan before the debate on the report but, in the interim, he announced that the Government was already ensuring that victims, victims' families, and vulnerable witnesses 'are treated more sensitively and fairly' and he turned in his support to the Youth Justice and Criminal Evidence Bill which was then before Parliament. He came to accede to all but a few of the recommendations,[212] and those few he promised to consider.[213] I shall list his responses below.

## Implementation and Impact

The report and the recommendations touching victims sustained the political momentum of the campaign to be fed diffusely and rapidly into the work of the Home Office, the criminal justice system,[214] and

---

[211] *The Times*, 18 February 2000.

[212] *Stephen Lawrence Inquiry: Home Secretary's Action Plan*, Home Office, London, March 1999.

[213] 'There were two recommendations that were regarded as controversial', he said, those touching on the criminalization of racist speech emitted in private (a response by Macpherson to the surveillance video of the suspects) and the abolition of double jeopardy (the *autrefois acquit* rule). 'The recommendation was that we should consider changing the law. You're all familiar with the English language. "Consider" is a very broad term. We are considering the matter very carefully...'. Jack Straw speaking at Foreign Press Association, London, 12 October 1999, my notes.

[214] McLaughlin observed that 'no part of the criminal justice system will remain untouched'. E. McLaughlin; 'The search for truth and justice', *Criminal Justice Matters*, Spring 1999, No. 35, p. 13.

the organizations in and around their boundaries.[215] They were of cardinal importance, the trilateral Ministers of the criminal justice system declaring in 1999 that 'One of the most significant challenges facing the criminal justice system over the next three years is tackling the agenda set by the Macpherson inquiry report into matters arising from the death of Stephen Lawrence.'[216]

Bodies confessed to their own institutionalized racism[217] and examined their practices in the light of what the recommendations had said[218] (the Victims Steering Group, for example, enlarged its own membership in June 1999 to include for the first time people from minority ethnic groups). Existing committees were entrusted with the report's progress, the Victims Steering Group being supplied at each meeting for some two years with a tabulated 'summary of progress on [the eight] recommendations in which VSG has an interest'. Existing programmes and timetables of work were scrutinized. When Ian Chisholm reported to a meeting of the Victims Steering Group held in November 1999 that 'the links are not always as consistent or tight as they should be. We need to make those mechanical links', he was told by its chairman, John Halliday, that 'the Home Secretary attaches the highest importance to the action plan so we must ensure here consistent agendas across

[215] The Magistrates' Association set up a race issues group after the report, for example. Meeting of RISC, 30 September 1999, my notes. And all criminal justice agencies, including the police, were expected to have an 'action plan on race and equality issues' in operation by Spring 2000 (see *Crown Prosecution Service, Annual Report for April 1998–March 1999*, 2 August 1999). All criminal justice agencies were obliged to set targets for ethnic minority recruitment. Voluntary sector organizations were reminded about the problems of institutional racism (see M. Blake; 'After Macpherson: issues for the voluntary sector', *Voluntary Voice*, June 1999) and so it went on.

[216] Criminal Justice System Strategic Plan 1999–2002—Foreword from the three Ministers. Touching a point I shall make below, it is instructive that an earlier, February 1999, draft of that plan had nothing to say about victims in the context of the Macpherson Inquiry.

[217] Victim Support, for instance, admitted that it was institutionally racist in April 2000. Draft minutes of meeting of Victim Support Trustees, 14 April 2000. It instituted 'diversity training' to sensitize its staff to issues of race and racism ('Promoting diversity in Victim Support—proposal to the Trustees', undated).

[218] Thus Beverley Thompson, employed by NACRO, a member of the Lawrence Steering Group, and added to the Victims Steering Group partly because she was from a minority ethnic group, asked the Victims Steering Group about a report on the restorative justice pilot projects: 'Why is there nothing about race and diversity issues in the report?' My notes of the meeting of the Victims Steering Group, 28 April 2000.

the action plans and things are taken forward quickly'.[219] Old committees were reconstituted[220] or awarded greater importance[221] and new committees and projects[222] were established to shepherd the recommendations to a conclusion. And all at first was marked by a sense of extraordinary and overriding urgency. When, for instance, a CPS official alluded to legal problems of confidentiality in the disclosure of information by the police to victims' families[223] at a meeting of the Racist Incidents Standing Committee in September 1999, John Grieve of the Metropolitan Police said simply 'Sir William did not take that line with us in his questioning and it was made clear to us that we should not raise too many difficulties'.[224] And the change was obvious to the recipients of information. Imran Khan said in November 1999 'what has happened is that there is a sea change, whether it's temporary, whether it's because it's me, I don't know. But certainly the approach from the senior police officers is "yes, we will, we're happy to work with you, co-operate with you, give you access to information, no problem".'

The Home Secretary took it upon himself personally to chair a new steering group charged with implementing the recommendations, saying 'when I published the report of the Stephen Lawrence Inquiry... I gave a commitment to publish an action plan setting out how the Government proposes that the report's recommendations will be taken forward... I will take personal responsibility for

---

[219] Meeting of the Victims Steering Group, 24 November 1999, my notes.

[220] For example, the Home Office's RISC (Racist Incidents Standing Committee since August 1998), formerly known as RAG (the Racist Attacks Group which had been established in 1986 in response to the Home Affairs Committee Report, *Racial Attacks and Harassment*), acquired an agenda largely dominated by the Macpherson recommendations, including recommendation 15 which required the preparation of the *Code of Practice on Reporting and Recording Racist Crimes*, Home Office, April 2000.

[221] Thus in 1999 the ACPO Community and Race Relations sub-committee became one of the six full ACPO Committees. In formulating its plans to develop an Action Guide to Race/Hate Crime, it marked that 'the document's standing must be explicit, i.e. Lawrence Inquiry Recommendations, Home Secretary's Action Plan'. Note of the first meeting of the Working Group, 1 June 1999.

[222] One was the Metropolitan Police Service's *Operation Athena*, targeted at racist crime, which was reported on one single occasion to have involved the mass arrest of 100 racists. *The Times*, 23 February 2000.

[223] Under the Data Protection Act and Articles 6 and 8 of the Human Rights Act.

[224] And see the report in the *Evening Standard*, 5 January 1999.

oversight of this programme.'[225] And his chairing was to be vigorous and vigilant,[226] conferring an extraordinary authority to an already commanding document.[227] It was reinforced privately by internal inquisitions[228] and publicly by new performance indicators[229] and annual reviews of progress and thematic inspections by the Inspectorates of Constabulary[230] and Probation[231] and other regulatory bodies. The Secretary of the Group commented that 'There was talk at the time about "whatever had happened to that excellent Scarman Report?", but the Home Secretary was very clear that he didn't want this to happen to that [Macpherson] report.'[232]

The initial composition of the Steering Group, with no victims' interests represented,[233] and its administrative supervision by the

[225] *Stephen Lawrence Inquiry: Home Secretary's Action Plan*, Home Office, March 1999, p. 1.

[226] When another CPS official complained in 1999 that resources were insufficient to introduce measures intended to inform victims about the progress of cases, he was very roundly rebuked in committee by the Home Secretary.

[227] He wrote in his formal response to *Winning the Race*, a report on the policing of race by the Inspectors of Constabulary that 'We are now at a watershed in police community and race relations—this is a time for permanent and irrevocable change.' Home Office Press Release 067/99, 1 March 1999. And see his comments reported in the *Evening Standard*, 25 February 1999.

[228] There was to be what was called 'a Council of War on Race & Criminal Justice' between officials in the Home Office in October 1999 to 'share information about what's happening in our neck of the woods and in CPS/LCD; Policy developments/ Lawrence agenda research; Front end planning/CSR/race equality; Monitoring—current state of play; problem; The big obstacles to getting a grip on race in the CJS.' Email to Ian Chisholm 14 October 1999.

[229] Home Office News Release: New Ministerial Priority for policing minority ethnic communities, 177/99, 14 June 1999. The new indicators were numbers of recorded racist incidents; use of stop and search and their impact on different ethnic groups; levels of recruitment, retention, and progression of minority ethnic staff; surveys of public satisfaction, where they are available, by different ethnic groups. None touched on victims *per se*.

[230] See *Winning the Race: Policing Plural Communities Revisited*: HMIC Thematic Inspection Report on Police Community and Race Relations 1998–9; and HM Inspectorate of Constabulary; *Policing London: 'Winning Consent:' A Review of Murder Investigation and Community and Race Relations in the Metropolitan Police Service*, Home Office, 2000.

[231] For example, HM Inspectorate of Probation; *Towards Race Equality*, Home Office, 2000.

[232] Patricia MacFarlane speaking at the Victim Support Seminar on Stephen Lawrence, 15 February 2000, my notes.

[233] The Steering Group was said, in conventional fashion, to have 'all key interests ... represented', being made up of members of the Race Relations Forum, the

Home Office Operational Policing Policy Unit, betrayed that it was taken principally at first to touch on matters of policing in an environment of race, not the treatment of victims and their families.[234] It was an impression reinforced by a briefing given to the Prime Minister on 'Law and Order' in October 1998 where it was said that there was a 'big agenda' about to flow from the Lawrence Report but the agenda was about policing ethnic minority communities, about the officers involved in the inquiry, and 'about the way police handle what they should be best at', the investigation of serious crime, not about victims.

That changed. The Home Secretary indicated before the very first meeting of the Steering Group in May 1999 that he wished to receive further background information about work being done around the report's recommendations, implicitly including, and as a matter of course, information on the recommendations about the treatment of victims. It was necessary, Ian Chisholm was told in April by the head of the Operational Policing Policy Unit, particularly to show good community consultation and that account has been taken of the interests of victims in the field of racist incidents and crimes. And that request for information was to lead to a more generous recognition of the scope of the report and a greater involvement of JVU. John Halliday told the head of the Operational Policing Policy Unit in May that Ian Chisholm was one of the heads of the units most directly involved and that a meeting would be appropriate: it was important to establish whether necessary detailed plans were in place; if not, when they would be; what arrangements should be made for monitoring progress; and an understanding about who was responsible for which part of the action plan. JVU was thus to be drawn in as the unit 'owning' some of the

Commission for Racial Equality, the Black Police Association, the Association of Police Authorities, ACPO, the Police Federation, the Superintendents Association, HM Inspectorate of Constabulary, the Metropolitan Police, and the Crown Prosecution Service.

[234] And that was mirrored by other formal responses anticipating or following the Stephen Lawrence Inquiry. For example, the report of papers presented at a conference held on 18 December 1998 and organized by the Metropolitan Police on 'Working together towards an Anti-Racist Police Service', said nothing about the treatment of victims. Neither did a paper by the General Council of the Bar: Race Relations Committee; *The Stephen Lawrence Inquiry Report: The Response of the Bar Council*, Considered by the GMC, 2 December 1999.

recommendations for victims. Herman Ouseley of the Commission for Racial Equality was also to propose the inclusion of members 'representing concerns of service users and victims, which may be critical to the group's public credibility.'[235] By the third meeting in October 1999, Ian Chisholm and a Grade 7 of JVU had joined as 'officials attending'.[236] Issues of implementation then rather more fully encompassed victims, although it is notable that the Home Secretary's forewords to his *Action Plan* and to the first and second annual reports of subsequent progress still made no explicit mention of victims: 'This plan', he said at the outset, 'is mainly about improvements in policing, because that was the focus of the Inquiry.' To be sure, improvements in policing do embrace the treatment of victims, but it was a fact not much trumpeted.

Quite predictably too, implementation was channelled through routine working practices in and around the committees of Government and the voluntary sector.[237] The uncommon politics of a 'racialised' victim may have taken the impact of the death of Stephen Lawrence to the offices and committee rooms of the Home Office (in Marc Wadsworth's phrase 'black people [had] been used as a battering ram') but, once there, they were inevitably to be 'normalized' and standardized; transplanted and modified from committee to committee;[238] made compatible with other policy and legal

---

[235] CRE response to the Stephen Lawrence Inquiry: Action Plan, 23 April 1999.

[236] Lawrence Steering Group: Minutes of Third Meeting, 13 October 1999.

[237] Coretta Phillips reminded me that the same process occurred with race and the social exclusion agenda.

[238] Before the Macpherson Inquiry report, the local Criminal Justice Strategy Groups had had no representation from victim service people and none from ethnic minority communities. A member of ACOP remarked to RISC in September 1999 'I couldn't believe what I was seeing'. And, in June 1999, Anne Viney of Victim Support talked about the growing consolidation of different committees around problems of race, policing, and victimization: 'the interesting thing about it is that really I think almost prior to the Lawrence Inquiry report, there wasn't that much of a linkup that was overtly visible between Justice and Victims Unit, who sort of make in quotes, "the victims policies" and OPPU [the Operational Policing Policies Unit] which had the police and race group. Then when I got onto [RISC], I started saying "well you know, others of my colleagues who go to the Victims Steering Group and there's the Victims Charter and that Charter should get into the work plan of this committee." And post-Lawrence, at this week's meeting, Justice and Victims appeared at RISC, so it's now starting to linkup much better.'

imperatives[239] and *vice versa*;[240] merged, reformulated, and generalized to embrace victims and witnesses at large;[241] exposed to the integrative and smoothing work of 'joined-up government';[242] and subjected, in effect, to a form of benign entropy.[243] Entropy certainly affected police work. Maria Wallis, then Deputy Chief Constable of Sussex, and a member of the ACPO Crime Committee, said in March 1999: 'I think the recommendations of the Macpherson Report are significant for policing generally in all avenues of what we do, in major crime investigation, how we respond on the streets . . . '. And, she added, in response to my question about how

---

[239] For example, and as a matter of course, the new code for the reporting and recording of racist incidents had to comply with data protection directives. Minutes of RISC meeting of 19 April 2000.

[240] Discussing the role of the victim in restorative justice, the Chairman of the Victims Steering Group asked at a meeting on 28 April 2000 'do issues of equality come up: where one is talking about these issues, do race, gender, sexuality come up . . . ?'. Again, in considering a special meeting to consider the specific needs of victims of rape and domestic violence in implementing *Speaking up for Justice*, the Chairman's brief asked 'are there any gaps? Should there be a separate paper on racial issues?' (VIW: IMPSG, chairman's brief for meeting No. 5, 10 March 1999.)

[241] And it was not to apply only to victims but also to employment practices as well. The Better Regulation Task Force; 2nd Annual Report, 1999 said that 'In the light of the Lawrence Inquiry, there is an understandable demand for more regulation to counter discrimination related to race, gender, disability and sexual orientation. There is plenty of evidence to suggest that endemic discrimination exists.'

[242] Thus the Attorney General wrote to the Home Secretary and the Lord Chancellor in June 2001 to propose 'a criminal justice wide conference on race concentrating on the needs of racist victims' to enable the three strands of the CJS, police, prosecutors, and courts to hear from those representing or supporting victims, and to promote "a joined-up approach on issues affecting victims of racist crimes"'.

[243] Interestingly, what might be considered a parallel process was also in train whereby an attempt was made to generalize the recommendations of the Lawrence Report to the larger sphere of race and racism in the criminal justice system of England and Wales. A paper presented to the Lawrence Steering Group, '7(3), Future of the Lawrence Steering Group, HO June 2000', referred to a meeting of the 14 March 2000 in which questions were raised about the future work and focus of the Group. The paper was to recommend what it called a more strategic approach and the broadening of its remit to cover race and criminal justice issues 'in the broadest sense and not limited to precise Lawrence recommendations'. It was proposed that there should be a change in the Steering Group's terms of reference to 'To oversee and audit the implementation of the Home Secretary's Action Plan published in March 1999 as the Government's response to the Report of the Stephen Lawrence Inquiry and to advise the Home Secretary on other issues relating to securing racial justice and equality in the criminal justice system.'

she was interpreting those recommendations: 'I'm reading it as a senior police officer to see possible likely national implications for policing, the implications for suspects and, as part of my role for the Crime Committee, looking at investigations generally and within that for all the sorts of crime that I take a lead on, including domestic violence.'

Entropy was visible to those who had campaigned. Imran Khan commented: 'what I've been doing is I've been saying to people "look, this is not simply about improving the lot for black communities, it's not special privileges, it's improving the system as a whole. So where we have improvements in terms of double jeopardy, if that can be called that, in terms of victims' liaison, in terms of all, it would improve the lot for everybody." And if you explain that to the majority community, you're not going to have the resistance to that.' Similarly, Davinder Lakkhar, a District Judge of Asian origin, Chair of the Criminal Justice Consultative Council's reconvened Race Sub-Group that met for the first time in July 1999 in response to the Inquiry,[244] and, also post-Macpherson, a member of the Victims Steering Group, said:

[the report has] actually kick-started a general victims [policy thrust] rather than just victims from ethnic minorities. I think it's a gain for everybody as a community because I don't think they can be treated, I mean don't think ethnic minorities expect special treatment. I think what they do expect is treatment as a human being . . . I think you can't say well actually it should only be the ethnic minorities because I think victims generally have been ignored to a large extent. And I think it's in the general interest of victims generally.

The report's recommendations were not then taken to extend solely to black victims and their families but to victims *tout court* (Ros Howells observed, 'I keep saying, when I'm sitting in the black community, I remind them that there are 54 million people here and only 4 million of them are people of colour. So this isn't about that. It's about having a just society'[245]). In so doing, two

[244] In doing so, it announced that 'It is important in the light of the Lawrence Inquiry report and the recent attacks in Brixton and Brick Lane that the criminal justice agencies should make every effort to gain the trust of the ethnic minority members of the community . . .' *CJCC Newsletter*, 15, May/June 1999.

[245] Janet Foster has reminded me that that and other like observations marked an interesting change in the rhetoric surrounding the aftermath of the Inquiry. What had

conventional, interlaced processes came into play: initiatives already in train could economically and efficiently absorb or anticipate the new work of the Macpherson Report,[246] on the one hand, and, on the other, the report's political authority would make it possible to sweep up other victims,[247] including those politically less favoured, such as the targets of homophobic attacks, who had been brought to a simultaneous prominence by the Admiral Duncan public house bombing of 30 April 1999.[248] John Grieve told a meeting of RISC in September 1999 that 'There's a need for a broad strategy around the broad subject of hate . . . When the nail-bomber comes to trial we're in for some nasty shocks. Work around race would give support to work around other forms of crime.' It was in this fashion that racist crimes evolved within the policing sphere to become a sub-category of a larger and increasingly unwieldy class of offence, hate crimes,[249] which were placed rather vaguely under the *aegis* of the Macpherson

begun as a campaign quite clearly centred on racial injustice was transformed almost imperceptibly into a series of recommendations that could be applied without loss to the population at large, irrespective of race. Where, Janet Foster wondered, 'were these voices and arguments earlier on in the process?'.

[246] Thus the implementation plan of *Speaking up for Justice* came to be described as 'dealing with vulnerable or intimidated witnesses including the victims of racist incidents' (Stephen Lawrence Inquiry report: Summary of progress of recommendations in which VSG has an interest (April 2000)).

[247] For example, measures to help the families of murdered victims at large were approved in December 1998 in anticipation of the Macpherson Report, the phrase being 'taken forward as part of the response to Lawrence'. Those measures included the payment of expenses to families attending trial in a fund to be administered by Victim Support.

[248] There was some integration of the various groups of potential victims of hate crime who coalesced at the time of the bombing (David Copeland, the man responsible, had also released a bomb in Brixton, London, a predominantly Black area). Jeff Brathwaite, the Deputy Director of the Racist and Violent Crime Task Force said at the time: 'we've got an officer who majors in family liaison issues and that really came to the fore in the Soho bombings, when the alliances between minority groups, gay and lesbian groups . . . was crucial in supporting families'. Copeland was convicted in June 2000 of the murder of three people.

[249] Thus the Metropolitan Police Fact Sheets on Understanding and Responding to Hate Crime, undated but distributed at an American Society of Criminology Conference, November 2002, listed as hate crimes domestic violence, homophobic crime, sexual assaults, and racial violence. ACPO argued that what hate crimes had in common was a high potential for harming the victim, harming the victim group, and for harming society (ACPO *Guide to Identifying and Combating Hate Crime*, Metropolitan Police, London, December 1999, p. 1).

Report. ACPO developed a 'Race/Hate Crime Manual'[250] in response to the Macpherson Report, that, in the hands of its Race and Community Relations Sub Committee, progressively changed title from 'racist incidents' to 'race/hate crime' (in April 1999) to 'hate crime' (in June 1999).[251] Under the Metropolitan Police 'diversity strategy', a Racial and Violent Crime Task Force[252] was estab-

[250] Anne Viney of Victim Support, a member of the Racist Incidents Steering Group, commented 'when something gets really into the public arena, it can lose its focus. And at the moment I'm having a discussion with them about what is hate crime. Because the manual is for race stroke hate crime . . . gay organisations are on the working group. Now that's fine but that almost creates a situation where we can't discuss what hate crime is because they're already there. And when it got to disabled people and domestic violence and this long list started appearing, I then started to say "well you know, I'm not so sure about this because if you're saying people with disabilities may be more vulnerable because of their situation, like if I'm sitting in a wheelchair, it's easier for someone to snatch my handbag, okay, fine. But is that a hate crime?" And then if you're disabled and have a carer, you may be abused by that carer. That's not a hate crime, that's a crime . . . where it doesn't transfer is into the treatment of those people as victims because some of the things that might be appropriate for race crime, would be very detrimental in domestic violence. And police forces have already got manuals for that anyway . . . I really sort of object to domestic violence being added into a manual that was supposed to be about race, you know. And I thought that the post-Lawrence work would be lost and lose some of its focus if that were to happen.' Domestic violence was to be segregated after September 1999. Victim Support itself chose not to adopt the term 'hate crime' (Victim Support's services to victims of racist incidents and crimes, September 2000).

[251] Anne Viney was to write to the Committee in June 1999 that 'the focus on responses after the Lawrence Enquiry is on racist crimes, and I have put forward the view that it would be a pity to lose that'. There was a need, she said, to emphasize the manual's provenance in the Lawrence Inquiry and concerns about racist crime.

[252] In response to what it called a recognition of the impact of racial and violent crime on the community, its brief was to provides oversight of the Metropolitan Police Service's response to all racial and violent crime, develop standards, involve lay people, increase awareness of ethnic minority victims, focus on training needs, set standards, raise awareness, improve communication with communities, and integrate intelligence (Racial and Violent Crime Task Force—Action Plan—Operation Athena—7 December 1998). The involvement of lay people (which was to have a troubled history) entailed the establishment of a lay advisory group in January 1999 in the interests of accountability and the restoration of confidence with 35 lay members and 7 police members. It allowed lay people critically to appraise police policies and practices; make dispassionate assessments; and improve police-community relations. Amongst the 'key issues' were the handling and resolution of critical incidents, including 'victim/family support/liaison'. (Lay Advisory Group of the Metropolitan Police Service Racial and Violent Crime Task Force, undated.) John Grieve reflected that the Independent Advisory Group was 'probably one of the most dangerous things

lished in August 1998 to enhance responsiveness and transparency,[253] but it significantly lacked immediate victim representation.[254] The Metropolitan Police formed Community Safety
Units[255] in the London boroughs and issued a leaflet on hate
crime.[256] Jeff Brathwaite, a Black police officer serving as the
Deputy Director of the Task Force in June 1999 said.

It is our expectation that that will be the case because this Task Force is not
only about the Lawrence case, it's about good professional policing. And
it's about officers being professional in their investigation, professional in
dealing with first steps at the scene. And that's all crime, right across the
board [although] special policy consideration, I suppose, is needed in the
case of minority groups because officers need to recognise their needs are
different and to work according to the needs of individuals...crime may
very well be different but the sort of care given to victims, witnesses, should
be of a similar high standard and it's also tailored around the need of that
particular victim or victims at the time, be they white victims or from
minority groups. So the expectation is that having attained that standard,
it will benefit everyone, not only minority groups.

The very first meeting of the Lawrence Steering Group devoted some
time to what such a transition from racist crime to hate crime might

I ever did. My independent advisors are hard to hear voices...selected from our
sternest critics...about coffee time things began to go downhill. Start hearing the
voices of the dispossessed, the angry, the unheard. They are certainly our most
knowledgeable critics.' 11th Eve Savile lecture, 27 June 2000, my notes. For a report
about the Group and its discontents, see the *Sunday Times*, 24 October 1999. Denis
O'Connor, a senior officer, recorded that 'We opened up our work to rigorous scrutiny
by community groups, journalists and academics; above all we sought to work in
partnership with others—including people who can expose us to values, beliefs, ideas
and perspectives that are inevitably lacking in an organisation which is still 97% white
and 15% female. These included lay advisers to our Racial and Violent Crime Task
Force...'. *Evening Standard*, 15 November 1999.

[253] The Deputy Director of that Task Force, Deputy Chief Superintendent Jeff
Brathwaite, said 'one of the main issues that came out of the report was one of
openness and transparency with the minorities communities and part of our remit is
to ensure that there's a mechanism for that to happen'.

[254] Ben Bowling, a member of the Advisory Group, said in 1999 'certainly the
victims themselves are not really represented in the task force'.

[255] The Lewisham Community Safety Team; Tackling crime and disorder in Lewisham, plan of action 1999–2002, was targeted at 'race and other hate crime. Our plan
of action...To reduce racial harassment and attacks and homophobic violence and
abuse by 6% in the first year and by 20% in three years.'

[256] MPS, *Tackling Hate Crime Together*, undated.

signify, concentrating in particular on the hate crime leaflet: 'Some felt that because it was generic it fudged the issue of race. There were other issues, but the major concern was race and the leaflet needed to be more explicit. A generic leaflet had the superficial attraction of a broad approach ... However, there were issues of imagery and messages for the particular groups concerned.'[257]

Let me turn briefly to the fate of the Inquiry's recommendations between their publication and November 2002, when the Lawrence Steering Group decided that the report had been substantially implemented, that the Group should be dissolved, and any remaining work (none of which expressly touched victims) should be entrusted to five sub-groups. I shall take each recommendation in turn, reporting in brackets the response of the Home Secretary's 1999 *Action Plan* to what was proposed. Recommendation 9 ('accept in part'), dwelling on freedom of information and the victim's right to know about the conduct of an investigation, would apply to all areas of policing, 'subject only to the substantial harm test for withholding disclosure' and the two exceptions of information relating to informers and information relating to an investigation or prosecution. There was to be no absolute right of access and would never be so.[258] Lord Williams, the Minister in charge of the Freedom of Information Bill in the 1990s, reflected:

The Lawrences would have had access to more information. Obviously they wouldn't have had access to the individual details of the investigation and that's quite right because I just point myself in the opposite position, assuming that somebody is murdered and he's a member of the National Front or something. Now they could create all sorts of havoc and mischief with the police investigation and terrorize witnesses and complainants. So I ... think it is perfectly legitimate to restrict matter which might prejudice the trial, prejudice the investigation or put people at risk. And certainly there's the blanket exemption for informers. And I don't think you can run an investigative or criminal justice system myself on any other basis.

Recommendations 12–14 ('accept'), touching on the new definition of a racist incident, had been adopted immediately by the police,

---

[257] Lawrence Steering Group: Minutes of First Meeting, 18 May 1999.

[258] The Campaign for Freedom of Information: Briefings on Freedom of Information, undated, complained flatly that the Government had rejected the freedom of information recommendation of the Stephen Lawrence report.

CPS, and other agencies[259] but, it was noted, they should not pre-judge the question of whether the motive was racist or not. That could only be resolved at trial and the definition would be used primarily to take account of the possibility of a racist dimension to an incident.[260] Recommendations 23–28 ('accept'), dwelling on the training and preparation of family liaison officers, brought about a major revision of ACPO guidelines; the development of the role of the family liaison officer as a specialism (although not as a specialism focused only on the care of minority ethnic victims' families[261]); and a new training curriculum which had been incorporated in courses offered by thirteen police services by early 2000. Before the Mac-pherson Inquiry, no training at all had been offered family liaison officers, but 'in the 16–17 months since Sir William reported we've trained some 1200 liaison officers', reported John Grieve.[262] Rec-ommendations 29–31 and 44 ('accept') on the better protection of victims and witnesses of racist incidents and crimes had been sub-sumed by the expanded initiative on vulnerable or intimidated wit-nesses and incorporated in Part 2 of the Youth Justice and Criminal Evidence Act 1999. Recommendations 35, 36, and 37 ('require further consideration') on the duty of the CPS to inform and consult with victims had been twinned with the proposals of the Glidewell Committee and their execution was considered by JVU to be 'ongoing' (and we have already noted what became of them in

---

[259] *Stephen Lawrence Inquiry: Home Secretary's Annual Report on Implementation of his Action Plan*, Home Office, February 1999. See *Code of Practice on Reporting and Recording Racist Crimes*, Home Office, April 2000.

[260] *Code of Practice on Reporting and Recording Racist Crimes*, Home Office, London, April 2000, p. 5.

[261] Mark Simmons of the Metropolitan Police, who had drafted the Commission-er's submission to the Macpherson Inquiry, remarked that most of its recommenda-tions affected 'crime in general. Family liaison is a clear example, a clear example, and the recommendations in the report don't relate . . . exclusively to family liaison on race crime cases . . . And the response to that, our response to that, is in the short term, we've got to focus on some of the issues, we've got focus on professionalising the family liaison role, which it never has been . . . there's a clear cross over into family liaison in general . . . With one of the meetings I was at this morning, part of the purpose of that was to look at what's the learning from our response to the Lawrence Inquiry and Stephen's murder in terms of domestic violence, homophobic attacks, repeat victimisation in general, all those sort of areas.'

[262] John Grieve; 11th Eve Savile lecture, King's College, London, 27 June 2000, my notes.

Chapter 4). Recommendation 41 ('accept'), touching on civil parties, 'came largely out of the blue',[263] but met with initial approval by the Home Secretary.[264] It was coupled with the unresolved and vexed matter of victim statements, and referred to the special Home Office conference in Macclesfield in September 1999 on 'The Role of Victims in the Criminal Justice Process', where it was discussed at length. An encyclopaedic survey of the treatment of victims in 22 European jurisdictions[265] was there reviewed by its authors, Brienen and Hoegen, two young Dutch scholars,[266] and their conclusion that, on the one hand, the *parti civile* procedure offered few benefits to victims[267] and was rarely employed,[268] and, on the other,

[263] Ian Chisholm at the Home Office Conference on 'The Role of Victims in the Criminal Justice Process', 13 September 1999.

[264] He was reported by Patricia MacFarlane of the Operational Policing Policies Unit to have been sympathetic, having noted what was then the recent demonstration of victim alienation in the legal developments in the Bulger case (Victim Support: Institutional Racism, draft of 31 May 2000: summary of a seminar on issues arising from the Stephen Lawrence Inquiry, February 2000). And Ian Chisholm told that self-same seminar that 'We haven't yet reached a conclusion, but there is a feeling in the adversarial system, it's a very hostile system, we're looking for ways of ameliorating it. The Home Secretary did say in response to the Thompson and Venables finding, he was tempted to give victims a more formal role.'

[265] M. Brienen and E. Hoegen; *Victims of Crime in 22 European Criminal Justice Systems,* Wolf Legal Publications, Nijmegen, 2000.

[266] Ian Chisholm told a Victim Support seminar in February 2000 on the repercussions of the Stephen Lawrence Inquiry that 'It was very helpful to have a couple of Dutch academics who looked at the victim's role in 22 countries. It is quite a radical proposal.'

[267] The 'biggest problem' of the *parti civile* procedure, they claimed, 'was that... you force victims to participate'. A civil party has a right of audience and a right to examine the papers, but intervention is limited solely to matters of compensation (whose collection is actually more problematic in foreign jurisdictions than in England and Wales), one must be the direct victim of a loss caused by crime to be eligible, and one may have restricted rights to testify because a financial stake in the proceedings makes the evidence tendered suspect. Introducing foreign institutions like the civil party, Brienen and Hoegen claimed, could have far-reaching implications. (Demurring slightly, Professor John Spencer said at the conference that 'people don't expect in France to get compensation but they want their say and the *parti civile* gives them that.')

[268] Marc Groenhuijsen, Brienen's and Hoegen's academic supervisor, reflected baldly that the *parti civile* model is virtually futile if enforcement is left to the victim, as it is in France. 'Trends in Victimology in Europe with Special Reference to the European Forum for Victim Services', 10th Annual Conference of the Japanese Association of Victimology, Kyoto, 26th June 1999. Later, in June 2000, Ian Chisholm

that the role of auxiliary prosecutor offered more promise, was to be adopted by the conference at large and thence initially by Ministers, including the Home Secretary in November 1999. Rather than the *parti civile* proposal being flatly rejected, the auxiliary prosecutor could be tendered in its stead as a better route to the same end.

But the notion of an auxiliary prosecutor did not find favour with the senior judges, who complained in April 2000 that it would compromise the integrity of a prosecutor who was not the mouth-piece of the victim but an 'independent and fair presenter of a case'. It was imperative, they said, not to weaken a dispassionate and independent role or introduce prejudicial material. It was a view to be endorsed by Sir Robin Auld, at that time compiling what was described as 'a wide-ranging, independent review of the criminal courts',[269] announced in December 1999,[270] a review which might possibly, it was thought at the time, prove to be yet another critical influence on the development of policies for victims.[271] In the summer of 2000, Sir Robin Auld argued that the Macpherson recommendations on the *parti civile* were too complicated, likely to be too under-used, and not worth the outlay. The same problems were posed by the auxiliary prosecutor: it was a role that was largely symbolic and passive, and, in awarding a special position to the

reported on the conference that 'the evidence was that where there were civil parties, victims were acquiring only part of the benefits envisaged'. But, he added, 'we also heard about auxiliary prosecutors'. They could bring victims closer to the heart of the criminal justice system. A paper was prepared for Lawrence Steering Group on 14 March 2000, and it was agreed that a consultation paper should be issued. 'We are now drafting that paper.' The best way forward, he concluded, would probably be to 'build up' CPS responsibility for victims.

[269] *A Guide to the Criminal Justice System in England and Wales*, Home Office, London, 2000, p. 21.

[270] Criminal Courts Review: Press Notice, 14 December 1999.

[271] Sir Robin Auld had solicited submissions very widely from 'anyone with experience to share their views with him. Do courts meet their needs?'. The Review embraced, *inter alia*, 'service to and treatment of all those who use or have to use the courts or who are the subjects of their proceedings' (Criminal Courts Review: Press Notice, 24 January 2000). One such memorandum was to be tendered by Mediation UK in May 2000. And Helen Reeves had been appointed an 'expert consultee' to the Review (Criminal Courts Review: Press Notice, 27 March 2000). However, a two day conference conducted by Sir Robin in September 2000 had, according to one participant, 'barely got through the agenda and had not talked about victims'. Robert Latham, chair of the Victim Support National Council, observed 'I don't think he is particularly sensitive to the victim's agenda'.

victim, in potential breach of Article 6 of the Human Rights Act.[272] Sir Robin Auld's report did not in fact come to discuss victims[273] (a member of JVU observed 'I get the impression he's fairly traditional on victim issues') but his was an authoritative voice in concert with other judicial voices at a time when ideas about changes in the victim's position were again being mooted. In the Spring of 2000, Ministers decided not to proceed with the *parti civile* proposal, it was 'not appropriate',[274] but it was noted that the Home Office was investigating other ways of involving victims procedurally.

It will be recalled from Chapter 4 that the CPS were at that time bidding for £20 m. from the Comprehensive Spending Review's 'unallocated reserve' or 'victims' pot' to finance their new obligation to communicate directly with victims under the recommendations of the Glidewell and Macpherson Reports[275] (that was why the Home Secretary had hesitated a little in his response to recommendations 35–37) and it was thought that they could incorporate action on the auxiliary prosecutor role in what they did. The proposal entered the consultation paper[276] on the revisions to the *Victim's Charter*[277] that stemmed from Recommendation 29 ('accept'), Ian Chisholm having told Ministers in June 2000 that 'it could bring victims closer to the

[272] R. Auld; 'Rights of Victims of Crime', Indo-British Legal Forum, 25 June to 1 July 2000.

[273] *A Review of the Criminal Courts of England and Wales*, published in September 2001, discussed, *inter alia*, the codification of the criminal law; a national criminal justice board as the strategic planning authority; a criminal justice council to replace existing advisory and consultative councils; a unified criminal court; the end of an elective right in triable either way cases; fewer jury exemptions; and the transformation and rationalisation of the law of evidence. Ian Chisholm said in September 2000 that the review was likely at a number of points to dominate the Home Office legislative agenda for the next few years, and would be the main framework document for policy in the areas it covers. 'The problem', he said later, 'is the relationship of that to existing initiatives'. The fact that the report did not make recommendations did not, of course, stop those who worked on policies for victims at the turn of the century trying to anticipate what his report might have to say.

[274] Stephen Lawrence Inquiry report: Summary of progress of recommendations in which VSG has an interest (April 2000).

[275] Announced eventually in the form of Press Release: New Code for Crown Prosecutors published, 11 October 2000.

[276] Ian Chisholm observed in a policy paper in June 2000: 'Difficulties have been highlighted but we have agreed to issue a consultation document to look at alternative models of victim involvement.'

[277] *Stephen Lawrence Inquiry: Home Secretary's Action Plan, Second Annual Report on Progress*, Home Office, London, February 2001, p. 21.

heart of the Criminal Justice System'. But the Government came in time to believe that there were what were called 'philosophical and practical difficulties'[278] even with that proposal and it did not look at all promising: 'we're going to stop short of victims being a full party to the dispute. We've had a strong steer to that effect', Ian Chisholm told the Victims Steering Group in June 2001.[279] I shall return to those matters in the next chapter.

Much of the remainder of Recommendation 29, touching on vulnerable witnesses, had already been 'taken care of', as Ian Chisholm put it, by the work of the Vulnerable or Intimidated Witnesses Committee,[280] and other work was underway with the one-stop shop and the introduction of victim statements. But, critically, it was the recommendation's second strand, calling for a revision of the *Victim's Charter*, already contemplated for 2000–2001 'in the context of the Stephen Lawrence inquiry and the context of other policy developments since 1996',[281] that was to prove a major catalyst whose repercussions will also be reviewed in the next chapter.

## Conclusion

The murder of Stephen Lawrence had had a belated but explosive impact on the workings of the criminal justice system. The mix of what the campaign had accomplished and what the politicians of the New Labour administration had *allowed* it to accomplish, amounted to a very major jolt to the politics of the victim. No

---

[278] G. Bradshaw; 'Article 36 Committee, Agenda Item 13, protection of victims in the European Judicial Area', undated.

[279] Victims Steering Group: meeting of 12 June 2001. My notes. The paper prepared for that meeting, 'Stephen Lawrence Inquiry report: Summary of progress of recommendations in which VSG has an interest (April 2000)', commented that the Home Secretary had agreed the implementation plan of *Speaking up for Justice* that refers to the production of guidance for the police on dealing with vulnerable or intimidated witnesses including the victims of racist incidents.

[280] In the Implementation Programme Plan for the *Speaking up for Justice* Report—Implementation of Part II of the YJCE Bill, it was declared that implementation would take into account the recommendations of the Macpherson Report in relation to vulnerable witnesses in the Home Secretary's *Action Plan*.

[281] Discussion Paper for the Meeting of the *Ad Hoc* sub group of the VSG—to consider the implementation of the recommendations of the Stephen Lawrence Report, JVU, February 2000.

other episode recounted in this book was to have the popular and
political force of the death of Stephen Lawrence. It gave victims a
political voice, authority, and platform to which they were unaccus-
tomed. It delivered a chance to re-negotiate who and what victims
were, what they might need and what could be done for them. John
Halliday told the Victims Steering Group on 28 April 2000: 'There's
a strong desire within this group to make things happen and that
message will be taken away by CPS and Home Office colleagues and
conveyed to the Home Secretary and Lord Chancellor especially in
the light of Macpherson' (which, as Ian Chisholm added, 'is a
published commitment').

Yet it should be noted that there was always a hesitancy or indecision at the core of the Campaign and the Inquiry. It had not been
the plight of a bereaved family or the unsatisfactory circumstances
of an investigation alone that had produced that political
response. Neither was it the result of the plight of victims
conceived in any conventional sense, and victims were often over-
shadowed in the report and its aftermath, re-instated only as an
*arrière-pensée*.

The political response had arisen instead from a peculiar concat-
enation of a murder, on the one hand, and, on the other, of politically
charged readings of policing and racism, that led to victimization
being defined substantially and perhaps metaphorically as the op-
pressiveness of *race*. The matter of Stephen Lawrence was not
focused on the problems of mundane crime victims at all. To be
sure, after the Inquiry had reported, the bolder politics of race,
racism, and victims did recede, and recommendations touching on
victims were to be diffused through the criminal justice system's web
of committees, melding with other processes then on the march
(including the Human Rights Act, the projected legislation on freedom of information, the consultation about the future of the Criminal Injuries Compensation Scheme,[282] the implementation of the
Glidewell Report, the execution of the two standards embedded in
the 1996 *Victim's Charter*, the impact of the representations made by
the parents of James Bulger, and much else). And proposals did
become stylized, adapted, synthesized, and generalized to cover

---

[282] The Criminal Injuries Compensation Scheme Consultation Exercise had asked
about whether there should be an 'additional award for racial element'. The summary
of responses in October 1999 reported that 3.8% had been in favour of the proposal.

virtually every victim of serious crime almost, but not wholly, re-gardless of race.[283]

There appeared yet again to be clear and absolute limits set on what could be done in the wake of the Inquiry. Like every other initiative of the 1990s, the Macpherson recommendations came in short time to confront the Maginot Line of judicial opposition to awarding victims a formal place in criminal procedure. In the next chapter, I shall discuss how, at a time when another general election was looming,[284] the convergence of the strong mandate conferred by the Inquiry, and the somewhat unorganized mass of policies that had accumulated in the victims' area, led to proposals first to review the *Victim's Charter* and then, more radically, to introduce legislation 'including consideration of legally enforceable rights for victims'.[285] 'In the normal course of events', Ian Chisholm observed in a paper about the need for a third *Victim's Charter,* 'we would have been seeking to have a new Charter at this point, but this has been given added impetus both by the considerable developments in victims' policy since May 1997 and the recommendations in the Stephen Lawrence Report for the Charter to be reviewed ...'.[286]

In showing how that was taken forward, I shall recount how Home Office officials came formally to propose substantive victims' rights for the first time, ingeniously devising a Schlieffen Plan to sidestep that Maginot Line and to content the judges and the Lord Chancellor's Department who defended it.

---

[283] Although victims of racist crime were still singled out as possessing special needs (in, for instance, the Metropolitan Police Service's 'Protect and Respect: The Met's Diversity strategy', Progress in Diversity, undated). One characteristic phrasing of the new approach was to talk about 'the handling of victims and witnesses, particularly in the field of racist incidents and crimes' (*Code of Practice on Reporting and Recording Racist Crimes,* Home Office, April 2000, p. 9).

[284] The JVU Labour Party Briefing for 2001 election reminded Ministers that they were committed to implement the Macpherson Report, for instance.

[285] Victims Steering Group meeting, 28 April 2000: project plan.

[286] 'Victim's Charter Review: Involvement of Victims in Criminal Legal Proceedings', 15 June 2000.

# 10

# Consummation

## Introduction

With some little repetition, I shall begin this penultimate chapter by exploring the state of play at the turn of the century, just before the politics of victims in England and Wales took off. The histories laid out in the previous six chapters had run more or less in parallel, administratively interwoven in the work of the politicians and more senior officials, but segregated in the work of others; transparent to some, but obscure to others. As I argued towards the beginning of this book, the shaping of knowledge in the Home Office rested in classic Weberian fashion on rank, structure, and function, information travelling upwards, and directives down, and there were different understandings of what was afoot.

The New Labour politicians had entered the Home Office in 1997 with an acknowledged interest in the victim of crime, and for reasons oblique or direct, their administration had worked to create an imposing structure of achievements; a perhaps somewhat distorted imagery of victims and victimization; a complicated web of some-times unresolved relations with other policies and prescriptions; and, with them, an array of opportunities and problems that re-quired increasingly ambitious answers. Their engagement had from time to time been immediate, and we have seen how the Home Secretary could intervene quite personally in what was being done. But theirs in the main was a necessarily edited world. They would periodically be offered what was in effect a carefully prepared review of events in the round. Together with the Permanent Secretary and directors of divisions, they had charge of great swathes of policy-making and, with certain exceptions such as the Home Secretary's involvement in the Lawrence Steering Group, they did not and could not learn about or direct every small detail. Ian Chisholm reflected about Ministers' knowledge and interest in

2000, the time when the events narrated in this chapter began to coalesce, 'it tends to be more of a steer... they were quite, quite keen on the idea of the victim having more of a role, without being too specific as to what that was. Fair enough.'

More intimate knowledge about victims was supposed to be vested in JVU, the Justice and Victims Unit. In conjunction with his colleagues, Ian Chisholm had himself personally attended to or supervised the progress of developments in policies for the vulnerable and intimidated witness, criminal injuries compensation, the looming impact of the Human Rights and Data Protection Acts, the evolution of Victim Support, the repercussions of the death of Stephen Lawrence, and all within the more *dirigiste* regime of the new performance management. He had, in short, figured in the histories of every one of the episodes recounted here, except the outlying area of restorative justice, whose progress had nevertheless touched tangentially on his own work and was reported to the Victims Steering Group. His had been a panoptic view although even he had had on occasion to receive special briefings from his staff about their more minute areas of expertise.

A number of his colleagues were as well-informed. One, a Grade 7 with long experience, acted from time to time as Ian Chisholm's deputy or surrogate and he was certainly as conversant as any with what was in train. Another, the secretary of the Victims Steering Group, attended meetings and saw and drafted papers across the field. But the victims area was segmented for many, and the more junior officials working in and around the JVU had tended to be shielded from one another and from a rounded knowledge of victims' policies. The Grade 7 said in mid-2000 'I don't think there was much joined-up policy-making and I think people did tend to plough their own furrows and were a bit surprised when they found something else is going on... I think traditionally it has been a plough your own furrows syndrome right across the Office.' Despite the existence of a Victims Steering Group where information was pooled every six months, and the need to co-ordinate departments when major initiatives were being formulated, his observation would have applied *a fortiori* to the work performed on victims and witnesses by officials outside the Home Office, in the CPS, the Cabinet Office, the Court Service, the Lord Chancellor's Department and elsewhere.

Yet an informed view was becoming elusive even to those who were structurally well positioned to follow events at close quarters. Very tps://githu4

different sources had thrust or coaxed a host of disparate projects into a common arena defined by the words 'victims and witnesses' (Helen Reeves said graphically in October 1999 'they're all separate histories, separate roots and separate objectives'[1]), and there they co-existed rather incoherently on the agendas of a number of master committees (and particularly the Victims Steering Group) and units[2] of Government (and particularly JVU), becoming increasingly, it was said, in need of reconciliation and organization. In the Grade 7's words in June 2000 there were 'dreadful conflicts': 'Freedom of Information conflicts with Human Rights Act. The victim data protection issues compete with police power issues. There are all sorts of conflicting issues which we're having, which are actually maybe mutually irreconcilable, well, at least, well they can't be 'cause you've got to make 'em, you've got to reconcile them somehow.'[3] And reconciliation had become more imperative and desirable still within the new structural arrangements dictated by joined-up government, the trilateral system and the need to prepare agreed bids for the Comprehensive Spending Review that was again looming in the Spring of 2000.[4] A senior official said:

[1] And, one might have added, different forms of development, a point to which I shall return in the final chapter.

[2] For example, the Prison Service declared in October 1998 that it was committed to the principles of the *Victim's Charter* and to meeting its charter responsibilities. In order to sharpen its focus on victims' issues, it said, it had committed itself in its 1998–9 business plan to establish a forum which would address those issues. 'Prison Service Work with Victims of Crime', Prisoner Administration Group, October 1998. Andrew Sinclair, a founding member of that forum, recalled in early 1999: 'I think it's actually something which the Prison's Board genuinely picked up as part of the way that the Home Office Ministers, the criminal justice system were moving. Recognising the Prison Service was somewhat behind. I mean I say this on the basis that I was at a meeting of Governors on another matter and I heard Richard Tilt [the Director of the Prison Service] talking about how the Prison Service needed to be right up there with victims... so I think that genuinely there was a feeling that this is something they wanted to be doing. It was also something which those working on it at the time won't deny the Prison Service should be looking to make improvements on.'

[3] In the field, working with the aftermath of the Lawrence Report, Assistant Commissioner Ian Johnston talked about contradictory advice tendered by lawyers about disclosure of information to victims: there are 'conflicts between you know freedom of information, human rights... we don't understand it... it's necessarily conceptually inevitably a mess... I think it's difficult for us to grasp who is going to be the arbiter around all of this and where the arbitration is going to be.'

[4] The Grade 7 observed 'the comprehensive spending review, Spending Review 2000, has been a particular driver for this with the Treasury, for example, quite rightly

I think [victims are] seen as having you know, very high political salience and they're all these issues, big cross-cutting issues that people worry about like confidence in the criminal justice system post-Lawrence and all that sort of thing, where you know, any action plan you're trying to put together, if it doesn't have both the good chunk of stuff on victims, then it's you know, something missing. So I think strategically that the placing is very favourable really.

Victims' issues may have been but a minor part of the criminal justice policy-makers' and politicians' world at the turn of the century but, in close focus, they appeared demanding and complex enough and only a few officials were still able to grasp them. Ian Chisholm told me in the summer of 2000 that they had 'got very complicated and only a handful of people [now] understand them'. And, the Grade 7 added, there was a problem of the 'sheer scale of what was going on. It is impossible to be on top of it.'

It was agreed by JVU staff on the eve of the special Home Office conference in Macclesfield in September 1999 that there was 'no master plan for victims'. To be sure, it was not necessarily the business of officials to devise such a plan. Neither might it have been feasible to construct one. How, after all, could one compress so complicated an area into a single scheme?[5] Officials may have only rarely engaged in schematic analyses of policy areas—they were not supposed to play the social or political philosopher—but they *did* have a duty to safeguard against practical inconsistencies of implementation or contradictions of presentation, and it was there that the difficulties lay. John Halliday said to me at a meeting of the Victims Steering Group a little earlier in April 2000 that there was a clear need for JVU to 'tidy up' all the proliferating provisions and

saying "look, there's no point in CPS making a separate bid and LCD making a separate bid, and you making a separate bid, let's have look at the totality of the bid." What are you trying to achieve globally in the criminal justice process and what are your priorities? And that's what we're doing.'

[5] After all, victims are not themselves a coherent or homogeneous population with uniform needs. Helen Reeves observed 'with all my experience, the one thing I do know is that people expect me to come along and give a talk about victims for twenty minutes but nobody would ever dream of asking someone to give a talk about offenders for twenty minutes. Because everyone recognises that offenders or crime is an absolutely vast subject with many, many facets and many aspects. And within the field of offender work, you get people with all sorts of different agendas...So it's always been a bit of a myth that victims should be any more simple or...that it's a subject in its own right.'

developments affecting victims, but, he emphasized, the need was to 'tidy up, not rationalise': 'rationalisation would be a mistake'. And a narrative did have to be on hand to make sure that what was done could be discussed in an intelligible form. In April 2000, Charles Clarke, the Minister responsible for victims' matters, said of what was afoot:

I think it's a story. Now Ian more than anybody else in the Home Office works on creating a story to tell on all this. And I think we've made massive progress even over the last, even in the time I've, not down to me by the way, but down to the initiatives that are already being pushed forward and moving forward. I think we've got an increasingly coherent story to tell and increasingly strong relationship with victims' organisations and I'd be very surprised, as I say, we're taking ten year time frames, I'd be very surprised if you didn't see that explicitly coming out as a strong theme of evolution in the criminal justice system over the coming period.

If there were more problems and more work to be done, if a narrative was emerging, there was also a growing will to act purposefully. Motives and meanings had changed as the work on victims evolved, although it was not always a change that was explicit or documented. The outward demeanour of a professional civil servant is supposed to be disinterested and calm, but it was difficult over time to keep one's stance towards working relations, colleagues, and tasks wholly impersonal and neutral. I have already described how work on victims, like any other policy area, was the foundation of a little social world and of a cluster of social histories that were embellished by gossip, banter, and casual conversation, punctuated by memorable landmarks and turning points, and animated by the personalities of those who figured in them. How could it have been otherwise? Officials, politicians, and the officers of voluntary organizations attended conferences together, drafted papers together, worked together, dined together, and formed relations which, while they lasted, had much of the look of friendship and reciprocity. Work so conducted was certainly more agreeable and efficient and there was a practical stake in cultivating congenial relations, trust, and goodwill. The flow of advice, information, and co-operation depended on it, and with it came a wish to please. The key staff of JVU, and Ian Chisholm and the one Grade 7 particularly, had had a long and uninterrupted history of working in an amiable manner with their counterparts in Victim Support, the criminal justice agencies, and Departments of State. Ian Chisholm had made, said Jeremy Corbett, the chair of Victim Support's National Council, 'an outstanding contribution. A lot of people will testify to that, that Ian's interest in victims went far beyond what could have been expected of someone in that post. It's been quite demonstrable in the help, advice and guidance he has given.'[6]

But I should emphasize that qualification 'while they lasted', because professional engrossments *were* inevitably and preponderantly professional, bounded, and contingent. They could sometimes extend beyond the work and walls of the Home Office, but it was by no means certain that they would do so. When Ian Chisholm finally left work on victims in 2001 to concentrate on implementing the Halliday[7] and Auld reports,[8] for example, he did so without manifest complaint. When later he announced his leaving the Home Office altogether in 2003, he again did so without manifest complaint.

There was more. Involvement in a particular area of policy over time, an area which one 'owned' within the division of labour, and in which one had invested oneself and one's reputation, could bring about symbolic attachments. One is what one does, and work constitutes a self just as a self constitutes work, professional identity being as important a signifier as any. The ability to be manifestly in command of one's subject, or to craft a neat solution to a policy dilemma, not only said something about a disembodied competence, but also about one's professional *persona*. 'Facts', Lafferty once remarked, 'are bits of biography',[9] and the salient facts of the policy-maker were the timely response, the well-drafted paper, the well-rehearsed argument, the ably-chaired meeting, and the problem successfully confronted. It was existentially rewarding to despatch work proficiently, defend a position, and achieve a result, and especially so when the material was victims of crime, a quite self-evidently deserving area of policy-making. Ian Chisholm reflected in an email to me:

---

[6] Meeting of Victim Support National Council, 18 September 2001, my notes.

[7] *Punishments Work: report of a review of the sentencing framework for England and Wales*, Home Office, London, 2001.

[8] *Review of the Criminal Courts of England and Wales*, Home Office, London, 2001.

[9] T. Lafferty; 'Some Metaphysical Implications of the Pragmatic Theory of Knowledge', *The Journal of Philosophy*, 14 April 1932, Vol. XXX, No. 8, p. 206.

I think it is one of my characteristics, a bit Celtic perhaps, that I tend to fight my case strongly. The Chisholm family motto is '*feros ferio*'. That is how I think it should be; as officials we should give advice without fear or favour. Sometimes that is less acceptable than at other times, depending on individual Ministers and the prevailing culture which is more 'Yes Minister' than it used to be. So my style is generally a bit more assertive than some. I will try and persuade Ministers of what I consider to be the right, evidence-based approach. Good Ministers accept that if they take a different view I, and my colleagues, will nonetheless carry out the Minister's wishes with all due commitment. I suspect you are right that in the case of victims I did come to believe what we wanted to do was in the best interests of victims and witnesses and developed a personal stake in the issues. It is fair to say the HO Ministers, Tory and Labour, have wanted to do good things for victims, subject to other pressures on resources etc. So to conclude my personal style has been a bit combative generally and even more so perhaps on victim/witness issues.

Sir Quentin Thomas, a retired, senior official who had himself worked long at the Home Office, regarded by many as a model civil servant, commented on that account of the marriage of the personal and the impersonal:

I entirely agree with the way he put it...I developed a high degree of commitment in all, or almost all of the jobs I did. It was certainly a key part of the job to challenge ministers, sometimes quite fiercely...More generally, I think one of my main tasks...was what I called swatting flies: namely seeing off bonkers Ministerial ideas and preserving the purity of the orthodox policy (as I saw it, of course). Heresy suppression, in short. The bottom line, on which Ian and I are in agreement is that if Ministers take, on advice, a considered but 'wrong' view, you have to accept it. (Though I would add it might not be enough for a junior Minister to do that; if it mattered enough you would certainly ensure the Secretary of State was drawn in.)

To take stock: what a member of the Prime Minister's Delivery Unit later dismissed as 'boutique projects'[10] had amassed in a confused but fairly imposing pile at the beginning of the century. Victims had begun to attain a small presence in the political world, and it was a presence that grew with every account, becoming in Charles Clarke's words the subject of a 'story', and acquiring with each recitation not only a set of concomitant motives but also the object-ive, self-justifying, objective and solid look of a nascent policy

[10] The phrase was used in October 2001.

that could convince a teller and an audience (as Graham Wallas once enquired, 'how do I know what I think until I see what I say?'). In late 1999, for example, a paper on 'Support for Victims of Crime' was prepared for the Ministerial Group on the Criminal Justice System. It employed what had become a stock narrative, repeated again and again, but with the necessary addition of increments over time, as if every thing that had been done was really part of some large, co-ordinated, and reflective venture (and indeed, it had become just so in the telling). There was the record of work in progress: the CPS undertaking to communicate directly with victims; speedier justice; the extension of the Victim Support witness services into the Magistrates' Courts;[11] the seventy-eight recommendations of *Speaking up for Justice*; a national telephone helpline for victims staffed by Victim Support; and the implementation of the Lawrence Report recommendations on the handling of victims and witnesses. There were the mandates authorizing action, and the narrative moved to the 1997 Labour manifesto commitments on victims and witnesses and a recital of Aim 2 of the March 1999 Strategies and Business Plans for the Criminal Justice System ('to meet the needs of victims, witnesses and jurors within the system'). The paper reported what victims wanted or expected: treatment with dignity, sensitivity and respect; to have the offender caught, charged, and convicted; support and assistance; information; simpler, clearer, and faster justice; 'decent treatment in criminal proceedings'; their views and special needs to be taken into account; and compensation and reparation for injury or loss. Evidence was adduced from research, evaluation studies, and the British Crime Survey; organizationally embedded experience; and work in progress on, for example, the *Victim's Charter* standards and youth justice pilots. And the paper concluded with an inventory of 'developments in process of implementation or under consideration', the most recent then being the consideration of the *parti civile* proposal (but, it was noted, 'The auxiliary prosecutor model looks a better option. Victims could put questions to witnesses and make statements to the court').

Victims, declared Sir Robin Auld in the summer of 2000, were 'obviously the flavour of the month'. Officials were busy, and there

---

[11] And that and the telephone helpline were two of the possible candidates for inclusion in the narrative of this book that were exempted on grounds of parsimony. In an already lengthy account, a number of events had to be neglected.

was a sense that so great, untidy, ramifying, and diffuse was the assembly of tasks focused on victims,[12] so lacking was its coherence,[13] that it had become what Smith and Freinkel would have called a 'ripe issue'[14] requiring appraisal, re-organization, and consolidation. The arguments about review may have been routine, having been deployed almost from the first,[15] but they were now buttressed by new and powerful injunctions from Sir William Macpherson to revise a *Victim's Charter* that had become quite obsolete, and from their offspring, the Lawrence Steering Group and its powerful Chairman, the Home Secretary,[16] not only to revise the Charter but also to embark on a consultation on the wider place of the victim in the criminal justice system.[17] Quite conventionally, the December paper had not furnished much of a master interpretive frame, but victims were certainly beginning to look like an area of concerted, coherent, and strenuous activity. Facts were beginning to

[12] Crawford and Enterkin wrote to telling effect about how 'Integrating victims within criminal justice has tended to take the form of a series of "initiatives"—often well-intentioned and launched to great fanfare—but lacking in coherence or coordination. One might go as far as to say that this has produced a tangle of overlapping competencies all seeking potentially to integrate the victim in different ways, at different stages and for different ends into the criminal justice process.' A. Crawford and J. Enterkin; *Victim Contact Work and the Probation Service: A Study of Service Delivery and Impact*, Centre for Criminal Justice Studies, University of Leeds, 1999, p. 7.

[13] Some members of the Victims Steering Group wondered whether there *was* a victims' policy or mere '*ad hockery*'. The term was that of the ACOP representative, Roger Ford, in conversation at a meeting of the Group in December 1999.

[14] S. Smith and S. Freinkel; *Adjusting the Balance: Federal Policy and Victim Services*, Greenwood Press, New York, 1988, p. 4.

[15] Very similar stock themes had been used to spur policy-making on for some years. For example, it had been argued in the Home Office's submission on 'Support for Victims of Crime' to the Comprehensive Spending Review in March 1998 that changes in the victim's role had been piecemeal rather than a response to coherent principles. There had been an increasing shift towards rights and role within the criminal justice system that might lead to a fundamental change. There were, it was said, many initiatives and the need for the adoption of a coherent approach to victims across all agencies.

[16] It was noted as plans to organize a consultation on the *Victim's Charter* unfolded in the summer of 2000 that 'the HS is taking a very close interest in this and will be keen to promote the new document'. 'The Victim's Charter—Draft Consultation paper', August 2000.

[17] The Steering Group came to agree with JVU's reservations about the *parti civile* and endorsed a recommendation for a wider consultation on the role of victims in legal proceedings. Minutes of the Lawrence Steering Group Meeting, 14 March 2000.

create facts and, continually urging the Home Office on from the wings, was Victim Support which, with its banner with a strange device, *Excelsior*, greeted every new fact and accomplishment as evidence of a growing recognition of the victim.[18]

If there was an accretion of facts, there was also a persistent, unresolved problem. It will be remembered that what had lain before the Home Office throughout the New Labour Government's first term of office was the barrier that had come to set limits on its every effort to change the formal place of the victim. All reforms had ultimately been hemmed in by the strong legal presumption that victims did not have, and could not have, a recognized standing in criminal procedure. There had been a succession of crises about 'automatic referrals', the victim's right to information about his or her case (and especially when set against the rights to medical confidentiality of 'mentally disordered' offenders), victim statements and the victim's right to privacy at trial. More than once, notions of compensatory legal rights for victims and the transformation of Victim Support into a statutory agency had been floated as a solution, although the floating had been short-lived and tentative, only to be abandoned in the face of robust judicial opposition or with the discovery of alternative and simpler solutions. And, despite the Human Rights Act,[19] that tentativeness had been reinforced by the prospect of the costs of litigation and compensation which justiciable rights might incur and the still alien quality of a rights discourse in the Home Office at the turn of the century, especially in the victims' domain. The author of *CJ2010*, a strategy document that would touch on victims, said in February 2001 'We don't ... use the language of rights to discuss the way in which we think this issue needs to be developed ... but then we don't have a tradition of doing

---

[18] See, for example, H. Reeves; 'Comment', *VSM*, Victim Support Magazine, No. 76, Autumn 2000. Robert Latham, the Chair of the National Trustees, told the plenary meeting of Victim Support's 1999 annual conference that 'the challenge is providing a seamless service for victims and the mass of policy issues now confronting us'. I noted to myself at the time that it was as if people were trying to construct an imagery of overwhelming pressure for change to spur things on.

[19] I argued earlier that victims were beginning to obtain rights generally as part of the creation of a wider rights discourse and a more narrow dialectics as negative rights were set against the positive rights of defendants. But no direct rights were conferred. A senior official noted that 'The Home Secretary likes to argue that victims, the Human Rights Act's got victims' rights in it but that's not really true.'

that.' But the crises lingered and the characteristic outcome was uncertainty.[20]

Structurally defined positions had there been delineated and maintained. The judiciary, the Law Society, the Lord Chancellor's Department (acting as the political voice of the judges), and the Attorney General, their eyes fixed on the courts, defendants' rights, and the integrity of justice, had argued for balance in an adversarial system where issues were tried solely between two parties, the State, and the defendant. The Home Office (and its satellite agency, the police service) and Downing Street, with their eyes fixed on the plight of victims as witnesses and constituents,[21] concerned about attrition in the criminal justice system and the problem of reducing crime, mindful of the impact of the Human Rights Act, argued not only for balance but also for improved treatment and, increasingly after the Thompson and Venables case, formal recognition of the victim in criminal procedure.[22] The Bar had been divided. The Probation Service had at first been uneasy but later became reconciled to working with victims. And Victim Support, the only victims organization of political consequence ensconced in Government (although its voice was small and not always heeded), not only argued for balance but also championed the minority of victims whose crimes reached the courts, and the much greater mass of victims who did not. Such was the equilibrium of that field of forces, and such was the negotiated character of relations, aiming always at consensus between the agencies of the criminal justice system, on the one hand, and, on the other, between Ministers under the trilateral arrangements[23] and in Cabinet, that what had happened so far had

[20] For example, at a meeting of ACOP's Victim Network in June 2001, a member commented on the probation service's new responsibilities for informing victims: 'Throughout the whole process, the question being asked is what rights does the victim have. It's not clear. Everyone struggled with this issue of disclosure... Has anyone done anything on this whole issue of victims' rights? ... it's an area where we have no expertise. It's completely unknown territory.'

[21] The discovery had been made that victims were, as Liz Lloyd, the Prime Minister's policy adviser, put it, 'poor and live in the poorest estates, they are "our people"'.

[22] Ian Chisholm informed the Victims Steering Group meeting of 28 April 2000, for example, that the Home Office conference in Macclesfield in the previous September had been 'fairly sceptical but ministers wanted us to do some further work about victim involvement in the criminal process'.

[23] The author of what was called *CJ2010*, a long-term strategy document for the criminal justice system, containing some material on victims, destined to be approved

had something of the character of a stalemate: there had been undoubted gains for victims, but the contenders were so evenly matched that there had been no clear or final determination of the issue of victims' rights.

The judiciary, Attorney General, and Lord Chancellor's Department may have long succeeded in warding off attempts to award formal rights to victims, but the Home Secretary and, later the Prime Minister, still pressed their case, both speaking, for example, about enhancing the position of victims at the important September 2000 Labour party conference,[24] the last before the 2001 general election. Indeed, the more robust the stance adopted by judges and lawyers in resisting victims' rights, the stronger the case for rights was believed by officials such as Ian Chisholm to have become. He told me in September 2000, for instance, that 'things were coming to a head' because it was necessary to confer rights on victims precisely to confirm a role in the criminal justice system that the judges were otherwise ill-prepared to cede. Perversely, he said, all the lawyers' opposition was helpful because it only emphasized the need for a Victims' Bill of Rights ('... one of the difficulties is getting the judiciary and bar, legal profession, to take all this seriously but if you put things on a statutory basis, they're forced to do something'). In this chapter, I shall show how that balance of power shifted and a clever gambit promised to resolve that *impasse*. In a changed and clichéd metaphor, if victims' policies were the Gordian knot, JVU became something of an Alexander.

## Downing Street

It would be useful before I proceed further to put in place a few other matters that were to shape and give added impetus to the

by the three trilateral Ministers, said that 'it is a trial actual document. So what comes out in this document, all three departments, Attorney General, Lord Chancellor and us, Home Office, will have signed up to it. So if there are large areas of disagreement, they won't be in the report.' I shall discuss the document below.

[24] Tony Blair talked of 'Standing up to criminals. Standing up for victims. Another big project for the second term of a Labour government.' Jack Straw said that 'An effective criminal justice system must provide more than justice for the criminal alone... This means... First class treatment for the victims of crime... For too long victims have been left out in the cold. Their interests are at the heart of our reforms... I want to do more for victims, turning them from passive spectators to more active participants in our criminal justice system.'

politics of victims at the beginning of the century. First, there was around 1999 a palpably greater interest in crime and, in its wake, victims and witnesses, that emanated from the very centre of power in Downing Street,[25] crime having been apportioned to the Prime Minister in a broad division of supervisory labour with the Chancellor of the Exchequer.[26] 1999, said Rawnsley, was deemed by the Prime Minister to be the 'year of delivery'.[27] The image developed in one journal was that of Mr Blair wanting to 'replace the percolator with a *cafétière*: strong pressure from above, infusing the policies and actions of the departments below' by means of an expansion of his secretariat, and particularly the Policy Unit that was virtually a Prime Minister's Department, that would suck 'power away from individual departments'.[28]

The Prime Minister, a former Shadow Home Secretary and barrister, married to a barrister, began personally and urgently to seek new ways of affecting the volume and effects of crime.[29] Victims themselves, it must be remembered, were seen by the Labour Party,[30] the No. 10 Policy Unit,[31] and Prime Minister as less of a discrete

---

[25] We have already seen, for instance, that from an early date a number of the new initiatives for victims were announced by press releases in the Prime Minister's name or quoting what he was purported to have said. An early instance was Home Office News Release 142/97 'Stopping Witnesses Being Scared Into Silence', 13 June 1997, which contained a statement by Tony Blair. Particularly important was to be the association by press notice of No. 10 with the launch of the Charter review in February 2001. Newspapers would regularly report the Prime Minister's interest in new ventures for victims. See, for example, *Sunday Telegraph*, 30 July 2000.

[26] See P. Hennessy; 'The Blair Style of Government', *RSA Journal*, December 2002, p. 43.

[27] A. Rawnsley; *Servants of the People*, Penguin Books, London, 2001, p. 292.

[28] *The Economist*, 21 August 1999.

[29] Some of which were to be dismissed as a little *ad hoc*, for example, the proposal that 'on the spot fines' should be levied on drunken youths. The president of ACPO said: 'The collection of cash is not a practical idea and we don't have that provision in the British police force.' See *The Times*, 4 July 2000.

[30] Matthew Seward, a Labour Party home affairs specialist, said 'The main issues at the top of the list are always going to be, you know, the level of crime, you know, police, drugs and then sort of victims and justice things. But I mean that's just the way the political debate works.'

[31] When I spoke to a No. 10 Policy Unit home affairs adviser in February 2000, a time when issues were beginning significantly to coalesce, she lacked detailed knowledge about the politics of victims and it was evident that they were only of marginal

issue than as part of a larger bundle of policies principally centred on crime reduction. Charles Clarke remarked that 'I think the internal logic of it in terms of our own policy ambitions, is very, very strong. Tony's commitment in particular is to getting a criminal justice system and policing in which we can have confidence. And that means, you know, reducing crime and all the rest of it, and he would see victims as a step on that road rather than, he's not coming and saying "it's victims and don't worry about the police numbers or something like that." He would just see victims as an important part of the package.'

Although crime rates were decreasing, there were predictions they would rise again, and, indeed, they *were* rising in the popular imagination. The fear of crime was static and about to fall, but it remained marked and consequential.[32] There were political anxieties voiced about the cramping effects of the new data protection legislation and the possibility that the new Human Rights Act might 'be wrongly used to throw out cases or limit police powers'. And the politics of crime and crime reduction were beginning to shape anticipations of the general election campaign to come in the Spring of 2001: the Government could no longer so readily blame the previous administration for the state of law and order,[33] and there was a growing trepidation that it was becoming seen as 'vulnerable'[34] and 'soft on crime'[35] at a difficult political time. In August 2000, and in some desperation, the Prime Minister invited an

interest. Her contention was that victims' policies did not loom very large in Government thinking. Victims were seen largely as parts and beneficiaries of wider reforms to the criminal justice system, not as policy targets in their own right. Victims would 'be alright' if other objectives, such as crime reduction, were realized. There was an interest in victims but it was 'not outstanding': 'when we were in opposition, we were saying more to do about victims, not that that's been flushed out. What does that mean in practice?'

[32] Although crime rates measured by the British Crime Survey had fallen by 12% between 1999 and 2000, 33% of respondents reported that they believed that crime had risen 'a lot more', and 34% 'a little more'. 19% said they were 'worried' about burglary in 1998 and 2000; 21% were worried about the theft of a car in both years; 18% were worried about being mugged in 1998, and 17% in 2000; and 31% of women were worried about rape in 1998, and 29% in 2000. C. Kershaw *et al.*; *The 2001 British Crime Survey*, Home Office, London, 2001.

[33] See *The Times*, 2 September 1999.
[34] See *The Times*, 13 July 2000.
[35] See *The Times*, 17 July 2000.

outsider,[36] Lord Birt, the former director general of the BBC and no criminologist, to review the Government's long-term strategy for reducing crime, examining, *inter alia*, data on crime, offenders, and victims; the 'levers of crime reduction'; and methods of improving programmes and the use of resources.[37]

At the very core of criminal justice policy-making, the Home Office itself was thought by an impatient Prime Minister's office[38] to be failing and defeatist.[39] Said the Prime Minister in November 1999 in response to the Home Secretary's prediction that crime rates would probably again increase with a changing demographic structure and the growing availability of portable property:[40]

We don't accept that [crime] has to rise, which is why we are taking a whole series of measures on burglaries...tougher measures on rape and assaults, tougher measures on youth justice, but also a whole range of

[36] He was appointed in part precisely because he was an outsider: 'The idea of getting Lord Birt in was to get a fresh perspective and to see whether there were any insights he could offer which might be valuable in the future...We had acknowledged that he did not have years of received wisdom in the area of crime.' 10 Downing Street Newsroom: Lobby Briefing, 10 July 2000.

[37] Work on the review lasted for some eight months and was never published. See the *Guardian*, 20 December 2002.

[38] Richard Wilson, then head of the civil service, reported that 'The Prime Minister said that he needed a stronger centre...Over the past year, the thing that has been coming through No 10 and departments is the realisation that they are well into their second year and they want to see more results. There is a real dialogue about the speed at which things can happen.' *The Times*, 24 September 1999.

[39] The Prime Minister later recalled that 'Shortly after the 1997 election, I received a presentation from our Home Office. It said that due to demographic and other factors, crime was set to rise sharply in the next few years. Some wearily thought it was inevitable. I didn't accept it then and I don't now.' Speech on the Re-balancing of criminal justice system, 18 June 2002.

[40] The Home Secretary had said on 29 November 1999: 'The models suggest that there is a strong historical association between changes in the level of recorded property crime and some of the key economic and demographic factors. The economists have made projections of what effect they believe this would have on the level of recorded property crime, assuming no positive intervention by the police, local authorities or Government. I want to emphasise that the projections are not forecasts of what we as Government believe will, or should happen. Criminal behaviour is wrong, and the model provides no excuse for it. There is nothing inevitable about the trend in the models.' Home Office news release, 383/99, 29 November 1999. His projection was based on an analysis performed for Lord Birt's strategy paper which had predicted in July that recorded property crime could double to 6.5 m. by 2010 and recorded violence rise by 50% (Policy Unit Crime Project—Phase 1: Understanding the Data).

measures on crime prevention as well. This is a situation where we can't allow ourselves to be defeatist about it. Crime has been coming down for two years, we have got to keep it coming down.[41]

Criminal policy was thus fitfully salient in the political mind, and it was scrutinized from the centre, and attended by a flotilla of performance targets, some of which had been proposed by the No. 10 Policy Unit, and by expenditure bids and public service agreements that were perused by the No. 10 Policy Unit.[42]

The Prime Minister himself declared that he wished more fully to be associated with what was being done.[43] As a matter of course he had 'bilaterals' with the Home Secretary and larger meetings with the criminal justice Ministers, and, from time to time, he demanded an accounting about what was in progress and how things could be bettered. Ministers, Permanent Secretaries, and others[44] were upbraided[45] or routinely summoned to what were called 'Law and Order Stocktakes' at Downing Street to explain how they proposed to improve services and performance in the criminal justice system. The aim of one such 'stocktake', in the words of a Home Office Director of Criminal Policy, was to demonstrate 'how [we] are responding to crime trends [and] make it clear that the current programme is directed to countering those trends'.

The interest of Prime Minister and Policy Unit counted. It spurred activity and conferred authority. It led in one of the Prime Minister's meetings with the Home Secretary to the inclusion of radical proposals for victims in CJ2010. And it could be cited as a warrant in the many exchanges that took place across the divisions of the criminal justice system. In September 2000, for example, Ian Chisholm was able to remind a colleague in the CPS that 'There are strong political

---

[41] BBC News On-Line: 30 November 1999.

[42] The Public Service Agreements for the Criminal Justice System were, for instance, perused by the Policy Unit before approval.

[43] Guidance for the public expenditure round in 1999 noted that the Prime Minister was apparently keen to help departments in their communication strategy if they could identify effective things for him to do.

[44] For example, Chief Constables were summoned to Downing Street in 1999 to explain what was seen as their deteriorating performance. *Evening Standard*, 12 October 1999.

[45] See the report which recorded how the Prime Minister proposed to hold Permanent Secretaries personally to account for the delivery of the Government's aims. *The Times*, 24 August 1999.

pressures from here [the Home Office] and no 10 for giving victims a role in criminal proceedings.' It was a warrant that did not guarantee compliance. The Lord Chancellor and the judges were too independent for that, but it was not without influence and it traced lines of engagement.

## The General Election

Much of this activity took place in the foreknowledge of a general election that would have to be called by the spring of 2002, but which was at first promised for April,[46] then May,[47] and finally, after considerable havering[48] because of a rural crisis centred on animal foot-and-mouth disease, for June 2001.[49] Although the campaign formally started at the very beginning of April, the mass media had been riddled with speculation about its timing and prospects throughout the end of 2000 and the greater part of the first half of 2001, and the effect created was that of an unusually protracted campaign that long concentrated the political mind, shaping speeches, papers,[50] and manifesto commitments[51] at the turn of the century. There were repercussions for the issue of victims, Ian Chisholm reflecting in February 2000 that 'Victims Rights Act stuff and new charters and all this stuff is quite good manifesto stuff'. Party conferences were especially important display cases for policies in the making, and we shall see that in due course the Labour Party's two national conferences before the election, taking place in September 2000 and February 2001, would exert a powerful teleology. The prospect of a big speech about to be delivered by the Home Secretary in the shadow of a general election induced political

---

[46] See *Evening Standard*, 29 November 2000.

[47] *The Times*, 24 November 2000 and *Guardian*, 8 January 2001.

[48] See, for example, *The Times* of 14, 15, and 26 March 2001.

[49] The announcement was made on the 2 April.

[50] Victim Support, for instance, elected in March to issue its own election manifesto to stir the politicians. See Victim Support: *March News 2001*. On of its principal themes was prevailing victims' policy attended only to the 3% of victims whose crimes arrived at the courts, neglecting the rest.

[51] Although officials suddenly found themselves thrust into something of a political limbo. There were strong conventions about what they could and could not do, and involvement in the overtly political was certainly proscribed. Home Office officials would not know (because of 'a Chinese wall between policy and politics') about the contents of the election manifesto until they were published.

advisers and Labour Party officers to search around for months in
advance for new and memorable matters to disclose, it was a timely
period for the birth of new initiatives, and one would be directed at
victims.

It is important to retain descriptive proportion. Crime generally
may have bulked large in the election,[52] forming what Justin Russell
called one of the three or four big themes, but, despite a reference to
victims' rights[53] in the Labour Party manifesto, and a number of
speeches, including the Home Secretary's[54] and Prime Minister's[55]
addresses to the Labour Party Conferences, victims came actually to
represent only one minor electoral issue among many,[56] not always
considered of independent importance by politicians[57] and their

[52] A. Rawnsley; *Servants of the People, op. cit.,* p. 500. The first poster issued by
the Conservative opposition after the announcement of the election date focused on
the theme of 'Violent Crime is Rising' (BBC News web site, 9 May 2001).

[53] Those allusions constituted in the words of a Labour Party policy officer 'fairly
routine references to victims must be at the heart of the criminal justice system'.

[54] For example, he addressed the ACPO conference only days before the election,
on 29 May 2001, and said 'To help witnesses to give the most accurate evidence they
can we will give them greater access to their original statements in the witness box and
will look at the scope for giving juries the opportunity to review interview transcripts
and other materials. And to put victims back where they belong, at the heart of the
criminal justice system, we are giving them the opportunity to make a statement on the
impact that crime has had on their lives. And a Victims' Rights Bill to ensure that every
victim gets the protection, support and information they need.' The Prime Minister
mentioned the proposed Bill of Rights in a speech on 30 May.

[55] He said on 26 September 2000: 'We have increased funding for victim support,
and given special help to victims of rape and sexual offences, but we need to do more—
They should get full information about the progress of the case—about the sentence,
and about the release of the criminal—Proper compensation, backed by a Victim's
Ombudsman. And I believe that the victim of crime should be able to give a written
assessment of the impact of the crime upon them, which should be presented in open
court, and taken into account when sentencing decisions are made. Standing up to
criminals. Standing up for victims. Another big project for the second term of a Labour
government.' *The Times* heeded that message, reporting the next day that 'He promised new help for the victims of crime . . .'.

[56] But, thought Ian Chisholm in March 2001, beginning to consider briefing the
incoming Government, they had attained more importance than before: 'compared
with where they've been, they are much more central. We're talking about a Victims'
Rights Bill in the next session. I mean that is a bit of a change and will probably change
the culture you know, once the statutory rights are there, lawyers will [respond].'

[57] Robin Corbett, the then Chair of the Home Affairs Select Committee told me in
March 2000 that he had not discerned any political interest in victims and his
Committee had not considered them for some three years, he got 'the odd letter but

advisers, possibly still stigmatized as a political cause,[58] and sometimes a little lost in the wider talk about criminal justice policy and crime reduction.[59] In February 2000, Liz Lloyd, the Prime Minister's home affairs policy adviser, certainly knew of no plans for legislation on victims, and took it that crime reduction and attrition rates were the overarching problems, not the treatment of victims: 'we should catch the people who do you harm rather than change the position of the victim in the criminal justice system' she said.

To be sure, elections cover a very broad span of competing issues, and victims could never have been especially prominent.[60] Politicians would have wished to convey only a limited point in each speech and policy paper, they tailored their arguments for particular audiences and particular times, and they certainly did mention victims, albeit sometimes perfunctorily. Thus a briefing paper on crime and policy for the September 2000 annual Labour Party conference touched lightly on past achievements but conveyed few of the more important victims' policies that were then *in utero*.[61]

---

that's all', and the Home Office, the usual instigator of the Committee's agenda, had not intimated that that inattention should change. Victims were marginal indeed: 'I think there needs to be more debate about this whole area you know, the role of the victim in the criminal justice system . . . and I think we never get time to think, I mean that's the problem.'

[58] Chris Nuttall, then Director of the Research and Statistics Directorate, a man familiar with the genesis of victims' policies not only in England and Wales, but also in Canada, reflected at the beginning of the new Government's term of office: 'I think the problem for victims is absolutely visceral. I think that human beings really don't want to associate with losers. Because these are losers. And it's not just that, which you know I think is on a very fundamental level, I mean, they're also against the whole of the criminal justice system, which is not victim-oriented. You cannot get people to say anything other than "we've got to do more for victims, victims are the forgotten, victims are doubly victimised". You cannot get people to do anything other than that. But my feeling is, that once they've said it they forget it. You never work up, you never work up the same emotional, you think of the emotional attachment to offenders' rights . . . '.

[59] For example, in a speech on 'key policies on crime' by Barbara Roche, a Home Office Minister, on 18 May 2001; and a speech by Jack Straw on 20 May 2001.

[60] When, for instance, in the immediate wake of the election announcement, *The Times* newspaper conducted what it called an audit of New Labour's record during the first term, it reviewed achievements in the realm of crime and criminal justice, but made no mention of victims and witnesses. *The Times*, 5 April 2001.

[61] The 9-page paper, 'Building a future for all: crime', talked summarily about the provisions for witnesses under the Youth Justice and Criminal Evidence Act, and the introduction of Victim Impact Statements [*sic*] from April 2001, and concluded

When the Labour Party Election web site first reported the launch of the election manifesto on 16 May, it alluded to crime and crime reduction, but not to victims, although later versions of the web site were to do so.[62] When the Home Secretary fielded questions on a 45 minutes BBC programme, 'Election Call to Jack Straw', on 31 May, there was no discussion of victims.

For their part, the Conservative Party flagged the politics of victims in a modest fashion,[63] having issued a number of iterative policy statements from August 1999 on,[64] and especially in its 'law and order initiative', *Common Sense on Law and Order*, launched on 16 November 1999, that promised, in the words of its election web site, to 'overhaul the law so that it is on the side of the victim, not the criminal', and calling for 'victims' rights'.[65] Like Jack Straw, Ann

'Victims' rights, more offenders brought to justice, new measures to tackle anti-social behaviour. We are embarked on nothing less than a radical reform of the criminal justice system.' But it did not specify those rights or make it clear whether they were intended to refer to past accomplishments or accomplishments to come.

[62] For example, on 1 March 2001 it referred to the achievements wrought since 1997, including 'better support for victims', the introduction of victim personal statements, and consultation with victims of violent or sex offenders sentenced to more than 12 months for consultation and notification about release.

[63] There was much talk about the Conservatives 'putting victims first' in contrast to the Labour Party's pampering of the criminal. Characteristic was a BBC interview with William Hague on the 5pm Radio 4 News on 6 June 2000: Hague said 'But it is those attitudes, attitudes of paying more attention to the victims of crime, more attention to the perpetrators of crime than to the victims, more attention to the school bully than to the vast majority who want to get on with their education. It is those sorts of attitudes that I'm talking about when I'm talking about the liberal elite.'

[64] See Conservative Party Press Release: Conservatives Put 'Victims First', 5 August 1999. It was time, the release said, time 'to put victims first'. The system was 'letting them down' and the Government was doing nothing to stand up for their interests. There was a need for a greater openness on the part of the police and CPS; victims of crime should be given direct access to police officers investigating their case through introduction of a named officer scheme; to one of the lawyers considering their case when it had been referred to the CPS; regular progress reports from the CPS and police; and a power to inspect witness statements on file. Those themes were to be reiterated in a number of succeeding papers and speeches, for example, A. Widdecombe; *Building a More Secure Society*, 6 October 1999; *Common Sense on Law and Order*, 16 November 1999; and Ann Widdecombe's speech to the Conservative Party Spring Forum (Conservative Party News, 1 April 2000).

[65] Speaking at the LSE on 28 February 2000, she had concentrated on law and order and immigration, focusing on police and prisons, but not mentioning victims until I asked her a question. At that point she said that 'Last summer we issued a policy document in which we promised victims statutory rights for the first time. Victims

Widdecombe chose to speak robustly about victims at the Conservative Party's Autumn annual conferences in 1999 and 2000.[66] And victims entered the Conservative Party's manifesto, *Time For Common Sense,* with the general promise that the justice system would treat them fairly, a more specific commitment that named police officers and CPS officials would provide continuous points of contact and information for victims, especially when cases were dropped or charges changed (echoing the extant but yet to be implemented standard introduced by John Major to the 1996 *Victim's Charter*); and two other commitments on a law on double jeopardy (already recommended on a restricted basis by the Law Commission in October 1999) and a law 'on self defence' in deference to the case of Tony Martin that had attracted the gaze of Conservative politicians a year before. The Party's web site reported in May 2001 that William Hague, the Leader of the Opposition, had said 'I will fight for the rights of the victim not the criminal' (and he was again pointing at Tony Martin), but those rights proved on that occasion to be little more than a redressing of the failure to insist on a legal requirement on the CPS that they should inform victims about decisions, a measure that was already in hand. It also reported a statement by the Shadow Home Secretary, Ann Widdecombe, that Labour is 'soft on crime and tough on victims', and that the Conservatives would introduce a Criminal Justice and Police Bill

appear to be forgotten: They don't know what's happening to them, they disappear into the black hole of the criminal justice system. When they're dissatisfied and want to mount a private prosecution, they can't get prosecution papers. They should have by law a police officer keeping them up to date. One official from the CPS. They must be given reasons if a case is dropped. Often victims can't understand why a case has been dropped. They write to their MP, the MP gets reasons and passes them on to the victims. Finally, save for any sensitive information, prosecution information should go to the victim. Statutory rights would consist of a right to written information, a right to have named officials responsible for providing that information.'

[66] She said: 'Jack Straw gives the criminals a party every day while victims wait outside in the cold . . . It's not that they're short on rhetoric when it comes to victims. Remember what Tony Blair said in his speech last week? Tony Blair said that one of the big projects for the second term of a Labour government—and I quote—would be "standing up for victims". Why is he waiting for a second term? It's not as if he's going to get one. What a sense of priorities. They've spent the first term getting prisoners out of jail early, cutting the police force, multiplying red tape, and dreaming of drunks at cashpoints. The victim has to wait for the second term. By contrast, my first pledge as Shadow Home Secretary, the very first policy I announced, was new rights for victims enshrined in law.'

giving victims a right to be informed of the progress of their case, and a right to see the files if the CPS decided not to proceed, so that they could consider the prospects of private prosecution. She gave a speech to the Police Federation, the body representing junior ranks, in which she said, again perhaps with the image of Tony Martin before her:

Criminals are not the victims. Victims are the victims. Criminals are criminals. They choose to commit crime and there is no excuse for what they choose to do. I want victims to feel they have had justice. I want the law-abiding people of this country to feel free from fear in their homes and on the street. I want to overhaul the law so that it is on the side of the victim, not the criminal. Such as the legal right to know why the CPS may have dropped or downgraded a case . . . we will further extend the powers to appeal against unduly lenient sentence. And we will reform the Double Jeopardy rule for the most serious cases . . .

But victims were never the less largely marginal to the election, they did not figure very conspicuously in the Labour Party's own political scheme and, despite the surface recriminations, they were almost certainly a matter of broad bipartisan political consensus. The Conservative Party had laid the groundwork for the development of policies for victims in England and Wales virtually from the first. They had been the sole party in power when most of the formative decisions had been taken between 1979 and 1997. And much of what had been done *since* 1997 (with the certain exceptions of the Macpherson Inquiry and the Human Rights Act, and the uncertain exceptions of the introduction of restorative justice and more lavish expenditure) was consistent enough with what had gone before. John Greenway, a Conservative Member of Parliament, and then a front bench spokesman on home affairs, said at the end of 1999:

I would think that to a large extent [victims] are probably a bipartisan issue and I have got a very strong suspicion that what we have put in our own *Victim's Charter* as part of our relatively sketchy but nonetheless important common sense on law and order initiative which we launched on the 16th of November, Ann Widdecombe, William Hague launched on the 16th of November, we've made two clear points about this and I think one-half of it in some respects, I'd be amazed if the Government doesn't try and take up. The first is that we say that victims should be given a named police officer who's working on their case as a point of contact. And they will be able to approach that officer directly if they need information and no longer have to navigate what we call anonymous bureaucracy before they can find someone to tell them what's going on.

Elections are at once fought on a grand scale, with strategic object-ives and themes,[67] and on a more modest scale as issues arise day by day, and sometimes unexpectedly, as a result of events, interjections by opponents or the mass media that demand a rapid response. Justin Russell said of crime as a general election issue, 'it's not something you can control, the degree to which the media will pick up on crime as the story of the day. I mean I think there'll probably be two or three election press conferences with a crime theme ... it depends on whether, how the Tories, whether the Tories can get a handle on something where they can create some blue water between us. And so far they haven't been able.' Victims were not in major contention, the Conservatives were not thought to have 'got a handle' on them, and Labour politicians and their advisers were not conscious of their having entered electoral debate unplanned,[68] although, as I have argued, there could have been a presence to detect[69] had they chosen to look hard. But discernible or not,

[67] Justin Russell talked about 'a campaign grid [that] will be drawn up for the campaign which will pencil in very roughly the sort of themes that they want to cover on each day. And I presume there'll be two or three days in the campaign where crime will be our positive theme for the day and Jack will do a press conference ...'.

[68] A member of the No. 10 Policy Unit could not recall in February 2001 either Ann Widdecome or William Hague having talked about victims, and there was, as a result, no need for what she called a 'balancing act politically'. Perhaps she and her colleagues had not for very good political reasons been attending hard amidst all the tumult before an election campaign, and that was itself significant. Justin Russell said at the same time that 'I haven't noticed [Ann Widdecombe] going particularly on about victims. I think ... very early on she said something but it hasn't been more recently as far as I can tell.' Their lack of focus was supported by a review of the record of the major parties conducted by the *Sunday Times* newspaper on the 13 May 2001: in the realm of crime, it said, there had been fewer police and fewer crimes under the Labour Government, the introduction of closed circuit television surveillance and 'strong anti-truancy measures', and, significantly, a 'promise to give victims a greater say'; but the Conservatives and the Liberals were associated with no electoral policies or promises on victims.

[69] For example, Ann Widdecombe, the Shadow Home Secretary, repeatedly re-proached the Home Secretary for not having enacted a Victim's Rights Act. In a House of Commons debate on the 12 December 2000, she asked ' What has the right hon. Gentleman to offer? There is no Bill to end the crisis in policing—just further burdens on the patrolling officer. There is no Bill to tackle last year's rise in sexual offences; no Bill to enhance the rights of victims in the justice system ...'.

the politics of victims was at the end to be lent context by an election that elicited accounts, defences, and commitments, and one such commitment would centre on victims.[70]

## The European Framework Decision

Things were also stirring in Europe. The United Kingdom was a member state of the European Community and was bound by its decisions and, at the turn of the century, the Community was turning towards victims of crime. Once of little importance,[71] Justice and Home Affairs measures, consolidated in what was called the third pillar of the European Framework, had become ever more driven by the globalization of crime and of crime markets, and by the prospects of a process of enlargement that would encompass the Baltic states and the states of Eastern and Central Europe,[72] and they were beginning to catalyse what was called European integration (about a third of the papers passing through the United Kingdom permanent representatives touched on the area at the turn of the century[73]). A decision was consequently made to incorporate co-operation on Justice and Home Affairs into the Treaty on the European Union, signed in Maastricht on 7 February 1992, and entering into force on 1 November 1993, with the effect of introducing what Walker called 'an elaborate policy-making and policy-implementing structure of steering groups and working parties ...'.[74] Later still, the 1997 Amsterdam Treaty 'transferred some of the fields covered by "police and judicial cooperation in criminal matters" (third pillar)

---

[70] It is more than conceivable that there would have been talk and action about a Victims' Bill of Rights without an election, but the election was nevertheless something of a catalyst.

[71] Home affairs Ministers rarely met together formally before 1986, at which time they discussed the abolition of internal border controls. In 1991, a new third pillar, the Justice and Home Affairs Pillar, was formed and all JHA policy-making took place within the framework. In 1996–7, 'free movement issues' and judicial co-operation in civil matters was shifted into the first pillar.

[72] See, for instance, *Reinforcement of the Rule of Law: Final Report of the First Part of the Project*, Phare Horizontal Programme on Justice and Home Affairs, European Commission, published by The Centre for International Legal Cooperation, Leiden, the Netherlands, 2002.

[73] B. Hall; *Policing Europe*, Centre for European Reform, London, undated, p. 1.

[74] N. Walker; 'The pattern of transnational policing', in T. Newburn (ed.); *Handbook of Policing*, Willan Publishing, Cullumpton, Devon, 2003, p. 119.

into "free movement of persons" (first pillar). Under the first pillar, a new title IV—visas, asylum, immigration and other policies related to free movement of persons was added to the European Communities Treaty (EC Treaty).'[75]

At the same time, the New Labour Government had become by inclination and necessity more closely tied to the politics of the European Community. In the 1970s and 1980s, its predecessors had treated Europe (and the United Nations) as far-off places about which little needed be known for the purposes of criminal justice policy making (the 1985 United Nations Declaration of Basic Principles of Justice for Victims of Crime and Abuse of Power, for example, had made no impact at all on domestic politics[76]). But the international elements of crime[77] and criminal justice systems were growing,[78] every Department of State had become, in David Held's words, 'a home affairs office and foreign affairs office',[79] the external world pressed in on Government,[80] and the Home Office

---

[75] L. Pereira; 'The Origins of the Framework Decision: Victim's rights from a policy viewpoint', Dublin, October 2002.

[76] See my *Helping Victims of Crime, op. cit.*

[77] The Labour Party's web site was later to state that 'As markets and borders have opened around the world and new technologies abound, new opportunities for sophisticated criminals have emerged. We are working with our European partners in the fight against crimes such as money laundering, people trafficking; drug trafficking and other crimes by organised gangs. The Government has put in place a wide range of anti-terrorist and security measures.' The Home Office delegation to the 10th United Nations Congress on the Prevention of Crime and the Treatment of Offenders, 10–17 April 2000, was concerned primarily to promote the making of an international declaration on the suppression of transnational crime, and crime involving the illegal trade in arms, drugs, and people in particular.

[78] See J. Nijboer; 'Comparative Perspectives on the Judicial Role', in S. Doran and J. Jackson (eds.); *The Judicial Role in Criminal Proceedings,* Hart, Oxford, 2000, p. 19. The State, said David Held and his colleagues, 'is confronted by an enormous number of intergovernmental organizations... international agencies and regimes which operate across different spatial reaches, and by quasi-supranational institutions, like the European Union... [there is ] an enormous problem of policy coordination such that often the state appears not so much as a single actor on the world stage but as a multiplicity of actors in many different forums'. D. Held *et al.*; *Global Transformations,* Polity Press, Cambridge, 1999, pp. 50, 55.

[79] Speaking at a seminar on globalization and new forms of crime, London School of Economics, 18 May 2001.

[80] It is interesting that Andrew Ashworth should have attributed the growth of political interest in victims in England and Wales at the turn of the century wholly to pressures emanating from international obligations. See his *The Criminal Process: an evaluative study.* 2nd edition. Oxford University Press, 1998, p. 31.

pursued politics in Europe as well as in England and Wales. 'We are working actively to secure our objectives in Europe'[81] declared the Permanent Secretary in 2000.

At the very moment a domestic politics of victims was beginning to take shape in England and Wales, plans were afoot to generate a politics of victims within the European Commission and Parliament,[82] and they were to culminate in the European Framework Decision on the Standing of Victims in Criminal Procedure that came into effect in March 2001. A Framework Decision is in Ian Chisholm's words, 'not a Commission document. It's a framework decision by the member states, collectively'. It was binding, and it was to lend modest definition to the course of events in England and Wales.[83] 'If this is adopted', said Giselle Vernimen of the Justice and Home Affairs Commission's secretariat in Brussels, 'it is a framework decision. It means that member states must introduce changes in their criminal procedure and it's not just wishful thinking, they have to do it . . . It's binding.'

The lineage of the Framework Decision may be traced back to the publication in 1996 of a policy statement of the European Forum for

---

[81] Foreword to *The Home Office—A Guide, October 2000*, p. 3.

[82] In May 1999, for instance, *Cittadinanzattiva*, an Italian non-governmental organization, organized an international conference under the European Commission's Grotius Programme on the rights of victims, and one of its aspirations was to 'promote various proposals regarding Italy, the European Union and Europe at large . . . At the European level, the main proposal could be to draft and disseminate a European Charter on the rights of victims . . . [that] should not only be a declaration of principles but it should include provisions that could immediately be assimilated in the different European legislations . . . '. M. Constantini; Presentation, 27 May 1999.

[83] Title VI of the 1992 Maastricht Treaty, Provisions on Police and Judicial Cooperation in Criminal Matters of the EU Treaty, called for closer co-operation between police forces, customs authorities, and other competent authorities in Member States; closer co-operation between judicial and other competent authorities of the Member States, both directly and through Europol; and approximation, where necessary, of rules on criminal matters in the Member States. Under Article 34, it laid down that 'the Council of the European Union, using the appropriate form and procedures as set out by Title VI, shall take appropriate measures and promote cooperation, thus contributing to pursuit of the objectives of the European Union. To that end, among others, the Council may . . . adopt framework decisions for the purpose of approximating laws and regulations of the member states. Framework Decisions are binding upon member states as to the results to be achieved, but leave to the national authorities the choice of forms and methods.'

Victims Services,[84] *The rights of victims in criminal justice*[85] that
had been drafted by Helen Reeves of Victim Support in early 1995,
launched at a special meeting of the European Parliament in Brussels,[86] and then presented to the Swedish Commissioner, Anita
Gradin, who was then Head of the Commission for Security, Justice
and Freedom. The Commission proceeded to establish a Committee
of Experts that met during 1998[87] and 1999, with a membership
drawn from the European Forum and including Helen Reeves, and,
said Giselle Vernimen, the European Forum for Victims Services'
'statements of rights was very much on the table when we prepared
the communication and its report'. That report, *Crime victims in
the European Union: reflexions on standards and action,*[88] was
in effect a consultation paper. Supported by the United Kingdom

---

[84] Members of the European Forum for Victims Services had met on a regular basis
since 1987 to 'exchange ideas and benefit from the principle of best practice'. It was
established formally in 1990 as a federation of victim support organizations in and
around the European Community. (M. Groenhuijsen; 'Trends in Victimology in
Europe with Special Reference to the European Forum for Victim Services', 10th
Annual Conference of the Japanese Association of Victimology, Kyoto, 26th June
1999, p. 7.) By June 2000, it was composed of 17 member organizations from 15
countries.

[85] The Statement laid out what has become a familiar set of standard rights to
respect and recognition, to communication with the justice authorities, to protection,
and to compensation.

[86] Much of this section is based on *New rights for victims of crime in Europe,*
Victim Support UK/Ireland, 2002.

[87] In December 1998, too, the Commission floated victims' rights for the very first
time in the Action Plan of the Treaty of Amsterdam.

[88] COM(1999) 349 final. It talked, *inter alia*, about the growth of travel and the
need to ensure European citizens had to secure access to justice and adequate legal
protection wherever they were. Compensation had been the subject of a plan by the
Council of the European Union in 1998, but it did not exhaust the provisions which
victims should receive. It was necessary to introduce crime prevention measures,
mitigate problems of language; supply special measures for tourists (such as a special
police detail in Amsterdam Airport that focused on pickpockets); offer material
assistance to victims away from their home country; and support from non-governmental organizations that were regulated by guidelines laid down by the European
Forum for Victims Services; equip the police to deal effectively with foreign nationals
when reports of crime were made; and consider the standing of victims in 'the criminal
procedure'. Under that last heading, there was a review of opportunities for foreign
nationals to participate in proceedings; including 'fast-tracking' procedures; the need
to follow the progress of a case, perhaps through a telephone 'hot-line'; the making of
representations; being offered safe waiting areas in courthouses; recovering stolen
property promptly; and undergoing mediation.

Government,[89] it was destined for and adopted by the Commission in July 1999 under Article 31 of the 1992 Maastricht Treaty and endorsed by the regular, thrice-yearly Heads of State meeting at Tampere, Finland, in October 1999.[90]

There had been doubts about the constitutional legality and propriety of the Commission deliberating the treatment of victims at all. It could be argued that the scope of the Justice and Home Affairs portfolio was limited to co-operation in matters affecting international crime and migration, and not the national workings of the Member States' criminal justice systems. The extension of Article 31 of the 1992 Maastricht Treaty, which talked about harmonization of practice, to the protection of victims was considered by some to be *ultra vires*.[91] The United Kingdom Government's legal advisers in London and the European Parliament's Legal Affairs Committee in Brussels certainly argued that none of the areas listed in Article 31 of the Treaty of Rome covered provisions for victims and they 'remained to be convinced that the list was not exhaustive'. But

---

[89] Justice and Home Affairs Council, Agenda Item 1B, 28 September 2000. It cleared scrutiny in the House of Commons on 25 November 1998. Ian Chisholm's advice had been that 'none of the items is politically contentious and we can offer our broad agreement to what is proposed. We are the European leader in support for victims', and he recommended signing. More generally, the view of JVU as the Unit briefing Ministers and British representatives in Brussels was that the Government should be keen to play a full part in discussions within the EU about how to respond to needs of victims and to participate fully in taking forward the draft decision. But it also had reservations about the implications for court procedure in view of the very different legal systems involved and the conclusions of the review of the civil party procedure.

[90] The agreement reached by the Council of Ministers at Tampere was that the 'enjoyment of freedom requires a genuine area of justice, where people can approach courts and authorities in any Member State as easily as in their own...minimum standards should be drawn up on the protection of victims of crime, in particular on crime victims' access to justice and on their rights to compensation for damages, including legal costs. In addition, national programmes should be set up to finance measures, public and non-governmental, for assistance to and protection of victims.' Tampere European Council 15 and 16 October 1999, Presidency Conclusions.

[91] Article 31 of the 1992 Maastricht Treaty laid down that 'Common action on judicial cooperation in criminal matters shall include—(a) facilitating and accelerating cooperation between competent ministries and equivalent authorities of the Member States in relation to proceedings and the enforcement of decisions; (b) facilitating extradition between Member States; (c) ensuring compatibility in rules applicable in the Member States, as may improve such cooperation; (d) preventing conflicts of jurisdiction between Member States.'

those driving the politics of victims were determined, and they
sought to circumvent the problem of jurisdiction by arguing that
the French version of the Article allowed greater interpretive latitude
and by applying the requirement under Article 31 to ensure consistency in criminal justice procedures to the treatment of European
Union travellers and tourists who were victims of crime in countries
other than their own.[92] Giselle Vernimen recalled that the then
Swedish Commissioner, Anita Gradin, 'was quite interested and
concerned by the different approach in different member states and
the lack of correct assistance and compensation. So what we, what
we did at the time, we elected to take the perspective of someone
travelling in another member state but bearing in mind of course,
that many of the proposals and suggestions which were contained in
the communication, would be to the benefit of any kind of victim.' It
was an effective enough device to allow victims to become subjects
of Community policy-making. Victims were, it could be argued,
entitled to 'true access to justice' and 'adequate legal protection
irrespective of where they find themselves'.[93] 'People travelling
about have fewer rights than nationals when they are victimised.
We want to rectify that',[94] said the Home Secretary immediately
before the meeting in Tampere.

Three months after the Tampere meeting, in January 2000, Portugal assumed the six-month long Presidency of the Commission,
and Luis Miranda Pereira, representing the Portuguese Government,

[92] Legal advice from within the Commission argued that under Article 34(2) of the
EU Treaty, 'Framework Decisions contribute to the pursuit of the Union's objectives,
and one such objective was to provide a high level of safety by developing common
action in the field of police and judicial cooperation. Article 29 says that was to be
achieved by preventing crime through closer cooperation in accord with Articles 31
and 32. Framework decision does not deal with transnational cooperation but domestic matters, but the Council have power to deal with the criminal justice system
because there is a wide latitude of interpretation; helping victims mitigates and
therefore combats crime and may enhance trust in the criminal justice system.'
Council of the European Union; Opinion of the Legal Service on the initiative for a
Framework Decision, 14 July 2000.
[93] Commission of the European Communities; Communication from the Commission to the Council, the European Parliament and the Economic and Social Committee: 'Crime Victims in the European Union, Reflexions on Standards and Action',
Brussels, 14 July 1999. *Inter alia*, the report recommended the need for information,
the need for training of staff dealing with victims, and, for foreign victims, problems of
language.
[94] Jack Straw speaking at Foreign Press Association, London, 12 October 1999.

became the chair of the European Judicial Co-operation Working Group, one of the Justice and Home Affairs groups that examined criminal law procedure and would become engaged in considering proposals for a Framework Decision. Luis Miranda Pereira was a former Chair of the Probation Department of the Portuguese Ministry of Justice, the Chair of *APAV*, (*Associação Portuguesa de Apoio à Vítima*), the Portuguese sister organization to Victim Support, which had 250 volunteers and thirteen local schemes, and he had strong links with the European Forum for Victims Services. He was described by a member of JVU as a man who had 'spent much of his time championing elements of the draft framework decision'. Luis Miranda Pereira himself declared that the Framework Decision was a combination of 'the right man, the right time and the right subject'.

On Portugal's succession to the Presidency, a group was convened by its Ministry of Justice, one of whom was Luis Miranda Pereira, and the official in charge went round its members asking for items for a justice agenda, and it was Luis Miranda Pereira who suggested victims. Marc Groenhuijsen, former President of the European Forum for Victims' Services, and a Professor of Law at the University of Tilburg, recalled:

We were working on the Executive Committee [of the European Victims Forum] for quite a long time about how to influence policy in European terms and shaping a foundation for a budget line for the European Forum. Against that, when Portugal was president of EU, the Portugese Government asked Luis Pereira—who used to be the chair of probation in the Ministry of Justice—a very serious policy adviser—he had been set aside and promoted away to an innocent corner of the building doing nothing [because of a change of Government]—but then they recalled him and charged him to prepare the Portugese Presidency on Justice and Home Affairs, and he proposed a Framework Decision on victims. The only part of his professional background was *APAV* but he lacked legal competence and experience—an honorary role—so he turned to us and asked me as President of the European Victims Forum to comment on the first draft submitted informally... Lots of drafts followed. He co-operated with people in Brussels, Giselle Vernimen, me invited as an expert in my own right to give credibility to the paper... It was a breakthrough. The main obstacle over a long period was that the EU did not accept competence in criminal law matters—that only changed with the Tampere conclusions...

There had been problems about 'fitting it in but it did seem to conform to Pillar 1'. The text of Article 31 was sufficiently elastic

to make out a reasonably persuasive case[95] (and, for its part, the
Home Office reminded itself that 'We have to remember the PM
signed up to work in this area in Tampere. We cannot therefore argue
now that it does not fall within EU competence. (No other state has
raised objections.).' Meetings were organized by the Portuguese
Embassy with France, Sweden, and Belgium, the countries next in
succession for the Presidency, and they contracted to continue the
work on the Decision when in office. The Framework Decision on
the standing of victims in criminal proceedings was drawn up and,
after being submitted to the Commission[96] and approved during the
Portuguese Presidency[97] under the urging of *APAV*, accepted by the
European Parliament during the French Presidency in the latter half
of 2000, under the urging of its own victim support organization,
*INAVEM*, (*Institut National d'Aide Aux Victimes et de Médiation*),

[95] It was noted in the Home Office that the 'French text of Article 31 shows the list
of activities to be illustrative rather than exhaustive and does not contain the ambiguities of the English text. We still remain doubtful but acknowledge scope for argument
either way. Measure is supported by Government and other member states and is
beneficial to victims of crime, so little purpose would be served by withholding
clearance at this stage.'

[96] The submission read: 'With reference to the United Nations Declaration of Basic
Principles of Justice for Victims of Crime and Abuse of Power; With reference to the
work of the European Union for Victim Services, in particular the Statement of
Victims' Rights in the Process of Criminal Justice. Whereas...the fact that the provisions of this Framework Decision are confined to looking after victims' interests under
criminal procedure; the fact that, for that reason, leaving aside any future addressing
of the whole issue of compensation for crime victims within the EU, the provisions of
this Framework Decision regarding compensation, as well as those regarding mediation, relate to criminal procedure and thus do not concern arrangements under
civil procedure;...the importance of affording victims the best legal protection
and defence of their interests, irrespective of the country in which they are present...has adopted this Framework Decision.' Council of European Union, 14
April 2000, communication from Vasco Valente, permanent representative of
the Portuguese Republic, to Javier Solana, Secretary General of the Council of the
European Union. Proposal by the Portuguese Government for a Framework Decision
on the standing of the victims in crime procedure to place on the agenda for the
appropriate bodies.

[97] The Commission stated that it 'welcomes the commission communication...
calls on member states as a matter of urgency to strengthen forthwith the introduction
of a harmonised system of cross-border protection of victims at Union level'. European Parliament; Report on the Commission Communication to the Council, the
European Parliament and the Economic and Social Committee on crime victims in
the European Union, Reflexions on standards and actions, 25 April 2000.

cleared by the House of Lords Sub Committee E[98] on 11 October 2000, it was approved and published in the Official Journal of the European Communities, during the Swedish Presidency, on the 15 March 2001. It would thereafter be incumbent on the British Government to make certain that 'it has the necessary laws and regulations to ensure compliance [of most of the provisions] in twelve months'.[99]

The chief difficulties encountered during negotiation had been the payment of compensation (of concern particularly to Germany—not all States had schemes in place and they were expensive[100] but, said Marc Groenhuijsen, compensation had only been planted as a 'bargaining chip' to be withdrawn if necessary); the payment of legal expenses to victims (unwelcome to the United Kingdom Government[101]); the extent to which the Decision should be prescriptive or binding;[102] and the way in which, if at all, victims' rights could be introduced into an adversarial system, a matter of particular concern to the representatives of the Irish and British Governments. As Ian Chisholm remarked in June 2000 at the height of the discussion:

Of course the Portuguese come from actually, you know, a Continental civil code tradition where the victim has a role and all sorts of assumptions, and the problem that the Anglo-Saxon countries, the Irish and ourselves

[98] Responsible for vetting European legislation. The Framework Decision, it was held, would have no impact on United Kingdom law; the relevant measures were already in place or in hand; and the Decision complied with the subsidiarity principle.

[99] Victims Steering Group: meeting of 12 June 2001: European Framework Decision on the Standing of Victims in criminal proceedings.

[100] L. Pereira; 'The Origins of the Framework Decision: Victim's rights from a policy viewpoint', Dublin, October 2002.

[101] The British representative was advised in January 2001 to argue that legal aid was not available to victims and there were no plans to make it so; documents in all EU languages would be too expensive; it was not feasible to extend provisions to civil process; that she should resist the amendment giving recognition to the legal standing of the victim: the victim had no legal standing in the criminal justice system and there were no plans to change this arrangement.

[102] A participant recalled that the core issue was the difference between statutory law and statutory guidelines. The Irish representative did not like being dictated to. She did not want informal policy measures being enforced by formal rules. They were afraid that there would be an obligation to upgrade the decision to statute, an objection in principle rather than of substance. Luis Miranda Pereira was asked to intervene. He went to Ian Chisholm, and the upshot was that the Irish representative was recalled.

have had, is this is very different. It is quite difficult, this area on the role of the victim in proceedings. So that's quite lively at the moment. they've got a very sort of much more active role for the victim... It's a matter of teasing one's way through that... My own view I don't think that's a problem. There are bits of draft that suggest that but when we had the discussion, there was a general willingness by everyone to try and draft something that everyone could live with, agree on general principles.

What strengthened the hand of Britain and Ireland was the convention that deliberations about drafts of documents such as the Framework Decision must arrive at a consensus. The United Kingdom representative in Brussels told her colleague in JVU in January 2001 that 'We work on the basis that if anyone has a substantive concern about a change proposed by the European Parliament it will not be accepted, but we also accept amendments in the interests of inter-institutional affairs.' A reluctance to accept a draft could be powerful indeed. At the instigation of the Irish and the British, the Framework Decision no longer defined victims as legal parties in procedure (representatives were reassured in May 2000 by Luis Miranda Pereira, the Chair of the Working Group, and by the Commission that the Framework Decision would only be binding on member states 'in overall objectives rather than the means of achieving them'[103]). And victims would have no rights of litigation under their newly acquired rights ('It creates obligations for member states but it's not, it does not have direct effect for the individuals', said Giselle Vernimen).

It had been Article 6 that was the principal rubbing point. In an early draft of July 2000 that article occasioned considerable difficulty in London. It had then read 'Irrespective of the possibility of victims participating in procedure as a witness or a party, Member States shall ensure an opportunity for victims to participate as such, in accordance with the provisions of this Framework Decision. Member States shall ensure that all victims, regardless of their means, have access to legal advice, provided free of charge if need be.' That version, a JVU official flatly told the United Kingdom representative in Brussels, 'is unacceptable'. A later draft of September 2000 then exacerbated the difficulty by talking about an obligation to 'maximise the involvement of victims in the criminal

---

[103] Note of Meeting, European Judicial Co-operation Working Group, Brussels, 15–16 May 2000.

procedure'. The United Kingdom representative urged its removal altogether, although she recognized that such a measure would not be favoured by the thirteen States in whose criminal justice systems victims could well have standing. By the end of October 2000, however, the Irish and British had succeeded in ensuring that victims would not be treated as parties, and a final version of Article 6 was agreed which laid down that victims should be afforded rights only 'when they are able to have the status of parties to criminal proceedings'.

Luis Miranda Pereira recalled that it 'wasn't smooth but there was a bit of a moral blackmail exercise against Ministers. They were put in a spot where they did not want to be seen hard on victims.' However, according to Marc Groenhuijsen, the acceptance of the Framework Decision had been relatively uncomplicated. He said in October 2002 that wide endorsement was possible because:

Member states felt that they had all already complied with the framework decision... The Dutch representatives, for instance, were given a very broad mandate from their Government to agree to the Decision providing there would not be much legislative change... They were wrong. Most of the states do not comply with the framework decision. This document is the first one on a supranational level which is legally binding. First to acknowledge the role of victim *as* a victim—it is very rare for a criminal justice system to acknowledge a victim *as* a victim, a person who is usually recognised by the role of reporter of crime, testifier, never as a victim *per se*. Not a single member state has legislated a comprehensive victims' bill. National reports confirm the self-confidence of member states in their assertion of full compliance. I disagree with that assessment.

Described by the President of the European Parliament as a 'very significant publication',[104] the Framework Decision[105] opened by rehearsing what international bureaucrats are wont to call the 'whereases' or the 'recital', the ceremonial litany of precedents and authorities that give a measure history and legitimacy: the 1985 United Nations Declaration, the initiative of the Portuguese Republic, the opinion of the European Parliament, the Action Plan of the Council and the Commission, the conclusions of the European

---

[104] Preface to Victim Support; *New rights for victims of crime in Europe, op. cit.*
[105] Council Framework Decision of 15 March 2001 on the standing of victims in criminal proceedings (2001/220/JHA).

Council Meeting in Tampere, and so on.[106] Recalling the mandate
residing in Article 31, it called on Member States 'to approximate
their laws and regulations to the extent necessary to attain the
objective of affording victims of crime a high level of protection,
irrespective of the Member State in which they are present'. And
then, drawing (in Luis Miranda Pereira's words) 'on the documents
that were available, the UN declaration etc', and echoing the European Forum of Victims Service's own statement of rights, respecting
what is described as 'subsidiarity'[107] (the principle of deference to
local arrangements or, as Ian Chisholm put it, 'sufficient national
variation'), the main rights to be enforced were listed: respect for
dignity, the right to provide and receive information, the right to
understand and be understood (referring in part to the need for
interpreters and translations in criminal procedure), the right to be
protected, and the right to have 'allowance made for the disadvantage of living in a different Member State from the one in which the
crime was committed'. After the representations of the two Governments with common law systems, there was little reference to the
victim as a party to legal proceedings, although Article 3 did talk
about the 'possibility for victims to be heard during proceedings and
to supply evidence';[108] Article 6 stated that victims should have
access to advice 'concerning their role in proceedings ... when it is
possible for them to have the status of parties to criminal proceedings', and Article 7 laid down that each 'Member State shall,
according to the applicable national provisions, afford victims who
have the status of parties or witnesses the possibility of reimburse-
ment of expenses incurred as a result of their legitimate participation
in criminal proceedings.' It had been, the Victims Steering Group
were told in June 2000, 'quite a tricky document to negotiate because of the difficulty of marrying common law and other systems of
law. Thirteen of the states give victims a role in criminal proceedings.

[106] Luis Miranda Pereira wrote that the Framework Decision 'already mentions
developments concerning the EU, the role of international organisations, as the United
Nations and the Council of Europe, is also essential as it "pushes" the countries into
accepting international agreements'. 'The Origins of the Framework Decision:
Victim's rights from a policy viewpoint', Phare Conference, Dublin, October 2002.

[107] Council of the European Union; Opinion of the Legal Service on the initiative
for a Framework Decision, 14 July 2000, emphasized the importance of subsidiarity.

[108] It was uncertain, some officials thought in June 2000, whether victims have a
right to be heard. It would be more accurate to say they will be heard.

As one of the leading countries in the EU, we felt we should take a leading role.'

The Home Office view was that compliance would not be problematic: English and Welsh victims' policies already conformed to the rights laid out in the Framework Decision.[109] The chief utility of the Decision would be to lend context and authority to domestic proposals, and it was to be cited as a matter of course in, for example, discussions in and about the review of the *Victim's Charter.*[110]

## Consultations

In a process that Marxists would have called over-determined, the prospects of a big policy push on victims were beginning to be considered across related sectors of Government from late 1999 onwards, having their formal origin in a series of parallel deliberations inaugurated by No. 10 and feeding on work under way principally in the Home Office. There were undoubted differences of nuance, content, and timing but, running in parallel, the committees in which the deliberations took place were inevitably interleaved.[111] They drew on the same members, considered very similar drafts usually written by the same authors, and discussed similar projects and proposals. To be sure, processes could get out of joint. Decisions taken in one forum would affect the work of another, and such was the volume of activity that there was scope for a confusion of co-ordination, timing, and presentation. In November 2000, for instance, it was not at all evident how the phasing of the *CJ2010* document, the Charter review, the Auld Review and the review of the place of the victim in criminal procedure should be

---

[109] Ian Chisholm's successor as head of JVU told me in June 2002, for instance, that 'We're in compliance and just strengthening what we've already done.'

[110] A summary statement offered in the Charter Review document, published in February 2001, just before the endorsement of the Framework Decision, recited that 'Early in 2000, the then Portugese Presidency of the European Union introduced a draft framework decision... Although the draft remains subject to approval by EU member states, the final framework decision would provide outline rights for victims for the first time across the EU...'.

[111] For example, a review of policy development work prepared for the *CJ2010* initiative listed the final revisions to be performed on the Charter review, the subject of a quite discrete chain of activity.

organized (and Sir Robin Auld was reported to be dismayed that the *CJ2010* paper had duplicated the ideas of his courts' review before his own report could be published[112]).

One chain of work started in discussions about 'a trilateral strategy paper' for proposals for the Comprehensive Spending Review's 'unallocated reserve' in early October 2000 (which, it will be recalled, had been established to promote 'joined-up government' between the three criminal justice ministries), where a member of the No. 10 Policy Group indicated that she wanted a 'package of joined-up work' on victims and witnesses. It was to lead, as we have seen in Chapter 4, to the CPS receiving funds for 'bronze level' communications with witnesses, the staggered implementation of the *Speaking up for Justice* report, and the funding of the extension of the Victim Support Witness Service into the Magistrates' Courts.

Another chain had its genesis at the end of October, when Ministers were reminded that the Prime Minister wanted 'a note' on the reform agenda as they saw it for a new long-term strategy review, and that reference should be made to the treatment of victims and to possible changes to the *Victim's Charter*. Briefed by Ian Chisholm, that short note was prepared by Justin Russell, the Home Secretary's policy adviser, and its second paragraph dwelt on victims and the 'huge problems' remaining: 'Our priority for the next Parliament must be to radically reform the criminal justice system [with] crime reduction and the needs of victims and witnesses (not just offenders) at the heart of the CJS.' It led to a meeting that was to bring about the commissioning of another 'long-term strategy paper', at first locally called *CJ2010*[113] but eventually published as *Criminal Justice: The Way*

[112] *The Times*, 21 February 2001. An official remarked on 15 February that 'we've obviously seen the interim findings that are on the web site, like everybody else and we're in close contact with LCD, indeed with Sir Robin Auld's secretariat. But that's an independent review. And while we may be making some fairly broad statements about maybe we would be considering a unified court, you know, the three tier idea, I don't think, we're not going to steal Sir Robin Auld's thunder, at the same time we're not going to pre-empt what the government might say about it which wouldn't be appropriate.'

[113] The official responsible for editing and drafting much of the paper recalled that 'we were doing these two projects, immigration and police. We did these for about four weeks and then we were called in to see the Permanent Secretary, and he told us to drop everything. And the whole team would be concentrating on providing a long-term strategy on criminal justice which became known as Criminal Justice 2010. A ten

*Ahead*, that was supposed to follow the 'NHS model' and determine 'what is wrong and what needs to be put right', composed of some fourteen strands ('some on which the PM would like personally to get involved'[114]), with descriptions of specified objectives for each strand, milestones, key risks, and key policy decisions, and accompanied by a number of linked seminars conducted personally by the Prime Minister. The seminars would encompass the criminal courts (in the context of the Auld review); the sentencing framework; attrition (in the context of John Birt's review and the idea that there were '100,000 young offenders at risk'[115]); police reform; and serious and organized crime. Also warranting seminars was the seventh strand on 'radically better treatment for victims, with information at every stage, service standards/ombudsman/revised charter'. The lead official would be the Director of Criminal Policy at the Home Office, Sue Street, with Ian Chisholm in support. And a paper was prepared on 7 December 2000 on what might be done, including, in the short term, the creation of a Victims Ombudsman, a new Charter of Rights, and, in the medium term, Internet access to the progress of one's case, on-line crime reporting and booked trial dates.[116]

In preparing those proposals, Ian Chisholm had explored how other adversarial criminal justice systems, including New

year strategy a little bit along the lines of the National Health plan and the transport plan, both of which are ten year plans but slightly different because this wouldn't be tied to resources in the way in which they were. So somewhat more aspirational, somewhat more speculative. And since October when we started that, what we did was we seconded in someone from CPS and two people from LCD because it's very much a trilateral initiative with a steering group chaired by the Home Secretary.'

[114] Note on *CJ2010* project delivery from Director, Strategy and Performance, 1 November 2000.

[115] And that figure flowed from cohort analyses undertaken by Marvin Wolfgang in the United States and Donald West and David Farrington in England that showed that some 60% of recorded crimes were committed by about 6% of offenders. See M. Wolfgang *et al.*; *Delinquency in a Birth Cohort*, University of Chicago Press, Chicago, 1972 and D. West and D. Farrington; *The Delinquent Way of Life*, Heinemann, London, 1977. For a discussion of some of the empirical problems of that notion, see A. Hagell and T. Newburn; *Persistent Young Offenders*, Policy Studies Institute, London, 1994.

[116] Minutes of the Lead Ministers' Meeting on Criminal Justice 2010, 7 December 2000.

Zealand,[117] Australia, the United States,[118] and Canada[119] had managed the problem of awarding rights to victims, and the Ombudsman seemed to be a suitable *deus ex machina.* He recalled:

The idea of a Victims Ombudsman was originally my idea. I was aware of the various victim support initiatives particularly in Canada, the USA and Australasia. This was the result of meetings and discussions both here and abroad, e.g. at International Victimology Conferences in the Hague in 1997[120] and Montreal in 2000 and at the UN meetings where we drafted the victims' handbook.[121] The meetings here included discussions with politicians/officials passing through London. [There was a] meeting

[117] Indeed, the Home Secretary had met the New Zealand High Commissioner in early 2000, and the briefings for that meeting anticipated some of what was later to be proposed. An official had earlier asked her counterpart in the New Zealand Ministry of Justice to inform her about current developments in that country, and she recalled that there had been talk about a Victims of Offences Bill. Had it, she wondered, been passed or was it still in the planning stage? She was to be informed on 16 December 1999 that the Bill contained provisions for victims to make submissions at sentencing, parole hearing, and in relation to final release conditions. A new Government had, however, 'called for other new and enforceable victim rights'. Although a Victims Commissioner had been proposed by the Victims Task Force; *Towards Equality in Criminal Justice* (Report to the Minister of Justice, Private Box 180, Wellington, New Zealand, 1993), in December 1999, Ian Chisholm was shown a copy of proposals from the New Zealand Ministry of Justice designed further to enlarge the role of the victim in criminal procedure in that country. And a Victims' Rights Act was indeed enacted in 2002 (2002 No. 39), but it made no provision for a Commissioner. What it contained instead was provision for the supply of information to victims, the protection of victims' privacy, the introduction of victim impact statements for sentencing purposes, and other sundry measures.

[118] A number of American States, including Minnesota and South Carolina, had established an Office of Crime Victims Ombudsman with responsibilities for investigation of rights violations, advocacy on behalf of victims, and the provision of information. Other States, like Connecticut, had Victim Compensation Commissioners.

[119] The Office of Victims Ombudsman of Canada was established by Bill C-457 of 2001–2 to 'conduct investigations, reviews of . . . policies, and studies into the problems of victims related to decisions, policies, acts or omissions . . .'. Matthew Seward, working at Labour Party headquarters, reflected 'the Ontario Government had some sort of Victims Bill of Rights thing there which I think they've drawn on a bit as well'.

[120] The Conference theme was 'Caring for Victims' and its proceedings were published under that title and edited by J. van Dijk and others.

[121] *Handbook on Justice for Victims,* Centre for International Crime Prevention, United Nations Office for Drug Control and Crime Control, New York, 1999. Ian Chisholm was named as one of the 40 or so contributors. There was a fairly comprehensive review of measures in that handbook, including discussion of victim impact statements and fine surcharges, and the duties of the criminal justice agencies, but I could find no reference to the idea of a Victims Ombudsman or Commissioner.

between Jack Straw and officials from the Govt. of New South Wales. The NSW Victims of Crime Act 1996[122] was discussed and was one of the models, but only one, of discussion here about a Victims' Rights Act here. I was most active in Montreal at the IV [International Victimology] Conference,[123] and after the conference in Ottawa, in 2000 in discussing victims' rights legislation, particularly with Canadian provincial and federal Govt. officials.

There were also to be separate consultations on the *Victim's Charter* and on the place of the victim in the criminal justice system. Criminal Justice Ministers met as part of their regular trilateral consultations on 15 December 1999, and they had before them the paper of 9 December on 'Better Services to Victims' which I have already summarized. 'Better Services to Victims' prompted the Home Secretary to enquire how work might further develop in 'the next couple of years': should there, he wondered, be a victims' advocacy service; a community chest of fine revenues which could fund support for victims;[124] or a safety package for victims at risk? John Halliday, in his turn, emailed Ian Chisholm:

---

[122] That Act, the Victims Rights Act 1996 No. 114, contained a number of measures that were later to be adopted or mirrored in the Home Office proposals, including a Charter of Victims Rights and a Victims Advisory Board (although the composition of the English and Welsh Panel was to be different from the New South Wales Board). There was no reference to an Ombudsman or Commissioner, but the Act did establish a Victims of Crime Bureau under a Director as a branch of the Attorney General's Department with duties to provide information to victims; co-ordinate the delivery of services to victims; promote and oversee the implementation of the Charter; receive complaints from victims about alleged breaches of Charter rights and attempt to resolve them; and report to the Minister for presentation to Parliament 'on any matter arising in connection with the exercise of its functions.'

[123] It was not of course a new proposal. Not only were there Victims Ombudsmen in post overseas but the JUSTICE committee had floated the idea of a Victims Ombudsman and a Victims Commissioner in its 1998 report.

[124] The bulk of revenues for victims' services in Canada (see Federal Legislation Strengthening the Voice of Victims of Crime, Department of Justice, Canada, 4 November 1999) and the United States stemmed from what were called 'fine surcharges' (in 1996, for instance, the US federal Office for the Victims of Crime received $528 m. in this way under the Victims of Crime Act Crime Victims Fund, July 1984), and Michael Howard and Jack Straw had both broached the prospect of such a scheme in England and Wales. The Prime Minister had expressed cautious support in January 2001, but was anxious about the elaboration of bureaucracy which any such fund might entail. Once again, however, the proposal was balked by the prospect of a veto from the Lord Chancellor's Department and a Treasury anxious about costs and reluctant to forego revenue ('If in the past the proposal for a Fund had been

when we meet I should like to focus on the wider picture, including the prospect for the sort of attractive package we have discussed informally from time to time, and how we might build on this for Ministers.

Ian Chisholm's paper received Ministerial endorsement and a commission to draft a consultation paper under the *aegis* of a new subgroup of the Victims Steering Group. There was much that was unresolved, particularly the probable costs of the bolder new proposals before the next Comprehensive Spending Review, and much that could be contentious, including the question of whether 'significant new measures on victims' "rights" might benefit from being put on a legislative basis in a Victims Rights Act'[125] (note how the word *rights* had been placed in double quotation marks to reinforce its tentative and untested quality). Following a meeting of the Crime Strategy Group in January 2000 on the next Comprehensive Spending Review, John Halliday wondered what might be done 'to follow up key messages for Aim 2', and reported the Home Secretary's political adviser's prediction 'that Ministers would like to see more recognition of the potential for a new victims' package, including a

rejected because of the cost, why were we looking at it again?'). By February 2001, the JVU phrasing of the issue had become 'we would have to give considerable thought to the creation of any fund, to ensure that it did not lead to an unsustainable charge to public funds'. The fund was finally mooted in public on 27 July 2003 under the *aegis* of a new Home Secretary, David Blunkett, where it was represented by the *Sunday Times* rather unkindly as yet another 'stealth tax'. Undeterred, the Home Office issued a consultation paper on 12 January 2004, *Compensation and Support for Victims of Crime*, in which, on p. 6, fine surcharges were again proposed to 'support those who are victims of crime, including the many people—often the poorest in society—who are repeatedly victimised and who may not even have the confidence to report the crimes committed against them. Supporting victims and witnesses throughout the criminal justice process will help bring more offenders to justice—which many victims want to see just as much as receiving support.' The formal launch was conducted by Baroness Scotland at the Bedfordshire Road Traffic pilot scheme, a pilot project designed to 'test options on support services for road crash victims', and it was lazily reported in the mass media as a project that would impose fine surcharges on speeding motorists (see, for example, *Evening Standard*, 12 January 2004). The headline in *The Times* of 13 January 2004 was 'Outrage over £5 "tax" on speeding fines'. Victim Support itself was not well disposed towards the scheme because it believed that it would introduce the potential conflict between offender and victim that the organisation had studiously avoided.

[125] 'Better Services for Victims and Witnesses', 6 December 1999.

victims' advocate scheme': costings were of a lesser importance and 'precision may not be essential'.[126]

Ian Chisholm's paper having been cleared by the meeting of criminal justice Ministers in December, it was submitted as 'a slightly updated [version] of the same thing' and at the request of the Cabinet Office's Economics and Domestic Affairs Secretariat to a meeting held by the Prime Minister with Ministers in February 2000.[127] Of all the developments, Ian Chisholm concluded, 'The most important area of new work under consideration is the idea, recommended for consideration by the Stephen Lawrence Inquiry and others, that victims should have a more recognised, formal role during trials.' He recalled in that month of February, 'I was asked to do a little bit of a think paper, "well this is what we're doing and where we go" . . . I did a paper for the Ministerial Group on victims back in December and there was a meeting with the PM and the Home Sec and the Lord Chancellor and the Attorney General this week actually, on the base of the paper. . . And obviously the victims' advocacy thing is the most important. But I thought if we're bringing it together in a charter, some of this, then maybe we should underpin it even more with some sort of victims' rights.' He added later, 'I went to ministers feeling fairly sort of neutral about it and they seemed quite enthusiastic about it, both the Home Secretary and Number 10 as well, about looking at this a bit further.'

Charles Clarke, one of the recipients of that paper, said in April 2000:

We're just looking at what are the ways in which we can support victims: what, how effective are organisations in ensuring that victims get the actual support that they need. . . There is secondly the question of have victims a stake in the criminal justice system itself so that how can victims have a voice in the trial, in the legal process. And third is, and how do you do that without it being fantastically bureaucratic?[128] And following Lawrence,

---

[126] Letter of 3 February 2000.

[127] The Prime Minister had become progressively more engaged in victims' matters during this period. For example, it was reported in July 2000 that he had become attracted by the notion of the auxiliary prosecutor role (although the report did not use that term). It could be, the article continued, that prosecutors will come to represent the victim rather than the State. *Sunday Telegraph*, 30 July 2000.

[128] What he was almost certainly alluding to was the anxiety attending proposals to establish a new victims' fund, based on fine surcharges, which was believed to be at risk of becoming unduly cumbersome organizationally.

which was I suppose you could describe as an externally driven event. But the whole issue of the relationship of the agencies, and particularly CPS and police, with victims is there. And then you've got things like legal costs . . . But I wouldn't say we had an entirely coherent position as yet about what we're doing about all these.

Ian Chisholm had reminded a meeting of the Victims Steering Group in April 2000 that a new Charter was necessary because 'so many things have been going on'.[129] There was talk about a 'challenge . . . to improve the Charter, taking into accounts developments over the last years both domestically and internationally and to reflect the increasing priority that Government attaches to help for victims and witnesses'.[130] But, as the 2001 general election loomed, as committees proliferated and Ministers began to exert more pressure to place victims at the 'heart' or the 'centre' of the criminal justice system,[131] as the need grew to demonstrate to the European Commission that rights were being considered,[132] so the emphasis shifted from a simple revision of the Charter to the possibility of something more substantial, perhaps even a Victims' Bill of Rights, and officials were uncertain whether what they were discussing should even still be called a Charter. There was a dawning sense that a turning point might have been reached and that the policy domain occupied by victims of crime was about to change, if only under the impact of the European Parliament:[133] 'The European Framework Decision will give rights anyway', said Ian Chisholm, it 'is essentially an EU Victims Charter of Rights . . . I thought if we're bringing it together in a charter, some of this, then maybe we should underpin it even

---

[129] Meeting of Victims Steering Group, 28 April 2000, my notes.

[130] Victims' Charter—draft consultation paper.

[131] See *Criminal Justice System Business Plan 2000–2001*, May 2000, Lord Chancellor, Home Office, Attorney General, p. 15.

[132] Ministers were reminded by Ian Chisholm in June 2000, 'We are not so strong on procedural issues. Consultation exercise would show European partners we are looking at ways of addressing the issue.'

[133] References would routinely be made coupling the European Framework Decision with the Charter review. For example, the man responsible for victims' research in RDS, said at a conference organized by the RDS on 8 February 2001, that 'strengthening of the *Victim's Charter* is tied up with the Decision'. Not only did the Framework Decision give weight to victims' rights, but it had appeared in March 2001, and events taking place at much the same time may be linked rhetorically and causally in people's accounts.

more with some sort of victims' rights.' At the very centre of things, a
JVU Grade 7 said in June 2000:

It is, it is beginning to come together. There is, I don't know whether it's
planned or it's just happening, but it's the sense that Ministers do keep
talking about bringing victims close to the heart of the criminal justice
system, it's happening. I mean all sorts of moves that we're now making are
doing this. And in a more joined-up way than has been common in the past.
I mean victims' statement is one clear example. The consultation we're
going to have about whether victims should have a more formal role in the
criminal justice process is another... Who knows what the combination is
going to be? This really is, this really is a consultation exercise without any,
without any particular agenda. I mean this is really 'let's see what we can
do'. The aim is to improve the role of victims within the criminal justice
system to the extent that that is possible without tipping the balance too far
in favour of victims and away from defendants. You've still got to have a
balance. That's the issue, that is crucial and therefore, the role of you know,
of the judiciary will not, again not be determinative but will be clearly very
important in the business of getting the balance right. Because after all
you know, you need the judiciary to operate the bottom end of the
system, you know, the extreme end of the system. And you clearly need
consensus and goodwill all along the line. So, and, this is all tied up of
course with the review of the *Victim's Charter* which is just about to be
kicked off... what is the charter actually going to be? Is it going to
be another set of service standards? Is it going to be a Bill of Rights? Is it
going to be legislation? In other words, what sort of *Victim's Charter* do
you want to finish up with at the end of the day? Are you looking for
another one like we've got at the moment which is just an expression of
good intention and a mechanism to complain but no enforceable rights?
Well do you actually want enforceable rights backed up in a charter of
human rights or underpinned by legislation?

Responding to the request to take matters forward and develop a
'package', and mindful of the unavoidable and insurmountable
judicial obstacles to full-blown victims' rights, Home Office Ministers were asked by Ian Chisholm in June 2000 whether they wished a
new Charter to entail 'fully fledged rights underpinned by legislation'; a Charter 'using the language of rights, but not underpinned by
legislation'; or 'a straightforward redraft of the current Charter
taking the same "standards of service" approach'.[134] The criminal

---

[134] 'Victim's Charter—Review: Involvement of Victims in Criminal Legal Proceedings', 15 June 2000.

justice agencies had, he reported, 'become more self-confident about the sort of services they are able to deliver... While it would be far simpler administratively to regard the review of the Charter as a straightforward redrafting exercise of the current document, we would recommend a rather more ambitious approach':

In our view, there are two options to consider. The first is to legislate to provide enforceable rights for victims, to make it clear what they could expect from the criminal justice system and, further, what penalties could be levied against those agencies which failed to deliver in individual cases. However, to broker this with the three main players in the victims' field— the police, the Crown Prosecution Service and the courts—would not be easy, and inevitably and immediately issues about resources would be raised... The other clear disadvantage of the legislative route is the length of time it would take... The second option may therefore be both more attractive and pragmatic. This would consist of an overarching 'Bill of Rights', highlighting perhaps 8–10 key rights to which victims should be entitled. This would be backed up by a more comprehensive document breaking down each of the 'rights' into a number of sub-headings.

Ministers were also briefed about how victims might become more formally involved in legal proceedings. They were reminded about the proposals to establish a *parti civile* procedure under Recommendation 41 of the Stephen Lawrence Report, the doubts raised by Brienen and Hoegen at the September 1999 conference, and the alternative proposal of an auxiliary prosecutor role. The Lawrence Steering Group had agreed in March 2000 to commission a consultation paper on the role of the victim, 'ranging from a provision of "victim advocates" at its fullest, to a guaranteed seat in the court room at the minimum'. But there were barriers that might not readily be overcome: 'the most promising approach is to build up CPS responsibility to look after the interests of victims... There is likely to be little enthusiasm for the more far reaching measures in some influential quarters. The Lord Chief Justice has already counselled against importing measures from other jurisdictions which he thinks would be inappropriate for our own criminal justice system', and by that, it will be recalled, he had had in mind the auxiliary prosecutor role. Ian Chisholm concluded by recommending a consultation exercise to be launched at the end of September.

Complementary draft documents and consultation papers then began to circulate in parallel in the summer of 2000, one for Lord Birt, another for the *CJ2010* exercise, yet another for practical administrative purposes having emanated from the Lawrence Steering Group,[135] and a fourth destined for the Victim's Charter Review Working Group,[136] the new sub-group of the Victims Steering Group charged with revising the *Victim's Charter*.[137] The two consultation papers were, in Ian Chisholm's words 'so cross-referenced' that 'they will be done together'. The former, commissioned by the Lawrence Steering Group and titled 'Formal Involvement of Victims in Criminal Legal Proceedings' was an unusually graphic document that began by discussing the structural imbalances of criminal proceedings: 'Some talk rather loftily about the might of the Crown taking on a sometimes pathetic, sometimes drug addicted, sometimes temporarily wicked and sometimes rotten to the core offender. The might of the resources commanded by the police and the Crown Prosecution Service ... are pitted against the often legally aided defendant with his High Street solicitor and junior counsel.' But a greater imbalance still was to be discerned between the rights of the defendant and of the victim, the one having legal representation, the other none; the one entitled to appeal, the other not; the one awarded a formal role, the other none; the one awarded access to justice, the other denied it. Turning to its mandate in the Stephen Lawrence Report, the paper proposed that a consultation should 'seek views on how the criminal justice system can better look after the needs of victims once the CPS have decided to lay a charge ... '.

All this was simple enough albeit relatively florid reporting. What *was* new and radical was the consideration of a gamut of new formal roles for the victim. The deliberations of the September 1999 conference in Macclesfield were again aired, the defects of the *parti civile* system exposed,[138] and the merits of the auxiliary or assistant

[135] As late as February 2001, it promised that a consultation paper would be issued at the end of the month to invite views, amongst other matters, on statutory rights for victims, the establishment of a Victims Ombudsman, and the contents of a revised *Victim's Charter*. See *Stephen Lawrence Inquiry: Home Secretary's Action Plan, Second Annual Report on Progress*, Home Office, London, February 2001, p. 21.

[136] Its members were drawn from the Victims Steering Group.

[137] Minutes of Victims Steering Group meeting of 28 April 2000.

[138] If a victim chooses not to be a *parti civile*, 'his or her rights to information and compensation are forfeit; the *parti civile* procedure is less effective at securing compensation than the existing mechanisms available in England and Wales; there may be a loss of rights to testify at certain stages because the victim is taken to be an interested party; there are few legal or administrative supports for the *parti civile*; and grafting

prosecutor role listed (it being noted that 'it is the additional services it provides that are particularly interesting'). Occupancy of the role of auxiliary prosecutor would supply much of what victims were said to need in legal procedure: being informed about the dates of proceedings, present during hearings and seated next to the public prosecutor, putting questions to witnesses directly or indirectly through the prosecutor; bringing evidence into the proceedings, and making statements to the court. In some jurisdictions, it was noted, the auxiliary prosecutor was also entitled to legal representation. And then there was the Home Secretary's notion of 'victim advocates', a role independent of the CPS and devised solely to represent the interests of the victim. Advocates would not have the power to examine or cross-examine witnesses, but they could act:

as an intermediary between victim and prosecuting counsel, providing advice about particular questions or a particular line of questioning. In turn, they could explain to the victim why a particular line... was being pursued, and why the rules of evidence prevented some matters being brought before the court. A more active role would come after a plea or finding of guilt. The Victim Advocate would have the power, on the instruction of the victim, to challenge any false or misleading claims made on the offender's behalf... In turn, s/he could draw the court's attention to the victim's personal statement and provide an oral update if necessary.

The twin draft consultation paper on the *Victim's Charter* was also at first modest enough in scope, being described as '95% mirror and 5% signpost'. Outline questions centred on the definition of victims: should they extend to shops, businesses, and corporations? And should they include those involved in 'road traffic incidents'? (a perennially vexed issue, given prominence by the consultation on criminal injuries compensation and discussions of victim personal statements,[139] and subject to persistent lobbying by organizations such as RoadPeace and its allies in Victim's Voice, the federation of activist victims' groups which championed the bereaved survivor). They centred on the selection of the broad principles that might underpin any new Charter, borrowing, as such documents do,

---

elements of an inquisitorial system on to an adversarial system may lead to problems...'.

[139] *Victim Personal Statement Scheme: Annex A: Road Traffic Offences*, 17 November 2000.

from the sheaf of other declarations already approved and in currency: the 1985 United Nations Declaration of Basic Principles of Justice for Victims of Crime and Abuse of Power;[140] a substantively similar 1985 Council of Europe report on victims' rights;[141] and statements of rights issued by Victim Support[142] and the European Forum for Victims Services[143] that were being copied into the European Framework Decision. The principles had already been substantially ratified, involving injunctions to treat victims with dignity and respect, provide protection and support, compensation or reparation, and accurate and timely information; offer an opportunity to state how victims had been affected by crime; and establish a transparent system of justice. What was new (but rejected *ab initio*) was the proposal that a sentence should match the severity of the victim's experience of crime. Those to be canvassed were to be asked whether any other principles should be added.

There was next a catalogue of the measures that might be listed in a new Charter and which should already have become familiar with the progression of this book,[144] including the recommendations of

[140] The declaration asserted some very general principles, some so general that they lacked the prospect of useful application, others a little more precise. They included the recommendations that victims should be treated with compassion and respect; that they should be given access to justice; that they should be informed about proceedings; allowed, under A.6.2. of the Annex, to have their 'views and concerns . . . presented and considered at appropriate stages of the proceedings where their personal interests are affected, without prejudice to the accused and consistent with the relevant national criminal justice system'; that they should be given proper support; assistance, compensation, and restitution; and the like. It nevertheless engendered (or was coaxed into engendering) a number of policy initiatives, including those in Canada (which I discuss in my *A View from the Shadows*) and in New Zealand. See Victims Task Force; *Towards Equality in Criminal Justice*, Report to the Minister of Justice, Private Box 180, Wellington, NZ, 1993, p. 5.

[141] *The Position of the Victim in the Framework of Criminal Law and Procedure*, The European Committee on Crime Problems, Council of Europe, Strasbourg, 1985.

[142] Victim Support declared that victims should be entitled to compensation that would ensure that they were not materially the poorer because of the crime they had suffered; to protection from intimidation and harassment; to respect, recognition, and support; and to information about the progress of their case. *The Rights of Victims of Crime*, Victim Support, London, 1995.

[143] *Statement of victims' rights to standards of service*, European Forum for Victim Services, London, 1999.

[144] Although there were a few others, including the European Framework Decision, which I am about to cover, some which I will not (including the Auld review and a review of the workings of the Coroner's Courts) and others still whose impact was

*Speaking up for Justice* and the Macpherson Report; victim personal statements, the review of the criminal injuries compensation scheme, and the like, and those to be consulted would be asked if those or other measures should be accepted. But there were also questions inviting comments about the Home Secretary's idea of fine surcharges and about the provision of special measures for hate crimes, traceable back to the shifting definitions within RISC that had stemmed from *Speaking up for Justice*. There followed a section on the format of the existing Charter, said to be an obscure document whose standards were difficult to measure. A new and clearer version might include an opening section with 'headline standards' based on the new agreed guiding principles; a summary of what victims could expect from agencies; and, finally, a section describing how complaints might be made.

Thus far, the draft had been routine in form and non-contentious in substance,[145] but its next few sections began importantly and candidly to broach the position of the victim in procedure and the taxing question of rights, declaring that the first Charter's ostensible rights had been aspirational and that the second Charter had 'avoided any mention of rights'. It asked about the provision of legal advice for victims, and 'options to enable victims to have the opportunity to be more involved in legal proceedings when their case comes before the court'. And it announced that the title of the third Charter would almost certainly return once more to the language of rights;[146] there was reference to policy papers by Victim Support and

a little tangential—for example, the use of new technology to enhance communication between agencies.

[145] For example, it retained many of the typifications and recipes for victims that had become embedded at different points in organizational practices. There was the well established: recipients of criminal injuries compensation should be the 'blameless victims of violent crime'; and the recent: 'special concern should be shown to the victims of very serious crimes, such as homicide, rape and sexual assaults, racial and homophobic crimes, and where the victim is vulnerable by reason, for example, of age, disability, sexual orientation, or minority ethnic background'; the right to be more fully informed about what had become of an offender, a charge, and a court hearing; and the right of victims to 'state how they have been affected by crime'. And the responsibilities of different criminal justice agencies, including Victim Support, were enumerated.

[146] Those consulted were to be asked whether they preferred as a title *The Victim's Charter—Rights for Victims of Crime*; *Rights for Victims—A Guide for Victims of Crime*; *Victims First—A Guide/Rights for Victims of Crime* or some other variant of the consulted persons' own choosing.

the Parliamentary All Party Penal Affairs Group on victims' rights ('This paper draws on both these documents in the sample new Charter...'); and comments were invited on the prospect of creating justiciable rights for victims:

> There is some hesitation about using the language of rights in a specific way because of the increasing expectation of litigation or financial compensation if those rights are not met... The Government is not convinced that legally enforceable rights, with attendant rights to take civil action to sue and to receive compensation if they are not met, is the route to take. We are, however, prepared to listen to contrary views and do not rule this route out either in response to this review or in the longer term... We have considered the more radical step of a victims' ombudsman as an arbiter of last resort should complainants remain unhappy with an organisation's response. S/he would be unable to comment or intervene with judicial or other legally based decisions, but would be able to investigate and comment on the way a case or an individual victim has been handled with the additional power of being able to award small sums of compensation. However, in view of the impending appointment of a joint Prisons and Probation Ombudsman, the existence of the Police Complaints Authority, and the fact that Victim Support is a non-governmental organisation outside the scope of the ombudsman system, it would seem the territory is already fairly well covered.

A two-part consultation on the Charter had originally been planned to take place in September,[147] and then, as timetables slipped, between October and November 2000, but the draft document was still with Ministers in November. It had collided with the Maginot Line erected in defence of the integrity of criminal procedure and the balancing of rights. The sections on the place of the victim and victims' rights, forming its second and more venturesome and controversial half, met with opposition from the Lord Chancellor's Department and the CPS. In his response to the draft paper on the Charter, written in August, an official of the Criminal Justice Division of the Lord Chancellor's Department declared his reservations about the proposal that victims should be endowed with rights in any new Charter. '[A]ny Government will find it difficult to resist the idea of victims' rights', but rights had to have substance: 'There must be a remedy. Otherwise we are not taking the rights seriously.' The remedy did not necessarily have to be through the courts, but it had

[147] A Grade 7 to Victim Statement Working Group, 13 July 2000.

to be available, and it would almost certainly encroach on vital rights held by others: 'In my view the real problem with victims' rights as a concept is that they are inevitably closely circumscribed by others' rights—most notably those of people accused of crime, and the right of the community to control lawbreaking behaviour whatever the victim's view.'

The official was more trenchant still about the second paper on the formal involvement of victims that had been commissioned by the Lawrence Steering Group. Victims were not, he said, universally deserving but morally diverse, ranging from 'those for whom every-body feels sympathy to those who claim to be victims but who are found by a court to be liars or at least unreliable'. Affording victims rights would compromise their own and others' rights: the paper 'needs to get away from the idea that there is a balance to be struck between the rights of the victim and the rights of the defendant... Strengthening the ability of the prosecution to obtain convictions against defendants may well mean that innocent defendants are convicted and the guilty remain undetected and unpunished. This does not enhance the rights of victims; on the contrary, it puts them at greater risk.' He was persuaded by the case against an introduction of the *parti civile* procedure, but was not enamoured of the idea of auxiliary prosecutors ('experienced prosecutors will say that to allow [victims to present evidence and make direct statements to the court] would repel juries and make securing a conviction more difficult'). The proposed victim advocate role could, however, 'avoid most of the pitfalls' although it would be very limited in practice, there being little conflict between the interests of the victim and the prosecution. His conclusion was blunt: 'there may not be much scope for enhancing victims' rights or providing more support at hearings'. The following month, the Lord Chancellor himself lent his considerable weight to that dissent. Rights for victims would be costly, unnecessary and wasteful:

We should not set up a new comprehensive tier of legally enforceable rights for victims. This would establish a new category of litigation calling for legal aid [and] highly attractive to civil rights lawyers who would be enthused by opportunities to assert deficiencies in the criminal trial pro-cess... There should be no legally enforceable right to representation for victims... I am opposed to victims being 'consulted' about <u>decisions</u> on cases...

The Director of Policy at the CPS also replied to the drafts in August, and he too demurred about the renewed talk of rights. He was unhappy about the use of the word 'rights' in the paper on the *Victim's Charter* ('should there be some alternative titles which avoid that phrase?') but was content for the draft consultation to go to Cabinet. On the other hand, the Lawrence Steering Group's paper on the role of the victim was more troubling. It raised 'funda-mental issues' which could affect the independence of the pro-secution[148] and the very role of the criminal courts and he could not agree its submission to Cabinet. An inter-agency working group was about to meet on 26 September to discuss the two draft documents but it was his view that much more work needed to be done before there could be agreement on a draft. And his trepidation was echoed by a CPS colleague who wrote to Ian Chisholm on the 6 September to remind him of his agency's 'anxieties about the second of the two papers . . . There are some pretty fundamental issues involved and whilst this is only a consultation exercise there is still a great importance on how the consultation document is phrased and presented.' The colleague continued, 'I'm not enthused about getting into an inter-Departmental debate on the fundamental issues in front of externals. Could we [including the official of the Lord Chancellor's Department who had also written] perhaps meet before? Or could the second draft consultation document come off the agenda for the 26th? The latter option may be the way forward since I see little prospect of sufficient re-drafting in advance of then.'

Recall that it was a matter of etiquette that conflict should wherever possible be mediated in private and avoided in public. The promise of a row between departments and before 'externals' made it almost certain that the second, more radical paper could not proceed as it stood. Ian Chisholm wrote to the Head of the Criminal Justice Policy Division of the CPS on 7 September that 'we agreed [yesterday] that in view of LCD and CPS reservations about the draft on the role of the victim in the CJS, we should restrict discussion at the meeting to the first Draft Consultation Document on the Victim's Charter . . . we shall have to give further thought to the draft of the second

---

[148] A colleague of his was flatly to remark later at a seminar on the Charter that 'we're not interested in victim advocates on grounds of costs and practicality'.

paper'.[149] And the members of the Victim's Charter Working Group were informed in their turn eleven days later that the original plan to issue a twin consultation paper had been suspended ('we are not yet in a position to proceed with this paper as further discussion is required within Government'). What came before the Working Group instead was a revised draft consultation document on the Charter, substantially similar to its predecessor, still flagging the question of rights, and with very modest amendments suggested by the Lord Chancellor's Department. It was newly observed that the case for rights had been enhanced by the doubts raised by the Law Officers about the lawfulness of some aspects of the 1996 Charter: 'most notably the disclosure of information, of any kind, about offenders by criminal justice agencies to victims'. The arguments about a Victims Ombudsman were still hedged about with doubts about problems of overlap with the jurisdiction of other ombudsmen. And a consultation about rights was still mooted but it had been pushed back in time: 'a related consultation paper is being prepared exploring options to enable victims to be more involved in legal proceedings when their case comes before the court. We expect that this paper will be issued later this year' (but that paper was later jettisoned altogether[150]).

The *impasse* on victims that had long divided the criminal justice system thus remained intact in the Summer of 2000 and, at the very least, more protracted diplomatic work had to be done. A JVU Grade 7 observed in June that:

I mean there's going to be difficulty in actually clearing the terms of the scope of the consultation exercise within Government before it actually goes out to the wider public and not least because of the very strong views the Lord Chief Justice has already expressed about giving victims a more formal role. You know, he's very much on the basis, look, the State prosecutes, they do not have a role, you know, the State is the prosecutor and it relieves them, you know, it's a *quid pro quo*. So we'll need to do that,

---

[149] But, he added, 'There are strong political pressures from here and No 10 for giving victims a role in criminal proceedings.' And the Law Officers had advised that it was unlawful to disclose to victims the details of a person involved, or suspected of involvement, in their case. That would certainly require a legal solution, possibly by giving the victim some standing in criminal procedure.
[150] That was a decision taken at a meeting of Ministers with the Prime Minister on 22 January 2001 to discuss *CJ2010*.

and then, and even then, quite frankly, you come up to the summer session and you can never get a hold of anybody.

In September, it was proposed that the consultation on the *Victim's Charter* should proceed, and, in the act of consulting others, it was hoped that it would reassure the judges and others that matters were not being done in dictatorial fashion. It would not only be unaccompanied by any other consultation but would also be shorn of its more controversial proposals about enforceable rights. A Bill of Rights would in any event have been impossible to legislate before the end of the administration's term of office in April 2002. Something else would be preferred: 'If we were to choose a half way house between the standards and rights, it would probably be an ombudsman for victims (although this too would require legislation).'[151] Whichever model was chosen, there were a number of 'headline rights', more akin to principles and not justiciable in practice, that had already been identified in the inventory circulated in the draft paper. Simultaneously, a JVU Grade 7 noted:

We are preparing a separate consultation paper to consider ways to involve victims more formally in criminal proceedings. The groundwork on this is being carried out. The outcome, subject to agreement from the CJS partners, is likely to be a fairly radical paper which might include reference to the introduction of Victim Advocates (with a right of address to the court) or a change in the role of the CPS ... Ideally, we want to ensure that victims have better opportunities to both give and receive information, and feel that they have better access to justice. At the same time we need to ensure that the rights of offenders are unaffected.

If the Lord Chancellor's Department and the Crown Prosecution Service had responded gingerly to the draft Charter review, No. 10 Downing Street was enthusiastic. Liz Lloyd of the Prime Minister's Policy Unit wrote on 22 September that it was 'comprehensive and well written'. She did, however, comment that 'We also need to say more about the motivation for revisiting the charter from the victim's point of view—ie what an improved charter can do for victims.' And set within the Home Office, JVU remained reasonably staunch but was also seeking a way of bypassing obstacles that had refused to yield.

[151] 'Review of the Victim's Charter/Victims' Rights', JVU, September 2000.

In September 2000, then, and at the request of 10 Downing Street, JVU was obliged to stop and think, and it laid out the contending positions as it understood them. On the one hand, it wrote, the creation of victims' rights would be supported by most victims' groups;[152] heighten the 'legal establishment's perception of victims' issues'; provide a 'court based remedy should the CJS or its constitu ents fail to deliver the services promised'; and 'Symbolically, might be perceived as a counter balance to the Human Rights Act (which is largely seen as being of benefit to suspects or offenders)'. On the other hand, it could be argued that rights were not necessary ('current services to victims are evolving rapidly and there is no lack of commitment on the part of CJ agencies'); 'Most disgruntled victims are in the very serious cases, and their concerns are often about judicial decisions... which new rights would not touch upon'; and they would make 'a further contribution to an increasingly litigious culture. A potentially increased burden for the courts.'

What might constitute a pragmatic compromise between the service standards of the 1996 Charter and 'fully fledged rights' would be the appointment of a Victims Ombudsman to consider complaints when 'the procedures of the individual agencies had been exhausted', and 'provide a neutral assessment of the performance of the CJ agencies and have the power to award compensation when s/he was satisfied that maladministration had taken place'.

Two matters of note were embodied in that paper. The first was that JVU had employed its own distinct analytic frame, appearing to give little weight to the arguments against the introduction of rights that had been levelled by other criminal justice agencies, officers, and departments. And the second, and more important by far, was that the seeds of a negotiable settlement were there sowed. If conventional legal rights could never be secured with the agreement of the judiciary and the other Ministries in the criminal justice system, leaving intact the older formulation of standards as aspirational near-rights, then some other stratagem altogether had to be devised, and that stratagem in the guise of a Victims Ombudsman had become much more attractive.

---

[152] Although Victim Support, the largest group, had its reservations. Express rights, thought Teresa Reynolds, were liable to the risk that 'you can end up with the lowest common denominator'.

In anticipating the meeting of the Victim's Charter Working Group meeting of 26 September, a JVU Grade 7 wrote that the draft review should now contain new text, including the statement that 'The Government proposes that headline rights for victims should be put on a statutory basis. The "guiding principles" . . . are the most likely to be framed as rights . . . The Government proposes to create the new post of Victim's Ombudsman, the duties of whom will also be defined in legislation.'[153] Observe that what might be 'framed as rights' had become principles rather than enforceable claims, and that the mechanism for their enforcement was not to be victims taking actions to court but a dedicated champion acting on the victim's behalf,[154] a Victims Ombudsman, who would have powers to investigate and recommend but not to prosecute. Victims' rights were to be entrusted to a new official who could, it was thought, neatly take the issue out of contention altogether.[155]

Ombudsmen were a proliferating solution to problems of regulation in public and private services in the latter half of the

---

[153] 'Working Group Meeting—Likely Issues', 25 September 2000.

[154] The word 'champion' had been employed by, for example, Ross Cranston, the Solicitor General, in November 2000 in his address to the annual general meeting of Victim Support.

[155] Victim Support were less enthusiastic about the proposal for an Ombudsman. It cast back to the JUSTICE report and its prescient proposal for a Victims Commissioner (see JUSTICE annual report 1998 which summarized the May 1998 publication of *Victims in the criminal justice process* and its recommendation of a Commissioner for Victims of crime to take on key functions such as reporting to Parliament, undertaking thematic reviews of the experiences of victims and witnesses, and being the ultimate point of reference for complaints. The JUSTICE Committee on the Role of the Victim in the Criminal Justice Process had discussed the possibility of a Victims Ombudsman but had decided that the example of the Prisons Ombudsman was 'not satisfactory' (minutes of the meeting of 2 December 1996) and it opted for a Commissioner at its meeting of 27 January 1997. Victim Support noted that an Ombudsman could not intervene with judicial or other legally based decisions, but would be able to investigate and comment on the way an individual had been treated. Most victims do not reach the criminal justice system and need help with health and social welfare. It recommended a Commissioner instead to examine legislation, procedural guidance, and codes of practice (Meeting of Victim Support Trustees, 20 October 2000, New Victim Policies: Paper for the Trustees meeting on 20 October 2000). New Zealand was to adopt the Commissioner model (see Victims Task Force; *Towards Equality in Criminal Justice, op. cit.*). In Northern Ireland, Victim Support groups proposed the idea of a Victims Champion rather than a Commissioner or an Ombudsman (Victim Support; Regional Meeting Spring 2001, 26 April 2001, Region 9, Northern Ireland).

twentieth century.[156] The first ombudsman in England and Wales, the Parliamentary Ombudsman, had been appointed under the Parliamentary Commissioner Act of 1967, and was neither a civil servant nor a Government official but formally an officer of the House of Commons appointed by the Queen. He or she could only consider complaints of maladministration against central Government departments, and was unable to investigate the judiciary, police, or local authorities. The Parliamentary Commissioner had powers to investigate complaints, determine whether they were well founded, and recommend remedies, but had no power to enforce recommendations (although the Government was said almost invariably to accept them) or conduct independent inquiries. Other Ombudsmen followed. A Prisons Ombudsman was first appointed in October 1994 as a result of the Woolf Report into the disturbances at Strangeways Prison, and the post was expanded to become the Prisons and Probation Ombudsman in September 2001. By 2003, there were greater and lesser Ombudsmen covering some nineteen different areas of activity in Great Britain and Gibraltar, including legal services, the police, and public services.

The new office of Victims Ombudsman might, it was thought, have two roles, the investigation of complaints by individual victims and a 'broader remit covering victims' interests in general'. It could be created by statute to be independent of Government and accountable to a Select Committee; engage in recommending improvements in agencies' procedures, conduct independent investigations, encourage the spread of good practice, and scrutinize legislation and policy; publicize recommendations (including cases of non-compliance), issue an annual report, and, inevitably, be regulated by aims, objectives, and performance targets.[157]

It had been agreed that the Home Secretary's speech to the Labour Party conference should be used to advertise the *Victim's Charter* review, and for some time beforehand the prospect of that major speech to be delivered before a general election and at the very time

---

[156] According to the International Ombudsman Institute, the first ombudsman was the Swedish Justitieombudsman (ombudsman for justice) who was appointed in 1809. The Office was subsequently adopted in other Scandinavian countries: in Finland (1919), Denmark (1955), and Norway (1962) and then spread elsewhere.

[157] Ian Chisholm; draft of 'Victims' Ombudsman: Key Issues', April 2001.

the European Framework Decision was under review,[158] had concentrated the mind and illuminated the politics of victims. The Home Secretary's political adviser, Justin Russell, reflected in February 2001:

It's the classic thing that happened in the lead up to party conference, two or three months beforehand, you're looking around for themes for the conference, you're looking around for possible announcements and what's out there in the department that you could be drawing on. And you, you're normally looking for something, I mean not in a cynical way but I think [something had to be said] about victims in a big speech like that, you can't just be seen to be ignoring them. And that it was a good time to start, I mean, across all sorts of policy areas. Those are the times when policies get made... For people like me, they're quite useful occasions because things go a bit more fluid and you can push things through a bit more harder than you could normally because the officials accept you've got to say something.

And Jack Straw did indeed make promises in his speeches to the conferences on 24 September 2000 and 17 February 2001.[159] To the former, he said:

Soon we will be publishing proposals for a new Charter of Rights for victims setting out the gold standard of service and support which every one of them should expect. With a new Ombudsman to deal independently with complaints, and act as a true champion for victims interests.

The next step was to remind the Home Secretary in October 2000 about what he had promised at the Party Conference. He was invited by Ian Chisholm to write to the Prime Minister with routine copies to his colleagues, the Attorney General, and Lord Chancellor, about

[158] A Grade 7 said on 28 September, that the announcement of a Bill of Rights had been 'prompted by the European Framework Decision which is being considered by European ministers today'.

[159] At that second conference in Glasgow, he said: 'We have to go a stage further, to level the balance of the system between victim and criminal. So, in the next few weeks, I will be publishing proposals to give victims of crime an enforceable bill of rights laying down the treatment which they can expect from the criminal justice system... The right to be treated with respect, to receive support and recognition. And a new Victims Ombudsman who would have the power to investigate complaints, to seek redress and to act as a champion of victims' interests within the criminal justice system and beyond. Together, this package of measures should finally begin to bring victims in from the cold—to put their interests at the heart of the criminal justice system...'.

what had become rather syncretically called a 'Victim's Charter of Rights' that now fused ideas of a *Victim's Charter* and a Victims' Bill of Rights.[160] There would be a consultation paper to review the *Victim's Charter* and seek views on establishing statutory rights for victims, together with the appointment of a Victims Ombudsman to investigate unresolved complaints and champion the interests of victims. The Prime Minister, in his turn, was to be reminded of the support that would stem from victims' organizations, including Victim Support, and the fact that victims' rights had already been introduced in the context of probation work in the Criminal Justice and Court Services Bill. What was now proposed was not 'detailed legislation for other aspects of victims' interaction with the system [but] the possibility of declaratory or headline rights to be enshrined in legislation, backed up by a revised Victim's Charter of Rights'. The idea of an ombudsman, he was told, had emerged in earlier stages of the review process and 'For the purposes of the consultation, we are seeking responses to the principle of an Ombudsman rather than presenting detailed proposals...'. It seemed to be a clever *finesse*.

Ministers were content, as officials had anticipated ('they've made up their minds on this' and, 'particularly, on the idea of a Victim's Ombudsman') but they did suggest minor amendments including greater attention being paid to the variety of victims' and community organizations that had a stake in the proposals and which should be consulted. The consultation would be allowed to proceed and its ideas were to be inserted in the victims' section of what was still called *CJ2010*,[161] the forthcoming criminal justice

---

[160] Although Downing Street would still refer to what was being proposed as a Victims' Bill of Rights. No. 10 press release, 27 February 2001.

[161] It was eventually presented to Parliament as *Criminal Justice: The Way Ahead*, Cm. 5074, February 2001. Its aims for victims, said the Home Secretary, were 'Protecting the needs of victims and witnesses: court familiarization visits and improved court waiting facilities for prosecution witnesses; introduction of Victim Personal Statements, so victims (including bereaved relatives in homicide cases) can give a statement in their own words saying how the crime has affected their lives; a new role for the Crown Prosecution Service in keeping victims informed about the progress of cases; a possible "Victim's Fund" to ensure victims are more swiftly compensated; consulting on a new Victim's Charter, to include whether to establish a Victims' Ombudsman to champion victims' interests; and the opportunity for victims to report minor crime online.' 10 Downing Street Newsroom [a web site]; Modernising the Criminal Justice System, 26 February 2001.

strategy paper[162] that was also to be published at the beginning of 2001. *CJ2010* might even be used to launch the consultation process in March.[163] 'Assuming the government's returned', said its author in February 2001, 'this document will be used in order to set the debate to where the criminal justice system might go over the next five years. I mean I think the Government's quite determined to modernize the criminal justice system if it gets back in again. I think it sees that there are all sorts of problems that need to be tackled like decline in clear up rates, low conviction rates, lack of public confidence. Those kinds of issues do need to be tackled.'

Although *CJ2010* had already received JVU briefings,[164] it had been noted, in the words of Justin Russell, the Home Secretary's political adviser, that it would need 'some strong new ideas on victims if we are to support one of the central themes about placing the victim at the heart of the CJS'. Timetables there meshed: the two papers would be published almost simultaneously in the new year lest the consultation paper otherwise pre-empt *CJ2010*'s section on victims, leaving nothing new to recommend. And a general election

---

[162] An official of the Strategic Policy Team, its principal author, said: 'the project started in October 2000, a difficult task. A high policy piece of work over a very short space of time. Need for consultation, for road-testing. Trying to produce a long-term strategy for the CJS—it comes out of other areas of policy modernisation, such as the NHS and the transport system in their 10-year plans. Their plans were tied to resources, ours isn't because it take places after the CSR, so there's no new money. The strategy document covers the next ten years. Three years are more or less fixed. Three years after that will be decided by the next CSR. A lot of content will build on what's been done so far. This is the next stage—what we can do to modernise the CJS.'

[163] In the event, it promised a consultation on the *Victim's Charter* from February 2001 with a view to implementing a revised charter by November 2001. There would be a new charter of rights, establishing statutory rights and a Victims Ombudsman 'to champion victims' interests' who would work with Government and the criminal justice service to introduce services to benefit victims. *Criminal Justice: The Way Ahead*, op. cit., pp. 69, 72.

[164] For example, under the meeting of *CJ2010*: on 7 December 2000, Agenda Item 2—Annex A: 'new ideas' included a Victims Ombudsman and a Charter of Rights for Victims; a guaranteed lock-fitting service within 24 hours for burglary victims in high crime areas; 'on-line case listing and case results for all courts by 2003'; on-line crime reporting, stolen goods and missing person enquiries; and an ongoing review of need for further reform, 'for example, a victim's advocate service to represent the victim in court'.

was pending in the first half of 2001.[165] The Charter review, the strategy document, the manifesto and pre-election speeches, especially in September 2000 and February 2001, would all appear within a short space of time, each able to bolster the others.[166] Justin Russell said of the latter speech in Glasgow on 17 February, 'By keeping victims, going on victims you know, a week and a half early in Glasgow, I think we hoped it would get a decent run . . .'.

The consultation on the Charter was finally launched on 27 February 2001[167] with a focus, a JVU Grade 7 said, on the 'introduction of statutory rights for victims in headline form and a victims ombudsman in background: depending on the election we'll be in a position to take things forward in the Summer' and, he added, 'The extra time we've got allows us to consider the extra matter of the victim in criminal justice proceedings.'[168] The launch had been presaged by a speech by the Home Secretary at the Labour Party spring conference on the 17 February, only days before, in which he had promised 'a bill of rights and an ombudsman [as] the key parts of a new government package to help victims of crime'.[169]

---

[165] Ian Chisholm said in February 2000, 'I get the impression that they're worried the opposition might be making quite an issue on victims, so they want to sort of pre-empt that a bit. And I can see, I mean Victims' Rights Act and new charters and all this stuff is quite good manifesto stuff. I get the impression . . . victims' rights, no, we can't do anything before the election, it might be quite useful in an election manifesto thing.'

[166] An official reflected, 'I'm sure the fact that an election is imminent is connected to the fact that we were asked to do that [the *CJ2010* strategy document]'.

[167] And in being so launched, it was the first of the three Charters that complied with what were supposed to be the standard requirements for revision: Peter Kilfoyle, then the Minister for Public Service, had declared in 1998, that the Government was 'committed to improving public services and making them more responsive to their users . . . in the past, too many charters were drawn up from the top down, and there was little or no consultation with those who used the services . . .'. *How to draw up a national charter: A guide to preparing national charters*, Service First, the Cabinet Office, London, 1998. It was important, Service First stated, 'to build consultation with outside interests into plans for policy development, both on specific proposals and services, and more generally.' *How to conduct written consultation exercises: An introduction for central government*, Service First, the Cabinet Office, London, 1998, p. 2.

[168] Victims Steering Group meeting, 8 December 2000, my notes.

[169] A marked element of electioneering had begun to appear by then. Ann Widdecombe, the Shadow Home Secretary, retorted that the Conservatives had been proposing victims' rights two years ago. It was all 'just another piece of new Labour cynicism'. The rights envisaged by the Conservatives were actually rather meagre.

The Charter review was issued in the names of the trilateral Ministers, it cited as an authority the European Framework Decision,[170] and it followed the draft described earlier, defining victims as personal victims and the families of homicide victims, but not corporations or the witnesses of offences. It wondered whether the Charter should extend to cases of death and serious injury in road traffic incidents. It laid out as before the general principles which should guide how victims were to be treated by criminal justice agencies. It asked which of the measures introduced since 1996 should be included in the new Charter. And it moved to the question of 'Standards or Rights?', marking the equivocation of the first two Charters and the recommendations made by Victim Support in 1995 and the Parliamentary All Party Penal Affairs Group, noting the proposal made by some[171] that there should be a Minister for Victims, and then asking 'whether the "service standard" approach in the current Charter should be continued in the new Charter or be replaced by a "rights" approach: and, if the "rights" approach is taken, should the rights be put on a statutory basis; [and] should the rights be enforceable.' The *parti civile* procedure was again raised only to be dismissed, and none of the difficult alternatives in the guise of a victim advocate or auxiliary prosecutor were floated: 'In our view, the essential point is that victims should receive better treatment when they attend court, but stopping short of being made a party to those proceedings.' The review also observed that 'We have considered the alternative or additional step of the appointment of a Victims' Ombudsman [who] would be an arbiter of last resort... [and who] might also act as a champion of victims interests in general.'

Whilst *A Review of the Victim's Charter* made provisional proposals, the Home Secretary and *Criminal Justice: The Way Ahead*, published the day before[172] and endorsed personally by the Prime

[170] It reported that 'Early in 2000, the then Portuguese Presidency of the European Union introduced a draft framework decision... Although the draft remains subject to approval by EU member states, the final framework decision would provide outline rights for victims for the first time across the EU.'

[171] And originally by the small activists' campaigning group, Justice for Victims, whose history and reasoning I describe in my *After Homicide*.

[172] It had been decided politically that on the day of its launch on Monday, 26 February, the emphasis should be on themes and recommendations that did not bear on victims, but that, on the next day, and with the announcement of the Charter

Minister,[173] seemed more emphatic. 'We are', *Criminal Justice: The Way Ahead* said firmly, 'revising the Victim's Charter and consulting with the aim of establishing statutory rights and a Victim's Ombudsman to champion victims' interests.[174] A new Victim's Ombudsman would have the power to investigate individual complaints and would act as a champion of victims' interests . . . '.[176] No little ambiguity was there introduced by what was necessarily a much curter and more emphatic statement about victims[176] (although the national press were uninterested in those proposals, and, as we have seen, victims' policies actually featured very modestly in the general election itself).

## End Game

I now move beyond the period of time properly covered by this book, but the Charter review and its aftermath extended into the New Labour administration that was returned to power with a majority of 167 on the 1 June 2001, and there are important loose threads to

review, *Criminal Justice: The Way Ahead* would also be flagged as a vehicle containing provisions for victims. Justin Russell said on 23 February: 'I mean it's a pretty substantial thing. It pulls together a lot of work that's been going on across Government and victims was something that was likely to maybe get lost on the day because of all the discussions about sentencing and rules of evidence. I mean I think on the day it's going to be much more of an offender type focus . . . Well I mean we'll try and get it a bit more coverage by doing it the day after. So it will essentially be Tuesday.' In the event, some newspapers did pick up the victims' policy themes. See, for instance, *The Times*, 27 February 2001.

[173] He was reported to have said that 'there used to be an air of fatalism in any debate about crime. Whatever the policies, nothing seemed to work. Crime rose inexorably. Today's Crime Plan marks the end of that fatalism. In fact, we have a clearer idea of what works than ever before . . . There are new rights for victims, better protection for witnesses . . . '. 10 Downing Street Newsroom; Speech by the Prime Minister at the Peel Institute, 26 February 2001.

[174] It mapped out a consultation on the Charter from February 2001 with a view to implementing a revised Charter by November 2001.

[175] *Criminal Justice: The Way Ahead*, Cm. 5074, Home Office, February 2001.

[176] Its author said 'don't forget that when you see this report, you'll see that we're talking, it's a fairly broad brush. I mean what we say about victims is much, much less than what Ian will be saying in the charter itself when that goes out to consultation. So it will have much more detail in it, you know, we're talking like a couple of paragraphs.'

be tied, threads which are, in effect, the logical culmination and
Aristotelian end of all that has gone before.

At the direct instigation of Justin Russell, the Labour Party election manifesto had touched on victims' rights,[177] and had done so
rather cursorily, in the manner of all manifestos.[178] Anticipating its
contents, a Labour Party policy officer working in the area of home
affairs said 'obviously manifestos aren't very long, it would probably
say something along the lines of you know, victims are you know,
very important whatever and then maybe mention a couple of
things, personal statements or something like that...'. The forty-
four page manifesto, *Ambitions for Britain*, laid out ten ten-year
goals, the eighth of which was 'a modern criminal justice system'.
Under the heading 'Strong and safe communities,' it promised a Bill
of Rights for victims: 'We now propose further action. First, victims
will be given the legal right [to state] their views on the impact of
the crime to the court and other criminal justice agencies before

[177] The development of the Labour Party election manifesto was a complicated
process that resided principally in internal deliberations within Cabinet and the policy
units. Inside the party, eight 'policy commissions' (one being the Crime and Justice
Policy Commission on which the Government was represented) would make recommendations to two bodies, the Joint Policy Committee, responsible for 'strategic
oversight in policy-making' and chaired by the Prime Minister, and a steering group
for the National Policy Forum with its 175 members (*Making policy*, The Labour
Party, 2000). Each policy area was considered over a two year period, there having
been two waves by the 2001 election. The first, 1998–9 wave covered crime, health
and welfare, and it had led to the production, *inter alia*, of the 1999 Labour Party
Crime and Policy Document, 'Delivering Justice', which had been approved by the
1999 Annual Conference. That document talked about victims and witnesses,
repeating the phrases that 'Labour is committed to ensuring that the victim is at the
heart of the criminal justice system' and that emphasis had been placed on 'aiming to
rebalance the justice system so that the needs and rights of victims are protected'. It had
proceeded to talk about the protections that would become available under the Youth
Justice and Criminal Evidence Act, and stated that 'Many victims or witnesses are
either too frightened to come forward or are unable to give evidence easily. This allows
criminals to go unpunished.' Matthew Seward, working on home affairs at the Labour
Party's headquarters, said 'obviously in terms of the detail of things to do with the
victims' policy, I mean these documents don't go into a great deal of detail... it just had
that little bit there... in terms of looking forward to what was going to be in the next
Parliament, it was still an early stage, which is why there's not a lot of detail there.'
'Delivering Justice' had been revised since the 1999 Conference but, it was noted in an
undated paper, 'Crime and justice policy commission report', 'very little had been
raised directly with the commission', and certainly nothing on victims and witnesses.
[178] At its launch in Birmingham, the Prime Minister had talked about crime and
justice, but had had nothing to say about victims or the Bill of Rights.

sentencing decisions. Second, prosecutors will be able to challenge defence pleas in mitigation of the crime. Third, we will legislate for a Victims' Bill of Rights to give support, protection and rights to information and compensation and information to victims.'

A new term of office introduced a new array of principals and responsibilities, a new political emphasis, and a *caesura* in policy-making. Departmental functions shifted[179] and people changed position. There were new Ministers and a new Home Secretary,[180] David Blunkett,[181] whose new priorities were declared to be security, order,[182] crime, and asylum laws,[183] and who displayed a marked interest in community development.[184] Ian Chisholm was replaced as head of JVU. The first Queen's Speech of the new administration touched on the abolition of double jeopardy and 'triable either way cases'; it stated that juries would be allowed to consider defendants' previous convictions; but it said nothing about victims.[185]

The election manifesto commitment to a Bill of Rights in 'this Parliament' led to the preparation of a report for the new Ministerial team[186] and the initiation of 'a small group . . . to take matters

---

[179] *Inter alia*, the Home Office gained responsibility for work permits from the DEE and the UK Anti-Drugs Co-ordination Unit from the Cabinet Office. It lost the Fire Service; electoral law, liquor and public entertainment licensing; and Human Rights and contingency and emergency planning to the Lord Chancellor's Department. Responsibilities for victims' policies were unaffected. Home Office web site: Machinery of Government: Changes to Home Office responsibilities, 8 June 2001.

[180] Jack Straw having become Foreign Secretary.

[181] The announcement was made on 9 June 2001.

[182] See his speech, 'Security and justice, mutuality and individual rights', delivered at John Jay College, New York, 3 April 2003.

[183] *The Times,* 9 June 2001.

[184] See his speech at the NCVO Conference, 12 February 2003, in which he talked about what he called 'the citizenship agenda' that draws 'in people from the bottom up to be able to deliver for themselves . . . through mutuality, through interdependence, through people being prepared to share together the challenge of the problems they have around them'.

[185] *The Times,* 21 June 2001.

[186] The new Ministers were reminded in their briefing that they had promised to legislate for a Victims' Bill of Rights and of the accomplishments of their first term of office. 'The proposed Bill of Rights is intended to enshrine many of these achievements in legislation, for example, the right to give and receive information, the right to protection and support, the right to be treated with dignity and respect.' (Criminal Policy Group: Victims' Bill of Rights.)

forward',[187] the Victim's Charter Review Implementation Group, which met for the first time in October 2001 to consider the replies to the consultation. JVU had, in Ian Chisholm's words, acted as a 'mailbox' for the consultation and analysed the 119 responses that had been received[188] (not a single one, it should be emphasized, from the groups who had mobilized the political aftermath of the murder of Stephen Lawrence,[189] but SAMM and eleven activist victims' groups *had* replied,[190] reinforcing once again the differences in significance and ownership of the Macpherson Inquiry and the Charter review). Eight replies had been received from Members of Parliament; eleven from the police; eight from the courts; six from probation services; two from 'other Government departments'; and fifty from 'members of the public'. The Members of Parliament had evidently been heavily lobbied by RoadPeace: with identical phrasing, all eight reported themselves to be in 'full support' of its work and its plans to include victims of road traffic incidents in the new Charter, and they echoed its demands for fuller participation by victims in decision-making in criminal justice policy-making and for the creation of a Minister of Victims. The police supported proposals for a Victims Ombudsman and new statutory rights for victims but paradoxically preferred the title 'The Victim's Charter—New Standards of Service', the only such title *not* to allude to rights. The Criminal Bar Association preferred a 'standards approach' and welcomed the creation of an Ombudsman. The probation service were said to support the idea of a Victims Ombudsman and statutory headline rights. Victim Support declared its preference for a Victim's Commissioner who would ensure that all agencies implement changes in their policies and procedures to take account of victims;[191] advise victims on how to seek redress; deal with individual complaints; scrutinize legislation; and conduct inquiries. It

---

[187] Victims Steering Group: meeting of 12 June 2001, my notes.

[188] Review of the *Victim's Charter*: Summary of the Responses, 17 July 2001.

[189] RISC, minutes of meeting 10, 15 October 2001, Statement by Geoff Bradshaw.

[190] *Inter alia*, SAMM sought a life-long tariff; and more generous information and involvement at the various stages of the tariff setting process. The *Victim's Charter*, it said, should include road traffic victims. SAMM *Newsletter*, June 2001, p. 13.

[191] Its Trustees had decided that they would not only propose a Commissioner for Victims but would want him or her to go further than the review envisaged, approaching victims 'holistically' and not just in the context of the criminal justice system. Meeting of Victim Support National Council, 20 March 2001, my notes.

welcomed statutory, enforceable rights that would define specific
entitlements rather than broad or 'headline' principles and be transparent about which agency was responsible for compliance. The
other victims' organizations replying were the Rape Crisis Federation which criticized the Government's reliance on Victim Support
as a monopoly supplier of services to victims; and Victim's Voice (the
activists' federation[192] that include RoadPeace) and its constituent
organizations, the North of England Victims Association, the
Victims of Crime Trust, Justice for Victims, Brake Care, and the
Marchioness Action Group, which supported, amongst other
matters, a Ministry of Victims. The Cabinet Office Women's Unit
proposed revisions to the 'Break the Chain' leaflet first issued in
1999 and a breakdown of data by gender in the British Crime
Survey; and supported the idea of a victims' fund, an Ombudsman
and service standards rather than rights (rights could, it was argued,
lead to 'costly court cases'). Local authorities in the main expressed
support for standards rather than rights, the notion of an Ombudsman, and the recognition of victims of road traffic incidents. The
Cyclists' Touring Club and the London Cycling Campaign supported the work of RoadPeace and the inclusion of victims of road
traffic incidents. And almost all the 'members of the public'
appeared to be members of RoadPeace or its sympathizers, and
they too endorsed the inclusion of victims of road traffic incidents.
Ninety-seven responses had touched on the theme, more than any
other. In his survey of responses, a Grade 7 remarked on the 'strong
lobby from the road deaths group so that their requirements are
included in any arrangements'.[193]

[192] Regarded by officials as 'prickly, abrasive and confrontational'. They had long
demanded a Minister for Victims, a post that existed in Northern Ireland but regarded
by officials as inappropriate in England and Wales because his or her responsibilities
would not include other matters that would affect development of victims' policy.

[193] RoadPeace had organized a particularly effective show of strength in the
consultation, noting that the Charter review had excluded 'road Victims' but asking
whether any new Charter should include road traffic incidents which lead to death or
serious injury. RoadPeace 'find it incredible that road victims could be excluded from
the stated aims' and advised its members to inform the Grade 7 that road victims are
victims of crime, 'they require equal treatment with other victims of crime, including
statutory funding[;] RoadPeace should be funded for their vital work on behalf of road
victims'. (*RoadPeace Newsletter 19*, Spring 2001, p. 5.) RoadPeace itself stated that
road crash victims are 'victims of violence, but in addition experience a casual and
dismissive treatment of their tragedies by the authorities and society. The fact that

In some senses, those victims of road crashes had been long at the margins,[194] subject to 'major policy and resourcing problems',[195] not always unambiguously the subjects of crime, and liable to increase the costs of measures to support victims. Victim Support had agonized about whether its own schemes could afford to embrace them although, as so often happened, a number had already spontaneously elected to do so. But so strong had been the representations, supported by instruments and declarations produced by the European Community and United Nations, that it was decided that they should at last be treated as victims in the deliberations that followed the consultation.[196] Even without a campaign, the new Implementation Group was told by JVU, 'we would have been broadly in sympathy', and BRAKE[197] and RoadPeace were invited to join the Group's Road Death and Injuries Working Group.

The first meeting of the Implementation Group in October 2001 was uncertain about the precise structure of what might be in the making: it talked about a Victims Ombudsman, although a paper submitted to it was titled 'Victims' Ombudsman/Commissioner',[198]

road victims were excluded from both previous charters and still continue to be excluded from the present one, is evidence of the bias with which road victims have been hitherto treated.' It then submitted a number of specific recommendations, most revolving around the proposition that road crash victims should routinely be included in counts of victims, policies for victims, and the provision of information for victims. Victims themselves should more fully be represented in deliberative bodies considering policy. It was announced in June 2001, that the Home Office [had] decided that road traffic accidents could be included in the *Victim's Charter* and the Victims' Rights Bill. Meeting of Victim Support National Council, 19 June 2001, my notes.

[194] Towards the end of the first administration, Ministers were also wondering whether the morally undeserving victim, ('in light of the Tony Martin case'), might not be excluded from the provisions of a new Charter, but they were reminded that to reject victims on such grounds would breach international conventions, including the European Convention on Human Rights, to which the United Kingdom Government was a signatory.

[195] There were estimated to be 3,500 deaths and 40,000 serious injuries *per annum* from road crashes.

[196] Andrew Sanders wondered at a private seminar why, if road traffic incidents were to be included, those dealt with by the Health and Safety Executive, involving the victims of industrial 'accidents' should be excluded.

[197] BRAKE describes itself as 'a road safety charity dedicated to stopping deaths and injuries on roads through awareness-raising campaigns, including Road Safety Week and educational resources including leaflets, posters and advertisements'.

[198] For example, in 'Options Paper on the Victims' Ombudsman/Commissioner', Victim's Charter Review Implementation Group, December 2001.

a Victims Ombudsman/Commissioner Working Group was formed,[199] and the minutes refer to both titles.[200] But after that meeting, there was to be a conversation between the Home Office, the Cabinet Office, and the Parliamentary Commissioner who maintained that the Charter review's model of a Victims Ombudsman was something of a hybrid that was quite contrary to the Government's own June 2000 review of public sector ombudsmen,[201] risked encroachment on existing terrain, and, in its role as champion, was incompatible with the impartiality and the adjudicative functions proper to an Ombudsman. It would be impossible, said the Parliamentary Commissioner more formally in January 2002, 'both to be a champion of a particular group and accepted as an impartial investigator of disputes between members of that group and other persons or organisations', and ombudsmen had to be impartial. The Home Secretary was obliged to reply that the office of a Victims Ombudsman would, of course, be developed in accord with agreed principles and the terms of the Colcutt Review. And the second meeting of the Victim's Charter Review Working Group in January 2002 duly noted that, whilst at its inaugural meeting it had decided that the ombudsman/commissioner's role would be to investigate complaints and champion victims' interests, it had subsequently been discovered that there were plans to legislate for the implementation of the Colcutt Review in 2003/4, one of whose recommendations was clearly inconsistent with the proposed model of the Victims Ombudsman.[202]

[199] Meeting of Victims Steering Group, 26 November 2001.
[200] Minutes of First Meeting of Victim's Charter Review Working Group, 2 October 2001.
[201] The review, written by Phillip Colcutt and Mary Hourihan, published on 13 April 2000 and conducted as part of the 'Modernising Government' programme, recommended a 'radical re-structuring' of the public sector ombudsmen in England and Wales that would respond to 'the changing face of public service delivery'. Those ombudsmen were named as the Parliamentary Ombudsman, the Health Service Ombudsman, and the three Local Government Ombudsmen. The key recommendations were the creation of a college or commission of ombudsmen; the abolition of the requirements that the public could approach the ombudsmen only through their Member of Parliament; and the formation of a more 'joined-up' system of working. The review gave rise to its own consultation exercise, announced on 15 June 2000 (Cabinet Office Press Release CAB 223/00).
[202] Recommendation 6.15 of the Review had stated that 'An ombudsman's function must remain grounded in addressing injustice caused an individual and own-initiative investigation appears inconsistent with impartiality.'

The original proposal was evidently unworkable, and it was now intended to split the role into two separate posts. A Victims Ombudsman would play the arbiter and investigator in disinterested fashion, brought into being when the Colcutt recommendations were made law; a member of the new collegiate structure; who would find a place within the new division of labour that would be negotiated with his or her new colleagues; and be bound to impartiality as they would be bound. And there would be a complementary Victims Commissioner, established by statute in the Bill of Rights, again perhaps in 2003/4, who would act the victims' champion without a pretence of disinterestedness.[203] Ian Chisholm recalled:

Where I was too simplistic was to think a Victims Ombudsman would be acceptable here operating as in other common law jurisdictions. British Ombudsmen give primary emphasis to the investigation of individual complaints, often being confined to procedural issues (excepting the Prisons/Probation Ombudsman) whereas other jurisdictions tend to have powers to look at the merits of a case. In addition more emphasis is placed in North American/Commonwealth jurisdictions on provision of information and advice to victims. Generally speaking Ombudsmen in these jurisdictions give equal prominence to both individual complaints and general administrative difficulties. In order effectively to perform this broader role most overseas ombudsmen are empowered to instigate their own investigations into general issues of maladministration and may have considerable enforcement/investigation powers. The Cabinet Office Review of Public Sector Ombudsmen published in June 2000 was firmly of the view that the Ombudsman's primary function should continue to be the addressing of individual grievances so the climate was not propitious for a broader role for the Victims Ombudsman. Accordingly the role was split into Victims Commissioner and Victims Ombudsman.

The other principal issue discussed at that second meeting was the matter of victims' rights.[204] There was said to be a provisional slot for a Bill of Rights in 2003/4. The key issue, a Grade 7 reminded the group, was enforceability. Legal advisers had argued that direct recourse to the courts would be unprecedented and the new Home

---

[203] And it was also agreed that ideas about a victims' fund and a Victims Advisory Panel, representing victims' organizations, were to be taken forward.

[204] Although it should be noted that at no point in the consultation or subsequent review (although raised by Helen Reeves on at least one occasion) were the rights of victims in restorative justice formally discussed, reflecting again perhaps the structural accident of responsibility for victims having been placed in a body other than JVU.

Secretary, David Blunkett, and the Lord Chancellor had expressed
reservations. What therefore would be offered instead was a right of
redress through the Ombudsman, and the Group agreed that that
would be an appropriate way forward.[205] And, as a concomitant, a
new power would be created for the Home Secretary, in consultation
with the Lord Chancellor and Attorney General, to issue a statutory
code of practice for the treatment of victims, binding on criminal
justice agencies[206] and, subject to their views, Victim Support, that
would represent, in effect, a tighter version of the *Victim's Charter.*

## Epilogue

1997–2001, the period I was supposed to cover, has now lapsed, but
it would not be right to conclude without a brief epilogue to describe
the state of affairs in the summer of 2003, the time at which I am
writing. My knowledge of the events that occurred between then and
June 2001 is necessarily relatively thin, and it will be offered in only
the most summary form.[207]

The germs of a new regime and its accompanying rhetoric had
been planted, and, during the next three years, their influence
remained visible in plans for arrangements which have yet to be
legislated. What had been proposed as a Victims' Bill of Rights in
2001 was to be re-named a Victims and Witnesses Bill and then a
Domestic Violence, Crime and Victims Bill, and legislation was still
being promised in 2003 'as soon as parliamentary time will allow'.
The germs were to be seen in a criminal justice White Paper, *Justice
for All*,[208] published in 2002 under the names of the three criminal

---

[205] Second meeting of Victim's Charter Review Working Group, January 2002,
minutes.

[206] A move that was not wholly welcome. A CPS official said, for instance, at one of
the meetings that accompanied the consultation that pressure should not be applied to
'an independent prosecuting authority'.

[207] There were developments separate from the evolution of proposals for victims'
rights: chief amongst them was the experimental extension of restorative justice to
adult offenders in a number of Crown Court centres in 2002; the provision of information to the victims of 'mentally disordered offenders' (see Department of Health:
Press Release 2002/0284: Publication of Draft Mental Health Bill, 26 June 2002); the
floating of a fine surcharge for victims, identified by newspapers as a new 'stealth tax';
and the ever-staggered introduction of measures under the Youth Justice and Criminal
Evidence Act 1999 (see *The Times,* 16 July 2002).

[208] *Justice for All*, Cm. 5563, July 2002.

justice Ministers, that opened with the statement that 'The people of this country want a criminal justice system that works in the interests of justice. They rightly expect that the victims of crime should be at the heart of the system. This White Paper aims to rebalance the system in favour of victims, witnesses and communities...'. *Justice for All*'s first substantive section dwelt on 'A better deal for victims and witnesses' in which proposals were again offered to establish a new office of Commissioner for Victims and Witnesses (but note the addition of witnesses), supported by a National Victims Advisory Panel;[209] a *Victims' Code of Practice* and, in a new turn, to 'a right of complaint to the Parliamentary Ombudsman for victims and witnesses who are not satisfied that the Code has been followed'[210] (and again note the new presence of witnesses). Under the still forthcoming restructuring of the Ombudsman system that had been induced by the Colcutt Review, the array of separate Ombudsmen was to be replaced by a new omnicompetent single entity, a 'collegiate structure'[211] or 'unified and flexible ombudsman body to which the public would have direct access'[212] through a single 'route for complaints', and victims too would be able to approach the Ombudsman through that one route[213] rather than resort to what would have been their own new, dedicated Victims Ombudsman.

Within a year, the White Paper was to be followed by a 'national strategy for victims and witnesses' emanating from what had been the Victims Steering Group. Ian Chisholm had left the supervision of

[209] The panel was to be established in June 2003. The victims sitting on the panel were those who had been affected by serious crime, including, *inter alia*, members of SAMM, Victim's Voice, and The Zito Trust, rather than the victims of volume crime, and their role was to report directly to the Home Secretary to 'identify good practice and promote a culture where all victims and witnesses are treated fairly and with respect'. (10 Downing Street news release, 21 June 2003.) The then Home Office Minister, Lord Falconer, speaking to the North of England Victims association on 7 June 2003, said that 'The Panel is a chance for those seriously victimised to speak directly to Ministers and senior officials about the issues that are of most concern. He also floated (rather controversially) the possibility of victims becoming involved in parole decisions.

[210] *Justice for All, op. cit.*, p. 37.

[211] P. Collcutt and Mary Hourihan; *Review of the Public Sector Ombudsmen in England: A Report by the Cabinet Office*, April 2000.

[212] Cabinet Office web site: Public Sector Ombudsmen, September 2002. The proposal for change had been made in July 2001.

[213] See Cabinet Office Press Release, 164/00, 13 April 2000.

victims' and witnesses' affairs to work on other aspects of criminal justice reform, and a major new Criminal Justice Bill in particular, and his successor at once announced a characteristic piece of stock-taking at a meeting of the Victims Steering Group in November 2001: 'this group needs to focus . . . [on] what are the gaps, and what is the best use of resource? . . . The overall aim is to make sure things happen, that the plans are in place, and that we think ahead.' She proceeded to change the Group's name to the Victims and Witnesses Strategic Task Force and embarked on formulating a 'national strategy' to lend order to what would be done. The ensuing new paper, *A new deal for victims and witnesses: National strategy to deliver improved services*,[214] was submitted to the Strategic Board of the Criminal Justice System in May 2002 (where it still retained proposals for a separate Ombudsman and a Commissioner[215]) and was then published in July 2003.

The national strategy's ancestry in the histories narrated in this book remained apparent, but there were changes too. There was a retreat from the difficult language of rights and a return to the less demanding and less contested language of needs, responsibilities, and service, part of the continual oscillation between rights talk and standards talk that had begun in 1990. And it followed that there was no inventory of core principles or so-called 'headline rights'. There was a radical recommendation to unpick the established relation between Victim Support and the State, and introduce what appeared to be the beginnings of a market in victims' services, possibly representing an attempt to break the monopoly of Victim Support that had been recommended earlier by the National Audit Office,[216] stemming from a more general drift in Government

[214] *A new deal for victims and witnesses: National strategy to deliver improved services*, Home Office, London, July 2003.

[215] JVU; A New Deal for Victims and Witnesses—A National Strategy to Deliver Improved Services, Draft Outline, to Strategic Board of the Criminal Justice System, 27 May 2002.

[216] The Home Office had told the National Audit Office that any new services to victims would be subject to competition, starting with the provision of support for road traffic victims. The report's final recommendation was that 'The Home Office should review the current arrangements for funding voluntary sector activity in the field . . . and ensur[e] that the opportunity to bid to run new services is available to all potential providers.' (*Helping victims and witnesses: the work of Victim Support*, Report by the Comptroller and Auditor General, HC 1212, Session 2001–2002, 23 October 2002.)

towards a controlled localism[217] and, specifically in the Home
Office, towards the local funding of the voluntary sector,[218] and
possibly reflecting the less intimate relations that prevailed between
Victim Support and the new Home Secretary. Funding for the Witness Service would be devolved from central government to Local
Criminal Justice Boards 'for them to contract locally within a national standards framework' (although none of the national agencies
represented on the Boards was well disposed to the recommendation
and the Boards themselves were not accountable bodies empowered
to undertake such funding). There was to be a continuation of the
growing emphasis on the witnesses of crime that had started
seven years before in the Julia Mason case and the work of Warwick
Maynard and Andrew Sanders.[219] The review of victims' problems
and remedies was more schematic and wide-ranging, tied, for instance, into 'Community Legal Service Partnerships' and 'Community Justice Centres', restorative justice programmes, and anti-social
behaviour orders; more alert to the special needs of distinct
populations of victims rather than to victims *en masse*, including
children, the members of minority ethnic communities, repeat
victims, and the victims of domestic violence; and centred more
squarely on the problems faced by victims before they ever entered
the criminal justice system, embodying Victim Support's preoccupation with the neglected 97 per cent, and injecting what Victim
Support would identify as the 'social rights' of victims to
health, social service, and similar services.[220] Road traffic victims
had come more fully into their own, a product both of local

[217] See S. Richards; 'The odd couple', *Prospect*, October 2003. Richards' argument
is that that drift represented a solution to the 'great conundrum: national standards
versus local flexibility'. p. 38.

[218] See *Voluntary and Community Sector Infrastructure: A Consultation Document*, Active Community Unit, Home Office, September 2003, p. 11.

[219] That increased emphasis was to take something of a stern turn in certain
quarters. Proposals were to be floated in a consultation paper that witness attendance
at trial should be accompanied by a greater threat of compulsion. See *Securing
the attendance of witnesses in court: A consultation paper*, Home Office, London,
October 2003.

[220] See, for example, Victim Support; *Criminal Neglect: No justice beyond criminal justice*, 19 February 2002. *A new deal for victims and witnesses* noted on
p. 9 that 'More needs to be done to provide help to victims who do not report
crime, but still need support... Many victims (and some witnesses) have needs
beyond those that can be met by the criminal justice system. Crime can leave victims

victim support schemes' ever greater involvement with crash victims and their families[221] and of the energetic campaigning of Road-Peace.[222]

But the bones of the 2001 Charter review still clearly showed, and all the mechanisms for securing 'headline rights' remained in place even if those or any other rights were no longer expressly named. There was still to be a Commissioner for Victims and Witnesses but, following the White Paper, the proposal for a discrete Victims Ombudsman had disappeared with all the other discrete Ombudsmen into the new 'resilient and flexible' single collegiate entity proposed by the Colcutt Review.[223] The Parliamentary Ombudsman would, in the interim, take responsibility, in a Grade 7's words, 'for policing the victims' code of practice . . . How this will pan out in practice remains to be seen (it is impossible to estimate how many complaints she might receive as, when the code is published, it will be the first time we will have given extensive publicity to "how to complain")—although the intention is for complaints to be handled by a specific team within the PCA's office so that knowledge and expertise about the code is built up.'[224] The *Victim's Charter* was never to be revised or re-issued, still awaiting replacement by proposals for a statutory code of practice for criminal justice

physically injured, emotionally traumatised, frightened, and with potentially long lasting psychological trauma, all of which can be compounded by severe financial difficulties.'

[221] Victim Support had long been preoccupied by the issue of whether it should recognize local schemes' initiatives in the area. In April 2000, some 140 schemes were taking referrals of families bereaved by road death, 41% of the total. One problem was whether road deaths were always and everywhere the result of crime, and if they were not, they did not properly generate victims of crime. Helen Reeves observed at a meeting of the Victims Steering Group: 'we've been very exercised by road deaths. About 10% are the results of pure crime, the rest are accidents, and it would be interesting to see how you're going to deal with the issue . . . there's a difference between the case where there's a crime and where there's not.' An ACPO representative told a meeting of the Victim Statement Group Meeting, 8 December 2000, 'Victims can suffer appalling injuries to the psyche as well as the body. Bad driving is a *crime* and there's no going away from it.' (My notes.)

[222] See Home Office Press Release 6 June 2002: Improved Support Services for Road Traffic Victims.

[223] The phrase was 'the Bill will . . . for the first time propose a right of access to the Ombudsman for victims and witnesses, and a statutory code of practice for criminal justice system agencies.' *A new deal for victims and witnesses, op. cit.*, p. 7.

[224] Email, 21 August 2003.

agencies, the *Victims' Code of Practice*,[225] that would also be encased in a new Bill. Eventually, and manifesting again the capacity of a Home Office initiative to meld parallel policies on the move,[226]

---

[225] A Grade 7 of JVU told me in July 2002 that 'The Code of Practice will place service obligations on all criminal justice agencies with regard to victims of crime. For example, under the current Victim's Charter the police are to be obliged to keep victims informed of significant case developments, under the Code of Practice these current obligations and several new ones will be placed on a statutory footing. The victim will have an opportunity to seek redress through the Parliamentary Commissioner for Administration, if he/she feels that an agency has breached the Code and they are dissatisfied with the response to their complaint from the agency themselves. The legislation may also make provision for a Victims Commissioner to champion victims interests and to make sure that victims' voices are heard, this role will be distinct from that of the Ombudsman and will not investigate complaints. When the Victims of Crime Bill is legislated for it will replace the current Victim's Charter, with statutory rights for victims of crime, with criminal justice agencies under statutory obligation to adhere to their obligations.' A draft version, issued in 2003, covered all the major agencies and officials touching the victim, including Victim Support, but it excluded the judiciary and the magistracy. There were cumbersome features in its provisions for enforcement. Victims would be obliged first to make a complaint through the internal procedures of the agency, then, if still discontent, to their Member of Parliament who would be able to refer the matter to the Parliamentary Commissioner for Administration. Victims themselves were defined somewhat awkwardly: for instance, a 'family spokesperson' would be eligible where the victim had died, but other members of the family were not expressly included as beneficiaries. Individuals or businesses employing fewer than nine employees would be eligible, but those with more would not, leaving bank employees and others exposed. Vulnerable victims included those under 17, people deemed to be suffering from mental disorder, the survivors of domestic violence and those liable to intimidation, but not the physically disabled or the elderly. Most of the provisions flowed directly out of the episodes recounted in this book, including the European Framework Decision, and touched, *inter alia*, on the right to information about the progress of cases before, during, and after trial, including, importantly, incidents where no progress had been made; the right to make a Personal Statement; the right to meet a representative of the CPS in serious cases and 'where circumstances permit' to receive an explanation of significant charge reduction or the abandonment of a charge; and safeguards introduced in restorative justice procedures, but not the right of a victim to be accompanied by a supporter.

[226] The notes accompanying the Home Office press release announcing the new Bill reminded editors that 'Safety and Justice,' the domestic violence consultation paper, was published in June 2003 (Home Office press notice 168/03). They were also told that the provisions for victims in the Domestic Violence, Crime and Victims Bill built on the *Justice for All White Paper* and the booklet *A Better Deal for Victims and Witnesses* of July 2002 (Home Office press notice 201/02), and the 'National Strategy for Victims and Witnesses', published on 22 July 2003 (Home Office press notice 212/03).

one foreign to the chronology and substance of this history, the other central to it, plans for a Commissioner for Victims and Witnesses, recourse to the Parliamentary Commissioner and a Code of Practice[227] were announced in the 26 November 2003 Queen's Speech and introduced into the House of Lords the following day as a new omnibus Domestic Violence, Crime and Victims Bill, so presented for 'legislative convenience'.[228] Ministers and policy frameworks had changed after 2001, and the word 'victims' had not even been part of the title at first, reflecting vigorous lobbying and the new ascendancy of domestic violence in the new Government's scheme of things.[229] Quite characteristically, the new proposals for victims[230] created very little stir in the larger media coverage of the Speech, attention being concentrated on the raising of fees for university students and provisions for asylum-seekers. And what Government press releases and reporting there were on the new Bill tended to focus wholly on plans to control domestic

[227] And, significantly, that Code would establish Victim Support as a statutory agency for the first time.

[228] The words are those of a Justice and Victims Unit official.

[229] The emphasis on domestic violence was imported by the Baroness Scotland, QC, the new Minister of State for the Criminal Justice System and Law Reform, who was a member of the Bar of Antigua and the Commonwealth of Dominica; was appointed a Recorder in 2000, and approved to sit as a Deputy High Court Judge of the Family Division.

[230] A press release issued on 2 December 2003 presented the proposals for victims and witnesses in a form that should by now have become more than familiar: titled 'Putting Victims First: Publication Of The Domestic Violence, Crime And Victims Bill, CJS011/2003', it talked about '[p]roviding a code of practice, binding on all criminal justice agencies, so that all victims receive the support, protection, information and advice they need. Allowing victims to take their case to the Parliamentary Ombudsman if they felt the Code had not been adhered to by the criminal justice agencies. Setting up an independent commissioner for victims to give victims a powerful voice at the heart of Government and to safeguard and promote the interests of victims and witnesses, encouraging the spread of good practice and reviewing the statutory code.' The wording of the Bill itself was perhaps somewhat more tentative: under paragraphs 15(1) and (2) it laid down that 'If a person fails to perform a duty imposed upon him by a code under [this Act], the failure does not of itself make him liable to criminal or civil proceedings. But the code is admissible in evidence in criminal or civil proceedings and a court may take into account a failure to comply with the code in determining a question in the proceedings.' A Justice and Victims Unit official commented on the question of enforcement that 'The Code of Practice will be statutory—and has the effect of giving "rights" to victims. Enforcement is via the Parliamentary Ombudsman.'

violence[231] (leading the *Evening Standard* of 2 December to become
so confused that it alleged that 'A "victims' commissioner" will be
established to speak up for people affected by domestic violence').
Members of the newly constituted Victims Unit were more than a
little dismayed. And their dismay was consolidated because, although the argument of the new strategy was ambitious and schematic in its imposition of a greater coherence on the provision of
services and support for victims across and beyond the criminal
justice system, it lacked a timetable, targets, a programme of action,
and a co-ordinating committee, the Victims and Witnesses Strategic
Task Force having been disbanded and not replaced.[232] More, it also
lacked dedicated resources, and there was no prospect of new money
coming forth in the future other than from the Victim's Fund that
was flagged speculatively in the January 2004 consultation paper.
Attempting to plan its implementation would be more than a little
fraught, bedevilling the Victim Unit's work.

   In a slightly veiled and now much more obscured form, then, the
Chisholm version of the Schlieffen Plan remained more or less intact,
still allowing victims to take a serpentine 'avenue of complaint to the
Parliamentary Ombudsman' and bypass the Maginot line that had
been erected against victims' rights. If the Bill's proposal to establish
a commissioner, a code, and a dedicated ombudsman does become
law, English and Welsh victims will yet have won rights of a sort even
though they are rights that no longer dare speak their name.

---

[231] The proposals included more powerful injunctions to control abusive men, the
ending of the defence of provocation in murder cases, the establishment of a register of
previous offenders, and reviews of domestic violence murders modelled on those that
follow child murders.

[232] Although new arrangements were installed to continue meetings between the
Home Office and Victim Support.

# 11

# Conclusion

What conclusions should one draw? I have offered a running series of observations as this book progressed, but it would be right to end by trying to make summary sense of what happened between 1997 and 2001, the period when a peculiarly English and Welsh version of victims' rights became an imminent possibility.

Try as I might, I was unable to offer a grand narrative about policies for victims in this history. I do not believe there was any such narrative to be had. It is tempting to talk about post-modernism and the collapse of foundational narratives, but matters were much more simple and mundane than that. Victims for the most part did not possess the political weight to qualify as the subjects of large historical gestures in their own right. Most of the components of this book were instead parts of other stories about race, gender, human rights, and the like, and that was to be their significance, interest, and role. The imagery of victims that ensued did not have to coalesce until the formulation of the national strategy described in the last chapter, a strategy that was a typical piece of reflexive work at a time of transition when one head of JVU was replaced by another. But coherence was not needed to convey, first, that a problem of administrative ordering existed, and that, second, the elusive issue of victims' and witnesses' rights had to be resolved, and resolved almost certainly by elliptical means.

Let me give a brief reprise of what happened. Victims, and later witnesses, it will be recalled, had come to the fore in the affairs of the first New Labour Parliament in a number of guises. In 1997, at the time of the general election, 23 per cent of victims known to the British Crime Survey were burglary victims; 23 per cent were the victims of 'other theft'; 25 per cent of vehicle crime; 20 per cent of other property offences; 8 per cent of violent crime, and 1 per cent of 'other offences'. Of that lesser category of violent crime, numbering

350,000 offences, the police recorded 18 per cent as robberies; 10 per cent as sexual offences; 65 per cent as 'less serious offences of violence'; and 7 per cent as homicide and more serious offences of violence.[1] To be sure, those figures should be read with caution, and rape and murder do have profound repercussions out of all scale to their absolute numbers, but reactions to crime are never wholly predictable or locked neatly within offence types, and the figures do reinforce the discrepancy between the distribution of victimization at large and the forms of victimization that were to bulk large in the politics of victims. Most victims and witnesses were not at first regarded as important subjects of policy-making, and what was done was not undertaken in their name, responsive to their demands or proportionate to their volume or distribution. They had, after all, made no demands, and only a few were allowed to 'materialize' as subjects for official action.

There was at first, in other words, a huge reservoir of victims eligible for political attention, some quite new, marginal,[2] and unconsidered.[3] Who and what actually came to be considered, and in what manner, was to be a contingent, idiosyncratic, and sometimes contested[4] matter. It did not necessarily rest on the arguments

---

[1] Taken from *digest 4: Information on the criminal justice system in England and Wales,* Home Office, London, 1999.

[2] When Marc Groenhuijsen addressed a session on Victims and Offenders at the *Tenth United Nations Congress on the Prevention of Crime and the Treatment of Offenders: Crime and Justice: Meeting the Challenges of the Twenty-first Century,* Vienna, Austria, 10–17 April 2000, he noted to himself the 'Host of new victim categories—victims of computer related crimes, environmental crimes and corruption.'

[3] More than once, individuals and organizations floated the proposal that victims should also include those who had suffered accidents at work at first or second hand, an area policed chiefly by a body, the Health and Safety Executive, that had not featured at all in the histories I have described. But the idea never took off. There were debates about which relatives of what victims could also be included as victims (discussed, for instance, in Victim Support's evidence to the Macpherson Inquiry, 7 July 1998). Boundary changes did occur. One fascinating definitional switch occurred at the end of 1998 when it was decided that child prostitutes were no longer to be treated by the criminal justice system as offenders but as victims (Home Office/DH: Draft Guidance on Children Involved in Prostitution, 17 December 1998; Home Office Press Release 508/98: Child Prostitutes to be treated as victims, 29 December 1998).

[4] There were heated debates in victims' circles about whether men could be the victims of domestic violence or rape, for instance. See C. Mirrlees-Black; *Domestic Violence: Findings from a new British Crime Survey self-completion questionnaire,*

of victimology, on accumulating research or on evidence about the victim's plight (although there were certainly occasions when policy-making was 'knowledge-based'). It was not an instance of blue book policy-making. Rather, the process of definition and selection was tangential and piecemeal. It depended on the manner in which wider structural changes in management constructed victims as service recipients. It reflected a new dialectic of human rights in which victims acquired rights by negation. In some reaches, and especially in the Criminal Injuries Compensation Scheme, it still centred on financially-modulated judgments about moral desert[5] and blame,[6] and, for many practical purposes, victims were those whom the State was prepared to support economically,[7] reminiscent of Barbara Wootton's *dictum* that social problems are what governments spend money on. It embodied accidents of administrative organization,

Home Office, London, 1999; and N. Naffine; 'Possession: Erotic Love in the Law of Rape', *Modern Law Review,* January 1994, 57:1, pp. 10–37.

[5] And certain movements were interesting in consequence. For instance, after May 2001, partners in same sex relationships were to be fully recognized as the next of kin and treated in the same way as heterosexual victims for purposes of the probation service's 'victim contact work'. National Probation Service; 'Victim Contact Work, Guidance for Probation Areas', May 2001.

[6] But those judgments were influential elsewhere as well. There were frequent allusions to the Tony Martin case. And one member of the Victims Steering Group declared himself averse to the proposal to award victims statutory rights because 'the problem is that not all victims are good. The second biggest drugs dealer shoots the first biggest drugs dealer and he becomes a victim.' The Prison Service representative's reply was that, even if the victim was the author of his own misfortune, he could still be in danger.

[7] Recall the debates about 'cutting out drunks' in the review of the Criminal Injuries Compensation Scheme. Victim Support's 2001 election manifesto called for State funding for work with the families of road deaths, victims of domestic violence, the families of homicide victims attending Coroners' Courts, and witnesses at courts martial. Extra money would have extended the practical reach of Victim Support and its Witness Service, ratifying new populations as victims and witnesses, giving them standing, discovering new areas of problems, and expanding the boundaries of need. When ACPO revised its training for family liaison officers after the Macpherson Inquiry, it defined the victim's family as 'partners, parents, siblings, children, guardians and others who have had a direct and close relationship with the victim' (ACPO Crime Committee: Homicide Working Group, Family Liaison Officers Strategy, 7 October 1999). It is inconceivable that such a definition would have been extended to the families of burglaries, thefts, or malicious damage. No police service could have afforded it. Andy May, then the ACPO representative on the Victims Steering Group, said about the general question of defining victims that 'My view would be that we're only ever likely to be able to cope with immediate victims.'

and victims in restorative justice, domestic violence, and violence against children were on the structural margins of the politics of victims (although, at a very late stage and as a result of a change of Ministers, victims of domestic violence threatened to swamp all others). It was shaped by elementary decisions about practice,[8] victims and witnesses being those who were made known in and around the routine work procedures of criminal justice agencies[9] (and, so defined, problems loomed about the identification of victims thrown up in other ways[10]). It encapsulated the working imperative of the criminal justice system to reduce crime by encouraging reports of offences from victims and bystanders, securing telling testimony from witnesses in court, and creating subjects who could make offenders accountable for their actions in restorative justice.[11] In one instance, it demonstrated the ability of a highly organized and persistent group, RoadPeace, to elbow its way into the political forum.[12] Above all, perhaps, it depended on the

---

[8]    Probation circular PC62/2001, for instance, defined victims for the purpose of contact work as the direct victim or family if the offence resulted in death or incapacity or 'where it seems sensible to approach the family'.

[9]    Recall how the category of victims was enlarged to deal with problems of poor response in the *Victim's Charter* standards pilots. See D. Stone; 'Causal Stories and the Formation of Policy Agendas', *Political Science Quarterly*, Vol. 104, 1989, p. 281; and Peter Manning who observed that 'Culture and the organizational culture are ways of restricting the range of relevant events and processes, pinning them down to routines. Events in the external world have meaning conferred upon them, and do not have intrinsic features and intervention points.' P. Manning; 'Managing Risk: Managing Uncertainty in the British Nuclear Installations Inspectorate', in J. Short and L. Clarke (eds.); *Organizations, Uncertainties, and Risk*, Westview Press, Boulder, 1992, p. 257.

[10]    See Victim Support response to 'The New NHS Modern and Dependable', White Paper, December 1997, 26 March 1998, which discussed the many victims who were known to hospital accident and emergency units but not to the police.

[11]    And pertinent here is the statement by Holstein and Miller that ' ... descriptions—as when we describe someone as a "victim"—are not disembodied commentaries on ostensibly real states of affairs. Rather, they are reality *projects*—acts of constructing the world ... We can conceive of "victimization" as *descriptive practice*—the interpretive and representational process for assigning victim status to ourselves and others ... Describing someone as a victim is more than merely reporting *about* a feature of the social world, it *constitutes* that world.' J. Holstein and G. Miller; 'Rethinking Victimization: An Interactional Approach to Victimology', *Symbolic Interaction*, Vol. 13, No. 1, 1990, p. 5.

[12]    The three criminal justice Ministers had been perfectly candid in 2002 in saying that those hurt or killed in road traffic incidents were not then regarded as victims (Lord Chancellor, Home Secretary, and Attorney General; 'A Better Deal for Victims

dramatization of an identity politics centred on gender and race,[13] because it was that politics, more powerful by far than any undeveloped, unexciting, and less appealing politics of victims, which gave the final propulsive thrust to policy-making (and nearly engulfed it at the climax[14]). For some time, anything done in the name of race and its attendant politics of public confidence was unbrookable.[15]

If the origins of the representations of victims gathered together in the work of JVU were contingent, so too, in some measure, was the diversity of administrative responses mobilized to deal with them. No single policy problem was thought to be represented. It was the view of the new head of JVU in June 2002 that there was a spectrum of unlike positions and 'drivers', 'sometimes pushing in the same direction, sometimes not':[16] Helen Reeves and Victim Support, she said, were focused on caring for the one million victims who were known to their volunteers but possibly unknown to the courts; RoadPeace was moved by a sense of anger and secondary victimization; and Ministers were arrayed on a continuum extending from Helen Reeves' position that victims should be made to feel better to one that sought to make the criminal justice system work more effectively by improving the performance of witnesses and securing

and Witnesses', November 2002). David Faulkner wrote to me with the observation that there was a 'problem that if boundaries are extended to road accidents, why not other accidents as well? Would that loosen the hold of the CJS on victims issues?' Letter of 4 March 2001.

[13] Jacobs and Potter wrote of the United States that ' . . . we argue that the passage of hate crime laws enacted in the 1980s and 1990s is best explained by the growing influence of identity politics. Fundamentally, the hate crime laws are symbolic statements requested by advocacy groups for material and symbolic reasons and provided by politicians for political reasons.' J. Jacobs and K. Potter; *Hate Crimes: Criminal Law & Identity Politics*, Oxford University Press, New York, 1998, p. 65.

[14] And that, ironically, was the very reverse of what had happened over 20 years before with the Canadian Federal Government's Justice for Victims of Crime Initiative, which had, in effect, used political interest in domestic violence as a Trojan horse to gain approval and modest funding for a portfolio of measures for victims at large. See my *A View from the Shadows: The Ministry of the Solicitor General of Canada and the Justice for Victims of Crime Initiative*, Clarendon Press, Oxford, 1986.

[15] For example, suggestions that the 'ethnic booster sample' be omitted from the 1998 British Crime Survey were greeted with the observation that 'the timing could not be worse'.

[16] And it was at that point that Helen Reeves entered the room and asked who had said that victims ever wanted to be at the heart of the criminal justice system?

a greater number of convictions. And accompanying the different drivers and positions there was for a long while a multitude of co-existing accounts about what was happening, what it boded and who and what had been responsible for change.[17] Helen Reeves herself said at the end of 1999 'I think there are lots of stor-ies... there's a lot of people who can only see the legal problem, which is why some of the initiatives such as the Victims Statement immediately gets translated in everybody's mind into a sentencing tool because nobody can see any other purpose for it. And the idea of being nice to victims or recognising other needs, the victims' need, and making sure they get the services they need, doesn't occur to a lot of people.' Authorship and ownership could be claimed quite prop-erly by Victim Support and the European Forum for Victims Ser-vices; by the Prime Minister and Home Office Ministers, advisers, and officials; by those who had campaigned in the politics of race and criminal justice; by those who had championed women sur-vivors; and by others still.

Neither was one pattern of policy-making applied. Some victims received the close political attention of Ministers, others took their place as anonymous service-recipients in the unfolding work of performance management, and others were the subject of quite routine consultations and reviews. Inspected closely, there was no standard formula for translating problems into recipes for action and one wonders whether any generalization could be possible. Yet, at a greater remove, there was also a routinization of response that flowed from the subjection of victims' issues to the stylizing proced-ures and absorptive propensities of policy-making in the Home Office and Government at the turn of the century. If victims entered the policy process in motley and individual form, and received disparate attention whilst in transition, they emerged at the other end as more or less standard subjects, the everyman or everywoman of criminal justice, to whom universal procedures should be applied.

---

[17] Victim Support could quite properly claim major responsibility for the emergence of a rights discourse, and particularly through the medium of the European Framework Decision (see H. Reeves and K. Mulley; 'The new status of victims in the UK: Oppor-tunities and threats', in A. Crawford and J. Goodey (eds.); *Integrating a Victim Per-spective Within Criminal Justice: International debates,* Ashgate, Aldershot, 2000, p. 130). But other bodies also asserted their impact on policy-making: organizations centred on race and gender; the Labour Party and its advisers; those in the restorative justice movement; and, with substantial justification, the officials of JVU.

The significance of the Stephen Lawrence murder may have begun in the anguished politics of race, but it evolved into a wider category of hate crime and ended in prescriptions for victims and their families irrespective of race. The Julia Mason case may have taken its form in the suffering of one woman, but it culminated in very broad proposals for witnesses at large. And so it went on. The State bureaucracy of England and Wales is, after all, regulated by formal rationality, broad laws and regulations, very general administrative routines, and the need to enforce impartial and equal standards.

So much had been done for and with victims during the first administration that problems of mass, conflict, contradiction, and unwieldiness came to demand action from a cluster of officials and politicians who were themselves increasingly disposed to act. Yet the divisions of the criminal justice system, themselves extrusions of the structurally embedded conflicts of the adversarial process, were bound always by conventions about the need to negotiate agreement between the principals, and proposals did not and could not withstand determined resistance. Time after time, actions mooted by the Home Office and 10 Downing Street met with stout opposition from those in the judiciary and the Lord Chancellor's Department who guarded defendants' rights, the maintenance of professionally controlled and emotionally unencumbered trials, and the doctrine that crime is at heart an offence against Society, State, or Sovereign.[18] However much talk there may have been at various times about victims' rights, the personal victim was finally to be afforded almost no formal role in criminal justice processes. He or she would never again be allowed to become more than a witness and an alleged

[18] For a shoal of examples of lawyers and others from very different positions vigorously defending the Maginot Line, see J. Fitzpatrick; 'The Macpherson Report in the Dock', *LM*, 119, April 1999, pp. 19–20; D. Miers; 'The Responsibilities and Rights of Victims of Crime', *The Modern Law Review*, July 1992, 55:4, pp. 482–505; T. Aldridge; 'No role for victims', *Solicitors Journal*, 28 November 1997; and C. Brennan; 'The Personal Statement Scheme', *New Law Journal*, Vol. 150, 6943, 7 July 2000, p. 1021. The author of that last article berated the Home Secretary for introducing the 'fallacious or novel idea that the criminal trial is about an opposition between the defendant and the victim'. Traditionally the sides have been conceived as the State and the offender, and there was, the argument ran, a risk of importing emotional and subjective appeals. J. Cooper wrote in *The Times*, 5 December 2000, 'Surely the most important individual in a trial is the defendant. Defendants, after all, face penalties, even loss of liberty, if found guilty. In one view, at least, it seems that this legislation puts the interests of witnesses—prosecution witnesses especially—ahead of defendants.' There are many similar instances.

victim until the trial had concluded, when, it may be supposed, support would be too late. By the time the United Kingdom was embroiled in discussion about the phrasing of the European Framework Decision in 2001, there was no doubt at home that victims should have no legal standing (and that was the very same stance taken, sixteen years before, when the United Kingdom had negotiated the wording of the United Nations Declaration on the Rights of Victims). The Maginot Line remained firm. Victims would for the foreseeable future have no clear formal rights and no right to litigate in England and Wales. Neither would they be allowed to become full-blown principals in the criminal justice system.

Yet the notion of victims' rights never disappeared: the problems which had engendered it were still pressing; it was clearly visible in the legislative portfolios of other jurisdictions with very similar adversarial systems such as Ireland,[19] Canada,[20] the United States,[21] New Zealand,[22] and Australia[23]; it was vigorously promoted by the European Forum for Victims Services;[24] and it was impressed upon the British Government by the intergovernmental policy-making organizations in which officials and politicians participated and by whose judgments they were often bound—the United Nations, Council of Europe, and European Community.[25]

---

[19] See Irish Independent, 18 September 1999.

[20] Federal Legislation Strengthening the Voice of Victims of Crime, Department of Justice, Ottawa, Canada, 4 November 1999.

[21] National Crime Victims' Rights Week, 9–15 April 2000: Victims' Rights: Dare to Dream, Office for Victims of Crime, US Dept of Justice, Washington, 2000.

[22] Victims Task Force; Towards Equality in Criminal Justice, Report to the Minister of Justice, Private Box 180, Wellington, NZ, 1993.

[23] See P. Grabosky; Victims of Violence, Australian Institute of Criminology, Canberra, 1989, p. 37; New South Wales Law Reform Commission; Discussion Paper 33—Sentencing, Sydney, 1996—Ch. 11.

[24] M. Groenhuijsen; 'Trends in Victimology in Europe with Special Reference to the European Forum for Victim Services', 10th Annual Conference of the Japanese Association of Victimology, Kyoto, 26th June 1999.

[25] See C. Hood; 'Beyond the Public Bureaucracy State? Public Administration in the 1990s', Extended text of an inaugural lecture delivered on 16 January 1990. Hood talked about 'the internationalisation of public administration—the shift of focus, at least in policy formulation, away from the national unit towards transnational institutions.... [That includes] [a] move towards joint policy-making through transnational institutions. A dramatic change in the European policy environment is the growth of the EC from an initially small and simple operation to place formerly separate states in a new network of "intergovernmental" policymaking.'

What emerged as the resolution of a seemingly intractable problem was the Chisholm *finesse*, later taken forward in *Justice for All* and *A new deal for victims and witnesses*, which proposed, on the one hand, the imposition of statutory duties on criminal justice agencies and the granting of access to an Ombudsman, and, on the other, a National Victims' Advisory Panel that would afford victims a symbolic voice, and a symbolic champion, a Commissioner for Victims and Witnesses. If victims could not litigate, they were certainly promised a novel legal remedy and a form of rights *sub rosa*, and it will be intriguing to learn how that machinery will evolve in the years to come.

# Index

574    Index